ERPA International Congresses on Education 2017 (ERPA 2017)

SHS Web of Conferences Volume 37 (2017)

Budapest, Hungary
18 - 21 May 2017

Editors:

E. Masal
I. Onder
S. Besoluk
H. Caliskan
E. Demirhan

ISBN: 978-1-5108-4707-1

Printed from e-media with permission by:

Curran Associates, Inc.
57 Morehouse Lane
Red Hook, NY 12571

Some format issues inherent in the e-media version may also appear in this print version.

Printed by Curran Associates, Inc. (2017)

For additional information, please contact EDP Sciences – Web of Conferences at the address below.

EDP Sciences – Web of Conferences
17, Avenue du Hoggar
Parc d'Activité de Courtabœuf
BP 112
F-91944 Les Ulis Cedex A
France

Phone: +33 (0) 1 69 18 75 75
Fax: +33 (0) 1 69 28 84 91

contact-edps@webofconferences.org

Additional copies of this publication are available from:

Curran Associates, Inc.
57 Morehouse Lane
Red Hook, NY 12571 USA
Phone: 845-758-0400
Fax: 845-758-2633
Email: curran@proceedings.com
Web: www.proceedings.com

TABLE OF CONTENTS

SHS Web of Conferences
Open access conference proceedings
in Human and Social Sciences
A flexible, fast and efficient
publication service,
for an open access recording
of your event
and a wide dissemination of
your proceedings
www.shs-conferences.org
edp open Open Access Publishing from EDP Sciences

edp sciences

SHS Web of Conferences

Statement of Peer review

In submitting conference proceedings to SHS Web of Conferences, I certify to the Publisher that I adhere to the **Policy on Publishing Integrity** of the journal in order to safeguard good scientific practice in publishing.

1. All articles have been subjected to peer review administered by the proceedings editors.
2. Reviews have been conducted by expert referees, who have been requested to provide unbiased and constructive comments aimed, whenever possible, at improving the work.
3. Proceedings editors have taken all reasonable steps to ensure the quality of the materials they publish and their decision to accept or reject a paper for publication has been based only on the merits of the work and the relevance to the journal.

Title, date and place of the conference

ERPA International Congresses on Education 2017
(18-21 May 2017, Budapest / Hungary)

Proceedings editor(s):

Dr. Ercan Masal
Dr. Ismail Onder
Dr. Şenol Beşoluk
Dr. Hüseyin Çalışkan
Dr. Eda Demirhan

Date and editor's signature 28.07.2017

Editorial: Special issue on education

Ercan Masal [1a], İsmail Önder[1], Hüseyin Çalışkan[1], Şenol Beşoluk[1] and Eda Demirhan[1]

[1]Sakarya University, Faculty of Education, 54300 Hendek, Sakarya, Turkey

Abstract. This special issue consists of selected proceedings presented in ERPA International Congresses on Education 2017 which was held in Budapest / Hungary, 18-21 May 2017. Studies are related to educational sciences, science and mathematics education, social sciences education, health and sports science education, music and fine arts education, computer education and instructional technology, language education and management of education. There are eighty valuable studies in this special issue. In sum the results of studies will contribute to the field.
Keywords: Special issue, Education, ERPA Congresses

Preface

It is the great honor for us to edit this special issue of SHS Web of Conferences for the selected proceedings presented in the ERPA International Congresses on Education 2017 which was held in Budapest / Hungary, 18-21 May 2017. Each paper submitted to the conference has been peer reviewed by the reviewers and at the end of the review process, a total of 84 high quality papers were selected and accepted for this publication.

It is with great pleasure seeing this impressive special issue of the SHS Web of Conferences going viral. As the following short description shows, it is an impressive collection of papers that are related to educational sciences, science and mathematics education, social sciences education, health and sports science education, music and fine arts education, computer education and instructional technology, language education and management of education.

Proceedings related to educational sciences in the issue are; [5], [11], [16], [20], [26], [27], [52], [53], [74], [77].

Proceedings related to science and mathematics education in the issue are; [12], [14], [17], [21], [24], [25], [38], [39], [40], [44], [50], [51], [57], [73], [75], [76].

Proceedings related to social sciences education in the issue are; [80], [84].

Proceedings related to health and sports science education in the issue are; [1], [2], [3], [4], [6], [7], [9], [18], [19], [22], [23], [29], [30], [31], [32], [34], [41], [42], [43], [45], [46], [47], [49], [54], [55], [56], [58], [59], [60], [61], [62], [63], [64], [65], [66], [70], [71], [72],[82],[83].

[a] Corresponding author: emasal@sakarya.edu.tr

Proceedings related to music and fine arts education in the issue are; [10], [28], [35].

Proceedings related to computer education and instructional technology in the issue are; [15], [33].

Proceedings related to language education in the issue are; [48], [67], [69], [78], [79], [81].

Proceedings related to management of education in the issue are; [8], [13], [36], [37], [68].

We hope that this special issue contributes to the field. Special thanks are given to all the reviewers, the members of the Scientific Committee and Organizing committee. We hope that you enjoy reading the papers of this issue.

References

1. Ruiz-Ariza, S. López-Serrano, S. Suárez-Manzano, E. J. Martínez-López. Looking for new active methods to improve the school performance: Physical Activity! SHS Web of Conferences, XX. (2017)
2. Ruiz-Ariza, M. de la Torre-Cruz, S. López-Serrano, E. J. Martínez-López. What is the relationship between parental supports, self-efficacy and physical activity in young students? A pilot cross-sectional study. SHS Web of Conferences, XX. (2017)
3. S. López-Serrano, S. Suárez-Manzano, A. Ruiz-Ariza, E. J. Martínez-López. Nintento Wii as an educational implement. Reality or fiction? SHS Web of Conferences, XX. (2017)
4. J. Martínez-López, S. López-Serrano, S. Suárez-Manzano, A. Ruiz-Ariza. Is the body composition equal or more important in physical fitness variables than other features like age or sex within physical education classes? A theoretical-practice study. SHS Web of Conferences, XX. (2017)
5. C. Fernández, C. M. A. C. Cortés. Alternative teaching practices for inclusive education. SHS Web of Conferences, XX. (2017)
6. M. A. C. Cortés, C. C. Fernández. Emotional and social representations of future teachers about sexually transmitted diseases. SHS Web of Conferences, XX. (2017)
7. S. U. Leong. Promoting healthy musculoskeletal function by applying regular exercises education and physical activities in senior activity centers. SHS Web of Conferences, XX. (2017)
8. El-Hmoudova. CB language competences testing methods in the class of tourism management. SHS Web of Conferences, XX. (2017)
9. Blidariu, D. Giurea. TETRAPOLIS - an exercise in building the complexities of proximity space. SHS Web of Conferences, XX. (2017)
10. Giurea, C. Blidariu.Working with mass and light: a challenge for architecture students. SHS Web of Conferences, XX. (2017)
11. Luchaninov, R. Bazhenov, N. Bazhenova. Student's information competence development: experience and prospect. SHS Web of Conferences, XX. (2017)
12. Tvarohová, S. Hybelbauerová. Education of organic chemistry at the grammar school - problem parts of subject. SHS Web of Conferences, XX. (2017)
13. Pikhart. Managerial Communication and its Changes in the Global Intercultural Business World. SHS Web of Conferences, XX. (2017)
14. Puig-Gutiérrez, M. Cruz-Guzmán Alcalá. The design of free activities for teaching science. A study with preservice teachers. SHS Web of Conferences, XX. (2017)
15. M. Majorek, M. du Vall. Civic technology for education. Analysis and evaluation of selected initiatives. SHS Web of Conferences, XX. (2017)
16. M. Majorek, J. Wojniak. Responsible Research and Innovation: Promoting a Scientific Career among Young People. SHS Web of Conferences, XX. (2017)

17. M. Ivan, R. Šulcová. Mathematics, chemistry and science connection as a basis of scientific thinking. SHS Web of Conferences, XX. (2017)
18. P. G. Leal, N.-J. Torres, D. Baracaldo. Analysis of the Pedagogical Components of 24 Significant Experiences in Sports Interest Centers in Bogotá, Colombia. SHS Web of Conferences, XX. (2017)
19. W.I. Pang. Promoting integrity of shift report by applying ISBAR principles among nursing students in clinical placement. SHS Web of Conferences, XX. (2017)
20. P. Moreno-Crespo, O. Moreno-Fernández. Do educators in initial training have stereotypes about adult education? SHS Web of Conferences, XX. (2017)
21. P. Moreno-Crespo. Perception on Mathematical Difficulties in Senior Adults. SHS Web of Conferences, XX. (2017)
22. T. Laurentiu-Gabriel, M. Veronica, I.-E. Mircea. Study regarding the use of movement games and relays in order to improve primary students' strength qualities. SHS Web of Conferences, XX. (2017)
23. T. Laurentiu-Gabriel, M. Veronica. Study regarding the use of physical exercise in order to prevent school-age children from being overweight. SHS Web of Conferences, XX. (2017)
24. V. Baños-Martínez. Application of the European Quality of Life Survey (EQLS) to the students of the University Program for older adults of the University of Burgos (PIE). SHS Web of Conferences, XX. (2017)
25. V. Baños-Martínez. Health-related Quality of Life of the students of the University Program for older adults of the University of Burgos (PIE): comparative study. SHS Web of Conferences, XX. (2017)
26. D. D.Sungatullina, E. O.Murtazina, Y. N.Gorelova. Graduate curriculum: A need for a change. SHS Web of Conferences, XX. (2017)
27. Y. Loginov, I. Kovalev. Formation of research competence in university project-oriented training. SHS Web of Conferences, XX. (2017)
28. S. Artut. Incorporation of computational creativity in arts education: creative coding as an art course. SHS Web of Conferences, XX. (2017)
29. M. S.Erzeybek, F. Kaya, O. Yüksel, M.B. Karavelioğu, H.Harmancı, A. Ersoy. Studying hand grip strength development among students who have taken tennis and massage courses. SHS Web of Conferences, XX. (2017)
30. M. Ilkım, M. Özdemir, H. Tanır. Evaluation of some physical and motoric characteristics of athletes with down syndrome. SHS Web of Conferences, XX. (2017)
31. M. Özdemir, H. Tanır, M. Ilkım, M. Özmaden. The effects of 8 week exercise program on reaction time performance of hearing impaired students at 11-14 years of age. SHS Web of Conferences, XX. (2017)
32. T. Kızılet Bozdoğan, A. Kızılet, B. Biçer. The effect of morphological characteristics on the physical and physiological performance of Turkish soccer referees and assistant referees. SHS Web of Conferences, XX. (2017)
33. S. Yildirim, M. C. Bölen, G. Yildirim. Learners' views about cloud computing-based group activities. SHS Web of Conferences, XX. (2017)
34. B. Taş, H. Akdeniz, G. Sekban, F. Öztürk. The awareness level of the parents about the benefits of the physical education lesson in secondary grade of the primary education schools. SHS Web of Conferences, XX. (2017)
35. Ü. Gezer. The definition of success in education and new approaches. SHS Web of Conferences, XX. (2017)
36. N. Çiftçi, A. Bedük. The relationship between organizational commitment and whistleblowing tendency: An empirical research. SHS Web of Conferences, XX. (2017)

37. N. Çiftçi, E.Ertürk, B. Doğanalp, E. Kızıloğlu. The effects of academic mentoring perceptions of research assistants on their organizational commitment. SHS Web of Conferences, XX. (2017)
38. H. Polat, F.B. Emre. Misconceptions about the particulate structure of science teacher candidates. SHS Web of Conferences, XX. (2017)
39. S. Demir Kaçan, F. Şahin. Levels of prospective science teachers' ability to structure 5E model. SHS Web of Conferences, XX. (2017)
40. S. Demir Kaçan, D. Çelikler. Importance of pre-school science education. SHS Web of Conferences, XX. (2017)
41. C.Ç. Ötkan, G. Tekkurşun Demir, A.Halıcı. Examination of group cohesiveness levels and goal orientations of basketball players
42. Tekkurşun Demir, A. Halıcı, C. Ç. Ötkan. Examination of burnout levels and academic procrastination of university students. SHS Web of Conferences, XX. (2017)
43. S. Selvi, E. Karagün. An analysis of decision making strategies of Kocaeli region football referees. SHS Web of Conferences, XX. (2017)
44. N. Aydogan, H. Polat, O. Cankaya, F. B. Emre. Effect of learning approaches of pre-service science teachers on the argument create skills. SHS Web of Conferences, XX. (2017)
45. Arslan, M. Atlı, Z. Özkan, Ş. Kaplan. In Turkey, factors which urge physically handicapped sporters to start badminton sport and their expectations. SHS Web of Conferences, XX. (2017)
46. Z. Özkan, M. Atlı, E. Arslan. Evaluation of attitudes of university students for handicapped individuals. SHS Web of Conferences, XX. (2017)
47. Kaya, M. S. Erzeybek, B. Biçer, T. Meral. Effects of in-water and dryland warm-ups on 50-meter freestyle performance in child swimmer. SHS Web of Conferences, XX. (2017)
48. Güvenç. The effect of awareness raising about using cognitive strategies in foreign language teaching on students' development of reading comprehension skills. SHS Web of Conferences, XX. (2017)
49. Kaya. The Effects of One Day Wrestling Tournament on Muscle Damage and Delayed Onset Muscle Soreness of Male Wrestlers. SHS Web of Conferences, XX. (2017)
50. Ö. Özcan. Examination the pre-service physics teachers' cognitive structure about the concept of "torque". SHS Web of Conferences, XX. (2017)
51. C. Gercek. An analysis of students' cognitive structures in relation to their environmental sensitivity. SHS Web of Conferences, XX. (2017)
52. C. Şahin, H. Kumcağız. The relationship between critical thinking disposition, problem solving and empathetic tendency in counsellor candidates. SHS Web of Conferences, XX. (2017)
53. Kumcağız, C. Şahin. The relationship between quality of life and social support among adolescents. SHS Web of Conferences, XX. (2017)
54. İ. Yalçın, F.Çalık, F. Ramazanoğlu, Ö. F. Tutar. Research on the Achievement Motivation Levels of the Amateur Football Players. SHS Web of Conferences, XX. (2017)
55. Gü. Uysal, D. Sönmez Düzkaya, A. Karakoç. Knowledge and Opinions of Parents of Children Hospitalized in Hematology/ Oncology Units Regarding Complementary and Alternative Medicine. SHS Web of Conferences, XX. (2017)
56. A.Damar, E. Eskiler. The impact of spiritual leadership on empowerment and work procrastination. SHS Web of Conferences, XX. (2017)
57. Yağcı, M. Çevik. Predictions of Academic Achievements of Vocational and Technical High School Students with Artificial Neural Networks in Science Courses (Physics,

Chemistry and Biology) in Turkey and Measures to be Taken for their Failures. SHS Web of Conferences, XX. (2017)
58. Ersoy, O. Yüksel, M. Erzeybek, H. Harmancı, M. B.Karavelioğlu. Effects of Different Strength Training Methods on Dynamic Balance in Basketball Players. SHS Web of Conferences, XX. (2017)
59. R. Eynur, A. Eynur, M. S. Erzeybek. Studying Attention Levels of the University Students from Various Sport Branches. SHS Web of Conferences, XX. (2017)
60. R. Eynur, A.l Eynur. Studying the Intended Uses of the Social Networks by the Students of the Department of Physical Education and Sport. SHS Web of Conferences, XX. (2017)
61. Taşvuran Horata, S. Erel. Evaluation of Low Back and Neck Pain and Disability of Interns at Physiotherapy and Rehabilitation Department of Afyon Kocatepe University. SHS Web of Conferences, XX. (2017)
62. Taşvuran Horata, S.Erel. Evaluation of professional awareness in physiotherapy and rehabilitation students of Afyon Kocatepe University. SHS Web of Conferences, XX. (2017)
63. N. Akyurt. An innovative approach study "Health students example". SHS Web of Conferences, XX. (2017)
64. N. Akyurt. Smoking of health students "State and Foundation University Example". SHS Web of Conferences, XX. (2017)
65. O. Kavi, H. Akdeniz, F. Y. Kömrükçü. The Factors Effect the Venue Selection and Joining to Physical Activity of the Users Visit 'Özgürlük Park and Recreation' area for Physical Activity. SHS Web of Conferences, XX. (2017)
66. Pedrero-García. Health education in the spanish education system. SHS Web of Conferences, XX. (2017)
67. E. Ticha. Teaching vocational subjects in a foreign language. SHS Web of Conferences, XX. (2017)
68. E. Zhuravleva, R. Mardanshina, M. Kudryavtseva, A. Khusainova. Extension activities of Kazan Imperial University in the 19th century. SHS Web of Conferences, XX. (2017)
69. Kalganova , Z. Kirillova. A brief history of the Tatar language teaching in universities in the 1920s and 1930s. SHS Web of Conferences, XX. (2017)
70. T.-M. Iconomescu, V. Mindrescu, L.-G. Talaghir. The Importance of Motion Games in the Psychomotor Development of Pre-schoolers during the Physical Education Class. SHS Web of Conferences, XX. (2017)
71. T.-M. Iconomescu, M. Ciapa. The development of spatial orientation and laterality in physical education classes from the countryside - pilot test. SHS Web of Conferences, XX. (2017)
72. Loginova. Two focus interactive learning: improving the quality of vocational training and the possibility of life self-fulfillment. SHS Web of Conferences, XX. (2017)
73. Tříska, H. Čtrnáctová. The Verification of Educational Objectives in the Chemistry Education of the Czech Republic. SHS Web of Conferences, XX. (2017)
74. Wojniak, K. Orzeł-Dereń. Preschool and Early School Education of Migrants and Minorities in Poland. Teachers' Competences in the Light of Regulations and Practice. SHS Web of Conferences, XX. (2017)
75. Kiss. Measuring the ICT Competencies in Slovakia and in Serbia in The Higher Education. SHS Web of Conferences, XX. (2017)
76. G.Kiss, P. Csiba. Analyzing of the Self Reported ICT Literacy Level of Slovakian and Serbian Students in the Higher Education. SHS Web of Conferences, XX. (2017)

77. S. Hamón, F. Casani, Je.Rodriguez-Promeda, R. O. Albacete. Project-Based Learning in the teaching-learning process University. A longitudinal study. SHS Web of Conferences, XX. (2017)
78. R. Ismagilova, I. M. Solodkova, E. V. Grigorieva. Cultural aspect in the course materials for the vocational training programs. SHS Web of Conferences, XX. (2017)
79. E. M. Galishninkova, L. V. Khafizova. The model of the first-year students' adaptation to vocational training: the example of foreign language . SHS Web of Conferences, XX. (2017)
80. Al-Qudah. The Jordanian terms of address: Asocio-pragmatic study. SHS Web of Conferences, XX. (2017)
81. V. Panfilova, A.Panfilov, A.Gazizova, N.Samarina. Professional and communicative foreign language competence of future teachers. SHS Web of Conferences, XX. (2017)
82. Y.D. Merih, K.D. Beydağ. Integration of health service with electronic nursery care process. SHS Web of Conferences, XX. (2017)
83. N. Gökbulut, K.D. Beydağ. The effects of women's satisfaction with their birth experience on breastfeeding sufficiency. SHS Web of Conferences, XX. (2017)
84. S. Ulutas, S. Groth, W.Thiems, M. Niehaus. Participation of academics with disabilities in science using the example of AKTIF project. SHS Web of Conferences, XX. (2017)

Looking for new active methods to improve the school performance: Physical activity!

Alberto Ruiz-Ariza[1a], Sebastián López-Serrano[1], Sara Suárez-Manzano[1], and Emilio J. Martínez-López[1]

[1]Faculty of Humanities and Education Sciences, University of Jaen, Campus Las Lagunillas s/n, Jaen, Spain

Abstract. The practice of physical activity (PA) has recently been used as a stimulant to improve the cognitive performance in young people and to have positive repercussions on the academic performance [2]. The aims of this research were to conceptualize the relationship between PA and cognition, as well as to associate different physical qualities with better or worse school performance, and thus to be able to make decisions about the kind of PA more adequate to foment from the educative and familiar areas. Our findings are in line with previous literature, and show that a higher physical fitness is associated with better school performance. In conclusion, our study suggests that it is necessary to strengthen the daily PA practice within school context, as well as to raise awareness among families and society about PA promotion.
Keywords: Physical activity, families, school performance.

1 Introduction

The practice of physical activity (PA) is presented as a great opportunity to improve health, prevent diseases or increase life expectancy [1]. In addition, in recent years, a new neuroscience stream is being focused on studying the effects of PA on the brain and its performance, either short-term or long-term [2]. These findings have reached schools and there are increasing studies that also link PA practice with improvements in academic performance (AP) of children and adolescents [3].

The PA is a very broad term that encompasses several kinds of activities. Among these activities is the physical fitness (PF). The level of PF, especially aerobic fitness, has been associated with better cognition in numerous studies [4]. In the last decade there has been a great increase of studies studying the relation between PF and cognition, however the results are still not conclusive, since few studies analyze the differences in function of the different components of PF, and there are few proposals about these components based on the real educational context [5, 6].

[a] Corresponding author: arariza@ujaen.es

2 Objective

The present research aims to conceptualize the relationship between PA and cognition, as well as to associate different physical qualities with better or worse school performance, and thus to be able to make decisions about the kind of PA more adequate to foment from the educative and familiar areas.

3 Sample

788 adolescents between 12-18 years participated in the present pilot study. The parents, directors and teachers of PE were informed about the study. Informed consent was obtained from parents or legal guardians.

4 Methodology

A mixed method was used through bibliographical review, quantitative analysis and theoretical-practical educational proposal.

4.1 Bibliographic review

Two specialized databases were used and the search was limited to the last 10 years. The search terms used can be seen in Table 1. The search was conducted in English.

Table 1. Search strategies in databases.

SportDiscus (EBSCO)	TX ("physical fitness" OR fitness OR "physical education") and TX ("cognitive performance" OR "academic performance" OR "academic attainment" OR "academic achievement" OR "academic outcomes") and TX (adolescent* OR children OR childhood OR teenager*)
Web of Science	("physical education" OR "physical fitness") AND ("cognitive performance" OR "academic performance" OR academic attainment OR academic achievement OR academic outcomes) AND (adolescent OR teenager OR children OR childhood)

4.2 Empirical research

A cross-sectional design was used. The ALPHA-Fitness battery was used [7], and academic qualifications in Mathematics and Language were used for AP [8].

4.3 Controlled confusion variables

The socio-educational level was obtained through the educational level of the mother, with the following options: without studies, primary education, secondary education, university education. Mothers were asked directly using a questionnaire [9]. In addition, gender and age were taken into account [8].

4.4 Statistical analysis

Data are presented as mean and SD or n (%). Differences between genders were compared by one-way ANOVA for continuous variables and the $\chi 2$ test for nominal variables.

Preliminary analyzes showed no significant interaction between variables (all p> .05); Therefore, we decided to carry out the analyzes with the total sample. The association of PF and AP was analyzed by linear regression. The regression model was controlled by sex, age, BMI and educational level of the mother. The analyzes were performed with the statistical software SPSS version 22.0 for Windows (SPSS Inc., Chicago). The criterion for statistical significance was set at p <.05.

5 Results and discussion

The flow of articles in the search for results can be observed in fig. 1.

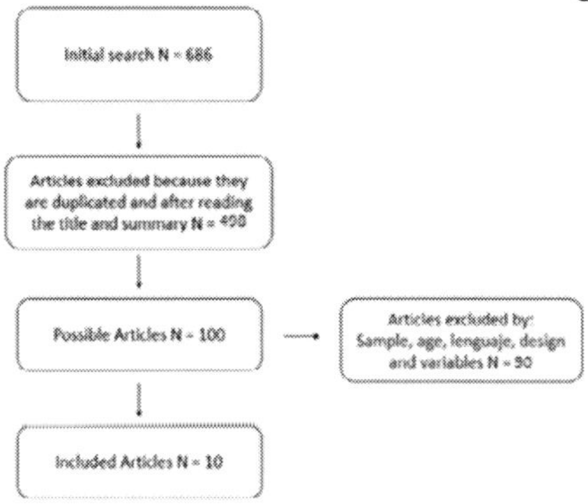

Fig. 1. Flow of articles through the search process.

10 articles were selected. 5 of them were cross-sectional [9-13], 3 interventional [5, 14-15], 1 longitudinal, and 1 had a double design (cross-sectional and longitudinal) [16]. PF variables were aerobic capacity, muscle strength, motor ability, coordination and flexibility. Over sixty percent of the studies included covariates, including socio-educational level of families, BMI, sex, and age. Most of studies showed a positive relationship between PF and cognition. Aerobic capacity, motor ability, coordination and perceptual ability are the components that are mostly associated with cognition in young people, however, the relationship to muscle strength or flexibility is unclear.

On the other hand, our own empirical cross-sectional research, has also shown that PF is associated with AP after adjusting by sex, age, BMI and maternal education. Specify, aerobic and motor ability were associated with Mathematic and Spanish Language. However, muscular strength is no related with any AP variable.

Previous studies have shown that it is related to better performance in several cognitive abilities, such as inhibitory control, working memory and attention [7]. In this sense, proposing intervention programs that include aerobic and motor training may improve PF, and therefore have positive effects on the brain. Some explanations may be the neurogenesis, angiogenesis or synaptogenesis that could increase the brain activity and the number of neuronal synapses, leading to increased BDNF and the reorganization of motor representations of motor cortex [17], with direct effect on cognitive performance and academic achievement.

6 Educational proposal

Based on our findings and the studies of [5, 6], and [3], we intend to include the practice of PA as a tool to increase cognition in the Educational Center. To this one, we propose:

- In PE classes: To create didactic units that have as objective the increase of the aerobic capacity. For example by including the HIIT method [18]. In addition, include the training of motor skill and coordination through agility circuits and the use of implements.

- Just before each class: 10 minutes of coordination exercise and motor skill improves attention and concentration, so we recommend that you spend that time before each class to activities of this type [14]. This would lead to an approximate daily increase of 60 minutes of PA practice (minimum recommended by WHO).

-Between classes: Include breaks of 5-8 minutes in the middle of the classes to make some coordination or motor skill play with the aim of arousing attention and concentration, for example: The ten passes with the non-dominant hand with a tennis ball, and having than keeping a leg still as a pivot.

- Just before and after the school day: Encourage active commuting to and from the Educational Center. Previous studies have already demonstrated its benefits at the cognitive level [19].

- Extracurricular PA: The practice of aerobic or motor PA during out-of-school hours may also be beneficial for the cognitive performance of young people [9], so fostering this practice from the public and family sectors is crucial.

7 Conclusion

In conclusion, aerobic capacity, motor ability and coordination may have a potential influence on the cognition of adolescents. We suggest that PE teachers give more importance to the aerobic and motor component in their classes and we encourage the promotion of joint actions in a multidisciplinary way between PE subjects and the instrumental subjects, as well as to promote an increase in aerobic fitness and motor skills during adolescence, from the educational, political and family spheres.

References

1. World Health Organisation. Extracted on 02 march 2017 in http://www.who.int/topics/physical_activity/es/ (2015)
2. A. Ruiz-Ariza, A. Grao-Cruces, N.E.M. de Loureiro, E.J. Martínez-López, International Review of Sport and Exercise Psychology, **1**, 108 (2017)
3. M.J. Mullender-Wijnsma, E. Hartman, J.W. de Greeff, R.J. Bosker, S. Doolaard, C, Visscher, Journal of School Health, **6**, 365 (2015)
4. M.A.I. Aberg, N.L. Pedersen, K. Torén, M. Svartengren, B. Bäckstrand, T. Johnsson, … H.G. Kuhn, Proceedings of the National Academy of Sciences of the United States of America, **49**, 20906 (2009)
5. D.N. Ardoy, J.M. Fernández-Rodríguez, D. Jiménez-Pavón, R. Castillo, J.R. Ruiz, F.B. Ortega, Scandinavian Journal of Medicine & Science in Sports, **1**, 52 (2014)
6. J.E. Donnelly, K. Lambourne, Preventive Medicine, **52**, 36 (2011)
7. J.R. Ruiz, J. Castro-Pinero, V. Espana-Romero, E.G. Artero, F.B. Ortega, M.M. Cuenca, …M.J. Castillo, British Journal of Sports Medicine, **6**, 518 (2011)
8. A. Ruiz-Ariza, J. Ruiz, M. De la Torre-Cruz, P. Latorre-Román, E.J. Martínez-López, Revista Latinoamericana de Psicologia, in press, (2015)
9. I. Esteban-Cornejo, C.M. Tejero-González, D. Martinez-Gomez, J. del-Campo, A. González-Galo, C. Padilla-Moledo, …O.L. Veiga, The Journal of Pediatrics, **2**, 306 (2014)
10. R.W. Bass, D.D. Brown, K.R. Laurson, M.M. Coleman, Acta Paediatrica, **8**, 832 (2013)

11. D.P. Coe, T. Peterson, C. Blair, M.C. Schutten, H. Peddie, The Journal of School Health, **7**, 500 (2013)
12. J.C. Janak, K.P Gabriel., A.O. Oluyomi, A. Peréz, H.W. Kohl, S H. Kelder, The Journal of School Health, **8**, 533 (2014)
13. L.B. Sardinha, A. Marques, S. Martins, A. Palmeira, C. Minderico, BMC Pediatrics, **1**, 176 (2014)
14. H. Budde, C. Voelcker-Rehage, S. Pietraßyk-Kendziorra, P. Ribeiro, G. Tidow, Neuroscience Letters, **2**, 219 (2008)
15. A.K. Travlos, International Journal of Sport and Exercise Psychology, **3**, 302 (2010)
16. L.J. Chen, K.R. Fox, P.W. Ku, C.Y. Taun, The Journal of School Health, **9**, 631 (2013)
17. D.L. Adkins, J. Boychuk, M.S. Remple, J.A. Kleim, Journal of Applied Physiology, **6**, 1776 (2006)
18. S.A. Costigan, N. Eather, R.C. Plotnikoff, D.R. Taaffe, D.R. Lubans, British Journal of Sports Medicine, **19**, 1253 (2015)
19. D. Martínez-Gómez, J.R. Ruiz, S. Gómez-Martínez, P. Chillón, J.P. Rey-López, L.E. Díaz, …A. Marcos, Archives of Pediatrics & Adolescent Medicine, **4**, 300 (2011)

What is the relationship between parental support, self-efficacy and physical activity in young students? A pilot cross-sectional study

Alberto Ruiz-Ariza[1a], Manuel de la Torre-Cruz[1], Sebastián López-Serrano[1], and Emilio J. Martínez-López[1]

[1]Faculty of Humanities and Education Sciences, University of Jaen, Campus Las Lagunillas s/n, Jaen, Spain

Abstract. This study examined the relationships between parental support for physical activity, weekly Physical Activity (PA) practice frequency, and self-efficacy expectations to overcome barriers to participation. A total of 335 adolescents took part in this pilot cross-sectional study. The results show that boys and girls who attribute parents to a high level of instrumental support, modeling and behavioral limitation are allocated to higher number of days per week to perform the physical-sport activity during a minimum interval of sixty minutes and were more self-efficacious in their practice. Likewise, the frequency of practice of the activity and self-efficacy were higher in the case of boys.
Keywords: Physical activity, parental support, self-efficacy.

1 Introduction

The practice of physical activity (PA) maintains a positive relation with the physical and psychological health of children and adolescents [1]. Despite of these benefits, the percentage of young people who perform the recommended account of 60 daily minutes of physical-sport activity at moderate to vigorous intensity, has decreased in the last two decades [2, 3].

In this regard, Bandura's [4] cognitive-social theory, suggests that the provision of social support increases the self-efficacy to overcome obstacles and the possibility to be physically active. One of the main sources of support is in the family [5]. The different kinds of parental support (logistic, modeling, establishment of limits) could differentially affect the practice of PA, and the examination of their influence could further clarify these relationships [6, 7].

Thus, the objective of this study was to examine the relationships between parental support, weekly frequency of PA and expectations of self-efficacy.

---

[a] Corresponding author: arariza@ujaen.es

2 Method

A total of 335 students (girls = 175, 52.3%) with ages between 12 and 17 years (M = 13.8; SD = 1.36) participated in this pilot cross-sectional study.

2.1 Process

The parents, directors and teachers were informed about the purpose of this study. Informed consent was obtained from parents. The different questionnaires were applied during Physical Education classes. Participants had 50 minutes to perform the tests. The procedure for obtaining data took into account the current Spanish legislation for research in humans (Royal Decree 561/1993 on clinical trials), the law on protection of personal data (Organic Law 15/1999) and the Declaration of Helsinki.

2.2 Instruments

To assess parental support, a Spanish version of the "Activity Support Scale, ACTS" proposed, by Davison [8], was used. This scale is composed of nine items grouped into three factors: instrumental support ("It took me to places where I could perform PA"), modeling ("It encouraged me to be physically active / acting as an example and being a model") and establishing limits to sedentary behavior ("I have limited the daily amount of hours playing video games"). The participants had to indicate along a Likert four-point scale the degree of agreement (1 = total disagreement, 4 = total agreement). The reliability indexes obtained for this study sample were .73 for the instrumental support dimension, .71 for the modeling dimension, and .79 for the limit dimension to sedentary behavior.

The MVPA "Moderate-to-Vigorous PA" scale [9] reports the number of days during the previous week and any one week in which participants performed moderate to vigorous intensity PA for at least 60 minutes. A value of five or higher corresponds to the inclusion of the young person in the physically active category. The reliability index of the two items in the study sample was .84.

Self-efficacy for the practice of PA was evaluated using an eight-item questionnaire developed by Dishman et al. [10]. Some examples of the items included were: "I am able to engage in PA in my free time regardless of how busy or busy the day" and "I am able to ask my parents or other adults to engage in PA with me during my free time". The items were valued along a Likert scale in which the participant had to indicate their degree of agreement with the different affirmations. The range of values ranged from 1 (totally disagree) to 5 (totally agree). A single factor was obtained that explained 49% of the variance of the scores obtained. The reliability index for this study sample was .84.

3 Results

3.1 Relationship between parental support and frequency of PA

Three univariate analyzes of covariance (ANCOVAs) were performed to know the relationship between perceived family support for the practice of physical-sport activity and the reported frequency of weekly practice of MVPA. Because previous research reveals that body mass index and chronological age have a negative relationship with the enjoyment and frequency of PA practice, these two variables were included as covariates.

The first of the analyses revealed a statistically significant main effect of instrumental parental support, $F_{(1,38)} = 51.18$, $p <.001$, $\eta 2 = .13$ and the participant's gender, $F_{(1,389)} = 26.79$, $P <.001$, $\eta 2 = .07$ and the weekly frequency of PA.

On the other hand, the participants who attributed a greater practice of physical-sport activity to their parents showed a higher frequency of weekly practical activity (M = 3.59 vs M = 2.79). Likewise, boys were more frequently involved than girls in this type of activity (M = 3.58 vs M = 2.83).

The third of the analyses revealed, as in the previous cases, that the frequency of practice of PA was higher in young people who attributed to their parents a greater restriction to sedentary behavior (M = 3.41 vs M = 2.97).

3.2 Relationship between parental support and perceived self-efficacy for the practice of PA

The analyses revealed that the highest perceived self-efficacy scores for PA were observed in those participants who attributed to their parents a high degree of instrumental support (M = 29.38 vs. M = 24.01).

The second analysis showed the existence of a statistically significant main effect of the modeled variable, $F_{(1, 371)} = 46.25$, $p <.001$, $\eta 2 = .1$. Adolescents who considered that both mothers and fathers were frequent models of PA to imitate reported higher self-efficacy expectations for PA (M = 29.15 vs M = 24.03).

Finally, the last of the analyses showed a statistically significant main effect of the parental limitation of the sedentary behaviors, $F_{(1, 412)} = 13.48$, $p <.001$, $\eta 2 = .04$. The self-efficacy perceived for the practice of PA was greater in the group of adolescents who perceived in their parents a greater imposition of limits on the performance of sedentary behaviors (M = 27.56 vs M = 24.45).

4 Discussion

The results show that boys and girls who attribute parents to a high level of instrumental support, modeling and behavioral limitation are allocated to higher number of days per week to perform the physical-sport activity during a minimum interval of sixty minutes and were more self-efficacious in their practice. These results are in line with those reported by previous research [6, 11-12]. Likewise, the participants who considered their parents a greater modeling of behaviors associated to the practice of PA expressed to be more active and more self-efficacious in relation to their equals whose attributed parental modeling was smaller. In consonance with this finding, several authors examined the relationship between parents and children weekly PA by accelerometers [13]. The results revealed that modeling showed a positive relationship, although weak, between the practice of PA performed by parents and children. However, the relationship was higher when parents were divided between those who met the international recommendations of daily PA practice (at least 30 minutes at moderate to vigorous intensity) and those who did not this PA amount.

5 Conclusions

It is possible that the socialization processes analyzed in this study have a bi-directional nature where the parental practices associated with PA affect the attitudes and behaviors of the children while the latter offer certain keys to their parents who regulate the types and levels of family actions aimed at promoting participation in activities of a physical and sports nature. On the other hand, the use of self-report measures is an additional limitation

DOI: 10.1051/shsconf/20173701002

to this study. Evaluating possible associations by including objective measures of PA (for example, using the use of accelerometers) could become an interesting route of new researches.

References

1. F.K.W. Ho, L.H.T. Louie, C.B. Chow, W.H.S. Wong, P. Ip, BMC Pediatrics, **15**, 48 (2015)
2. K.K. Davison, G.D. Deane, Social Science Medicine, **70**, 518 (2010)
3. D.J. Graham, K.W. Bauer, S. Friend, D.J. Barr-Anderson, D. Neumark-Sztainer, Journal of Physical Activity and Health, **11**, 51 (2014)
4. A. Bandura, *Self-efficacy: The exercise of control.* (New York, Freeman, 1997)
5. Y. Laird, A. Fawkner, P. Kelly, L. McNamee, A. Niven, International Journal of Behavioral Nutrition and Physical Activity, **13**, 79 (2016)
6. S.J. Sebire, A.M. Haase, A.A. Montgomery, J. McNeill, R. Jago, Journal of Physical Activity and Health, **11**, 734 (2014)
7. K.K. Davison, R. Jago, Medicine & Science in Sports and Exercise, **41**, 1816 (2009)
8. K.K. Davison, Journal of Physical Activity and Health, **1**, 363 (2004)
9. J.J. Prochaska, J.F. Sallis, B. Long, Archives of Pediatrics and Adolescents Medicine, **155**, 554 (2001)
10. R.K. Dishman, D.P. Hales, J.F. Sallis, R. Saunders, A.L. Dunn, A.L. Bedimo-Rung, K.B. Ring, Journal of Pediatric Psychology, **35**, 72 (2010)
11. S.G. Trost, P.D. Loprinzi, American Journal of Lifestyle Medicine, **5**, 171 (2011)
12. M. Verloigne, J. Veitch, A. Carver, J. Salmon, G. Cardon, I. Bourdeaidhuij, A. Timperio, BMC Public Health, **14**, 996 (2014)
13. J. Jago, J.L. Thompson, S.J. Sebire, L. Wood, L. Pool, J. Zahra, D.A. Lawlor, International Journal of Behavioral Nutrition and Physical Activity, **11**, 54 (2014)

Nintento Wii as an educational implement. Reality or fiction?

Sebastián López-Serrano[1], Sara Suárez-Manzano[1], Alberto Ruiz-Ariza[1a], and Emilio J. Martínez-López[1]

[1]Faculty of Humanities and Education Sciences, University of Jaen, Campus Las Lagunillas s/n, Jaen, Spain

Abstract. The current society is in constant evolution in search of new methodologies that allow an integral formation of the students. The current scientific evidence has corroborated that one way to stimulate cognitive function is through the usual practice of physical activity (PA). It has been shown that the inclusion of play activities such as exergames (EX) during the academic day, helps to increase the amount of daily PA, as well as to improve socialization and cognitive performance. The aim of this research is to review if PA practice through the use of the Nintendo Wii console positively influences on cognition of children and adolescents. In conclusion, the practice of EX, and specifically the Nintendo Wii, can be key in the improvement of cognitive and academic performance.
Keywords: Nintendo Wii, cognitive performance, socialization.

1 Introduction

Recent studies have shown that the systematic practice of Physical Activity (PA) can contribute to the improvement of Cognitive Performance (CP) in children [1] and adolescents [2]. PA produces physiological adaptations such as increased blood flow by increasing levels of brain-derived neurotrophic factor (BDNF) that promotes neuron growth and survival by improving learning ability [3]. In addition, the practice of PA helps to reduce the high levels of sedentary that we are currently a great resource for improving health, disease prevention or increased life expectancy [4].

In relation to the above, active video games like the Nintendo Wii, appear as a key opportunity to increase the daily amount of PA in a playful way. These active video games present great popularity among young people, and their interactive dynamics generates a connection between the player and the game. In this way, the body movements are interpreted reflecting the activity carried out during its development in the device. In addition, this type of video game mode favors peer social relations [5] and increases caloric expenditure [6]. On the other hand, the potential that the Exergames (EX) present in the

[a] Corresponding author: arariza@ujaen.es

transformation of sedentary time into physically active time is known [7]. Therefore, knowing the relation of the use of the EX in the educational framework could favor to increase the levels of PA, the reduction of the sedentary time that children currently spend in the classroom [8] and favor their personal and social development, with direct consequences on school performance.

2 Objective

To carry out a current bibliographic review that associates the effect of the Nintendo Wii with the academic performance in children and adolescents.

3 Sample

Four interventional studies were included. The total sample of articles analysed ranged from 6 to 19 years. The total number of participants was 252 children and adolescents.

4 Methodology

Two specialized databases (SportDiscus and Web of Science) were used and the search was limited to the last 7 years. The search terms used can be seen in Table 1. The search was conducted in English.

Table 1. Search strategies in databases.

SportDiscus	Topic: (Exergames OR Nintendo Wii) AND Topic: (cognitive OR academic performance) AND Topic: (Children OR adolescent)
Web of Science	TX (Exergames OR Nintendo Wii) AND TX (Cognitive OR academic performance) AND TX (children OR adolescent)

The selection criteria used were:
1º) The study was performed with a healthy population.
2º) The population outside children and adolescents between 6 and 18 years.
3º) The EX and the variable of academic performance were clearly described.

5 Results

The flow of results obtained after the completion of the search is shown in Figure 1. After elimination of duplicates, excluded by title or age, a total of 126 articles were reviewed. These studies followed the review criteria discussed above. Finally, 4 articles were included for analysis.

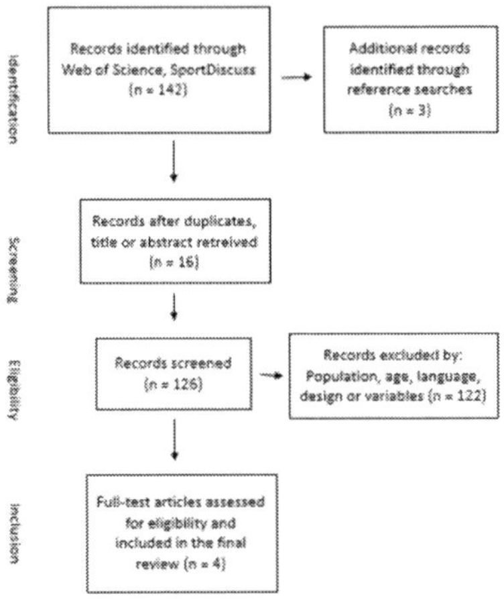

Fig. 1. Flow of articles through the search process.

The four studies selected were intervention studies [9-11]. 2 studies conducted the groups randomly [11,12] and 2 did not randomize groups [9,10]. They present a total of 252 subjects. All of them belong to the American continent (USA). The PA variables that were controlled were the heart rate [9], strength [11], the score given by the game after the practice session [10] and the time to go one mile before and after the intervention with the Nintendo Wii [10]. Performance measures at the cognitive level focused on executive functions. These studies included covariates, including socio-educational level of families, BMI, sex and age.

The studies showed a positive relationship between the PA level performed during EX and cognition. Best [9] demonstrated that with an EX session they improved the cognitive functions of children. Staiano et al. [11], after ten weeks of intervention, indicated that young people who practiced EX competitively and cooperatively improved their executive functions more than the group that did not perform any type of activity through these devices. On the other hand, Flynn et al. [12], showed that children who played for five weeks at EX improved their cognitive performance, and as they played more, they gained greater benefits. Gao et al. [10], following a six-week intervention, concluded that children undergoing EX practice performed better in terms of executive function and effort.

6 Discussion

The results of this review are related to the majority of previous research that relates a positive association between the play of any modality of EX and the improvement of cognition [8]. These studies showed benefits in cognitive aspects -attention, understanding and motivation- as academic achievement. Other studies focused on the benefits of active video games on health [6, 13], positively influencing an increase in caloric expenditure and a better level of fitness. On the other hand, information regarding the amount and intensity of exercise that is necessary to positively influence cognition is very scarce. Analyzing the degree of intensity (low / high) as a predictor of a better or worse cognitive response is the most appropriate, it would help the integration of this type of activities for its development in schools.

DOI: 10.1051/shsconf/20173701003

7 Conclusion

In conclusion, the use of the Nintendo Wii presents great potential for the development of activities during the school day. The PA that is needed during the development of this video game favors an improvement of the cognition in the children and adolescents. Therefore, the inclusion of this type of activities in the educational framework would help a greater motivation on the part of the students, having a positive effect on their academic performance. In addition, it highlights its social factor, benefiting the relationships between peers and teachers, as well as the health benefits associated with the practice of PA itself.

References

1. E.A. Haapala, Journal of human kinetics, **1**, 55 (2013)
2. D.N. Ardoy, J.M. Fernández-Rodríguez, D. Jiménez-Pavón, R. Castillo, J.R. Ruiz, F.B. Ortega, Scandinavian Journal of Medicine & Science in Sports, **1**, 52 (2014)
3. L. Chaddock, Heyman, C.H. Hillman, N.J. Cohen, A.F. Kramer, Monographs of the Society for Research in Child Development, **4**, 25 (2014)
4. World Health Organization (2015). Extracted on January **2**, 2016 in http://www.who.int/topics/physical_activity/es/
5. V.M. Nurkkala, J. Kalermo, T. Jarvilehto, Journal of Communication and Computer, **11**, 403 (2014)
6. N. Dutta, M.A. Pereira, Journal of Physical Activity and Health, **6**, 890 (2015)
7. A.G. LeBlanc, J.P. Chaput, Preventive Medicine (2016)
8. E. Norris, M. Hamer, E. Stamatakis, The Journal of Pediatrics, **172**, 40 (2016)
9. J.R. Best, Developmental psychology, **5**, 1501 (2012)
10. Z. Gao, J.E. Lee, Z. Pope, D. Zhang, Games for Health Journal, **5**, 318 (2016)
11. A.E. Staiano, A.A. Abraham, S.L. Calvert, Developmental psychology, **2**, 337 (2012)
12. R.M. Flynn, R.A. Richert, A.E. Staiano, E. Wartella, S.L. Journal of educational and developmental psychology, **1**, 209 (2014)
13. Z. Gao, S. Chen, D. Pasco, Z. Pope, Obesity reviews, **9**, 783 (2015)

Is the body composition equal or more important in physical fitness variables than other features like age or sex within physical education classes? A theoretical-practice study

Emilio J. Martínez-López[1], Sebastián López-Serrano[1], Sara Suárez-Manzano[1], and Alberto Ruiz-Ariza[1a]

[1]Faculty of Humanities and Education Sciences, University of Jaen, Campus Las Lagunillas s/n, Jaen, Spain

Abstract. The aim was to quantify the influence of body composition on the strength and cardiovascular endurance in adolescents. 858 Spanish adolescents participated in this pilot study. BMI values, standing jump test and Course Navette test were analyzed. The degree of influence of BMI was calculated by effect size. In the standing jump test, only between 18-25% of boys and between 17-36% of overweight girls got a distance equal or greater than those with normalweight. In Course Navette, only between 9%-19% of the boys and 23%-35% of overweight girls got equal or greater scores than those with normalweight. It is concluded that only a small percentage of adolescent overweight reach outcomes in strength and cardiovascular endurance equal or greater than the normalweight students. These results suggest that it would be necessary to include the body composition variable within the scales of scholar physical fitness test in young people.
Keywords: Physical education, body composition, adolescent.

1 Introduction

Health-related physical fitness is defined as the ability of a person to perform daily activities with vigor [1]. One way to assess physical fitness through the test or battery test of fitness. These are the different components of the same and individually as a whole, are related to sports performance or to the specific health and future of a person [2].

At present, there are more than 15 batteries and dozens of tests to assess physical fitness in children and adolescents [11]. Different researches have shown that physical fitness is higher in boys than girls [1, 3-5], Ortega et al. [5], have shown that levels of strength,

[a] Corresponding author: arariza@ujaen.es

speed/agility performance, and aerobic capacity are greater in adolescent boys, except flexibility where girls obtain higher results [5-6].

Another important fact is that adolescent boys increase physical fitness levels with increasing age, while in girls it is observed a maintenance level [2, 5-6]. Despite of these important variables, in the last years there is another variable that could mediate in the physical fitness scales in adolescents. In developed societies, obesity has been developed as the most frequent nutritional disorder during childhood and adolescence, and its prevalence has increased progressively during the last decades [7].

In relation to the developed countries, Spain presents very high values of obesity. In recent years, trends indicate an increase in the prevalence of overweight and obesity in children and adolescents [8], and the low levels of physical activity practice are some of the most determinant factors [9]. This increase in overweight can lead to significant limitations in physical fitness tests among young people and significantly affect the performance of adolescents during Physical Education classess [10-11]. In other words, physical fitness in adolescents is significantly better in normalweight than in overweight or obese people [2, 11].

2 Objective

Based on the above, this study aimed to quantify the influence of body typology (normalweight or overweight + obesity) on strength and cardiovascular endurance, measured with physical fitness test, in Spanish adolescents.

3 Methodology

3.1 Participants

The present descriptive-cross-sectional pilot study involved 858 adolescents (453 boys and 405 girls) and a BMI of 22.3 ± 3.9 kg/m2. The sample was for convenience. Data were collected from 8 Spanish secondary schools. The study was approved by the Bioethics Commission of the University of Jaén (Spain), with the consent of the parents or legal guardians. Participants were categorized into normalweight and overweight (overweight + obesity) adolescents, according to the specific cut-off points for each sex and age proposed by the Orbegozo Foundation's Research Institute on Growth and Development [12].

DOI: 10.1051/shsconf/20173701004

Table 2. Anthropometric characteristics and physical fitness parameters of the study sample according to sex.

	All (n= 858)	Boys (n= 453)	Girls (n= 405)	Sex Differences	Trending Age
Age	14.5 (1.3)	14.3 (1.3)	14.4 (1.3)	=	-
Wight (kg)	59.6 (13.6)	63.12 (14.7)	56.3 (11.42)	>	>
Height (m)	1.6 (0.2)	1.7 (0.2)	1.6 (0.2)	>	>
BMI (kg/m^2)	22.1 (4.1)	22.2 (4.3)	21.9 (4.1)	>	>
Normalweight (%)	72.4	73.5	71.3	=	>
Overweight (%)	27.6	26.5	28.7	=	>
Longitudinal Jump (cm)	153.3 (33.6)	172.8 (30.6)	132.5 (22.4)	>	>
$VO2_{Max}$ course navette (ml/Kg/min)	41.9 (7.1)	45.2 (6.6)	38.3 (5.1)	>	<

Data are expressed as mean (SD). The> symbol in "sex differences", means that the variable is significantly higher in men than in women (p <0.05); On the contrary; =, There are no significant differences. The> symbol in "trending age" refers to that variable tends to increase with increasing age (p <0.05); On the contrary; - not applicable.

3.2 Process

The level of muscular strength and cardiovascular endurance was assessed following the battery of physical health-related tests in young people, ALPHA-Fitness (Assessing Levels of Physical Activity) [1]. The muscular strength was measured with the long jump test. Cardiovascular Endurance was measured with the 20-meter shuttle-run test (Course Navette). The number of completed periods was transformed into maximal oxygen uptake (VO 2 max, ml / kg / min) through the Lèger equation [13]. In addition, weight (kg) and height (cm) were measured according to the protocols established in Ruíz et al. [1]. Both measures were carried out barefoot and in light clothing. As a derived variable, the BMI was calculated using the traditional Quetelet formula [weight (kg) / height2 (m)].

3.3 Static analysis

Anthropometric and fitness characteristics are presented in mean and standard deviation (SD) values unless otherwise noted. Differences between age in physical fitness variables (test) were analyzed by analysis of variance. To analyze the differences between sexes, by age group and body type in each of the physical fitness tests, the Student's T test was used. The degree of influence of body typology (overweight + obesity) on strength and cardiovascular endurance was calculated by the effect size analysis, which was quantified using the Hedges g statistic. The accepted level of significance was p <0.05. The data were analyzed with the SPSS program, version 22.0.

4 Results

Anthropometric characteristics and fitness parameters are presented in Table 1. Descriptive analysis showed that boys had significantly more weight, height and BMI than girls ($p < 0.05$). Physical fitness is better in boys and these variables tend to increase with increasing age.

The results obtained in the standing long jump test showed significant differences between normalweight and overweight adolescents (all $p < 0.05$). In boys with overweight ($p < 0.001$), only between 18% (g = 0.927; 0.803) and 25% (g = 0.677; 0.748) jumped a distance equal to or greater than normalweight students. However, in girls ($p < 0.01$) the differences were more heterogeneous, accentuating during the 17 years, where only 17% (g = 0.95; 0.819) of them obtained a score equal to or lower than the normalweight students.

The results obtained in the 20-meter shuttle-run test showed that there are significant differences between normalweight and overweight adolescents ($p < 0.02$), in all ages and both sexes. Only between 9% (g = 1,21, 0.91) and 19% (g = 0.913; 0.82) of overweight boys obtained a VO2 max. equal or higher than normalweight students. However, in overweight women, only between the 23% (g = 0.75; 0.78) and 35% (g = 0.41; 0.66) obtained a VO2 max. equal to or higher than normalweight students.

5 Discussion

This study aimed to quantify the influence of body typology on the results of strength tests and cardiovascular endurance in adolescents within each age range. The results of the present study have shown that the level of fitness is greater in boys than girls. It has also been shown that there are significant differences between adolescents of both sexes with normalweight and with excess of weight in the results of strength and cardiovascular endurance. In standing long jump test, only between 18%-25% of overweight boys get a distance equal to or greater than normalweight students, while in girls it range was from 17% to 36% . In the 20-meter shuttle-run test, only 9-19% of overweight boys had a VO2 max. equal to or higher than normalweight peers, while in girls this range from 23% to 35%. Therefore, the results suggest that it would be necessary to include the body type variable within the scales of assessment of strength and cardiovascular endurance in adolescents.

Our findings are similar to those obtained by previous studies that show that the body typology is determinant for the results of physical fitness. For example, Fogelholm et al., [10], indicated that overweight adolescents from Finland showed worse results of muscle strength and cardiovascular endurance than normalweight. However, excess of weight was associated to a lesser extent with motor skills. Similarly, Hsieh et al. [14], and Hanifah et al. [15], showed a high negative correlation between BMI and cardiovascular endurance in young men from Taiwan, Iran and Malaysia, respectively. In Spain, both muscle strength and cardiovascular endurance are negatively associated with total body fat and central body fat. However, strength was greater in overweight adolescents [16]. For some authors, overweight and obesity significantly affect the physical fitness level in adolescents [11]. Thus, it is especially important to establish adjustment measures in fitness batteries. So far, there are physical fitness scales based on sex and age in US youth [17], Australia [18], in some Asian countries [5, 14] and in Spain [6]. However, we have not found scales that include the body typology, therefore we cannot compare our findings with previous studies. Thus, the present study would be presented as an effective tool to improve the quality of the scales for Physical Education classes and thus, to improve the quality of teaching.

6 Conclusion

It is concluded that only a low percentage of adolescents between 13-17 years, with overweight and obesity, obtain a result of strength and cardiovascular endurance equal to or higher than the normalweight students. Thus, these results suggest that it would be necessary to include the body type variable within the physical fitness scales in adolescents.

References

1. J.R. Ruiz, V. España Romero, J. Castro Piñero, E.G. Artero, F.B. Ortega, M. Cuenca García,..., M.J. Castillo, Nutrición Hospitalaria, **26**, 6 (2011)
2. J.D. Secchi, G.C. García, V. España-Romero, J. Castro-Piñero, Archivos argentinos de pediatría, **2**, 132 (2014)
3. J. Castro-Piñero, E.G. Artero, V. España-Romero, F.B. Ortega, M. Sjöström, J. Suni, J. R. Ruiz, British journal of sports medicine, **13**, 934 (2010)
4. J.R. Gómez-Puerto, C.J. Berral de la Rosa, B.H. Viana Montaner, F.J. Berral de la Rosa, Archivos de medicina del deporte, **90**, 273 (2002)
5. F.B. Ortega, E.G. Artero, J.R. Ruiz, V. España-Romero, D. Jiménez-Pavón, G. Vicente-Rodríguez,..., M.J. Castillo, British journal of sports medicine, **1**, 20 (2011)
6. F.B. Ortega, J.R. Ruiz, M.J. Castillo, L.A. Moreno, M. González-Gross, J. Wärnberg, Á. Gutiérrez, Revista española de cardiología, **8**, 898 (2005)
7. L.A. Moreno, M.I. Mesana, M. González-Gross, C.M. Gil, F.B. Ortega, J. Fleta, ..., M. Bueno, International Journal of Obesity, **12**, 1798 (2007)
8. L. Serra-Majem, L. Ribas Barba, J. Aranceta Bartrina, C. Pérez Rodrigo, P. Saavedra Santana, L. Peña Quintana, Medicina clínica, **19**, 725 (2003)
9. S. Plachta-Danielzik, B. Landsberg, M. Johannsen, D. Lange, M.J. Müller, Public health nutrition, **11**, 1870 (2010)
10. M. Fogelholm, S. Stigmanl, T. Huisman, J. Metsamuuronen, Scand J Med Sci Sports, **18**, 162 (2008)
11. G. Botelho, M. Aguiar, C. Abrantes, Journal of Physical Education and Sport, **1**, 19 (2013)
12. C. Fernández, H. Lorenzo, K. Vrotsou, Curvas y tablas de crecimiento (estudio transversal) (Bilbao: Fundación Faustino Orbegozo Eizaguirre (2011)
13. L.A. Leger, D. Mercier, C. Gadoury, J. Lambert, Journal of sports sciences, **2**, 93 (1988)
14. P.L. Hsieh, M.L. Chen, C.M. Huang, W.C. Chen, C.H. Li, L.C. Chang, International Journal of Environmental Research and Public Health, **7**, 7275 (2014)
15. R.A. Hanifah, H.A. Majid, M.Y. Jalaludin, N. Al-Sadat, L.J. Murray, M. Cantwell, … A.M. Nahar, BMC Public Health, **14**, S5 (2014)
16. D. Moliner-Urdiales, J.R. Ruiz, G. Vicente-Rodriguez, F.B. Ortega, J.P. Rey-Lopez, V. España-Romero, L.A. Moreno, British Journal of Sports Medicine, **2**, 101 (2011)
17. J.C. Eisenmann, K.R. Laurson, G.J. Welk, American Journal of Preventive Medicine, **4**, S106 (2011)
18. M. Catley, G.R. Tomkinson, British Journal of Sports Medicine, **2**, 98 (2013)

Alternative teaching practices for inclusive education

Celia Corchuelo Fernández [1a], and Carmen María Aránzazu Cejudo Cortés[1]

[1] University of Huelva, Faculty of Educational Sciences, March 3 Avenue, 21071 Huelva, Spain

Abstract. The research that we carried out in this article tries to demonstrate how the good practices that the teachers of the Second Chance Schools have in their centers (significant learning, propinquity and support) are effective pedagogical tools to reduce rates of school failure and dropout and, in other cases, to eliminate those two hurdles that the education system has and which is exacerbated in certain social contexts. Basically, this research is articulated in a theoretical framework, a research process or methodological framework, results from that research and the establishment of conclusions.
Keywords: Inclusive education, alternative teaching, teachers

1 Introduction

This article go deep into school failure during the secondary education stage, with special emphasis in the context of social exclusion, due to the marked incidence of conditioning factors leading to poor performance, non-achievement of objectives, repetition of course and early school-dropout in adolescents between the ages of 12 and 15 at risk of exclusion, led to a possible insertion which will not be achieved due to not be qualified for it.

In order to turn this situation back, on the one hand we find studies [5] that analyze the possible causes of the increasing rate of schooling flaws and school failure in a poor area where the main objective is the labour integration of young people. Today generation has been beaten by early school leaving and the absence of degree or qualification given as a result the swap from the marginal area to the area with good social and economic prospects, which definitely brings, according to this study, is a new brand community that moves from reflection to action and accompanies adolescents in their transition from School to work.

On the other hand, we find projects like «Alternativas al fracaso escolar, prácticas pedagógicas para la inclusión» [4] centered on the research carried out by an interdisciplinary and interinstitutional team of teachers, linguists and psychologists, who went deep in the study of the causes and indicators of the phenomenon of school failure in contexts of social exclusion, with the aim of reversing it. In this study, special importance was given to pedagogical alternatives based on diversification and the proposal of a new

[a] Corresponding author: celia.corchuelo@dedu.uhu.es; carmen.cejudo@dedu.uhu.es

school model high social vulnerability environment, the so-called school with a community teacher program.

2 Significant learning, propinquity and support

It is inevitable to focus on the secondary stage in dealing with school failure, because it is the educational period in which its consequences become evident, although it has also been proven that their roots can be found in primary school. In most cases, due to the chance of joining the labor market and quitting schoolwork which the student, may not feel very comfortable, it is in the last cycle "or the last two years of compulsory secondary education" when students begin to "walk on the tightrope", considering early school dropout.

Due to this reason, there are three basic foundation that all students should have in mind if he is planning to join the Second Chance School. Firstly, to support those students who achieve their academic success [9]. Secondly, in order to achieve meaningful learning there must be a predisposition of the student to this type of assimilation and finally, there must be some kind of material that is potentially significant (so as to speak, that can be related in a non-arbitrary way with the cognitive structure of the student or with preconceptions).

The research about the theory of meaningful learning which was done a year before helps to elucidate the cases in which the assimilation is not significant, but repetitive or mechanical [10]. First, the author highlighted two main characteristics of meaningful learning whose absence cannot be just given: the receptive attitude or predisposition to learn significantly, and the preexistence of concepts of anchorage in the cognitive structure that can serve as a basis or contrast to the new information.

Based on the observations in the different secondary schools where support and reinforcement programs were developed, good teaching practices materialize when all the professionals who are part of the program are integrated in their framework, remaining in direct and continuous contact with students at risk of exclusion, evaluating results and introducing the changes they deem necessary, planning new practices and scheduling the teaching-learning process [8].

Teachers who are fully involved in these tasks are promoting educational engagement and, in this specific context, a series of values that include citizen education and solidarity learning.

3 Objective

The objective is to carry out a research process in which the teaching practices performed by a group of teachers of a second chance school are exposed.

Thus, this study aims to expose students to an alternative. In this sense, the research intends to present other options in which it is understood that each student is different, authentic, unique and disrespectful and that each of them can and have the capacity of achieving any goal that they want to accomplish.

4 Method

The methodological framework describes and shows the design of the research as a case study centered on the Institute of Secondary Education of Andalusia. In order to carry out this research, we have opted for a descriptive method, used to collect, organize, synthesize, present, analyze, generalize and conclude the results that arise from the different information collection instruments. This method involves the collection and systematic presentation of data to present a clear idea of a particular phenomenon or situation, evaluating the proposed objectives.

4.1 Sample

We have carried out our research based on the descriptive method from a multi-method approach, understood as a research strategy in which more than one method is used for the investigation of the same phenomenon or object of study. Their use is justified due to their flexibility to adapt to the demands of understanding and explanation of our reality, improving the research processes and products. That is the reason why, we have used the qualitative method through the interview and the quantitative method by means of the observation record.

The sample is based on twenty subjects, which were selected from a total of thirty subjects and reflects an excess number for such a case study.

5 Results

Regarding the results, on the one hand, an analysis of the interviews has been carried out. as well as a description of the families of codes and the frequency of occurrence in the interviews. Code families refer to the nomenclature that brings together a group of categories that have resulted from the analysis of the interviews conducted to the twenty subjects belonging to this research. The classification of families has been based on the model of social competence for students at risk of school failure [1], [11], [3], being the codes the descriptors of roles, profiles, skills, interactions, ideas, ways of acting, strategies, interventions, organization of the center.

On the other hand, a descriptive analysis of the observations. Using the conceptual model extracted from the principles that some authors have called "alternative instruction" [6], [7], or "authentic instruction" [2]. The underlying model identified after factor analysis identifies three factors: significant learning, proximity and support.

In order to identify possible relationships between variables, in the analysis of the observations, we proceed to perform an analysis of Spearman correlations, given that these are qualitative variables of an ordinal nature. This analysis allows to identify the significant correlations that are discussed below. In general, the analysis of correlations corroborates, in part, the underlying model.

That is, a strong direct correlation ($r = 0.481$, $p < 0.01$) was found between the variable "substantive conversation, substantive with his/her classmates" and "teacher-student relationship", both variables are identified with the denominated factor "proximity".

Secondly, a direct correlation ($r = 0.254$, $p < 0.05$) between "student participation" and "connection with students' experiences outside school" was verified, both variables being aspects of the so-called factor "significant learning". In this sense, "material coherence" correlates directly ($r = 0.186$; $p > 0.05$), but not significantly with "student participation", the third variable of the "meaningful learning" factor.

In the variable "reinforcement of personal aspects", it correlates directly and significantly ($r = 0.248$, $p < 0.05$) with "teacher-student relationship". It also maintains an inverse but not significant correlation with "student participation", which is reasonable evidence.

Finally the bivariate analysis of interviews and observations. We combine the data from the encodings of the interviews with those coming from the observations. Codes from both category systems are combined into the same database. The objective is to identify if there are relations between the teacher profile, codified through the interviews, and the didactic actions, codified through the observations. As already indicated, observed behaviors are

DOI: 10.1051/shsconf/20173701005

recorded on an ordinal scale with values ranging from 1 to 4, while codes related to the teaching profile will be presented in the database on a nominal scale indicating presence or absence of the code, in this case of teaching trait.

For the combination of product codes of different instruments (interview and observation) a contrast of means is made, identifying as independent variables the interview codes that define teacher attitudes, while the dependent variables are those that define the didactic action in the classroom of teachers. Therefore, the following attitudes are considered as independent variables: discipline-affection balance, accompaniment, empathy and involvement.

Likewise, as dependent variables, the following are considered: Material coherence, connection with student experience, substantial conversation, student participation, higher order thinking skills, teacher-student relationship, reinforcement of personal aspects and leadership.

6 Conclusions

We have tried to know the educational responses that teachers display in Second Chance Schools through a case study focused on secondary school in Andalusia, but whose conclusions could be extended to other centers with similar characteristics. To this end, we have compiled a model of educational attention that is put into practice with students characterized by a trajectory of school failure and the risk of social exclusion. In our study, we have compiled and defined good teaching practices emphasizing those that in this particular center are obtaining positive results and have again attracted the education system to boys and girls who had abandoned it or at least perceived it with large doses of Skepticism, getting them not to resign, give themselves a second chance and find a motivation that opens new horizons and personal and educational expectations.
About:

6.1. Pedagogical practice

6.1.1 Significant learning

- Teachers of Second Chance Schools deal in depth with key concepts or ideas, basic to teaching, presenting topics in an integral, non-fragmented and offline.
- Students seem to respond to this work methodology, since when applied properly, they focus on the task to be developed, significantly decreasing attention loss and disruptive behaviors.

6.1.2 Proximity

The preponderant attitude in the Second Chance Schools is to maintain a strong relationship of trust between the teaching staff and the majority of the students. There is also often a very positive support. This is reflected in the conversations held between teachers and students, which allow establishing friendly relations and are capable of generating mutual trust.

6.1.3 Support

Teachers of Second Chance Schools use positive reinforcement, working on self-esteem/motivation and personality characteristics of students. At the same time, specific leadership characteristics are observed in these schools, since most of the teachers maintain, as a form of leadership, a certain balance between authority and democratic consensus.

6.2 Pedagogical alternatives from Second Chance Schools

6.2.1 Motivation, one of the keys

In order to face this situation, the teacher starts from the idea of understanding motivation as one of the keys in the teaching-learning process, since its lack causes a good part of the school failure and the premature abandonment of the classrooms, besides generating conflicts within them.

6.2.2 Teacher-student relations

Dialogue and closeness, supported by the action of the center's psychological and pedagogical team, make it possible to diagnose gaps, as well as detecting the strengths and weaknesses of each student separately, and in this way to design and plan the individual and collective didactic strategy. Therefore and despite the levels of self-esteem and motivation are low, there will always be a small door to enter and "awaken" the students of the disengagement, making him see that he can change his career and take charge of his own growth as a person through the education.

6.2.3 Importance of class climate

To cope with this situation, an suitable class atmosphere will generally begin; establishing limits during the first weeks of the course, keeping them intact throughout the academic year, providing rules that are visualized in the classroom in panels or walls, maintaining a relationship of empathy and trust with students, training in reciprocity relationships.

6.2.4 Presence in the tutorials

In this regard, the subjects of the sample consider detrimental and counterproductive to strengthen the habits of reciprocity and mutual respect especially in Secondary and in educational contexts in which diversity becomes fundamental, the change of tutors and teachers that annually takes place.

References

1. Comer, J. P. The Yale-New Haven Primary Prevention Project: A follow-up study. Journal of the American Academy of Child and Adolescent Psychiatry, **24**, 154–160 (1985)
2. D'Agostino, F. Interpretación y hermenéutica. Revista de fundamentación de las Instituciones Jurídicas y de Derechos Humanos, **35**, 39-56 (1996)
3. Dumas, J. E., Prinz, R. J., Smith, E. P., Laughlin, J. The EARLY ALLIANCE Prevention Trial: An Integrated Set of Interventions to Promote Competence and Reduce Risk for Conduct Disorder, Substance Abuse, and School Failure. Clinical Child and Family Psychology Review, **2,** 1, 37-53 (1999)
4. Gabbiani, B., y Kachinovsky, A. El fracaso escolar. Prácticas pedagógicas para la inclusión. (2010). Retrieved from http://www.psico.edu.uy/sites/default/files/cursos/ps-educacional_alternativas_al_fracaso_%20escolar.pdf on 16.03.2017

5. Gallardo, M.C., y Nieto, C. El fracaso escolar y la exclusión social en una zona de transformación social, zona sur de Sevilla: causas, actuaciones, estrategias y perspectivas futuras de intervención social. RevistaRets, **14**, 11-117 (2009)
6. Knapp, M., Cambridge, P., Thomason, C., Beecham, J., Allen, C., Darton, R. Care in the Community: Challenge and Demonstration. Avebury, Aldershot. (1992)
7. Newman, F. M., Wehlage, G.G. Five standars for authentic instruction. EducationalLeadership, **50,** 87, 15-19 (1993)
8. Ritacco, M.J., y Amore, F.J. Buenas prácticas educativas ante el fracaso escolar en los programas de apoyo y refuerzo en contextos de exclusión social. Revista de currículum y formación del profesorado, **15**, 118-137 (2011)
9. Rodríguez, M. La teoría del aprendizaje significativo: una revisión aplicable a la escuela actual. Revista Electrònicad'Investigació i InnovacióEducativa i Socioeducativa, **3**, 29-50 (2011)
10. Rodríguez, M.L. La teoría del aprendizaje significativo en la perspectiva de la psicología cognitiva. Barcelona: Editorial Octaedro (2010)
11. Smith, E.P., Connell, C. M., Wright, G., Sizer, M., Norman, J. M., Hurley, A., Walker, S. N. An ecological model of home, school, and community partnerships: Implications for research and practice. Journal of Educational and Psychological Consultation, **8**, 339–360 (1997)

Emotional and social representations of future teachers about sexually transmitted diseases

Carmen María Aránzazu Cejudo Cortés [1a], and Celia Corchuelo Fernández[1a]

[1]University of Huelva, Faculty of Educational Sciences, Campus el Carmen, Avenida 3 de marzo s/ n, 21071 Huelva,Spain

Abstract. Health Education programs for young people have drastically increased in recent years in Spanish universities. In part, this is due to the fact that new cases of infection of a sexually transmitted disease continue happening, especially at this stage, and universities as an educational space in which a large number of young people are concentrated, must address this problem. Training young students in promoting healthy sexual habits will prevent not only new infections, but also facilitate the acquisition of competences in the students of the health and socio-educational areas, necessary for their later professional development. This research provides some information about the knowledge and attitudes of students of educational qualifications about HIV/AIDS, with particular relevance to the emotions and social representations that the students have about this fact and that can interfere in their lack of information making them more vulnerable to the disease.
Keywords: Diseases, sexual habits, young students.

1 Introduction

Despite the obvious progress made in scientific research, antiretroviral therapy and dissemination of information on HIV/AIDS, there is still a long way to go, especially in preventing new infections and the consequent need to maintain and strengthen Social and educational actions. Over the world, but particularly in countries with more economic resources, access to pharmacological treatment has led to a dramatic decline in AIDS mortality [1]. However, even in these countries, there are still problems to control this pandemic, with worrying data such as the stability of the number of new cases per year, mostly in young people, and the late diagnosis in many of them [2].

At present, the young population is the world's most vulnerable due to risky sexual practices, which is the main route of contagion. In addition, a great number of infected people are unaware of their serological status, which favors the progression of infection and

[a] Corresponding author: carmen.cejudo@dedu.uhu.es; celia.corchuelo@dedu.uhu.es

the spread of the virus [3-5]. For all these reasons, they insist on the need to promote and develop socio-educational prevention and intervention policies.

Multisectoral plan against HIV infection and AIDS in Spain [6] points out that for years our country has maintained infection rates above the EU average, despite efforts to prevent new infections. This report indicates that there are between 120,000 and 150,000 Spanish citizens infected with HIV and that more than a quarter of them are unaware that they are. And that each year there are between 2,500 and 3,500 new diagnoses that mainly affect young people. This fact, that is to say, the vulnerability of young people to HIV, basically due to their risky sexual practices, led us to ask ourselves about the level of knowledge and the type of attitudes they have in relation to this disease, as a starting point to support effective socio-educational intervention. This intervention can only be implemented with conscious and well-educated educators in relation to this problem. Do our current students have, I mean, those who will become teachers the perception of having that training? What are your attitudes towards HIV/AIDS?

The Teaching Innovation Project titled "*Mejora de la acción tutorial individual y grupal en programas de educación para la salud y prevención del VIH/SIDA*" of the University of Huelva and whose main investigators are the authors of this article, aims to address not only the attitudes, but also the knowledge and representations of this student population. Our study, as will be seen below, tries to find out by means of a thoroughly elaborated questionnaire, which was applied to a sample of more than six hundred subjects, as well as several groups of discussion and analysis of documents elaborated by the subjects of the sample.

2 The promotion of health in Spanish universities

The importance given to the promotion of healthy habits as a form of prevention of diseases and addictions has been progressively increased over recent years, finding one of its ideal frameworks in universities [7]. The main reasons for this formation are due to the fact that higher education institutions are the places where future professionals are prepared, who will play a relevant role in the public life of the country to which they belong and spend much of their time there during their student years. For this reason, the university is undoubtedly the site as well as the temporary space of life adequate to transmit good health practices, which will be consolidated in later years, impacting on the immediate environment, taking into account, the future impact that can have this training when dealing with students who in the near future will be education professionals [8,9].

It is also significant to choose precisely this stage of life of the individual for the intensive promotion of healthy habits, because that is when at greater risk is exposed in terms of sexuality and drug abuse. However, the intention of those who promote preventive and awareness-raising actions is that the attitude adopted by them is perpetuated and has a positive impact on the workplace, on social and family relations, on integration into a community and even at the citizen level. Not surprisingly, the university student must combine his knowledge and academic skills with those referring to health, since they will have to put them, in the same way, in practice in their personal and work future [10]. In the research presented in this article, the subjects who participated in the study will be in the near future, teachers and educators who will have to give an effective response to situations that may occur in a given educational context.

To sum up and in a global view, the conjunction of the objectives, the strategic lines and action, and the philosophy of the Universities Promoting Health, is described as much both as by the Spanish Network of Healthy Universities and by the research that supports the Movement and try to make improvements in it, and all of it is concluded the following:

«A Health Promotion University is concerned with developing institutional regulations that generate a healthy culture within the walls of the university, while offering educational activities, literacy and communication in health and prevention and care services.. It also integrates professional academic training in Health Promotion and Health Education into its university education programs and fosters research and evaluation in these fields from. It also seeks partnerships with other health promotion centers at community, national and international levels. And lastly, he gives an example of the reconstruction of his own infrastructures in pursuit of healthy habits» [11].

3 HIV / AIDS and social stigmatization

Since the first cases of seropositive children were known within the school environment (the first documented discrimination in Spain occurred in 1987) it was observed how, as the spread of the disease progressed, discriminatory attitudes were produced in all the social contexts, being obvious that they would also be produced in the educational institutions.Unjustified discriminatory attitudes continue to be produced during these more than 30 years due to the fear that promotes the probability of transmission, motivated by lack of information in this regard. In the research we address, it has been intended to know, among other issues, what can those people who are planning to work in education, do to face the hard task of changing social preconceptions about AIDS/HIV and value if they are ready to face that challenge. The need to improve the fundamental pedagogical tools and resources to address these difficulties in our work as teachers justifies in large part the interest of this study.

This fear has been unfounded or based on irrational fears and social and cultural prejudices, to which these professionals, as active components of their own society and culture, cannot escape [12]. Therefore, the need to change social attitudes and behaviors towards HIV is ratified, a transformation that is inevitably due to the suppression of prejudices without a demonstrable basis and irrational fears [13].

The FIPSE study [14] that addresses the arbitrary discrimination of people living with HIV or AIDS, states that training must be focused on permanently eradicating attitudes of discrimination and stigmatization towards people with HIV/AIDS and, if effective, will result in a "radical change of attitudes". Moreover, teacher training in general, and not only that of subjects related to health and medicine, should contain educational programs that change the popular imaginary or archetypal about this fact.

It is easily deductible that stigma is one of the main sources of negative attitude towards HIV, making it a sine qua non condition for rejection and discriminatory behavior towards infected and at-risk groups. Already warned of the consequences of stigma, being an attribute that socially discredits the person who owns it, leaving the individual defenseless against reactions of rejection that, in turn, favor isolation and trigger feelings of guilt and self-rejection, which do no more that worsen the social situation of the affected [15].

There are countries, as in the case of Nicaragua, in which the struggle focuses on other, more localized, prejudices, for example, those caused by macho behavior towards sexual behavior. That is why it is confirmed that higher levels of studies have not yet succeeded in eradicating the indisputable male predominance in the decision making on sexual habits and prophylaxis [16]. This form of discrimination causes a woman to lose her right to take care of herself and to decide on her health, with her own partner coming to blame and stigmatizing her if, as a result of the described attitude, she contracts the virus.

The possibility of providing this information to the most affected population group in the developed countries, the young population, and the choice of socio-educational qualifications to train these students in skills that develop healthy habits in their future educational centers, will help prevent risky sexual relations from the beneficiary students and also to develop their competences as professionals of the education. Education must respond to the social needs that occur in our environment and, therefore, the students of the different educational qualifications should develop in the not too distant future, projects that improve the quality of life of their students, implementing programs health education at school and promoting healthy sexual practices.

4 Methodological aspects and context of the research

The research work presented in these pages has a general objective to know the attitudes of students of educational qualifications to HIV/AIDS, to offer diverse socio-educational responses if it proves necessary. This study was developed in the Faculty of Education Sciences of the University of Huelva. Of a total of 2,076 students enrolled in this faculty, a sample of 613 subjects was selected for the completion of the questionnaire. Taking into account that 79.8% of the students surveyed are less than or equal to 25 years of age, we are looking at a valuable sample for the purpose of this study, since not only do we try to know how future teachers, teachers/as well as educators face such a stigmatized disease, we also gain an important record of knowledge, perceptions and attitudes of one of the most affected groups by the HIV epidemic in developed countries, young people. The participants in the discussion group were 11 students and 89 people studying Social Education have drawn up graphic documents on attitudes towards HIV. Therefore, a total of 713 students have been consulted on the subject that is addressed in this research work.

5 Results

Both in the review of the scientific literature and in the field study itself, we find that the attitude of future education professionals is an extremely important element in the prevention of new HIV and stigma contagion. Some of the results obtained in this study, reveal the need to continue training university students in health education. Some of the opinions of the subjects of the sample are collected in the following lines as examples.

One of the commonly widespread myths is that HIV is transmitted through saliva. 36.7% of the subjects of the sample think that two babies cannot share their dummies when one of them is HIV positive as there is a high risk of contagion. In the discussion group, we also discussed this question and we observe the doubts presented in this case when two babies share dummies or pacifier:

"But it has been said that by saliva but children often have blood on their teeth, you will lose a tooth. That swapping a pacifier is like when you exchange a toothbrush with your partner or something that causes you to get blood. Then it is already contact by the blood...So I think we should tell the parents because somehow they have to put them in the alternative or take the necessary measures to be aware of those things" subject 4 the discussion group.

On the other hand, 25.6% of the students express that they would change their son or daughter from daycare if they knew that there are children with HIV/AIDS as we see in the following graph:

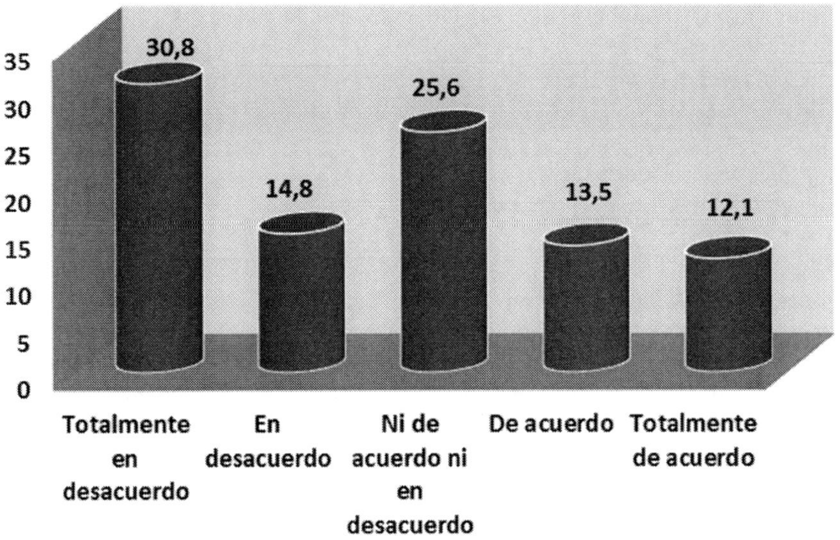

Fig. 1. Would you change your child's daycare if there were children with HIV/AIDS?

Another relevant fact is the one obtained when students were asked if they would "*take strict hygienic measures if they were teachers in a class where there are people with HIV/AIDS.*" 39.8% agree with this question as shown in the following graph:

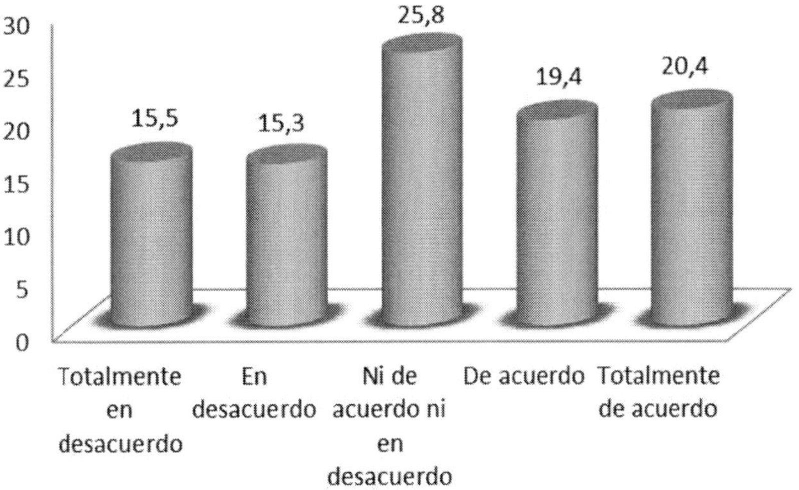

Fig. 2. Would you take strict hygienic measures if you were teaching in a class with HIV/AIDS people?

This fact encourages us to think that some of these strict hygienic measures carried out in a classroom could become discriminatory and possibly promote stigma. We already checked this fact in the questions that some of the subjects were asked when they participated in the discussion group, such as washing the clothes, or doubts about washing the dishes, cleaning the bathroom, etc. In the following lines we collect what the subjects of our discussion group thought if they should take special measures if there is an HIV positive child in a class:

"Do not intercalate in this case for example pacifiers, not take things to the mouth, be aware that if it falls, is that person who goes with adequate protection for that child "Subject 5 the discussion group.

"What protection?" Moderator

"For example gloves" Subject 5 the discussion group.

"That would be special treatment and we must treat all children equally." Subject 8 the discussion group.

*"Anyway in the hospitals with these people it is not that they use gloves is that it uses double glove"*Subject 2 the discussion group.

"That if they have a stepfather then they cannot be touched." Subject 9 the discussion group.

"This I do not know but take measures like the masks, in the sense that I might cough." Subject 6 the discussion group.

"I also think that a very important thing is also not taking too much care of us, we do not need to wear many gloves, face masks, because the other person ... is that they feel rejected. Subject 2 the discussion group.

42.4% of the students that were asked have the opinion that if they were parents, they would have the right to know if there are children or teenagers infected in their child's class. These results suggest the following question: If the chances of transmitting the infection by sharing a classroom with a classmate are nil, what is the information needed for? Then, this would result in the fomentation of discriminatory attitudes of other students or parents which have not been properly informed that subsequently would affect the normal integration of the minors.

The discussion group also discusses this issue and, as you can see, there is a diversity of opinions about this fact:

"The truth is that I think that if I were the father of a child and there is a partner who has HIV to me I would like to know." Subject 8 the discussion group.

"But it is very difficult because if they had the others, of course we would want to know but not if they were our children. That person deserves a little privacy". Subject 9 the discussion group.

When the students were asked "if, in the case of they were teachers, they think that the parents of the children of their classes should know if there are children with HIV/AIDS", we find that 41.4% fully agree or agree on the issue that we have addressed thinking that if they are teachers in a class with HIV positive children, the parents of the rest of the students, would have the right to know. We want to re-emphasize that if the chances of transmitting the infection by sharing a classroom with a classmate are null, it is not necessary to give that information, besides that we would violate the confidentiality of the data of the student in question, being able to provoke discriminatory attitudes by other students or parents not properly informed that would affect the normal integration of these HIV positive students.

With regard to the emotions and social representations that generate the subjects of this research the words HIV or AIDS, some express the following:

"People with HIV are marked for life" subject 36 document analysis.

"People with HIV should feel sad because they feel like a bird locked in a cage, which cannot fly freely or do anything that might appeal to them. Time passes and is consumed while he is not totally happy or has no solution to his problem "subject the 52 document analysis.

"I think people would flee from me if I had HIV/AIDS" subject 59 document analysis.

It can be seen how the social representations about HIV/AIDS (in almost half of the people that are part of this research) are still bound to a disease that provokes social rejection and isolation by the affected person. Disgrace, sadness, a truncated life evoked by death and loneliness, remains anchored in the representation of many people when referring to HIV.

Contrary to previous opinions, many of the students think that if they had HIV or AIDS, their daily lives would pass normally and they think they could do the same activities. Some examples of this are observed in the following narratives:

"Even if one has HIV, one can live in a positive way and lead a standardized life thanks to pharmacological treatment" subject 35 document analysis.

"But it would limit you, maybe, for example, when you have an accident and you stay in a wheelchair, you are really limited, but a person with HIV can lead a totally normal life" subject 3.

"You can live a normal life, where love, opportunities, support, affection, family, friends, treatment, fun and travel have room for you" subject 45 document analysis.

6 Conclusions

The data obtained in our research confirm that there is a large percentage of university students who, despite having received training in school institutions and in the university itself, still do not know basic aspects of HIV/AIDS. Providing more comprehensive, concrete and repeated information over time at an early age can contribute to the prevention of new infections and, in addition, avoid discriminatory attitudes towards people living with HIV.

It is necessary to insist on the development of educational initiatives to prevent the stigma that people with HIV suffer and try to change the imaginary and pejorative social representations that provoke such attitudes. This will prevent people with HIV from continuing to feel vulnerable and undervalued in their rights. But this can only be achieved through training that helps to shake the foundations anchored in disinformation and ignorance. The aim is to establish and develop educational programs that train students (professional education professionals) to empathize with people with HIV/AIDS, to make them agents that not only avoid discriminatory actions but actively contribute to change of attitude in the educational field preventing new infections.

Likewise, the results of this research warn us that there are plots in which to continue deepening in the scientific field, and in the proposals for socio-educational interventions that contribute to overcome the prejudices and stigma associated with HIV, as well as establishing a more effective prevention with the most vulnerable group in our country, young people.

References

1. ONUSIDA. El SIDA en cifras. Ginebra: Programa Conjunto de las Naciones Unidas sobre el VIH/SIDA (2015)
2. Maquera-Afaray, J., Cvetkovic-Vega, A., Cárdenas, M. M., Kälviäinen, H., Mejia, C. R. Diagnóstico tardío y enfermedad avanzada de VIH en pacientes adultos en un hospital de la seguridad social de Perú. RevChilenaInfectol, **33,** Supl 1, 20-26 (2016)
3. Rodríguez, M y Zamora C. Plan Andaluz frente al VIH/SIDA y otras ITS (2010-2015). Junta de Andalucía. Consejería de Salud (2010)
4. ONUSIDA. Informe de ONUSIDA para el día mundial del SIDA. Ginebra: Programa Conjunto de las Naciones Unidas sobre el VIH/SIDA (2016)

5. FIPSE (Fundación para la Innovación y la Prospectiva en Salud en España). Retrieved fromhttps://fipse.es/ on 18.03.2017
6. Ministerio de Sanidad y Consumo. Plan multisectorial frente a la infección por VIH y el SIDA: España 2008-2012. (2008).
7. REUS (Red Española de Universidades Promotoras de Salud). Retrieved fromhttp://www.msssi.gob.es/profesionales/saludPublica/prevPromocion/promocion/UniversidadesSaludables/REUS.htm on 12.03.2017
8. REUS. Declaración de Pamplona/Iruña. IV Congreso de Universidades Promotoras de la Salud. (2009) Retrieved from http://www.fundacion.unavarra.es/universidadsaludable/documentos/declaracion%20de%20pamplona.pdf on 18.03.2017
9. Arroyo, H. Desarrollo del Movimiento de Universidades Promotoras de la Salud. Centro Colaborador de la OMS-OPS para la Capacitación e Investigación en Promoción de la Salud y Educación para la Salud Escuela de Salud Pública, Universidad de Puerto Rico. (2012) Retrieved fromhttp://javeriana.edu.co/redcups/Hiram_Arroy_Movimiento_de_Universidades_Promotoras_de_la_Salud.pdf on 20.03.17
10. González Alfaya, M. E. Intervención de la Universidad en la promoción de la salud de sus estudiantes. (U. S. Compostela, Ed.) Innovación Educativa, **19**, 247-260 (2009)
11. Ministerio de Sanidad, Servicios Sociales e Igualdad. Gobierno de España. Universidades Saludables. (2013) Retrieved fromhttp://www.msssi.gob.es/profesionales/saludPublica/prevPromocion/promocion/UniversidadesSaludables/docs/AnexoI.pdf on 27.03.2017
12. Sábado J. T y Aradilla A. Actitud ante el sida en estudiantes de enfermería. ¿Cuál es el papel de la formación académica? Educación Médica, **6**, 2, 87-92 (2003)
13. Dihigo, M. Actitudes ante el VIH-SIDA de los estudiantes que ingresan a la carrera de Medicina. Facultad de Ciencias Médicas. Matanzas. Curso, 2007 (2006)
14. FIPSE. Discriminación y VIH/SIDA. Estudio Fipse sobre discriminación arbitraria de las personas que viven con VIH o SIDA. Fundación para la Investigación y la Prevención del Sida en España (2005)
15. Goffman, E. Stigma: Notes on the Management of Spoiled Identity. Garden City, New York: Anchor Books (1963)
16. Sanchiz, D.C., Marchena, J.A.M., Jarquín, E.J.L., Costales, E.M.R.A propósito del SIDA: un estudio cualitativo sobre percepción y actitudes de estudiantes y profesorado universitario en Chontales, Nicaragua. Población y SaludenMesoamérica, **10**, 2, 6-22 (2013)

Promoting healthy musculoskeletal function by applying regular exercises education and physical activities in senior activity centers

Cindy Sin U Leong[1a]

[1]School of Health Sciences, Macao Polytechnic Institute, Rua de Luis Gonzaga Gomes, Macao

Abstract. There are varied types of exercises that are beneficial to promoting healthy musculoskeletal function among older adults. The purpose of this study was to investigate the factors contributing to the health of the adults by having regular exercise education and physical activities provided by the senior activity centers in Macao. 56 participants aged 65 and over from four senior activity centers were interviewed in the past two years. Three senior activity centers were located in Macao peninsula and one senior activity center was in Taipa, another island of Macao. Adults in the two senior activity centers provided with regular exercise education and physical activities were having better quality of life with more satisfaction in physical, psychosocial and mental development. The other two activity centers provided less or zero exercise program showed more chances of falls and health problems.
Keywords: Activity centers, regular exercises, healthy musculoskeletal function.

1 Introduction

Regular and healthy exercise is essential for maintaining musculoskeletal function and consequence independence reached among older adults. A few intrinsic risk factors of fall may include gait, chronic illness and side-effect of medication as well as balance impairment [1]. While extrinsic risk factor is mostly related to environment, therefore a good, comfortable and safe environment available for frail older adults is very important. Therefore, the living environment for outdoor activity and senior activity center for indoor activity is very supportive for older adults to keep on being social active and mobile. According to WHO [2], older adults' physical activity may include walking, dancing, swimming, household chores, and planned exercise as list a few. To the ideas of WHO, physical exercises have many benefits to not only for older adults' body development such as less fall incidence, better mobility balance, and psychosocial development [3]. Many studies have showed that regular exercise, for example as simple as walking, helps much in

[a] Corresponding author:suleong@ipm.edu.mo

body organ development which improves respiratory system, circulatory system and immune system[3-4]. Furthermore, the chronic illness has much control with medication treatment together, especially the diabetic mellitus sugar level in the blood is way better in control [5-6]. Referring back to the title of this paper, musculoskeletal function is much promoted by regular exercise. Improvement in musculoskeletal flexibility and strength among older adults assists to balance and reduce pain as their normal body function declines alongside aging. In consequence, the healthy physical status helps to postpone the occurrence of illness or prevent their chronic illness from getting worse. Moreover, the "good healthy body" let older adults feel the sense of well-being from psychosocial view [6]. As older adults often state that they feel satisfied with very simple daily life activities, such as they can "walk, stand, eat, and sleep", and do not need grown-up children to "care" them, which is a very good traditional thinking of Chinese older adults.

1.1 Background of Macao

Macao, a moderately-sized city of 645,000 residents who are predominantly Chinese (97%), is approximately 35 km^2 in size [7], and is located in the southern part of Guangdong Province. There are approximately 66,340 older adults over 65 years of age, which is around 9.8% of the Macao population. The average life expectancy of people in Macao is 87 years old for females and 81 for males. The average life expectancy of Macao residents is 84 years old. Therefore, the high life expectancy stimulates the author's interest to explore the senior activity centers' function, including the kind of exercise education and physical activities provided in the centres, as well as any difference or effects for the older adults who attend different senior activity centres with different mission of the centres. According to [8], quite many older adults in Macao were cared by non-family caregivers. Non-family caregivers would even bring the older adults out to park pushing wheelchair in the morning or late evening. Therefore, this phenomenon reminded the author those active life older adults might not require home maids' caring. There are many senior activity centers in Macao, and the author has the experience of knowing that many older adults would like to attend their nearby senior activity centers for leisure. The centers might have many different kinds of activities such as physcial education, interested class such as singing, dancing and drawing, just name a few. From the author's long-time observation, the older adults seemed more good-looking, healthier and more educated after attending the activities. Furthermore, the better life expectancy is having relationship with regular physical education taking in senior activity center. The author would also like to explore how older adults felt about their activity centers.

The aims of this study were to explore how the older adults perceive their physical education and how they felt about their activity centers' activities. The older adults' perception of their musculoskeletal function after having physical activities practicing would also be explored. As expected, the senior activity centers might provide more helpful and useful knowledge and skills to assist older adults to obtain better well-being.

2 Method

In this study, the data was collected from older adults who are 65 or above. The data was gathered through a qualitative approach. Many interviews were conducted among older adults who have participated in activities provided by senior activity centers. This qualitative study was approved by the Management Board of Research Committee at the Macao Polytechnic Institute.

 DOI: 10.1051/shsconf/20173701007

2.1 Participants

The study involved older adults from four senior activity centres. At the onset of the study, invitation letters were distributed to those senior activity centers for the explanation of this study. A total of four senior activity centers agreed to have interviews. Those older adults interested in the interviews signed the consent and understood their interviews were audio-taped anonymously or had private information recorded. Older adults aged 65 and above were invited for participation. There were 56 older adults willing to participate in the interview. Their age was from 65 to 94 years old. There were 43 females and 13 males recruited. All participants were married and had grown-up children, grandchildren and some participants even had great grandchildren. There were 10 females (a total of 23) aged 80 and over lived alone. All male participants lived with their wives.

Table 1. Participants from four senior activity centers

Age group	Gender
65-69	8/1
70-74	5/4
75-79	7/4
80-84	14/1
85-89	4/2
90-94	5/1

F=female, M=male

2.2 Interview

The questions for the interviews (Table 1) were structured following literature reviews, past teaching observation and communication with the older adults. There are many reports mentioning that older adults having regular physical exercises and activities are less likely to have falls and more able to achieve physical balance. Accordingly, the questions explored what older adults had in their senior activity centers, how they felt and what they concerned the most during their physical exercises, such as pain, twist of their ankles and other concerns.

Table 2. Interview questions

1.	Do your senior activity center provide regular exercise education and physical activity? Please describe.
2.	How do you perceive your health? Please describe.
3.	How do you perceive your exercise activity with your health status? Please describe.
4.	Do you live with your family members? How do you make use of your time?
5.	Does your apartment have elevators or you need to walk upstairs? If no elevators for your building, how many times a day did you walk? Do you feel tired? Please describe.

2.3 Procedure

To achieve a representative response, older adults from four different senior activity centers were selected. To be even more representative, the older adults were selected from centers located in Macao peninsular and Taipa (Macao is made up of three islands). Most Macao residents were living in these two big islands. The 56 interviewees included 43 females and 13 males. All participants welcomed the audio-taping of the interviews. Interviewing began two years ago. The interviews were limited to summer months (June to August regarding the researcher is an academic staff). At the beginning of each interview, the participant confirmed that the interview would be recorded. Participants were assured that their recorded material would be kept confidential. The interviews were conducted in Cantonese, after each interview the transcripts were analysed immediately to capture the researcher's thoughts and feelings. The participants were coded as numbers P01-P056.

2.4 Transcription and data analysis

All the interviews were transcribed into verbatim to ensure that the expression of the interviews was accurately reported. After transcription, the results were examined using thematic content analysis. The number of times that the same sub-concepts or concepts occurred in the interview was grouped into the same theme. For example, codes P1, P2, P3, P4, and so forth, were assigned to the concepts noted in the interviews; these concepts were formed from the grouping of similar attributes [9, 10]. The attributes that were combined to form the concepts were given abbreviations such as P1.1, P1.2, P1.3, etc. For example, the concept of outdoor activity was composed of attributes such as 'fan dance', 'Tai Chi', 'sword dance' and 'jogging'. In order to achieve inter-rater reliability, a colleague independently coded 10% of the whole transcripts; and then, an English version of the report was written and recorded.

3 Results

From the analysis of the various concepts identified, one theme emerged: exercise among older adults who were attending senior activity centers (Figure1). The exercise theme from the interviews included three major concepts: outdoor activity, indoor activity, and other activity. All the older adults agree that their active life was greatly helpful in their daily life. The more exercise they performed, the more they liked and the more they would do which resulted that a group of older adults had two rounds of exercise (outdoor and indoor regular activity) in the morning in a senior activity center. Two groups of older adults living in Taipa and Macao peninsula, would have "Tai Chi" exercise in the outdoor garden. Then they would have their breakfast and returned to senior activity center for physical exercise again. The older adults were full of energy even they did not have any regular exercise attending in the senior activity center. They would go to the grocery early in the border of Macao and China where they could have less expensive food. They would buy lots of vegetables and meat two or three times a week. Some older adults would go to the grocery in the late evening as the food were cheaper for they were not so fresh. Some older adults not attending either indoor or outdoor activity, they had great responsibility. That was they needed to care their grandchildren. They had to prepare breakfast for grandchildren whom were primary children. Then they needed to take them to school in walk. In the afternoon, they had to fetch them back from school and prepare dinner for their adult children and grandchildren.

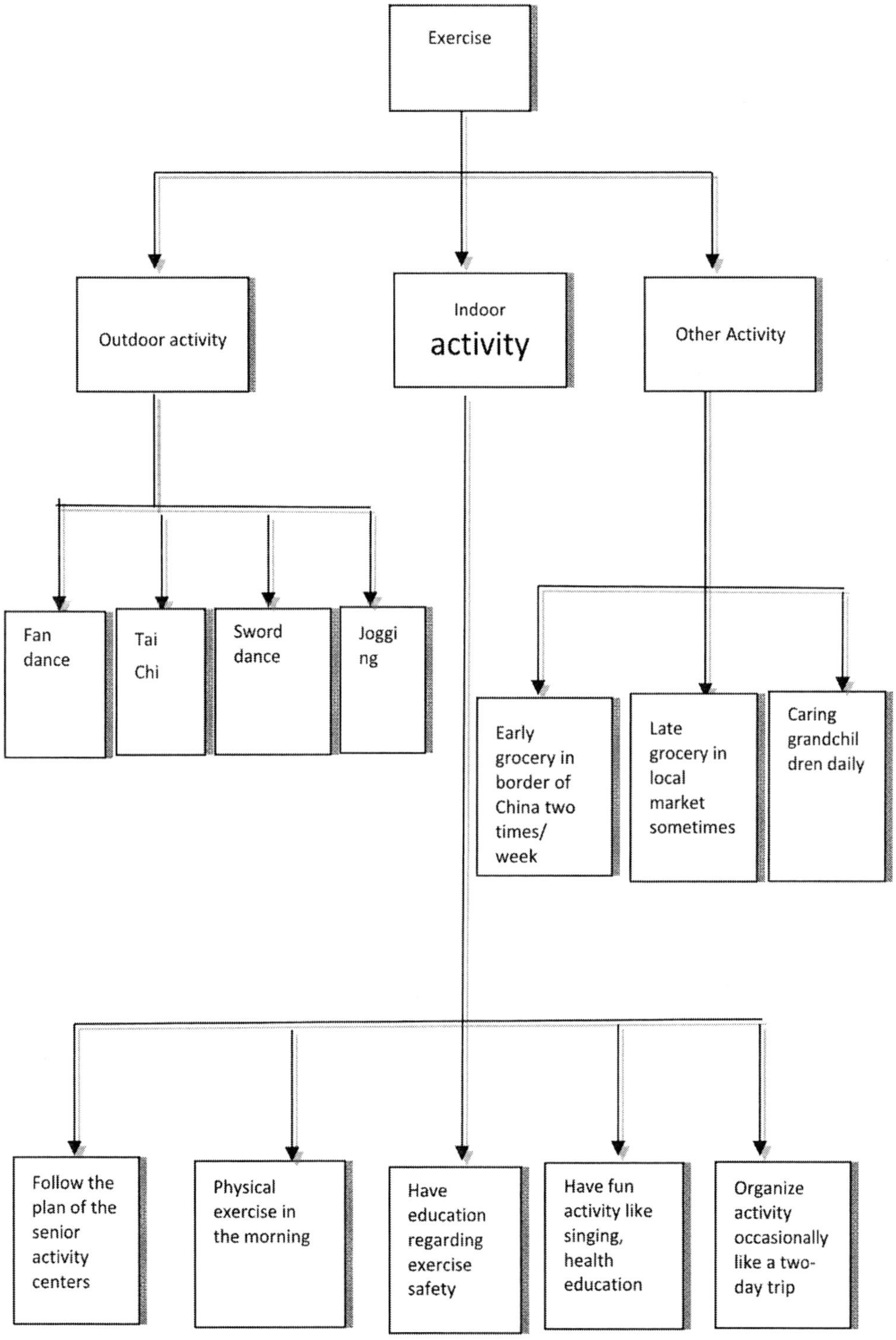

Fig. 1. Participation in healthy activity

3.1 Exercise

3.1.1 Outdoor activity

Outdoor activity was the most important concept forming theme 1 (figure1). Older adults preferred to have outdoor activities early in the morning around seven o'clock. Adults from a senior activity center in Taipa and another senior activity center preferred to have regular exercise outdoor and indoor twice per day. The senior activity center started activity around nine in the morning. Since adults regularly had early wake up schedule. Therefore, they had the following comments:

'I have been doing exercise regularly after retirement, Before retirement, I occasionally performed exercise, I was quite lazy, because after the whole day working, I preferred watching TV lying in the sofa'. (P01-male/71)

'When I was young, I only performed exercise when I had time. Now I am a Tai Chi teacher, teaching some adults in a public garden… After I have breakfast with my wife and some Tai Chi friends, my wife and I will go back to center for exercise again. Then in the afternoon, every Tuesday and Thursday, I will learn Latin dance. Sometimes, we will go for competition... just going to mainland China for dance competition'. (P08-male/86)

'I did exercise twice, early morning in the outdoor, then after going back to center for second round..of course I will have breakfast, center opens around 9. My first round of exercise is around 7'. (P015 - female/84)

'I have fan dance as outdoor activity with some friends, we also practice sword dance. Mostly two times of both dances takes approximately 40 minutes, our center does not have regularly exercise activity provided'. (P28 - female/88)

3.1.2 Indoor activity

A senior activity center provided interesting activities in the afternoon such as singing, dancing, health knowledge session by professional specialist. The second center occasionally provided gathering and short trip such as a day or two-day trip to mainland China. The third and forth senior activity centers provided morning regular exercise program. One regular exercise activity was from Monday to Saturday while the other provided three times a week. The rest of the days, they may provide useful knowledge regarding prevention of musculoskeletal harm. They regularly provided healthy education such as how to prevent risk of falls, how to do exercise in a correct manner, and how to prevent harmfulness during physical exercise. The center's physical therapist would regularly provide proper information or correct their myth of how to do healthy and not risky exercise and activity.

'I will do more exercise after my husband's retirement, I will come to the center only in the afternoon, I need to prepare breakfast and dinner for my husband, he is working even he is 70, he works in a private small business firm, so no retirement consideration, unless your boss thinks you are no more helpful'. (P22 - female/67)

'I like this center because they teach us what kind of exercise we can do, we know we are not young any more, risk of fall happens easily, we cannot bend like this… (stand up showing she cannot bend her upper body to legs while standing up'. (P30 - female/80)

'I seldom do extra exercise now, it is tiring to get up to this center (located in a top hill), I mean the outdoor exercise, here this center's exercise activity is simpler and easier, the staff will adjust our physical ability to match the level…'. (P34 - female/90)

'I occasionally have a jogging in the morning if it is not raining, however, I prefer going to swimming, I go to a swimming pool in Taipa, many adults swim there in the morning, I take bus, it is easy…in the afternoon, we have fun activity like singing, health education and discussion, or planning for activity and trip'. (P42 - female/82)

3.1.3 Other activity

These adults, whose center, mostly provided a short term trip for them and sometimes evening activity. So they are happy because they may be out of Macao for fun and do not have to care their family members and grandchildren. They were not having "sendary life". Their daily activity was caring family members, adult children and grandchildren such as going to grocery, doing meal preparation and taking grandchildren to school.

'I accompany my wife for grocery in the morning, grocery in the border is a good activity. We bought lots, my son and his family members live with us…'. (P40 – male/78).

'I now go to grocery in the late evening, but go to border buying meat and fish, there (border) is much cheaper and fresh'. (P48 – female/85).

'I have no time for activity, I have to bring my grandchildren (6 and 8 years old to school and back home in the afternoon. Their grandpapa will bring them back after school, sometimes. I have to climb up stairs to the 5th floor'. (P50 – female/68)

'I have to prepare three meals a day, how I can have time for activity. My grandchild lives with us'. (P54 – female/72)

3.2 Discussion

The interviews conducted with 56 older adults provided a great number of insights into factors that may be contributed to their daily activity which might have effect to their choice of regular exercise. In addition, the senior activity center the older adults attended due to closer to their living area. However, the activity provided for the older adults also affected the favour of the older adults to healthy exercise. Continuously moving and having physiologic function is very important to the older adults [11]. The well-being of physical function significantly has great impact on older adults' quality of life. Physical functions mostly have the domains of daily activities such as self-care, bathing, dressing or walking and instrumental activities of daily living such as cooking, grocery and laundry [12]. Basically, walking as one wants or the higher level of doing exercise as one likes would be the top level of an older adult's independence and feeling of psychosocial wellness too. For many older adults, risk of falls and consequence of fractures play a very essential part to their intention of healthy physical activity.

As mentioned by participants, they would like to "move as they prefer". The activity center is a good venue providing an opportunity, environment and atmosphere for older adults to share and enjoy, and get useful healthy knowledge. Since the older adults have more time for learning and participating in their interested plans in comparison to their non-retirement status. A 78-year-old male participant stated: "I am more concerned about my health than before, I spend two hours doing exercise in the center, I use their activity instruments in the afternoon as there are not many people using. I also spend 30 minutes to massage my head, I can see things very well, no cataract in my eyes". The physiotherapist in the senior center always reminds and corrects the older adults' improper exercise or myth during activity. There the importance role of the senior activity did much support to older adults' physical and physiological development. It is because after learning the professional knowledge, they gained happiness, comfort and no harm after physical activity. They have more topics shared with their peer groups. They can sleep well after physical activity [13]. An 86-year-old female participant mentioned that if there was rain, she could not go and only practice "indoor activity". She felt uncomfortable as she mentioned. Other older adults

DOI: 10.1051/shsconf/20173701007

felt they used to have exercise and felt good every day. So if there was rain for a few days, they stated that their bodies "did not feel easy and body is "itchy".

However, even some older adults have to take care of their grandchildren. That is one of the Chinese traditional cultures, a very good and tied union family support [14]. However, they do not lack walking and running up and down. Actually, walking and climbing upstairs and go to grocery or shopping is a good practicing of exercise [15]. It is interested to note that a senior activity center has the history of a couple of fall incidents of older adults. Maybe this is coincident to this study. The center rarely provides musculoskeletal function knowledge to the older adults. No matter what, the more we know, the more we benefit. The musculoskeletal function is also important during physical activity. Having proper exercise performance helps improves the flexibility of the strength of the muscle, tender, blood circulation and body system [16]. Older adults even have good benefit for mobility balance as well as muscle tone up. All the participants whom having regular exercise, mentioned that they felt happier, relaxed, energetic and not much body pain such as back or knee or foot [17]. They learned not to over use their joints and know how to protect them as they learned from center teaching class. However, those older adults caring grandchildren and performing much of household chores complaint of back pain and knee pain [14]. They need to carry heavy food or grandchildren whom were very small kids. Plus they lacked proper working body behaviour.

The 13-male participants all lived with their spouse, however, their spouses were typically no longer young themselves. They may have chronic illness or are very frail either. Therefore, there is a push for these male participants urged to be healthy and in return assist their spouses to care the family matters. From the qualitative approach, the results show that regular and proper exercise not only give the benefit to the older adult himself or herself, but also to the family members. In addition, with more formal physical activity knowledge provided by professionalism, the older adults enjoy more in physical and psychosocial development.

3.3 Conclusion

Healthy older adults usually have regular activities in the morning either outdoor or indoor or both after each other. Because of different family background, some older adults did not go for physical activities, they went for "other activity" for grocery, either in Macao border in the morning or late afternoon in local market as the vegetables were less expensive. The senior activity center also has great impact on them. If the center is more active in providing physical activity and educate the older adults how to involve suitable and healthy exercise, the older adults would be more enjoyable. They would not easily put them in risk of musculoskeletal twist and harm. As they mentioned they were more bravely to do exercise and were not afraid of hurting themselves. Therefore, providing regular health education regarding the exercises for older adults involved as mentioned above is very helpful in maintaining and improving gait, and balance. In addition, safety of exercise is very important. Repetition of education on the function of musculoskeletal, such as how to protect the joints and bones, and musculoskeletal-related physical excise is vey essential. The old way of thinking needs to be replaced by new scientific thinking slowly.

Acknowledgements

The author would like to thank all the older adults for kindly participation in the interviews as well as the director of senior activity centers providing a comfortable and quiet area for interview. The author would also like to thank Macao Polytechnic Institute for funding this study ((RP/ESS -03/2014).

References

1. M.E.Z. Estes, Health Assessment & Physical Examination. Publisher: Cengage Learning (2014)
2. WHO Physcial Activity and Older Adults. Retrieved on 2017/06/10 website: http://www.who.int/dietphysicalactivity/factsheet_olderadults/en/ (2016)
3. UK Chief Medical Officers' Guidelines: Physcial activity benefits adults and older adults. Stay Active, Stay Active (2011)
4. R.J. Shephard, T.J. Verde, S.G. Thomas, P. Shek, Physcial activity and the immune system Can J. Sport Sci. (1991)
5. inMotoin, The Role of Physical Activity in Diabetes Prevention and Control, **17**, 2, March/April (2007)
6. Centers for Disease Control and Prevention, Be Active! Why is it important for people with diabetes to be physically active?
7. Statistics & Census Service, Demographic statisitics: Government of Macao special administrative region (2016)
8. S.U.C. Leong, L.B. Clutter M.W. Ho, Empowering Non-family Caregivers of Older Adults in Macao Chinese Society: Combining Theory Knowledge Lesson and Basic Care Skill Laboratory
9. J. Corbin, A. Strauss, Basics of Qualitative Research (2nd ed). Los Angeles, CA: Sage Publication (2008)
10. E.V. Cruz, G. Higginbottom, The use of focused ethnography in nursing research. Nurse Researcher, **20**, 4, 36-43 (2013)
11. C.A. Miller, Nursing for wellness in older adults. Publisher : Wolters Kluwer (2015)
12. J.T. Stone, J.F. Wyman & S.A. Salisbury, Clinical Gerontological Nursing: a guide to advanced practice. Publication: W.B. Saunders (1999)
13. M. Mendelson, et al., Low Physical Activity Is a Determinant for Elevated Blood Pressure in High Cardiovascular Risk Obstructive Sleep Apnea, Resp Care, **59**, 8, 1218-1227 (2013)
14. J. Sun Chinese Older Adults Taking Care of Grandchildren: Practices and Policies for Productive Aging, Ageing Int ,**38,** 58-70 (2013)
15. Y.H. Chang, R.C.Y. Chen, M.L. Wahlqvist & M.S. Lee, Frequent Shopping by Men and Women Increases Survival in the Older Taiwanese population, J Epidemiol Community Health, **66**, e20 (2012)
16. M.R. Franco, A. Tong, K. Howard, C. Sherrington, P.H. Ferreira, R.Z. Pinto & M.L. Ferreira, Older People's Perspective on Participation in Physical Activity: a Systematic Review and Thematic Synthesis of Qualitative Literature, Br J Sports Med, **49**, 1268-1276 (2015)
17. E. Sitthipornvorakul, P. Janwantanakul, N. Purepong, P. Pensri, A.J. Beek, The Association between Physical Activity and Neck and Low Back Pain: a Systematic Review, Eur Spine J **20**, 677–689 (2011)

CB language competences testing methods in the class of tourism management

Dagmar El-Hmoudova[1a]

[1]Univerzita Hradec Kralove, Rokitanskeho 62,500 03 Hradec Kralove, Czech Republic

Abstract. Computer-based testing is a method of administering tests in which the responses are electronically recorded, assessed, or preferably both. The assessment is a testing tool which checks student´s knowledge, measures their progress and gathers information from students. The most important attributes to consider when creating an assessment in computer-based environment is threefold; the structure and types of questions included, deployment and setting options, and grading assessments and availability of multiple attempts. The paper focuses on computer-based testing methods applied in online English language course of Tourism Management in the Blackboard LMS. The aim of the presented paper is to monitor and assess the bachelor students´ proficiency of key language competences progress. The key language competences defined by the Common European Framework of Reference for Languages (CEFR) are tested with a special view on students´ individual learning styles.
Keywords: Computer-based testing methods, key language competences, Blackboard learn environment, individual learning styles.

1 Introduction

In a decade of researching digital education there have been fundamental changes in our culture, education paradigms and thinking about human capacity. The terms like divergent thinking, creativity, variability, and interactive skills have been discussed widely in the field of educational process. Professor Philip Zimbardo claims that young people today will never fit into a traditional analogue classroom as their brains are digitally re-wired [1]. In the attempt to reflect the new revolutionary changes in educational process we have decided to convert the traditional paper –based testing into computer - based assessment of second language ability in Professional English language courses at the Department of Applied Linguistics, Faculty of Informatics and Management, University of Hradec Kralove. As is well known, intelligence is distinct, diverse and dynamic, and thus creativity and variability have been main priorities when designing Professional English language on-line courses in university Blackboard learn environment.

[a] Corresponding author: dagmar.elhmoudova@uhk.cz

DOI: 10.1051/shsconf/20173701008

1.1 Computer-based testing methods

Computer-based (CB) testing of second language competences has been increasingly used as a part of assessment and consequently teaching process in the academic environment. It is an instrument which provides both students as well as teachers with information on students′ language ability, feedback on how they have progressed and what they have achieved. According to kind of information assessed we distinguish many types of tests e.g. proficiency tests (prepared by professional institutions, based on what student have to be able to do in language to be considered proficient); achievement tests (related to language course and divided into final and progress tests); placement tests (used to assign different level students to classes);objective and subjective tests (if no judgment is required on the part of scorer, scoring is objective – multiple-choice tests with correct answers); communicative language tests(emphasis is mainly on meaning and form, progress, creativity, authenticity) [2]. In our on-line language courses prevail achievement tests as they perfectly correspond with the need to evaluate students′ language progress and achievements in the course of one semester.

In relation to assessing language competences we distinguish two major categories – “macro-skills”: productive skills (speaking, writing) and receptive skills (listening, reading). This is in contrast to the "micro-skills"(see Table 3), e.g. grammar, vocabulary, pronunciation and spelling, which cross-cut the four major language competences, see Figure 1. Alongside with these skills, a lot of classroom progress testing focuses on testing grammar and vocabulary. Unfortunately, a lot of tests, which concentrate on these areas exclusively and ignore assessment of the four major language skills, give students wrong message that their overall progress in language performance is good [3].

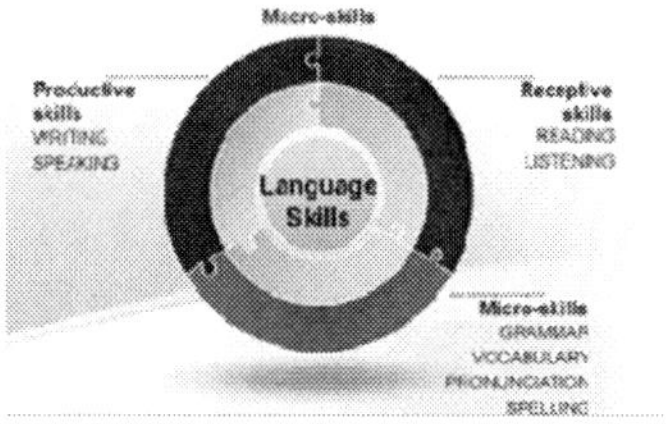

Fig. 1. Language skills

When testing receptive skills (reading, listening) the key element is authenticity which means that the oral and written texts are taken from real sources (TV and radio shows, news, advertisements, newspapers and magazines, social network, etc.). The main objective of assessing reading and listening is to check whether students are prepared to function successfully in real-life reading and listening situations (instructions, interviews, conversations, etc.). A lot of testing methods – techniques used in assessing reading can be adapted to assess listening as well, although cognitive demand has to be taken in account, see Table 1.

The assessment of productive language skills (writing, speaking) is very difficult as it involves the ability of student to interact in foreign (English) language in written or spoken form and comprehension as well as production is required. Selecting appropriate testing formats is crucial. Ideally the tasks involve integrated (combined) and independent skills (read, listen and then speak in response to a question; listen and then speak in response to a question; read, listen and then write in response to a question), see Table 2.

Table 1. Receptive skills testing techniques

Competence	Activity	Methods/Techniques	Purpose
Reading	reading for detail reading for specific information understand the structure	multiple choice, true/false statements gapped text short answer questions multiple matching	understanding of a long and short text; effectively scanning text for key facts, understanding the general topic including details; the ability to follow text development; understanding vocabulary in context
Listening	listening for specific information stated opinion ;listening for gist ;attitude and opinion interpreting context	multiple choice sentence completion multiple matching jumbled sentence	focus on gist; interpreting context; listening for basic comprehension; listening for pragmatic understanding; connecting and synthesizing information

Table 2. Productive skills testing technique

Competence	Activity	Methods/Techniques	Purpose
Writing	writing essay: responses based on reading and listening tasks support an opinion in writing	writing one of the following: an article, a report, a proposal, a letter, a competition entry, a contribution to a longer piece, an essay, an information sheet, a review; writing one of the prescribed reading texts	focus on evaluating, expressing opinions, hypothesizing, persuading, comparing, giving advice, giving opinions, justifying, persuading
Speaking Test	short exchanges with the interlocutor and with the other candidate;	general introduction, socializing, talking over the picture, a two-way conversation between the candidates, a discussion on topics related to the collaborative task	general interactional and social language; comparing, describing, expressing opinions, speculating, exchanging ideas, justifying opinions, agreeing and/or disagreeing synthesizing information

Table 3. Micro-skills testing techniques

Competence	Activity	Methods/Techniques	Purpose
Use Of English Vocabulary	different types of exercise which test grammar and vocabulary	multiple-choice cloze open cloze word formation gapped sentences key word transformations	emphasis on vocabulary and grammar; focus on gist, attitude, main points, interpreting context

DOI: 10.1051/shsconf/20173701008

As Powers [4] claims: "The language skills of listening, reading, writing, and speaking are distinct from one another. Although testing one language skill individually may provide indirect information about a test taker's ability to perform the others, it cannot provide a comprehensive assessment of one's overall communicative ability, which frequently involves the use of multiple language skills in combination with each other."

2 Blackboard learn environment and individual learning styles

1.2 Blackboard learn environment (BB)

The efficient CB testing methods, see Tables 1; 2; 3, are incorporated and used in university CB course tests in the frame of the Blackboard Learn environment, which has been used in Faculty of Informatics and Management, University of Hradec Kralove, where the studies are facilitated by the fact that most teaching materials are readily available in electronic form. The advantages of CB credit test are quite obvious. The test can be only started when it is needed for duration of few days or months depending on the specific request of the teacher. If needed, it is protected by a password. The instructions which contain information about the length of test, number of questions, evaluating and passing levels at the beginning of the test, see Figure 2, are very short and clear which reduces careless errors to minimum. Students are alerted in case that they have not answered any of the test questions before downloading and confirming their answers. Well-designed test examines wide range of language competences within a predetermined timeframe. The test is immediately corrected and evaluated and therefore both, students and teachers can see the results just few seconds after the answers have been downloaded and verified. This type of testing is very well assessed, primarily for this reason, by students of both full-time and combined form of study [5].

The only disadvantage of the computer based tests in the Blackboard Learn environment, which has occurred lately, is that they are key sensitive, which can cause some minor problems (e.g. writing apostrophes in short versions of English language) in the process of evaluation. However, based on our experience, we can confirm that CB testing in the field of assessing language competences is beneficial in all respects.

2.2 Individual learning styles and their reflection on English language on-line course design

In the attempt to improve the testing techniques professor Felder´s ILS (Index of learning styles), an on-line instrument detecting students´ individual learning styles preferences, was implemented into the English language on-line course in BB. At the beginnings of the semester are students asked to fill in the ILS and their preferences are collected in BB in the form of preference graphs, see Figure 2. The Felder-Solomon´s Index of Learning Styles (ILS) is a self-scoring web-based instrument that assesses preferences on the Sensing/Intuiting, Visual/Verbal, Active/Reflective, and Sequential/Global dimensions. The forty-four multiple choice questions in the questionnaire reflect the psychological and behavioral characteristics of four dichotomous dimensions of learning styles mentioned above. Questions in this questionnaire are written in English and the two choices in each question reflect the two dichotomous learning styles. For example, in the question "When I am learning something new, it helps me to (A) talk about it, (B) to think about it", this question is trying to distinguish whether the student is more an active learner or a reflective learner.

Students indicate their preference to either of these two answers depending on their normal practice. After submitting their answers, students are provided with Learning Style Results, where if their score on a scale is 1-3, they are considered fairly well balanced on the two dimensions of that scale. If their score on a scale is 5-7, they have a moderate preference for one dimension of the scale and will learn more easily in a teaching environment which favors that dimension and if their score on a scale is 9-11, they have a very strong preference for one dimension of the scale and are classified as purely a single style learners, which may cause struggling and suffering when learning in an environment which does not support their preference.

The main objective is to create a balanced course, including achievement tests with relevant testing techniques. The knowledge of students learning style preferences can help the language instructor to adapt their instruction to address preferred poles of students′ learning style dimensions, so that optimal learning and testing environment is provided [6].

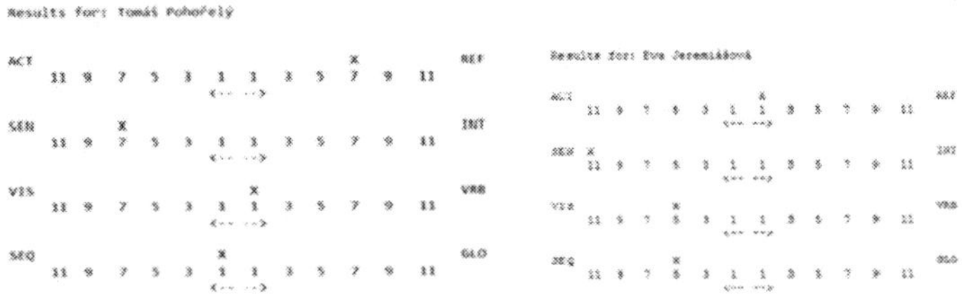

Fig. 2. ILS graph with preference dimensions

2.3 The focus group and LS preferences

3rd year Tourism Management students (No: 83; 61 F, 22 M) proved to be mostly sensing and visual, which supports the teaching strategy reflecting the adaptive testing and personalization, see Fig. 3.

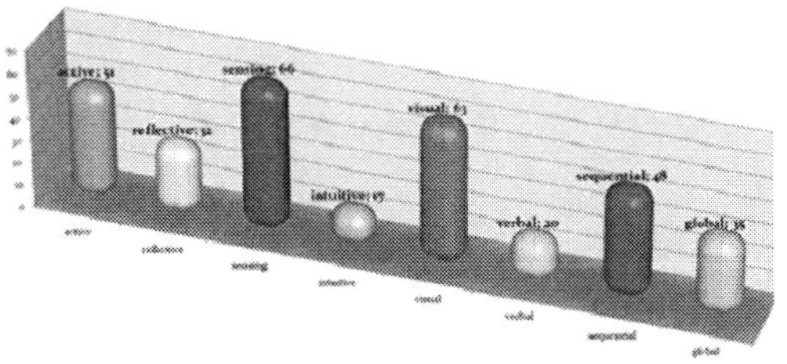

Fig. 3. LS preferences in a focus group of tourism management students

The students were also asked to indicate their preferences in assessment tools. Based on the questionnaire we can deduce that most of the students prefer multiple matching and multiple choice exercises and they favor testing of professional vocabulary (88%), grammar (66%) and professional communication skills (64%), see Fig 4.

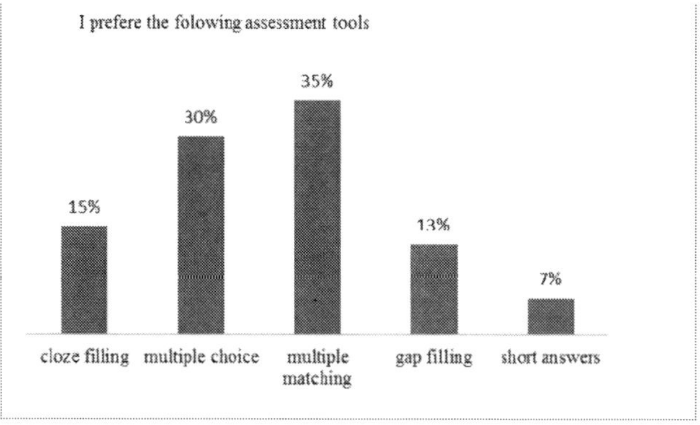

Fig. 4. Students' preferences in assessment tools

3 Implications

The students of focus group do vary in their preference for particular learning style preferences. This gives instructors and teachers closer understanding of how the students perceive the new study materials, as well as the preferred assessment models. Our students are mostly visuals and sensors, preferring multiple matching and multiple choice types of CB testing.

Assessment for Learning is one of the teaching approaches that enables personalization of learning and provides frequent assessments [7]. Computer-adaptive testing is another efficient approach – that can increase our students´ motivation and to some extent eliminate certain concerns (testing language skills). The aim is to create balanced tests in cyber environment which would answer the subject knowledge requirements [8], [9]. This is in accordance with the principles of adaptive educational systems, which leads to holistic understanding of the subject matter. CATs are one of the ways in which technology-enhanced assessment is used at our faculty. We collect the information about a student´s performance X the language skills, tested separately, are not isolated in reality it is important to think very carefully about the validity of a test despite all the drawbacks of technology for assessment - we believe that if students are motivated to learn, they can turn any experience with technology into a language-learning opportunity.

4 Conclusion

In the paper we have stated that alongside with several types of language tests there are two main categories of language competences – skills which are assessed by relevant testing methods – techniques. Due to technological innovations incorporated into educational process and with respect to the preferences of nowadays generation of university students, traditional paper-based testing is converted into computer-based assessment in the academic environment [10], [11]. In the Faculty of Informatics and Management, University of Hradec Kralove, most of the subjects thought presently are available also in the form of on-line courses in Blackboard learn environment, which allows instructors to implement a multiple style approach and variety of relevant testing methods. To achieve effective English language learning and testing, professor Felder´s ILS was implemented into the Professional English language course.

DOI: 10.1051/shsconf/20173701008

Acknowledgement

The paper was supported by the IGA Project 2017run at the Faculty of Informatics and Management, University of Hradec Kralove No: 1903/1210/024302017.

References

1. Zimbardo,P. *The Time Paradox: The New Psychology of Time That Will Change Your Life,* Free Press, NY, (2008)
2. Common European Framework of Reference for Languages Council of Europe. Cambridge: Cambridge University Press (2001)
3. Douglas, D. *Assessing Languages for Specific Purposes.* Cambridge: Cambridge University Press (2000)
4. Powers, Donald E, The Case for a Comprehensive, Four-Skills Assessment of English-Language Proficiency, R&D Connections, n14, May 2010 Document Type: Periodical Page Count 2 (2010)
5. Milkova, E., El-Hmoudova, D. Computer-based testing in the field of foreign language assessment. Efficiency and responsibility in education 2012 : proceedings. Prague : Czech University of Life Sciences Prague, ISBN: 978-80-213-2289-9 (2012)
6. Arce-Ferrer,Alvaro J. Standard Progressive Matrices Test Educational and Psychological Measurement October 1, **69**, 855-867 (2009)
7. Coffield, F., Moseley, D., Hall, E., Ecclestone, K. Learning styles and pedagogy in post-16 learning: A systematic and critical review. London: Learning and Skills Research Centre (2004)
8. Felder, R. M., Spurlin, J. Applications, reliability and validity of the Index of Learning Styles. International Journal of Engineering Education, **21**, 103-112 (2005)
9. Felder, R. M., Silverman, L. K. Learning and teaching styles in engineering education, Engineering Education, **78**, 674-681 (1988).
10. Schroeders,Ulrich. Equivalence of Reading and Listening Comprehension Across Test Media Educational and Psychological Measurement October 1, **71**, 849-869 (2011)
11. Paciorek, J. Internet, computer and communication technologies in modern e - learning methods, Journal of Technology and Information Education 3/2012, **4**, 3, 115-119 (2012)

TETRAPOLIS - an exercise in building the complexities of proximity space

Cristian Blidariu[1], and Diana Giurea[1a]

[1]Faculty of Architecture and Urbanism, Politehnica University of Timisoara, Timisoara, Romania

Abstract. It is often said that the precarious state of Eastern European public space is a direct consequence of the poor communal and social bonds that the communist governance of space inadvertently put forth. Communal spaces belonged to all and to no one at the same time- were, and many times still are, devoid of anyone's responsibility towards them. With this premise, we experimented with our first year architecture student's intuitive ways for understanding these vicinities, their physical and symbolic proximities, through participatory tactics and certain poetic/architectural tools required in the phenomenological build-up of space. We thus devised the TETRAPOLIS game, through which, our students were able to work both autonomously as well as in teams, with the task of building a communal setting. Our paper discusses the methods used by this community building game and our findings regarding the student's abilities to intuitively understand the complex nature of proximity.
Keywords: Tetrapolis, architectural tools, students.

1 Problem statement

In Architecture schools, more so then in other academic fields, the first year of studies is the moment where the groundwork for entire curricular study is laid. For students coming mostly from the standardized branched training so typical for high school curricula's, this can turn into a really confusing experience. Their expectations of what it means to be an architect and how architecture is to be understood and practiced are from what we surveyed mostly at odds with the practice itself. Mostly perceive architecture as a marriage between art and engineering which although true to a point is an incomplete definition. Fascinated by the concept of architect as demiurge few have any ideas of how architecture affects the life of the user/users, or its cultural, social, and political discourse. Although all these aspects are covered in the five or six years of study, considering our new social economical paradigm of a post crisis world, we noticed the need for a better understanding of these topics even from the first projects that students are faced with.

[a] Corresponding author: diana.giurea@yahoo.com

In a typical architecture school, as was in the case of our only a few years ago, the first year projects usually tackle the abstract and philological problems specific for the architectural vocabulary, morphology and syntax. These linguistics exercises, though important in their own right are however many times devoid of real world problematic. Their outcome is often times purely formal, teaching the young architect to perform within a universally accepted set of linguistic rules. How do they fair when put in context, when related to the realities of the world? As we have by now only too often seen, even in the case of the most talented students, they can create the myth of the architect as Artiste, of architecture as a purely expressive formal discipline, devoid of any responsibility toward the social aspects of its context. This only exacerbates the image of architecture that the students are equipped with in the first place. It is by all means an architecture that operates solely on the principle of figure ground relations, where the expressive architectural figure is set against a neutral background whose sole purpose from now on is to emphasize the first one. In this mode of understanding so typical for modernism, where architecture assumes the role of the figure the background or surrounding space becomes the negative. How does one make this surrounding space a positive and why does it matter in the first place?

As stated above in this papers abstract, Eastern European post-communist public space, the space we all publicly and socially inhabit is mostly negative space, a direct consequence of the poor communal relationships and mentalities that the communist model inadvertently put forth through poorly designed modernist schemes. Following the intense welfare building programs of the sixties and seventies Romania quickly turned from a mainly agrarian society into an urban one [1]. In this artificial transition both rural as well as urban community bonds and their typical spatial use patterns were lost. The new urban dwellers unaccustomed to urban dwelling were unable to truly make their own the spatial structures envisaged for them by the state. In a society with no real private space where public space belonged in theory to everybody, no one really wished ore dared for that matter to appropriate anything. As no man's lands [2] communal spaces and especially micro vicinities, spaces that ironically belonged to all and to no one at the same time, were and many times still are, devoid of anyone's responsibility towards them. Furthermore this lack of communal appropriation was made worse in the transitional, post-communist years of Turbo-Urbanism, so typical for the Balkans, when the private property and private developments manifested themselves with total disregard of any societal, administrative or cultural norms. Once the subdued desires of individuality where released, new shows of identity building, status and power came to be, mostly at expense of the few remnants of unity and clarity that public space still possessed.

It is an undercurrent of thought that unfortunately still flows in perception that many Romanians have towards architecture and space, being them either private or public. It is no surprise then, that the typical first year architecture student has a cultural predisposition towards this line of thought. From the questionnaires that we hand out in the beginning of the academic year we noticed that in most cases their experiences with space are profoundly vitiated by this status quo. As Bourdieu would put it [3], most of them are the victims of an illusio, the illusion of either the cultural group or social strata of which they are a part of, towards architecture's role in this type of culture. To only and to this, one might argue that architectural training itself was until not so long ago the victim of just such an illusion, the illusion that oftentimes the aesthetic quality of architecture itself has miraculous healing powers, that localized infusions of greatness can by means of trickle down tactics change the context in a good way. Though sometimes successful this strategy has none the less proven to be ineffective, actually widening the gap between the so called good and the bad, between the planed and the organic, between the conceived, the perceived and the lived space [4]. So how does one plan for the lived qualities of space without using his own theoretical or linguistic predispositions [3] towards that space. Understanding the language of this space is not just about syntax and grammar, but mainly about the cultural and social parameters that define the context. One needs to know and understand these parameters if he is to operate within the context. Are they as students aware of how these parameters have shaped them thus far? We argue that in the case of first year architecture students these parameters can be tweaked towards an intuitive response to architecture's problems. This can be best achieved not necessarily through the abstract exercises of a newly acquired language but through a guided play highlighting the multiple meanings of the already known language.

2 Purpose of study

First year students are ideal for just such an exercise for they can provide the context. It is they who can create the social milieu that can be subsequently modelled intuitively into an architectural model. Their lack of any in depth theoretical knowledge concerning either architectural theory, urban planning, economy, sociology, or the more subjective issue of the phenomenology of space, can be turned on its head by applying these concepts through means of intuitive study, without the need of ever directly postulating any of the known dogmas specific for each of these fields. Bourdieu notices [3] that often times the illusions that we project upon concrete realities are born from the predispositions of the field from which we operate. These predispositions often lead to solutions that are right only when viewed from that specific operating field, and incomplete when viewed from all others. We thus consider that in order to compensate for the distortions typical for these viewpoints, even before they are well established by the acquisition of specific theoretical knowledge, one can experiment intuitively, without a clear field type goal in sight. In this respect the method and the process of learning, and not necessarily the final outcome, become the dominant undercurrent of the whole experiment. What we wanted is to see how much of the individualist cultural model already described above translated into their work, if this affected it, and in which way. How are they going to shape space, both private and public, using only intuitive methods, past experience, channeling their unbridled desires? Will the individualist cultural model already described above translated into their work, will it affect it, and how?

Moreover by working in teams as opposed to individually, ideas and findings are shared democratically between the participants, just as they are in real life situation. Ideally a process of maieutic searching is ensued, where ideas flow freely from one peer to another. Participants are however left to their own choice weather they wish to cooperate or not, and at what intensity. We were thus able to see in what manner the students were accustomed to collaborative design processes so far, and their willingness to do so not necessarily for their immediate own benefit but for the benefit of their teams. It has to be stated that the potential success of their individual outcome depended in equal measure on the group's total response. In this respect we consider that laying the groundwork of their negotiation and collaborative skills is not only important their practice in the future but mainly for establishing methods of understanding and empathizing with the needs of their end-users/ clients.

By abandoning the framework of the typical philological abstract study of space, materiality and form, we experimented for three consecutive years with our students within the game world of the city of Tetrapolis. Although it is built like any game around a few fixed principles that serve as guidelines, the final and most important parameters of the resulting game world are dependent on the type of response each group of students puts forth. So how does it work?

3 Methods

The premise is the following. The year is split into four groups of roughly 25 students. Each group has to build one of the four neighborhoods that encompass the town of Tetrapolis. They do so using a gridded board upon which each student places his lot. The lot has four 5 by 5m squares shaped like Tetris bricks : L, T , I, Z. Out of the four squares allotted to each plot at least one must be given to the neighbourhood as public space (Fig.1). The rest are to be used as intermediary space and as private space.

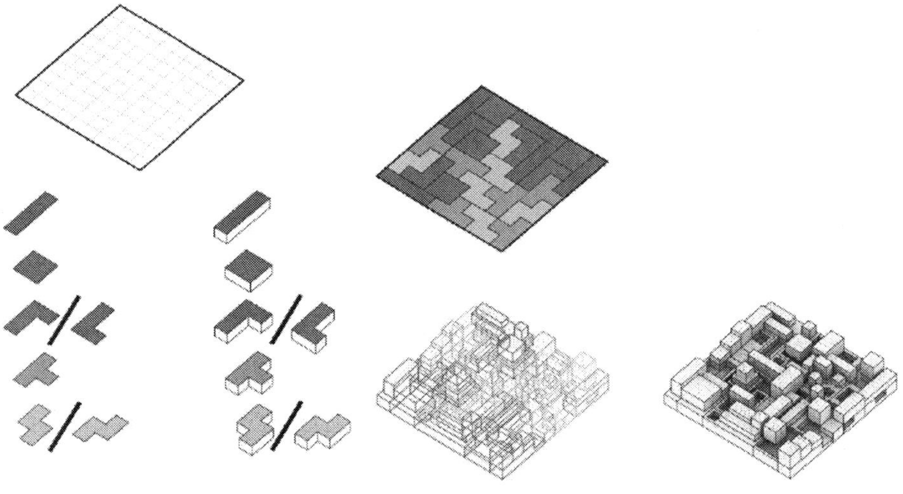

Fig. 1. The allotted plots and the game board

The students are also assigned two of three possible artefacts: a bench, a tree, and the element of water (fountain, pond, spring). Out of the two one must be given to the neighborhood one must be kept private. The neighborhood is built by using the material found on site, meaning that each student can produce building materials by digging on his plot for stone or clay but no deeper than five meters. This has to be carefully planned between them since uncoordinated digging can collapse their plot borders. Considering the tightness of the plots and their shapes the students are faced with the problem of finding the best possible position for their plot, in regard to one another, taking into account the terraforming process, the need for roads, the possible larger public areas, as well as the direct physical contacts between the built object. Thus the students are forced to cooperate in one form or another if they are to build a coherent structure. However once these general decisions are made they will work individually on their plots coordinating with their immediate neighbors. A chain reaction follows, as each individual decision has the potential to alter the context. What is particularly important is the way in which they relate to the public space that they thus generate, since the artefacts dotting this space can generate places of certain interest. This is in fact the basic theory behind the artefacts, since each one of them has imbedded multiple purposes: functional, symbolic, poetic, compositional. A bench is a place for socializing, or for resting and observing just as a fountain can be, or the shade of a tree for that matter. Since the spatial, functional and symbolic qualities of these elements are often neglected by the general population in present day Romania, these artefacts are in many ways testing our students understanding of the principle of commons. These elements are thus to be used as place generating tools.

In order to understand the importance of such features, in preparation for this project students are given a two week assignment in which they are supposed to make a critical analysis of three different public spaces from Timisoara, our schools hometown. Following DeCerteau and Debord advise to walk the streets [5], [6], to view the city from the pedestrian perspective of the flaneur students are encouraged to experience these spaces during different times of the day, in order to distinguish the relations between the forms of the architectural space, and how it is affected by light, texture, complexity or simplicity, patterns of movement, daily use, sound, noise and other phenomena. These studies are also based on Pallasma observations on the nature of perception [7], and emphasize a multi-sensory experience. The methods of observation are similar to the ones implied by the situationist derive. In fact the whole hidden purpose of the Tetrapolis game is to produce a situationist city, akin to the one envisaged by the situationist architect and artist Constant Nieuwenhuys as a city of play and movement, free of physical borders and fences [8].This is especially important since Romania as much of Eastern Europe is also a country o strict fences and limits, where private property is clearly defined- perhaps one of the many reasons for the dissolution of public space.

The Tetrapolis game ensues afterwards and lasts for six weeks. Students work in groups for most of the game, finishing their project individually in the final two weeks. It is at that time that they apply onto their solution the basic elements of architectural language acquired thus far, focusing on form, light, the materiality of space, while solving the links between the public and the private area. The game is arbitered by 8 teaching assistants, two for each group. The arbiters are seeing that the rules are respected, but mainly help in the exchange of ideas and concepts. In the final stages they oversee the detailing of the individual solutions.

4 Findings and results

The findings of our exercise where from certain aspects surprising, especially in the first and the third year of the game. We will continue by describing separately the results for each year since there are important differences. We must also note here that this is exercise takes place in the second semester of the academic year. This is important since by that time we already have an idea as to how each study group performs in general. Some of the groups already had academic leaders, other charismatic leaders, and there were a few without clear leadership. Some of the groups where already clearly defined as micro-communities with an internal hierarchical structure, others were not.

What we noticed in the first year of the exercise was the different approach each of the four groups had toward the assignment. Some of the groups left the process of decision making to its leaders, while others produced an anarcho- syndicalist mode of decision making (Fig2). The ones that based their decisions solely on their academic leaders were to our surprise unable to produce a viable working model, since the weaker links felt left out, working by solely the numbers, not caring of the outcome. Cooperation between the higher strata of power and influence and the lower tier was weak. These neighborhoods were subsequently disjoined and split up between different factions and modes of work, as was the case of group B and C. In one case that of group D two of the students with better academic results were left out of the general plan due to their lack of social skills and somewhat stubbornness toward other ideas. In all these cases the qualities of the public space and immediate vicinities depended on the ability of each of these factions to interpret it. Much to our surprise the most interesting result came from what proved to be the less per formative group of the first semester. In the case of this group there was only one clear academic leader, and many charismatic leaders. More over this group, that immediately adopted the anarchic model of participatory decision making, was well aware of their inherent weakness. This however proved to be the engine of the group as a whole. Their level of involvement and participation was at such high such levels that other groups felt somewhat beaten halfway through the exercise. To our surprise we found out that this experience tightened this group so much that in the following years it became somewhat of a brand, others trying to emulate its spirit. The neighborhood that they produced, although not having the best individual solutions, was however the most complex and grounded in the requirements of the game. Public spaces where well distributed and vicinities carefully micromanaged among neighbors.

During the second year the experiment produced somewhat similar results, but unfortunately no group managed to surpass the success of the previous' year group A. What happened was a clarification of the relationships between public and private spaces. What we noticed was that in spite of actually playing some of the students were simply simulating their response trying to emulate what was already done, or at least what they thought that was expected of them. A level of conformity became evident as some solutions where simply treading on known ground. This might explain to a certain degree the modes in which certain tried and tested features and typologies are transmitted throughout generations, as was clearly the case here. However due to this issue nothing really stood out as original.

We tried to correct this in the third year introducing a new element in the logic of the game. Now each student had to build a "house" for a fictional literary character of his own choosing. Thus the city was inhabited by a more complex set of characters each with his own specific back story and atmosphere. The houses and the physical relationships they maintained between them had to somehow reflect the nature of the chosen characters. This was a good decision since again the students were forced to find new justifiable means of expression. It was in many ways a renaissance of the exercise. Again it produced surprises since what we considered to be one of the best group of students that we had seen in the past few years performed poorly. It was the case of group B this time, a group filled with personalities and notable students that once faced with the task of cooperating choose to downgrade their skills to some sort of common denominator. Thus none shined and all solutions looked similar, so much so that you could not clearly perceive the different narrative of their characters. Much to our surprise the group wilfully chose to produce a unitary formal concept that practically annihilated what gave them strength in their first place: their personalities. And again, the group that performed poorly in the first semester managed to outperform its competitors, this time not through grand scale common strategies but through successful micromanagement among individual neighbors. They were thus able to maintain their narrative stances individually while achieving complexity and order on a large scale. It was the most altruist mode of operation that we had seen thus far, perfectly describing the tit for tat logic of the prisoner's dilemma. Despite not getting along with one another, as prisoners of this game, they cooperated to get the best possible outcome.

Fig.2. Working on the game board and detail of the model

5 Conclusions and recommendations

We draw our conclusions by observing the progress of our witness students through the following academic years. We were thus able to see how this experience affected their performance in the second and third year of studies. We noticed that the students with good cognitive skills, manifested even from before the game, continued to show good responses towards their subsequent academic tasks. Upon individual questioning they considered the game as positive experience. Only one student from our first batch had mixed impressions since he felt ostracised by his group following his poor communication skills with what he considered to be inferior peers. In general we consider that these students would have performed well in any circumstance, with or without the game. The most surprising results came in the median area, where we noticed the forging of strong bonds between students. As we have already shown the students who were able to properly understand their individual weaknesses, were able to outperform others simply by combining their skills. This peer to peer exchange was the not only detrimental in their learning processes but in the final outcome of their projects. Through cooperation and micromanagement towards a common goal, these projects supplied the most adequate solutions for the public/ private space problematic. As a general observation we can thus conclude that in the case of our experiment the most engaging learning processes were observed with the groups that chose a participatory *modus operandi*. The trickle down tactic, or top down approach, where an established elite somehow gives the tone of the entire setting has produced poorer results that expected. In this respect this gives an interesting interpretation on the insular nature of the built environment. It also give some measure of a response to the question Lefebvre raised concerning the right to the city [9], on who is more entitled to symbolically appropriate the communal effort, the resulting neighborhood, its public and private spaces. In this respect we can argue that individual quality and singular expressions are not enough to establish or maintain a complex and democratic larger context. Participation can be achieved between similarly skilled peers, but is best manifested when all strata communicate on the top down / bottom up vector of decision making.

References

1. Culiciu, C. Romanian Cities and Socialist Urbanism. Consequences on the Aspect of the Cities and on Everyday Life. In W. J. Jedynak Kinal, From Post-Industrial to an

Information Society (pp. 33- 45). Rzeszow: Wydawnictwo Uniwersytetu Rzeszowskiego (2015)

2. Jurghiu& Costea, A. C. The Neither-nor Space, the Either-or Space. In D. C. Ina Stoian, The Would- Be City, Interventions in the post-comunist urban space (pp. 68-72). Cluj Napoca: Tact. (2012)
3. Bourdieu, P. Les regles de L'art, genese et structure du champ litteraire. Paris: Edition du Seuil (1992)
4. Lefebvre, H. *The Production of Space.* Oxford: Basil Blackwell .Debord, G. (2006) Theory of the Derive in Internationale Situationniste #2 1958. In K. Knabb, Situationist International Anthology (pp. 62-67). Berkley: Bureau of Public Secrets (1991).
5. DeCerteau, M. *The Practice of Everyday Life.* Berkley: University of California. (1984)
6. Debord, G. Theory of the Derive in Internationale Situationniste #2 1958. In K. Knabb, Situationist International Anthology (pp. 62-67). Berkley: Bureau of Public Secrets. (2006)
7. Pallasma, J. The Eyes Of The Skyn, Architecture of the Senses. Chichester: Wiley&Sons (2009)
8. Sadler, S. *The Situationist City*. Cambridge, Massachusetts: The MIT Press (1999)
9. Lefebvre, H. *The Right to the City.* In K. E. Lebas, Writing on Cities (p. 158). Chichester: Wiley- Blackwell (1995)

Working with mass and light: A challenge for architecture students

Diana Giurea[1a], and Cristian Blidariu[1]

[1]Faculty of Architecture and Urbanism, Politehnica University of Timisoara, Timisoara, Romania

Abstract. The distinctiveness of architecture education raises understanding issues and adaptation difficulties of first-year architecture students because of the abstract visual language they must become familiar with. Thus, a special attention should be given to the way in which the basics of architectural language are taught and implemented in particular design projects. The aim of this research is to test the efficiency of an intuitive-based didactical method through a specific design exercise. Therefore, in order to facilitate the shift from concrete elements to abstract ones we propose an exercise which will enable architecture students to design high-quality interior spaces. Starting from a personal space, each student will develop his/hers environment according to natural light needs, functional necessities and spatial relations between three main interior places, while working with an imaginary stone mass on which only subtractive operations are allowed. The illustrative part of the paper contains some of the students' work that we consider to be successful responses to the proposed exercise. This type of teaching method can trigger students' creativity by using only means which the students are already accustomed with: looking, searching and analyzing.
Keywords: Architecture students, mass, light.

1 Introduction

The need to study the architectural form is defined by the major changes occurring in the current anthropic environment through a variety of socio-cultural phenomena and interconnected processes. Diversity and differentiation are the main features of this environment [1] found in a continuous process of change and, thus, the recalibration of the built environment plays a crucial role. This has led to the need to think and act creatively and innovatively according to the new parameters. The architect now has the task of providing high performance solutions capable of meeting this level of complexity. Accordingly, architectural form should provide an answer to many problems whose causes will be sought in the changes in contemporary society, environmental conditions, technological progress, etc.

[a] Corresponding author: diana.giurea@yahoo.com

In Romania, the vast majority of people live in homes without architectural qualities, such as collective housing units intensively emerged during the communist period [2]. This type of buildings is characterized by standard living spaces built with regards to achieving high performance in economical and functional terms, but low attention to user's space experience and to his/hers real needs. This has led to a misconception of what architecture is and what can be achieved through it, constantly altering the way its inhabitants, including architecture students, perceive their surrounding built environment.

The task of architecture education, especially in the first year of studies, is to provide an experimental and effervescent environment able to stimulate the imaginary power of individuals and to establish the foundations of architectural language in students' conscience. The difficulty of managing this process is experienced beginning with the first year of study because each student has a certain amount of knowledge and experiences that can influence substantially their performance during the education period and in architectural practice. This paper tries to identify to what extent previous experiences can affect the creative performances of the architecture students.

The assimilation of a language does not always start with learning initial letters, but with perceiving its specific sounds. In architecture, the discussion is about the formal language whose alphabet is made up of the primary elements in which it can be decomposed [3]. But which is the counterpart of sound in architecture? It can be stated that the experience itself is the answer – a process by which the individual perceives the characteristics and general nature of the architectural object through physical referencing and in the light of previous experiences that may limit or intensify his/hers perception. The specificity of this present study consists in its focus on experience, where experience presumes movement in time and space such as in the case of the concept of burrow [4].

The didactic approach in this study uses a design experiment which proposes the return to the foundations of systems of thinking specific to man's primitive dwellings (Fig. 1) by imagining a situation that has only raw building material and one modeling tool. The choice of such a circumstance is explained by the low level of complexity of the material and its means of operation.

Fig. 1. Primitive dwellings in Cappadocia, Turkey

2 Aims and objectives

The main purpose of the proposed experiment is to test the influence of the background of first year architecture students, semester 1, on their imaginative abilities and the extent to which perceptive stimulation is capable to shape skills of detachment from the context in which they developed as individuals. The purpose is to develop a flexible thinking system that will ensure the transition from concrete components taken as they are to the specific formal abstracted language of architecture. To achieve this goal, we used a teaching method based on intuitive processes related to their own experience that, as Christopher Budd remarked, could stimulate the novelty, and the understanding of feelings and meanings [5].

Andrew Roberts estimated that individuals who tend to practice successfully intuitive thinking manage to see the big picture, in a holistic manner [6], an approach which is desirable in the architectural field. In this regard, the experiment "Working with mass and light" was born, aiming to provide students with the opportunity to express themselves creatively in their own space by increasing the spatial qualities using a single constructive material and a unique way of operating – subtraction. This experiment contains a number of objectives which participate in determining the influence the background of each student has on his/her formal expression means, such as: the definition and operation with a unitary formal language, the development of a imaginative three-dimensional thinking, the expression of differentiation by unity, the ability of correct dimensioning and spatial configuration according to the needs, etc.

3 The design experiment "Working with mass and light"

The experiment's starting data relates to the types of spaces where students spent most of their existence, space that has more or less left its mark on their perception of what architecture is, its composition and operating means. Thus, a survey was conducted on a number of 98 students, which revealed the following:

• 72 students live in urban multi-unit housing apartments built during the communist era, characterized by minimal and standardized spaces;

• 18 students live in urban single-family houses built during the post-revolution period (after 1989), an architecture characterized by resuming largely to functionalist and economic features of the collective dwellings described above;

• 8 students live in rural single-family homes, homes with low levels of interior comfort, but with access to a large outdoor space.

As an overview, the experiment consists of two major parts, structured in stages: analysis and implementation. The first part consists of three phases that will provide the base information for the design process. Starting from a perceptive analysis of the architectural elements with regards to the five senses (hearing, sight, touch, smell, taste), the student will focus on in-depth understanding of the specificity of personal space. In addition, he/she will try to familiarize him/herself with the notion of natural light and its effects on the perception of the character of interior spaces. The second part refers to the application of these information in the design of an architectural multispatial ensemble similar to the "burrow" type habitat, as it appears in the vision of Rudolf Arnheim [4].

3.1 The perceptive analysis of the architectural elements

The first stage of the experiment involves exploring the city of Timisoara in terms of the five senses, a process focused on identifying contrasts between various elements of the built environment, for example: vertical / horizontal, silence/noise, textured/plain, new/old, bright/dark, etc. This involves training thinking towards synthesizing visual information by three conscious actions: looking, searching and capturing. The anthropic environmental component analysis phase aims to establish the nature of architectural objects, but more importantly, the intuition of the means by which this character is defined. Furthermore, the student attempts to translate and interpret own feelings and experiences through the visual information extracted from the urban environment. It is worth mentioning that this is the student's first deliberate action of investigation and of understanding of parts which furnish urban space.

3.2 The analysis of personal space and the identification of its characteristics

Once the previous stage passed, representing a first step in intuiting the qualities and the character of architectural objects, towards which the students did not previously displayed a particular interest, it felt natural for the next step to be the application of the knowledge gained in the previous phase on their own personal space. The selection of personal space as a subject has emerged from the idea that each individual has an interior space that he perceives as his, that "my room", a micro-universe populated by "my objects", "my atmosphere", "my activities" which defines that person's individuality.

The analysis manner of this space proposed to the students consists of determining its specific physicality and phenomenology. For example, by drawing the space's survey, the student will realize the influence of physical boundaries on perception and the possible presence of obstacles. On the other hand, the phenomenological analysis of the personal space is related to the relationship between actions and place. Preference for a particular area of personal space may be the result of spending a considerable time in that place or a predisposition to undertake various activities in a subarea of personal space. For example, the place of study may serve as a place to stay or socialize therefore the overall size is directly influenced by multifunctionality, by the objects that actively participate in these functions, but also by the physical and spiritual needs that involve some activities.

Thus, the information that the student acquires from the study will meet both quality data of space and his/hers favorite place, and a list of things he considers to be shortcomings, complemented by a series of goals that could participate in increasing comfort in terms of spatial experience.

3.3 Natural light and the comfort of interior space

Daily activities are directly influenced by the comfort offered by the interior space in which they take place. By eliminating all means of amplifying the interior comfort and quality of life (furniture, technology, ambient elements, etc.), regarded as functional and aesthetic additions, all that remains is space itself. But this space interacts with environmental phenomena. Of these, natural light plays an essential role in perceiving objects, spatial boundaries or directing movement and flow.

Of course light is not the only factor that leaves its deep mark on the spatial experience specific to architecture but, to avoid overloading with variable elements and simplifying the analysis process to a single phenomenon through reduction, step 3 of the experiment focuses on identifying the means of introducing daylight indoors, the effects of plastics that it can get through and, not least, the influence exerted by this user's behavior in terms of spatial experience. The requirement for this phase is to look for examples of indoor natural light that actively participate in defining recognition along with their impact on spatial perception of the user.

3.4 Augmenting the reality of personal space

All information collected in the steps listed above, together with the theoretical part, represent working tools for advancing to the creative phase of the approach. The emphasis is on the individual and his/her quest to identify own needs, and the shortcomings arising from the interaction with personal space that will turn into something embedded into the project imagined.

3.4.1 The context

Starting from John L. Culkin's idea according to which "We shape our tools and therefore our tools shape us" [7] we can already see that the world consists of objects and phenomena, that we see the world concretely both through sight, hearing, smell, touch, and sensitively, based on experience and subjective interpretations of these experiences. Architectural space is both objective and subjective because it is built by what French philosopher Michael Foucault called the prosthetic god, that is, a man endowed with tools and technology. "Gods" have shaped the natural world, people have anthropized it by tools. A man maneuvering a hoe, a hammer, a chisel extends his will through the prosthetic tool. The chisel becomes an extension of the arm, just like today smartphones are becoming auxiliary organs of the mind. How many of you have not felt incomplete, cut off from the world, in its accidental absence? This is the power of tools. They transform us.

Equipped with tools that have enhanced his abilities, man transformed the world according to his measurements, has conquered and mastered it. Architectural space is thus a measure of man but also of these tools. As a consequence of these very tools, homes today are different from homes dating one hundred years ago, just as they in turn are different from homes dating a thousand years ago, and, regressing to the beginning of history, from the first caves occupied by man. Spatial archetypes however have remained unchanged because personal space has retained its functions: protection against the elements, protection against others, and a meeting place with them, place of individual study and reflection, as well as of hosting and receiving. Each of us wants to build this space according to our own desires.

3.4.2 Design assignment

The assignment puts the student in front of his/her own space. Until now, space was presented through words and objects, and dimensions it revealed. The student studied the qualities of spaces, saw how these spaces can interfere by tangents and overlaps, and had observed the qualities they acquire through light. Next he/she will use all these elements analyzed to redefine the room in an ideal representative variant. To do this, the student will start from his/her room's dimensions. It will be considered as the support-empty space around which he/she will have to redeploy a given built mass so as to generate subspaces and places only within this new material. The amount of mass that can be used and distributed around this given space cannot exceed six times the air volume of the existing room. In these new spatial limits with variable thicknesses, the requirement is to generate a place to sleep, a place to study and a place with a function to be chosen by each student according to own needs. The current capacity of the room shall remain recognizable until the end and can be formally changed only up to a maximum 25%. It will remain as a distribution and meeting space, a semi-public area to which other spaces are attached. The material making up the mass is rock. It can be built in blocks of different sizes or excavated from a single block. The tool will be the chisel. In spatial positioning, the student will have to operate with natural light and with light gap marks left both on the outer surface area (facade) and on the inside. The student will have to determine how one enters this space, what is seen and unseen, and if this process is an experience in itself.

3.4.3 Evaluation criteria

The evaluation criteria of the projects are designed to measure the levels of attainment of the objectives by each project. The main issues that have influenced the appreciation of final proposals were:

- creating a cursive and consistent spaciousness;
- the ability to interpret and generate a clear expression in a space;
- understanding the relationship between the excavated void and mass seen as a cover;
- the ability to negotiate in the same formal language with spaces with different functions;
- treating the epidermis as a mediator between the inner and outer space in the relation to the conditions of penetration of natural light and understanding the role the cover plays;
- the relationship between space, material and texture;
- clarity of concept expression by means of graphic and layout drafting.

Depending on the degree of fulfillment of these criteria, the projects relate to the minimum locative character from which the study started; by compared, we established whether the project has managed to overcome the "burrow" type organization through a complex spaciousness shaped according to wishes and needs.

4 Findings and results

Following the evaluation of the projects drawn, we have considered as positive responses to the experiment undertaken only 38 of the 95 works handed-in. Each of these has managed to fulfill most of the evaluation criteria stipulated above. Formally, there is a number of variables that participated in customizing each project, resulting in works that use various elements of more or less uniform architectural language. The main factors responsible for the differentiation and influence exerted by them on projects are listed in the Table 1.

Table 1. Variables and effects

Variables		Effect
Initial personal space dimensions and volume	→	Increase or decrease of the maximum of 6 times mass addition
The proposed function of the new interior spaces and connection means	→	According to the activities which would take place in that space, the overall size and interior configuration
Student personal preferencies	→	Vertical or horizontal project development, different types of introducing natural light in interior spaces
Quality and means of drawing and representation	→	The project is / is not easy to understand and is/is not
Guidance and discussions with two teachers, alternatively	→	The student tries to understand and apply into hir/hers project all the information gathered durring the discussions - a process which can be more or less accurate

It should be noted that the nature of the variables is found at different levels: variables related to actual data of the design assignment, preferences and imaginative capabilities of the student, and, not least, the type of guidance given by teachers and the understanding and assimilation of the aspects discussed during a project correction.

The images below depict some examples of the students' works (Figure 2) developed in this exercise that we have considered to be positive responses to the great complexity of the design assignment. As it can be seen, representation was left up to each student, which has highlighted even more the individuality of each project. Materials used for the layout and the operating technique represent the students' personal option, with the mention that the final result should be consistent with the drawn pieces and the general nature of the project.

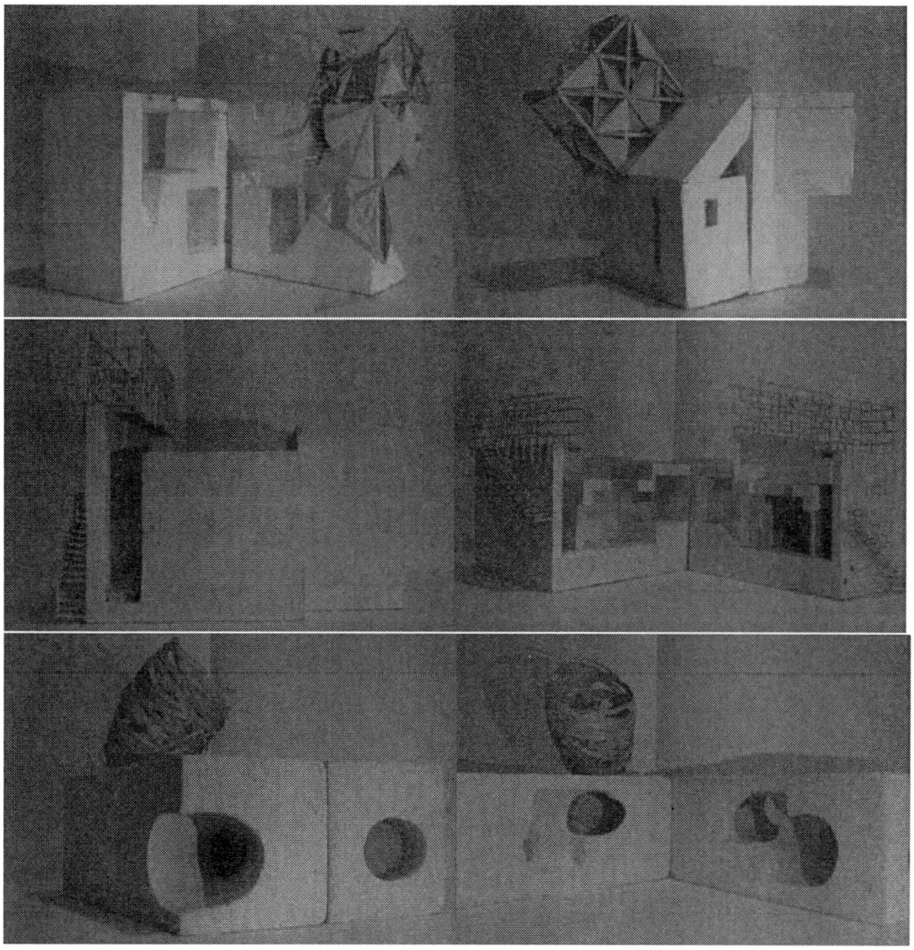

Fig. 2. Student work

This experiment however does not related to the architectural object resulted, but to testing the influence a student's previous experience can have on his/her imaginary and abstraction capability. The 38 projects evaluated positively relative to the current habitat of each architecture student translate numerically as follows:

-36 projects were developed by students who live in apartments in standardized collective dwellings;

-1 project belongs to a student living in an urban single-family home built in the early '90s;

-1 project was created by a student who lives in a rural modest single-family home.

It should be noted that if the two first categories of projects focused on interior space and the outer configuration remained parallelopipedic, for the third case increased attention to the expression of the interior space to the outside figure of the massive was observed.

5 Conclusions and recommendations

In conclusion, we believe that this intuitive-cognitive approach of the educational process in architecture for first year students can be considered a viable alternative to stimulate students' capacity for abstraction, a preamble in learning the architectural language's alphabet. The results confirm that the environment in which an individual carries out his/her daily existence can influence the perception on architectural spatial experience but not in an irreversible manner, as evidenced by the 38 positive results obtained in the experiment "Working with light and mass" which managed to exceed their possible limitations caused by the indoctrination produced by purely functionalist architecture and dictated by socio-economic factors.

In addition, it should be noted that the last project draws attention to the importance of access to the outer space for understanding the needs of external perceptual experiences in relation to the interior ones. From a teaching perspective, in order to improve outcomes for this type of exercise, we recommend the following:

- Ensuring the theoretical study necessary for each stage by outlining the elements of architectural language, concepts, focusing on the presentation of relevant case studies;
- In developing a design assignment, enunciation of data in the design assignment must consider presenting a clear framework for the conduct of the study;
- Increasing fixed character requirements and decreasing variable elements, where the latter will eventually focus on the means of architectural expression;
- Emphasizing the importance of dialogue between content and container, that is, in this case, mass and interior space;
- Considering the fact that in general design workshops in architectural education imply an extended collective of teachers, in which each member has certain preferences and sensitivities, we propose that revision sessions to alternate between revisions made by only one teacher with sessions with more teachers to establish common guide denominators;
- Developing a questionnaire able to reveal the quality of the backgrounds of each student.

References

1. F. Moussavi, *The function of form*. Cambridge, SUA: ACTAR, Harvard Graduate School of Design (2009)
2. C. Culiciu, *Romanian cities and socialist urbanism. consequences on the aspects of the cities and on everyday life. In From post-industrial to an information society,* Rzeszow: University of Rzeszow. p.39 (2015)
3. F.D. Ching, *Architecture: form, space and order*. Hoboken: John Wiley & Sons, Inc. (2007)
4. R. Arnheim, *The dynamics of architectural forms*. Berkeley: University of California Press, p.148 (1977)
5. C. Budd, *Valuing the Intuitive: Reintroducing Design Into Interior Design Education*. Journal of Interior Design, **36,** 3, v-xi (2011)
6. A. Roberts, *Cognitive styles and student progression in architectural design education*. Design Studies **27**, 161-181 (2006)
7. J.L. Culkin, *A Schoolman's Guide to Marshall McLuhan*. The Saturday Review , 51-53 (1967)

Student's information competence development: Experience and prospect

Dmitry Luchaninov[1a], Ruslan Bazhenov[1] and Natalia Bazhenova[2]

[1]Sholom-Aleichem Priamursky State University, Department of Information Systems, Mathematics and Training Methods, 679015 Birobidzhan, Russian Federation
[2]Sholom-Aleichem Priamursky State University, Rector, 679015 Birobidzhan, Russian Federation

Abstract. In the article the pedagogical interaction effectiveness for student's informational competence development within informational-educational environment is analyzed. The concept of pedagogical interaction, interactive tools of informational-educational environment, training methods for student's informational competence development are described. Sholom-Aleichem Priamursky State University served as an experimental base. The purpose of the experiment is to analyze effectiveness of interactive informational-educational environment tools used to create pedagogical interaction for the development of student's information competence. Two groups were selected for research: experimental (66 students) and control (69 students). Quantitative indicators of the dynamics testify the effectiveness of the experimental work: control group shows 4.4 percent progress while the experimental have 22.7 percent.
Keywords: Information competence, pedagogical interaction, university informational-educational environment

1 Introduction

The main peculiarity of higher education at this stage of evolutionary development is the availability of a large number of hardware and software tools to support the educational process. This is due to the emergence of modern educational concepts, such as Ubiquitous learning (U-learning) [1]. It implements the availability of training everywhere using any device capable of working with the web or its locally implemented components. Accordingly, faculty members devising the way of teaching their subjects increasingly use tools that provide an indirect access to educational material, assignments, consultations, that is, through specially organized interactive tools. The majority of documents regulating such an organization of the educational process use the term "Informational-educational environment", in which the student is immersed in the process of learning. However, the meaning of this term is too broad to describe the tools used to organize the training;

[a] Corresponding author: dvluchano@mail.ru

therefore, the more precise concept of "interactive tools of the informational-educational environment" is introduced. These tools give professors and lecturers an opportunity to organize an out-of-class activity of a student in a discipline, including the processes of indirect interaction, group work, etc., that is the processes of pedagogical interaction.

Learning management systems (LMS), i.e. ready-made kits (Moodle, Canvas, Edmodo, etc.) as well as specifically developed ones for a particular educational organization are often singled out among the interactive tools of the Informational-educational environment (IEE). LMS usually take the central place in the IEE because of some reasons connected with fulfilling the greater part of functions which are necessary for organizing pedagogical interaction. However, when a professor or a lecturer has an idea of conducting some classes in an informal way, these LMS happen to have defects, which cannot be repaired even with the help of extensions (plug-ins). Besides, many students do not actively seek socialization within the "imposed" system, preferring social networks to it. These problems help to recognize the fact that LMS being undoubtedly one of the most important elements of the interactive tools of the IEE need additional software to ensure the effectiveness of the learning process.

Moreover, while organizing pedagogical interaction, one should remember about the student's competence, which has to be formed as a result of training. There is an informational environment around the person in the modern world, all his life and professional activities abound with various pieces of information. Thus, the importance of the information competence of a person increases, as well as his ability to process, search, analyze, and synthesize information using different techniques and technologies. A lot of secondary schools begin to teach students to work with information using interdisciplinary teaching tools and e-learning environment [2].

There are many research works devoted to the usage of elements of IEE interactive tools, such as social network [3], student's rating system usage [4], development of interactive learning web-based environments [5], and other learning tools based on Web 2.0 technology [6]. In addition, systematic analyses of e-courses effectiveness [7-8], an assessment of students' satisfaction with their studies [9] are carried out. Besides, the analysis of using information technologies is made to support this concept [10]. All instruments claimed as tools for organizing and supporting training are located in the IEE.

The organization of pedagogical interaction is used to form professional competence in applied information sciences [11], engineering [12] and chemical [13] fields of study, when training how to use information technologies in the future professional activity of students majoring in Humanities [14].

The aim of this paper is to analyze interactive IEE tools used to create pedagogical interaction for the development of student's information competence.

2 Methods

We consider the information competence to be a set of knowledge, skills and experience in different areas of study when employing information technologies in future professional and educational activities of a student in the context of information interaction and information activities between subjects of the educational process.

Correspondingly, students' information competence will be defined as the possession of information competences, which enable to implement value and motivational components while doing future professional activities.

Pedagogical interaction is a purposeful interaction between professors / lecturers and students of the University, providing, through mutual influence, quantitative and qualitative changes in the form of improving existing knowledge, skills, and competences and increasing new ones.

The university informational-educational environment is a complex of program, technical, educational, organizational, administrative components of the university system, providing an immediate access to necessary information and organizing subject-subject communication between participants of the educational process.

According to the more precise definition of the IEE, it is necessary to describe the content of complex components. So, the software used for the IEE consists of different platforms to support the educational process. These platforms comprise official and educational sites of the university, LMS (in this paper LMS tools Moodle), tools for indirect pedagogical interaction (e-mail, social networks). Technical tools of the IEE are the equipment of the university (local university networks, servers and computers of the organization). Educational components include educational materials which help to organize the educational process (teaching materials, methodical systems of subject teaching, etc.). Organizational and management components belong to the system of the administrative organization of the IEE and are governed by normative documents of the federal and local levels, namely the Federal Law on Education, state standards of higher education, the Regulation on the Usage of the University IEE, etc. in the Russian Federation.

Interactive tools of the University IEE are a complex of components of the University IEE, providing an immediate access to necessary information, organizing indirect pedagogical interaction of a professor / lecturer and students, as well as actively and diversely reacting to their actions.

Interactive e-learning provides a powerful set of tools to stimulate the educational process, taking into account the needs and the training level of participants of the educational process. The usage of this approach is able to fulfill specific tasks, such as raising students' motivation, supporting with original materials, providing the clarity of basic concepts, increasing the intensity of training, as well as avoiding unnecessary workload.

For the organization of pedagogical interaction different interactive tools within the IEE were used to develop the student's information competence in 2015-2016. We used these tools taking into account the usage of U-learning. Sholom-Aleichem Priamursky State University was an experimentation facility of the research. 76 people took part in the research at its various stages. There were students and members of the faculties of Pedagogics and Psychology - Center for Pedagogical Education, Sociocultural Activity and Service, Mathematics, Information Technologies and Technics, Philology, History and Journalism. E-courses were developed for the subjects engaged in the research. Those e-courses helped to implement methods of pedagogical interaction and support the intramural educational process by tools of several tools available in the Informational-educational environment:

- electronic documentary tools;
- databases and knowledge databases;
- Moodle training management system;
- social networks (communities);
- rating system for recording students' academic achievements;
- free and licensed application software packages.

Electronic and documentary tools are usually included in the IEE as a necessary theoretical basis. Digital libraries, Internet resources for educational purposes, digital educational materials of a lecturer or a professor are often used for this purpose. Their usage is directly related to the knowledge component of the student's competence, his mastering of theoretical positions, technologies, methods, etc.

Databases and knowledge databases are used in two ways:

1. As an electronic resource, its usage is similar to electronic and documentary tools.

2. As an element of preparation, in this case students develop a knowledge database about the principles of an academic discipline, a system of theoretical guidelines. In particular, Wiki-technology, a system of glossaries, etc. are employed.

LMS Moodle is used to fulfill the following functions:

– developments of tasks which give a possibility to send a report in a file format, for example the program code for laboratory works with the attachment of the report;

– a consultation forum for discussing problems that a student can have during his studies, a chat system can also be used for this purpose;

– a forum for carrying out assignments, such as "feedback session", for example students can evaluate each other's projects and advise how to improve them;

– subject testing system used for intermediate and final testing of students;

– questionnaires and surveys that help to analyse the development of students' competences, which cannot be assessed by academic achievements;

– surveys employed to choose topics for student articles, reports, essays.

Communities of social networks are used to organize group work of students over a given problem under the guidance of a professor / lecturer. The usage of communities is an activating tool that transfers learning into an all-permeating one, due to the usage of mobile applications with the help of which a system with delayed communication can be transferred into an online communication system. The usage of mobile applications to inform about new emails also allows intensifying the support of the educational process.

The main function of the student's rating system is to inform students about the current state of their academic progress. When using this system, the competitive component of the educational process is employed, creating a situation of success or failure for students. These situations motivate them to make additional efforts.

Free and licensed software packages are used as tools for training information technologies. When choosing software, the following factors are taken into account:

1. Software localization should be in Russian, if there is no other way, e.g. absence of analogues, the English version is used.

2. The completeness of the functionality is also taken into account; software should offer all the possibilities that students need to master a subject successfully.

3. Teaching subjects with the help of information technologies has some peculiarities. It is necessary to have educational software on the student's computer. It determines the choice of freeware.

Students should do practical assignments on their own or in groups using computers and the Internet. For the organization of a group interaction of students, there was provided a branch of the forum to share information. Reports on practical assignments were made by each student in the form of an electronic document and uploaded for a professor's review in LMS Moodle. The rating system was used to inform students rapidly about the credits scored. This system is included in the University IEE. For illustrative purposes we will describe several techniques for improving the information competence of a student.

The seminar on the materials of original research works carried out by students under the guidance of a professor. At the beginning of the training, students were given an assignment to make a report on a selected topic. For instance, examples of machine translation systems were offered for students majoring in Linguistics. They made reports on each system and uploaded them with the help of the forum to be discussed by the group. The discussion began after getting an assignment in a month. In the course of the work, the professor assessed the activity of each student, his reaction to the comments of his/her classmates, the level of activity in defending his work, and in studying works of other students.

The system of "feedback session". A student is given an assignment (making a report, writing an essay, filming a video, etc.). After completing the given assignment the student uploads it onto a special branch of the forum. His groupmates evaluate this work, pointing at its drawbacks and recommending some improvements. Thus, the student has to defend his work, and then correct it taking into account groupmates' recommendations. The aim of this task is to be able to analyze the works which have some elements of project activities, to take criticism of various kinds, to interact with group members. IEE interactive tools in this case act as a necessary link between the students uploading their works for evaluation and a group of students evaluating these works.

The methods of creating positive competence motivation are employed in organizing and conducting in-person classes such as "dispute seminar", "conference seminar". First of all, students receive a broad topic for their performances. A student has to narrow the topic and choose a subtopic for his performance, to make a report and a presentation and speak at a studying conference.

Methods of organizing interactive cognitive and practical activities of students are arranged in the form of online learning and represent a complex of problematic and research tasks aimed at independent cognitive activity with supervisor's minimal support, which is realized with by tools of organizing indirect pedagogical interaction.

Each student was given an assignment that he was doing during the academic term. While carrying out this task (for example, inventing algorithms for publishing activities), a student could consult a supervisor by tools of a chat once a week. Other types of receiving advice on how to do this assignment were not available to him. The student handed in his work at the appointed time. Then it was checked according to the established criteria.

The assessment of students studying these subjects took place in two stages. The first stage was to test students with the help of LMS Moodle. Each student had an opportunity to be tested on the appointed day and was given one attempt. The second stage was to develop and defend one's own project in a subject. The defense of projects took place during the final class in the classroom.

The monitoring and measuring stage was implemented through the organization of the measurements of the students' information competence. These measurements were carried out for each subject under study during the first and last class.

3 Results and discussion

The main task of studying students' information competence was to observe and record the dynamics of indicators. The object of the research is the process of developing the student information competence, and the subject is the dynamics of changing the level of the student information competence which helps to overcome obstacles in the usage of information technologies.

Table 1. Students' information competence levels

Students' Information Competence Level	Level Characteristics
Low	When a student does an assignment with the help of information technologies, he independently reproduces and uses the algorithms of the learnt basis for carrying out this work
Middle	When the student does an assignment with the help of information technologies, he produces subjectively new information in the course of an independent synthesis of a known basis
High	When the student does an assignment with the help of information technologies, he creates new algorithms for each new situation / task, i.e. objectively new information

Two groups of students were selected for the study. The first control group was trained according to the system of mixed training. LMS Moodle was employed as the site which contained materials and assignments to carry out. The most part of classes was conducted in the classroom. The second experimental group was trained with the help of the pedagogical interaction system. Test measurements showed quantitative changes in the levels of students' information competence in the control and experimental groups.

Table 2. Students' information competence levels dynamics in control group

Groups	Number of students	Students' information competence levels					
		Low		*Middle*		*High*	
		No.	*%*	*No.*	*%*	*No.*	*%*
Before	69	56	81.2	9	13.0	4	5.8
After	69	43	62.3	19	27.5	7	10.2

Table 3. Students' information competence levels dynamics in experimental group

Groups	Number of students	Students' information competence levels					
		Low		*Middle*		*High*	
		No.	*%*	*No.*	*%*	*No.*	*%*
Before	66	32	48.5	20	30.3	14	21.2
After	66	13	19.7	24	36.4	29	43.9

The analysis of the research results allows us to speak about the effectiveness of the usage of pedagogical interaction, realized with the help of interactive tools of the informational-educational environment. At the same time, the transition of students from the low level of the information competence to the average level is especially significant. It indicates that there is a shift in the competence, an appearance of a vector for the further development of a student. In addition, the usage of pedagogical interaction has significantly increased the level of the information competence of students who already had prior knowledge.

Quantitative indicators of the dynamics testify the effectiveness of the experimental work, i.e. pedagogical interaction in IEE conditions contributes to the development of the student information competence.

4 Conclusion

The control measurement according to the indicators after the forming experiment showed quantitative changes in the student information competence. The dynamics of these data indicates to the effectiveness of the experimental work. The study shows that pedagogical interaction can be an essential part of the educational process if we change the forms of education. A distinctive feature of pedagogical interaction is the organization of intensive interaction of students with various elements of the IEE. It helps to master students' information competences.

This research does not completely clear up the problem under consideration, offering only one of the variants of its solution. Prospects for further research may be related to the in-depth development of diagnostic techniques and the expansion of pedagogical activity forms in the interaction of the informational-educational environment that forms the information competence of students.

References

1. Lopez, G. A., Builes, J. A., & Villamil, S. C. Overview of u-learning. Concepts, characteristics, uses, application scenarios and topics for research. IEEE Latin America Transactions,14(12), 4792-4798., (2016). doi:10.1109/tla.2016.7817013
2. Kim, Y., & Smith, D. Pedagogical and technological augmentation of mobile learning for young children interactive learning environments. Interactive Learning Environments,25(1), 4-16., (2015). doi:10.1080/10494820.2015.1087411
3. Meishar-Tal, H., & Pieterse, E. Why Do Academics Use Academic Social Networking Sites? The International Review of Research in Open and Distributed Learning,18(1), 1-22., (2017). doi:10.19173/irrodl.v18i1.2643
4. Reeves, T. Evaluating what really matters in computer-based education. Computer education: New perspectives, 219-246., (1994).
5. Albertos-Marco, F., Penichet, V. M., & Gallud, J. A. Distributing Web Interaction: The Web Interaction Hub Capabilities. Proceedings of the XVII International Conference on Human Computer Interaction - Interacción 16, 37., (2016). doi:10.1145/2998626.2998654
6. Greenhow, C., Robelia, B., & Hughes, J. E. Learning, Teaching, and Scholarship in a Digital Age: Web 2.0 and Classroom Research: What Path Should We Take Now? Educational Researcher,38(4), 246-259., (2009). doi:10.3102/0013189x09336671
7. Mwalumbwe, I., & Mtebe, J. S. Using Learning Analytics to Predict Students' Performance in Moodle Learning Management Systems: A case of Mbeya University of Science and Technology. The Electronic Journal of Information Systems in Developing Countries, 79(1), 1-13., (2017).
8. Umek, L., Keržič, D., Aristovnik, A., & Tomaževič, N. An assessment of the effectiveness of Moodle e-learning system for undergraduate public administration education. International Journal of Innovation and Learning, 21(2), 165-177., (2017). doi:10.1504/IJIL.2017.081939
9. Clawson, S. L. Does quality matter? Measuring whether online course quality standards are predictive of student satisfaction in higher education (Doctoral dissertation, Capella University), (2007).
10. Smeureanu, I., & Isaila, N. Information technology, support for innovation in education sciences. Procedia - Social and Behavioral Sciences,15, 751-755., (2011). doi:10.1016/j.sbspro.2011.03.177
11. Nazarova, O., Maslennikova, O., Davletkireeva, L., & Novikova T. Modeling and factor analysis of efficient increase of bachelors and masters' training connected with applied informatics. ARPN Journal Of Engineering And Applied Sciences, 11(3), 2030-2036., (2016).
12. Maldague, X., Kuimova, M., Burleigh, D., & Skvortsova, S. Information and Communication Technologies in Engineering Education. MATEC Web of Conferences, 79, 01044., (2016).
13. Busstra, M. C., Hulshof, P. J., Houwen, J., Elburg, L., & Hollman, P. C. Nutrient analysis explained for non-chemists by using interactive e-learning material. Journal of Food Composition and Analysis,25(1), 88-95., (2012). doi:10.1016/j.jfca.2011.07.003
14. Luchaninov, D.V., Bazhenov, R. I., Shtepa, Y. P., Kazinets, V. A., & Ledovskikh, I. A. Student Information Competence under Conditions of the Realization of Interactive Pedagogical Interaction. Global Media Journal, (S2), 1-7., (2016).

Education of organic chemistry at the grammar school - problem parts of subject

Eliška Tvarohová[1a], and Simona Hybelbauerová[1]

[1]Charles University in Prague, Faculty of Science, Department of Teaching and Didactics of Chemistry, Prague, Czech Republic

Abstract. In teaching of chemistry, every teacher can enumerate some topics of the chemistry curriculum, which are hard to understand or to memorize for grammar school students. These topics were defined as a problematic parts of subject. There was a qualitative educational research conducted with teachers of chemistry at grammar schools. The goal of the research was not limited to determinate the difficult parts of curriculum in organic chemistry but also included methods of the teaching. Finally the research also encompassed the reason behind the root causes misunderstanding of organic chemistry topics. Based on the results of this research there were new learning materials designed. They show the problematic topics of organic chemistry in different ways using other teaching methods. These materials will be consulted with teachers and theory will be proved in chemistry lesson at grammar school.
Keywords: chemistry curriculum; problematic parts of curriculum; learning materials in organic chemistry; educational research, grammar school

1 Introduction

Chemistry education at the grammar school level is defined in educational objectives which are laid down by Framework Education Programme for grammar schools [1] and further detailed by the grammar school. Experiences of teachers and their long-standing practice show the educational areas which are repeatedly hard to understand for students. This could have a bad impact to the achievement of educational objectives. There was a research conducted to discover the problem parts and their causes focused on organic chemistry at grammar school. It is the first goal of the project. Based on the results of the research there were the new learning materials developed, which explain the problem areas and their educational content another way and they can probably more easily achieve the educational objectives. This was considered as the second main goal of the project.

[a] Corresponding author: eliska.tvarohova@gmail.com

2 Methods

All goals of the study were reached by several methods, which depend on each other. The results of one were used as an input of the next.

The qualitative educational research was made in 2015. There were 15 teachers with an average length of their practice of 17 years, who got involved in the research. A questionnaire and controlled interview were chosen as tools for the research [2]. Teachers could answered the questions by themselves or selected from various possibilities of answers. These results were the most important step in the research, because they presented the problem parts of organic chemistry an their causes at grammar school and also their supposed causes. Teachers have expressed the interest of various materials and provided valuable advices and ideas.

After finding out the problem areas there was made a short comparative analysis of these parts in the six most frequently used chemical textbooks [3]. The analysis was based on defined criteria, which were evaluated by point scale from 1 = minimum to 3 = maximum. Analysis of textbooks monitored the content, range, intelligibility, text structure, difficulty of topic, selected reactions, their mechanisms, examples of compounds, explanation of new words, pictures, graphs, motivational text, questions and tasks for students. All these informations were useful for design of new learning materials and worksheets [4].

3 Findings

The qualitative educational research results show four the most problematic topics in organic chemistry at the grammar school. The first topic is inductive and mesomeric effects. Teachers said, student don't comprehend the main substance of effects. The second topic are reaction mechanisms. Teachers are missing comprehensive and systematic materials which simplify and better explain the topic to students. The third topic is organic nitrogen compounds. Students supposedly don't understand different properties of the compounds, nomenclature and also don't take interest in this topic. The fourth problematic part are heterocyclic compounds. This topic is probably too abstract and difficult which caused demotivation to study.

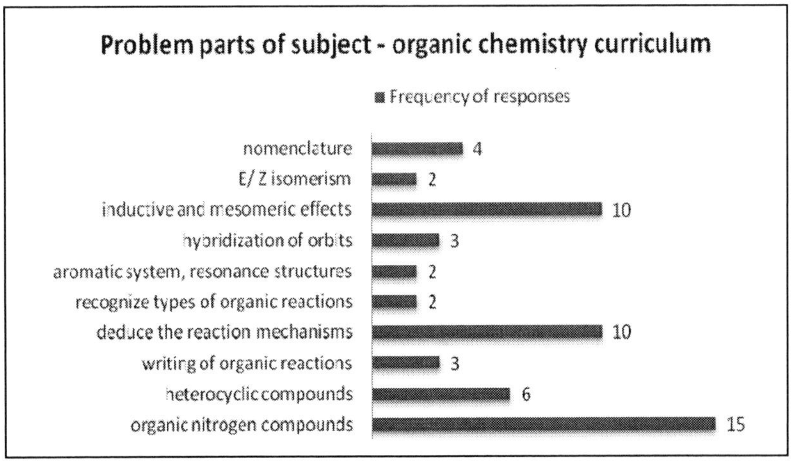

Graph 1. Problem parts of subject – organic chemistry curriculum

Teaching methods of these topics are usually lecture method, demonstration of a chemical experiment and continuesly repeating and explain of problem parts of curriculum.

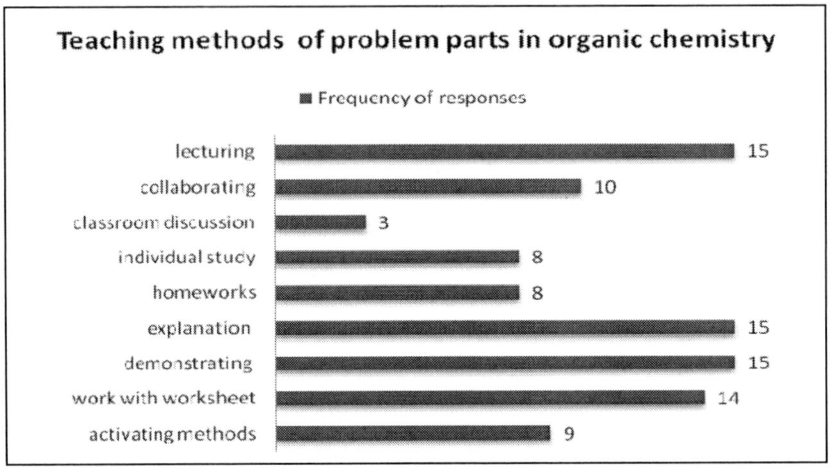

Graph 2. Teaching methods of problem parts in organic chemistry

Teachers also admitted they almost don't use the books so they would appreciate any other materials for teaching eg. worksheets, examples or interesting synthesis or things from daily life.

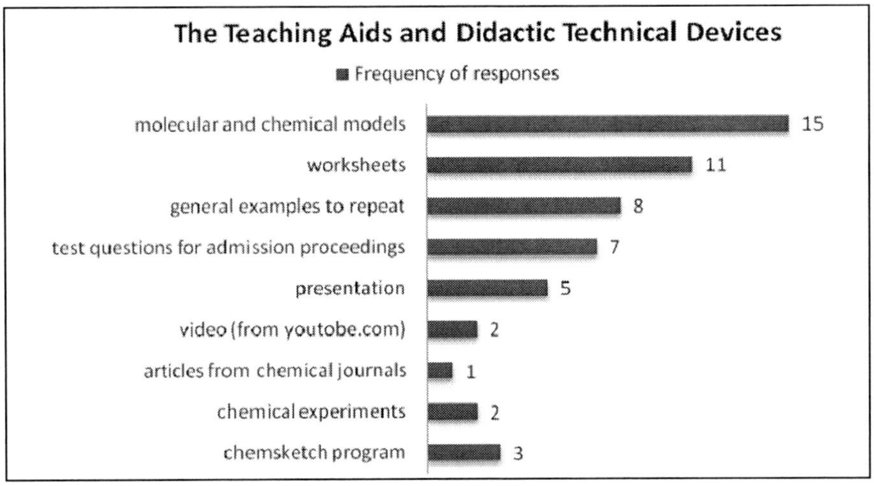

Graph 3. Teaching aids and didactic technical devices

4 Discussion and conclusion

One of the goal of the project was to design new learning materials [5], which can improve the teaching and could be helpful to teachers and their students as well. We tried to use other teaching methods and didactic technical devices. New learning materials explain the problem areas and their educational content another way and teachers with students can probably more easily achieve the educational objectives.

The topic inductive and mesomeric effects is presented as learning tasks for group lesson. All tasks should expand chemical thinking and stimulate thinking about the influence of the substituent on the whole molecule. The main aim of this material is steer students towards logical thinking, deduce from the properties of effects and explain that to the others in the group. They are responsible for the schoolwork and they can choose the way, how to explain that. The role of the teacher is just to be a kind of support for students in the group. Teacher is not the only one, who explains everything. There was designed the methodological guidelines for teachers, which contain the goals of the group lesson, realization part and the possibility of evaluation including some feedback questions.

After analysis of chemical textbooks and from the results of the research, there are seven the most teaching mechanisms of organic reactions. All of them were depicted to the powerpoint presentation. Firstly the reaction, next slide is the mechanism of the reaction. Below mechanism there are informations about the single steps and their causes. The presentation is including motivation tasks and interesting synthes. This material could be useful for teachers and students as well, considering that it is comprehensive overview of selected reaction mechanisms.

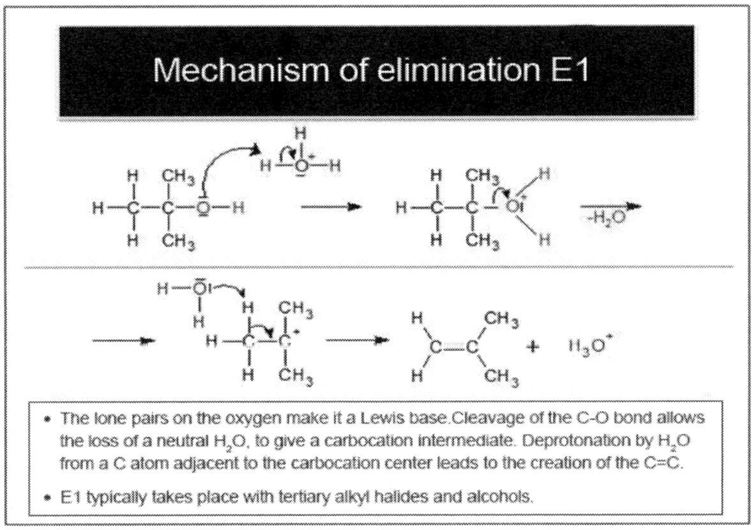

Fig. 1. Reaction mechanism of elimination (E1)

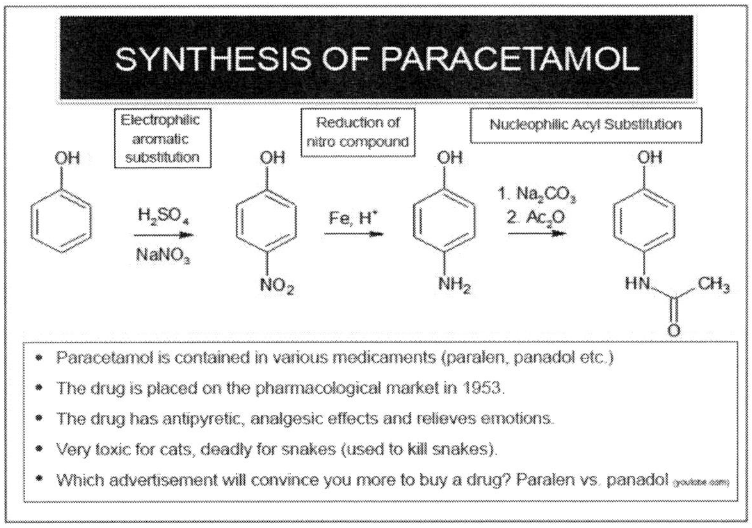

Fig. 2. Interesting synthesis of paracetamol

Different properties of the nitrogen compounds and nomenclature are explained by the worksheet. Students are working with incentive text, adds new information down to the

DOI: 10.1051/shsconf/20173701012

teacher's interpretation and fulfil learning tasks, which are based on newly acquired knowledge. The worksheet is rich in compelling information and curious tasks from daily life. It should motivate the students and make the topic more interesting. The worksheet was created for students and also for teachers including solution of all tasks and questions.

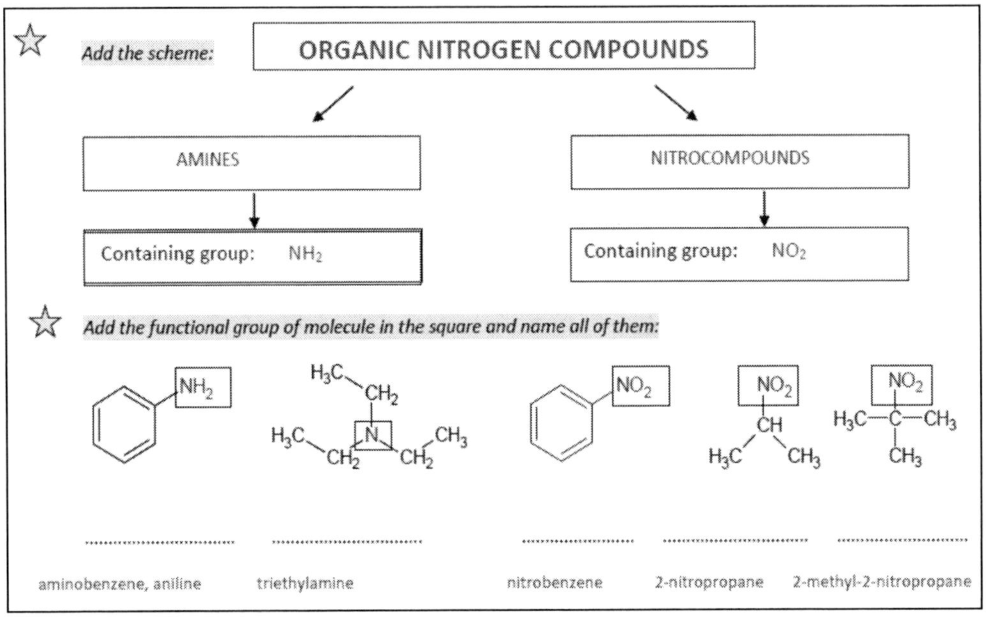

Fig. 3. Part from worksheet – Nitrogen compounds

Heterocyclic compounds are presented by project method of teaching with focus on motivation and interesting compounds from daily life of students. The intention of the project is to give students insight into the topic by themselves. There were chosen some compelling topic e.g. vitamins, medicine, drugs, hormones. The project method is demanding for teachers and organization of the lesson. Therefore there was designed the methodological guidelines for teachers, which could help them to organize the time and student´s work.

The research found out the problem parts in organic chemistry curriculum at the grammar school, their causes and teaching methods of these topics. Established results were used as starting point for new designed learning materials. All materials were discussed with teachers and will be verify at grammar school.

During the educational research teachers have expressed the interest of accomplishment in the same research across whole chemical curriculum at the grammar school. The extended research is taking place and should introduce an overview to the problem parts of curriculum in chemistry. The output of the research is going to be an overview of problematic parts of chemistry curriculum and the set of learning materials which will ease the lectures and students understanding.

References

1. MŠMT. *Rámcový vzdělávací program pro gymnázia: RVP G.* Praha: Národní ústav pro vzdělávání, 2007. ISBN 978-80-87000-11-3
2. Skalková, J. a kol. *Úvod do metodologie a metod pedagogického výzkumu.* Praha: SPN,

1983
3. Huvarová, M. *Nejpoužívanější středoškolské učebnice chemie na gymnáziích* [online]. Olomouc, 2010, [cit. 2015-7-12]. Bakalářská práce. Katedra anorganické chemie, Přírodovědecká fakulta, Univerzita Palackého v Olomouci. Vedoucí práce doc. RNDr. Marta Klečková, CSc.
4. Mrázová, L. *Tvorba pracovních listů: metodický materiál* [online]. Brno: Metodické centrum muzejní pedagogiky, 2012, [cit.2016-4-12]. Dostupné z: HTTP://MCMP.OMEGADESIGN.CZ/FILEADMIN/USER_UPLOAD/VZDELAVANI/METODICKE_TEXTY/10_PRACOVNI_LISTY_S_ISBN_1._11..PDF. ISBN 978-80-7028-403-2.
5. Lepil, O. *Teorie a praxe tvorby výukových materiálů* [online]. Olomouc: Univerzita Palackého v Olomouci, 2010, [cit.2016-4-12]. Dostupné z: http://zvyp.upol.cz/publikace/lepil.pdf. ISBN 978-80-244-2489-7

Managerial communication and its changes in the global intercultural business world

Marcel Pikhart[1a]

[1] University of Hradec Kralove, Faculty of Information Technology and Management, Department of Applied Linguistics, Hradec Kralove, Czech Republic

Abstract. The current business world is experiencing significant changes in the way people communicate in the global intercultural environment. The presented paper summarizes the most common trends and attempts to find invariants of this communication so that it could possibly facilitate business communication in the global world leading to increased efficiency and thus profitability. The communication tools used in this communication have seen unprecedented changes which influence not only the means of communication but also its contents and pace at which the information is transferred. To understand these phenomena will help us to enhance the business communication but also to eliminate misunderstandings which can potentially create serious problems.
Keywords: Managerial communication; business world; communication tools

1 Introduction

The current business world is experiencing significant changes in the way people communicate in the global intercultural environment, and thus, the author attempts to focus on these changes inasmuch they can influence business communication and company profitability. The presented paper summarizes the most common trends of business intercultural communication and tries to find invariants of this communication so that it could possibly facilitate business processes in the global world leading to increased efficiency and therefore even profitability.

1.1 Literature review

The topic of global changes in business and communication has already got enough attention from the scholars [9]. There has also been a lot of research into business communication [4, 7, 12, 18], into global business communication [1, 11, 18] and intercultural communication [2, 5, 8] in the last two decades due to the increased

[a] Corresponding author: author@e-mail.org

interconnections among companies since the beginning of the new millennium. The introduction of the Internet as the new medium of communication has changed the way the information is transferred and the way the companies communicate so that the need for the research from linguistics [10, 15, 19], sociopragmatics [6], managerial and communication studies was very urgent. However, we still lack a combination of these approaches which would look for synergy of these analyses. We claim that it is not very useful to describe business communication from a merely linguistics point of view, and similarly, the pure managerial approach to business communication is not sufficient either to explain properly the trends and the consequences. Therefore, we are trying to find a symbiosis of these approaches [14].

1.2 Current trends in business communication

The communication tools used in business communication have seen unprecedented changes which influence not only the means of communication but also its contents and pace at which the information is transferred [3, 16]. To understand these phenomena will help us to enhance the business communication but also to eliminate misunderstandings which can potentially create serious problems in the business market [13, 17].

The modern communication tools are widely used not only in everyday communication but also in business communication, and more and more people from various cultural contexts use these tools to exchange information. First, it is the modern communication tools, and second, intercultural business environment which create the background and platform of our communication. These two phenomena significantly influence the nature of our business communication and the paper tries to find how they interfere with each other.

There are a few new issues emerging from the global nature of current business communication as described by Hua [7]. She talks about the difficulties when looking for a common language, problems with inadequate translations into the subsidiary language, difficulties with spoken language and its varieties, centralisation of the power to the hands of a few people who lead the company through the official language, and the people lacking the language and communication skills may feel isolated. It is possible to spot these trends and therefore our research tries to find out if these issues are still under way.

2 Research

The presented study is significant for all companies as basically all of them do some international business, i.e., they must communicate in the global business environment when using modern communication technologies. However, as the research shows, the managers are not aware of potential communication problems arising from the situation. The aim of the research was to find out what the current trends of business communication are and how these trends can be described so that they can be better understood. The research also looked into the connection between globalization and technical changes in communication in intercultural management.

2.1 Research methodology

The methodology used in the research was observations and questionnaires, as the author has access to several Asian and European multinational corporations and small and medium enterprises as a consultant, therefore, the data collected are both quantitative and qualitative. The researched companies do business both in the European and the Asian markets in areas of insurance, banking but also industrial production and machinery. The top management is both European and Asian, and the employees are mostly European.

Several interviews were conducted with the top and middle management of these companies or the company owners as well, to evaluate and find out the level of awareness of the situation in the global market regarding the communication principles and standards. The data obtained were processed using standardised techniques of statistics and further used in implications and discussion part of the paper.

2.3 Research results

The research results led us to several findings which can prove useful not only for the academic world but also for the people who are responsible for communication strategies in the companies, i.e., the top management, middle management, sales people responsible for external communication, and HR employees who are responsible for internal communication setting.

The people responsible for intercultural business communication are usually not aware of the potential pitfalls and the results of the research can also bring important ideas for improvement of the communication strategies in the companies. Almost everyone has agreed that the quantity of transferred information has increased dramatically versus the quality of the information.

The language competencies of the middle and top management of these companies were on a good level or even very good levels, however, the intercultural communication competencies were somehow neglected. Just a few companies offered training of intercultural communication skills for the management. The business communication has changed radically as confirmed by the majority of respondents usually complaining about the unprecedented increase of the volume of information, the quantity versus the quality of information is perceived in a very negative way.

The virtual electronic communication, now dominating over traditional mail, has led to quantitatively unlimited stream of dozens to hundreds of emails a day, which causes significant problems in maintaining the communication in a manageable way. The significant part of information is lost during the process of the transfer of the information due to the improper use of the modern communication means. The majority of the researched managers would welcome the change if all the people involved in business communication would be aware of the current trends.

3 Discussion

The author tries to show that managerial training of intercultural communication abilities is a must for anyone who does international business and that is also the reason why the paper calls for this kind of training which should be implemented in the university curricula for the students who study business and economy, international trade and business related study programmes. The research results clearly show the urge of the current world to be able to communicate in the intercultural world efficiently and use modern communication tools so that they facilitate the communication and not blur the message which is intended to be transferred.

All the described changes also caused many organisational alterations leading to core business thinking, major use of outsourcing, increased specialization, and thus, increased cooperation in the form of joint ventures and global alliances. Communication therefore becomes the key topic as the pace of globalization is very fast and it supports making networks and cooperation with partners from various cultural backgrounds.

4 Conclusion and implications

Communication plays a crucial part in modern business and is probably one of the most important issues when doing business globally. Neglecting the communication and its proper function would have fatal consequences which would inevitably lead to the loss of the market, current or potential. The presented study is significant for all companies as basically all of them do some international business, i.e., they must communicate in the global business environment using modern communication technologies. However, as the research shows, the managers are not aware of potential communication problems arising from the situation.

When predicting the future development, we have to take into account that multicultural and intercultural communication will take the lead in the global communication, Discourse and communication will create the space for competitiveness and innovativeness. The global companies are created as networks of people from multicultural environments and the top and middle management must be aware that there are specific competencies for them to manage these people. Intercultural competencies and the right solving of problems in this environment will be a must for anyone who wants to be successful in the global market. The role of trust will also be taken into account as it will be more and more important in managing people. Their involvement and engagement will be connected to the way the management communicates with them, and this communication will always be intercultural due to the nature of the current world.

References

1. M. J. Gannon, K. L. Newman. *The Blackwell Handbook of Cross-cultural Management.* Oxford: Blackwell Publishers Ltd, (2002)
2. A. Firth, *The Lingua Franca Factor. Intercultural Pragmatics* **6**-2, 147-170, 1612-295x/09/0006-0147, (2009)
3. T. L. Friedman, *The World is Flat: A Brief History of the Twenty-First Century*, (2007)
4. M. Geeritsen, C.Nickerton, *BELF: Business English as a Lingua Franca.* In *The Handbook of English Discourse*, (2009)
5. A.Holliday, M. Hyde, J. Kullman, *Intercultural Communication. An Advanced Resource Book for Students,* (2010)
6. J. House, Introduction: The Pragmatics of English as a Lingua Franca. *Intercultural Pragmatics* **6**, 141-145, (2009)
7. Z. Hua, *Exploring Intercultural Communication. Language in Action,*(2014)
8. J. Jackson, *Introducing Language and Intercultural Communication,* (2014)
9. A. Koblizkova (Eds.), R. Kucha, H.Cudak, *Intercultural Communication through International English.* p. 101 – 115. In *European ideas in the works of famous educationalists. Internationalization, globalization and their impact on education.* Studia i Monografie nr. **41** (2013). Łódź, Społeczna Akademia Nauk, pp. 558, (2013).
10. W. P. Lehman, The role of Intercultural Studies in the Development of Linguistics. *Intercultural Communication Studies* XV: **3** (2006)
11. R. D. Lewis, *When Cultures Collide: Leading Across Cultures*, (1996)
12. L. Louhiana-Salmien, *Business Communication.* In *The Handbook of English Discourse.* Ed. Francesca Bargiela-Chiappini, (2009)
13. A. Luzio, *Culture in Communication: Analyses of Intercultural Situations,* (2001)
14. M. Pikhart, *Interkulturní komunikace v globálním obchodě. Perspektivainterkulturního managementu*, (2013)
15. I. Piller, Linguistics and Intercultural Communication. *Language and Linguistics Compass* **1**/3 (2007) 208-226 (2007)

16. L. A. Samovar, R. E. Porter, *Communication Between Cultures*, (2007)
17. H. Spencer-Oatey, *Culturally Speaking. Culture, Communication and Politeness Theory,* (2008)
18. P. Tan, R. Rudby, *Language as Commodity. Global Structures, Local Marketplace.* (2008)
19. H. G. Wolf, F. Polzenhagen, *Intercultural Pragmatics* **3**-3 285-321, (2006).

The design of free activities for teaching science: A study with preservice teachers

María Puig-Gutiérrez,[1a] and Marta Cruz-Guzmán Alcalá[1]

[1]Departmet of Didactics of Experimental and Social Sciences, Faculty of Education Sciences, Seville University, C/ Pirotecnia s/n, 41013,Seville, Spain

Abstract. This paper studies a science teaching problem related to students in the Bachelor of Preschool Education at the Seville University, Spain. Preservice teachers face difficulties when designing child-guided activities (also called, free activities). This type of tasks is desirable in preschool classrooms, because they promote creativity, observation capacity, inquiry and children autonomy. With the aim of improving the formation in the Bachelor, two university teachers have asked 136 preservice teachers of the third course to design a 'children´s corner in their future classroom' about a specific issue related to the science area in preschool education, according to the Spanish legislation. It is shown the headings of the students´ report as a result of their work. It has been analyzed the quality of the child-guided designed activities. It has been observed the need of improving the explicit instruction about the design of free activities for the first educational level.
Keywords: child-guided activities; preschool education; preservice teachers

1 Introduction

To design free activities that allow students to explore the world around them and begin their learning in the scientific area is a key aspect of the formation of preservice teachers. Thus we consider that the corners of work are a good opportunity to carry out these activities and to develop in children basic scientific skills as inquiry thinkining, reasoning or creativity

For this reason, we believe that preservice teachers should have the possibility to design activities with which students reach a more autonomous and independent learning. This could help them in some way to overcome the traditional model of teaching. So in this paper we focus on the quality of the activities preservice teachers design when they are asked to plan free activities.

[a] Corresponding author: mpuig@us.es

2 Theoretical background

Several authors claim teachers need to balance both child-guided and adult-directed activities [1]. That is the reason why preservice preschool teachers need to know how to plan both types of activities. In this paper we want to know the quality of the child-guided activities preservice preschool teachers design. Our hypothesis is that there is an educational problem, related to the science teaching, in the Bachelor of Preschool Education at the Seville University, Spain. Preservice teachers could face difficulties when designing child-centered activities (also called, free activities). This type of tasks is desirable in preschool classrooms, because they promote creativity, observation capacity, inquiry and children autonomy.

Child-centered activities have been studied in preschool research. It has been seen [2] that teachers' use of child-centred approaches affected pupils' acquisition of science skills in schools. Also, child-centered classroom strategies, as thinking routines, develop positive attitudes in children toward thinking and learning. In literature there are examples of child-centered activities [3] that grounded children's understanding.

It could be difficult for preservice teachers, who have lived a traditional teaching model, to design effective free activities in the learning process of their pupils, as teachers tend to teach in the same way they have been taught [4]. This could be one of the reasons why teachers avoid the inquiry activities in the kindergarten class. Besides, it is usual to find preschool preservice teachers thinking children aged 4 to 6 years old are not able to initiate and follow process of science inquiry, although nowadays it is well known that these children are able to build science process skills such as asking questions, formulating hypothesis, observing, classifying, or sorting [5]. Instead of designing high quality free activities, they could plan playful activities, leaving the learning process for further teacher-directed activities. However, a successful free activity is able to promote a meaningful change in the children's ideas, besides to enhance intellectual capacities as important as creativity, or scientific skills as the formulation of hypothesis, planning an inquiry, data analysis, reach conclusions, teamwork, etc. Also, some researchers [6] have found evidence that too much teacher-directed activity undermines young children's self-confidence and motivation to learn.

In this context, we need more research about the difficulties preservice preschool teachers could face when planning child-guided activities, to be able to give them an adjusted quality formation on how to plan child-guided activities, which develop science process skills.

The aim of this paper was to analyze the free activities designed by 136 preservice preschool teachers, who study at the Seville University, in Spain. We wanted to know the quality of these planned activities, searching their potential as children meaningful learning.

3 Method

3.1 Participants and context

The participants of the study were 136 preservice preschool teachers grouped in small teams. All of them were coursing two coordinated subjects of the third course of the Preschool Bachelor 'Teaching about the Natural Environment (0-6 years old)' and 'Knowledge of the Social Environment'.

3.2 Data collection tool

For data collection, it was used a report made by preservice students. It had seven questions to be answered. The fifth one asks for the design of a minimum of three child-centered and three teacher-directed activities. In this communication, authors analyse the free activities planned by students.

Table 1. Data collection tool.

Guide for the children´s corner design.
1. Name of the children´s corner
2. Age of children
3. Importance of the corner´s subject, and its learning sense and value
4. Setting: Description, materials and resources you need
5. Activities (Name, objectives, description, duration, resources) a) Teacher-directed ones (3 or more). A group of pupils are guided by the teacher b) Free activities (3 or more): They are able to be developed without the teacher´s guide.
6. References (APA 6th Edition)
7. Books and stories (3 -4) for the children´s corner

3.3 Data analysis instrument

For the qualitative analysis, it is presented the second instrument, which is based in the child-guided learning characteristics [1]. It has been stablished seven items to assess the quality of every free activity, using a 1 to 4 scale for each item, where 1 shows the greatest disagreement and 4 the greatest agreement. The two authors applied the analysis rubric independently, with the goal of crossing data and reaching consensus on the evaluated items in cases of missing agreement. In this way, it was reached a 100% of agreement on every item.

Table 2. Data analysis instrument.

Corner´s name	Activity Nº. Activity description				
Items	**1**	**2**	**3**	**4**	**Comments**
1. It does not need the adult intervention (the teacher can describe the activity, but he/she is not required in the development of it).					
2. It is related with any issue of the selected subject in the science area of preschool curriculum					
3. It requires inquiry and/or actively materials, actions or ideas exploration					
4. It enables pupils to formulate and test new inquiry questions. Children apply and extend existing knowledge in new ways.					
5. Children are motivated to solve problems on their own					
6. Turn to one another for assistance					
7. Challenge themselves and one another to master new skills					

4 Results

We show the obtained results for each of the evaluated items. Firstly, in Figure 1 are collected the percentages obtained in the first four items.

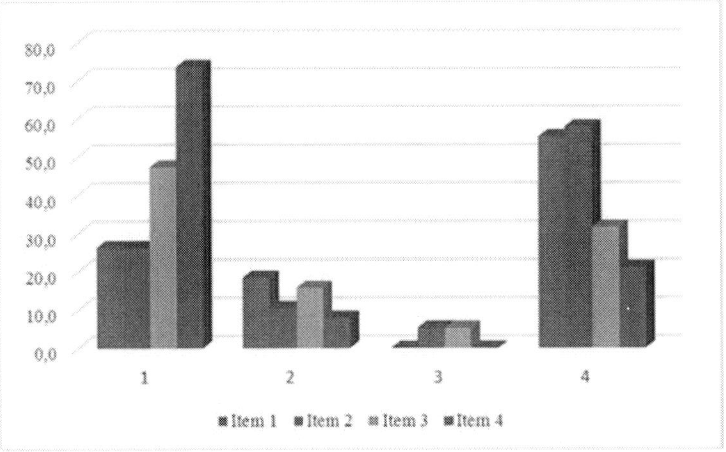

Fig. 1. Results Item 1, 2, 3 and 4.

About the item 1, it is found that the majority of the designed free activities did not meet requirements to be considered as high quality activities. Indeed, just the 50% of the activities did not require an adult intervention. Therefore, designed free activities showed a high degree of directionality.

On the other hand, the designed free activities not always worked the selected science subject matter from the preschool curriculum stablished by the Spanish educational law (Item 2). More than a 30% of the activities did not work these selected subject matters, they worked another ones or none.

Another important date is that nearly the 50% of the cases did not promote the inquiry or material, actions, or ideas exploration (Item 3).

In relation to the possibility that the activity give to pupils to formulate new research questions and apply in new ways the exiting knowledge (Item 4), the results show than 70% did not encourage pupils to get this goal.

Then, Figure 2 shows the percentages obtained in items 5, 6 and 7.

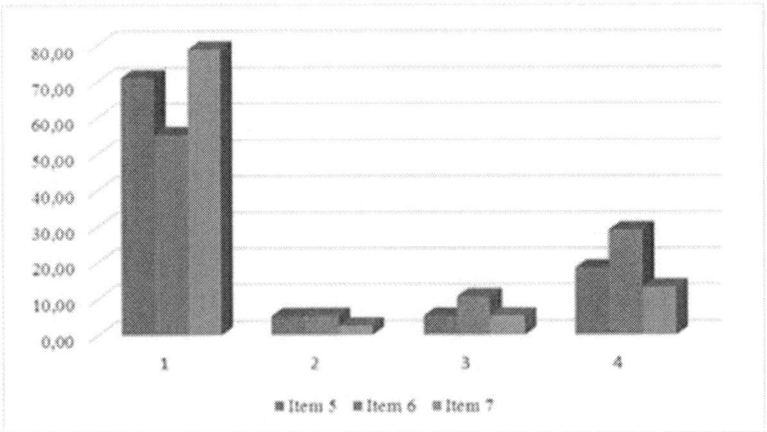

Fig. 1. Results Item 5, 6 and 7.

As we can see, the results in these three items are not too favourable. Thus, more than 70% of the activities not motivates children to solve problems by themselves (Item 5). In addition, more than 50% of activities don ´t promote the establishment of relationships (Item 6). Finally, the results show that most of the activities (80%) did not challenge pupils to reach new skills (Item 7).

5 Discussion and conclusion

The studied Spanish preservice preschool teachers tend to plan teacher-directed activities when they are asked to plan child-guided activities, as they have high degrees of directionality in their proposals. The planned activities give children limited possibilities of inquiry or exploration, with serious difficulties for the autonomous learning. In addition, they don ´t promote the establishment of relationships between children or the development of new skills in them. This data confirms our initial hypothesis, as preservice teachers have difficulties to design high quality free activities. This could be due to the fact that teachers are reproducing the same model with which they learned [4], using a traditional teaching model where the student is given little chance of experimenting or inquiring independently. On the other hand, the belief of many teachers about the constraints that early-age children have to develop skills linked to scientific research processes [5] may be influencing. Therefore, it is necessary to get deeper in this issue, making specific teaching approaches to guide preservice teachers to design high quality free activities.

References

1. A. S. Epstein, *The Intentional Teacher: Choosing the Best Strategies for Young Children's Learning* (2014).
2. N. C. Andiema, JEP, **7**(27), 1-9 (2016)
3. M. L. Rönkkö, J.A. Aerila, S. Grönman, IJEC, **48**(1), 17-32 (2016)
4. R. M. Pringle, JSTE, **17**(3), 291-307 (2006)
5. H. Eshach, M.N. Fried, JSET, **14**(3), 315-336 (2005)
6. R. Barnes, *Teaching Art to Young Children,* (2015)

 DOI: 10.1051/shsconf/20173701015

Civic technology for education: Analysis and evaluation of selected initiatives

Marta Majorek[1a], and Marta du Vall[2]

[1]Andrzej Frycz Modrzewski Cracow University, Poland
[2]Andrzej Frycz Modrzewski Cracow University, Poland

Abstract. Civic Technology is defined (in general) as the use of information technology to engage local government and community residents in behaviors that improve the quality and accountability of public services, facilitate resident-driven improvements to local quality of life, and deepen participation in public decision-making and infrastructure maintenance. The drivers of Civic Technology in communities include technology-business entrepreneurs, civic hacking and local government efforts such as labs or think tanks. Authors present what civic tech actually is and confront theory with civic tech initiatives in education field. The main goal of the article is to explore the links between Civic tech and Education.
Keywords: Civic technology; education; civic tech initiatives

1 What is civic technology?

"For many, civic tech is the bridge between government's mission and modern technology's potential" [1]. Generally, civic tech is defined as use of information technologies to involve citizens, local communities and public administration bodies into operations that are intended to - among others - improve quality and clarity of public services, facilitate and improve citizens' life quality, increase the citizens' contribution to the public decision-making process, promote information sharing to develop the feeling of community, belonging and ownership. Civic tech's development is driven by entrepreneurs who operate in the tech industry, information activists and civic hackers, various think tanks and public authority entities [2]. It is the easiest to describe civic tech as the use of technology for the public benefit. "The underlying idea is that civic tech shares many of the characteristics of 21rst century movements. That includes such elements as being mission driven, focusing on creating change that benefits the public and enabling more citizen input into decision making" [3]. Since such notions as an enterprise, public authority or think

[a] Corresponding author: marta@majorek.com

tank should bring no doubts in terms of their definitions, it is worth taking a longer look at information-activism and civic hacking.

Currently, the term hacking should be employed to describe a phenomenon that embodies basic values of a networking society, i.e. passion, freedom, social value, openness, activity, concern and creativity [4]. It might be assumed that during development of any knowledge (in art, science, philosophy, culture, etc.), "everywhere where data can be collected, information can be compiled thereof, providing the world with new opportunities, there will be hackers hacking the new from the old" [5]. Along with development of new technologies and an increase in access (or even unlimited access) to the Internet, possibilities for use of hacking tactics and concepts have broadened [6]. It has been observed that they might be applied more widely than just the computers and networks. This fact brings extensive social consequences. A networked environment is a perfect platform for all actors, i.e. third sector's organizations, hobbyists, business environments, etc. It also ensures some space for new mechanisms allowing dispersed units to adopt decentralized strategies for cooperation. In such a system, the progress is of an incremental character, resulting from collection of (frequently) minor achievements of many persons, who decide independently what their subject of interest and actions is [7]. People may become a part of that "digital community" at a relatively small cost (it is enough to have a computer connected to the Internet, some initiative and creativity), thanks to which such an action becomes even more attractive [8]. "Civic hacking is nothing more as a way for social and economic advancement. It has already been known for some time that bottom-up, networking actions have the power to change the world, influence lives of others, among others through a direct contact established between a donor and an individual in need of support, help (according to the principle of mutuality). Currently, we are dealing with intensification of interactions and continuous development of communication related to development of a network society. This multiplicity of mutual relationships reduces the risk of alienation and anxiety, defeating the egoism of individuals. The more often people get in touch, the more common initiatives they undertake, and the more trust they put in each other. Changing and influencing the surrounding world is an activity that frees individuals and their potential. It combines two more natural needs of a man, which on one hand are the freedom of individual actions, and on the other the freedom to combine one's own efforts with those of other people and cooperate with them as a result" [9].

Information-activism, as stated in an article by Marta du Vall, should be comprehended as the ability to use the technology for creation, selection and sharing of information [10]. The information activists' objective is to provide people with information that help them make decisions in a conscious manner. Thus, it seems justified that information-activism is a sort of a form for informal education which adopts the democratic potential of the Internet, of other information and communication technologies and of new-type (i.e. virtual) societies, hence transforming the previously centralized social structures. Therefore, it is an activity that consists in improvement of awareness and advocacy through digital media [11].

Information-activism helps to mobilize individuals and motivate communities, thus revitalizing the notion of "community", changing its character and broadening the cognitive horizon. This is an action that forces involvement, participation in a civic society, social and political life. The activity is characterized with mutual trust, restraining from violence and respecting human rights. The main motif for inclusion of citizens into the social development is recognition of the right of all citizens to take part in the decision-making process related to their surroundings, as well as their opportunity to make independent decisions. The objective of information activists is to develop some varied media space, where you can hear different voices, and where everyone can report an event or express their opinion with a minimum editing intervention [12]. According to USDN Civic

Technology Scan, there are three levels, which the civic-tech operates within: geospatial (global, regional, national, local), urban system (transport, energy, facilities, waste, water, safety, health, education, etc.), development of communities - neighbors, electorate, activists, service users, students, etc. [13].

We may also point to three categories of the civic tech users: public administration of various levels (e.g. local governments, state authorities), citizens (various communities), hackers (specialists that develop new tools, often making use of open data sources) [14]. "Investors, philanthropists, and the media see a gathering force, convergence of trends. The technology industry is increasingly interested in societal impact. Governments are developing the capacity to leverage advanced technologies. Communities are being expected to accomplish more with fewer resources" [15].

Therefore, we can state that Civic tech is where the public lends its talents, usually voluntarily, to help government do a better job [16].

"<<Hackathons>>, meetings of software developers, entrepreneurs and government officials looking for new solutions to established problems during the course of a day or maybe a long weekend — are perhaps the most common example of civic tech, but the definition can be stretched to include any intersection of government cooperation with the public where the goal is to expand the role of the citizen in government's operations" [17]. Microsoft Corporation gathered hundreds of up-to-date examples of civic tech, and divided them into categories according to their functions. The result is a list of functional categories: crowdfunding platforms, benefit navigation tools, campaign organizing platforms, check-in tools, constituents of Government communication tools, crowdsourced data collection, data schemas and standards, data visualisation tools and platforms, event organizing tools, freedom of information tools, group communication tools, group decision-making tools, ideation tools, issue reporting platforms, mapping platforms, marketplaces and clearinghouses, neighborhood forums, online petition sites, open data publishing platforms, opinion matching platforms, resource matching/ sharing sites, sensors, service alerts, watchdogging and transparency projects [18].

Civic technology constitutes a change-making step, aiming to serve today's societies' sustainable progress and well-being [19]. It's clear that Civic Tech and education share many challenges and that Civic Tech should be adopted to improve education, and considered in activities undertaken by all actors responsible for educational projects. As we can read in post-event report from the CRI Open Class EdTech #8—What education for what democracy? with François Taddei (Founder and Director of Centre for Research and Interdisciplinary), held on 10th of November 2016 - "Many of the existing educational systems remain limited; they only reproduce and <<teach>> the solutions of the past. However, our world's evolution follows a rather dynamic, nonlinear curve, within which new conditions create new challenges and needs. For this purpose, finding the solutions of tomorrow requires education that will train cooperative problem-solvers who think critically, re-combine, adapt and evolve existing knowledge, but most importantly <<invent>> a new approach that contributes to a sustainable solution for all" [20].

The problem with centralization and standardization is that they constitute objective rationality, which does not leave much space for reflecting upon action or for enabling teachers and students to explore issues through different perspectives. Such rationalization of education is specifically problematic in democratic countries, since it equates education with training students to achieve a mastery level in several subject matters, but neglects the need to develop autonomous individuals, who will have the capacities to make their present and future decisions in a critical and reasonable manner. There is an obvious need to prepare students for the 21st century and move beyond standardization to develop creativity, civic values, and critical skills [21].

Due to the growing access to the Internet, new technologies and services, it is clear that today the younger generations are becoming more active in the online environment, and the use of the Internet does not bring any difficulties for them [22]. While thinking of the next generation's needs we should take into consideration the priorities of the re-invented education, and civic tech tools could act as facilitators and catalysts of this progress. As François Taddei pointed out: "one of the oldest and best "technologies" available to foster both engagement and education is discussion. Civic-tech tools inherit ideals of consensus and collective decision-making processes from the antique Greek "polis" through virtual discussions" [23] and "If one can build a Civic-Tech, EdTech, Open Science-Tech tool, one could invent new collective solutions, a much more open, fluid and inclusive debate. If it works, the mission will have contributed to creating a hybrid between Civic-Tech, EdTech and the future of knowledge technologies" [24].

2 Civic tech applications in field of education

According to Lea Douhard, civic tech is mainly considered as a tool for improvement of the "political fabric" (debates, concertation, legislative process, elections, etc.). She claims that "these new tools provide real empowerment of the civil society regarding the political system and the decision-making process; but they remain focused on the "traditional fields" of politics". She also proposes a hypothesis that "the democracy revolution will be sustainable and inclusive if and only if we go beyond the political agenda. Civic tech opened the door to a continuing citizen activity, over the long term, which imply new ways of teaching, learning, sharing and creation" [25]. Here, we should highlight and discuss some examples of applying the civic tech in education, with particular focus on discussing educational platforms ran by recognized university units, such as Harvard or MIT.

Civic tech can be first seen as the future of libraries. It's all about thinking wisely about those things that librarians know for certain, i.e. what a community wants and how to create an ideal place for everyone. This can happen when libraries "dig deep to understand community needs at the local and neighborhood level, and develop collections, programs, facilities and services to meet those needs" [26]. That's why libraries of all sizes serving all types of communities should choose civic technologies as one of their main tool. Civic tech experts "can help use libraries data that can support libraries in their getting connected with customers, finding more of them, and providing them with what they need and want" [27].

An example of civic technology that works for libraries is CommunityConnect. It "is a web-software solution that integrates data from (...) a library with market segmentation, demographic, and other data so [it] can better understand (...) community, predict what people are interested in, and deliver relevant services to them". [28].

As we can read on the web page, use of the above-mentioned software allows "customers to effectively execute cardholder development campaigns, make smarter decisions on collection expansion, determine the need and find the best sites for new locations, plan programs and services, match staff to meet community needs, plan facility improvements, develop consumer technologies, and invest in effective marketing and communications campaigns" [29].

CommunityConnect website offers some examples for using its service. Libraries staff report that "they have learned much about their communities and that what they've learned is reflected in actionable activities" and that "the more they study the data the more they learn". Users pay attention to the fact that CommunityConnect software provides the opportunity to present critical insights into community literacy conditions [30].

Another example of a civic tech app is Rafter [31]. It adopts cloud-based e-textbooks and course materials, helping campus bookstores digitize their offerings and keep their prices low, allowing them to regain the market share they were losing to other stores and course-materials marketplaces. In this solution - it the school wins because store revenues rise and the students win because course materials are cheaper. We cannot forget about Rafter itself who wins boasting with the results in convincing win-win customer testimonials [32]. Rafter is an all-inclusive solution that allows schools to include textbooks as an item on the student's bill. By adopting Rafter, colleges provide students with all of their assigned course materials on day one for a low and predictable flat rate[33].

As Paul Toler, Vice President of Finance at Avila University, pointed out "Rafter gave us the freedom to select both on-campus pickup and direct-to-student distribution, enabling us to put books in the hands of all students. We're looking forward to seeing the improvements we anticipate in the results." [34].

It is worth mentioning some other civic tech projects in the field of education like Quizlet, Coursera, edX, Udacity and many others that are excellent illustrations for implementation of innovative projects aimed at adapting the learning process to today's requirements. Quizlet is a popular platform that enables teachers to design quizzes, which provide several options to help students to memorize terms and concepts. For example, teachers can add flash cards for a specific class unit. The students review the concept, and once they click on a flashcard, an explanation of a given concept appears. A common use of Quizlet is a match game, in which students need to match the concept with its correct definition. This can be used for competing between individual students or groups. During classes I observed that teachers used this tool mainly for group competition. University of Michigan offered courses published on a start-up platform called Coursera. The company promotes massive online open courses — known as MOOCs. An interesting initiative is also a nonprofit venture founded by the Harvard and the Massachusetts Institute of Technology - edX that features 26 classes, including "Quantum Mechanics and Quantum Computation". Learning Labs for Cities: A Virtual Civic Tech Series is an initiative which is developing a virtual learning platform where government leaders can learn and share content as peers focused on civic technology and emerging areas of innovation. The Learning Labs will provide communities with specially curated resources from the higher education ecosystem via a relationship with edX. The main goal of the project is to facilitate an online learning environment where best practices about emerging innovation can be shared [35].

Another competitor among civic tech initiatives is Udacity. Backed by venture capitalists, it was established by Sebastian Thrun, an acclaimed computer science professor, after more than 160,000 students had taken part in his online artificial-intelligence course at Stanford University. He thinks Udacity will ultimately increase enrollment at brick-and-mortar institutions by preparing more underserved high school students for college [36]. For the universities that create free online courses, mainly major colleges with A-plus brands, relationships with Coursera, Udacity and edX could be beneficial. Mega classes, which can draw hundreds of thousands of students, may aid faculty retention, providing a perk for star professors. And all MOOC marketers promise to share revenues with partner universities, although the path to profitability is murky. The future is brighter for students, whether they choose to continue education or not. As colleges start to give loans to students who complete MOOCs, market forces will pressure many other institutions to liberalize their credit-transfer policies, bringing educational costs down [37].

Most of the popular sites charge a subscription fee while leaving some portion of their offerings free to the public. Course Hero collects a charge of $20 monthly from students, who are willing to access its offerings, although they can skip the monthly charge by uploading at least 30 documents useful to peers, such as class notes or graded tests. Most of Cramster's offerings are free of charge, but the site collects about $10 a month or $50 per year for a premium membership entitling students to gain broader access and have a shorter response time on message boards. In some cases, even professors used the sites. For example, professor David Choi, who gives entrepreneurship classes at Loyola Marymount University College of Business in Los Angeles, conducted a course on product development devoted to students enrolled at two different colleges. He uploaded class materials to the Course Hero platform, so students from both schools could easily access the same files. This shows that information technology dramatically affects how we do business now, including teaching. In academia nowadays, the sharing of information is generally much more ubiquitous, as more professors shift to open courseware publishing or wiki models where multiple writers can contribute. Yale and MIT now post all course materials online. The traditional model of university teaching assumes that we are the givers of information, so we need to move to a model where different sorts of information available are addressed and students need to learn to be critical consumers of information [38].

3 Conclusion

Fostering democratic citizenship and having informed citizens requires public education that advocates public interests and prepares students to be critical, reflective, sensitive, and active citizens. For example, students ought to understand how the legal, political, and economic systems work, as well as become aware of the ways in which they can and should be involved in issues concerning the public good [39]. Cultural discourses aim to reconsider hegemonic cultural assumptions, such as "the common culture," and suggest that acknowledging cultural difference is essential for attaining an inclusive and vibrant democratic society [40]. The meaning of this in terms of digital technology is that rather than reproducing cultural conventions, digital technology holds the potential for students to be exposed to and to experience different cultures.

Today, we are living in the world where culture is mediated through the Internet, blogs, social media, video communication software, and other communicative platforms. Instead of reinforcing predetermined cultural narratives, educators can help students to encounter cultural differences, reflect upon them, and realize the cultural challenges, as well as the possible opportunities open for them as individuals and as members of society. In addition, teachers and students need to recognize the potential of digital tools to engage in transformative online spaces, which struggle for equity, equality, and the betterment of the common good. Moreover, the discussion can continue beyond the limited time of the class. Students can discuss the issue in the class forum or in social media beyond the boundaries of the classroom. They can also compare how other countries treat similar issues. The key here is to avoid (resist directing students towards) an instant answer after a short class discussion that hardly scratches the surface. The purpose is rather to challenge students to encounter different views and to reconsider the issue through various lenses. This can help students to link the curricular content with the world, gradually helping them to develop their critical and reflective understanding of different situations, to shape their positions about them, and to imagine what might be the desired society in which they aspire to live. Digital citizenship involves the nexus of inclusive democracy, critical literacy, and realization of the nature of digital technology. I deem this framework useful for moving beyond technical and functional understanding of digital technology and for supporting teachers and students in utilizing digital devices in a more complete and meaningful way. Recognizing the nature of technology is necessary for demystifying the biases of digital design and placing them in a social context. Becoming aware of social conditions is an inevitable step to create active agency and move towards social transformation [41].

Undoubtedly, the impact exerted by the strong advocates on development of civic tech is limited to countries with advanced technological development, with highly developed instruments and democratic institutions. Majority of presented examples come from

DOI: 10.1051/shsconf/20173701015

countries such as the USA, UK, the Netherlands, where Civic Tech is an environment where only individuals but also many national and local NGOs are strongly engaged. Significant involvement is also evident at the universities of different specializations, in representatives of government agencies and plenty of different levels of government, representatives of organizations and institutions that care about specific parts of the public domain such as information, education, environment, social support. The most famous place in Poland that brings Civic Tech together is the Code for Poland, run under the aegis of the Foundation of the Republic. The first is the large and resilient American Code for American organizationa. There are also smaller groups that can collaborate on specific projects. There may be many informal groups that are small enough to still be difficult to identify. Unfortunately, so far, the Polish environment is hardly represented by the academic world and public administration, but it is also slowly changing. This clearly demonstrates that only the integrated actions of numerous institutions can exert significant and noticeable impact on modifying educational assumptions and changing the existing model that is currently unable to meet the challenges of the 21st century.

References

1. C. Wood, What is Civic Tech?, http://www.govtech.com/civic/What-is-Civic-Tech.html (29.05.2017)
2. The Civic Technology Landscape: A Field Analysis and Urban Sustainability Directors Network Recommendation,(A USDN Innovation Fund Scan, 07.2015)
3. A.Field, Why There Isn't More Of A Hullabaloo About Civic Tech https://www.forbes.com/sites/annefield/2016/06/11/why-there-isnt-more-of-a-hullabaloo-about-civic-tech/#3b60ed322989 (30.05.2017)
4. T. Jordan, *Hakerstwo*, (Warsaw, 2011)
5. W. McKenzie, *A Hacker Manifesto* (Cambridge 2004)
6. A. Harper, *Gray hat hacking: the ethical hacker's handbook* (New York, 2011)
7. Y. Benkler, *Bogactwo sieci. Jak produkcja społeczna zmienia rynki i wolność* (Warsaw, 2008)
8. D. Tapscott, A.D. Williams, *Wikinomia. O globalnej współpracy, która zmienia wszystko* (Warsaw, 2008)
9. M. du Vall, *Obywatelski hacking jako implikator zmian społecznych w XXI wieku,* [in] *Demokracja elektroniczna. Kontrowersje i dylematy*, ed. M. Marczewska-Rytko (Lublin, 2013)
10. M. du Vall, *Infoaktywizm. Strategie komunikacyjne społeczników ery cyfrowej*, [in] *Haktywizm*, ed. M. Marczewska-Rytko (Lublin 2014)
11. J. Nowak, *Aktywność obywateli online. Teoria i praktyka* (Lublin, 2011)
12. L.A. Lievrouw, *Media alternatywne i zaangażowane społecznie* (Warsaw 2012)
13. The Civic Technology Landscape: A Field Analysis and Urban Sustainability Directors Network Recommendation, (A USDN Innovation Fund Scan 07.2015)
14. Ibid.
15. Towards a taxonomy of civic technology https://blogs.microsoft.com/on-the-issues/2016/04/27/towards-taxonomy-civic-technology/#sm.0000npt3rosvxfn2t9g11oloc8iwh (1.06.2017)
16. C. Wood, What is Civic Tech?, http://www.govtech.com/civic/What-is-Civic-Tech.html (29.05.2017)
17. Ibid.
18. Towards a taxonomy of civic technology https://blogs.microsoft.com/on-the-issues/2016/04/27/towards-taxonomy-civic-

technology/#sm.0000npt3rosvxfn2t9g1loloc8iwh (1.06.2017)
19. E. Maraitopoulou, Civic Tech and tomorrow's Education, https://medium.com/open-edtech/civic-tech-and-tomorrows-education-e79a87eedcf0 (1.06.2017)
20. Ibid.
21. D. Mamlok, *Digital Technology and Education in the Age of Globalization* (Doctoral dissertation, Miami University 2017)
22. J. Wojniak, M. Majorek, Children in internet space – the European Union policies on children's safety online, SHS Web of Con. **26**, 01048 (2016)
23. A. Jahn, Civic-Tech and tomorrow's education: An Open Class with François Taddei https://medium.com/@anthony.jahn/civic-tech-and-tomorrows-education-an-open-class-with-fran%C3%A7ois-taddei-91f76b735529 (30.05.2017)
24. Ibid.
25. L. Douhard, When Civic Tech meets Education & Culture (2016) https://forum.etalab.gouv.fr/t/when-civic-tech-meets-education-culture/2250
26. http://civictechnologies.com/
27. Ibid.
28. Ibid.
29. Ibid.
30. Ibid.
31. Rafter http://www.rafter.com/ (2.06.2017)
32. I. Mochari, 16 Startups Poised to Disrupt the Education Market https://www.inc.com/ilan-mochari/16-startups-that-will-disrupt-the-education-market.html (2.06.2017)
33. Jenzabar Partners with Rafter to Prepare Students for Success, https://www.jenzabar.com/blog/2016/05/25/jenzabar-partners-rafter-prepare-students-success/ (2.06.2017)
34. Avila University Partners With Rafter to Provide Students With 100% of Required Course Materials to Improve Student Outcomes http://www.marketwired.com/press-release/avila-university-partners-with-rafter-provide-students-with-100-required-course-2163711.htm (2.06.2017)
35. Civic Innovation Project, http://www.civicinnovationproject.com/contact
36. D. Wallis, Colleges assess cost of free online-only courses. The New York Times, 18 (2013)
37. Ibid.
38. A. Chaker, Do Study Sites Make the Grade. The Wall Street Journal (April 9, 2009)
39. K. Robinson, *Creative schools*. (2015)
40. K. Knight-Abowitz, *Publics for public schools: Legitimate, democracy, and leadership*. (2013)
41. D. Mamlok, *Digital Technology and Education in the Age of Globalization* (Doctoral dissertation, Miami University, (2017)

Responsible research and innovation: Promoting a scientific career among young people

Marta Majorek[1a], and Justyna Wojniak[2]

[1]Andrzej Frycz Modrzewski Krakow University, ul. Herlinga-Grudzińskiego1, 30-705 Krakow, Poland
[2]Pedagogical University of Krakow, ul. Podchorążych 2, 30-084 Krakow, Poland

Abstract. Responsible Research and Innovation is a project initiated by the European Commission in 2014, involving 26 institutions from 30 European countries. Its main purpose is to create science and innovation with society and for society by developing harmonious relations between science and society in Europe. One of the most important dimensions of responsible research and innovation is to make young people aware of scientific specificities of the different aspects of social life and the relationship between science and society. The next step would be encouraging them to choose science as a future path of their career. Therefore it raises the question of the extent to which modern educational systems, not only in Poland, are ready for this kind of challenge. In education strategies or reform projects these issues are firmly underlined. It remains however doubtful whether these are not just idle declarations devoid of real dimension. The paper presents leading European project IRRESISTIBLE aimed at promoting science among young people and making them interested in scientific career. This will be confronted with the Polish young people's views on science education and their attitude towards scientific career.

Keywords: Scientific career; young people; irresistible

1 Introduction

One of the main reasons for emergence of Responsible Research and Innovation emergence was the unsatisfactory contribution of scientific institutions in economic development, solving the contemporary world's problems, developing solutions intended to get rid of economic barriers and technological limitations that restrain the contemporary economy. More active contribution of the sad institutions was assumed to improve life quality. Examples of effective involvement of the scientific environment in solving the above-

[a] Corresponding author: marta@majorek.com

mentioned issues show the scope of possibilities in that range. However, political decision-makers and publicity are dissatisfied with improper use of this potential. This gives further possibilities of actions and encourages to develop priorities in terms of scientific practice and remove barriers in cooperation of the scientific environment and other social actors.

2 RRI concept – its origins and development

It seems necessary here to answer a question on what the above-mentioned Responsible Research and Innovation concept - abbreviated to RRI - are. The first definition was developed by Rene Von Schomberg in 2011 who assumes that we should understand it as: "a transparent, interactive process by which societal actors and innovators become mutually responsive to each other with a view on the (ethical) acceptability, sustainability and societal desirability of the innovation process and its marketable products (in order to allow a proper embedding of scientific and technological advances in our society)" [1].

A common feature of all initiatives carried out under the auspices of Responsible Research and Innovation is active development of the future. These actions consist in solving so-called complicated problems what requires plenty of data to be collected and new algorithms for their analysis to be developed for the need of decision making and social contribution to scientific research. Hence, there must be actions undertaken intended to identify the methods that ensure efficient cooperation with local communities and openness towards diversified recipients.

The European Commission's opinion is that development of scientific activity should go hand in hand with researchers' social responsibility, but at the same time with the society's awareness. To achieve such a state of affairs it becomes indispensable for the scientific and social spheres to cooperate. This requires a dialog between representatives of both those environments occupying equal positions. Keeping a high level of the scientific research and technological innovation requires continuous recruitment of talented researchers, but also inspiration. The researchers come from a broadly understood society, and the impulse for development of research problems is posed by social needs and expectations. However, it must be kept in minds that the scientific environment should restrain from treating publicity in a paternalistic manner and perceiving it as a poor recipient of scientific activity's results. Thus, the element of social control over such activity gains on importance, i.e. legal and ethical aspects of its performance as well as the mentioned social needs and expectations, grasped in the system of values context, significant from the perspective of the society as a whole. Such an approach is related to particular democratization of the science development process. It is worth adding that democratization perceived in such a manner has its relatively practical justification, arising from the fact that financing of the scientific and research operations comes from public resources.

"The ultimate goal is bring into being a European community of practice that draws together all people and organisations that are active in this new vision of scientific and social development" [2].

The European Commission, to achieve the goal in cooperation with multiple entities representing scientific, economic and social sectors, has developed a project named RRI Toolkit. It covers concepts and examples of good practices in several major spheres. One of them is sex equality, i.e. exclusion of all premises of discrimination based on sex, when it comes to access to possibilities, resources or advantages provided thanks to the science sector development [3]. This perspective provides special importance to the possibility of revealing the full societal potential, which can be thus employed for developmental purposes. Apart from that, RRI Toolkit also covers the already mentioned social contribution into the process of research and innovation development, which is seen through participation of scientists, industry and representatives of the civic environment. Another area is facilitating access to research results what is especially important in case of research financed from public funds. Following ethical standards in the process of research development and innovative solutions implementation is attached with the same importance. In this case, a fundamental reference point is social significance and acceptability of the obtained results. There is also a need to mention management in the scientific and research sector, which is to be characterized with responsibility of decision-makers for development of harmonious RRI models [4]. Eventually, there is an educational area mentioned, both in its formal and informal form, construed in such a manner so it poses a path of promoting a scientific career among young people as a potential path of the future professional development [5].

These are the elements that compose the core of assumptions, which were highlighted as crucial within the Horizon 2020 programme. Therefore, it is obvious that in order to allow effective introduction of those assumptions, it is necessary to grant the operations intended for their implementation. Nevertheless, the whole process will bring expected results only if financing plans for particular RRI actions were given some thought. It was assumed on one hand that there is a need to distinguish a group of funds intended for implementation of RRI projects within the already existing programmes realized by European Union member states, especially those, which assume financing of the scientific and research operations. The existing programmes were provided with catalogs of rules that should be followed while assigning funds for research [6]. These actions were intended to improve awareness about RRI in an indirect manner, although introduction of such solutions into the already existing programmes seems insufficient. Hence, a decision was made to undertake more direct actions, which would cover particular funding instruments with a purpose to implement particular projects meeting the RRI criteria [7].

An example of direct actions may be Joint Programming Initiatives, which is intended to direct resources of particular states, allocated solely to implementation of innovative research, which would pose a response to the challenges that contemporary societies must face. A decision was made to develop a pilot phase of the project as a reaction to small recognizability of the RRI concept in particular member states. This phase adopts a form of dedicated financial instruments included in the Horizon 2020 programme. An example of direct support for RRI implementation is also the European Innovation Partnership, intended to focus on support for improvement in European competitiveness. The concept assumes introduction of a strategic approach for development and implementation of innovation what is rooted in the European Union strategy for 2020. According to those assumptions, RRI is to become its integral part [8]. It is assumed that introduction of the RRI concept will allow realization of undertakings both on a local and supralocal scale through implementation of new technological solutions.

When it comes to possibilities brought by technologies to the area of solving contemporary problems, attention is focused on the need to improve social awareness in that scope. This is also related to recognition of potential threats and risks that can be noticed here. Thus, it is impossible to bring notions related to science and technology closer to publicity without adequate preparation of the recipients. Therefore, education, both in the formal and informal manner plays a crucial role here. On one hand, it provides individuals with the most elementary knowledge on phenomena or processes that pose the research subject in an obvious manner. On the other hand – its role should be to trigger interest in that area and achievement that emerge within it. However, it is equally important to shape some critical attitudes during the educational process, directed to some forms of scientific operations or its potential effects.

3 RRI in education

In the educational area, RRI means not only the change in the manner young people perceive innovative technologies and their use, but also encouragement for participation in scientific projects [9]. Hence, actors involved in RRI Toolkit development felt it was appropriate to get young people acquainted with specificity of the scientific profession. This is justified because a lot of stereotypes arose around it, among which the most popular is the belief about its tightness and inaccessibility for an average recipient. On the other hand, bringing the scientific profession closer to young people is a condition necessary to make them interested enough in that sphere so the gifted and talented students can locate their professional future in that sector.

Undoubtedly, this though may be improved by initiatives and activities carried out on all educational levels, especially in primary and lower secondary schools, where young people will not only obtain knowledge in sciences, but also get familiar with possibilities and consequences of a research process. Shaping of attitudes that are open to challenges that are brought by scientific work is another step for development of the society of knowledge, and triggering the individuals' willingness for direct participation in the innovation process.

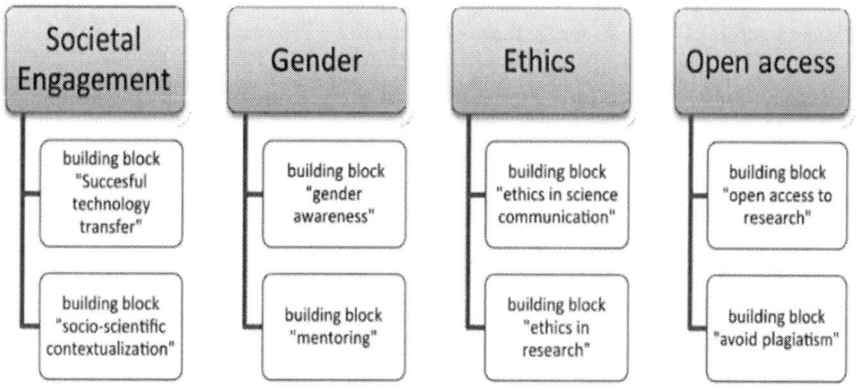

Fig. 1. Key-specific building blocks that form the educational RRI training program (source: [6])

From the educational perspective, especially in its formalized dimensions, one of the most interesting initiatives that implement the RRI assumptions seems the IRRESISTIBLE project (Including Responsible Research and Innovation in Cutting Edge Science and Inquiry-Based Science Education to Improve Teacher's Ability of Bridging Learning Environments). It combines the elements of formal and informal education, directed towards responsible research and innovation.

In Poland, the project was implemented within the scope of actions coordinating and supporting the FP7-SCIENCE-IN-SOCIETY-2013-1 Activity 5.2.2 entitled Young people and science. Topic Sis.2013.2.2.1-1. Improvement of young people's awareness in terms of responsible research and innovation through education in the scope of sciences and scientific inquiry. In this scope, the aim of IRRESISTIBLE has become to develop actions intended to support involvement of students and society into the process of responsible research and innovation [10].

In the context in question it is worth paying attention especially to one of the above-mentioned elements, namely on education in the scope of sciences. There are not many European states that have developed particular strategies intended to improve the position of sciences in education and within the society. However, it does not mean that states do not implement initiatives aimed at improvement in educational quality in the STEM system. It is hard to measure the impact of those unitary activities, thus the need for in-depth research in that scope, allowing to review and assess the undertaken initiatives. Strategies popular in Europe assume cooperation between schools and scientific organizations, while the areas of partnership are highly differentiated what is reflected also in different manner of organization and implementation of such practices.

At least one of the following objectives is embedded in all kinds of partnerships: promotion of sciences, knowledge and research among students; improvement in students' understanding of practical use of science; improvement of didactics of sciences in schools, and improvement of recruitment for mathematic, scientific and technical majors. Scientific centres assume at least one of the above-mentioned goals, and make their contribution into improvement in teaching of sciences through implementation of student-oriented actions, which go beyond the schools' offer. Two thirds of interviewed states inform that there are no scientific centres on the national level. Wherever general strategies for promotion of sciences are prepared, their integral part is usually the student-oriented counseling. However, there are not many states that introduced counseling practices that would especially consider sciences, and only in few were the girls encouraged to choose such a professional career. There are few states, where programmes and projects intended to provide special support for students that are gifted and have talent for science were introduced [11]. The mentioned facts justify promotion of postulates put forward within the RRI, and point to the need for improvement in awareness of that concept and strengthening promotion of scientific development directions included in STEM.

Within the discussed project IRRESITIBLE, awareness of RRI was developed in two manners:

- improvement of scientific research knowledge by introducing latest achievements into the curricula for sciences, encouraging and supporting discussions about RRI among students;
- formal (in schools) and informal (in science centres, museums, during scientific festivals) education; students learn about the world of science.

Each state that declared its participation in the project created Community of Learners (CoL), the task of which was to develop didactic modules. Those teams were composed not only of teachers but also of university lecturers and designers of interactive exhibitions. The Community of Learners develops materials intended for work with students. Furthermore, students of the teachers involved in CoL visited university laboratories, and based on that they prepared exhibitions that pictured the relationship between scientific research and the society [12].

Implementation of the project was divided into two main stages. 1st stage of the project resulted in 10 modules about various types of RRI, tested in 5-10 classes.
Topics of the modules:

- Healthy aging
- Genomics and oceanography
- Climate change
- Sustainable renewable energy
- Solar energy
- Nanomaterials
- Nanotechnology
- Catalysis in protection of the environment

During the 2nd stage of the project, 7 teachers that took part in the 1st stage had the task to train other five persons. The modules are also available on a special website available in various languages. The best exhibits developed within the project were

DOI: 10.1051/shsconf/20173701016

presented to the public during the project completion ceremony. As a result, within the project, almost 10 thousand students were sensitized to social effects of scientific research.

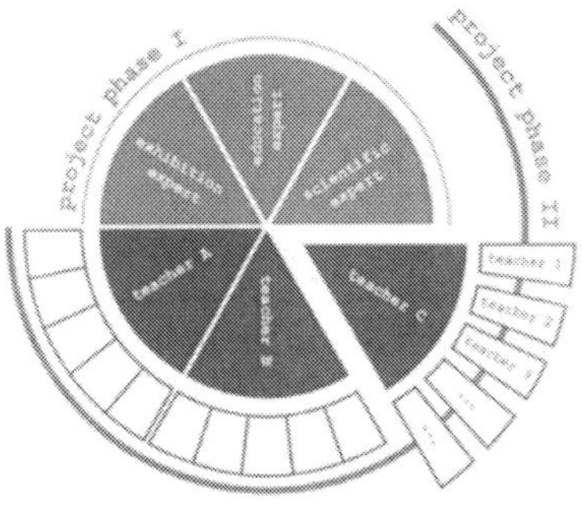

Fig. 2. Project approach (source: [10])

RRI Toolkit assumptions, which were planned for implementation in the education areas and the actions undertaken in that scope based on an example of a particular initiative in a form of the project IRRESISTIBLE provided the authors of this article with a field for analysis of the young people's attitude towards sciences as an object of education and as a sphere of social and professional activity. The performed research also allowed to attempt to evaluate the implemented solutions related to promotion of responsibility in the research and innovation operations, according to assumptions adopted by the European Commission.

4 Procedure and findings

The research was carried out in 2017 on 16-year-old students of 3rd grade of a lower secondary school, finishing their education on that level. Selection of a sample group was of a purposeful character not only because of the possibility to reach the respondents. From the perspective of the analyzed problem, it was also significant to cover a particular group with the research, namely the students, who took part in the discussed project IRRESISTIBLE.

The research was carried out with the diagnostic survey method, adopting a tool in a form of a survey questionnaire. The survey was of an anonymous character. The answers were collected from 69 persons, out of which 21 were students of a school where the project IRRESISTIBLE was carried out.

Questions included in the questionnaire were intended to identify how the students perceived science education. Majority (60%) of respondents from the group that did not take part in the project IRRESISTIBLE responded that this was a difficult sector. The students who had a chance to get familiar with the scientific notions in a broader scope thanks to their participation in the said project, the proportions were opposite, as 62% of respondents claimed that science education is a tough field. Such a scheme of answers may result from deeper and broader description of the scientific notions to students from the group IRRESISTIBLE. In their case, not only classic expository methods were employed as it happens in case of the obligatory educational process, where often - regarding time limitations - realization of core curriculum is focused on theoretical aspects, not always accompanied by illustration in a form of an experiment or practice.

Afterwards, the students were asked to determine the degree of science education knowledge usability in comparison to other subject, among others social sciences. Here, in the group of students not covered by the project IRRESISTIBLE, 25% of respondents claimed it was more useful, 58% said it was useful to the same degree, and 17% pointed it was less useful. In turn, it was surprising in the group IRRESISTIBLE that only 5% believes science education is more useful, while as many as 81% pointed that it was useful to the same degree. The group stating that science education is less useful was 14%. This may lead to a conclusion that students, who had a chance to participate in the project bringing the sphere of science closer believed that such activity should not be attached with features that would distinguish it from other spheres of a human intellectual activity. It might be related to being aware that social life along with individual needs and expectations require differentiated strategies for solving specific problems and undertaking challenges that are adequate for a given situation. Therefore, science and solutions it offers may be one of numerous proposals that should be used in a flexible manner, without the desire to treat it with superiority.

The opinion that understanding science education and moving freely within its notions exerts positive influence on individual career possibilities was expressed by 65% of students from the group non-IRRESISTIBLE, when compared to 52% from the group IRRESISTIBLE.

Quite interesting results were also provided by answers to the question about an image of a researcher that dominates within the minds of young people, without dividing them into non-IRRESISTIBLE and IRRESISTIBLE groups. The respondents could select 3 positions out of the proposed answers: Creative (A), Extremely intelligent (B), With passion (C), Detached from the reality (D), Bookworm (E) and Enterprising (F).

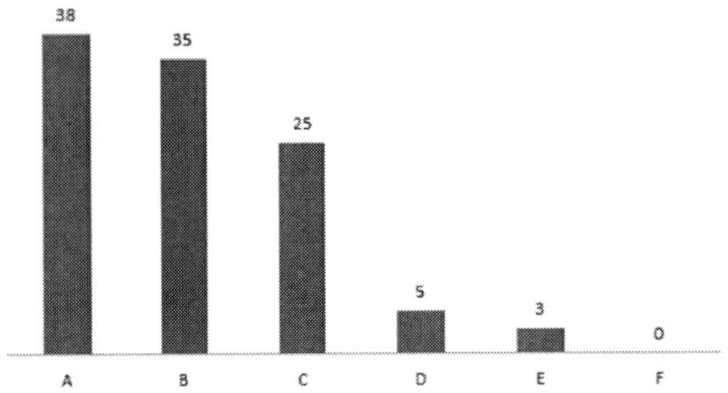

Fig. 3. Image of the researcher

As it may be noticed, the dominating features are those that can be thought of as positive in case of a researcher's image. Definite minority pointed here to features associated with researchers stereotypically or ironically, i.e. detached from reality or remaining in the world of books and scientific papers. None of the students pointed to enterprising what may suggest that scientific practice is still associated with a sort of a mission, actions for common good, not gaining profits. Such a belief should grow some thought for decision-makers, both on the European and national level, who definitely stress the significance of the link between science and innovation within various developmental strategies, along with the need for deep commercialization of scientific research results.

Further, the students were asked about attractiveness of the scientific profession. The following were proposed as its determinants: Contribution to the human development (A), Fascinating (B), Financially attractive (C), Boring (D), Financially unattractive (E), Harmful to people and environment (F).

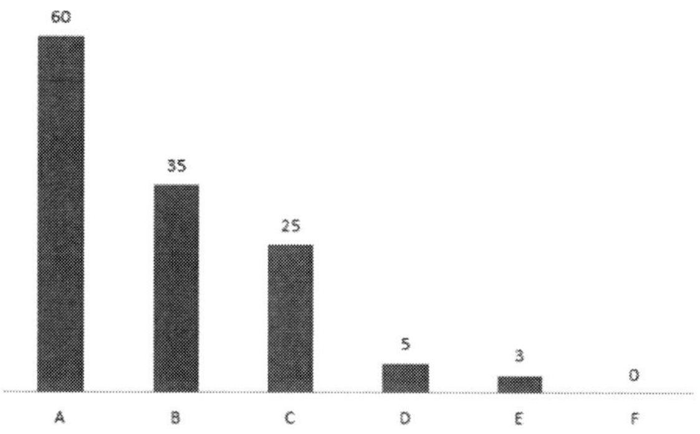

Figure 4. Attractiveness of the scientific profession

Here also the positive aspects dominate, with a definite belief in its role from the perspective of contribution to humanity development. What may be surprising is the fact that the respondents did not even think about the risk element that the scientific and innovative activities' results may bring to people or environment. This may prove limited level of criticism and scale of imagination what is surprising as the popular culture, first of all the movie, delivers a lot of examples of dangerous activities of "mad" scientists. Such a positive attitude towards a social role of a researcher may be also linked to the question asked previously, for which the students provided the answer suggesting that their minds have strongly adopted a belief that scientific practice has no premises of enterprising, so it should be combined with the previously mentioned mission for realization of the common good.

What is more, a relatively large group thought of a scientific profession as financially attractive, thus providing a certain scope of life stability what according to the respondents probably does not support risky or ethically doubtful behaviors that would result in negative impact on the researcher's life situation.

At the end, it is worth mentioning answers for the question on whether the respondents have any professional plans related to science. The results were identical in both researched groups:

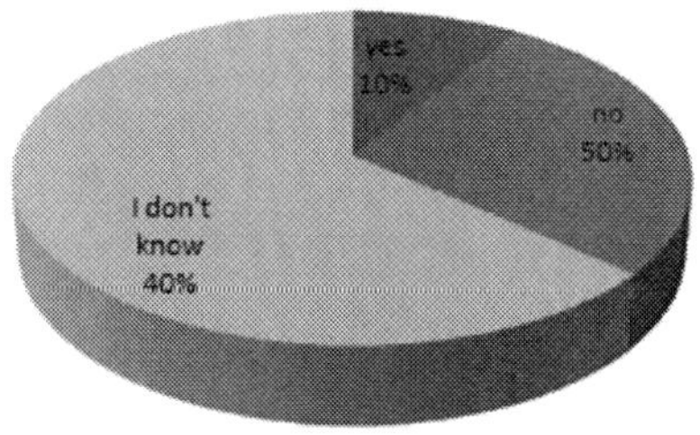

Figure 3. Professional plans related to science

Most probably, the small share of affirmative answers results from limited awareness of what the profession is connected with, and what the duties of a researcher are. Undoubtedly, it is not a job that – in colloquial meaning – is related to a particular sector or position. Knowledge about remuneration or employee entitlements is also strongly limited. On the other hand, a justification for as many as 40% of those undecided may be the fact that a 16-year-old individual is not yet old enough to make more particular decisions on their professional future. On this stage, young people tend to focus on choosing an upper secondary school, and from their perspective it might be too early, to already decide on the major in academic or direction in vocational education.

5 Conclusion

To sum up the results it must be added that schools as institutions, also the employed staff, do not prove their understanding of the Responsible Research and Innovation. Reports compiled by the European Commission, as a body responsible for all community initiatives related to education and courses suggest that a condition for implementation of the RRI Toolkit's assumptions in all areas mentioned by the Commission is modernizing science initial teacher training programmes, particularly by updating of initial teacher training courses, as well as establishment of national quality standards for science initial teacher education - 49 students as a reason for the lack of interest in the field of science mentioned a poor teacher. There is also a need to update the skills of in-service teachers to motivate learners, which demands the development of new dedicated degree programmes and close cooperation between schools and universities [13].

References

1. R. von Schomberg, *Prospects for Technology Assessment in a framework of responsible research and innovation*, in: *Technikfolgen abschätzen lehren: Bildungspotenziale transdisziplinärer Methode*, Springer VS, Wiesbaden, 39-61 (2011)
2. European Commission, *RRI Tools: building a better relationship between science and society*, retrieved: http://www.rri-tools.eu/project-description (2014)
3. Ibid.
4. Z. Gontar, *Odpowiedzialne badania i innowacje – nowy paradygmat w budowaniu współpracy między nauką i społeczeństwem*, Collegium of Economic Analysis Annals, **40**, 325 (2016)
5. G. A. Anghel, G. Gorghiu, *Considering Responsible Research and Innovation in Science Education Teaching Approaches at Primary Level*, International Journal of Teaching and Education, **5** (1), 9 (2017)
6. D. Elster, T. Barendziak, J. Birkholz, *Science Education as a Trigger to Attain Responsible Research and Innovation (RRI) in Biosciences*, in: *Conference Proceedings. New Perspectives in Science Education*, 402 (2017)
7. European Commision, *Options for Strengthening Responsible Research and Innovation Report of the Expert Group on the State of Art in Europe on Responsible Research and Innovation*, retrieved: https://ec.europa.eu/research/science-society/document_library/pdf_06/options-for-strengthening_en.pdf , 32. (2013)
8. Ibid.
9. J. Apotheker, R. Blonder, S. Akaygun, P. Reis, L. Kampschulte, A. Laherto, *Responsible Research and Innovation in secondary school science classrooms: experiences from the project Irresistible*, Pure and Applied Chemistry, **89**, 2, pp. 211-219 (2016)
10. IRRESISTIBLE, *Project Approach*, retrieved: http://www.irresistible-project.eu/index.php/en/approach (2017)
11. European Commision – Eurydice, *Nauczanie przedmiotów ścisłych i przyrodniczych w Europie: polityka, praktyka i badania naukowe*,

retrieved:
http://eacea.ec.europa.eu/education/eurydice/documents/thematic_reports/133PL.pdf, 9 (2012)
12. Jagiellonian University – Programme Irresistible, retrieved: http://www.zdch.uj.edu.pl/irresistible (2017)
13. European Commission *Indicators for promoting and monitoring Responsible Research and Innovation Report from the Expert Group on Policy Indicators for Responsible Research and Innovation*, Publications Office of the European Union, Luxembourg, 41-43 (2015)

 DOI: 10.1051/shsconf/20173701017

Mathematics, chemistry and science connection as a basis of scientific thinking

Matúš Ivan[1a]; and Renata Šulcová[1]

[1]Charles University, Faculty of Science, Department of Teaching and Didactics of Chemistry, Prague, Czech Republic

Abstract. Scientific thinking is a basic skill that can support problem-solving of interdisciplinary tasks in science. Our research is leading us to creation of materials and resources that will support this interdisciplinary approach to education. The research includes interviews with high-school teachers of mathematics, chemistry and science, item analysis of extensive testing of knowledge and skills of high school students in chemistry in Czech Republic, follow-up survey of students' problem-solving processes in tasks requiring the use of combined knowledge of mathematics and chemistry and the creation of educational materials. The article contains a few examples of proposed educational materials. The effectiveness of created materials is verified in high-schools. Students have got the most difficulties applying algebraic calculations in chemistry, using proportions, solving equations, expressing the unknown, the spatial imagination, geometry and stereometry and the resulting arrangement of atoms and shapes of molecules, chemical analytical tasks with logical thinking, interpretation of information from graphs and tables, plotting measured values into graphs and statistical evaluation.
Keywords: Scientific thinking; high-school teachers; interview

1 Introduction

It is very difficult for the students to comprehend phenomena in chemistry if they lack proper mathematical apparatus. It is also not very simple to show the students practical applications of theoretical mathematical knowledge without referring to natural sciences, especially chemistry and physics.

This problem could be solved by leading the students towards scientific thinking. Scientific thinking could be defined as knowledge seeking [1]. This definition encompasses any instance of purposeful thinking that has the objective of enhancing the seeker's knowledge. One consequence that follows from this definition is that scientific thinking is a skill that the students can gain. This skill can be referred to as scientific understanding. When conditions are favourable, the process of scientific thinking may lead to scientific

[a] Corresponding author: ivanma@natur.cuni.cz

understanding as its product. Indeed, it is the desire for scientific understanding – for explanation – that drives the process of scientific thinking [1].

2 Theoretical background of research

2.1 Experts' opinions

The problems of interdisciplinarity in science subjects and mathematics have been mentioned in many research publications around the world. Authors of these publications are considered to be specialists on subject didactics, they are mostly academic educators, education researchers and high-school teachers of not only natural science subjects. The sources for solving the indicated problems can be found in statements of renounced specialists in science and education.

Mathematician, university educator and academic researcher Jindřich Bečvář: [2]: "*Many people are convinced that they do not need the mathematics in their everyday life. The partial reasons for this are overuse of technologies in daily life and overall atmosphere in the society. It is common to emphasize the importance of mathematics and science in many curricular documents and development plans. In spite of this the reality of education is very different because mathematics and science 'do not bring any direct economic effect'. The change in this situation depends on teachers – their qualification, methods of education and sufficient amount of appropriate educational materials.*"

Educationalist, university educator and chemist Vincentas Lamanauskas [3]: *"One of the most probable causes of such situation is, that at school it is not shown or (insufficiently shown) the importance of science and technologies for future career possibilities. Why isn't this shown? Again, a lot of things determine such situation. First of all, science subjects and especially math are taught at school referring to formulas, theorems, blindly following the textbooks. Apparently, there is a lack of practical examples, real situations and problem solutions. It is understandable, that this requires much bigger resources – both material and intellectual. Thus, it is necessary to increase the possibilities for students to get acquainted with the practical appliance of sciences and math.*

The problem is that teachers usually work individually; there is little of integrated activity. A wider and deeper collaboration is noticed in the science teachers' group. Math and science subject teachers collaborate much less."

University educators: Sedat Karaçam, Volkan Bilir, Azize Digilli Baran [4] *"Nowadays, since the importance scientific activities and knowledge are increasing, enhancing students' scientific process skills and epistemological beliefs are more important than before. In this view, science curriculums have been revised to enhance students' scientific process skills, views about nature of science and scientific knowledge in several countries."*

University educator, chemistry didactic Małgorzata Nodzyńska [5]: *"Recently, the graphical communication has been essential part of all information surrounding us every day. It is necessary to consider whether the graphical information and visualisation (not only in science) is really providing simplification for understanding of messages. Not all of the people are able to comprehend the meaning of visual information without former experience. When we consider the chronology of learning through images, the older experience with graphical information is always stronger than the new one. This is the reason why even the first visualisations of the phenomenon must be factually correct."*

University educator, chemist, chemistry didactic Martin Bílek [6]: *"Visual perception, processing of visual information and creation of adequate conceptions in students' minds are essential parts of science education. Functional, visual and graphical literacy, modelling and visualisation in chemistry, education based on observation, measuring, experimenting, and data evaluation represent connection of mathematics and science,*

DOI: 10.1051/shsconf/20173701017

especially chemistry. However in reality of our school system the transmissive approaches dominate over the constructivism. Since the end of the 20th century many educational studies including educational materials have been created for more active approach to education (problem solving, constructivism, project-based education and inquiry-based science education – IBSE)."

Mathematician, university educator, psychologist Alena Šarounová [7]: *"Intentional teaching in school is mostly performed using speech and images. The ability to comprehend and extract the information from the visual elements of education (models, images and schematics) and to understand the meaning of symbolic language in these aids is commonly referred to as symbolic function of a brain. We have to teach our students how to read and comprehend the images (this is not very common in our schools)."*

2.2 Conclusions from literature search

We can conclude that scientific thinking and visual literacy skills are the main tools for comprehension and understanding the science in general. These skills cannot be constructed and properly used without adequate knowledge of mathematics. The mathematical theories can be simultaneously demonstrated on phenomena from natural sciences. We can demonstrate the interdisciplinarity of mathematics and science especially on relations of chemistry and mathematics. The interdisciplinary approach to education in schools is a necessary condition for further complex problem-solving of everyday issues in professional life.

3 Research methodology

3.1 Interview

To pinpoint the areas of education content of chemistry that are the most problematic for the high-school students, we used the method of personal interviews with qualified high-school teachers of mathematics, chemistry and science. Our investigation currently includes 11 interviews.

According to the answers of the interviewees the students are able to comprehend the definition of a certain chemical phenomenon but are unable to describe it and formally or graphically express the steps of the solution. In other words students cannot apply their mathematical skills to interdisciplinary problem-solving and make the correct conclusions in chemistry. For us it is the main reason to put our efforts into creating sets of materials and educational tasks appropriate for acquiring the skills for development of scientific and visual literacy.

3.2 Item analysis of tests

An extensive testing of knowledge and skills of high-school students in chemistry was conducted in Czech Republic in 2014 and 2015 [8]. Item analysis of this testing was second source for our research. The evaluation of analysis revealed the difficulties in the procedures of solutions and discovered the most difficult parts of the logical thought processes of students. The sample range of tested students was 1079 overall, 396 students have taken the test in general chemistry, 337 in inorganic chemistry, 243 in organic chemistry and 103 in biochemistry. The sample was composed of 656 girls and 423 boys.

The areas of close connections between chemistry and mathematics have been determined according to this analysis. The first step to successfully solve every task is to choose the appropriate part of the mathematical apparatus. The revealed connections are summarized in the Table 1. The mathematical skills are divided into four basic groups.

Table 1. Mathematical skills and their applications in chemistry

Mathematical skill	Application in chemistry
Application of algebraic calculations	•Use of direct and reverse proportion in general chemistry calculations, mass fraction, solution concentration •Determining the stoichiometry of a reaction •Expressing an unknown from a physical chemistry formula
Spatial imagination and the use of geometry and stereometry	•Determining the structure of molecules and crystals •Modelling and construction of structural particles •Graphical interpretation of structures and formulae
Analytical logical thinking, charted and tabled data interpretation	•Identification of a compound according to given properties •Plotting a graph out of experimental measurements •Practical application of laws of physical chemistry
Application of functional analysis	•Spatial shapes of orbitals and bond formation •Functional dependencies of quantities in physical chemistry

The logical thinking in chemical interpretation of conclusions gained during the problem-solving is the essential prerequisite for the inquiry-based approach to education. The scientific thinking has to be unconditionally based on applications of mathematical procedures and logical thought processes.

3.3 Follow-up testing

The preliminary research was the basis for creation of the follow-up test that should prove the assumptions made from previous conclusions. To verify our ideas we conducted a smaller survey in 2017. The sample range of this local survey (in Prague) was 104 students. This new test consists of 14 chemical tasks focused on the areas that naturally and appropriately require the usage of mathematics to comprehend the chemical principles and vice versa. Certain inquiry procedure, logical deliberation or mathematical skill and knowledge were necessary to solve each of the test items. The validity of the new test was discussed and verified by independent competent high-school teachers and academics.

The test was taken by two groups of students. One group consists of 73 high-school students in the last year of their studies (so they have the knowledge about the whole chemical curriculum) the second group are the first year university students of bachelor studies in chemistry teaching, molecular biology and general biology. Number of university students was only 31.

The results of the testing can be summarized in a few conclusions. Overall it is certain that the success rate of high-school students is higher than the university students. The main reason for this strange outcome could be the factor of forgetting, but also insufficient interdisciplinary connection between mathematics and science subjects and logical applications of knowledge and skills in science into practical problems. The interest of the students in the subject of chemistry could also be next reason for the difference between the high-school students and university students. The analysis of test items has shown the main differences between the two groups of tested students (see Table 2).

Table 2. Comparison of results between groups of students

	3.3.1	3.3.2	3.3.3	3.3.4		3.3.5	
High school	56 % 16 % EoI	48 %	26 %	78 % GC	84 % BC	77 % (models of structures)	69 % (allotropes)
University students	22 % 39 % EoI	17 %	0 %	61 % GC	78 % BC	70 % (models of structures	0 % (allotropes)

3.3.1 Comprehensive reading

16 % of high-school students and 40 % of university students have not read the instruction properly and so they have solved the task only partially, although their procedure of solving the task was correct (errors of inattention EoI – see Table 2).

3.3.2 Logical reasoning using mathematical principle of a concept in physical chemistry

48 % of high-school students and only 17 % of university students have solved the task concerning half-life of radionuclide. This task can be solved by simple logical mathematical reasoning or using the exponential function.

3.3.3 Data analysis and evaluation

26 % of high-school students were able to analyse the data from a chart to determine the formula of an organic compound according to the results of a certain set of chemical reactions. The students from university have not solved the task properly at all and only 9 % of the students have solved the task at least partially. This task demonstrates the lack of ability of students to logically connect chemical knowledge with data interpretation.

3.3.4 Interpretation of tabulated data

The success rate of tasks concerning the reading with comprehension of data from charts were different depending on the area of chemistry. Overall success rate of the task in biochemistry (BC - see Table 2) was higher than the success rate of a similar task in general chemistry. The task concerning about the finding out the proper sequence of amino acids depending on the sequence of nucleotides in m-RNA according to the codon table was solved successfully by 78 % of university students and 84 % of high school students. This proves the sufficient knowledge and ability to work with the tabulated biochemical data and also a good connection with the knowledge of biology. Similar task in the area of general chemistry (GC –see Table 2) concerning the ionisation energy of elements was successfully solved by 61 % of university students and 78 % of high-school students. The success rate in general chemistry task is lower.

3.3.5 Structure of compounds and spatial imagination

Spatial imagination about the shapes of molecules and structures of chemical compounds is sufficient in both groups (success rate of high-schools students was 77 % and success rate of university students from university was 77 %). A similar task about the allotropes of the carbon had a similar success rate in high-school group. The university student group had much lower success rate (complete solution – 0 %, partial solution – 35 %). The task that requires the comprehension and application of knowledge of chemical structures had a higher success rate than the task that required simple remembering of terms about the spatial structure.

4 Possible system solutions of survey issues

There are two main approaches to solve the problem that was uncovered by our research. These solutions are not mutually exclusive, on the contrary their effectiveness is based on their synergy. Synergy could be defined as a wholesome approach to problem solution in which the sum of effects of individual parts is lesser than the whole effectiveness [9].

4.1 Change of curriculum

The first of the possibilities is a system change of the subject curricula. This change could concern the logical arrangement, appropriate selection and modification of the subject content. The newly gained knowledge of content in different subjects has to be in a mutual logical correspondence. This approach requires the team collaboration among the teachers of related science subjects with mathematics and interdisciplinarity in every area of education. The topics in science subjects should logically connect to the corresponding theoretical mathematical skills.

4.2 Educational materials

The second part of the proposed solution is to create educational materials and make the available to the teachers via the educational websites. The created materials are supposed to naturally accent the connections between mathematics, chemistry, physics, biology and science in general. The inquiry-based science education (IBSE) is the most suitable method for this interdisciplinary approach.[10]

Our educational materials include worksheets containing interdisciplinary and inquiry-based educational tasks for students. The worksheets are accompanied by the methodological commentary for teachers. The materials are being used and verified in common high-school education during this school year.

One of the worksheets concerns about chemical structure. The pupils are supposed to discover the structure of molecules of simple inorganic compounds and elements (see Figures 1-3).

Fig. 1–3 Models of P_4 molecules created by students (including the misconceptions) – modelling clay and skewers

Similar activities concerning about the structure of simple organic compounds can be seen in Fig. 4-5. The students were independently creating and inquiring about the tetrahedral structure of organic and inorganic molecules. The Figure 4 shows the process of creation of correct arrangement of atoms in tetrahedral structure of methane. The Figure 5 shows the similarity in structures of molecules of white phosphorus (P_4) and methane (CH_4).

Fig. 4–5 Models of molecules (including the misconceptions) CH_4 and P_4 – chestnuts, rosehips, toothpicks and skewers.

The other worksheets concern about the mathematical modelling of physical-chemistry phenomenon – the disintegration of nuclei of radionuclides. The pupils use coin-tossing as a way to model this phenomenon. Fig. 6-7 shows the activity and its' evaluation and statistical analysis performed by students.

Fig. 6-8 Coin-tossing and evaluation of results

5 Conclusion

The research of using the mathematical principles in chemistry has lead us to the idea of rearranging the parts of chemistry curriculum so the explanation of the phenomena in chemistry would be easier. This requires cooperation of high-school teachers of related fields during the creation of the school curriculum. At the same time it is necessary to create appropriate education materials that accent and support the interdisciplinary approach to education. These materials should simplify the process of preparation of lessons by the teachers. The methods most suitable for this approach are project-based education, inquiry-based education and other methods of active student learning. It will be easier for the teachers of science without focus on the mathematics to implement the mathematical principles into solving the practical educational tasks.

Nowadays, the effectivity of our created materials has been verified with the high-school students in common lessons during this school year.

Acknowledgement

This work is supported by research project PROGRESS Q 46.

References

1. D. Kuhn, S. Pearsall Journal of Cognition and Development **1**, 113-129, (2000)
2. J. Bečvář *Matematika Aktivně, aktuálně a s aplikacemi,* 43-60, (P3K, Praha, 2012)
3. V. Lamanuskas *Problems of Eduation in the 21st century* **62**, 5-7, (2014)
4. S. Karaçam, V. Bilir, A. D. Baran, *ERPA* **4**, 129-134, (2016)
5. M. Nodzyńska *Wizualizacja w chemii i nauczaniu chemii* (Wydawnictwo naukove Uniwersytetu Pedagogicznego, Kraków, 2012)
6. M. Bílek *Vybrané aspekty vizualizace učiva přírodovědných předmětů* (M&V, Hradec Králové, 2007)
7. A. Šarounová *Matematika Aktivně, aktuálně a s aplikacemi,* 5-24, (P3K, Praha, 2012)
8. R. Šulcová, T. Cífková *BECH* **20**(4), 11-18 (2016)
9. R. B. Fuller *Synergetics: Explorations In The Geometry Of Thinking.* (Macmillan Publishing Company, Inc., New York, 1975)
10. R. Šulcová, M. Ivan *Aktuální aspekty pregraduálne přípravy a postgraduálního vzdělávání učitelů chemie* (Ostravská univerzita, 2017)

Analysis of the pedagogical components of 24 significant experiences in sports interest centers in Bogotá, Colombia

Pedro Galvis Leal[1a], Nidia-Judith Torres[2], and Deisy Baracaldo[3]

[1]Faculty of Education, Department of Science Education, Libre University, Colombia.
[2]Physicak Education Faculty, National Pegagogical University, Colombia.
[3]Faculty of Education, Department of Science Education, Libre University, Colombia.

Abstract. The regulatory framework of Bogotá proposes an education that will combine academic excellence and holistic training, which will ensure better, well-being, opportunities, and quality of life for individuals, families, and groups [1]. One of the strategies used for this purpose was called Sports Interest Centers (SIC), an extracurricular space in which Bogotá public school students could select a sport to practice. The objective of this study is to recognize, integrate, re-order and express the pedagogical elements that compose the educational dynamics of 24 schools that used this strategy, as participants in the city's Sports Interest Centers Festival (SICF). A collaborative hermeneutical study was carried out to understand the educational dynamics and consciously develop the description, analysis, and interpretation of the component elements of a system of pedagogical and didactic actions and their relationships, through school sports. The results demonstrate different emerging pedagogical categories geared at the acquisition of essential knowledge for good living and therefore implicating methodologies that favor the body, displace the mechanical gaze of sports, and bring their transcendence and complexity to school life.
Keywords: School sport; pedagogical components; sports interest centers

1 Introduction

Educational research has recently generated a new focus in analyzing the non-traditional spaces of schools, especially those which do not prioritize "academic achievement", to discuss central themes in the holistic development of the students like social affectivity [2], emotional intelligence [3]; the power of citizens [4], ethnic education [5], and body consciousness [6].

[a] Corresponding author: pepegale@gmail.com

In the same way, the education secretariat of Bogotá established, the Developmental Plan, which foresaw "a city that reduced segregation and discrimination with the human being at the center of the focus of development" [7], and with the goal of improving the educational quality in District Educational Institutions (DEIs). Consequently, the strategy - Curriculum for academic excellence and holistic development in elementary and secondary education-[8], was implemented. Its primary goal is holistic training "as a lifelong process, in which the school is just one more setting for its development" in a diverse, integrative, evolving, and promising way. It offers students essential knowledge that reinforces their learning and cultivates their being through arts, sports, and civil participation, with the goal of incentivizing the development of "essential knowledge for better living" [9]. Thus, from the integrative perspective of physical education, recreation and sports are a catalyst for "being" (developing a citizen conscious of their physicality), for "living together" (developing aptitudes and attitudes for relationships with others), for "doing" (presenting challenging practices and harmonious interactions in playful environments), and for "learning" (developing higher-level thought processes through physical experiences).

With the goal of honoring the experience of the Sport Interests Centers SICs and recognizing the process carried out by teachers, children, and young adults, the DSE held an event in 2015 called the Meaningful Experiences Festival. It called the DEIs to register and participate in the event. The experiences written in the integrative area of "Physical Education, Recreation, and Sports" were selected and evaluated by experts, and later systematized by the team at the Pedagogical and Social Observatory of the Body.

2 Method

The systematization of pedagogical experiences [10], [11], [12], is based on Action Research [13], and therefore it is in the socio-critical investigative paradigm. It is performed through the ordering and reconstruction of lived experience and it permits the discovery and the explanation of important takeaways, with the goal of evaluating, sharing, and debating them, while contributing to the body of pedagogical knowledge through emerging "lessons learned".

2.1 Participants

24 teachers from different SIC of the DEIs that implemented this strategy in the city of Bogotá, registered and selected by the Sport Interest Centers Festival 2015, located in 12 districts of the city of Bogotá, and 100 students (selected at random) who were interviewed in the selected SICs.

2.2 Equipment and data

Three types of data collection methods were used. 1) an online sign-up form administered by the Sport Interest Centers Festival, 2) semi-structured interviews of the teachers and 3) semi-structured interviews of the students. Additionally, video recordings were taken in some Sport Interest Centers, to complement the information obtained. The narratives of the teachers and their students, for example, what was written on the registration form, was transcribed in Rich Text Format (RTF) documents to later be entered into a database or "hermeneutical unit" in the Atlas Ti system.

2.3 Procedure

In accordance with Jara's proposal, the study consisted of the following steps: 1) define a plan for the Systematization of Significant Experiences from which the framework of the SICF was designed, 2) ask the initial questions: leading questions to establish the basis for systematization; 3) recover the lived process: reconstruct what happened in an orderly manner, classify the available information and identify the stages of the process; and then 4) carry out deep reflection: the question "why did what happened happen?" emerges. The information is synthesized and analyzed, in addition to a critical interpretation of the process, and 5) Formulate conclusions and communicate new learning.

3 Results

3.1 Sport interests' centers and their orientation towards essential learning for better living

"When I am angry, I come, I work and I spend the whole day relaxed"
Student DEI Simon Rodriguez

The sport Interest Center SIC´s aim was to develop ways of essential learning for better living, as sports done in different classes were integrated with other areas, cross cutting themes in the school were proposed to establish a comprehensive education. This is essential, due to the fact that, in accordance with the guidelines of the area, "Physical education training, Recreation and sports can only be considered training when it contributes to the holistic development of children and young people" [1]. The teachers interviewed stated that their practices "not only consisted of teaching them a sport" but "of respecting each other [...] and improving our integral education" and a reflection "on the transformation of the student´s life" as well. This was a position with which parents agreed by saying "we believe that it is good, because it helps us to be better in mind and body". This wholeness is realized in two dimensions: individual and social which take shape in a few developments that allow the students greater awareness of themselves and of others. This position is consistent with Dacica´s approach, which argues that sport and physical education represent components of a global education, taking into account that its content influences the health, growth and development of children; their developmental movement, psychological and socialization processes ([1], p.1243)

Teachers and students highlight aspects such as self- control, safety, emotional expression, and autonomy as characteristics of the individual dimension in their "being", when referring to specific themes in their development, like punctuality, serenity, discipline, autonomy, and self-esteem. These "values", "[...] begin to generate a new culture" that "very certainly, will lead us to great things, as people and sportsmen". As Carreiro said, "the purpose of physical education, recreation and sport is to prepare children and youth for participation, rewarding the culture of movement through life" ([15], p.27). With regards to "living together", the SICs highlight the social interaction displayed and manifested in coexistence and social skills such as empathy, peer respect and social responsibility.

In addition to the aforementioned, there is a series of references that teachers and students make regarding respect, solidarity and commitment. This view of the SIC "allows participants to learn how to respect and value themselves and others, so that, it is indispensable to the variety and experience of the different activities in the game, leisure, recreation and sport to be implemented continuously", setting the scene for the purposes of

Physical education at the national level, which is "to support the formation of civil culture and fundamental values for coexistence and peace" [25]. In short, it focuses on the transformation of reality itself, becoming visible in "the language we now use", and the "reduction in the rates of violence at school and in their neighborhoods". Thanks to the opportunity provided by the schools to prevent children from "loitering in the street", they live, on the contrary satisfying bodying experiences that strengthen "the notions of sense, meaning and significance that are so essential to the dynamic human relationship." ([14], p. 177). If we consider what proposes "the relationship with the world is fundamental bodily, because the body is the external element that first makes contact with the world and the human is positioned inside of it, then the pedagogical practice in P.E will be based on an inquiry of the body's ability to relate to others and to the world."

3.2 Transformative citizenships

"Our dream is for a transformative citizenship in its context, an active citizenship that thinks about where we came from and where we are going"
SIC Karate Teacher DEI La Estancia San Isidro.

Citizenship is understood as the condition from which people participate in defining their destiny as individuals and as a society [25]. To do this, the subject must understand that it is part of a context (family, village, society) in which the forms of interaction and communication of those who make it up are mediated by values, customs, traditions, and standards supported by their members. In the SIC, teachers and students refer to the live-in space as a secure welcoming, inclusive environment, that promotes the development of students "into positive leaders". For the DSE, the SIC constitutes learning environments, where students from dynamic pedagogical processes explore and play collectively established roles and generate systems of knowledge that facilitate their practical experience, these environments allow the student to exercise and develop citizenship, beyond a civil status by belonging to a geographical site, because, as claimed by Herrera, " citizenship refers to the exercising of multiple skills in the context of the practiced democracy that is dynamic and creative" [21].

In this sense, the SIC will promote the development of skills, attitudes, motivations and practices, essential skills proposed by the District Secretariat of Education in the Comprehensive Plans for Citizenship and Coexistence: Identity, dignity, and rights, duties and respect for the rights of others, sensitivity and emotional management, a sense of life in the body and nature, and participation and coexistence.

3.3 Building territory

"My mother is very proud, she came to see me compete and she likes what I do"
SIC Karate student. DEI la Estancia San Isidro.

According to the DES, "we are the territory that we inhabit, that is to say, the ways of being, understanding, living, feeling and sharing meaning, in a space that we specify, and makes us belong to something" [1]. According to this approach, the SIC allowed the processes of appropriation of spaces in the areas of school, family and community. This experience "opened up and allowed a greater number of participants in all educational cycles of all the districts of Bogotá. This caused in some cases, the free-time projects to adjust their work to the Institutional Educational Project, where each teacher articulated their proposal, not only related to the sport, but also to the proposal of the IEP to the school.

Given the dynamics of these conditions, the general community had the necessary tools for its development, with the necessary administrative support.

Regarding the role of the family, the DES gives relevance and meaning to the SIC in two ways: one in which parents approve their child's participation, and the other through participation and support. In summary, the SIC enriches environments using sports, allowing participants to have meaningful experiences that are open to the school environment, family and social fabric, in order to: "transform the collective imagination that has been rotated around the town, (...) to demystify violence, violent actors, transformers of lives" (DEI la Estancia San Isidro), as mentioned by a teacher of a Sport Center.

3.4 Didactics

Understanding the SIC as enriched learning environments ([1], p. 30), teachers and students gave account of its development as a meaningful experience thanks to certain features in the sphere of the didactics. Didactics is understood as the theory of teaching: "our discipline is an inherited teaching theory, and indebted to many other disciplines, its destination. However, when dealing with education, it should be constituted, reciprocally in the offering of theoretical analysis in the social field, and of knowledge". Thus, we are able to observe the teaching of harmonization, understood as the process of articulation of the SIC with the dynamics and purposes of the DEI. Consequently, we performed a work set which prompted the exchange of knowledge and communication between the different areas and teachers of the school.

In relation to the specific Didactics of the discipline, it was found that, although the objective of the performance engine is not abandoned, there are spaces in each session to dialogue, share knowledge, set goals, design joint strategies and assess performance. All of this is done "on a needs basis keeping in mind the potential and interests of those affected" [1]. This generates other dynamic interest that promotes learning environments as significant. Decisions about teaching are based on the interests, tastes, needs, motivations, and dispositions of students. Thus, they spoke of practices based on approaches to critical and participatory thinking that highlight all their skills to the school. From this basic practice comes the response to how to teach the teachers, whose main features were: going from the easy to the complex, relying on the example, making use of the inter-learning, promoting self-learning, the enjoyment, the self-control and motivation for achievement, in a scenario of "courtesy, integrity, perseverance, self-control and an indomitable spirit". At this point, the role of the teacher was determinate, being the leader of the educational process and the dynamics that they are currently experiencing, directing them under the above principles and agreements established collectively as the dialogue. Good treatment, the capacity for listening, the demand, and the respect for the rhythms of learning and, especially, its reflexive capability: "as a lesson as one which always needs correcting and improving. I'm making a journal of this work of writing that I'm failing [...], one begins to raise expectations in the sense of leaving training and going forward because it is not there as the training of one is a challenge so improvements must be made to be able to offer students something better."

3.5 Reflective bodily practices.

"Doing many things halfway balances my body" SIC Cheerleading student DEI Porvenir

It is observed that the bodily practices have favored the autonomous work and the co-operative tasks as a form of organization in the activities, and that such possibilities have allowed the development of the learning of life essentials, promoting the transformation of the interactions of the participants with themselves and with others, as interpreted in "the desire of students to be discovered". Reviewing the expressions of the participants tells of the way in which the proposed actions allowed the interweaving of cooperative work, understood as "that activity undertaken equally and proportionally by two or more persons jointly to achieve the objectives and, ultimately, learn." [20].

The SIC helped to establish new relations among students, improve their attitude toward the group, and improve the relationships based on trust. The bodily practices and experiences allowed body recognition in children and young people from the participating Schools, facilitating multidimensional experiences, that is to say, that only through the corporeal nature, the subject accesses the world of the senses, motor, social, emotional, intellectual, cultural, that, in this case, is achieved by the transfer of the "physical body to the symbolic body" [27], a conscious and thinking body that "is primarily a tool of meaning and symbolization key –a corpus– that is expressed and communicated in society in the form of corporeity" [16] to LIVE TOGETHER, because, as Martin Barbero [22] says "there is no life experience or access to knowledge of the self or of others, which is extra-corporal".

4 Discussion

Attending the phenomenological approaches stated by Merleau Ponty [24] who argues that corporeality, as bodily experience (embodied), involves emotional, social and symbolic dimensions, it is understood that in the SIC we worked intentionally in favor of the construction of learning about "being" and "coexistence", which are the proposals from the Secretariat of education of Bogotá for the implementation of such strategies.

Merleau Ponty, as opposed to the mechanical dual vision of Descartes, posits that where the mind and the spirit are understood as separate from the body (res cogitans and rest extensa), in which he expresses a total denial of the validity of the senses; proposes "being all one", i.e., that man is the indissoluble union between body and soul, inside and out, because, as he says in his book, humans "don't have a body, they are a body" [23].

The SICs have faced the reigning and dichotomous model from the traditional schooling, according to which the human body and movement are a hindrance to "important" "intellectual" learning, because, among others, they are measured based on national and international standardized tests. Proof of this is the specific weight that every area of the curriculum at the school has. These significant experiences made corporeal experiences that involved students (alumnus: those who are breastfeeding - feed - and grow) in its entirety: "a human being who feels, thinks and does things in relationship with each other and with the world that surrounds him, and from those relationships he builds a world of meanings that give meaning to his life".

From the perspective of Merleau Ponty, according to each ego (what I think of myself) is only achieved when sharing with others, what has been done in the SICs is to combine the expression of their own to be subjective as an intentional act and self-conscious (its sameness), with the act of expressing an idea of corporeal form to the other (otherness). It is to say that, as proposed by Sergio is an intentional staging that "is a concrete form of relationship of the human being with himself, with others and with the world through its corporeality," because, in the end "humans' acts are performed in and to the world" [24].

For the DSE, that sense of "world" construction is not anything other than the construction of the "territory". If "Petting, smelling a flower or play [...] are not the effect of a cause called world, but a dialectical and unfathomable relationship in its entirety between who I am and my environment", the dynamics in the SIC's objective of this study comes to enrich this relationship, thanks to the generation of a new conceptual net crossed by the body, in the Merleaupontian combination of incarnate awareness and conscious body , and the abandonment of the claim body-machine or body-gadget process in which, the elaboration of an own corporeality is made, necessarily, recognizing the others corporeality in the play of inter subjectivity, its spaces, times and actions.

In short, the SICs, value the body in relation to other bodies (self-aware and respectful of others) "as a point of reference through which the world is articulated, where come into play throughout the constellation of subjective and intersubjective relations of human beings in society" [19].

It is worth combining careful observation with this type of strategy in the classroom. Taking from its analysis, those lessons that may well guide the work of the classroom, in a country that urgently requires to the rebuilding of the social tissue with strong social and emotional threads, mediated by the body.

References

1. Secretaría de Educación del Distrito. "Reorganización curricular por ciclos.Acompañamiento Pedagógico 5", Bogotá: Alcaldía Mayor de Bogotá, **205**, (2015)
2. C. M. Castañeda, Competencia socio-afectiva en el marco escolar colombiano". Bogotá: Escenarios, **12** (2), Jul., 19-34, (2014)
3. J. Ciarrochi, J.Forgas, J. Mayer, Emotional Intelligence in Everyday Life: a Scientific Inquiry. New York: Psychology Press. 251-260, (2006)
4. Solano, R., Alpargatero. L. Orientaciones para el área de Educación para la Ciudadanía y la Convivencia. Bogotá: Secretaría de Educación, 20-38, (2014)
5. P. Enciso, Estado del Arte de la etno-educación en Colombia con énfasis en política pública. Bogotá: Ministerio de Educación Nacional, (2004)
6. J. Castro, Pedagogía de la Corporeidad y Potencia Humano. Medellín: Educación Física y Deporte, **8**(17), 23, (2004)
7. Alcaldía Mayor de Bogotá. Plan de Desarrollo 2012 – 2016 Bogotá Humana, (2012) http://www.canalcapital.gov.co/images/planeacion_pdf/Plan-de-Desarrollo-2012-2016.pdf
8. Secretaría de Educación de Bogotá. Currículo para la excelencia académica y la formación integral 40 x 40. (2012) https://issuu.com/secretariadeeducacionbogota/docs/0_pantalla
9. Secretaría de Educación de Bogotá. "Orientaciones curriculares para el área de Educación Física, Recreación y Deporte". Bogotá: SED, (2014)
10. O. Jara, Sistematización de experiencias, investigación y Evaluación: Aproximaciones desde tres ángulos. Educational Research Global, **1**, 156-70, (2004)
11. A. Ghiso, Sistematización: Un pensar el hacer, que se resiste a perder su autonomía. Decisio, **28**, 3-8., (2011)
12. M. Barnechea, M. Tirado, La sistematización de experiencias: producción de conocimientos desde y para la práctica. Tendencias y Retos N **15**, 97-107, (2010)
13. R. Ávila, La producción de conocimiento en la investigación acción pedagógica (IAPE): Balance de una experimentación. Revista Educação e Pesquisa, **31**(3), 503-519, (2005)
14. A. Almonacid, La educación física como espacio de transformación social y Educativa: perspectivas desde los imaginarios sociales y la ciencia de la motricidad humana. Estudios Pedagógicos **38**(1), 177-190., (2012)
15. F. Carreiro, La gestión del currículo a través de competencias: un enfoque desde el contexto portugués». Tándem. Didáctica de la Educación Física, **29**, 27., (2009)
16. L. Cencillo, J. García, Antropología y cultura. Guadiana (1973)

17. L. Dacica, The formative role of physical education and sports. Presentation at: The 6th International Conference Edu World 2014 "Education Facing Contemporary World Issues", (2014). http://ac.els-cdn.com/S187704281501602X/1-s2.0-S187704281501602X-main.pdf?_tid=e73fa562-5026-11e5-859f 0000aab0f01&acdnat=1441056552_0e598fc42716ef12102f533360a0818d.
18. J. Fernández, La importancia de la Educación Física en la escuela. Digital Magazine EFDEPORTES.COM, 13 · (130), (2009). http://www.efdeportes.com/efd130/la-importancia- de-la-educacion-fisica- en-la- escuela.htm
19. C. Godina, La teoría de género desde la perspectiva fenomenológica del cuerpo vivido. La Lámpara de Diógenes Magazine. 6, 203-209., (2001)
20. Gutiérrez Del Mora, M. El Trabajo Cooperativo, su diseño y su evaluación. Dificultades y Propuestas. (2009). In conference: Univest 09. http://dugi-doc.udg.edu/bitstream/handle/10256/1956/217.pdf?sequence=1.
21. J. Herrera, R., Rodríguez, Citado en Secretaría de Educación. Educación para la ciudadanía y la convivencia. Módulo 2: Ciudad, sociedad y territorio. CINEP, 68., (2014).
22. J. Martín Barbero, De los medios a las mediaciones. Gustavo Gili., (1987)
23. Merleau-Ponty, M. Sens Et Non-Sens. Gallimard., (1966)
24. M. Merleau Ponty, Fenomenología de la percepción. Translation: Jem Cabanes(1993).Translation by Ediciones Península®, Proyectos Editoriales y Audiovisuales CBS, S.A., (1945)
25. Ministerio de Educación Nacional. Documento No 15: Orientaciones Pedagógicas para la Educación Física, Recreación y Deporte. MEN, Viceministerio de Educación Preescolar, Básica y Media. Bogotá, 1, 14., (2010)
26. Ministerio de Educación Nacional. Programa de Educación para la Sexualidad y Construcción de Ciudadanía. (2008). http://www.mineducacion.gov.co/1621/article-173877.html
27. Morera de Guijarro, J. Problemática del yo en Maine de Biran. Logos. Anales del Seminario de Metafísica, 22, Universidad Complutense de Madrid, pp. 185- 198., (1988). http://revistas.ucm.es/fsl/15756866/articulos/ASEM8788110185A.PDF
28. Secretaría de Educación. Lineamiento Pedagógico Educación para la Ciudadanía y la Convivencia. (2013) http://www.redacademica.edu.co/archivos/redacademica/proyectos/pecc/centro_documentacion/caja_de_herramientas/serie_1_orientaciones/02_lineamiento_pedagogico_educacion_para_la_ciudadania_y_la_convivencia.pdf
29. Secretaría de Educación De Bogotá. Educación para la ciudadanía y la convivencia. Módulo 2: Ciudadanía, sociedad y territorio. CINEP. Bogotá: 2014.
30. A. Sicilia, Educación Física y transformación social: implicaciones desde una epistemología posmoderna. Estudios Pedagógicos, **38,** 47-65 (2012)
31. Y. Silveira, Miedo a equivocarse en educación física y deporte. Universidad Miguel Hernández De Elche, Departamento De Psicología de la Salud. 15-32 (2013)

Promoting integrity of shift report by applying ISBAR principles among nursing students in clinical placement

Weng Ian Pang[1a],

[1]PHD student, Faculty of Health Sciences, Macau University of Science and Technology. Lecturer, School of Health Sciences, Macao Polytechnic Institute, Rua de Luis Gonzaga Gomes, Macao

Abstract. Shift report is an essential method for nursing staff to carry out health care communication. The most important purpose of the shift report is to ensure the safety of patients and to provide continuous care. Nursing students are inadequate of clinical experience and rational organization during patient care. They may not be able to handle the critically ill patients and pass the messages to the following nursing staff. ISBAR (Identify, Situation, Background, Assessment and Recommendation) tool is increasingly being utilized as a format for structured shift report communication. In this study, a scale of ISBAR principles is designed to provide students with self-assessment and teachers with evaluation, in a way to improve nursing students' self-awareness of shift report. Hopefully, with the use of the scale of ISBAR, nursing students are able to complete shift report in systemic integrity and orderliness during clinical placement.
Keywords: Shift report; nursing students; ISBAR principles

1 Introduction

Good communication is recognized as essential to quality and patient safety, and good communication skills are integral part of health professional expertise [1]. It has long been recognized that shift report is an essential method for nursing staff to carry out health care communication. Clinical handover refers to the transfer of professional responsibility and accountability for some or all aspects of care for a patient, or group of patients, to another person or professional group on a temporary or permanent basis [2]. Handovers can only be achieved through linguistic exchange. So, when this communication is suboptimal, patient safety is compromised [3,4]. Incident and complaint data provide strong evidence for the critical role of lack of appropriate communication in adverse events [5]. Australian and international agencies recognize the imperative to act to improve clinical communication [6]. Its effectiveness has been demonstrated in clinical using a standardized format, which can assist the transfer of information, improve the quality of clinical communication and

[a] Corresponding author: author@e-mail.org

prevent subsequent medical errors. [4, 7-9]. Therefore, the most important purpose of a standardized format shift report is to ensure the safety of the patient and to provide continuous care.

The Joint Commission and the Institute for Healthcare Improvement recommend the SBAR (situation, background, assessment, recommendations) communication technique to improve communication and reduce medical errors [10]. JCAHO [4] recommend that ISBAR (Identification, Situation, Background, Assessment, and Recommendation) is a tool, which may improve communication within multidisciplinary teams. ISBAR tool be utilized as the model that all healthcare staff use to structure clinical communication, and ensuring accurate handover of information between shifts [4, 7]. The ISBAR framework can organize this information in a clear and concise format (Table 1), which includes a summary of the patient's medical history, illness history, pathophysiology, laboratory data, current situation and nursing care information [7,11].

Nursing students lack experience in interprofessional communication skills, being overwhelmed with organizing and are unable to accurately presenting their patient's information in clinical. They may not be able to handle the critical ill patients and pass the messages to the following nursing staff. Also, students are fear of making mistakes, making learning difficult and lose self-confidence. A study of Davis [12] found that the time for preconference was shortened during the clinical placement, while discussion was focused on pertinent information. Students also reported less anxiety when presenting with the modified SBAR format. However, nursing students' clinical learning experiences are important components of their professional development [13].

Table 1. ISBAR https://www.inmo.ie/tempDocs/ISBAR_PAGE46-47%20feb13.pdf

Items	ISBAR
Identify	Identify yourself, who you are talking to and who you are talking about
Situation	What is the current situation, concerns, observations, etc.?
Background	What is the relevant background? This helps to set the scene to interpret the situation above accurately
Assessment	What do you think the problem is? This requires the interpretation of the situation and background information to make an educated conclusion about what is going on
Recommendation	What do you need them to do? What do you recommend should be done to correct the current situation?

Faculty are challenged continuously to improve communication skills among nursing students preparing them for safe clinical practice. ISBAR principle can improve the relevance of teaching and management strategies. Regarding the improvement in both clinical practice preparation and communication competency of nursing students, Skaalvik, Normann, & Henriksen [13] found that oral shift reporting can stimulate learning if it includes consultation and discussion between nursing students and the nursing staff. Therefore, to enhance students' organizational skills and ability to assess patient, students are educated the learning strategy as a measurement for integrity of shift report after they have finished their shift handover. Through using assessment form with a standardized rubric as the learning strategy for teaching and evaluating communication in clinical handover, it will then provide quality and safety in students' education.

Communication is a complex phenomenon and includes skill, cognition, emotion, and value [9]. Raya [14] stated nursing practice requires not only scientific knowledge, but also interpersonal, intellectual and technical abilities and skills; this means a composition of knowledge, clinical work and interpersonal communication. Although there is a standardized ISBAR format to help student to transfer information, nursing students also need shared responsibility for timely, relevant, clear, and concise exchange of patient information with a cadre of disciplines often in hectic, chaotic environments in order to assure good communication among them [9]. Hence, there are four parts in the assessment criteria including SBAR, professional attitude, nursing knowledge and communication skills.

The author of the present study took a qualitative research approach to explore the promoting integrity of shift report by applying ISBAR principles among nursing students in clinical placement. The aims of this study were to provide an evaluation method for shift report among nursing students during clinical placement, to develop the standards for guiding their efforts to target, to develop students with self-improvement, and to facilitate clinical preceptor to focus on students-to-nurse communication evaluation.

2 Method

A pilot study was initiated with designed evaluation methods among nursing students to assess the outcomes of the application of ISBAR. Evaluation of professional attitude, SBAR skill, knowledge and communication skills were the focus of the study assessment criteria.

2.1 Participants

The study was recruiting nurse managers and advanced nurses from a government hospital who were baccalaureate, licensed clinical nurse specialist with a minimum of five years' teaching experience in nursing who also took part in grading the students. A total of five participants voluntarily and anonymously took part in this study, with four nursing preceptors and one head nurse (Table 2).

Table 2. Participants in the interviews

Participant	Gender	Ward	Education	Experience (Year)
1	Female	Medical	BSN, CNS	>30
2	Female	Medical-Surgical	BSN, CNS	>30
3	Female	Surgical	BSN, MSN with CNS	>15
4	Female	Critical	BSN, MSN with CNS	>15
5	Male	Critical	BSN, CNS	>10

BSN: Bachelor of Science in Nursing; CNS, Clinical Nurse Specialist
MSN with CNS: Master of Science in Nursing (MSN) with Clinical Nurse Specialist (CNS)

2.2 Procedure

Data collection took place in the government hospital. Interview with the five advanced nurses that included one head nurse and four nursing preceptors began in mid-March and ended in mid-April 2016. At the beginning of each interview, the participant confirmed that the interview could be recorded. The interviews were conducted in Cantonese.

Data collection and analysis of clinical preceptors and head nurses focused on the shift reports requirements for the nursing students. The interview questions (Table 3) were structured following literature reviews, mainly indicating nursing students' professional attitude, nursing knowledge, communication skills and narrative thinking as the development and application of the evaluation criteria.

Table 3. Interview questions

Interview questions
1. What are your comments regarding the shift handover of nursing students?
2. Are you satisfied with the handover of nursing students? Why?
3. From a professional attitude point of view, which items of handover are important? Why?
4. What are your comments/suggestions regarding the organization ability of nursing student to shift handover? Please explain.
5. Do you think nursing students need to have sufficient nursing knowledge to shift handover? Why?
6. What do you think about using assessment criteria of ISBAR for nursing students? Please explain.
7. Do you think the nursing student's communication skills are related to the handover? Why?
8. Do you have any case about the shift handover of nursing student? Please explain.

3 Results and discussion

The transcribed data of all participants were read and organized into categories or selection of themes. When similar or identical items were found in most or all of the individual transcriptions, they were grouped into concepts, which were then examined to determine themes.

The interviews of all five nurse managers and advanced nurses were identified and analyzed in four major concepts (Figure 1): (1) Professional attitude of students. (2) SBAR (Situation, Background, Assessment, Recommendation). (3) Knowledge of nursing care and medications. (4) Effective communication skills. The details of each concept are further explained below under the four themes.

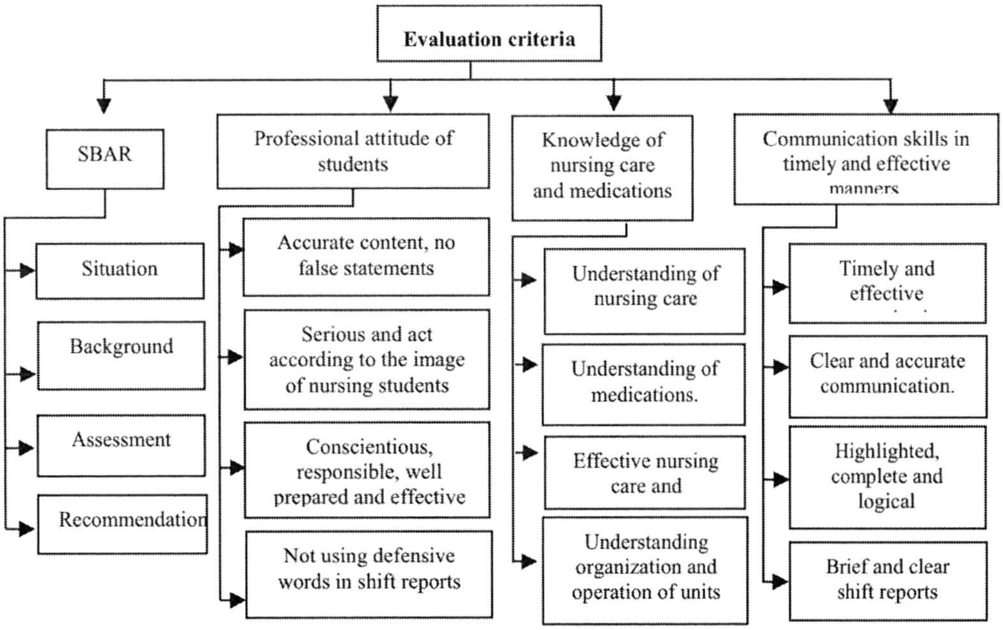

Figure 1. Evaluation criteria

3.1 SBAR

ISBAR is the most important concept in the theme that included Identification, Situation, Background, Assessment, and Recommendation. The ISBAR approach holds great promise to enhance communication as a simple, portable and memorable tool which can be used by anyone to optimize communication, especially for nursing student [8].

In the first concept, the interviewers explored this area in detail. The nurse manager and one of the advanced nurses stated that there are usually a lot of students who could not understand and failed to grasp the patient's situation, especially being neglectful in considering the patient's background and lack in providing recommendation for patients. Some of the participants' comments on students using the ISBAR principle to clinical handover are:

> 'What are your comments regarding the shift handover of nursing students? The year 3 students cannot understand how to complete description of the patient's situation. The students do not understand what patient's data is needed to be expressed, they also often ignore the patient's history and recommendations. If there is a systematic form for guidance on how to handover, that will help improve students' ability to express and organize.'

> 'ISBAR is a good way for students to shift and can help improve students' self-confidence, as well as to help students better understand the patient's condition.'

In terms of judgment for the score of this assessment criteria, as ISBAR is the most important concept among the themes, it comprises 40% of marking in this form and a 10-point system was applied to assess students' understanding. The "I" in ISBAR which is "Identification" refers to "Identify yourself, who you are talking to and who you are talking about". However, all participants commented that it was not suitable to use the 10-point system on "Identification", and they agreed to transfer the "Identification" score to professional attitude of students in assessment criteria. Therefore, the format (Table 4) for the preparatory work were changed to a modified version that became Situation, Background, Assessment, and Recommendation (SBAR).

> 'The "Identification" in ISBAR, which is a basic requirement in handover, should not be included in the 10-point system; the scores arrangements should be considered more appropriate in the professional attitude of students.'

Table 4. SBAR

Performance	Excellent		Good		Fair		Acceptable		Poor	
Situation: Able to describe the current situation, concerns, observations, etc.	10	9	8	7	6	5	4	3	2	1
Background: Able to give a summary of information relevant to the current problem: medical history, medications, laboratory results, diagnostic tests, etc.	10	9	8	7	6	5	4	3	2	1
Assessment: Able to provide background information, found on examination of the patient, progress and results.	10	9	8	7	6	5	4	3	2	1
Recommendation: Able to provide follow-up action, direction, prevention, etc.	10	9	8	7	6	5	4	3	2	1

3.2 Professional attitude of students

From the respondents' descriptions, the professional attitude of students in clinical handover is mostly concerned by the nurses. All advanced nurses in the interviews reported that the demand from clinical handover involved professional attitude as they requested students to be serious, rigorous and responsible for their action.

> 'Nursing students should be serious when passing the messages to the following nursing staff during shift reports.'

Question 4 dealt with the comments/suggestions regarding the organization ability of nursing student in shift handover (Table 3). The nurse manager and one of the advanced nurses stated that the patient's report content must be accurate, so the item "no false statement" is very important when composing the shift report. One of the advanced nurses indicated that students should not use offensive words, complain nor attack someone in the shift reports.

> 'A student used offensive words in shift report; the student blamed a male patient who did not finish lunch by himself, and then she also criticized her patient for being useless and needed help to finish his lunch. '

In terms of judgment for the score of this assessment criteria, as professional attitude is an important concept in the themes, this part comprises 20% of total marking in this form. This time we used a 5-point system to assess the students' understanding. All participants mentioned that nursing profession must acquire professional attitude. Each nurse needs to understand the responsibilities and concerns that are integrated to the nursing profession [15]. The professionalism in the nursing field is defined as non-biased care for patients, integrity, respect for patients, attitude, appearance, willingness to help others, team work, honesty, responsibility and discipline [15]. These are the core values of nursing professional that are expected and appreciated. Nurses should possess responsibility, honesty, integrity, belief in human dignity and patient equality [15].

Ascano-Martin [16] stated that omission of vital patient information including the patient's age, sex, race and medical history is common when transferring information from one professional to another. It also reflects the lack of professional attitude during clinical handover. Therefore, the modified format (Table 5) included no false statement, Seriousness, responsibility, preparedness of shift reports, effectiveness of introduction and free of offensive words, etc.

Table 5. Professional attitude of students

Performance	Excellent	Good	Fair	Acceptable	Poor
Accurate content, no false statement	5	4	3	2	1
Serious and act according to the image of nursing students	5	4	3	2	1
Conscientious, responsible, well-prepared in shift reports and effective introduction	5	4	3	2	1
Not using offensive words in shift reports such as criticism, blaming, complaining and attacking someone, etc.	5	4	3	2	1

3.3 Knowledge of nursing care and medications

According to the participants' descriptions and their experience in teaching students, students who lack knowledge are more likely to make mistake when transferring critical information during clinical handover. Question 5 dealt with the need of nursing students to have sufficient nursing knowledge for shift handover (Table 3). For the interviews of all 5 nurse managers and advanced nurses, information indicated that the students should enhance their nursing knowledge in order to identify the clinical problem and to effectively deliver the messages for following nurses, particularly in pathophysiology, pharmacology, critical care, medical and surgical care. Clarke [17] suggested that understanding handover improvement complexities can enhance problem recognition and increase the likelihood of achieving successful outcomes in subsequent stages of change. The nurse manager has more detailed sharing on this issue:

> 'Students and recent graduates still need to further develop their vital knowledge, especially in medication. Usually, students do not understand why the patients are taking the drug, and not understanding the precautions for the medication, so, they cannot verbally explain the situation of patient about the drug when they undergo clinical handover.'

In terms of judgment for the score of this assessment criteria, as the knowledge of nursing care and medications is an important concept in these themes, this part comprises 20% of total marking in this form. A 5-point system was used here to assess the students' understanding. Smith and Kaluzny [18] stated that solution identification follows problem recognition in a process that is influenced by characteristics of both the organization and of the solution. It is therefore important to understand the organization and operation of ward to ensure that solutions will be successful in overcoming handover complexity and context variability. Therefore, the most major considerations or factors in this format (Table 6) included understanding of medication, understanding of nursing care, effective nursing care and treatments and understanding of organization and operation in wards.

Table 6. Knowledge of nursing care and medications

Performance	Excell ent	Good	Fair	Acceptable	Poor
Understanding of nursing care	5	4	3	2	1
Understanding of medications	5	4	3	2	1
Effective nursing care and treatments	5	4	3	2	1
Understanding organization and operation of units	5	4	3	2	1

3.4 Effective communication skills

As the clinical care environment has progressively become more complex, there are needs to reinforce the belief that the improvement in students' communication during clinical handover are best for managing complex environments. Manning [9] stated that communication skills included listening, assimilating, interpreting, gathering, and sharing information. Question 7 dealt with the nursing students' communication skills that are related to the handover (Table 3). The nurse manager mentioned that students' verbal handover of the content is not logical, not highlighting the patient's problem, and not clear in the shift report. According to WHO Patient Safety Solutions [19], these gaps in communication can cause serious breakdowns in the continuity of care, inappropriate treatment, and potential harm to the patient. All participants agreed with the necessity of communication skills for safe transfer of information. They also believed that the transfer of messages should be timely and effective, and that the content should be clear and accurate. One of the advanced nurses stated about some issues found in the communication skills in students:

> 'Students often forget the important message when they orally present the shift reports. The students did not timely inform to the nurses the need to follow the situation, which implies the lack of organizational capacity of students' communication.'

In terms of judgment for the score of this assessment criteria, as communication skills is an important concept in these themes, this part comprises 20% of total marking in this form. A 5-point system was used to assess the students' understanding. Kourkouta and Papathanasiou [1] observed the results of their study and stated that good communication also improves the quality of care provided to patients. There is a strong emphasis in identifying the communication skills of students during clinical handover that can contribute to, or protect against, preventable medical errors. Therefore, good communication of assessment criteria in shift report can ensure patient's safety and reduce error susceptibility. The most major considerations or factors in this format (Table 7) included timely, effective, complete, logical and clarified communication in shift reports.

Table 7. Effective communication skills

Performance	Excellent	Good	Fair	Acceptable	Poor
Timely and effective communication	5	4	3	2	1
Clear and accurate communication	5	4	3	2	1
Highlighted, complete and logical communication	5	4	3	2	1
Brief and clear shift reports	5	4	3	2	1

4 Conclusions

This study demonstrated that expected outcomes improves student communication that using a scale of ISBAR principles that may improve student shift report in systemic integrity and orderliness. The concerns expressed by our interviewees about the students lack the ability to transfer the important information during clinical handover, if not addressed properly compromise student's ability to transfer in oral shift reports while adding to the serious breakdowns in the continuity of care. Therefore, the assessment criteria as a learning strategy and measurement for integrity of shift report after they have finished their shift handover. It can be provides a guidance for student in shift handover and promotes a scoring scheme for teacher to recognize shortage of student in shift reporting.

References

1. L. Kourkouta, L.V. Papathanasiou, Communication in Nursing Practice. Mater Sociomed, **26**(1), 65-67., (2014)
2. Australian Medical Association. Safe handover: safe patients. AMA Clinical Handover Guide. Sydney, (2006).http://ama.com.au/node
3. C.C. Greenberg, S.E. Regenbogen, D.M. Studdert, S.R. Lipsitz, S.O. Rogers, M.J. Zinner, A.A. Gawande, Patterns of communication breakdowns resulting in injury to surgical patients. J. Am. Coll. Surg. **204**: 533-540. (2007)
4. JCAHO. Sentinel event statistics. (2006). http://www.jointcomission.org/sentinelevents/statistics/
5. K. Hill, R. Aldrich, D. Lawson, T. Easton, Enhancing Clinical Communication: Characterizing the Role of Communication in Clinical Incidents and Complaints International Society for Quality in Health Care Conference, Boston. (2007)
6. Australian Commission on Safety and Quality in Health Care. The OSSIE Guide to Clinical Handover Improvement. Sydney, ACSQHC, (2009). https://www.safetyandquality.gov.au/wp-content/uploads/2012/01/ossie.pdf
7. M. Horgan. ISBAR stickers may improve communication within multidisciplinary teams, ensuring accurate handover of information between shifts. (2013). https://www.inmo.ie/tempDocs/ISBAR_PAGE46-47%20feb13.pdf
8. R. Aldrich, A. Duggan, K. Lane, K. Nair, K.N. Hill, ISBAR revisited: identifying and solving barriers to effective clinical handover in inter-hospital transfer – public report on pilot study. Newcastle: Hunter New England Health (2009). https://www.safetyandquality.gov.au/wp-content/uploads/2012/01/ISBAR-PSPR.pdf
9. M.L. Manning. Improving clinical communication through structured conversation. Nurs. Econ., **24**(5), 268-271. (2006).
10. Institute for Healthcare Improvement. Web and action: using SBAR to improve communication. (2006).http://www.ihi.org/ihi/fbmms/Sh()wForum^spx?ForumID:97
11. Medical Audits. Medical Audits ISBAR Audit Tool. (2015). http://www.medicalaudits.co.uk/sepsis_isbar.aspx
12. R.L. Davis, Using SBAR as a Preconference Reporting Tool for Nursing Students. Nurse Educ. **41**(2). Copyright * 2016 Wolters Kluwer Health, Inc. All rights reserved
13. M.W. Skaalvik, H.K. Normann, N. Henriksen, To what extent does the oral shift report stimulate learning among nursing students? A qualitative study. **19**(15-16), 2300-2308. (2010)
14. A. Raya. Nursing of man as a unique person Nosileftiki. **45**(1): 19-24. (2006)
15. Health eCareers. How important is professionalism for a Nurse? (2011).https://www.healthecareers.com/article/healthcare-news/how-important-is-professionalism-for-a-nurse
16. F. Ascano-Martin. Shift report and SBAR: strategies for clinical post conference. Nurse Educ. **33**(5), 190. (2008).
17. C.M. Clarke, D.D. Persaud, Leading Clinical Handover Improvement: A Change Strategy to Implement Best Practices in the Acute Care Setting. J Patient Saf. **7**(1):11-18. (2011)
18. D. B. Smith, A.D. Kaluzny, The White Labyrinth: A Guide to the Health Care System. 2nd Edition. Ann Arbor, MI: Health Administration Press, (1986)
19. WHO Patient Safety Solutions. Communication during patient hand-overs (2007) http://www.who.int/patientsafety/solutions/patientsafety/PS-Solution3.pdf

Do educators in initial training have stereotypes about adult education?

Pilar Moreno-Crespo[1a], and Olga Moreno-Fernández[2]

[1] University of Huelva, Faculty of Educational Sciences, March 3 Avenue, 21071 Huelva, Spain
[2] University of Seville, Pyrotechnic St.., 41013 Sevilla, Spain

Abstract. The initial training that future educators receive must be prepared for the education of adults, which includes knowing the characteristics of the group and overcoming the stereotypes towards them. However, not always achieved. The purpose of this communication is to approximate the stereotypes that early educators (elementary school teachers and social educators) have about adult education. To this end, 110 students of teachers in the specialty of Primary Education and 151 of social education responded to a Likert scale questionnaire in which eight items related to stereotypes towards adult education. From the results obtained, the most outstanding stereotypes are present in issues related to the management of new technologies and the learning capacity of this group.
Keywords: Initial training; stereotypes; adult education

1 Introduction

In the last decades the population of adults and older adults has increased. This increase means that institutions begin to focus resources on promoting the quality of life of this group ([13], [6], [7], [10], [11]). Among the measures taken is the increase in the educational offer for this group in the formal and socio-cultural spheres. The trainer profile of adults in the formal field is represented by the Primary school teacher, for being a generalist professional (can teach diverse subjects). On the other hand, the profile of adult educators in the socio-cultural area is represented by the Social Educator. We consider that from the formation of educators for adults, it should be prepared understanding the characteristics of the collective and overcoming the stereotypes towards them. However, we find that in future educators there are stereotypes that we must face.

Continuing to be educated continually implies maturing as a citizen throughout the life cycle. Likewise, it implies assuming rights and obligations that allow the person to be an active part of society ([2], [10]). For this reason since the mid-twentieth century has been

[a] Corresponding author: author@e-mail.org

recognized and strengthened Life Long Learning (LLL). Proof of this are the World Conferences held by UNESCO (Elsinor in 1949, Montreal in 1960, Tokyo in 1972, Paris in 1985 and Hamburg in 1997), as well as the actions of the Council of Europe, OECD, ILO or UN ([4], [12], [14], [15]). These international meetings have been crucial for the development of lifelong education.

[14] emphasize that the dimensions of these encounters are: 1) Basic or academic training; 2) Technical and vocational training; 3) Personal and cultural training; and 4) Social formation and citizen participation.

[3] indicate that adult education is conceived at all stages of education, including basic education and non-formal education, which we refer to here as "socio-cultural".

However, we prefer the definition of adult education that makes [16], "all formative action that tends to provide knowledge and skills to the people of post-school age, as well as to promote in them valuable attitudes and behaviours aimed at fostering their personal and professional development, and social participation" (p. 44).

However, this definition takes on a broader aspect with the words of [8] on lifelong education:

> [...] recognizes the foundation of adult education that goes beyond compensatory education, since it raises the question that the individual must remain active throughout his or her life, which has implications for the education system and for policies developed by institutions (p. 114).

Among the principles of lifelong education, we find that it is a continuous, comprehensive, global, democratic, dynamic and flexible process, among many other issues [12]. On the other hand, [16] emphasize the lifelong character, unity, globality and universality of Lifelong Education.

2 Method

Among the professional exits of the Primary Education teacher and the Social Education professional, is the adult educator profile. Therefore, the objective of the research is to approximate the stereotypes that primary school teachers and early childhood educators have about adult education. To this end, 261 questionnaires have been collected (110 students of teaching in the specialty of Primary Education and 151 of Social Education) Likert type which contains eight items related to stereotypes towards adult education. It is a descriptive, quantitative, transverse and non-probabilistic study ([1], [5]).

3 Results

It is noteworthy that the management of ICT and the reduction of learning capacity are the stereotypes that are represented more strongly in the data obtained. Thus, we can affirm that 75% of the respondents disagree with the statement "People over 65 do not have the ability to start studying at these ages". However, 21% agree, and 4% fully agree. That is, 25% of the respondents consider that some people over 65 are not trained to study, the predominant factor being the fact of age. It is striking that a quarter of the educators in formation have this stereotype, being this group that will have to attend at some point in their professional life, especially in the field of social education (graphic 1).

People over 65 do not have the capacity to start studying at these ages

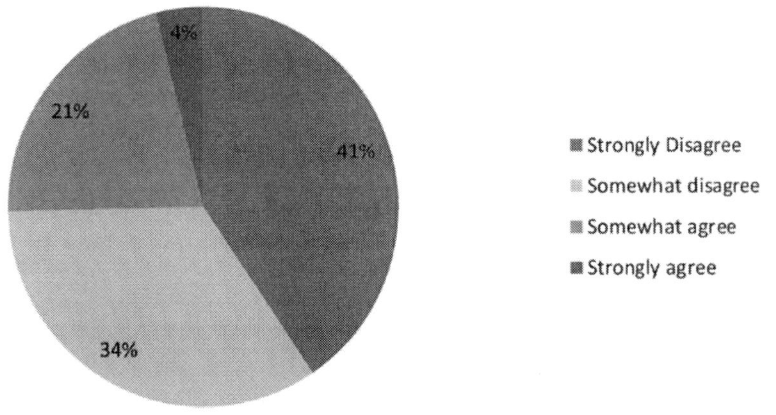

Graphic 1. People over 65 do not have the capacity to start studying at these ages.

As for the perception that the future professionals of the education have on the possibility that certain ages are learned new things, 95% of the respondents indicated that they did not agree with the statement "it´s almost impossible for older people to learn new things". However, 5% consider that at certain ages acquiring new learning is almost impossible (graphic 2).

It is almost impossible for older people to learn new things

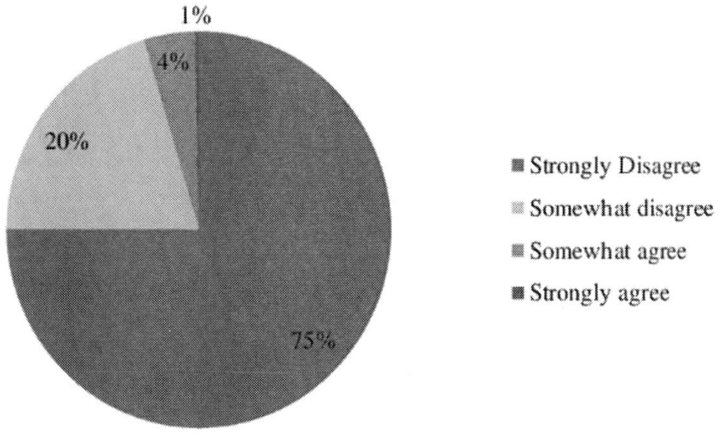

Graphic 2. It is almost impossible for older people to learn new things

As for the use of new technologies, it is noteworthy that only 5% consider that the elderly have no problems with ICT, along with 28% who indicate that they are somewhat at odds with the statement "older people have problems using new technologies". On the other hand, 51% of educators in training point out that they are somewhat in agreement that older people have problems with ICT. 15% of respondents consider older people to have problems with ICT. We can say that in relation to the use of ICT, 66% of educators in training show stereotypes (graphic 3).

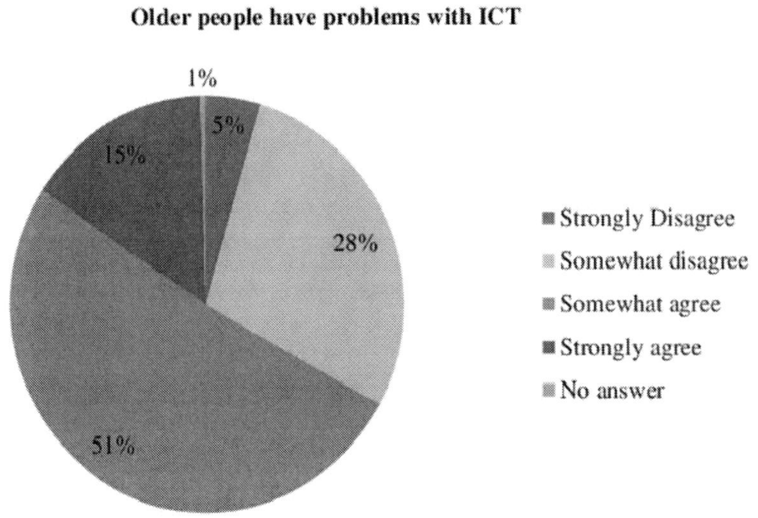

Graphic 3. Older people have problems with ICT

It draws attention to only 8% believe that learning ability does not decrease with age, along with 24% who indicate they are somewhat at odds with the statement. A total of 32% is against the claim. However, 45% are in agreement and 23% totally agree. This means that 78% of respondents show stereotypes regarding learning abilities and age (graphic 4).

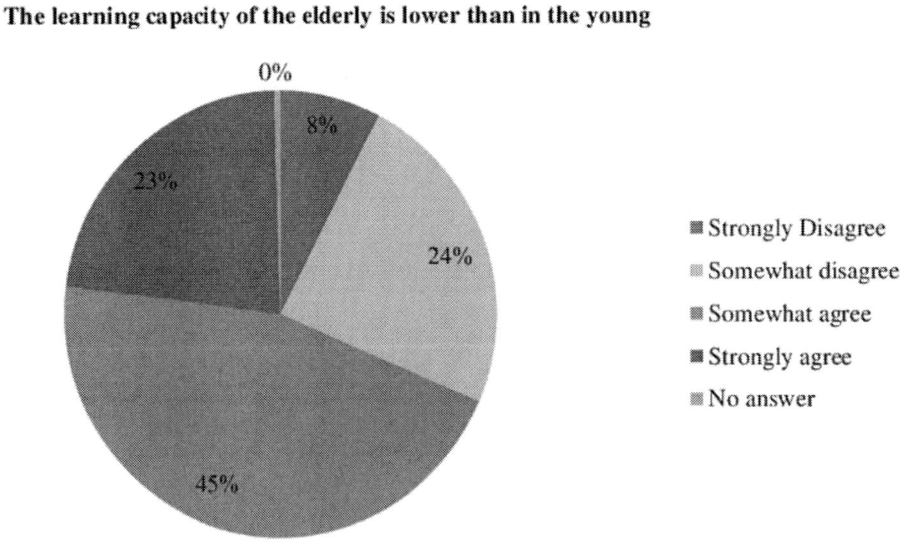

Graphic 4. The learning capacity of the elderly is lower than in the Young.

As for the statement, "as an educator I can work easily with the group of older adults", 15% of respondents consider that as educators will not work easily with older adults. Faced with 31% who are somewhat in agreement and 54% who totally agree (graphic 5).

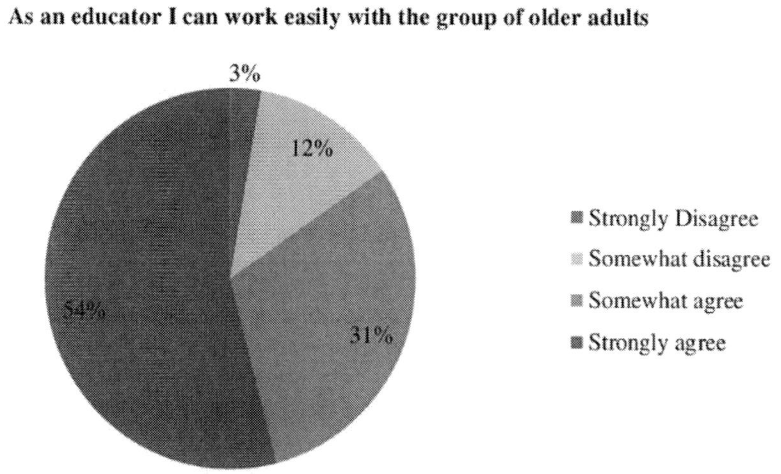

Graphic 5. As an educator I can work easily with the group of older adults

If we refer to the report, 50% indicate that they disagree with the statement referring to "the majority of people when they reach the age of 65 begin to have considerable memory impairment", although there is 42% who are somewhat in agreement, and 7% who fully agree. Only 1% chose not to answer the question raised (graphic 6).

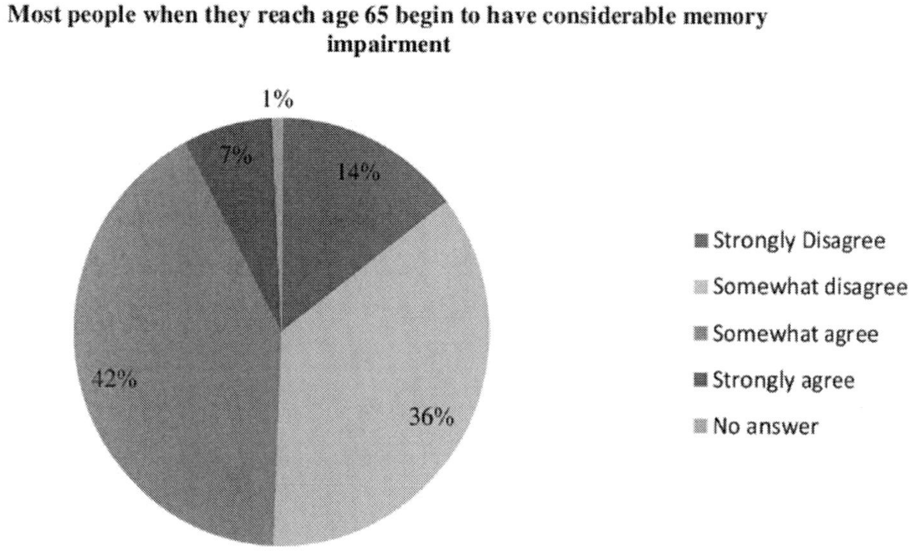

Graphic 6. Most people when they reach age 65 begin to have considerable memory impairment.

And, as we grow older we lose interest in things, or at least 54% of respondents agree with this statement, which we consider in a significant percentage taking into account the group with which we are working in this research (graphic 7).

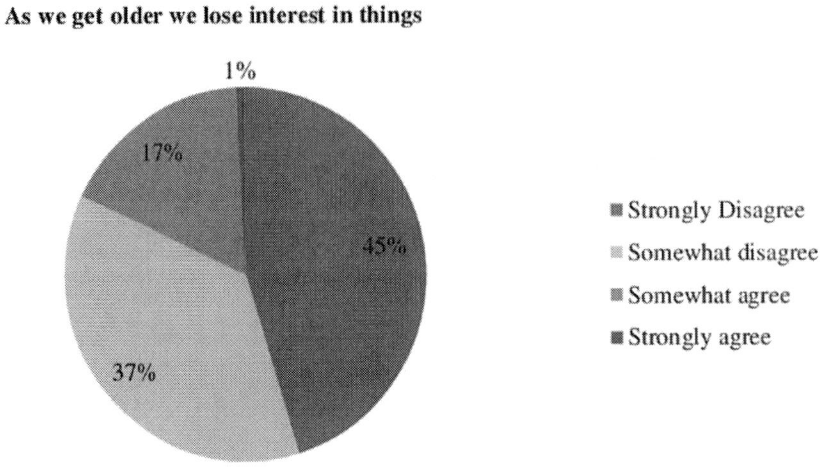

Graphic 7. As we get older we lose interest in things.

As for the last question, the statement "as we age we lose the ability to solve problems," we find that 80% disagree, compared to 20% who agree with the statement (graphic 8).

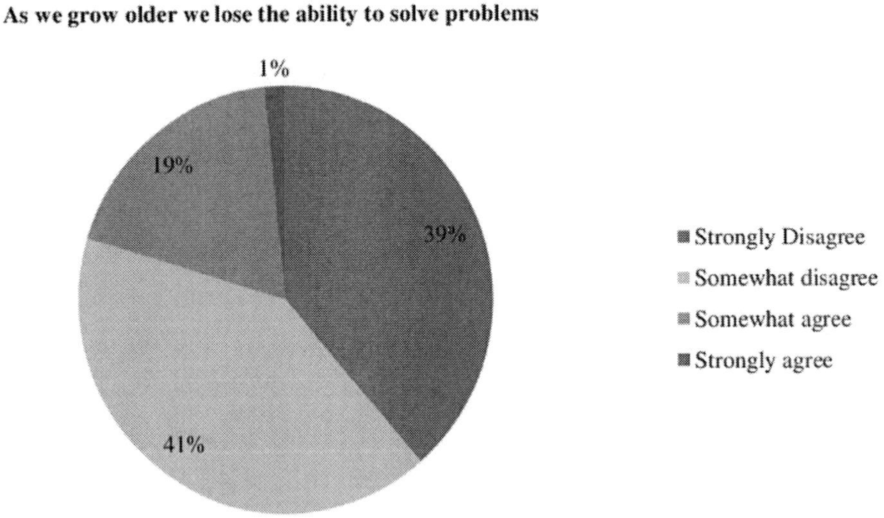

Graphic 8. As we grow older we lose the ability to solve problems.

4 Conclusion

Educators in training have a series of stereotypes that the institution must face in order for future educators to have the skills needed to deal with a group with its own characteristics. The great learning that must prevail is that the education professional should approach any group without prejudice, adapting any curricular content to the needs and expectations of the group with which it will work. From the University it is imperative that there are subjects of each degree where adults can freely participate, providing the perspective and experience necessary for future educators to break the stereotypes towards the collective.

 DOI: 10.1051/shsconf/20173701020

Similarly, University Programs for the Elderly, as well as Adult Education Centers, should support the collaboration of future educators for the same purpose.

References

1. M. Canales, Metodologías de la investigación social. Santiago: LOM Ediciones. Córdoba, (2006).
2. Mª.R., Cruz Díaz, P. Moreno-Crespo, T. Rebolledo, El alumnado universitario mayor ante los recursos tecnológicos y los medios de comunicación social: El caso del Aula Abierta de Mayores, en I Simposium Internacional sobre envejecimiento activo y solidaridad intergeneracional. Madrid: UNED, 1-14 (2012)
3. J. M. Fernández-Batanero, M. M. Reyes-Rebollo, Competencias emprendedoras del alumnado de educación permanente de Andalucía. Percepción del profesorado. Educación XX1, **20**(1), 253-275 (2017)
4. C. Guerrero-Romera, Principales aportaciones de las conferencias internacionales de educación de adultos de la UNESCO al campo de la formación ocupacional. Educatio, **20-21**, 185-212 (2003)
5. R. Hernández, C. Fernández, P. Baptista, Metodologías de la Investigación, (2006)
6. Moreno-Crespo, P. Mayores y formación: Aprendizaje y calidad de vida. En J.C. Gómez (Coord.), I Congreso Científico de Investigadores en Formación (281-283). Córdoba: Universidad de Córdoba, (2010)
7. P. Moreno-Crespo, Mayores y Formación. Aprendizaje y Calidad de Vida. Tesis Doctoral (no publicada). Sevilla: Universidad Pablo de Olavide, (2011)
8. Moreno-Crespo, P. Educación a lo largo de la vida: aula de mayores. Revista Fuentes, **17,** 113-133 (2015)
9. G. Pérez-Serrano, Aprender a lo largo de la vida. Desafío de la sociedad actual. Ágora Digital, **1**, 1-17 (2001)
10. P. Moreno-Crespo, M. R. Cruz Díaz, Promoción de la calidad de vida a través de los programas socioeducativos para mayores: Universidad y mayores. En D. Cobos; A. Jaén, E. López, A.H. Martín y L. Molina (Coords.), I Congreso Virtual Internacional sobre Innovación Pedagógica y Praxis Educativa INNOVAGOGÍA. Sevilla: AFOE, (2012)
11. P. Moreno-Crespo, E. Prieto Jiménez, L. Amador Muñoz, La necesidad de proyectos socioeducativos para mayores: el caso del aula abierta de mayores. Universidad Abierta: Revista de Estudios Superiores a Distancia, **29**, 141-152 (2009)
12. G. Pérez Serrano, Aprender a lo largo de la vida. Desafío de la sociedad actual. En Ágora digital, **1,** 1-17 (2001)
13. E. Prieto-Jiménez, P. Moreno-Crespo, Diseñando programas para nuestros mayores: el caso del Aula Abierta de Mayores. En G. Pérez Serrano, J. García Gutiérrez y A. De Juanas Oliva (Eds.), V Jornadas de Calidad de Vida en Personas Mayores. Envejecimiento Activo y Participativo. Madrid: UNED, (2009)
14. Mª F. Ríos-González, El contenido de la Educación Permanente en las conferencias mundiales de la UNESCO. Pedagogía Social. Revista Interuniversitaria, **10,** 281-297, (2003).
15. C. Sabán-Vera, Educación Permanente y Aprendizaje Permanente: dos modelos teóricos-aplicativos diferentes. Revista Iberoamericana de Educación, **52**, 203-230, (2010).
16. M.L. Sarrate, M.V. Pérez, Educación de Personas Adultas. Situación actual y propuestas de futuro. Revista de Educación, **336**, 41-57, (2005).

Perception on mathematical difficulties in senior adults

Pilar Moreno-Crespo [1a]

[1]Universidad de Huelva, Spain

Abstract. The importance that Life Long Learning currently has, entails reinforcing educational policies in adults and older adults. We have studied the perception about the difficulties of calculation in older adults who are participating in educational activities. In the same way, we analyze which are the factors that influence to a greater extent in a negative perception on the mathematical difficulties. The sample is 448 subjects. The questionnaire is a Likert scale. On the data obtained, we point out that, in general terms, they consider that they are not slow in carrying out calculation operations and that they have no difficulty understanding the mathematical concepts. Likewise, we found correlation ($p < 0.001$) in factors that lead us to affirm that they perceive more difficulties in the calculation, as well as those who have carried out primary studies and whose occupation is focused on the housekeeping.
Keywords: mathematical difficulties, perception, senior adults

1 Introduction

Nowadays exist an "aging population" in constant growth, with an important interest in forming and involved in educational activities. The positive influence of a socio-educational environment on the elderly is linked to active aging and quality of life. The importance that Life Long Learning (LLL) currently has, entails reinforcing socio-educational policies in adults and older adults [1, 2, 4, 5, 6, 7, 8, 10]. In the words of Sabán-Vera [12, p. 204], the LLL: "From its different perspectives covers a great variety of objectives, pursues a high degree of well-being and is linked to multiple causes." Similarly, we can affirm that [6, p. 115]: "Permanent education is provided as an essential resource for the advancement of society."

The positive influence of these university programs on active aging and quality of life is evident in the increasing presence of these in the training landscape in developed and developing countries as well as in the enormous scientific production in this regard. In the last decade, the International Congresses have debated on this tripartite theme: education in the elderly, active aging and quality of life. A number of international conferences have

[a] Corresponding author: pilar.moreno@dedu.uhu.es

 DOI: 10.1051/shsconf/20173701021

been held that have influenced the recognition and strengthening of the concept of lifelong education [3, 9, 11, 12]. The current importance of LLL involves reforms in educational policies for adults and the elderly.

In relation to this evolution, we point to a series of determinants that make LLL necessary [9]: a) The explosion of knowledge and recent scientific advances present a challenge to the education; B) The ever deeper knowledge of a material; C) Scientific and technological changes have not only been quantitative but also qualitative; (D) Deep transformations are occurring under the horizon of globalization; E) The world of work presents new demands every time; F) The democratization of education is making it increasingly seen as an activity available to all.

The LLL includes adult education, which is where we focus on this article. According to Sarrate and Pérez[13, p. 44], adult education is "[...] all formative action that tends to provide knowledge and skills to people of post-school age, as well as to promote in them attitudes and valuable behaviors aimed at fostering Personal and professional development, and social participation."

LLL comprises adult education and the "senior's room". The "senior's room" are university programs that have their own character, move away from regulated education and approach "formal-educational" and "educational-sociocultural" [4, 5].

We will address those aspects related to the perception of older adults who participate in academic contexts rather than their mathematical difficulties. The "calculation" requires a series of cognitive processes that include the capacity for reasoning, the identification of numerical and operational meaning. In this sense, it includes aspects such as problem solving and the implementation of strategies that allow solutions to proposed mathematical problems in the classroom or in daily life. We also analyze the factors that influence largely a negative perception about mathematical difficulties.

2 Method

The purpose of our research has focused on studying the elderly in an educational context. We want to know your perception of your "calculation" skills. The research question is: What perception do older adults have about their personal cognitive dimension of "calculation"?

The objective of the research is to know the perception of the cognitive personal dimension of "calculation" of the older adult students that is in the "senior's room".

The specific objectives disaggregated are: a) Analyze the opinion that the older adults have on their "calculation" competences; B) To discover the relational magnitudes between the self-perception of the competences of "calculation" and the sociodemographic variables.The sample is 448 subjects, over 50 years, who attend courses and educational programs with a marked socio-cultural character. The questionnaire is a Likert scale, with the following conceptual range: "Strongly Agree", "Agree", "Disagree", "Strongly Disagree".

3 Results

Analyzing the data obtained, we can roughly state that it is a constructive, active and strategic process in which the older adult has obtained positive results.

1. They have been asked if they are slow to perform calculations. 65.4% believe that they are not slow in performing calculation operations (31.7% are Strongly Disagree and 33.7% are Disagree. To make calculation operations: "Agree" (22.5%) and "Strongly Agree" (9.4%).

2. They have been asked if they have difficulty understanding mathematical concepts. They respond "Strongly Disagree" 26.9%, "Disagree" 30.5%, "Agree" 28.5% and "Strongly Agree" 11.4%.

Broadly speaking, we can say that the older adult considers that it is not slow to perform calculation operations, as well as in the processes of understanding mathematical concepts, although sex and the level of studies are determining factors to be aware of. Next we will see the relational data.

We emphasize that in the difficulties calculation we have detected aspects that influence in a relevant way, such as sex (table 1) and the level of studies (table 2), the years worked (table 3) and age at which they started to work (table 4).

Among the most significant significant relationships in this sense, men have less "Difficulties of calculation" ($p < 0.001$) (table 1).

Table 1. Sex.

	Difficulties calculation (p<0.001)
Man	31,31
Woman	42,38

Those who have a basic level of education, mainly primary studies, have more difficulty in calculation ($p < 0.001$) (table 2). Those who have the greatest difficulty in calculating are those who have worked between 16 and 25 years.

Table 2. Level of studies.

	Difficulties calculation (p<0.001)
Primary	55,4795
High School / Baccalaureate	35,5191
Technical / FP	27,7778
Higher / University	26,1494

Those with the greatest language and calculation difficulties are those who have worked between 16 and 25 years (table 3).

Table 3. Years worked.

	Difficulties calculation ($p<0.05$)
Less than 5 years	40,4762
Between 5 and 15	43,8889
Between 16 and 25	59,4203
Between 26 and 35	31,3008
More than 35 years	33,4758

With a low degree of significance ($p < 0.05$), they have more difficulty in calculating those who started working after age 40 and before age 12. The rest of the sample does not reflect a great difficulty of calculation, nevertheless, those who began to work between the 31 and the 35 years find that they have less difficulties in this respect (table 4).

Table 4. Started to work.

	Difficulties calculation ($p<0.05$)
Before the age of 12	51,6667
Between the ages of 13 and 18	34,9638
Between the ages of 19 and 25	38,2353
Between 26 and 30 years	34,2105
Between 31 and 35 years	16,6667
Between 36 and 40 years	0
After 40 years	70

The purpose of our research has focused on studying the elderly in an educational context. We want to know your perception of your "calculation" skills. The research question is: What perception do older adults have about their personal cognitive dimension of "calculation"?

The objective of the research is to know the perception of the cognitive personal dimension of "calculation" of the older adult students that is in the "senior's room".

The specific objectives disaggregated are: a) Analyze the opinion that the older adults have on their "calculation" competences; B) To discover the relational magnitudes between the self-perception of the competences of "calculation" and the sociodemographic variables.The sample is 448 subjects, over 50 years, who attend courses and educational programs with a marked socio-cultural character. The questionnaire is a Likert scale, with the following conceptual range: "Strongly Agree", "Agree", "Disagree", "Strongly Disagree".

4 Conclusions

Women, directly related to a low level of study, are more vulnerable to calculation difficulties; as well as those who have worked between 16 and 25 years and who began to work before the age of 12. These factors analyzed could have influenced the educational and professional projection of the subjects surveyed.

Therefore, we affirm that quality of life and active aging are linked to the concept of lifelong education, which allows the development of higher capacities in the human being, together with the maintenance of cognitive, physical, social, psychological and Spiritual In this way, we make the following proposals: 1) To combat the existing myths and stereotypes in society from a series of target groups (the elderly themselves, students of professions linked to socio-educational intervention, 2) Bear in mind the determining aspects in this Population for the design of socio-educational intervention programs (sex and educational level, mainly); and 3) Promotion of lifelong education, as it is linked to quality of life and active aging.

If we follow the example of countries such as the UUEE or Japan, we must intensify policies in education and training, associating these actions with social welfare and improving competitiveness [6, p.115].

The challenges proposed by Sarrate and Pérez [13, p. 53] are: a) To respond to the demands of the knowledge society; B) Develop active and committed citizenship; C) Need to achieve a balance between the different dimensions involved - personal, cultural, civic, social, economic and labor - and democratic principles; D) To promote education in values as the axis of human development in all its dimensions.

References

1. M.R. Cruz Díaz, P. Moreno-Crespo, y Rebolledo Gámez, T. El alumnado universitario mayor ante los recursos tecnológicos y los medios de comunicación social: El caso del Aula Abierta de Mayores. En I Simposium Internacional sobre envejecimiento activo y solidaridad intergeneracional (pp. 1-14). Madrid: UNED, (2012)
2. J. M. Fernández Batanero, y Reyes Rebollo, M.M. Competencias emprendedoras del alumnado de educación permanente de Andalucía. Percepción del profesorado. Educación XX1, **20**(1), 253-275 (2017)
3. C. Guerrero-Romera, Principales aportaciones de las conferencias internacionales de educación de adultos de la UNESCO al campo de la formación ocupacional. Educatio, **20-21**, 185-212 (2003)
4. P. Moreno-Crespo, Mayores y formación: Aprendizaje y calidad de vida. En J.C. Gómez (Coord.), I Congreso Científico de Investigadores en Formación (281-283). Córdoba: Universidad de Córdoba, (2010)
5. P. Moreno-Crespo, Mayores y Formación. Aprendizaje y Calidad de Vida. Tesis Doctoral (no publicada). Sevilla: Universidad Pablo de Olavide, (2011)

6. Moreno-Crespo, P. Educación a lo largo de la vida: aula de mayores. Revista Fuentes, 17, Diciembre, pp. 113-133 (2015)
7. P. Moreno-Crespo, M.R Cruz Díaz, Promoción de la calidad de vida a través de los programas socioeducativos para mayores: Universidad y mayores. En D. Cobos; A. Jaén, E. López, A.H. Martín y L. Molina (Coords.), I Congreso Virtual Internacional sobre Innovación Pedagógica y Praxis Educativa INNOVAGOGÍA 2012. Sevilla: AFOE, (2012)
8. P. Moreno-Crespo, E. Prieto Jiménez, L. Amador Muñoz, La necesidad de proyectos socioeducativos para mayores: el caso del aula abierta de mayores. Universidad Abierta: Revista de Estudios Superiores a Distancia (Ciudad Real), **29,** 141-152 (2009)
9. G. Pérez-Serrano, Aprender a lo largo de la vida. Desafío de la sociedad actual. Ágora Digital, **1**, 1-17 (2001)
10. E. Prieto-Jiménez, P. Moreno-Crespo, Diseñando programas para nuestros mayores: el caso del Aula Abierta de Mayores. En G. Pérez Serrano, J. García Gutiérrez y A. De Juanas Oliva (Eds.), V Jornadas de Calidad de Vida en Personas Mayores. Envejecimiento Activo y Participativo. Madrid: UNED, (2009)
11. M. F. Ríos-González, El contenido de la Educación Permanente en las conferencias mundiales de la UNESCO. Pedagogía Social. Revista Interuniversitaria, **10**, 281-297 (2003)
12. C. Sabán Vera, "Educación Permanente" y "Aprendizaje Permanente": dos modelos teóricos-aplicativos diferentes. Revista Iberoamericana de Educación, **52**, 203-230, 2010
13. M. L. Sarrate, M. V. Pérez, Educación de Personas Adultas. Situación actual y propuestas de futuro. Revista de Educación, **336**, pp. 41-57 (2005)

Study regarding the use of movement games and relays in order to improve primary students' strength qualities

Talaghir Laurentiu-Gabriel [1a], Mîndrescu Veronica [2], and Ion-Ene Mircea [1]

[1]University Dunarea de Jos",Domneasca Street, no. 46, 800008, Galati, Romania
[2] Transilvania University, Bdul Eroilor, no. 29, 500036, Braşov, Romania

Abstract. The present paper is part of wider research carried out during 2015 – 2016 with primary school students from a primary school in Galati, Romania, which studied the possibility of increasing the motor skill manifestation indices. Within this research we wished to present the role that movement games and relays could play in developing strength as motor skill and we used 6 movement games and 3 relays for this purpose. Movement games were used within physical education classes whose topic was the development of strength as motor skill. Relays were used at the beginning or at the end of the PE classes as a means of engaging the body during exercise. For assessment, we used three specific trials for testing strength as motor quality: crunches, back extension and standing long jump. The results recorded in the final testing for all the trials revealed significant progress as compared to the initial tests. The statistical processing of data was performed with the help of the SPSS 23.0 software. The positive results proved that the use of movement games and relays is efficient for the increase of strength motor skill manifestation indices with primary school students.
Keywords: movement games, primary students, motor skill

1 Introduction

As in any activities performed by humans, in the education domain, too, there is an ongoing concern to improve methods so that the expected results be achieved in a faster and more efficient manner. Physical education, which is part of the general education process, follows the same guidelines of the structural and conceptual evolutions adapted to social realities and to the students' needs in line with technological progress.

In recent years, in this sense of evolution and adaptation, new curricula for PE for the Romanian primary school system have been drawn up [13, 14].

[a] Corresponding author: Gabriel.Talaghir@ugal.ro

This reality of adapting the curricula to the ever changing social reality is reflected in the specialists' concerns worldwide [5, 7, 8, 9, 6].

To meet the new conceptual guidelines, an adaptation of the practical activities' content to the general competences, encountered in the new primary school curricula, is required. The evaluation, as part of the instructive-educative process, must be in acord with its finalities. From this point of view it must be in acordance with the trends which are noticed at the international level [12]

Specialists such as [2, 11] consider that the physical education class is different from the other classes in terms of content, structure, methodology, dynamics, location and learning particularities. The learning rules are specific. They focus on forming perceptions and motor skills and on acquiring knowledge while practising physical exercise as well as on shaping motor and moral-volitional qualities.

In this context of re-thinking the PE classes, movement games, which are already known to specialists in the domain, acquire new formative and educational meanings, which contribute significantly to the growth and development of children. The game, as an activity for young children, also has an integrative role in the community, being thus in line with the competences that must be developed in primary school students.

School PE has two components, that is practical activity training and education as the assimilation of a set of rules, which regulate human behaviour [3, 4]. The problem of organising the educational process for the primary school PE class in an efficient manner has always been a main concern for specialists of all times. Therefore, specialists proved that, in order to produce lasting and performant results, the quality of the educational process mainly depends on the conscious selection of the training means, methods and procedures [15].

The development of motor qualities in primary school students represents a topical subject because the diversity of the actuating means at young ages can generate positive results in the growth and development process [10]. Also, a high degree of motor skill manifestation, in all its aspects, will determine the student to participate in the proposed activities within classes because he will be able to withstand a sustained effort. Another positive effect, generated by a high manifestation level of the motor skill indices, is the opportunity of acquiring some skills, which are specific to some sports, quicker.

The present paper is the result of the equal contribution of all authors.

2 Procedure

The experiment was conducted in the Secondary school no.18, in Galați. The length of the experiment was represented by school year 2015- 2016. In the experiment, there were 59 primary school students involved, who were in the third grade. Out of these, there were 29 boys and 30 girls.

In order to conduct the experiment under standard research conditions, we established class III A as the experimental group and class III B as the control group.

The aim of the experiment was to notice if, by using movement games, it is possible to improve the strength motor skill manifestation indices in primary school students.

In order to carry out the study within the experimental group, we used 6 movement games and 3 relays for the development of strength as motor quality.

The movement games and the relays were selected in such a way that they could correspond to the students' motor manifestation level and were used in the PE classes during which the development of strength as motor skill was planned in accordance with the planning documents, approved by the school management at the beginning of the school year.

We didn't interfere in the activities performed by the control group. For the control group, the planning documents drawn up by the PE teacher, and approved by the school management, were taken into account, and the activities regarding the development of motor qualities were performed with the help of specific means. In the case of the control group, the traditional teaching method was adopted for the learning units with specific content.

The data obtained at the initial and final testing of both groups (the experimental and the control group) was interpreted from a statistical point of view by means of a specialised software, named SPSS 23.0.

In order to create diversity within the PE classes, these games and relays were coded and combined. The content of the lessons was made up of two movement games and one relay or one movement game and two relays. The relays were also used at the beginning and at the end of the class and during classes whose subject was not the development of strength as motor quality, as means of engaging in effort.

For assessment, we used three trials which are to be found in the National School Assessment System for the Physical Education class [1]. They were: crunches, back extension and standing long jump.

The description of the trials is as follows:

- for the "crunches" trial, the student laid on his/her back, with the hands behind the head, with the legs bent and the soles on the ground, supported by a colleague, and he/she lifted the torso to a vertical position and, then, the student returned to the initial position; the number of repetitions was recorded.

- for the "back extensions" trial, the student laid on his/her abdomen, face down, with the hands behind the head, the feet being supported by a colleague, and he/she lifted the torso towards the vertical position so that his/her head was higher than the height of the gymnastics bench and, then, the student returned to the initial position; the number of repetitions was recorded.

- for the "standing long jump" trial, the student stood with his feet slightly apart, with the arms up, behind a line, and he/she took off and landed using both feet, swinging the arms and bending the knees to provide forward drive. The distance from the line to the heel was measured.

The trials were taken at the beginning and at the end of the school year.

3 Results and discussions

In order to decide if the movement games proposed by us within the experiment had the expected effects on primary school students, the data collected during the initial and final tests were statistically interpreted.

The statistical analysis was performed within the group and between the groups for each of the three trials in which the students participated.

In table no.1, we presented the results obtained by the control group and by the experimental group in the "crunches" trial.

Table 1. Results in the "crunches" trial

	The control group(**n=15**)				The experimental group(**n=14**)			
	T.I. $\overline{x} \pm m$	T.F. $\overline{x} \pm m$	t	p	T.I. $\overline{x} \pm m$	T.F. $\overline{x} \pm m$	t	p
Boys	6,73±1,10	8,33±0,90	-7,48	< .000	6,79±1,18	9,50±1,01	-13,98	< .000
Girls	4,79±0,69	6,71±10,72	-7,23	< .000	4,69±0,70	7,25±0,93	-16,29	< .000

It may be noticed that in the initial test, the control group and the experimental group obtained similar results, which indicated a similar level of physical training. The groups of boys had an average result value of 6.73 repetitions, the control group, and of 6.79 repetitions, the experimental group. In the final test we may notice that both groups of boys obtained better results and the recorded progress may be considered to be significant ($p < 0,001$).

In table no. 1 we may also notice the result evolution for the groups of girls. The girls had initial average performance values of 4.79 repetitions, in the case of the control group, and 4.69 repetitions in the case of the experimental group, fact which indicated a similar value of the groups for this age level. In the final test, both group of girls obtained average performance levels higher than in the initial tests ($p < 0,001$). This demonstrates the fact that the activity performed during PE classes is efficient and leads to an increase in the motor skill manifestation indices, by using various methods.

The statistical analysis performed between groups we may notice significant differences both for the group of girls and for the group of boys. The statistical interpretation is presented in table no.2.

Table 2. The statistical analysis between the control groups and the experimental groups for the "crunches" trial

	G.M **(n=15)** $\overline{x} \pm m$	G.E **(n=14)** $\overline{x} \pm m$	t	p
Boys	8,33±0,90	9,50±1,01	-3,27	<.003
Girls	6,71±10,72	7,25±0,93	-1,76	<.088

As shown for the "crunches" trial, all the groups involved in the research recorded positive evolutions in terms of performance, which are considered significant from a statistical point of view. In table no. 2 we may notice the fact that both the girls' and the boys' experimental groups had a superior evolution as compared to the control groups. This fact is due to the significant statistically proven progress, ($p < 0,003$) for the boys' experimental group and ($p < 0,088$) for the girls' experimental group. By highlighting these results, we can assert that the methods proposed by us within the experimental groups were efficient and led to an increase in the strength motor skill manifestation indices.

Further on in the statistical analysis, we wanted to see the evolution of the results recorded in the "back extensions" trial. These results are presented in table no. 3.

Table 3. Results in the "back extension" trial

	The control group**(n=15)**				The experimental group**(n=14)**			
	T.I. $\overline{x} \pm m$	T.F. $\overline{x} \pm m$	t	p	T.I. $\overline{x} \pm m$	T.F. $\overline{x} \pm m$	t	p
Boys	7,87±0,74	10,07±0,96	-8,40	<.000	7,86±1,23	11,29±1,43	-24,98	<.000
Girls	6,21±1,25	7,93±1,20	-10,49	<.000	6,31±1,13	9,13±1,02	-12,35	<.000

In order to render a unitary character to the research, we used the same type of statistical analysis for the analysis both within and between groups. The statistical analysis carried out between groups focused on the results obtained in the final tests between the control groups and the experimental groups.

From table no. 3 we may notice that the average values obtained by the groups involved in the research in the initial tests showed a similar level of physical training. The boys' control group recorded an average value of 7.87 repetitions, whereas the experimental group recorded a result of 7.86 repetitions. In the case of the group of girls, the control group had an average performance value of 6.21 repetitions, whereas the experimental group recorded an average performance level of 6.31 repetitions.

In the final tests for this trial we can assert that all the groups of boys and girls involved in the research recorded significant progress. This is because, from a statistical point of view, by analysing the data within the groups, the indicator p was established as having a highly significant value (p <0,001).

As a result, we continued the analysis from a statistical point of view between the boys' and the girls' control and experimental groups.

The results are presented in table no. 4.

Table 4. The statistical analysis between the control and the experimental groups for the "back extensions" trial

	G.M **(n=15)** $\overline{x} \pm m$	G.E **(n=14)** $\overline{x} \pm m$	t	p
Boys	10,07±0,96	11,29±1,43	-2,70	<.012
Girls	7,93±1,20	9,13±1,02	-2,63	<.013

As we may notice from the table above, the results recorded in the final tests by the experimental groups are superior to those recorded by the control groups. Thus, the experimental group of boys obtained an average performance value in the final test in the "back extensions" trial of 11.29 repetitions. This result is significant from a statistical point of view because p <0,012. As far as the girls' experimental group is concerned, it obtained an average performance value of 9.13 repetitions. This result is superior to the one recorded by the girls' control group (7.93 repetitions). The achieved progress is a positive one because it is significant form a statistical point of view (p <0,013).

The third trial used as assessment for the primary school students involved in the research was the "standing long jump", whose aim was to establish the improvement level of strength as motor quality at the leg level. The results for this test are synthetically presented in table no. 5. After tabulation, the results were also statistically interpreted.

Table 5. The results in the "standing long jump" trial

	The control group**(n=15)**				The experimental group**(n=14)**			
	T.I. $\overline{x} \pm m$	T.F. $\overline{x} \pm m$	t	p	T.I. $\overline{x} \pm m$	T.F. $\overline{x} \pm m$	t	p
Boys	1,05±10,03	1,14±0,03	-7,10	< .000	1,07±0,04	1,20±0,04	-11,75	< .000
Girls	1,01±0,03	1,11±0,03	-8,85	< .000	1,00±0,03	1,15±0,01	-30,02	< .000

In table no. 5 we may notice that, as with the other trials included in the research, the results recorded in the "standing long jump" trial, in the initial tests, by all the groups, were similar.

Significant differences were noticed within the final tests as compared to the initial tests. The boys' control group obtained an average performance level of 1.14 metres. This result led to a significant progress from a statistical point of view because (p <0,001). The experimental group of boys obtained in the final test an average performance level of 1.20 metres, which, as compared to the value of the initial test, of 1.07, is considered to be highly significant from a statistical point of view (p <0,001).

The girls' control group obtained in the final test an average performance value of 1.11 metres. In this case, too, the progress achieved was considered highly significant (p <0,001) as compared to the results recorded in the initial test. The experimental group of girls obtained in the final test an average performance level of 1.15 metres. The progress achieved was considered to be highly significant (p <0,001) as compared to the average value of the performance obtained in the initial test, of 1 metre.

The statistical analysis performed within the groups helped in revealing the fact that all the groups had positive evolutions in the final test as compared to the initial test. This shows that the practice of physical exercise in an organised manner, within the mandatory PE classes, has a positive effect on the improvement of the strength motor skill manifestation indices.

In order to see if the proposed movement games and relays significantly influenced the results obtained in the "standing ling jump", we performed a statistical analysis on the results obtained by the groups involved in the final tests. These results are presented in table no. 6.

Table 6. The statistical analysis between the control and experimental groups for the "Standing long jump" trial

	G.M **(n=15)** $\overline{X} \pm m$	G.E **(n=14)** $\overline{X} \pm m$	t	P
Boys	1,14±0,03	1,20±0,04	-4,31	< .000
Girls	1,11±0,03	1,15±0,01	-3,97	< .000

The boys' experimental group recorded a performance of 1.20 metres in the final test, which is superior to that recorded by the control group (1.14 metres). This positive result is also significant from a statistical point of view (p <0,001).

The girls' experimental group obtained an average performance value in the final test of 1.15 metres. This result showed significant progress within the group as compared to the initial test. Also, it is considered superior to the result recorded by the control group (1.11 metres) in terms of statistical analysis because the value of the significance threshold indicates this fact (p <0,001).

4 Conclusions

As a result of the analytical presentation of all the results obtained by the third grade students in the trials included in the research, we can draw several conclusions. The main conclusion is that the use of movement games and relays has a positive effect on the possibilities to influence the strength motor quality manifestation indices.

In conjunction with the requirements stipulated in the general competences that must be developed in primary school students, we can assert that this game-like PE class meets the new conceptual requirements from the PE curriculum.

The use of movement games and relays created a better dynamics during the PE class, thus achieving the competences proposed for this age group by integrating the students' motor skill manifestation.

We consider that movement games and relays used as practice within PE classes represent a method by means of which, on the one hand, the student enjoys the activities proposed and, on the other hand, he/she can independently play the same games and relays in different other groups. Therefore, the students will come to enjoy movement and this, in its turn, will determine the student to independently practise physical exercise as a means of maintaining health.

From the point of view of the performance-related assessment, we may assert that the idea of enjoying sports activities and their integrative role is diminished. We consider that, at the primary school level, at least, different criteria and assessment tests should be drawn up in order to evaluate students' activities that do not focus on competitiveness and on the perception of physical exercise as a means of achieving performance.

DOI: 10.1051/shsconf/20173701022

The attitudinal aspects, the integration of students in a group, the ability to communicate by using terms from the motor activity domain are only a few benefits brought by movement games and relays in students' evolution.

References

1. C. Filip et all., The National Assessment and Examination Department, The National School Assessment System for the PE class.Bucuresti: MNE, (1999)
2. D. Stojiljkovic, D. Pirsl, *Impacts of specific exercising on motor abilities development in junior elementary schoolchildren,* Acta Kinesiologica, **10** (2), 60-64 (2016)
3. G. Griggs, (Ed.), *An Introduction to Primary Physical education,* 151-161, (2012)
4. J. L. Currie, *Teaching Physical Education in Primary School - An integrated health perspective,* Publisher: ACER Press, 112-118 (2013)
5. J. MacLean, R. Mulholland, S. Gray, A. Horrell, Enabling curriculum change in physical education: the interplay between policy constructors and practitioners, Physical Education and Sport Pedagogy, **20**(1), 79-96 (2015)
6. M. Jess, N. Carse, J. Keay, The primary physical education curriculum process: more complex that you might think!!, *Education 3-13 International Journal of Primary, Elementary and Early Years Education*, **44**(5), 502-512 (2016)
7. M. O'Sullivan, New directions, new questions: relationships between curriculum, pedagogy, and assessment in physical education,, Sport Education and Society, Vol. 18(1), 1-5 (2013)
8. N. Carse, Primary teachers as physical education curriculum change agents, *European Physical Education Review,* **21**(3), 309-324, (2015)
9. P. Vlcek, Discourse on curriculum development in physical education, recent development in Europe, 9th International Conference on Sport and Quality of Life, 335-343, (2013)
10. T. Buszard, R Machar, S. W. Masters Rich, et all, *Scaling Tennis Racquets During PE in Primary School to Enhance Motor Skill Acquisition* Research Quarterly for Exercise and Sport, **87**(4), p. 414-420, (2016)
11. T. M. Iconomescu, Didactics of Physical Education and Sport – Course notes, Zigotto Publishing house, Galati, (2013)
12. T. M. Iconomescu,., D. I. Alexe., *Differences and similarities in curriculum and assessment in physical education in eastern european states,* Journal „Analele Universității Ovidius Constanța. Serie Physical Education and Sport - Science, Movement and Health, **XV**(1), 41- 46, (2015)
13. The Ministry of National Education, Curriculum for Physical Education, The preparatory grade, the first grade and the second grade, București, (2013)
14. The Ministry of National Education, Curriculum for Physical Education, The third grade and the fourth grade, București, (2013)
15. T. M. Iconomescu, L. G. Talaghir, Teaching approach to enhance motor skills for students in primary school, Procedia - Social and Behavioural Sciences, **152**, 746-751, (2014)

Study regarding the use of physical exercise in order to prevent school-age children from being overweight

Talaghir Laurentiu-Gabriel[1a], Mîndrescu Veronica[2]

[1]University „Dunarea de Jos",Domneasca Street, no. 46, 800008, Galati, Romania
[2] Transilvania University, Bdul Eroilor, no. 29, 500036, Braşov, Romania

Abstract. In the present study, we aimed at applying a physical training program with simple exercises, focused on two aspects: on the one hand, we intended to lower body mass index and, on the other hand, to increase the level of physical fitness. We considered that both directions converge towards the formation of a healthy lifestyle.
Keywords: overweight, physical exercise, school-age children

1 Introduction

The most frequent cause of obesity is the lack of physical activity, the excessive intake of calories from food, even if there are also particular cases in which obesity may be hereditary or it may occur as a result of endocrine disorders or medicine ingestion.

Physical activity is, next to a balanced diet, the basis of a healthy life-style [13, 14] and is also very important for keeping healthy. In addition, physical activity is the perfect remedy for stress because it helps us relax and have a good night's sleep [1, 4, 7]. Specialists from different field of science which are related with a healthy life-style provide a lot o varieties type of efforts to prevent overweight [2, 3].

Obese people have a much greater calorie intake than their thinner counterparts because they must maintain a high body mass [5].

In 2010, [12] carried out a study in the USA that concluded that obesity is probably the result of the interaction between natural selection, which favours those with an accelerated metabolism, today's consumer society, in which everybody has easy access to cheap, energy-dense food, and the lower energy requirements of everyday life.

The food energy supply per inhabitant varies significantly between different regions and countries [14]. This supply has also changed depending on the period of time. From the beginning of the 1970s until the 1990s, the average calorie intake per person increased worldwide (with the exception of Eastern Europe). The greatest increase was recorded in

[a] Corresponding author: Gabriel.Talaghir@ugal.ro

the United States, reaching 3654 calories in 1996 and 3754 calories in 2003. Calorie intake is closely connected to obesity.

This calorie intake increase mainly comes from carbohydrates. The primary sources of these carbohydrates are sweetened sodas and chips. The consumption of sweetened sodas is considered to have majorly contributed to the rising rates of obesity [15].

Because societies are increasingly dependent on meals which are rich in calories, because fast-food is more and more present in people's everyday life, the association between fast-food and obesity is becoming more and more alarming.

A sedentary lifestyle also plays an important role in obesity. There has been a major change worldwide because of the work that is physically less demanding and because, at present, at least 30% of the world population is taking too little physical exercise. The cause is mainly mechanised transportation, which is increasingly used, and the existence of technologies, which make work easier. The level of physical activity decreases in children because they walk less and they do not have as many physical education classes as they should [9].

Many children do not take physical exercises because they spend their time doing activities that do not involve movement like playing video games or watching TV. Technology is a great risk factor for children's physical activity. A healthy life-style means daily physical activity [9, 11].

The studies that focused on heredity models rather than on specific genes concluded that 80% of the children who had two obese parents also became obese, in contrast with less than 10% of the children who had two normal weight parents [6].

The thrifty gene hypothesis postulates that, because of the food shortage that existed during human evolution, people have a predisposition to obesity. Their ability to take advantage of the rare periods of abundance by storing energy as fat would be an asset in times of insufficient availability of food and people with higher fat reserves would be more likely to survive famine. Nevertheless, this tendency towards storing fat could be harmful in a society with stable sources of food [10].

Wellness is a complex concept, multifactorial and not very specific. Something, the lack of a healthy diet, sport practicing and a sum of other different factors (emotional and so on) could lead to sickness. Health issues occur and they affect our general metabolism, our osteoarticulatory / locomotion system, the endocrine and the nervous systems, and the bloodstream [16]. The present paper is the result of the equal contribution of both authors.

2 Methods

The research was carried out in Brăila, the county of Brăila, during school year 2015 – 2016, in the Pedagogical High school Perspessicius, on a number of 7 overweight subjects with ages ranging from 10 to 13. The children participated in physical activities for a period of 7 months, twice a week. For each subject, the program was customized from the point of view of effort intensity, duration and exercise complexity.

The main aim of the research was to apply a physical training program, which followed two directions: on the one hand, the intention was to lower body mass index and, on the other hand, to increase the level of physical fitness. We considered both objectives to be an integral part of a healthy lifestyle.

In order to achieve the aim of the research, the subjects' body mass index and physical fitness were assessed by means of the following tests: push-ups, squats, pull-ups, hanging exercises and crunches.

The body mass index represents the ratio between weight and height. With the help of this indicator we may notice the correlation between the fat tissue and the total weight of fat. This indicator is considered to be the most used one in determining obesity. When the value of the BMI ranges from 19 to 24, the person is considered to have an ideal weight. A value ranging from 25 to 30 means that the person is overweight, and over 30, the person is considered to be obese.

The statistical analysis was performed with the help of the program SPSS 23 and we used the statistical method entitled The Pair Students' Test, where the significance threshold is t<.05.

3 Results and discussions

Before the implementation of the physical training program, the subjects of the research were assessed in point of body mass index and physical training tests. We tested the students at the beginning of the program and after 7 months, at the end of the program. In order to be able to realize if the implementation of the physical training program was successful, we compared the obtained data by means of the statistical analysis described in table 1.

Table 1. The comparative statistical analysis regarding the initial and final test results of the researched subjects

TESTS	Subjects (no = 7)			
	TI $\overline{x} \pm m$	TF $\overline{x} \pm m$	t	p
BMI	28,14±0,78	23,53±0,78	12,15	<,000
Push-ups	1,14±0,26	8,00±1,30	5,79	<,001
Squats	9,57±0,99	17,29±2,37	7,45	<,000
Crunches	9,57±0,99	19,00±1,57	5,73	<,001
Pull-ups	0,71±0,18	4,14±0,55	6,49	<,001
Hanging exercises	2,14±0,40	8,86±0,63	7,31	<,000

The BMI indicated if, after implementing the physical activities, the subjects under research lost weight. In table 1 and figure 1, we may notice that there is a difference between the two tests. The average weight loss recorded in the final stage is of 50.42 kg, that is to say an average of 8.71 kg. less per person as compared to the initial stage.

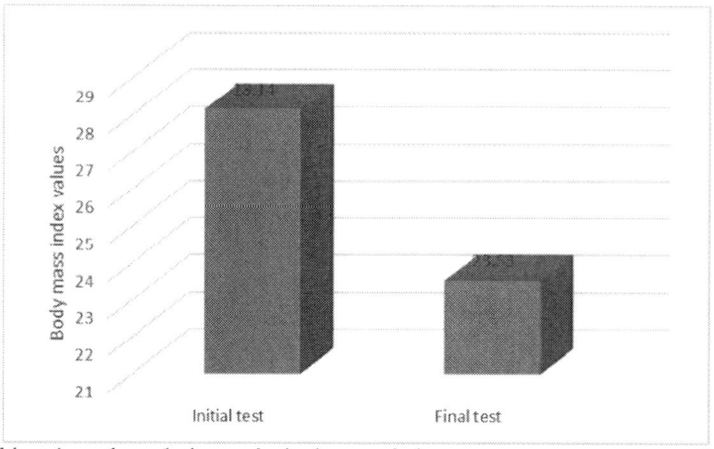

Fig, 1. The subjects' result evolution at the body mass index test

As a result of the performances obtained at the push-up test, we ascertain that the results obtained at the final test were better than those obtained at the initial test.

This demonstrates the fact that physical activity improved the level of physical fitness of the researched subjects, the average reaching 6.86 repetitions, according to figure 2.

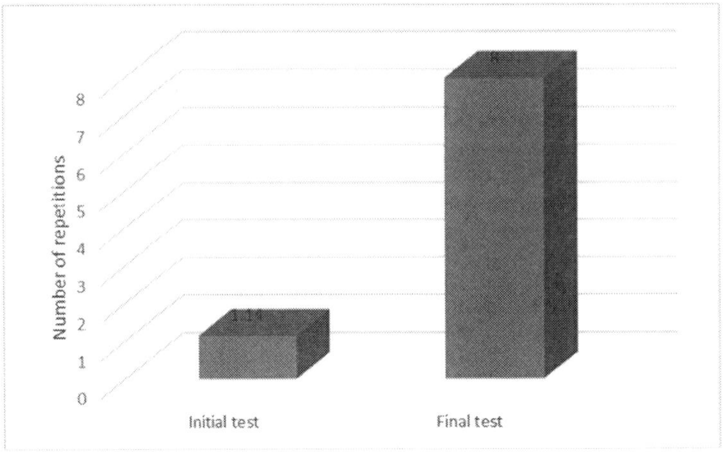

Fig. 2. The subjects' result evolution at the push-up test

Testing leg strength was achieved with the help of the squat test, where the subjects under research improved their performance at the final test, after implementing the physical activity program, with 7.72 repetitions, according to figure 3.These performances are not random, this fact also being demonstrated by the statistical analysis where the significance threshold is t<.001.

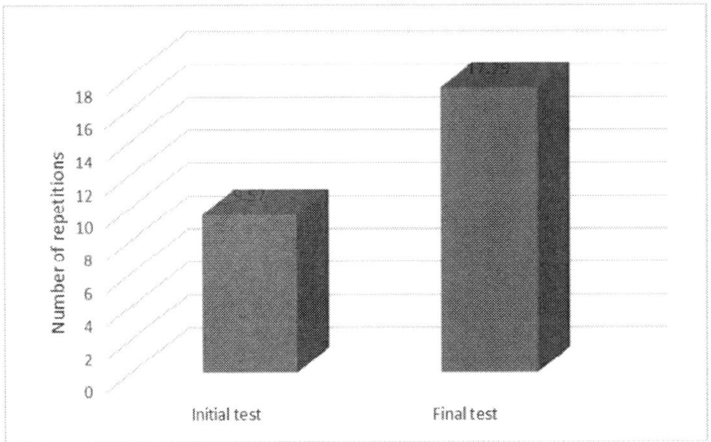

Fig. 3. The subjects' result evolution at the squat test

The values recorded at the crunch test indicate a low level of training at the initial test, which was improved at the final test with an average of 9.43 repetitions. The performance achieved at the final test is due to the physical training carried out by the researched subjects and is statistically supported by the results presented in table 1 and the performance averages presented in figure 4.

DOI: 10.1051/shsconf/20173701023

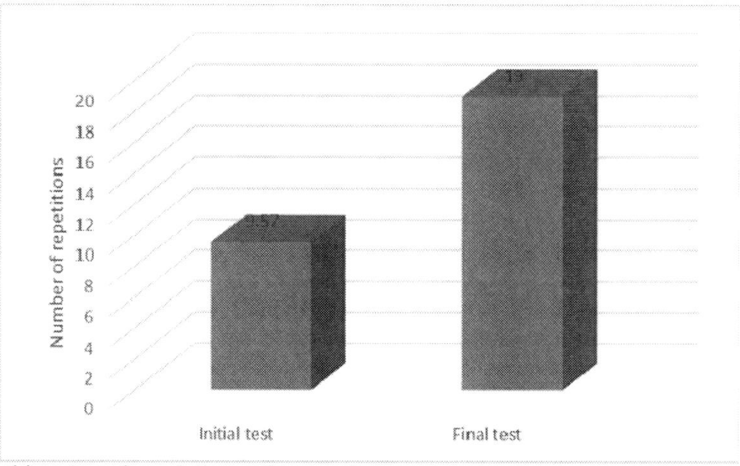

Fig. 4. The subjects' result evolution at the crunch test

At the arm strength test, significant progress was recorded, with an average of 1-3 repetitions, a good thing given the significant weight of the subjects. The progress is supported by the statistical analysis, where the significance threshold is of $t<.001$ and by the average of the results presented in figure 5.

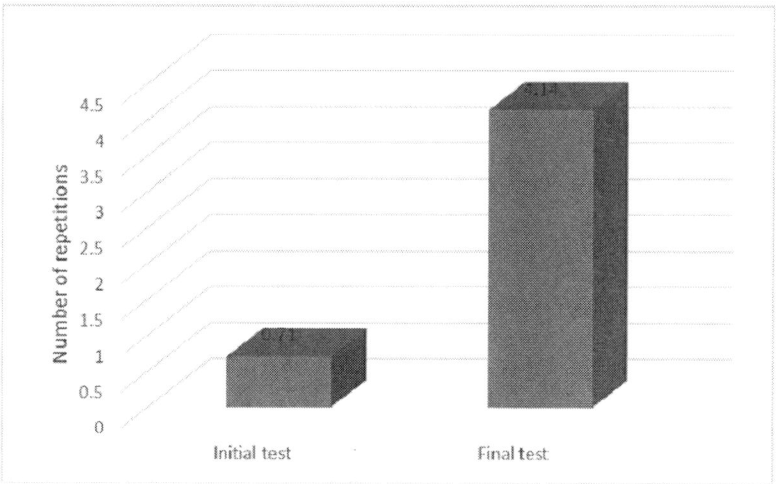

Fig. 5. The subjects' result evolution at the pull-up test

It is likely that this lack of significant progress is due to the lack, in our intervention, of a specific program dedicated to developing the muscle groups involved in this test or to the fact that certain fitness components weren't dealt with separately or, maybe, we should have focused on more weight loss.

In presenting the results obtained at this test, we checked muscle endurance and arm strength. As with previous tests, the subjects under research obtained an improvement of performance at the final test as compared to the initial test with an average of 6.72 repetitions. The improvement of the results confirms the fact that the physical training program applied to the subjects under research was well-applied and the content was well thought and organised.

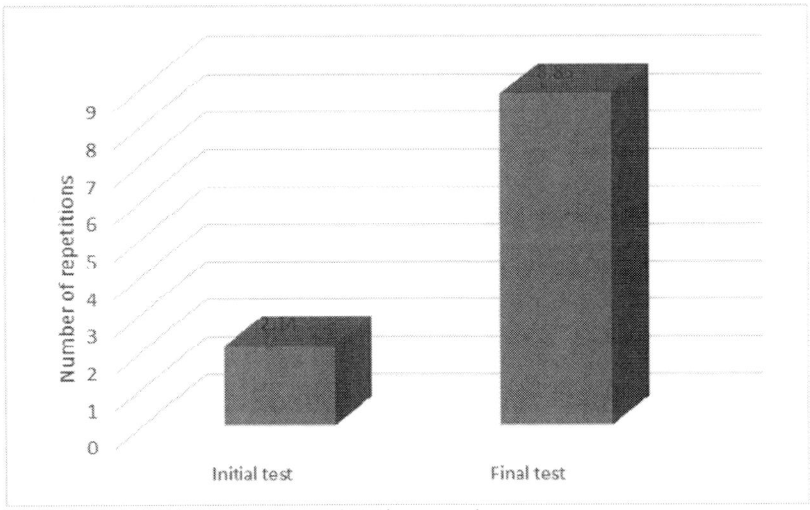

Fig. 6. The subjects' result evolution at the hanging exercises

The recorded progress is certain and obvious, being expressed in energy and strength, which, at the beginning of the training didn't exist. Even if, sometimes, the analysed tests didn't contain specific exercises, the proposed general physical training program was also positively transferred to the other body segments.

4 Conclusions

The main conclusion of our research was that physical exercises can be a great way to achieve an optimum body weight, which definitely represents a premise for good health.

At the same time, the pleasure of practising physical exercises will lead to better results obtained by the kids at their physical tests. Due to the fact that they increased their level of motricity, in the future, they would not avoid, to participate in physical activities, the foundation of a healthy lifestyle.

Another important aspect of the research is that, in order to fight childhood obesity, it is necessary both to see a nutritionist and to practise any kind of physical exercise.

We consider that kinetoterapy hasn't a significant effect in fighting obesity, especially in children. As long as they can perform voluntary specific motor activities, their practice represents the main element in burning the surplus of the daily intake of calories.

References

1. D. Bădău, A. Bădău, *The influence of various types of water gymnastics upon the exercise capacity*, International Journal of Science Culture and Sport (IntJSCS), Vol 3, No 4: Number: **14**(94-102) (2015)
2. D. Bădău, A. Larion, A. Bădău, D. Alexandrescu, *Experimental Study on Improving the Quality of Life through the Standardization of an Aerobics Program and of Effort Parameters Control using Pulse Tester,* Mathematic Methods and Applied Computing (Volume II), Mathematics and Computers in Science and Engineering, A Series of Reference Books and Textbooks, WSEAS Press, pp. 610-615 (2009)
3. D. Bădău, G. Prebeg, D. Mitic, A. Bădău, Fitness index and VO2max of physical education students, *Ovidius University Annals, Series Physical Education and Sport/Science, Movement and Health* 15.2 S1: 246-252 (2015)

4. E. Mcauley, S. Elavsky, GJ. Jerome, JF Konopack, DX. Marquez, Physical activityrelated wellbeing in older adults: Social cognitive influences. Psychology and Aging, **20**, 295-302 (2005)
5. F. Raymond, *Niciodată nu vei mai fi obez,* All Publishing house, Bucureşti, (2007)
6. G. Kolata, *Rethinking thin: The new science of weight loss – and the myths and realities of dieting*. Picador, (2007)
7. G. Ninot, D. Delignieres, M. Fortes, L'évaluation de l'estime de soi dans le domaine corporel. STAPS, **53**, 35-48, (2000)
8. J. Salmon, A. Timperio. "Prevalence, trends and environmental influences on child and youth physical activity". *Med Sport Sci*. Medicine and Sport Science, (2007)
9. Kr. Fox, The effects of exercise on selfperceptions and self-esteem. In: Physical Activity and Psychological Well-Being. Biddle J, Fox Kr, boutcher Sh (eds). Routledge, London and New York, b: 88-117, (2000)
10. M. V. Chakravarthy, F. W. Booth, Eating, exercise, and thrifty genotypes: Connecting the dots toward an evolutionary understanding of modern chronic diseases". *J. Appl. Physiol.* **96**(1), 3–10, (2004)
11. R. Valois, HE. Zulling, JW. Drane, Physical activity behaviors and perceived life satisfaction among public high school adolescents. Journal of School Health, **74**, 59-65, (2004)
12. S. W. Keith, DT. Redden, KPT. Katzmarzy, *A Plan for Measuring Progress,* Institute of Medicine Evaluating Obesity Prevention Efforts, The National Academies Press, Washington DC, USA, (2013)
13. T. M. Iconomescu, M. Ciapa, L.G. Talaghir, G. Badicu, , *Survey regarding the importance of education for health trough physical education,* The Annals of „Dunarea de Jos" University of Galati, Fascilce XV, Physical Education and Sport Management, no. **2**, 62 (2013)
14. T. M. Iconomescu, M. Ciapa, L. G. Talaghir, V. Popescu, , *Survey regarding the importance of sports to maintain a state of health good,* The Annals of „Dunarea de Jos" University of Galati, Fascilce XV, Physical Education and Sport Management, **2**, 67 (2013)
15. V. S. Malik, M. B. Schulze, F. B. Hu, *Intake of sugar-sweetened beverages and weight gain: a systematic review*. Am. J. Clin. Nutr., (2006)
16. Y. Netz, Mj Wu, B. J. Becker, G. Tenenbaum, Physical activity and psychological wellbeing in advanced age: a meta-analysis of intervention studies. Psychol Aging, **20,** 272-284 (2005)

Application of the european quality of life survey (EQLS) to the students of the university program for older adults of the University of Burgos (PIE)

Vanesa Baños-Martínez[1a]

[1]Faculty of Education, Department of Science Education, University of Burgos, Spain

Abstract. This study presents a complete analysis of the quality of life of a group of older university students of the University of Burgos. The emphasis has been placed on the quality of life from a subjective point of view without forgetting that it involves multiple dimensions that range from health and public services to social exclusion. On the other hand, the relationship between education, quality of life and active aging has been sought and a strong and positive correlation has been found. We can state that university students, despite their age, have better quality of life than their citizens and, in this sense. We can conclude that the future of societies with strong aging processes of their population is to develop and expand active aging, either from the university or from other institutions. the oldest students over their own health is worse than that of the youngest.
Keywords: quality of life, university students, older adults

1 Introduction

The aging of the population is one of the most important challenges that faces contemporary Europe [13]. Predictions leave no room for doubt, by the middle of the twenty-first century, one in three citizens will be over 60 years old [6].

Because of that, it is worthwhile to encourage older people to take part in educational activities in their free time and thus put into practice the idea of lifelong learning. In this sense, University Programs for older adults represent a very praiseworthy effort to improve the quality of life (QoL) of the elderly and to cope with the increase of longevity and thus respond to the erroneous assumptions that associate aging with physical and/or intellectual decline [8].

Kuykendall, Tay & Ng [12] argue that leisure activities promote subjective well-being in adulthood by their association with intrinsic motivations, perceived freedom and other psychological benefits. For example, a recent study concluded that leisure activities are

[a] Corresponding author: vbanos@ubu.es

positively related to subjective well-being among older Chinese and that they may play a leading role in promoting healthy aging [20].

According to García [9], education in the elderly favours a better adjustment and greater life satisfaction and maintenance of optimal levels of QoL. Learning can benefit, at the health level, all the people regardless of their initial levels of mental and psychological well-being [1, 10, 19]. Education improves the QoL by increasing subjective well-being and personal and social knowledge which allows students to feel part of society [5].

Some studies confirm that about 75% of older people value their QoL as good or very good and the great majority of them adapt satisfactorily to the consequences of aging and refer to a high level of satisfaction with life [15]. Fernández-Ballesteros [7] states that older people score slightly above average on life satisfaction and slightly lower than average on happiness.

Other studies have concluded that women are generally less satisfied with their lives and are less happy than men at all ages and in old age [11, 18].

Perceived social support is important too [2] either through family relations or friendships, the conservation of them and interest in the social and institutional environment prevent the appearance of pathologies and the negative effects on health [14].

The economic situation has been related to well-being and the QoL in old age [17]. A macro study published in the medical journal "The Lancet" states that poverty and social inequality are highly detrimental to health. Stringhini, et al. [16] conclude that the socioeconomic level has a decisive influence on health.

In short, this research is important because it helps to strengthen the need for older people education, justifying the same in which the QoL of the students is maintained. On the other hand, it seeks to understand which dimensions are the most influential for the quality of life of the elderly, which can help managers and any educational or social agents related to University Programs for older adults to better adjust programming to give response to real needs.

The main objective of this research is to analyse the quality of life of the students of the University Program for older adults of the University of Burgos (PIE) in the headquarters of Burgos and Aranda de Duero.

2 Method

The applied sampling technique is a non-probabilistic sampling for convenience, since the group of subjects that includes the students of the University Program for older adults of the UBU in the headquarters of Burgos and Aranda de Duero has been selected given the accessibility and suitability of the same. It is divided naturally into groups, which in this research are identified as venues and for which these venues have been selected as the first to launch the Program at the UBU in 2002.

2.1 Participants

The choice of this methodology allows us to gather the opinion and assessment of the maximum number of students possible, maintain the anonymity of the respondents, favour the freedom of response and obtain varied, useful, reliable and valid information. The sample used consisted of 332 subjects, older than 50 years.

The questionnaire was answered anonymously and voluntarily by 332 students in October 2014, at the beginning of the academic year 2014/2015. Of the total, 119 people study in Aranda and 213 in Burgos. The sample is representative because it gathers answers of 97.65% of the total students, which are 340 people, the statistical formulation tells us that we have worked with an error rate of 1.09% and with a confidence interval of 99%.

A large sample has been chosen to be able to access also the small differences or weak relationships that may exist between the multiple variables.

2.1 Instrument

The selected technique to collect the data about QoL of the students of the University Program for older adults of the University of Burgos is the transversal design survey denominated EQLS 2012 of the European Foundation for the Improvement of the Living and Working Conditions (Eurofound) [3]. It is a survey of European citizens aimed at obtaining a perspective on the objective conditions of life and their perception of QoL. The work of the experts allows the questions contained in the questionnaire to capture the phenomena that are intended to capture in the real world (validity).

The EQLS has a four-year nature, dealing with several issues, such as employment, income, education, housing, family, health and reconciliation of work and family life. It is also interested in more subjective issues, such as the degree of happiness of the people, their satisfaction with their personal life and how they perceive the quality of their societies.

Among the different instruments reviewed for the realization of the present study, we have been interested in the EQLS 2012 because it is designed for the general population and not for the elderly specifically, so the results allow us to make broader comparisons. Also, our interest is that it measures both positive and negative aspects related to the QoL and reproduces the multidimensionality of the concept. It has been sought to know the behaviour of the instrument with a sample that is not the usual one. On the other hand, it is backed by the European institutions and is adapted to the Spanish population and duly validated.

For the research presented here, three questions were added to the questionnaire, which serve as classification data: place of residence, enrolment course and, for graduates only, number of years of permanence in the Program.

In a total of 66 issues, the EQLS 2012 addresses the following dimensions: employment and work-life balance, family and social life, health and public services, home and local environment, quality of society, social exclusion and community involvement, standard of living and deprivation and finally, subjective well-being.

The scales of answers are varied, because some of the questions are closed dichotomous, that is, they give only two answers: yes or no and, if appropriate, do not know/no answer; others are closed categorized because they present as answers a series of alternatives among which the respondent must choose an alternative and finally, there are also numerical questions in which the answer is asked to be expressed in number form.

3 Findings

In a first approximation to the various elements that make up subjective well-being, we face to the following aspects: being optimistic about the future, feeling that life is worthwhile, being free to decide how to live the life or not having time to do things that you enjoy. In this sense, as reflected in Figure 1, UBU students have the best results among all their peers, both Spanish and European, being the difference bigger with respect to the latter. On the other hand, if the comparison is made between the elderly of the UBU and the total sample of Spain, the university students value with 1% more their decision capacity; an 11% more of the students disagree with the affirmation "I rarely have time to do things that I really enjoy" and 82% emphatically affirm that their life is worth it. There is only a 3% difference in favour of the total Spanish sample about optimism about the future. The Spanish results, beyond the sample used in this research, are better than those of the Europeans in every single question collected here. Among the older people, we also

DOI: 10.1051/shsconf/20173701024

observed that there are significant differences between the elderly of up to 64 years and those over 65 years old, the latter have slightly more negative results.

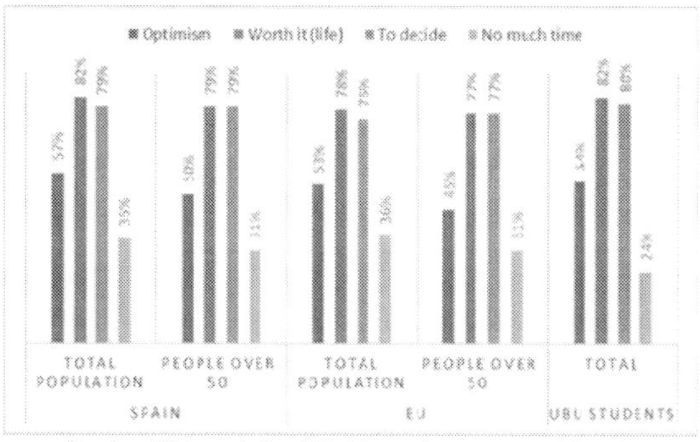

Fig.1. Comparison between Spain, EU and the UBU students on subjective well-being.

In relation to health as UBU students show a higher percentage of good health than the elderly of the Spanish sample (19%) and European. So, they are placed very close to the total of the Spanish average. The differences are significant among those over 65 years of age and those aged between 50 and 64 years, with the latter having a 24% increase in positive responses (Figure 2). Health is one of the most important factors in the perception of the quality of life and it can be confirmed that UBU student who take part in a University Program for older adults present high levels.

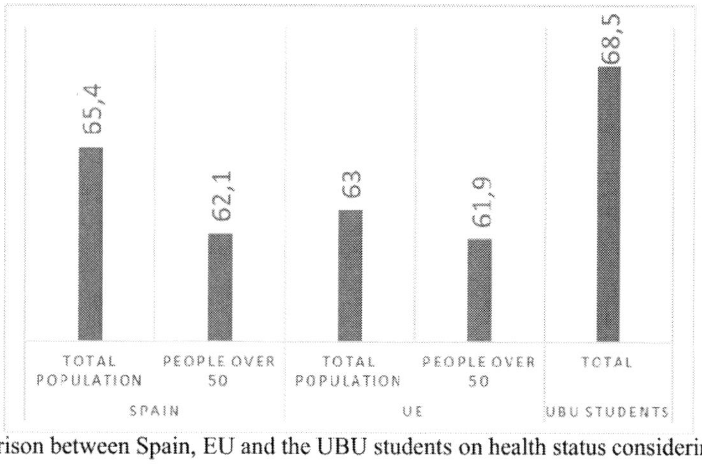

Fig. 2. Comparison between Spain, EU and the UBU students on health status considering the answers: "very good" or "good".

The analysis of the quality of the society leads us to the reflection that the UBU senior students have high levels of confidence in most people, more than the Spanish and European average and more than the elderly of the national sample. On the other hand, as shown in Figure 3, confidence in institutions is substantially lower for university graduates than for the rest of the population. This difference is clearly significant with respect to the legal system, where the PIE students are 6 tenths below and in relation to the local authorities, with about 1 point difference in favour of both, the general sample and the elderly of the global sample. In all aspects, those over 65 are more confident than those aged between 50 and 64 years. It seems that the younger ones are more critical of the institutions that represent, inform or protect them. There is scope for improvement in this sense and even more when we are aware that quality of society is an important aspect in the design of the overall model that has been made for the sample of the PIE.

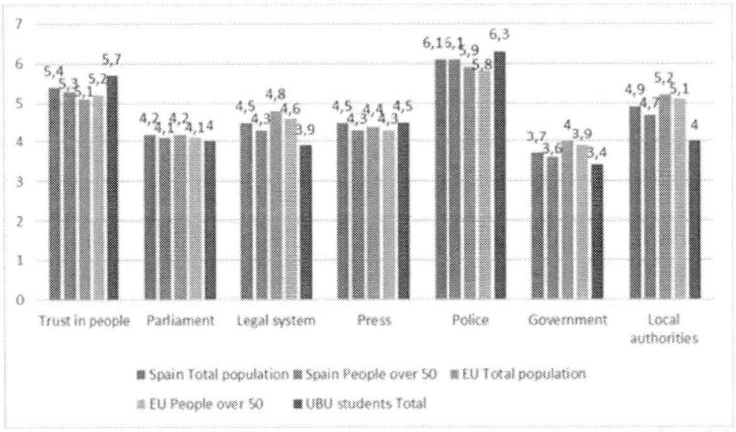

Fig. 3. Comparison between Spain, EU and the UBU students about the degree of confidence in different groups and institutions.

In relation to the perception of the quality about different services, university students are the ones that get a worse score, whether compared to the general sample or to those over 50 years of the total sample or even to the Europeans (Figure 4). Social housing, along with pensions or resources for the care of the sick or disabled, are the services that generate the most dissatisfaction.

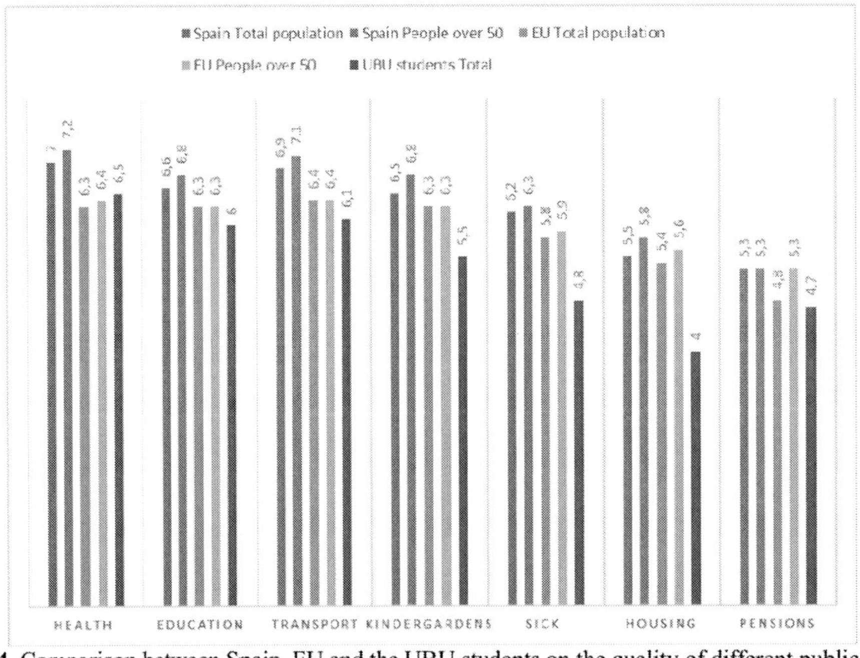

Fig. 4. Comparison between Spain, EU and the UBU students on the quality of different public services.

Broadly speaking, we can say that the UBU elderly students have good levels of health and mental well-being, with levels very similar to those of the general population. On the other hand, at the level of public services, although they do not find many factors that make it difficult, for example, medical visits, they consider that the quality of the most relevant public services in the country could be much higher.

4 Discussion and conclusion

The participation of UBU students in training activities has been relevant to their subjective well-being, as it has been shown in previous studies [12, 20]. We corroborate that in this context there are opportunities for socialization, cognitive stimulation, personal growth and, occasionally, physical activity.

The PIE of the University of Burgos, as a leisure activity based on training, contributes to the integral development of students and this fact has positive consequences on the quality of life. The health benefits of participants, both physically and mentally, have also been verified. These results coincide with those presented by Argyle [1], Yanguas [19] and Hammond [10].

Our research presents points in common with the study of Fernández-Ballesteros [7], as in both cases the most economically favoured students are those who also have better health [8, 16, 17] and that age influences the perception of health [11, 18].

In the case of the University of Burgos the elderly has strong social support, which although it positively influences their quality of life [2, 14], is not decisive. Some of the students take care of their grandchildren occasionally and they do not feel stressed by their responsibility.

Overall, the results reinforce the idea that the UBU students from Burgos and Aranda de Duero have an active and satisfactory aging profile, away from the much-feared dependence, free of serious health problems, with good life satisfaction and high levels of happiness. These circumstances may not be a direct consequence of the PUMs, although we can affirm that university education contributes decisively to the maintenance of a good health status (physical and mental) and high levels of subjective well-being associated with self-esteem, self-confidence, to personal relationships or the sense of personal identity as members of the university community.

The University of Burgos is an example where it is shown that aging actively and with quality of life is possible in a university training environment that satisfies the needs of their students and provides them with the resources and tools necessary to achieve their personal development. Activity is the key to good aging and to achieve this is key to promote actions that focus on prevention, through the promotion of healthy living habits, and effective intervention programs focused on the person.

All the literature on active aging, lifelong learning and quality of life is a concrete reality in the University of Burgos elderly students.

References

1. M. Argyle *The psychology of happiness*. Routledge, (2013)
2. J. Buz, P. Mayoral, B. Bueno, J. L. Vega, Factores sociales del bienestar subjetivo en la vejez. *Revista Española de Geriatría y Gerontología*, **39**(3), 23-29 (2004)
3. EQLS translated questionnaire. https://www.eurofound.europa.eu/surveys/european-quality-of-life-surveys/european-quality-of-life-survey-2012/eqls-2012-questionnaire/eqls-2012-questionnaire-translation
4. EQLS 2012 data. https://www.eurofound.europa.eu/es/surveys/data-visualisation/european-quality-of-life-survey-2012
5. P. Escuder-Mollon, R. Esteller-Curto, L. Ochoa, M. Bardus, Impact on senior learners' quality of life through lifelong learning. Procedia-Social and Behavioral Sciences, **131**, 510-516 (2014)
6. European Comission. Comunicación sobre "Asociación Europea para la Innovación sobre un Envejecimiento Activo y Saludable" (COM (2012) 83 final). http://ec.europa.eu/health//sites/health/files/ageing/docs/com_2012_83_en.pdf

7. R. Fernández-Ballesteros, *Psicogerontoloía: perspectivas europeas para un mundo que envejece*. Ediciones Pirámide., (2009)
8. M. Formosa, Lifelong learning in later life: The Universities of the Third Age. *Lifelong Learning Institute Review*, **5**, 1-12, (2010)
9. A. J. García González, *Variables psicosociales que inciden en la calidad de vida de los participantes en Programas Universitarios de Mayores*. Sevilla: Servicio de Publicaciones., (2011)
10. C. Hammond, Impacts of lifelong learning upon emotional resilience, psychological and mental health: fieldwork evidence. *Oxford Review of Education*, **30**(4), 551-568 (2004)
11. R. Inglehart, Gender, aging, and subjective well-being. *International Journal of Comparative Sociology*, **43**(3-5), 391-408 (2002)
12. L. Kuykendall, L. Tay, V. Ng, Leisure engagement and subjective well-being: A meta-analysis. *Psychological Bulletin*, **141**(2), 364-403 (2015)
13. J. Mackowicz, J. Wnek-Gozdek, "It's never too late to learn"–How does the Polish U3A change the quality of life for seniors? *Educational Gerontology*, **42**(3), 186-197 (2016)
14. J. J. Maldonado Briegas, M. I. Fajardo Caldera, F. Vicente Castro, S. González Ballester, Adulto mayor y envejecimiento activo. Caso de éxito de una iniciativa emprendedora. International Journal of Developmental and Educational Psychology. *Revista INFAD de Psicología*, **1**(2), 57-62 (2016)
15. M. Richart Martínez, J. Cabrero García, M.J. Cabañero Martínez, A. Reig Ferrer, Calidad de vida en la vejez. En Millán Calenti, J.C. *Gerontología y geriatría: Valoración e intervención* (pp 617-638). Madrid: Editorial Médica Panamericana, (2011)
16. S. Stringhini, et al. Socioeconomic status and the 25 × 25 risk factors as determinants of premature mortality: a multicohort study and meta-analysis of 1´7 million men and women. *The Lancet*. (2017)
17. A. Walker, Calidad de vida de las personas mayores. Análisis comparativo europeo. *Revista Española de Geriatría y Gerontología*, **39**(3), 8-17 (2004)
18. Y. Yang, Social inequalities in happiness in the United States, 1972 to 2004: An age-period-cohort analysis. *American sociological review*, **73**(2), 204-226 (2008)
19. J. Yanguas Lezaun, *Análisis de la calidad de vida relacionada con la salud en la vejez desde una perspectiva multidimensional* (No. 11002). Imserso. (2006).
20. W. Zhang, Q. Feng, J. Lacanienta, Z. Zhen, Leisure participation and subjective well-being: Exploring gender differences among elderly in Shanghai, China. *Archives of Gerontology and Geriatrics*, **69**, 45-54 (2017)

DOI: 10.1051/shsconf/20173701025

Health-related quality of life of the students of the university program for older adults of the University of Burgos (PIE): Comparative study

Vanesa Baños-Martínez[1a]

[1]Faculty of Education, Department of Science Education, University of Burgos, Spain

Abstract. It is shown in this research the analysis of the results obtained by a group of older university students of the University of Burgos when asked for their health using the European Quality of Life-5 Dimensions (EQ-5D-5L VAS) health questionnaire developed by the EuroQol Group. The study results show, always bearing in mind the limitations of the study, that men tend to assess their health with higher score than women. It also has been found that the score of the oldest students over their own health is worse than that of the youngest. Overall, these results support the idea that education can be an important pillar for active aging, which helps to maintain away the dreaded dependence.
Keywords: quality of life, health-related, university students, older adults

1 Introduction

The study of life quality of life (QoL) in the elderly has been analysed by multiple researchers [13]. In recent times, the interest in improving the QoL of older people has increased. A highly innovative approach that has been promoted within the framework of the European Union with the construction of the European Higher Education Area. In this paper, the training of European citizenship is explicitly linked to the thesis of lifelong learning, reinforcing the cultural dimension of universities [8, 9].

From the World Health Organization's conceptualization of active aging, this is "the process of optimizing opportunities for health, participation and security to enhance quality of life as people age" [14], actions aimed at promoting attitudes and behaviours that promote intellectual concern, scientific and cultural curiosity, will allow older people to face this stage of life. From this preventive perspective, University Programs for older adults are a very effective way to be active in the psychological, physical and social areas.

Research and experience have shown that training is possible and must be done throughout life. Lifelong learning is one of the best ways to contribute to promoting active aging, enhancing personal development in all directions, facilitating spaces where

[a] Corresponding author: vbanos@ubu.es

intergenerational relationships are a daily fact, motivating older people to continue growing and ultimately improving their QoL.

The justification for this research does not come exclusively from the socio-demographic factors and the policies on active and healthy aging in which University Programs for older adults are contextualized, but we can say that the QoL is related to indicators of health, well-being and needs satisfaction [6]. It is based on the potential of the elderly to adapt to their environment and thus lead a successful aging through accommodation strategies or instrumental activities such as training in a University Program [10].

The decade of the 90's of the last century prompted the development of the concept "Quality of Life Related to Health (HRQoL)" also known as perceived health. The study of HRQoL makes it possible to evaluate the effects of health, disease and treatment on people's quality of life [3], based on the individual's own perception and considering different dimensions. The concept of HRQoL that best fits the aims of this research is the one that conceives it as the individual's ability to do things, influenced by subjective perception. Quality of life is a unique human concept that is directly related to the degree of satisfaction that has the person as to his level of happiness. It is important to focus on this concept and its relationship with lifelong learning because developed countries and continents, especially Europe are facing a new era with many elderly people whose needs are changing. If we manage to provide them tools, as education, to maintain their health that would be a success.

Older people involved in educational experiences have benefits that include not only the development of coping strategies but also the development of interest in new activities, social integration and, above all, the development of new social networks; in other words, increased quality of life and well-being [7].

So, in this paper we aimed to analyse the Health-Related Quality of Life of the students of the University Program for older adults of the University of Burgos (PIE) at the headquarters of Burgos and Aranda de Duero. Thus, the specific objectives of the study are:

• To know the degree of association, if any, between HRQoL and different sociodemographic factors.

• To describe the general health status of the students of the University Programs for older adults.

Based on these objectives, the following hypotheses are expected to be fulfilled:

• There are statistically significant differences in the dependent variable (VAS – Visual Analogue Scale) caused by the independent variable (sex).

• Older students report having more health problems.

2 Method

To reach the objectives, we have opted for an exploratory and empirical methodology, being aware that it adapts to a great variety of situations in different contexts and to the human complexity.

The technique used for data collection has been the EQ-5D-5L EVA Health Questionnaire (2009) of the EuroQol Group [11] as a generic and standardized instrument used to describe and assess the HRQoL of a group or population and whose development has been possible thanks to the support of the European Union. In Spain, the questionnaire was validated by Badía et al. [1] and complies with the properties of cultural adaptation, validity, reliability and sensitivity to change. On the other hand, this instrument has also been the tool that has been used to evaluate HRQoL in the National Health Survey of Spain, in its latest edition of 2011/2012. We have added to this instrument a block of questions to obtain sociodemographic data such as age, sex, level of education, etc.

The instrument itself consists of two parts: on the one hand the questionnaire that is responsible for measuring the self-perceived limitations of health and on the other, the Visual Analogue Scale (VAS). The questionnaire traces the health status of the students through 5 dimensions [5]: mobility, self-care, usual activities, pain/discomfort and anxiety/depression. Each of them has 5 levels of response: no problems, slight problems, moderate problems, serious problems and total impossibility. With this data we obtain a simple descriptive profile on health. On the other hand, students also assess their health status through the VAS that is a kind of thermometer of 20 cm. which offers a value for health status between 100 (best state of health imaginable) and 0 (worst state of health imaginable). With respect to its psychometric properties, test-retest reliability ranges from 0.86 to 0.90 [12], and its validity and sensitivity to change has been demonstrated in numerous studies [4].

The questionnaire was answered anonymously and voluntarily by 332 students in October 2014, at the beginning of the academic year 2014/2015. Of the total, 119 people study in Aranda and 213 in Burgos. The sample is representative because it gathers answers of 97.65% of the total students, which are 340 people, the statistical formulation tells us that we have worked with an error rate of 1.09% and with a confidence interval of 99%.

The data were entered by double digitizing to the EpiData software, which is used by the World Health Organization in various projects and analyses. Subsequently, the database was exported to the statistical package Stata in its version 12 through which the descriptive statistics of the variables (means, standard deviations or percentages) were calculated as well as the statistical techniques and graphs recommended for each type of variable (t tests, ANOVA or correlations).

3 Findings

Table 1 gives a summary of the statistical relationship between the dependent and independent variables showing the p-value. From this information and using the different statistical tests the analysis of the results has been done.

Table 1. Contrast of hypotheses between dependent and independent variables.

Dependent variables	Independent variables							
	Place	Sex	Age	Cour-se	Level of studies	Employ ment situa-tion	Civil status	People in the household
EQ-5D-5L	0.010	0.031	0.048	-	<u>0.000</u>	<u>0.000</u>	0.012	0.018
VAS	-	0.033	-	<u>0.005</u>	0.025	<u>0.004</u>	-	-

The analysis of the questionnaire EQ-5D-5L in relation to the place of registration informs us that the students at the headquarters of Burgos show a difference with the students of Aranda of 0.036, that means that their health is slightly better than the health of their colleagues from Aranda, a small city in the south of the province.

Related to sex, we found statistically similar values in the p-value of both dependent variables. As can be seen in Figure 1, it is men who have higher scores on VAS. The difference is 3,633 points out of 100 and, although the median is equal in both sexes, in women the scores are concentrated below it.

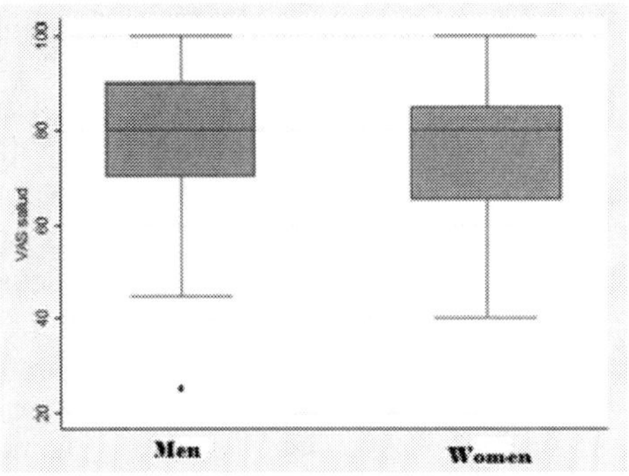

Fig.1. ANOVA of sex related to VAS.

On the other hand, the results of the students in the health questionnaire EQ-5D-5L also benefit men compared to women because their results are more grouped in the upper parts of the Figure (2). We conclude in this sense that sex is a variable that decisively affects the perception of health when we study the quality of life.

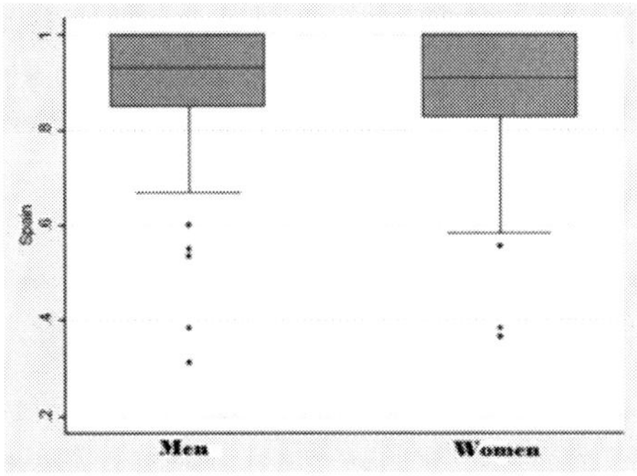

Fig. 2. ANOVA of sex related to the health questionnaire EQ-5D-5L.

The link between age and the perception of health collected in the EQ-5D-5L questionnaire is shown in Figure 3, which shows that the older the students, the lower the value offered by the health index. On the other hand, knowing that the results can vary between 1 and -0.654 we see that most of the students are in a range of high scores, higher than 0.844 and the older students are those who obtain lower values.

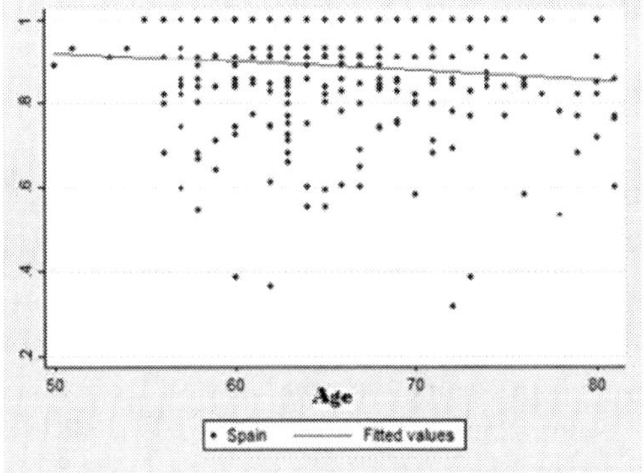

Fig. 3. Linear regression of the values of the health questionnaire EQ-5D-5L and age.

In relation to the course and the VAS we found that there is a slightly decreasing tendency that only manifests itself with the graduates. Regarding the level of studies, the analyses inform us of the existence of a relevant association with the health levels where they present an increasing tendency, the higher the formative level the better the health self-perception.

On the other hand, the association between the employment situation with both the VAS and the EQ-5D-5L questionnaire tells us that those who claim to have a better general health status are those who are active, and they are more likely to be in better physical and mental conditions than another person who, for example, is unemployed. Those who have poor health are clearly the disabled ones followed by the housewives.

To conclude, we address the variable on the number of people living in the household and we check that it has statistical significance with the independent variable EQ-5D-5L, we can affirm that those who live with a greater number of people have better results in the EQ-5D-5L questionnaire.

4 Discussion and conclusion

By the results obtained and always bearing in mind the limitation of the study by the size of the sample, we can conclude that:

- Male students express a more positive perception of their health in most of the dimensions in contrast to their female counterparts whose answers are more negative. On average, men on the VAS have obtained a score of 77.59 compared to 75.05 points for women, there is a difference of 2.54 points. We can say that men tend to value their health better than women and these differences between sexes are statistically significant.

-The older the students, the worse is the assessment of their own health. The students with the best results in VAS have been those who are in second grade, who have had on average 80.38 points and whose average age is the lowest, 62.79 years. On the other hand, we find that it is a trend that is maintained since the following students with the highest average scores on the scale are those of the first course who are the youngest (63.31 years) and those in the third course with an average age of 64.84 years. Finally, the graduated students, who are 6.33 years older than the youngest, get an average score of 73.84 in the VAS, which means a difference of 6.54 points with respect to their classmates than not only are the best positioned but also the youngest. We conclude at this point that age differences exist but are not statistically significant.

The results confirm the hypotheses raised in the research, being largely coincident with other studies of national and international character.

If we compare our results with those of the National Health Survey in Spain (ENSE) 2011/2012 [2], we see that there are similarities in the sense that both confirm that women report more health problems than men in most dimensions, and that is the pain/discomfort dimension in which both sexes claim to have problems more often. The older students of the University of Burgos show lower percentages of problems related to mobility than the general population, and we see that in the dimension related to self-care there are important differences, mainly from the age of 75, since our sample scores better in about 15% than the general sample. A similar situation to that described above occurs in the dimension related to the usual activities. On the other hand, in the dimensions of pain/discomfort and anxiety/depression, the situation is completely different to the ones described so far and we find that the UBU students obtain worse results than the population in general, being more accentuated this fact in male than female. These data show that the University Programs for older adults are a good remedy against certain problems because they can make the elderly with pain or anxiety/depression able to enrol in a program of these characteristics and benefit from all the advantages it offers. We can say that this kind of programs allow people who are not completely healthy to continue being part of what we call "active citizenship", can continue training and acquire guidelines and develop strategies that allow them to maintain, despite their personal health circumstances, high levels of happiness. As a summary, we can say that University Programs for adults contribute to improve the quality of life of those who participate in them.

On the other hand, the National Health Survey, which measures the HRQoL in the adult population in general, concludes that the mean VAS score is 77.53 and that the values decrease systematically with the age, a fact that is also reflected through the information collected and analysed in this research. In our study, the average VAS of the students is 77.32 points, a very positive value in our case since it is not only close to the average of the Spanish population but is practically the same value (76.34) as the one of our region, Castilla y León. On the other hand, and following the comparison with the region, we find that although the general population presents a higher percentage of problems in the dimensions of usual activities and mobility, in our sample these large percentages are reflected in the dimensions of pain/discomfort and anxiety/depression as in the general data of the Spanish population. These data inform us that the health levels of our university students are very like those of the general population, which includes people from 18 years to more than 85 years, which supports the idea that lifelong learning has numerous benefits both personal and social and contributes in a clear way to maintain or even improve health levels.

As a conclusion, we can affirm that the Spanish elderly perceive that their health is worse in comparison with the university students of the UBU, despite this data, we cannot conclude that this situation is a direct consequence of an educational intervention framed within some objectives of active aging. Our sample could be biased if health is a decisive factor to enrol in a training program that requires a trip to the place where the classes are developed, willingness to enter socio-personal relationships or a minimum well-being that allows paying attention to the topics. What we can affirm is that those students who remain enrolled in the Program after graduation, despite having a mean age of 69.12 years, present better results in VAS than their counterparts in the national sample. It seems clear that training at maturity is directly related to a better perception of health and that although HRQoL depends on age and sex [2] there are other variables that can influence.

References

1. X. Badia, M. Roset, S. Montserrat, M. Herdman, A. Segura, La versión española del EuroQol: descripción y aplicaciones. *Medicina clínica*, **112**, 79-85 (1999)
2. Encuesta Nacional de Salud. España 2011/2012. Serie Informes monográficos nº3. *Calidad de vida relacionada con la salud en adultos: EQ-5D-5L*. Madrid: Ministerio de Sanidad, Servicios Sociales e Igualdad., (2014)
3. C. E. Ferrans, J. J. Zerwic, J. E. Wilbur, J. L. Larson, Conceptual model of health-related quality of life. *Journal of Nursing Scholarship*, **37**(4), 336-342 (2005)
4. M. Herdman, X. Badía, Berra, S. El EuroQol-5D: una alternativa sencilla para la medición de la calidad de vida relacionada con la salud en atención primaria. *Atención primaria*, **28**(6), 425-429 (2001)
5. M. Herdman, C. Gudex, A. Lloyd, M. F. Janssen, P. Kind, D. Parkin, G. Bonsel, X. Badía, Development and preliminary testing of the new five-level version of EQ-5D (EQ-5D-5L). *Quality of life Research* **04**/2011 (2011)
6. P. M. Iglesias-Souto, A. Dosil, Algunos indicadores de percepción subjetiva implicados en la satisfacción del residente mayor. Propuesta de una escala de medida. *Revista Española de Geriatría y Gerontología*, **40**(2), 85-91 (2005)

7. R. J. Manheimer, La educación para mayores en los Estados Unidos: tendencias y programas de desarrollo. En VV.AA., *Los modelos marco de programas Universitarios para Mayores* (pp.111 -121). Alicante: Universidad Permanente de Alicante., (2002)
8. C. Orte, M. Gambús, *Los programas universitarios para mayores en la construcción del Espacio Europeo de Enseñanza Superior.* Palma de Mallorca: Universitat de les Illes Balears., (2004).
9. C. Palmero, A. Jimenez, The quality of university programs for older people in Spain: Innovations, tendencies and ethics in the face of active ageing and the European Higher Education Area. *Educational Gerontology*, **44**, 4., (2008)
10. H. Pillay, K. Irving, M. Tones, Validation of the diagnostic tool for assessing tertiary students' readiness for online learning. *High Education Research & Development*, **26**(2), 217-234., (2007)
11. The EuroQol Group. EuroQol – a new facility for the measurement of health-related quality of life. *Health Policy* **16**(3), 199-208., (1990) www.euroqol.org.
12. H. M. Van Agt, M. L. Essink-Bot, P. F. Krabbe, G. J. Bonsel, Test-retest reliability of health state valuations collected with the EuroQol questionnaire. *Social science & medicine*, **39**(11), 1537-1544 (1994)
13. M. A. Verdugo, L. E. Gómez, B. Arias, *La Escala FUMAT de evaluación de la calidad de vida de personas mayores y con discapacidad.* Salamanca: Universidad de Salamanca, Publicaciones del INICO, Colección Herramientas, 4 (2009)
14. World Health Organization. A*ctive Ageing-A Policy Framework. A contribution of the World Health Organization to the Second United Nations World Assembly on Ageing.* Madrid (ES): WHO, (2002)

Graduate curriculum: A need for a change

Dilyana D.Sungatullina[1], Ekaterina O.Murtazina[1] and Yuliya N.Gorelova[1a]

[1]Kazan Federal University, 420008, 18, Kremlevskaya str., Russia

Abstract. Over the last couple of years there was an increase in graduates' willingness to interleave their vocational careers with academic instruction at the university. Hence, the authors conducted evaluation and needs analysis of the skills crucial for graduate students to possess. The current study analyzed the attitude of 150 KFU IMEF graduates towards their core requirements within the framework of modern educational environment. The results showed that the majority of the respondents consider knowledge of teaching methodology (a new topic introduction, the material delivery, its further practice and revision, effective groupwork and public speaking) to be of great importance. The paper concludes with suggestions on the need for the development and the introduction of a cutting-edge course at a Master's level tailored to graduates to enhance the skills applicable not only in the professional field but the educational environment as well.
Keywords: modern educational environment, attitude, graduate students

1 Introduction

Education in the 21st century is undergoing significant changes due to profound modifications in the requirements to the University graduates set by business and industrial landscape. New educational paradigm determines the competences and skills which stakeholders, namely potential employers, consider essential for the graduates employability [1].

The current trend observed is that employers pay significant attention to the soft or transferable skills development, while the University still focuses on training the hard ones. Most employers believe that there is a competence gap between skills necessary for the successful employment in the company and the skills acquired by the graduates in the universities [2]. Unlike hard skills, which determine the person's ability to perform specific tasks, soft skills are more universal and applicable in almost all jobs. The European Union and OECD countries have done a considerable amount of work to define the "21st century skills" inducing many schools to review the stand-and-deliver model of teaching and learning, introduce technology in the education process, reshape pedagogy to answer new shift. Even though the curriculum design presupposes the inclusion of transferable skills

[a] Corresponding author: gorelovajuliya@gmail.com

development in the teaching process, the challenge is that they are difficult to test and control, therefore the practice shows that hard skills are still a priority for tertiary institutions. Thus, we may observe a contradiction that made the authors consider the problem of curriculum development and address the changes that it needs to undergo in order to meet the requirements of contemporary world.

Any university is an employer itself as a certain percentage of graduates holding master's degree, stays at the University as a tertiary teacher. Thus, the University experiences the same problem as other employers do - the lack of soft skills among graduates, who made their decision to go on with teaching career on a full-time or part-time basis [3]. Therefore, the problem doubles due to the fact that novice tertiary teachers are incompetent of building soft skills in other students. Traditional solution offered by Russian higher education system is the professional development programs (PDP) or advanced training courses, which are obligatory to be taken by novice tertiary teachers along with their more experienced colleagues every three years. Notwithstanding the fact that academics are free to choose the field and the mode of PDP, quite frequently the programs, sponsored by the state, are far from being efficient and do not satisfy the requirements set by the University.

All the assumptions mentioned above induced the authors to consider the stated problem at Kazan Federal University, namely the Institute of Management, Economics and Finance (IMEF KFU). Therefore, the goal of this research is to identify the skills that would fill the current gap in the curriculum to provide relevant and competitive qualification for the graduates.

2 Research questions

To achieve the goal of our research, we will address two questions:

1. What soft skills are essential for a university graduate applicable not only in the professional field but in educational environment as well?

2. How could the curriculum be altered to meet the requirements of soft skills development?

3 Theoretical background

3.1 Overseas soft skills development approaches

The relevance of soft skills development is indisputable and highlighted by all stakeholders. The review of employers' preferences has revealed that transferrable skills that are considered as a "must have" for a graduate include reliability, interpersonal skills (teamworking), problem-solving (accountability) communication, self-direction and creativity (innovation) [4].

As both universities and businesses acknowledge significance of the issue for the Russian community the authors analyzed the existing international and domestic approaches to soft skills development. The analysis revealed that HEIs basically implement the following measures:

1. Publish students' guidelines on the university official website recommending to pay enough attention to soft skills development (to take a professional course, to volunteer in the community, to participate in class or to teach a class, to become a mentor or to get involved in the students' organizations.)

2. Introduce zero-credit courses, where students have an opportunity of practicing their social skills.
3. Introduce mandatory soft skills course in the curriculum with particular attention paid to interpersonal, communication and leadership skills development (bolt on model) [5].
4. Develop soft skills within the campus surrounding.
5. Organize work-integrated learning or internships together with potential employers.
6. Include soft skills development component in the hard skills course syllabus (imbedded model) [6].

The international experience observed advocates the implementation of the imbedded model i.e. the inclusion of soft skills into teaching hard ones. This approach possesses an indispensable benefit - there is no need to introduce a new course into the already overloaded curriculum. However, this requires a complete revision of teaching methodology and teachers' attitude to the course delivery [7].

3.2 Home experience

Domestic tertiary education is built around federal state educational standards (namely FSES 3+), which implies the competence approach implementation while designing the course syllabus. The standard presupposes the division of all competences into professional (similar to hard skills), general cultural and general professional ones which have a wide application field and indirectly relate to soft skills development. Thus, we may conclude that Russian tertiary education system utilizes the imbedded model as well. However, the standard does not describe the tools for measuring the degree of competence development among graduates and, in fact, these general cultural and general professional competences are difficult to measure and assess inside the professional course syllabus. Moreover, most teachers in their 40s-60s lack the required soft skills and are ignorant of their importance. Therefore, we may conclude that the problem of soft skills development in Russian universities in general and in IMEF KFU in particular is acute, as the existing system does not bring the desired effect. It requires serious consideration from the point of the university management, course designers and policy makers.

The authors have analyzed the IMEF KFU current graduate curriculum designed according to the FSES 3+ and identified the general cultural / general professional competences or soft skills that are to be developed in the course of programs mastering [9].

The general cultural competences prioritize analytical thinking, adaptability, social responsibility; general professional competences include communication skills (oral and written in native and foreign languages), leadership skills, cultural awareness and tolerance. The main advantage of the graduate curriculum in IMEF KFU is that along with compulsory vocational subjects preparing students for their future qualifications, there is a range of soft skills developing courses, which are predominantly elective. However, the variety of such courses is rather low and in many cases they are not represented in all majors of Master degree programs. The top 5 most popular programs in economics, management and environmental engineering do not have elective courses on soft skills development, while state and municipal management program along with human resources management allow incorporate 5% of optional subjects which are free to be chosen by students.

Thus, the authors of current research assume that a new course introduction to the curriculum of graduate students of all majors within IMEF KFU is of an utmost importance. Furthermore, this course should provide students with soft skills applicable not only at a tertiary education level (in case they decide to merge their career in business with teaching prospects) but be transferrable in all the spheres of their professional development.

4 Research methodology

To identify the necessity of a new curriculum design for Master Students the authors subdivided the research into four stages.

Stage 1.

The primary objective of this stage in research was the quantitative analysis of the IMEF KFU graduates who preferred to continue their career path as a tertiary-level teacher within 2010 to 2016 timeslots out of 500 academic staff of the Institute.

Stage 2.

This stage was concerned with the calculation of costs that IMEF KFU spends annually from the Federal budget of the Russian Federation on PDP of its academic staff. At this stage we estimated the potential savings that the University can obtain by introducing the teaching methodology course into the Master's curriculum.

Stage 3.

In the third stage we collected the information on the skills, which are critical for students to burnish in case they wish to blend their vocational careers with teaching at the university. Our data are based on responses of the 162 IMEF KFU 22–24 year-old Master students who completed the online questionnaire. The research questions outline the issues concerning students' work experience, willingness/unwillingness to interleave their major qualification and option of teaching at a tertiary level; crucial skills to be obtained before embarking on the career in education, including teaching methodology, teamwork organization, interaction with the audience; desire to hold lectures and seminars in English for the international audience.

Stage 4.

At the final point of our research we used binary variables in various dimensions (high versus low): employment status/desire to teach at HEI, employment status/desire to enroll in the teaching methodology course, desire to teach at HEI/ students' assessment of teaching methodology relevance, desire to enroll in the teaching methodology course/desire to teach at HEI. The degree of correlation between the variables was calculated with Pearson correlation coefficient.

5 Results and discussion

At the first stage of our research we have identified that 11.6% of the tertiary teachers educating at IMEF KFU are novice teachers graduated from the Institute in the period of 2010-2016 (58 out of 500 faculty members). Thus, we could conclude that annually approximately 3 graduates stay at IMEF KFU to teach. Therefore, the issue of the graduates skills and qualifications is of an utmost importance.

In accordance with the expenditures from the federal budget of the Russian Federation in 2016 education accounts for 9.18% [10]. However, expenses on professional development programs and further vocational training programs constitute only 1.29% from total investments into the sphere of education. Thus, we have calculated that the introduction of the teaching methodology course into the Master students' curriculum of IMEF KFU may save 0.16% from the total amount of spendings to the PDP from the federal budget of the Russian Federation. Consequently, former graduates may attend any other PDP, which will be crucial for them at the start of their teaching career.

DOI: 10.1051/shsconf/20173701026

Having compared the soft skills requirements of potential employers, with the existing competences to be developed in the curriculum, the authors have identified the gap. To fill this gap we have explored the existing needs of current students about the skills and competences, which they consider vital to develop. According to the data provided in Figure 01, the majority of the respondents (87.6%) indicate that being aware of teaching methodology for academics at a tertiary level is of great relevance. What is more, Figure 02 illustrates that a significant number of graduates (61.4%) feel indispensability of a teaching methodology course implementation into their current curriculum.

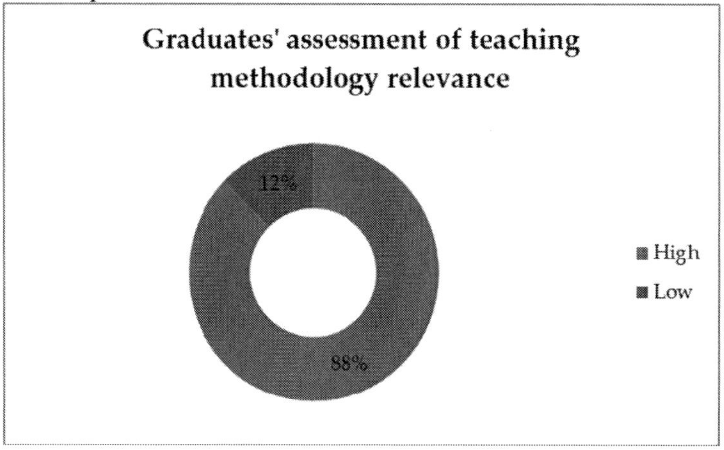

Fig. 01 [The importance of teaching methodology awareness as a tertiary teacher]

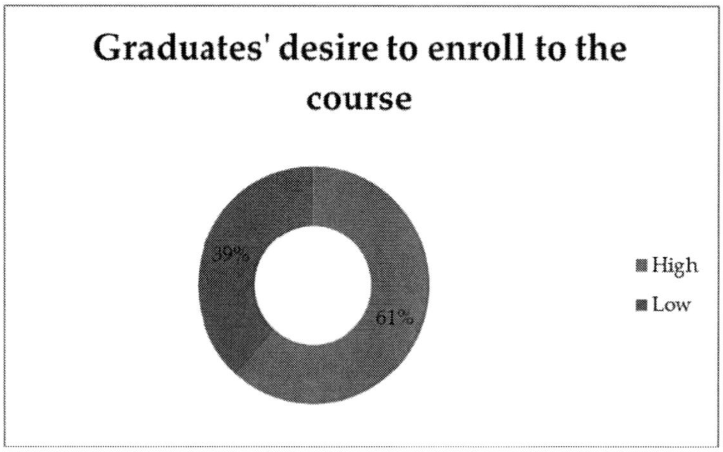

Fig. 02 [Teaching methodology course necessity within Master's curriculum]

The data collected from Figure 03 emphasize the most crucial and desirable skills for the graduates to obtain if the course described is taken into account when designing a curriculum. It is interesting to notice, that more than 58% of the respondents consider classroom management skills such as topic introduction or material delivery to be the most significant ones. Public speaking (51.7%), interactive teaching methods (50%) and ability to attract an audience attention (48.3%) seem quite meaningful to the participants of the survey as well. Besides, such skills as interaction with the audience (30%), knowledge assessment (13.3%), structuring presentations (11.7%) are of less valuable.

DOI: 10.1051/shsconf/20173701026

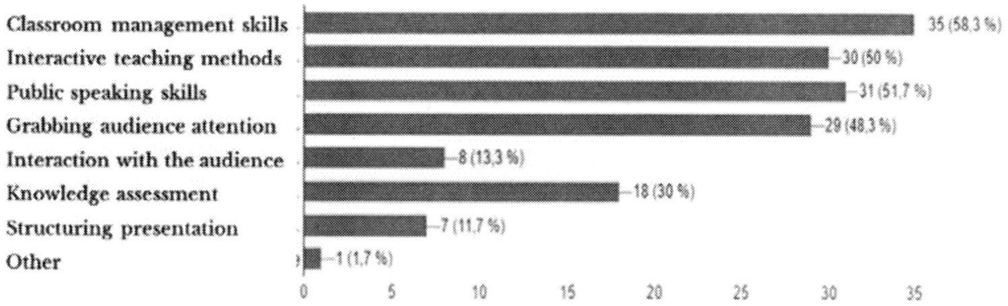

Fig. 03 [Targeted skills to be learnt within teaching methodology course]

Figure 04 demonstrates graduates' willingness and unwillingness to interleave their major qualification and option of teaching at a tertiary level. A relatively large number of respondents (43.4%) would wish to stay at the university for teaching practice and experience.

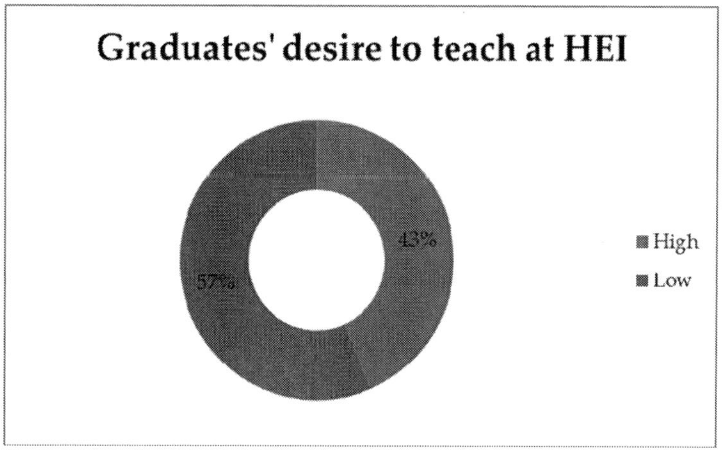

Fig. 04 [Graduates' desire to teach at a tertiary level]

Therefore, the results show that the majority of the respondents consider knowledge of teaching methodology to be of the highest priority, thus, confirming their wish to enroll in the course. The participants of the research demonstrate an encouragement towards learning the ways of effective groupwork organization, as well as new topic introduction, material delivery, its further practice and revision. Along with these, public speaking skills and interactive teaching methods are also in high demand.

The final step of our research revealed the correlation between employment status/desire to teach at HEI, employment status/desire to enroll in the teaching methodology course, desire to teach at HEI/ students' assessment of teaching methodology relevance, desire to enroll in the teaching methodology course/desire to teach at HEI (Table 1). As we can observe from the Table 1, there are no or very low cause-effect relations between the variables represented in the first 3 dimensions. However, the last variables correlation, namely "Graduates' desire to enroll in teaching methodology course / Graduates' desire to teach at HEI", is characterised by a negative trend, signifying the fact that the more students want to teach at HEI – the less they find a necessity of attending teaching methodology course. Nevertheless, the results of our previous research prove that teachers, as a rule, face the issues, which can be basically solved through a teaching methodology course [8]. Thus, the primary objective of a new course is to break the traditional viewpoint to the teaching methodology, transforming it into the vital soft skills development platform applicable in the educational and business landscape.

Table 1. Indicators affecting Graduates' desire to teach

Variables Correlation	Correlation Coefficient
Employment status / Graduates' desire to teach at HEI	0,26*
Employment status / Graduates' desire to enroll in teaching methodology course	-0,06*
Graduates' desire to teach at HEI/Relevance of teaching methodology	-0,016*
Graduates' desire to enroll to teaching methodology course / Graduates' desire to teach at HEI	-0,61*

(*p≤0,05)

6 Conclusion

Thus, in the course of our research we have identified that there is a significant gap between the skills and qualifications taught at the universities and the requirements of the labour market. The University as an employer itself is attempting to solve the problem by obligatory advanced training courses for its faculty members, which however provide doubtful effect. Therefore, the authors come up with suggestions on the urgency for the designing of an advanced course at a Master's level, which will positively impact the professional sphere and academic environment as well. Needs analysis performed, exposed that students focus on diverse labour market sectors requiring a combination of skills. However, the data obtained in the course of the research signify the fact that the education sector gains its strength and prestige demonstrating favourable ambiance for entry-level candidates to start their careers. Furthermore, new course design can diminish the governmental expenditures on tertiary teachers professional training due to the fact that the course offered can potentially be regarded as a base for the set of competencies development indispensable for the academics at a tertiary level.

References

1. E. M. Galishnikova, T. A. Baklashova, L. V. Khafizova, *Formation of Student's Tolerance in Multicultural Environment When Teaching a Foreign Language (KFU Experience, Kazan, Republic of Tatarstan, Russia)*. European Proceedings of Social and Behavioural Sciences, **12**, 38-44, (2016)
2. L. R. Ismagilova, O. V. Polyakova, *The problem of the syllabus design within the competence approach based on the course "English for Master Degree Students in Economics (advanced level)"*. Procedia Social and Behavioral Sciences, **152**,1095-1100, (2014)
3. I. M. Solodkova, L. R. Ismagilova, *Acquisition of Socio-Cultural Competence via Dynamic Learning Environment.* European Proceedings of Social and Behavioural Sciences, **12**, 389-395, (2016)

DOI: 10.1051/shsconf/20173701026

4. L. Rider, *Soft skills starter kit ...& guide.* Retrieved from http://wastatecouncil.shrm.org/sites/wastatecouncil.shrm.org/files/Soft%20Skill%20Survey%20Rpt%20-%20Sum%20of%20Findings%20-%20031615.pdf. (March, 2016).
5. S. Roselina *Soft skills at Malaysian institute of higher learning.* Asia Pacific Education Review, **10**, 309-315, (2009)
6. E. Dunne, *Personal transferable skills: Final report.* Exeter: University of Exeter, (1995)
7. B. Schulz, *The Importance of Soft Skills: Education beyond academic knowledge.* NAWA Journal of Language and Communication, 146-154, (June 2008).
8. Sungatullina D. D., Zalyaeva E. O., Gorelova Y. N. *Time for a change: defining the academic teacher's brand pillars.* III International Forum on Teacher Education, Kazan, (to be published), (2017)
9. Federal'nyye gosudarstvennyye obrazovatel'nyye standarty 3+ Magistratura (Federal state educational standards 3+ Master's level) (n.d.). Retrieved from http://cfuv.ru/federalnye-gosudarstvennye-obrazovatelnye-standarty-3-magistratura (Last update: 2017, April, 26)
10. Raskhody konsolidirovannogo byudzheta Rossiyskoy Federatsii po razdelu «Obrazovaniye» v 2016 godu (Consolidated budget expenditures on Education in Russia in 2016). Retrieved from http://fin.edu.ru/InfoPanel/min_obr1.html (Last update: 2017, April, 26).

Formation of research competence in university project-oriented training

Yuri Loginov[1a] and Igor Kovalev[1]

[1]Siberian State Aerospace University, Krasnoyarsk, Russia

Abstract. The aim of the study was to investigate the efficiency of research competence formation of aerospace university students in conditions of project-oriented training. The technology of project-oriented training of students in the form of a unique project for the development and creation of a series of student scientific-educational small satellites was implemented. To assess the effectiveness of the system of formation of research competencies a set of criterion-oriented test tasks was developed. In the experiment was attended by 130 students of the Institute of mechanical engineering and mechatronics, consisting of three control and three experimental training groups. The experiment was carried out step by step monitoring of the process of formation of research competence at the end of the third and fourth years of study. Comparative analysis of the results showed a positive trend in all indicators in the structure of research skills.
Keywords: project-oriented training, aerospace university students, efficiency of research

1 Introduction

The emergence of high-tech and science intensive industries, the dynamic growth of scientific and technical information, the creation of complex automated production systems requires the engineer a good fundamental training, the ability to quickly absorb the latest technology, the readiness to improve of facilities and means of engineering work. In this regard, the future of engineer training should be aimed at the formation of competences, focused on the development of creative thinking, inventiveness, the ability to solve research problems, skills of independent search activity.

One of the most important competencies is a research competence [1], which provides an opportunity for students with available to them the knowledge and skills to model, analyze, and transform (modify on a background of varying professional tasks) the objects of professional activities, showing the activity, the ability to make their own decisions and take responsibility for them, critically evaluate the results of their actions.

[a] Corresponding author: loginov@sibsau.ru

As a basic principle, which determines the approach to the process of forming of research competence, we used the principle of project-oriented modeling that defines the strategy for training and research activities as a system of increasingly complex simulated objects of professional activity, allowing a high degree of reliability to evaluate the objects themselves and identify their connection with other objects.

Competence is a complex system, which is based upon the three common and well-understood categories such as knowledge, abilities and skills. In our view, a separate sub-system in the structure of competence, which is a kind of an add-on knowledge and skills, is a subsystem of analysis and management of these categories in order to maintain the capacity of the knowledge according to the current state of the object of professional activity. In our understanding, the competence is formed exclusively as a result of interaction of the specialist with the real object of professional activity.

To determine the substantive content of the research competence structure is fundamentally important to proceed from the fact that it is specified in a set of interrelated personality characteristics [2], including:

– sustained motivation and high moral and ethical values;
– personal qualities (perseverance, persistence, responsibility);
– scientific, methodological and legal knowledge;
– research abilities and skills (cognitive, subject-specific, technological, communicative, organizational, design, creative);
– experience the famous and creative ways, creative methods of research.

The process of development the research competence of students should be focused on the implementation of their research and personal potential, formation of readiness for creative activity [3].

Here are the components of this process:

– Ability to organize own work, choose standard methods and ways to perform professional tasks, to assess their effectiveness and quality;
– Search and use of information necessary for the effective performance of professional tasks, professional and personal development;
– Use information and communication technologies in professional activity;
– Independently determine the problem of professional and personal development, self-education, consciously plan improvement of professional skill.

Formation of research competence involves the use of interactive teaching methods, not only in the preparation of course work, but also in the study of various disciplines during the passage educational and industrial practices, the results of which may also be submitted via electronic presentations. In demand are elective courses "Fundamentals of educational and research activities," "Search, analysis and presentation of textual information." It seems important and the involvement of students in the scientific community.

Important ways of research abilities of students are active learning methods. One of the leading places is occupied by the project method. The project-based method is the development of cognitive skills, abilities independently to use their knowledge and skills to navigate in the information space. Project-based learning requires the integration of knowledge, skills to apply knowledge from various fields of science and technology, technology and creative areas [4].

Project method is a flexible model of organization of the educational process that focuses on self-development, creative self-realization of the individual student and aiming at the formation of the research competence. Performance analysis on the formation of the research competence through project activities suggests that it provides an increase in the quality of theoretical knowledge and practical skills of students, formation of students' ability to apply research methods in the course of practice, orientation of students on creativity and autonomy.

Thus, the problem of the study is to find effective ways of forming of research competence of the future engineer on the basis of project-oriented modeling while studying at the Technical University.

The aim of the study was to investigate the efficiency of research competence formation of aerospace university students in conditions of project-oriented training.

2 Methods

To evaluate the efficiency of the system of research abilities formation a set of criterion-oriented test tasks has been developed. We used methods of pedagogical diagnostics and testing, pedagogical observation, conversation, questionnaire, statistical processing of results of experimental work and analysis.

Following research objectives have been identified:

– Study the effectiveness of research competence in a project-oriented training at university;

– Define the requirements to the educational environment which allow to effectively form the research competence of University students;

– Develop a set of research tasks, which allows students to develop research capacity and to propose a methodical approach its implementation;

– Develop criteria for evaluating the formation of research competence.

3 Results and discussion

The first stage of changes was implemented in the educational process to ensure the implementation of the principle of project-based learning.

For this purpose, the training process was implemented technology of project-oriented training of students in the form of a unique project for the development and creation of a series of student scientific-educational small satellites (Smallsat) [5]. The integrated system of training engineers for the aerospace industry using innovative technology project-based learning student is actively developing in the Siberian State Aerospace University for several years in cooperation with an industrial partner of JSC "Information Satellite Systems" (JSC «ISS»). Students from the third year take part in all stages of satellite production from the development of project documentation to the control satellite in orbit. Scheme of the project-oriented training of engineers is shown in Fig. 1.

The industrial partner of the University JSC "ISS" is a leading enterprise of the Russian space industry. The company works in all fields of satellite production – from spacecraft design to satellite flight path control at low circular and geostationary orbits.

Resource Centre of the University "Spacecraft and Systems" has been engaged in the design and assembly of a series of scientific and educational small satellites for a number of years. The project is carried out by a team of students, postgraduate students, young scientists, and specialists of JSC "ISS"; the team is also responsible for conducting scientific and technological experiments in space. The Centre's equipment enables the assembly and testing of satellite mechanical systems, electronic equipment prototyping, conducting vacuum and climate tests, researching spacecraft electronic equipment. Students take part in all stages of satellite production from the development of project documentation to the control satellite in orbit.

Implementing the project allows to identify the students who have shown their best effort and enjoyed laboratory work not only during their main curricula, but in related extracurricular activities. This experience shows that such students subsequently become the most qualified and responsible professionals.

Typically, the third, fourth, and fifth-year students simultaneously participate in the project. They specialize in the areas of aircraft control systems, rocket complexes and astronautics, geodesy and remote sensing. Students of other courses also have an opportunity to participate in the project, for example, students of marketing and high technologies management. Each student must undergo a research practice, find two research supervisors – one must be an academic staff member of the Siberian State Aerospace University; the other should be a leading specialist at JSC "ISS".

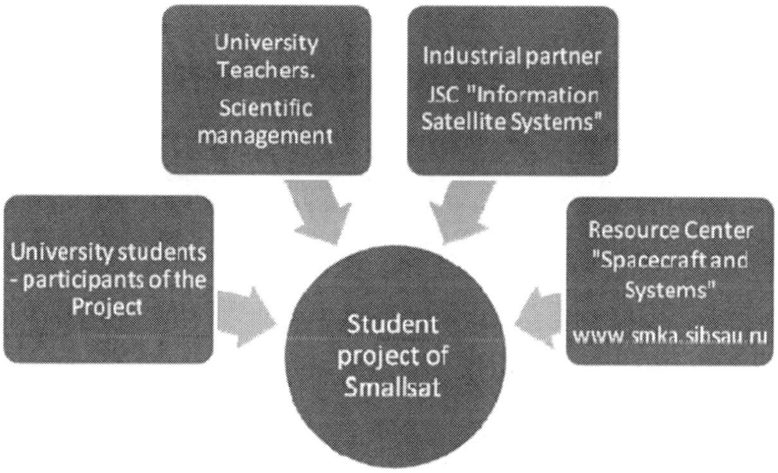

Fig. 1. Scheme of the project-oriented training of engineers

Resource Centre of the University "Spacecraft and Systems" has been engaged in the design and assembly of a series of scientific and educational small satellites for a number of years. The project is carried out by a team of students, postgraduate students, young scientists, and specialists of JSC "ISS"; the team is also responsible for conducting scientific and technological experiments in space. The Centre's equipment enables the assembly and testing of satellite mechanical systems, electronic equipment prototyping, conducting vacuum and climate tests, researching spacecraft electronic equipment. Students take part in all stages of satellite production from the development of project documentation to the control satellite in orbit.

Implementing the project allows to identify the students who have shown their best effort and enjoyed laboratory work not only during their main curricula, but in related extracurricular activities. This experience shows that such students subsequently become the most qualified and responsible professionals.

Typically, the third, fourth, and fifth-year students simultaneously participate in the project. They specialize in the areas of aircraft control systems, rocket complexes and astronautics, geodesy and remote sensing. Students of other courses also have an opportunity to participate in the project, for example, students of marketing and high technologies management. Each student must undergo a research practice, find two research supervisors – one must be an academic staff member of the Siberian State Aerospace University; the other should be a leading specialist at JSC "ISS".

The construction project of the students' satellite is divided into twelve directions. This models the number of main satellite subsystems – the thermal control subsystem, the electric power subsystem, the attitude determination and control subsystem, etc. The thirteenth direction comprises the design of payload equipment for the satellite. Further in the project, this direction is responsible for performing scientific and educational experiments in space. The scientific work of each member of the student team must be done in one of these areas. When the student accomplishes his first year on the project, he or she becomes a tutor for younger student of the same direction, sharing the acquired experience.

The final results of the student's scientific work in the selected direction, including the graduation project and diploma thesis, is the design and manufacturing of a functional satellite component or constructional element. This part will be installed inside an actual satellite, which will be then launched into space. The telemetry data from this device will be received and processed at the University's Satellite Control Center. After the defense of the diploma project the student is qualified for employment at JSC "ISS". He will be working with their scientific adviser at the same department. This ensures the student has already got a significant background and experience in practical design. Simultaneously, the graduates also can continue their studies in postgraduate course at University.

A specialized internet-portal has been developed at www.smka.sibsau.ru along with a projects management system for project monitoring. This enables the remote coordination of joint projects between different higher education facilities, bringing together students from different cities.

Technology project-based learning provides high quality training, ensures graduates a competitive advantage in the labor market and their effective work in the industry and other high-tech enterprises. Typically, to the end of training most of the graduates are employed on the profile of obtained specialty. The high level of preparation is also confirmed by team and individual prizes, regularly won by University students in contests and competitions on different disciplines, such as theoretical mechanics, strength of materials, programming, computer graphics, information technology security and management.

Direct involvement of students in practical works on designing, manufacturing, testing, preparation for launch and flight control of scientific and educational satellites significantly increases the level of training and developing research competence. The practical experience gained by students in the course of work on the creation of university satellites, significantly reduces the time of their adaptation to the implementation of specific production problems at the enterprises of space industry and the formation of young professional as an authoritative member of the labor collectives.

Great importance in the formation of research competences for our study had a control and evaluation of students' achievements. To assess the effectiveness of the system of formation of research competencies a set of criterion-oriented test tasks was developed. The study was carried out on the basis of the Siberian State Aerospace University.

In the experiment, was attended by 130 students of the Institute of mechanical engineering and mechatronics, consisting of three control and three experimental training groups of the third and then the fourth years.

During the training were held extra classes, which clarified the nature of research competence and the role of scientific and research activities, as well as to focus attention on the need for the formation of research competence, taking into account the specifics and problems of further professional activities.

In the fourth year of study in the design of research tasks main target setting has been made to maximize the autonomy of research activities, enabling learners to assess their research capabilities, thus learn to maintain cognitive component of future professional activity at the required level.

The experiment was carried out step by step monitoring of the process of formation of research competence at the end of the third and fourth years of study. Monitoring was carried out in three main features: the ability of planning, analysis and control, and readiness to study.

Figure 2 shows the results of analysis of formation of research competence in the course of monitoring on three main signs.

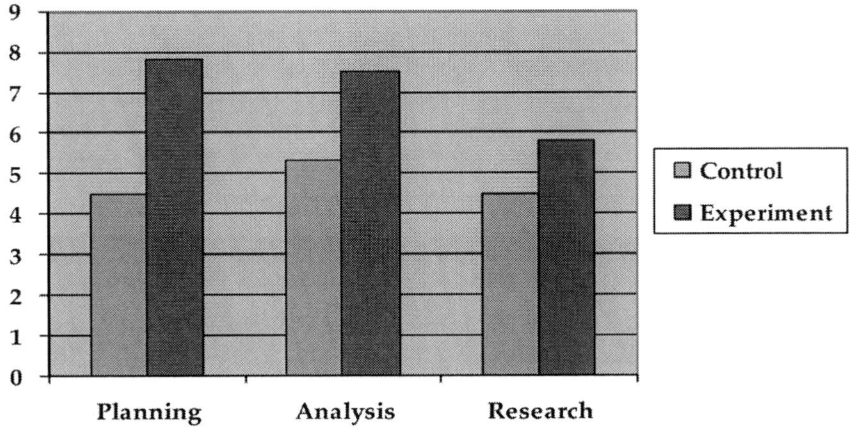

Fig. 2. Signs of research competence in students of the control and experimental groups at the end of the fourth year (averages on a ten-point scale)

Figure 2 shows that the experimental groups all signs observed excess values compared to the control groups.

Monitoring of the process of formation of research competence at the end of the fourth year showed that students of experimental groups have formed an idea about the study as a holistic event, containing planning, organizational-control and analytical components.

Comparative analysis of the results showed a positive trend in all indicators in the structure of research skills. So, the organization of proposed a package of measures within the framework of educational programs for the design and mathematical modeling have provided not only introduction to the scientific work and the implementation of the project, but also a significant increase in the level of work. For the formation of skills necessary for research the performance of works containing elements of research were included. Students received knowledge and skills the research orientation, which influenced the attitude to the profession, led to realize the necessity of mathematical methods development for future professional activities.

It was found that the percentage of students who meet the criteria of formation of research competence, according to experts in the control groups was 28%, while in the experimental group, the figure was 46%. It should be noted that in the experimental groups were the students with the research competencies are not only general and applied, but also of a professional nature. The percentage of students who have research competencies of applied nature in the experimental groups is significantly higher (15%) compared with the control groups (5.8%).

Implementation of student research and participation in research projects influenced the development of the intuition and the ability to assess compliance with the outcome predetermined benchmark requirements. Appeared ability to organize information and make generalizing conclusions, think logically.

Here are the main components of the method of project-based learning that allows arranging the research competence of technical universities students:

DOI: 10.1051/shsconf/20173701027

– Creating a space of interaction of the teacher and the student, allowing the student to take the most favorable model of professional activity and exercise early professional self-determination;

– Provision of student development opportunities in terms of competency, namely, in the formation and development of the components of the subsystem analysis and management as part of the student's competence;

– Creation of a clear understanding of students about the subjects and occupations;

– Possibility of versatile modeling of objects of professional activity.

Developed and experimentally tested structural and logical model of the student's research competence formation assumes prerequisites for further improvements, which are primarily seen in the development of technologies of the student's research competence formation, allowing carrying out this process on a more high organizational and methodological level.

4 Conclusions

Created and tested the educational environment in the form of project-based learning that allows to effectively generating research competence in students, the most favorable way to perceive the professional activity and exercise early professional self-determination. Technology of project-based learning ensures the development of research competencies, the high quality of the training of engineers, ensures graduates a competitive advantage in the labor market and their effective work at the industrial enterprises.

Experimental verification of the results of the study using a phased monitoring showed the effectiveness of the developed structural-logical model of the research competence formation of Aerospace University students.

As a part of general professional and special disciplines have been developed a set of research tasks of varying complexity, focused on the individual approach to the student, to unleash the research potential and show the ability of students to independent study of real and simulated objects of professional activity.

The practical significance of the study lies in the fact that the implemented project-oriented learning method allows to generate the research competence of students as the basis of professional competence of the future specialist.

References

1. A. A. Chervova, I. A. Yanyuk, Formation of research abilities of students of high schools. *Science and School*, Moscow: MSPU, **6**, 11-14 (2007)
2. Y. A. Komarova, Research competence of specialists: functional and informative description. Proceedings of the Russian State Pedagogical University. St. Petersburg, **11** (68), 69-77 (2008)
3. E. N. Lekomtseva, Scientific research competence of bachelor. Yaroslavl Pedagogical Gazette. **3**, 92-96 (2009)
4. E.S. Polat. Method of projects. Electronic resource // http //: wiki.iteach.ru (2003)
5. I. V. Kovalev, Y. Y. Loginov, P.V. Zelenkov, An integrated system of training engineers for aerospace industry in Siberia using innovative technology of the student project-and-team work. Procedia – Social and Behavioral Sciences, **174**, 537-543 (2015)

Incorporation of computational creativity in arts education: Creative coding as an art course

Selcuk Artut[1a]

[1]Visual Arts and Visual Communication Design, Sabancı University, Istanbul, Turkey

Abstract. In the lights of the Information Renaissance, like the unavoidable transformation of everyday practices, contemporary educational perspectives and principles are going through a state of change. Recently, the proliferation of computer aided art education is widening its doors, because the contemporary artists are using computers not only as an assistive apparatus, but as a collaborative platform to infiltrate far beyond their imaginations and expressions. Therefore, the notion of creativity cannot be limited only to a human-centred approach, rather there is a significant need for discussing the discourse of dialectic creativity that embodies human technology collaborations. In this article, Computational Creativity is explored as an educational content for contemporary arts education with its implications and its various dimensions in the creative thinking process. In this study, a new course content called Creative Coding which is included in the curriculum of Sabanci University, Istanbul is explored as a proposed model to shed lights on the Computational Creativity. The course content and its methodologies will be explained while examining the technological dimensions in the art education.
Keywords: creativity, creative coding, arts education

1 Introduction

Art stands as one of the oldest phenomena on earth with its ambiguous nature full of uncertainties. Its underpinnings and origins are concealed in the history of civilization. Therefore, emphasizing the history of art and its evolution in time becomes an essential component in comprehensive arts education. However, by its nature history evolves and it never suspends. When history takes over the contemporary, the establishment debate initiates itself. During addressing an art student to enhance his/her knowledge and skills with educational materials, it is certain that the content also needs to be adjusted to the changes occurring in the contemporary society. When art is observed in different periods of time, it is inevitable that its discourse has been considerably influenced by the social movements and technological developments. Especially after the modern period in art, art is walking close hand in hand with the latest technological advancements in various

[a] Corresponding author: sartut@sabanciuniv.edu

dimensions including kinetic art, video art, computer art etc. Several contemporary artists, whose numbers are notably increasing day by day, are creating unique art works with using new possibilities provided by technology.

Because of the Information Renaissance, with the use of Internet, we are exposed to a proliferation of information from various dimensions. Currently education systems are undertaking a structural transformation while considering the changing role of the educator as the primary source of influence. In this technological climate, to what extent should the art students be educated in this kind of technological exposition? How should the computational creativity be integrated in art education as a new apparatus to make distinct forms of art?

Today artists are not only using technology as an apparatus to enhance their artistic expressions, but to explore hidden dimensions in the formalization of art [1]. According to Flusser [2] we are going through a post-historical age with the extensive inclusion of Technical Images. As opposed to traditional paintings, by technical images Flusser includes works of photograph, films, videos, television screens and computer terminals of which all belong to a certain technological progress and innovation in recent history. These new forms of technological art disciplines have been widely acknowledged and utilized by the art scholars; therefore, the art education based on these disciplines have also been welcomed in art schools to a notable extent. While examining the contemporary methods in art education, the core subject of the ontological definition of art should be reconsidered under the existing conditions. We also need to address questions towards the role of the artist in the creativity process while using technological apparatuses.

2 Exposition of computational art

The computers become widely available to masses in the 1980s and onwards [3]. Back then there was a limited group of engineers and scientists who became experts in computer programming and their main purpose was to be dealing with solving complex problems in their field of expertise. In the following years when game industry was to take a leap towards becoming a powerful attraction for the computer users, computers became a medium of interest for expressing art into digital forms. Many game developers started to not only focusing on the game logic but also interested in building visually appealing elements. However, the game industry can be considered only as one component of the related influences on computational art. Additionally we may include some procedural art making examples in the forms of performance art, music, painting etc. that are taking place in the 1950s and onwards. As an example, in Alvin Lucier's famous performance (1969) "I am sitting in a room" we are observing Lucier to repeatedly recording himself inside a studio while replaying the previous recording of himself. This performance illustrates a recursive structure which is widely observed in most computational art pieces. In the same manner, recursive algorithms are widely observed in Computer Programming implementations such as fractals, l-tree systems, etc. [4]. Likewise, some computer programmers were interested in creating algorithms that would simulate and replicate a form of nature in a programming environment, and some contemporary artists were also significantly influenced by these automatic creative skills built by computational operations. Even though it is not possible to track the earliest, Frieder Nake, Manfred Mohr, George Nees, John Whitney are regarded as early pioneers in digital computer art who were exhibiting their art pieces in acknowledges venues. According to Francesca Franco, computer art was introduced in the mid-1950s to early 1960s as a mainstream genre [5, 6]. Individual examples of using digital computers and programming to create works of art may follow, but Cybernetic Serendipity exhibition that took place at the Institute of Contemporary Arts (ICA) in London (1968) would be considered as one of the early examples for a group show that gathers several artists who are affiliated with the use of computation in their creation of artworks.

With the influence of Information Renaissance, computational forms have been inserted in the traditional art forms. Therefore, some main art attractions such as biennials, art fairs and museums such as Art Basel, Art Hong Kong have started to welcome art works with computation influences. Alternatively, we may also observe the new formation of art foundations and events focusing around the theme of computational creativity with announcing names such as Computer Art, New Media, Electronic Arts, Media Arts etc. Here below is a brief list of most well-known events organized around the idea of computational art forms:

Table 1. Acknowledged computational art events, festivals and exhibitions.

Name of the Event	Location
ISEA International Symposium on Electronic Art	in various countries
Prix Art Electronica	Austria
Kikk Festival	Belgium
Enter Festival	Czech Republic
Transmediale	Germany
Dutch Electronic Art Festival	The Netherlands
Resonate	Serbia
Sonar	Spain
One dot Zero	UK
File	Brazil
Sight and Sound	Canada
New York Electronic Arts Festival	USA
Japan Media Arts Festival	Japan

When art is to be integrated with technological factors, physicality of art needs to be reconsidered within the limits of its reflections. For instance, if the art considered reflects its properties in the digital realm with using software only, it becomes immaterial to a certain degree. The artworks' exhibiting standards are to be reconsidered as well. According to Xiaobo [7] when we are talking about an interaction between a human and a system three aesthetic criteria needs to be elaborated; 1) Addressing to all senses, not only visually 2) Extension of Temporal Relations 3) Comprehensive Experience. As a result, if we are to be introducing use of technology or to be more specific use of computation, the traditional frameworks in art education needs to be reconsidered extensively.

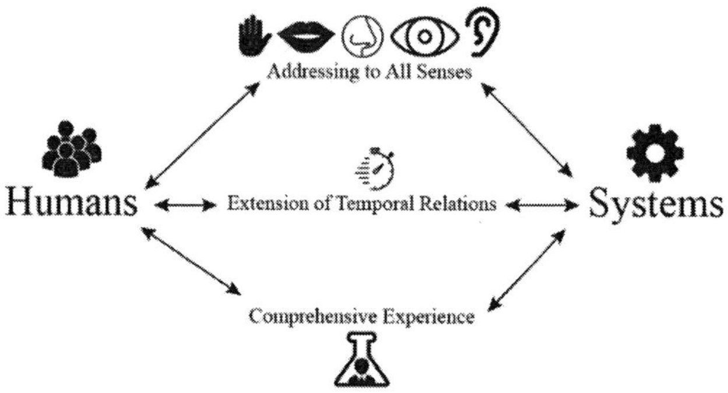

Fig. 1. Xiabo's interaction framework between a human and a system

3 Teaching computational skills for art students

In the recent years, there has been a wide interest in building interdisciplinary curriculums in the education programs. According to World Economic Forum's Report [8] on 10 skills you need to thrive in the Fourth Industrial Revolution, "Creativity" has been listed as the 10th in year 2015, successively "Creativity" has been listed as the 3rd for the year 2020. One aspect of such a need is that the new generations are heavily bombarded with technological tools, and computer becomes a common ground to integrate multiple skills in a single environment. Therefore, we have turned out to be rapid task switchers or multitaskers while working on our engagements. Students have eager to explore various interests and a standardized education system has difficulties in accommodating these demands. Same issues would be addressed to art education as well. Using computational skills in the process of art making is a contemporary issue. However, there is an increasing interest in teaching computational creativity skills in various schools of visual art, music, design and architecture [9]. Furthermore, creativity is not only treated as a means of human only production.

When Sabanci University in Istanbul was established in 1994 its philosophy was based on adopting an interdisciplinary approach of "learning to learn" to cultivate knowledge, support education and facilitate social advancement [10]. In the same manner, Visual Arts and Visual Communication Programme offers interdisciplinary courses to students from various disciplines including humanities and arts, social sciences, and natural sciences. Therefore, class environment becomes a medium where people from different interests are met and new explorations are to be foreseen. In this article, a new course opening titled VA345 Creative Coding is to be introduced and its content will be elaborated below.

4 Building a creative coding course

VA345 Creative Coding course explores code at a conceptual level with the aim of using computation as an expressive and creative tool. It addresses topics such as generative audio-visuals, computational art, scripting for common media tools. The structure is based on experiential learning with utilizing projects on themes. Students who have backgrounds and needs from various disciplines are treated equivalent in terms of their abilities and skills. Here below is the weekly course content;

Table 2. VA345 Creative Coding Weekly Contents.

Teaching Period	Course Content
Week 1	Introduction, Course Objectives, Students' Expectations
Week 2	Automatons
Week 3	Algorithmic Forms in Art
Week 4	Processing.org Programming Platform
Week 5	Conditions, Iteration, Looping
Week 6	Arrays, Lists, Classes
Week 7	Midterm Project
Week 8	Typographical Design by Coding
Week 9	Fractals / L-Tree Systems / Recursions
Week 10	Particle Systems
Week 11	Playing with Sound
Week 12	Computer Vision
Week 13	Exhibition Production
Week 14	Exhibition Production

VA 345 Creative Coding assumes coding not only as a programming paradigm on a flat screen, but rather it aspires to explore computational thinking in all reflections including even building physical systems with no use of computer at all. Each week a new Computational Artist's artworks are brought to class to familiarize students with contemporary examples. Works of artists such as Joshua Davis, Aaron Koblin, Casey Reas, Sougwen Choung, Joachim Sauter, Theo Jansen, Karsten Schmidt, Golan Levin and Alexandor Randon will be discussed during the class hours. As an introduction finding a proper definition for Creativity is examined, thus following questions would arise including "How do we incorporate creativity in computational disciplines?". To establish strong links to find out these inquiries, a history of Computational Arts is studied with watching Casey Reas' Gray Area Festival presentation "History of the Future, Art & Technology from 1965 – Yesterday". Second week focuses on Automatons as self-operating systems. Since automatons are built to be following calculated set of rules to succeed an operation, their systems are of interest for analysing the determination of a procedure to be utilized. History of Automatons is introduced by screening "Pierre Jacquet-Droz's Androids" documentary. Mark Sussman describes automatons as dramaturgical hybrid of theatre, magic, and science, similarly the subject is an essential component of how a mental labour is transformed into a mechanization [11]. To exemplify the creative process behind the automatons, the students are given a automaton project to be built with use of simple cardboards and handcraft tools. Next theme in the course content is Algorithmic Forms in Art. During this week students are introduced to several examples of how algorithm turns ideas into complex, abstract visuals. Even though examples presented will be outcomes of programming frameworks, the students will still not be introduced to computer programming environments until the fourth week. On the contrary, the students will be required to build a mechanical Harmonograph with use of wooden structures. With the use of oscillations in its movements, Harmonograph creates complex geometric images. In week 4, students are introduced to gain basic programming skills with the use of Processing Programming Framework. Processing embodies software paradigms to handle creation of visual form, motion and interaction [12].

Fig. 2. First steps in building a computational system

When basic insight is introduced, students will be motivated to construct more complex projects with the use of Loops, Iterations, Arrays, Lists and Conditionals. Next in the agenda typographic elements will be explored and an assignment based on building a design project will be provided. Students will be informed to learn the main principles and properties that construct a type-face so that they would be able to deconstruct and construct experimental approaches to accomplish artistic tasks. Later in the course Fractals, L-Tree Systems will be studied as a recursive approach towards creating complex forms with the use of simpler ideas. In week 10, the particle systems are elaborated with discussions evolving around multiplication and pattern registration. Basic sound use is included to facilitate students to experiment with use of sound via computational frameworks. Finally, how computers perceive the world with use of image processing is investigated with computer vision theories. As a result, participants will be able to use basic image processing skills such as motion detection, skeleton tracking, blob detection to hunt for ideas to create artistic projects. At the end of the course, a collective art exhibition project is organized to have the participants experience the process of exhibit preparation and display their artworks.

5 Conclusion

Computational Art has driven the art educators to question possible uses of computers in the arts. Even though artistic pieces have a certain kind of aesthetic framework, recently extensive use of technology has been enrolled as a major factor in determining the new aesthetical formations in solidifying artistic ideas into shapes and forms. In the light of all these discussions, an adaptive education system based on experiencing computational skills in art making needs to be considered in various dimensions. In this article, VA345 Creative Coding course has been exposed as an effort to examine the barriers and opportunities between art and computational sciences. Students participating this course will not only be acknowledging the field as a contemporary development to be aware of, but to gain experience in the making of the art projects.

References

1. Truckenbrod, J., *A New Language for Artistic Expression: The Electronic Arts Landscape*. Leonardo **21**(5) 99-102, (1988)
2. Flusser, V., *Into the universe of technical images*. **32**. U of Minnesota Press, 2011.
3. King, R. G., *Computer graphics and animation as agents of personal evolution in the arts*. Leonardo. Supplemental Issue 43-46, (1988)
4. Saupe, D., *Algorithms for random fractals*. The science of fractal images. Springer New York, 71-136, (1988).
5. Franco, F., *Computational art exhibitions in London*, 2014: A New Hope." Visual Resources **31**(3-4) 201-210, (2015)
6. Prince, P. D., *The Aesthetics of Exhibition: A Discussion of Recent American Computer Art Shows*. Leonardo **21**(5) 81-88, (1988)
7. Xiaobo, L., and Liu Y., *Embodiment, Interaction and Experience: Aesthetic Trends in Interactive Media Arts*. Leonardo **47**(2) 166-169, (2014)
8. https://www.weforum.org/agenda/2016/01/the-10-skills-you-need-to-thrive-in-the-fourth-industrial-revolution/ (Retrieved 14.05.2017)
9. Bergstrom, I., and R. Beau Lotto, *Code Bending: A new creative coding practice*. Leonardo (2015).
10. http://www.sabanciuniv.edu/en/about-sabanci/philosophy (Retrieved 14.05.2017)
11. Nake, F., and Susanne G., *Human–computer interaction viewed as pseudo-communication*. Knowledge-Based Systems **14**(8) 441-447, (2001)
12. Reas, C., and Fry, B., *Processing: a programming handbook for visual designers and artists*. No. 6812. Mit Press, (2007).

Studying hand grip strength development among students who have taken tennis and massage courses

Mustafa Said Erzeybek[1a], Fatih Kaya[2], Oğuzhan Yüksel[1], M.Barış Karavelioğu[1], Halit Harmancı [1], and Adnan Ersoy[1]

[1] Department of Physical Education and Sport, Dumlupınar University, Kütahya, Turkey
[2] Department of Physical Education and Sport, Faculty of Education, Erzincan University, Erzincan, Turkey

Abstract. In this study, the finger and hand force developments of the students who have taken selective/applied Tennis and Massage courses at the University have been examined. From the students of the Department of Physical Education and Sport, 19 healthy females and 73 healthy males (age = 21.25 ± 1.55 years (average ± SD) who have taken selective Tennis courses;51 healthy males (age = 22.00 ± 1.04 years (average ± SD) who have taken Massage courses; and as the control group,16 healthy womenand50 healthy males(age = 21.72 ± 1.47 years (average ± SD) have been participated to the study. The age, length, body weight, grip strength of both hands as well as the finger grip strength of the subjects have been recorded. The course schedule has been set as once a week four hours practice for both tennis and massage. Two weeks of the education and training program that takes twelve weeks in total were assigned for theoretical classes. The remaining period of ten weeks was for practice classes and the measurements were performed before and after this ten weeks period. The hand grip strength measurement has been carried out with a Takkei branded hand dynamometer whereas for the measurement of the finger grip strength, a Baseline branded pinch meter has been used .For both the pre-test and final test of the finger grip and hand grip strength measurements, the paired sample t test has been used in terms of in-group comparisons, whereas for the inter-group comparisons, one-way ANOVA has been used. For the significant F values, post hoc Tukey test has been used. The right hand and the left hand grip values of both test groups as well as the values of the control group have been significantly increased between the pre-test and final test. Particularly, preferring the exercises that improve the hand and finger grip strengths would enable a better racket handle grip as well as an improved shot efficiency for tennis. This would also enable masseurs/masseuses to apply an efficient massage therapy with higher pressure.
Keywords: hand grip strength, tennis course, massage course

[a]Corresponding author: msaid.erzeybek@dpu.edu.tr

1 Introduction

The hand skills are listed as follows according to the difficulty level: Gripping, Rolling, Throwing, Catching and Shotting. The hand is the most important component affecting the functionality of the upper extremity. Among the hand functions, gripping is an important factor for the continuity of the daily life activities [1]. Accordingly, the gripping strength is accepted as an objective measurement with regard to the evaluation of the upper extremity performance [2].The conducted studies have shown that the hand grip strength, besides being correlated with the muscle strength of the upper extremity, is also related with the overall body muscle strength [3].

It has been indicated that the fore arm volume, fore arm length, fore arm perimeter, hand sizes, age, Body Mass Index (BMI) as well as length are the estimation indicators of the hand grip strength [4]. The massage therapy is used to relieve the pain, to take down the swelling in a certain area, to relax the muscles, to accelerate the recovery of the strain and sprain resulted from injury and it is applied through manual manipulations. The masseurs/masseuses shall regularly practice in order to be able to use both hands with the same ability. S/he would be more efficient if s/he succeeds to use both right and left hands with equal skills. The masseur/masseuse would feel less tired personally. Currently, tennis is an olympic sport branch adopted by the civilized world that is exciting for the players and both exciting and admirable for the audience. This sport branch comprising both aerobic and anaerobic loads is also a performance sport that requires good biomotor skills such as strength, speed, endurance, flexibility and coordination [10, 11]. For an efficient shotting, all physical fitness parameters of a tennis player shall be at the top level. Tennis is an individual sport where the players do not contact each other and the game is based on the fast spins, fast arm movements, jumps and moves [12, 13, 14].

Tennis requires high aerobic and anaerobic strength, but also the muscles generating the strength shall be strong [15, 16].The most striking aspect of tennis education is to define the most appropriate working schedule for the athlete, to apply this schedule at the optimum level and consequently to obtain maximum performance [5]. At the tennis serve; the fine motor skills improve with the use of the Fore hand, Backhand, angle volleys, lob shot or other techniques' variations. With regard to the physical capacities, tennis improves strength, power, anaerobic performance, flexibility, agility as well as all coordination and conditional skills. These developmental characteristics of the children should be considered when planning their training programs [5].

2 Method

The study has covered 51 male students who have taken Massage courses, 19 female and 73 male students who have taken Tennis courses from Dumlupınar University, Department of Physical Education and Sport. The control group has consisted of 50 males and 16 females. This research is based on pre-test and final test approach. Nineteen healthy female and seventy three healthy male students (age = 21.25 ± 1.55 years (average ± SD) who have taken the tennis courses; and fifty one healthy male students (age = 22.00 ± 1.04 years (average ± SD) who have taken the massage courses have been participated to this study carried out within the Department of Physical Education and Sport, and the control group comprised of sixteen healthy female and healthy fifty male students (age = 21.72 ± 1.47 years (average ± SD).

The age, length, body weight, hand and finger grip strength of the subjects have been recorded. The course schedule has been set as once a week, four hours practice for both tennis and massage. Two weeks of the education and training program that takes twelve weeks in total were assigned for the theoretical classes. The remaining period of ten weeks was for practice classes and the measurements were performed before and after this ten weeks period. The hand grip strength measurement has been carried out with a Takkei branded hand dynamometer whereas for the measurement of the finger grip strength, a Baseline branded pinch meter has been used. The measurements of the athletes have been repeated twice and the average values have been used.

3 Results

Table 1. The variations in the finger and hand grip strength between pre-test and final test

Grup		Mean	Std. Deviation	t	sd	p
Tenis n=92	pinch_sağ_ön	9.54	2.60	-9.037	91	.000
	pinch_sağ_son	10.15	2.37			
	pinch_sol_ön	8.47	2.37	-7.530	91	.000
	picnh_sol_son	9.06	2.33			
	hadgrip_sağ_ön	51.41	5.71	-8.610	91	.000
	hadgrip_sağ_son	53.24	5.66			
	handgrip_sol_ön	47.32	5.52	-9.068	91	.000
	handgrip_sol_son	48.80	5.53			
Masaj n=51	pich_sağ_ön	11.74	2.30	-6.941	50	.000
	pinch_sağ_son	13.19	1.98			
	pinch_sol_ön	10.71	2.31	-7.068	50	.000
	picnh_sol_son	11.59	1.89			
	hadgrip_sağ_ön	54.12	3.41	-5.924	50	.000
	hadgrip_sağ_son	55.57	3.28			
	handgrip_sol_ön	51.26	3.05	-4.299	50	.000
	handgrip_sol_son	52.35	2.80			
Kontrol n=66	pich_sağ_ön	8.12	1.67	-17.186	65	.000
	pinch_sağ_son	8.87	1.76			
	pinch_sol_ön	7.20	1.84	-5.174	65	.000
	picnh_sol_son	7.80	1.85			
	hadgrip_sağ_ön	49.56	7.53	-7.860	65	.000
	hadgrip_sağ_son	51.67	7.85			
	handgrip_sol_ön	45.53	7.21	-7.417	65	.000
	handgrip_sol_son	47.07	6.98			

For both the pre-test and final test of the finger grip and hand grip strength measurements, the paired sample t test has been used in terms of in-group comparisons, whereas for the inter-group comparisons, one-way ANOVA has been used. For the significant F values, post hoc Tukey test has been used. Average and standard deviation have been used for all variables. The significance level has been set as $p \leq 0.05$.

The right hand and the left hand pinch values of both test groups as well as the values of the control group have been significantly increased between the pre-test and final test($p<0.05$). The right hand and the left hand grip values of both test groups as well as the values of the control group have been significantly increased between the pre-test and final test ($p<0.05$).

Table 2. The difference in the finger and hand grip variations between the groups

		Sum of Squares	df	Mean Square	F	Sig.
pincright_diff	Between Groups	23.913	2	11.956	15.671	.000
	Within Groups	157.175	206	.763		
	Total	181.088	208			
pinchleft_diff	Between Groups	3.177	2	1.588	2.202	.113
	Within Groups	148.607	206	.721		
	Total	151.784	208			
handright_diff	Between Groups	12.515	2	6.258	1.542	.216
	Within Groups	835.892	206	4.058		
	Total	848.407	208			
handleft_diff	Between Groups	6.732	2	3.366	217	.298
	Within Groups	569.628	206	2.765		
	Total	576.360	208			

The variations in the right hand pinch values were significant between the groups [$F(2, 208)=15.671$, $p<0.05$)], whereas the variations in the left hand pinch values were similar between the groups [($F(2, 208)=2.202$, $p>0.05$)]. The post hoc analysis has revealed that the significant difference is between the tennis and massage group ($p<0.05$), and between the massage and control group ($p<0.05$).Accordingly, the improvement in the massage group is higher compared to the tennis and control groups. The variations in the right hand and left hand grip values are similar between the groups [(sırasıyla $F(2, 208)=1.542$, $p>0.05$); $F(2, 208)=1.217$, $p>0.05$)].

4 Conclusion

Mostly, the thumb helps to perform the functional capacity and fine hand skills. A study by Peterson et al. has shown that the dominant hand's grip strength is 10% higher than the grip strength of the non-dominant hand. The 10% rule revealed by Peterson et al. is only valid for those people using their right hands dominantly whereas for those people with dominant left hand, the grip strength of both hands are equal [7].

Hand grip strength is very important in terms of carrying out most of the daily life activities. Mostly, the thumb helps to perform the functional capacity and fine hand skills. Another study regarding tennis, has revealed that playing tennis during a single academic term improves significantly the strength values as well as the forehand, backhand and serve speed of the male and female students using either right or left hands. It has been reported that the dominant hand or gender has no effect on these improvements [6]. For the generation of the isometric strength during gripping, the participation of the wrist extensors is necessary. Similar to the hand grip strength, the finger grip strength also indicates the efficiency of the hand functions [8].

In another study carried out about message therapy, it has been reported that among the manipulations carried out with both hands, particularly friction (circular movements; generally carried out with fingers) and petrissage (kneading; generally carried out with palm) improve the strength and that accordingly, giving massage regularly improves the hand and finger grip strength [9].The hand grip strength is very important for carrying out most of the daily life activities. Mostly, the thumb helps to perform the functional capacity and fine hand skills. In terms of human subjects, particularly for the young age groups, giving massage, tennis or other specific strength trainings in different branches should be correlated with the strength improvement. Particularly, preferring the exercises that improve the hand and finger grip strengths would enable a better racket handle grip as well as an improved shot efficiency for tennis. This would also enable masseurs/masseuses to apply an efficient massage therapy with higher pressure. Although giving massage regularly or playing tennis improve the finger and hand grip strength, in order to obtain significant improvement in the control group, specific strength trainings are needed for this type of branches.

In terms of human subjects, particularly for the young age groups, giving massage, tennis or other specific strength trainings in different branches should be correlated with the strength improvement. The right hand and the left hand grip values as well as the right hand and left hand pinch values of both test groups as well as the values of the control group have been significantly increased between the pre-test and final test. Particularly, preferring the exercises that improve the hand and finger grip strengths would enable a better racket handle grip as well as an improved shot efficiency for tennis.

References

1. Nicolay CW, Walker AL. Grip strength and endurance: Influences of anthropometric variation, hand dominance, and gender. Int J Ind Ergon **35**, 605-618, (2005)
2. Gabriel YF Ng, Andy CCF. Does elbow position affect strength and reproducibility of power grip measurements? Physiotherapy **87**, 68-72, (2001)
3. Sahin G, Ulubas B, Calikoglu M, Erdoğan C. Handgrip strength, pulmonary function tests, and pulmonary muscle strength in fibromyalgia syndrome: is there any relationship? South Med J **97**, 25–29, (2004)
4. Charles LE, Burchfiel CM, Fekedulegn D et al. Occupational and other risk factors for hand-grip strength: the Honolulu-Asia Aging Study. Occup Environ Med **63**, 820-827, (2006)
5. http://www.ttf.org.tr/tenis-eğitimi (Erişim Tarihi: 08.05.2017)
6. Erzeybek, M.S., Kaya, F., Eynur, R.B., Yildiz, S., Önen, M.E.The Investigatıon Of The Impact Of Hand Preference On The Servıce, Forehand And Backhand Hıttıng Speed And Strength Parametersamong Students Taking Tennıs Training At Unıversıty 19th Annual Congress Of The European College Of Sport Scıence, Amsterdam – The Netherlands e-poster PP-UD01 p. 721, 2nd - 5th July (2014)

7. Peterson P, Petrick M, Connor H, Conklin D. Grip strength and hand dominance: challenging the 10% rule. Am J Occup Ther
8. Sahin G, Ulubas B, Calikoglu M, Erdoğan C. Handgrip strength, pulmonary function tests, and pulmonary muscle strength in fibromyalgia syndrome: is there any relationship? South Med J **97**, 25–29, 2004
9. M.S.Erzeybek, F.Kaya, O.Yüksel ·Masaj Dersi Seçmiş Öğrencilerin El Kavrama ve Parmak kuvvetlerinin Masaj Manipulasyonlarından Friksiyon ve Pedrisaj Üzerine Etkisinin İncelenmesi, SHS Web Conference (2016)
10. Ferrauti A, Maier P., Weber K. Temlistraining., Meyer und Meyer Verlag, s.11-25,121-138,185-199, (2002).
11. Kermen O. Tenis Teknik ve Taktikleri. Ed: B. Yavuz, s. 42-50, Aşama Matbacılık, İstanbul, (1997).
12. Chu D.A: Power Tenis Training., Human Kinetics Champaign, p. 7-15, 3345, (1995).
13. Gullikson T. Teniste Fiziksel Uygunluk Testleri (Çev. Yavuz Yarsuvat B.),Spor Araştırmaları Dergisi, Cilt **7**, Sayı 1, s.135-156, (2003).
14. Weber K. Tenis-Fitness., BLV Verlagsgesellschaft, s. 58-68, (1982).
15. Ferrauti, A., Maier, P., and Weber, K. "Tennistraining", Meyer und Meyer Verlag, ss:11-25, 121-138, 185-199, (2002).
16. Zorba, E. "Herkes İçin Spor ve Fiziksel Uygunluk", GSGMYayınları, no:149, ss:96-159, 324-443, Ankara, (1993)

DOI: 10.1051/shsconf/20173701030

Evaluation of some physical and motoric characteristics of athletes with down syndrome

Mehmet Ilkım[1], Mehmet Özdemir[2], and Halil Tanır[3a]

[1] Physical Education and Sport High School, Inonu University, Turkey.
[2] Physical Education and Sport High School, Bingöl University, Turkey.
[3] Physical Education and Sport High School, Adnan Menderes University, Turkey.

Abstract. The aim of this study was to evaluate some physical and motoric characteristics of Down's syndrome athletes. The sample of the study consists of 60 athletes (n=30 experimetal group and n=30 control group) who are in the Malatya Sessiz Adımlar Sports Club, aged between 13 and 15. Athletes in the experimental group were subjected to a training program to improve the balance and flexibility of 2 hours of 3 days a week for 8 weeks. The athletes, in the control group continued their usual training programs. Before and after the 8-week training program that is applicated for the athletes in the experimental group, the balance and flexibility performances of the athletes in both the experimental and control groups were determined. It was used the flamingo balance test to determine the balance performance of the athletes; was used Sit & Reach test to determine flexibility performance. In favor of the athletes who are in experimental group a statistically significant difference ($p<0.05$) obtained between pre-test and post-test results that is applicated to determine the balance performance from statistical analysis however no statistically significant difference ($p>0.05$) obtained between pre-test and post-test results that is applicated to determine the flexibility performance. It was also found that there was no relationship ($p>0.05$) between the BMI values of the athletes and their balance and flexibility performances. In the study, it was found that the training program for 8 week training to improve balance and flexibility that was applied to dealing with athleticism 13-15 age group athletes with down syndrome improved the athletes' balance performance but did not contribute to the their improvement of flexibility performances.
Key Words: Down syndrome, balance, flexibilty, BMI

1 Introduction

Down syndrome (DS) is one of the most common genetic anomalies that result from chromosome 21 being one more than the normal number (trizomi 21) and which cause mental retardation, immunodeficiency, and congenital heart disease and observed in approximately 700 live births. One of the most common causes of Down syndrome is the problem in the separation of homologous chromosomes in meiosis (nondisjunction).

The non-cleavage event on chromosome 21 occurs largely during oogenesis, and thus the source of abnormal gametes in DS is usually egg cells [1].

[a]Corresponding author:halil.tanir@adu.edu.tr

When individuals with Down's syndrome are compared [5] with the general population, functional disorders may be seen in motor performance due to differences in cerebellum [4].Children with Down's syndrome can achieve postural control disorders through symmetrical activities. Coordinative skills can be developed with an appropriate therapeutic program. Thus, postural reactions, head, central region, and excretes of control can be provided [9]. Participation in competition-based activity programs for Down's syndrome athletes may contribute to their physical and metabolic development, gaining self-confidence and social development [3]. For this reason, it is important that the training program to improve the 8-week flexibility and balance performance of the 13-15 year old group who are dealing with athleticism not only can contributes to the development of motor skills in down syndrome individuals but also their the adaptation of daily life.

2 Methot

2.1 Participations

The sample of the study consists of 60 athletes (n=30 experimental group and n=30 control group) in the Malatya Sessiz Adımlar Sports Club, aged between 13 and 15, dealing with athleticism. Athletes in the experimental group were subjected to a training program to improve the balance and flexibility of 2 hours of 3 days a week for 8 weeks. The athletes in the control group continued their usual training programs. Before and after the 8-week training program that is applicated for the athletes in the experimental group, the balance and flexibility performances of the athletes in both the experimental and control groups were determined. The following measurements were made to determine some physical and motoric characteristics of the athletes forming the sample.

2.2 Anthropometric Measurements

In the scope of the research, height (cm) and body weight (kg) measurements were performed to determine some anthropometric characteristics of athletes. In length measurements was used FB 721 brand Body Analyzer. Before the measurement, students were asked to remove their shoes, socks and wear clothes that would not weigh as much as possible. During the measurement, students were reminded that they should assemble their heels after taking a deep breath, keep their body in a vertical, keep their head in frankfort position and protect their positions. When body weight (kg) was determined, it was noted that the athletes had to wear their feet naked and there would be clothes that would not weight on them. Measurements were made with Seca 727 digital scales. The body mass index (BMI) values of each athlete were calculated by the weight (kg) / height length (m2) formula from the measurements.

2.3 Sit & Reach Test

The flexibility levels of the athletes were determined by the Sit & Reach test. During the measurements from the athletes were asked to stretch their bodies as far as possible without twisting their knees over the stand of the Sit & Reach and remain immobilized at the farthest point they could flex. Better than two measurements were recorded as a test result.

2.4. Flamingo Balance Test

The Flamingo Balance Test was used to determine the static balances of the athletes. According to this test, the athletes; keep in balance by upping with their dominant foot to wooden balance device made of 50 cm. Length, 4 cm. Height and 3 cm. wide. He holds the other foot with the hand on the same side, bending it from the knee, by pulling it towards the hips. When the athlete is in this way balanced with one foot, the time starts and tries to stay balanced for 1 minute. The time is stopped when the balance is disturbed (if he leaves his foot while holding it, falls from the board, touches to ground with anywhere his body and etc.). When the athlete provides his balance again by upping to balance device, time continues from where it left off. The test continues by the way for one minute. When the time is up, the athlete's attempt to provide each balance is calculated and this number is recorded as the athlete's score when one minute is completed at the end of the test.

3 Findings

Table 1. Comparison of Balance and Flexibility Performances of Experiment Group

Variables	Tests	n	X	Ss	t Test	
					t	p
Balance (error)	Pre test	30	5.43	2.55	6.242	0.000*
	Post test	30	3.20	1.95		
Flexibilty (cm)	Pre test	30	5.37	3.44	1.769	0.087
	Post test	30	4.37	2.82		

** significiant of level 0.05*

It is seen that there is a significant difference between the pre-test and post-test results regarding the balance performance of the athletes in the experiment group ($p<0.05$). However, it is understood that there is no significant difference between the pre-test and post-test results regarding flexibility performance of athletes ($p>0.05$).

Table 2. Relationship Between BMI Values and Balance and Flexibility Performances of the Experiment Group

Variables	Balance		Flexibilty	
	r	p	r	p
BMI	0.130	0.494	0.074	0.699

BMI: BodyMass Index

There is no statistically significant relationship between the BMI values of the athletes in the experimental group and the balance and flexibility performance ($p>0.05$).

Table 3. Comparison of Balance and Flexibility Performances of the Control Group

Variables	Tests	n	X	Ss	t Test	
					t	p
Balance (error)	Pre test	30	8.70	1.98	-0.582	0.486
	Post test	30	8.90	2.03		
Flexibilty (cm)	Pre test	30	3.13	1.77	-0.660	0.514
	Post test	30	3.27	1.48		

It is seen that there is a significant difference in the balance performance of the athletes in the control group when the pre-test and post-test results are compared ($p<0.05$).

Table 4. The Relationship Between BKI Values of Control Group and Balance and Flexibility Performances

Variables	Balance		Flexibilty	
	r	p	r	p
BMI	-0.003	0.986	-0.089	0.640

BMI: Body Mass Index

There was no statistically significant relationship between the BMI values of the athletes in the control group and their balance and flexibility performances ($p>0.05$).

3 Discussion and conclusion

Individuals with Down's syndrome have weak muscle strength, low muscle tone and poor motor coordination [12]. The difficulties in motor skills can affect the ability of individuals with Down's syndrome to perform various tasks in their daily lives [6]. Furthermore, in children with Down's syndrome and adolescents due to obesity, flatfood [7] and visual and auditory functional disorders can lead to loss of balance [8]. In studies conducted to determine balance control in individuals with Down's syndrome, were found individuals with Down's syndrome to have a weaker balance than healthy subjects, and the likelihood of postural disturbances was higher in these individuals [2] and [10].

In this study, ıt could said that while the athletes in the experimental group contributed to the development of equilibrium performance, the training they performed to improve balance and flexibility performance for 8 weeks, ıt didn't not contribute to the development of flexibility performances. When the average values of the athletes' balance and flexibility performances in the control group are examined, it is understood that the athletes in the control group decrease their balance performances after 8 weeks of their usual training. In athletes of the control group, although have been seen improvement of the their flexibility performance after 8 weeks of training, this improvement doesn't mean statistically significant. In this study, it is understood that the BMI values of the athletes in the experimental and control groups did not affect the balance and flexibility performances positively or negatively.

In the study, it was found that the training program for 8 week training to improve balance and flexibility that was applied to dealing with athleticism 13-15 age group athletes with down syndrome improved the athletes' balance performance but did not contribute to the their improvement of flexibility performances. For this reason, athletes with Down's syndrome who are dealing with Athleticism could provided to participate of them in training programs to improve balance for 8 weeks or longer. Thus, depending on the development of balance performance in athletes with down syndrome, it may contribute to the increase of sportive performance or adaptation process to the daily life.

Referance

1. Eröz, R., Okur, M., & Berik, Ö. Down sendromlu çocuklarda AgNOR sayısı ile gelişim arasında bir ilişki var mı?. Düzce Üniversitesi Sağlık Bilimleri Enstitüsü Dergisi, **1**(1), 8-11., (2011).
2. Galli, M., Rigoldi, C., Mainardi, L., Tenore, N., Onorati, P., & Albertini, G. Postural control in patients with Down syndrome. Disability and Rehabilitation, 30(17), 1274-1278., (2008).
3. Gonzalez-Aguero, A., Vicente-Rodriguez, G., Moreno, L.A., Guerra-Balic, M., Ara, I., & Casajus, J.A. Health-related physical fitness in children and adolescents with Down syndrome and response to training. Scandinavian Journal of Medicine & Science in Sports, **20**, 716–724., (2010).
4. Lahtinen, U., Rintala, P., & Malin, A. Physical performance of individuals with intellectual disability: A 30-year follow-up. Adapted Physical Activity Quarterly, 24(2), 125-143., (2007).
5. Latash, L.P., Latash, M.L., & Meijer, O.G. 30 years later: On the problem of the relation between structure and function in the brain from a contemporary viewpoint (1996) part II. Motor Control, **4**(2), 125–149., (2000).
6. Marques-Aleixo, I., Querido, A., Figueiredo, P., Vilas-Boas, J. P., Corredeira, R., Daly, D., & Fernandes, R. J. Intracyclic velocity variation and arm coordination assessment in swimmers with Down syndrome. Adapted Physical Activity Quarterly, **30**(1), 70-84., (2013).
7. Pau, M., Galli, M., Crivellini, M., & Albertini, G. Foot–ground interaction during upright standing in children with Down syndrome. Research in developmental disabilities, **33**(6), 1881-1887., (2012).
8. Pitetti, K., Baynard, T., & Agiovlasitis, S. Children and adolescents with Down syndrome, physical fitness and physical activity. Journal of Sport and Health Science, **2**(1), 47-57., (2013).
9. Popa, C.E. & Ovidiu, G. (2012). Study regarding the improwement of postural control in children who have down syndrome through swimming, Scientific Journal of Education, Sports, and Health, **2**(13), 85-99., (2012).
10. Rigoldi, C., Galli, M., Mainardi, L., Crivellini, M., & Albertini, G. Postural control in children, teenagers and adults with Down syndrome. Research in developmental disabilities, **32**(1), 170-175., (2011).
11. Vuillerme, N., Marin, L., & Debû, B. Assessment of static postural control in teenagers with Down syndrome. Adapted Physical Activity Quarterly, **18**(4), 417-433., (2001).
12. Wu, J., Beerse, M., Ajisafe, T., & Liang, H. Walking dynamics in preadolescents with and without Down syndrome. Physical therapy, **95**(5), 740-749., (2015).

 DOI: 10.1051/shsconf/20173701031

The effects of 8 week exercise program on reaction time performance of hearing impaired students at 11-14 years of age

Mehmet Özdemir[1], Halil Tanır[2a], Mehmet Ilkım[3], and Murat Özmaden[2]

[1] Physical Education and Sport High School, Bingöl University, Turkey.
[2] Physical Education and Sport High School, Adnan Menderes University, Turkey.
[3] Physical Education and Sport High School, Inonu University, Turkey.

Abstract. This research is aiming to investigate the effects of 8-week exercise program on reaction time performance of hearing impaired students at 11-14 years of age. 32 students (n=16 girls and n= 16 males) aged between 11-14 years in the Malatya Akşemseddin Secondary School for Hearing Impaired Students were participated in the study by the consent of their parents. The students were divided into 2 groups as athletes (n=8 girls and n=8 boys) and sedantary students (n=8 girls and n= 8 boys). The athlete students are engaged in activities like "Turning to the front with the basketball ball with the ball and taking the pass, walking on the balance instrument which is 30 cm wide and 3 m long, making slight left and right bounces, 10 m short distance runnings, short distance rusting with a handball ball, throwing the basketball ball up about 2 m with a light, Sedantery students have not been subjected to any work during this period. The reaction time performances of all students participating in the 8 week were determined before and after workout program by the REACTION TIME HUBBARD - HAP brand device. It was determined that there was a significant difference between athletes and sedentary students in favor of the athletes in terms of pre-test and post-test results according to reaction time performance ($p<0.05$).To sum up it was found that the exercise program which was done for 3 days a week for 8 weeks, enhanced the reaction performance of hearing-impaired students aged 11-14 years.
Key Words: Hearing impaired students, reaction time, exercise

1 Introduction

There is more evidence that physical activity is beneficial to health and well-being, and it has a growing role in our life. It is suggested by some researchers that, regular physical exercises increase the physical and functional capacities of children as providing a strong and sheltered structure to the body. Sport is one of the best methods for social integration of disabled people. It also contributes to people's independence [16]. It is the most important factor that causes the disabled person to look at his life from different windows.

Today, sport is regarded as activities that are natural rather than leisure time sociology, and which should be done for the health of the individual in all fields. In addition to the supportive benefits of sports in the field of biological, psychological and social development, there is an encouraging aspect of belonging to a group and participating in group activities. Many studies show that the risk of heart disease in physically active individuals is lower than the sedentary ones [8,9].

[a]Corresponding author:halil.tanir@adu.edu.tr

Reaction time is one of the topics that scientists have been most interested in since the mid-19th century. Reaction time is defined as the period of preparation required to occur the movement by taking the stimulus [1,17].The reaction time as the internal timing between the taking of the stimulus and the response [22].The movement time is the time from the beginning to the end of the movement right after the reaction time [22, 19]. Reaction time is a positive effect of the organ systems, with the nervous system working regularly and coordinated work among the muscle groups [20].It is accepted that the reaction time can be shortened by training but it cannot be lowered to a certain level [11]. When examining the reaction time, it is necessary to distinguish the response time [19].The reaction time is considered to be a part of the reaction period in the true sense and the response time is the reaction time and the action time [3,19].Some researchers have suggested that speed is a factor lying under reaction and movement time. [10,19].Reaction time is a decisive factor in most sports and can be improved by regular training. Because the reaction time seen as the main component of many skills [18]. It has been reported in many studies that regular training in a given program, can improve the reaction time [4,7 and 15].

2 Methot

2.1 Participations

It is aimed in the study that, the effect exercise on reaction times of hearing impaired students aged between 11-14 years. A total of 32 students, 16 male and 16 female, who studying at the Malatya Private Anatolian Private School participated as volunteer in the study with permission of their parents.

2.2 Exercise Programme and Reaction Time Measurement

To the participated 8 students of each group of male and female, simple attention enhancing actions such as; turn back based on turnover and do chest pass with basketball ball, walking on the balance instrument which is 40 cm high, 30 cm wide and 3 m long from the ground (each athlete made 4 trials) slightly left and right jumps, 10 m short distance start runs, short distance passes with handball ball, throw and keep the basketball ball up about 2m with the lighted sign, were applied during eight weeks and three days in a week as Tuesday, Thursday and Saturday. The reaction times of the groups were measured before and after eight weeks of exercise with the REACTION TIME HUBBARD-HAP brand reaction meter. In the measurements, the best rating was recorded by giving three trials in the form of a light reaction in the hand-held reaction device of the hearing-impaired students.

Hearing-impaired students were identified in the Private Anatolian Private Education School (in the same school). Among the identified students, hearing-impaired students athletes and sedentary were identified. Students between the ages of 11-14 were participated. Eight students were identified in all groups (hearing-impaired students doing sports, hearing-impaired students not doing sports). Female and male students were evaluated among themselves. Sports groups were trained 3 days a week (Tuesday, Thursday, and Saturday). The study continued for 8 weeks. All groups were subjected to a reaction test with the REACTION TIME HUBBARD-HAP brand instrument before the study began and the results of these measurements were recorded. The reaction test was conducted in all groups over the hands of the students they used more frequently in daily life. Trainings such as; turn back based on turnover and do chest pass with basketball ball, walking on the balance instrument which is 40 cm high, 30 cm wide and 3 m long from the ground (each athlete made 4 trials) slightly left and right jumps, 10 m short distance start runs, short distance passes with handball ball, throw and keep the basketball ball up about 2m with the lighted sign, were applied to the hearing impaired students during eight weeks. Nothing was applied to the students who did not do sports and their measurements were taken again after 8 weeks. Reaction measurements of hearing impaired students who, do sports and did not do sports, were taken again after 8 weeks by the same methods. Measurements of hearing-impaired students who do sports were taken before training day. Measurements were taken by putting out the light that appears in the reaction tool by hand, which students used in daily life. Initial measurements and final measurements of all students were taken on equal terms and in the same environment. In all measurements, each student has 3 trials and the best recorded as the result. The results of the hearing-impaired students who do sports were taken into account between themselves and the results of hearing-impaired students who did not do sports were taken into account between themselves.

2.2 Exercise Programme and Reaction Time Measurement

SPSS 22.0 (SPSS 22.0 for Windows / SPSS® Inc, Chicago, USA) was used for the statistical analysis of the data. The Paired-Sample t test was used to compare the hearing-impaired students' differences according to the pre-test and post-test scores. A $p<0.05$ value was considered statistically significant.

2.3 Statistical Analysis

The sample of the study consists of 60 athletes (n=30 experimental group and n=30 control group) in the Malatya Sessiz Adımlar Sports Club, aged between 13 and 15, dealing with athleticism. Athletes in the experimental group were subjected to a training program to improve the balance and flexibility of 2 hours of 3 days a week for 8 weeks. The athletes in the control group continued their usual training programs. Before and after the 8-week training program that is applicated for the athletes in the experimental group, the balance and flexibility performances of the athletes in both the experimental and control groups were determined. The following measurements were made to determine some physical and motoric characteristics of the athletes forming the sample.

3 Findings

Table 1. Descriptive Statistics of Subjects

Variables		n	%
	Female	16	50
Gender	Male	16	50
	Total	**32**	**100**
	Yes	16	50
Athlete	No	16	50
	Total	**32**	**100**

In Table 1, descriptive statistics of the gender and athlete are shown.

Table 2. Descriptive Statistics of Student's Some Anthropometric Characteristics

Variables	Minimum	Maximum	X	Sd	Median
Height (cm)	1.38	1.74	1.53	0.08	1.51
Weight (kg)	36	65	47.7	8.39	45.5
BMI (kg/m²)	14.6	25.8	20.2	0.50	20.4

In Table 2, According to the statistical values obtained from some anthropometric measurements of the subjects participated in the study, the height mean 1.51 cm, weight mean 45.5 and body mass index means were determined as 20.4. The number of observations for all parameters is 32.

Table 3. Comparison of Pre-test and Post-test Values of Athlete and Non-Athlete Subjects

Groups	Pre-test			Post-test			T test	
	n	X	Sd	n	X	Sd	t	p
Athlete	16	33.5	5.03	16	27.19	4.11	5.614	0.000*
Non-Athlete	16	51.13	17.78	16	57.13	18.68	-1.798	0.092

* *Significant level of 0.05.*

When Table 3 is examined, although there is a statistically significant difference between pre-test values and post-test values of athletes ($p<0.05$); it is seen that there is no statistically significant difference between pre-test values and post-test values of non-athlete subjects ($p>0.05$)

3 Discussion and conclusion

Because of hearing impaired people have little or no sense of hearing, late development of balance and motor skills negatively affects their interaction with their peers. Hearing impaired individuals suffer from inadequacy of balance and motor response due to insufficiency of sensory stimulation due to damage to hearing sensation. Physical activity is beneficial for development of balance and motor skills [13].

Simple reaction times of visually impaired individuals participating in regular physical exercises can reach much better levels than non-exercise visually impaired individuals. The reason for this situation is thought as; besides the development of the muscle-nerve conduction ability which is important in the reaction time through the training of the individuals participating in the physical exercises, to be a lack of experience, by gaining the skill on the forms of movement that are revealed by the activities carried out [2].

Cağlar et al. [5] specified, in their study about physical fitness of hearing impaired individuals who are athletes or non-athletes, that; there is significant differences between athletes and non-athletes regarding their, height, resting pulse, elasticity, stretching, 20 m speed, reaction time, hand grip strength, back and leg strength, shuttle, vertical jump and body fat percentage values ($p<0.05$).

In the study which made by Cigerci et al. [6] it was stated that; while there were significant differences when hearing-impaired sedentary men and non-hearing impaired sedentary men compared according to the reaction time values of right and left handed light

($p<0.05$), there were no significant differences between hearing-impaired volleyball player men and non-hearing impaired volleyball player men, and hearing-impaired sedentary girls and non-hearing impaired sedentary girls ($p>0.05$). It is seen that the results are similar because the content of the work we have done is close to each other with this study is.

Çağlar et al. [5] specified, in their study about hearing impaired individuals who are athletes or non-athletes, that; there is significant differences between active athletes and non-athlete's reaction time values. Similarly, Karagöz [12] notes in his master's thesis that 12-week training has significantly improved reaction times among children in the 8-10 age group. The limited literature we obtained as a result of the researches carried out supports our research results and specify that according to hearing impaired individuals participating in sports activities, the hearing impaired individuals who do not participate in sports activities have shorter reaction times. Participation in sports or physical exercise has a positive effect on the physical and motor development of the disabled, as it is in unimpeded individuals. Şirinkan [21] reports that sportive educational games applied to hearing-impaired students contribute to their physical development in the study he made about impact on the physical development of sportive educational games on 10-15 year old hearing impairment students. It is reported that; individuals who regularly participate in the physical activity program have higher physical capacity than sedentary individuals of the same age and that the nervous system responses are faster.

Bakır and Doğan [2].reports in their study that, there is a significant difference in favor of participated in sport sight-disabled individuals in terms of auditory simple reaction times between the sight-disabled and non-sported sight-disabled individuals ($p<0.05$). Çağlar at al. [5].reports as a result of their study that; sportive activity contributes significantly to physical development, physical fitness characteristics and body composition of hearing-impaired individuals.

It has been determined that the sport contributes significantly to physical development, physical fitness characteristics and body composition of hearing-impaired [5]. In our study, although there was a statistically significant difference between pre-test values and post-test values of athletes ($p<0.05$), it is stated that there is no statistically significant difference between pre-test values and post-test values of non-athlete subjects (Table 3, $p>0.05$). Our study is similar with the study made by Koç et al. [14] which is; comparison of reaction time of hearing-impaired sedentary and hearing-impaired soccer players.

Bakır and Aydoğan [2] reports that in their study on visual impaired children; regular physical exercises shortened the auditory reaction time of children. As it is understood from this result which is, sportive exercise shortens reaction time, this study supports our study. It is known that the sport has contributed significantly to the physical development, physical fitness characteristics and body composition of hearing-impaired children.

To sum up it was found that the exercise program which was done for 3 days a week for 8 weeks, enhanced the reaction performance of hearing-impaired students aged 11-14 years. Accordingly, at least 8 weeks of exercise programs that can be implemented under the supervision of a physical education teacher or coach can enhance their performances and enable them to harmonise themselves with Daily life tasks more easily by improving their reaction time performances.

References

1. Anson, J.G. Effects of moment of inertia on simple reaction time. Journal of Motor Behavior, **21**(1), 60-71., (1989).
2. Bakır, S., Aydoğan, H. 12-14 yaş grubu Gençlerbirliği Spor Kulübü sporcuları ile spor yapan ve yapmayan görme engelli öğrencilerinin işitsel basit reaksiyon zamanlarının

karşılaştırılması. Selçuk Üniversitesi Beden Eğitimi ve Spor Bilimleri Dergisi, **13**; 151-160., (2011).

3. Bjorklund, R.A. Reaction time and movement time measured in keypress and a key-realese condition. Perceptual and Motor Skill. **72**, 663-673., (1991).
4. Bompa, T.O. Antrenman Kuramı ve Yöntemi. Keskin İ., Tuner A.B. (Çeviren), 1. Baskı, Ankara: Bağırgan Yayınevi, 357- 455., (1988).
5. Cağlar, Ö., Uludağ, A.H., Sepetci, T., & Çalışkan, E. Evaluation of physical fitness parameters of hearing impaired adolescents who are active and non-active in sports. Turkish Journal of Sport and Exercise, **15**(2); 38-44., (2013).
6. Ciğerci, A.E., Aksen, P, Cicioğlu, İ. & Günay, M. 9-15 Yaş Grubu İşitme Engelli ve İşitme Engelli Olmayan Öğrencilerin Bazı Fizyolojik ve Motorik Özelliklerinin Değerlendirilmesi. Selçuk Üniversitesi Beden Eğitimi ve Spor Bilimleri Dergisi, **13**,41., (2011).
7. Çolakoğlu, M., Tiryaki, Ş., & Moralı, S. Konsantrasyon çalışmalarının reaksiyon zamanı üzerine etkisi, Hacettepe Üniversitesi Spor Bilimleri Dergisi, **4**, 32-47, (1993).
8. Dowdy, B.D., Cureton, K.J., Duval, H.P., & Ouzis, G.H. Effects of Aerobic Dance on Physical Quark Capacity, Cardiovascular Function and Boy Composition of Middle Aged Women, Research Quarterly for Exercise and Sport, **56**,(3) 227-233., (1985).
9. Elmacı, S., Gürpınar, D., Erdinç., T., İşleğen Ertat, A., Durusoy, F. & Gediz, A., Sedanter şahıslarda egzersizle kilo kaybının bazı kardiak risk faktörlerine etkisi, IV. Spor Hekimliği Kongresi, Bildiri Kitabı 17-19 Eylül, ss:263., (1993).
10. Groves, R. (1973). Relationship of Reaction Time and Movement Time in A Gross Motor skill. Perceptual and Motor Skills, 36: 453-454., (1973).
11. Jokela, J, & Erai P. Reaction and Movement Times in Men of Different Ages Perceptial and Motor Skills USA., **63**,111-124, (1986).
12. Karagöz, Ş. 8-10 yaş arası çocuklarda 12 haftalık tenis antrenmanlarının görsel ve işitsel reaksiyon zamanına etkisinin incelenmesi. Afyon Kocatepe Üniversitesi Sağlık Bilimleri Enstitüsü. Yüksek Lisans Tezi. 42-51, (2008).
13. Keskinkılıç, B., Yardım, N, & Vardar, C. Türkiye fiziksel aktivite rehberi; engellilerde fiziksel aktivite; Kuban Matbaacılık ve Yayıncılık, Ankara, 26-31, (2014).
14. Koç, H., Tekin, A., Sitti, S., & Akçakoyun, F. İşitme engelli sedanterler ile futbolcuların reaksiyon zamanının karşılaştırılması. Selçuk Üniversitesi Beden Eğitimi ve Spor Bilim Dergisi, **13** (3), 364–367, (2011).
15. Nöcker, J. Physiyological der Leibesungen, Ferdinand Enke Verlag, Stuttgard, 262., (1971).
16. O'Connell, M. The effect of brailling and physical guidance on the self-efficacy of children who are blind. Unpublished master's thesis: State University of New York College at Brockport, NY., (2000).
17. Rosenbaum, D.A.Human Motor Control Psyiological Foundations Acedemic Pres., London. (1991).
18. Rudısıll, M.E., & Thoole, T. The effect of pysical activity programme on reaction time an movement time for the older adult. Jour. Hum. Mow. Stu, **22**, 205-212, (1992).
19. Schmidt, R.A. Motor Learning Anda Performance. Human Kinetics Pub. USA., (1991).
20. Sevim, Y. (2000). Antrenman Bilgisi. Ankara Nobel Yayınları, s: 112, (2000).
21. Şirinkan, A. 10-15 yaş işitme engelli öğrencilerde sportif eğitsel oyunların fiziksel gelişimlerine etkisinin araştırılması. Selçuk Üniversitesi Beden Eğitimi ve Spor Bilimleri Dergisi, **13** (3), 74-80, (2011).
22. Sullivan, S.J, & Hayes, K.C. Changes in short and long latency strech reflexes prior to movement intitation. Brain Research, 139-143, (1987).

The effect of morphological characteristics on the physical and physiological performance of Turkish soccer referees and assistant referees

Tuba Kızılet Bozdoğan[1a], Ali Kızılet[1], and Bilal Biçer[2]

[1]Sport Science Faculty, Marmara University, Istanbul, Turkey
[2]School of Physical Education and Sports, Mustafa Kemal University, Hatay, Turkey

Abstract. Physical fitness and physiological status play an important role in the referees' performance. Therefore, the aim of this study was to analyze the body structure and morphological characteristics of Turkish Ssccer refereesand assistant referees and to determine the effect of these variables on physical performance. A sample of 158 male referees and 55 asisstant referees (mean age 31.8 ± 4.2 and 37.4 ± 3.3 years)was evaluated. Physical assesment were conducted using the Yo-Yo Intermittent Recovery Test Level 1 (YYIRTL1) and Repeated Sprint Ability (RSA) for referees and Active Recovery Intermittent Endurance Test (ARIET) and the RSA for assistant referees. We analyzed heart rate assesments. The measures used to assess morphological characteristics were age, weight, body mass index (BMI), body fat (BF), body mass, and fat free mass.The ANOVA test (Tukey test)was used to determine the result. Correlations between the referees' fitness test performance and their morphological characteristics were examined using Pearson's correlation ($p<0.05$). To result of this study, point to the existence of a strong correlation between morphological and physical and physiological characteristics. According to the literature, we found that greater BF and a higher BMI may negatively affect areferee's running performance.
Keywords: Anthropometry; Soccer Referee, Heart Rate, HRload

1 Introduction

During the game of soccer, footballers and referees are both active in field. They are important because soccer is very popular sports all around the world [31] and developing of the economy. While researchon referees has beenrather insufficient in the past,studies about their physical and mental competencies have increased by considering the effect on the results of the game today. Some of these are; anthropometric states [11, 33], including referee motion analysis, heart rate measurements [7, 41], physical activity intensity,and distance covered [16, 18]. These studies have contributed to the creation and design of refereetraining programs.

[a]Corresponding author: tuba.kizilet@marmara.edu.tr

Referees' and assistant referees'body composition is important for their performance. In soccer, body mass index (BMI), fat free mass '(FFM)' and body mass '(BM)' is associatedwith field performance [25]. Previous studies have shown that regular exercise reduces the BMI, FFM and body fat (BF) [22, 28]. Body composition is assessed as BF and lean body mass.

Gregory et. al [10] has shown that increasing of fat negatively affects athletic performance. However, Ugarkovic et. al [38] has found no correlation between body composition and performance.

During the gameplay, a distance of the referee's point with the rule infringement is the compatibility indicator with the game tempo [30]. Researchers have reported that a referee runsan average of 9-13 km during a match [3, 35] and an assistant referee runs about 6-8 km, and 1.2 km of it is by side runs. An elite referee is running average 110 high-intensity runs that take 2 s on average. In addition, it has been shown that an experienced referee faces similar physical demands as a midfielder [2]. In a study of Danish soccer players, midfield players have run averaged 1950±130 m. in the Yo-Yo Intermittent Recovery Test Level 1 (YYIRTL1) test [32]. According to the literature, this result is similar to referees covered distance.

The Repeated Sprint Ability Test (RSA) is a test widely used by sports scientists for soccer players and soccer referees. It is used to measure the referees' ability to recover after anaerobic performances during short rest intervals [8, 45]. Weston et al [42] found a correlation between the referees and footballer'shigh-intensity conditions ($p<0.05$).In similar research has been reported that the referee's adaptation to the game is influenced by the number of high-intensity players during a soccer match [24].

Referees must keep up with the pace of gameplay. As the economic importance of football increases,referees' and assistant referees' physical and physiological conditions becomingincreasinlyimportant. Referees are generally older than footballers. The referees reaching the elite level in their 40s.This means that there is usually a 15-20-year age difference between footballers and referees. Referees therefore require excellent physical and physiological health. The continuity and pursuit of training programs are important to the positive management of their performance. Therefore, the aim of this study was to analyze the body structure and morphological characteristics of Turkish soccer referees and assistant referees determine the effect of these variables on physical performance.

2 Material and methods

2.1 Participants

This study examined 158 male soccer referees (mean age 31.8 ± 4.2 years; training duration 12 years), from the Turkish Super League, First League, and Second League and 55 male assistant referees (mean age 37.4 ± 3.3 years; training duration 12 years), from the Turkish Super League and First League.

2.2 Procedures

The participants were evaluated on November 10-15, 2015. The tests were conductedin the morning.The tests were conducted in Istanbul to ensure that environmental factors and travel-related fatigue did not interfere with results. Referees performed a standard warm-up consisting of 5 min of slow jogging followed by 10 min of mobility exercises and 5 min of dynamic stretching.

2.2.1 Field tests

The tests were conducted on an artificial grass. All participants were subjected to physical assessments consistent with the test battery protocols.Referees were evaluated using the

YYIRTL1 and RSA (6x40 m), and assistant referees were evaluated using the Active Recovery Intermittent Endurance Test (ARIET) and RSA (6x40m). The tests for each test battery were done in two days. The YYIRTL1 test consists of intermittent exercises with maximal consumption of the aerobic system. It also shows the ability to recover after intense exercises [13]. The RSA is designed to test the subject ability to perform short-duration sprints, which occur frequently during gameplay. Recent studies have demonstrated a significant correlation (r= 0.65, r= 0.60) between sprints during gameplay and RSA results [29]. We used a heart rate monitor (Polar Heart Rate Monitor,Finland) to analyze physiological abilities. We evaluated HRload,HRmean and HRmax of the physiological parameters.

2.2.2 Antropometric measurements

Assessments of the chosen morphological characteristics (age, BM, BMI,BF, and FFM) were conducted in the early morning before breakfast.A bioelectrical impedance analyzer (Tanita-bc 418-ma) was used.

BF evaluation criteria is used for finding differences of groups. The evaluation references for BF were <%10, 10-12%, 12-14%, 14-16 %, >16% (13,14).

2.3 Statistics

Results are presented as means ± standard deviations (SD). The results of the tests were moderated, and the differences in the mean values were appraised through variance analysis (ANOVA), followed by the Tukey test for the identification of statistically significant differences among the equal of means. Correlations between the referees' fitness test performances and their morphological characteristics were examined using Pearson's correlation(r; $p<0.05$). Data analysis was performed using the Statistical Package for Social Sciences (version 21.0 for Windows, SPSS TMInc, Chicago, IL, USA). Statistical significance was set at $p < 0.05$.

3 Findings

Tables 1 and 3 shows the sample characteristics with the values of the mean and standard deviations by age, BM, BMI, FFM and BF percentage from referees and assistant referees, respectively.

Table 1. Referees' morphological characteristics, pyhsical/ physiological performance

	Mean	Standart Deviation	Max	Min
Age	31.85	4.2	42	23
BM (kg)	77	6.5	92.7	57.9
FFM (kg)	66.9	4.93	80	54.3
BF (%)	10.6	2.97	21.1	5
BMI	23.5	4.29	73.3	17.5
YYIRTL1 (m)	1607.3	296.6	2400	920
HRload	61.6	12.1	76	40
HRmax (beat/min)	186.7	10.5	205	167
HRmean (beat/min)	166.2	11.2	184.0	148.0
RSA (6x40m; sec)	36.6	2.40	48.1	31.8

BM: Body Mass; BMI: Body Mass Index; BF: % Body Fat; FFM: Fat Free Mass; Hrmax: MaxiumumHeart rate; HRmean: Mean Heart Rate

Both BF and BMI were negatively correlated with YYIRTL1 (Total distance) for Rs ($p<0.05$). There was also a negatif correlation between HRmean and BF. Additionally, age was negatively correlated with physiological ability ($p<0.05$). However, BF was positively correlated to the RSA performance (total time) and there was a positive correlation between BF and BMI.Nocorrelation was found between FFM, BM and the physical and pyhsiological abilities (Table 2).

Table 2. Correlations between morfological characteristics and referees' physical /physiological abilities

		Age	BM	FFM	BF(%)	BMI
YYIRTL1		–0.032	–0.024	0.042	–0.224**	–0.186*
	HRload	–0.464*	0.139	0.237	–0.345	–0.037
	HRmax	–0.476*	–0.285	–0.140	–0.445	–0.423
	HRmean	–0.603*	–0.169	0.053	–0.465*	–0.397
RSA(6x40m)		–0.093	0.080	–0.010	–0.262**	0.092

*P<0.05

Table 3. Assistant referees' morphological characteristics pyhsical/ physiological performance

	Mean	Standart Deviation	Max	Min
Age	37.4	3.3	45	31
BM (kg)	75.4	5.80	85.5	61.9
FFM (kg)	64.4	4.58	75.7	51.6
BF (%)	11.6	3.3	20.4	5.5
BMI	23.2	1.51	25.7	20
ARIET (m)	1782.8	140.6	1920	1240
HRload	47.5	6.7	56.0	34.5
HRmax (beat/min)	193.8	10.3	219	181
HRmean(beat/min)	178.4	11.0	198	160
RSA(6x40m; sec)	33.7	1.17	36	30

BM: Body Mass; BMI: Body Mass Index; BF: % Body Fat; FFM: Fat Free Mass; Hrmax: MaxiumumHeart rate; HRmean: Mean Heart Rate

Assistant referees BF was negatively correlated with RSA result.But no correlation was found between their BF and ARIET test results.There was also acorrelation between ARIET total distance with HRmean and HRload and age factor. ($p<0.05$) However,no correlations were observed between FFM, BM, BMI and the physical and physiological abilities considered in this study (ARIET and RSA; Table 4).

Table 4. Correlations between morfological characteristics and asisstant referees' physical /physiological abilities

		Age	BM	FFM	BF(%)	BMI
ARİET		–0.256	0.050	0.117	–0.214	–0.048
	HRload	–0.557*	0.210	0.298	–0.175	0.047
	HRmax	–0.120	0.190	0.046	–0.370	0.043
	HRmean	–0.269	0.242	0.042	–0.484*	–0.017
RSA(6x40m)		–0.253	–0.064	0.068	–0.329*	–0.139

*P<0.05

A statistically significant difference between the <10 BF% and 14.1-16.0 BF% referees in terms of RSA. A statistically significant difference was found YYIRTL1 test total distance between the individuals with <10 BF% and those with> 16 BF% in the referees. Individuals with low-fat percentages were found to covered longer distances. Additionally, a statistically significant difference to the total duration of the RSA test was found between the referees with 10.1-12 BF % and 16 BF% and those with <10 BF% and >16 BF% (p<0.05). However, no significant differences were observed in the YYIRTL1, ARIET and RSA results referees and assistant referees with other BF percentages (p>0.05) (Table 5).

Table 5. Comparison of physical abilities according to body fat variables

		Referees		Assistant Referees	
BF%	BF%	YYIRTL1	RSA(6 x 40M)	ARIET	RSA(6 x 40 M)
<10	10.1-12	.783	.143	.809	.794
	12.1-14	.566	.401	.873	1.000
	14.1-16	.147	.022	.990	.572
	>16	.010	.000	.513	.019
10.1-12	<10	.783	.143	.809	.794
	12.1-14	1.000	.910	1.000	.945
	14.1-16	.790	.968	.998	.967
	>16	.183	.085	.150	.185
12.1-14	<10	.566	.401	.873	1.000
	10.1-12	1.000	.910	1.000	.945
	14.1-16	.824	.476	.997	.762
	>16	.160	.003	.228	.085
14.1-16	<10	.147	.022	.990	.572
	10.1-12	.790	.968	.998	.967
	12.1-14	.824	.476	.997	.762
	>16	.765	.260	.477	.707

P<0.05

4 Discussion and conclusion

In this study, we described the morphological characteristics of elite referees and assistant referees and analyzed the influence of these variables on the physical performance. Results for both of the groups that we studied demonstrate a significant correlation between morphological and physical characteristics.

The accuracy of a referee's decisions during a match is related to the optimal closeness to the position.The ability to maintain performance throughout the game is influenced by physical and mental competence. Previous studies support our findings that BF, BM,and BMI values influence athletic performance [12, 37].

Referees must make correct decisions during gameplay; therefore, their physical characteristics are extremetely important as they affect performance [5]. Excessive body weight causes too much energy to be consumed during movement, and the fatty tissue creates a thermal insulation effect. Thisleads toan increase in dehydration. Which can cause the referee's movements to deteriorate during the game. Studies have shown that the ideal BF percentage in soccer is 7-12% [9].

In a study of footballers, it has documented that the BF% values were 11.64 ± 1.61 [27]. In previous studies were reported that BF percentages were 16.7% [33] of Greek referees and 20.7% [34] of Santa Catarina referees. However, referees' BF ratios must be in the ideal range to work at an elite level (<12%). Recent studies have shown that BF content is 11.6% [24]. Studies have reported values of 19.3 ± 4.1 [6] for Brazilian referees and 12.63 ± 4.2 [19] for South African referees. The present study found that the average percentage

DOI: 10.1051/shsconf/20173701032

of BF in referees and assistant referees was 10,6 % and 11.6%, respectively. Respectively, which suggests that the average Turkish referee is in ideal BF range.

Wilmore et.al.[44] have shown that the BMI is reported as a rough measure of body compositionand a good indicator of relative BF. Helsen and Bultynck [11] reported BMI values of 24.2 ± 2.6 kg/ m2European referees in 2000. Rontoyannis et al. [33] reported 25.9 ± 2.1 kg / m2 of Greek referees. and Reilly & Gregson [30] found British referees to have a BMI of 27.1 ± 5.3 kg / m2 and Krustrup et al. [18] also showed as 23 kg / m2.It is suggested that top-class referee's BMI values should be<25 kg / m2 [33]. The presented study, BMI is 23.5±4.29 kg/m2for referees and 23.2±1.51 kg/m2for assistant referees. According to ourresults, Turkish referees' BMI values seem to be better when compared to the literatures.

Studies by Weston et al. [39] and Castanga et al. [4] have shown that age has no significant effect on physical fitness and performance.The present study finds no statistically significant correlation between referees' age and physical characteristics (p>0.05).

The YYIRTL1 test scores has been shown to be consistent with the physical performance of elite-level soccer referees [27]. Previous studies using the YYIRTL1 test have documented the maximum distance covered by referees in Denmark (1.420 ± 90 m; 1). Belgium (1.720 ± 276 m; 43) and Italy (1.503 ± 399 m; 4).The present study found that the referees' average running distance of the referees was 1.607 ± 296 m.Additionally, a negative correlation was observed between referees' YYIRTL1 running distance and their BMI and BF percentage (r = −224 and r = −186. respectively).However, no correlation between the morphological characteristics and ARIET running distance (p> 0.05).

Several studies on referees' heart rates during a match have been conducted. Which have measured averages of 162–165 beats/min [30]. 163 ± 2 beats/min [17]. 161 ± 9 beats/min (in Italian referees; 21) and 163 ± 5 beats/min (in English Premier League referees; 7).A study conducted on British referees showed no correlation between mean heart rate and average distance in the match [41]. In a similar study conducted by Morris [24] HRmax values were shown as 189±8.61 beats / min and HRmean as 160.32±10.42 beats / min according to the YYIRTL1 test results.In the presented study, the referees' and assistant referees' HRmax, HRmean and HRload values were 186.7 ± 10.5 beats/min., 166.2 ± 11.2 beats/min., 61.6 and 193.8 ±10.3 beats/min., 178.4 ± 11 beats/min. and 47.5 ± 6.7, respectively.According our study test results, HRmean andBF percentage were a statistically significant in referees and assistant referees (p <0.05). Also,there was a significant difference between BF referencegroups and heart rate values (p> 0.05).

In a study, Mallo et al. [20] reported that there was no correlation between RSA performance and the distance the referees covered at high speed. A recent study has found that sprints in a match indicated a significant correlation (r = -.65. r = - 0.60) between high intensity running and RSA [26].

Our study has found a significant negative correlation between RSA total time and BF percentage for referees and assistant referees(r= -262 and r=-329.respectively).In a similar study, there was a positive correlation with the decline in velocity performance between BM, FM and BF percentages [23]. This shows that an increase in total mass and fat mass is detrimental to speed [36].

In this study, we found that increases to BF percentage and BMI negatively affected referee running performance. Appropriate training strategies and nutrition should be recommended to the referees in order to promote optimal health and physical performance.

References

1. Bangsbo J. Mohr M. & Krustrup P. Journal of Sports Sciences.**22**(6): 524. (2004)

2. Bizzini M. Junge A. Bahr R. Helsen W. Dvorak J. Br J Sports Med.; **43**(7):490–7 (2009).
3. Castagna C. Abt G. D'Ottavio S. Sports Med.**37** (7):625–46 (2007).
4. Castagna. C. Abt. G. D'ottavıo. S. & Weston.M. Journal of Strength and Conditioning Research.**19**(4): 785-790 (2005a).
5. Catteeuw P. Helsen W. Gılıs. B. Wagemans. J. Journal of Sports Sciences; **27**(11): 1125–1136(2009).
6. Da Sılva. A. Fernandez. R. Paes. M. Fernandes. L. & Rech.C.Archivos De Medicina Del Deporte. (**144**): 238-246 (2011).
7. D'ottavıo. S. Castagna. C. J. of Srength and Conditioning Research. **15** (2). 167-171 (2001).
8. Fıtzsımons. M. Dawson. B. Ward D. & Wılkınson A. Australian Journal of Science and Medicine in Sport.**25**(4): 82-87 (1993).
9. Garret JR. William E. Kirkendall DT. Porto Alegre: Artmed(2003).
10. Gregory G. Haff. Travis Triplett N. National Strength and Conditioning Association 4. Th Ed. Human Kinetics (2016).
11. Helsen W. Bultynck JB. J Sports Sci; **22**: 179-89 (2004).
12. Housh TJ. Thorland WG. Johnson GO. Tharp GD. *Brit JSports Sc*.**2**:3-11 (1984).
13. Iaıa. F. Rampınını. E. & Bangsbo. J. International Journal of Sports Physiology and Performance. 4: 291-306 (2009).
14. Jackson AS. Pollock ML. Phys Sportsmed.**13**:76–90 (1985).
15. NevillA.M. MetsiosG.S.JacksonA.S. Wang. J. ThorntonJ. and GallagherD. Int J Body Compos Res. **2**; 6(3): 114–121 (2008)
16. Johnston. L.; Mcnaughton. L.Aust J Sci Med Sport.**26** (3-4): 67-72 (1994).
17. Krustrup. P. & Bangsbo. J. Journal of Sports Sciences.**19**(11): 881-891 (2001).
18. Krustrup. P.; Helsen. W.; Randers. M. B.; Chrıstensen. J. F.; Macdonald. C.; Rebelo. A. N. & Bangsbo. J. Journal of Sports Sciences.**27**(11): 1167-1176 (2009).
19. L.Lategan African Journal for Physical. Health Education. Recreation and Dance.**17**(4): 675-693 (2011).
20. Mallo. J.; Navarro. E.; Garcıa-Aranda. J. & Helsen. W. Journal of Sports Sciences.**27**(1): 9-17 (2009).
21. Mallo. J.; Navarro. E.; Garcıa-Aranda. J.; Gılıs. B. & Helsen. W. Journal of Strength and Conditioning Research.**22**(1): 235-242 (2008).
22. Marandi MS. Abadi BN. Esfarjani F. Mojtahedi H. Ghasemi G. Int J Prev Med.**4**. 125 (2013).
23. Moncef C. Said M. Olfa N. Dagbaji G. Asian Journal of Sports Medicine.**3**:2. 74-80 (2012).
24. Morris B. 'Doctara Thesis:Stellenbosch University https://scholar.sun.ac.za.(2015)
25. Oliver MJ. Lambert SB. Martin ES. Green SJ. Crouse FC.J Athl Train. **47**. 263 (2012).
26. Oliver.O. Armstrong. N. Williams. C. International Journal of Sports Physiology and Performance.**2**: 137-149 (2007).
27. Osiecki R. Glir FG. Fornaziero AM. Cunha RC. Dourado AC. Rev Edu Física/UEM;**18**.177-82 (2007).
28. Rahimi R. Physical Edu Sport.**4**. 101 (2006).
29. Rampinini. E. Bishop. D. Marcora. S.M. Ferrari. D. Sassi. D.Impellizzeri. F.M. Int. J. Sports Med..**28**:228-235 (2007)
30. Reilly T. Gregson W. J Sports Sci.**24**(7):795–801 (2006).
31. Reilly T.J Sports Sci;**15**(3):257–63 (1997).
32. Reilly. T. Bangsbo. J. Franks. A**18**. 669± 683 (2000).
33. Rontoyannis. G. P.; Stalikas. A.; Sarros. G.; Vlastaris. A. Journal of Sports Medicine and Physical Fitness. **38**. 208-14 (1998).
34. Schwingel. A.C.; Mıchels. G.; Petroskı. E.L.; Velho. M.N. Anais do XXIm Simpósio Internacional de Ciências do Esporte. São Paulo. p. 77(1998).

35. Stolen T. Chamari K. Castagna C. Wisloff U. Sports Med.;**35**(6):501–36 (2005).
36. Stuempfle. K.J. Katch F.I. & Petrıe D.F. J. Strength Cond. Res. **17**.238–244 (2003).
37. Swain. DP. 9th ed. Baltimore(MD): Lippincott and Wilkins. s.342 (2014).
38. Ugarkovic. D. D. Matavulj. M. Kukolj. And S. Jaric. J. Strength Cond. Res. **16**.227–230 (2002)
39. Weston M. Drust B. Atkinson G. Gregson W. Int J Sports Med.;**32**(3):190–4 (2011)
40. Weston. M & Helsen. W. (3rd Ed) (Pp 271-285). Routledge: New York (2013).
41. Weston. M. & Castagna. C. Journal of Sports Sciences.**23**(11): 1302-1303 (2005).
42. Weston. M.; Castagna. C.; Impellizzeri. F.; Rampinini. E. & Abt. G. Journal of Science and Medicine in Sport.**10**: 390-397 (2007).
43. Weston. M.; Helsen. W.; Macmahon. C.; Kirkendall. D. The American Journal of Sports Medicine. Vol. **32** (1). 54s-61s (2004).
44. Wilmore JH. Costill DL. Human Kinetics. Campaign 145-152 (1999).
45. Wragg.C.B. Maxwell.N.S.Doust. J.H. J. Appl. Physiol.**83:** 77- 83 (2000).

Learners' views about cloud computing-based group activities

Serkan Yildirim[1,a] Mehmet Cem Bölen[1], and Gürkan Yildirim[2]

[1]Atatürk University, Erzurum, Turkey
[2]Bayburt University, Bayburt, Turkey

Abstract. Thanks to its use independently of time and place during the process of software development and by making it easier to access to information with mobile technologies, cloud based environments attracted the attention of education world and this technology started to be used in various activities. In this study, for programming education, the effects of extracurricular group assignments in cloud based environments on learners were evaluated in terms of group work satisfaction, ease of use and user satisfaction. Within the scope of computer programming education lasting eight weeks, a total of 100 students participated in the study including 34 men and 66 women. Participants were divided into groups of at least three people considering the advantages of cooperative learning in programming education. In this study carried out in both conventional and cloud based environments, between groups factorial design was used as research design. The data collected by questionnaires of opinions of group work were examined with quantitative analysis method. According to the study results extracurricular learning activities as group activity created satisfaction. However, perceptions of easy use of the environment and user satisfaction were partly positive. Despite the similar understandings; male participants were easier to perceive use of cloud computing based environments. Some variables such as class level, satisfaction, computer and internet usage time do not have any effect on satisfaction and perceptions of ease of use. Evening class students stated that they found it easy to use cloud based learning environments and became more satisfied with using these environments besides being happier with group work than daytime students.
Keywords: Cloud computing, programming education, extracurricular learning activity, group work

1 Introduction

Learner-learner interaction that reflects the interaction between learners and their peers is as important as teacher-learner and learner-content interactions in an individual's learning processes. In this context, peers, who come together to proceed formal and informal learning processes, constitute various study groups. These groups provide development

[a]Corresponding author: serkanyildirim@atauni.edu.tr

opportunities to each individual, who creates the group itself, in a collaborative atmosphere as engaging both learning and teaching activities. Learning activities that peers perform with each other revealed the "collaborative learning" approach. Collaborative learning is described as a technic for students to help each other for a common purpose as constituting small mixed groups and also ensures them to learn in the process [1, 5]. Findings that collaborative learning has positive effects on student success and even that this technic is more effective compared to traditional teaching technics takes its place in literature [19, 31, 32, 40].

In-group communication is one of the effective conditions for individuals' learning activities in collaborative learning processes. Collaborative learning activities could be organized in class or different physical locations where healthy communication could be maintained, in traditional approach. Therefore, technological developments remove location borders of collaborative earning activities for today and provide opportunities for learners to participate in learning processes and group studies in different locations with computer and internet technology. Even today, computer supported collaborative learning platforms can not only be performed with computers but also with mobile devices and other platforms that use many internet-based technologies. One of these technologies is cloud computing [10, 24].

Basic philosophy of cloud computing is to enable for information and applications to be reached independently from location and time. With cloud computing technology, its users can benefit from infrastructure (i.e. server, network and storage), platform (i.e. operating system and middleware) and software (i.e. application programs) services that require high level of budget and qualified workforce investment by allocating lower level of monetary and labor force source compared to localized service types [9, 37]. With these specifications, cloud computing technologies include internet-based applications in itself that allow users to benefit from generally physical sources and application software independently from location. Physical sources and software can be reached through web browser, and special application software [14] or through user interface of a software that is currently used, with communication and integration opportunities of cloud computing technologies.

Unlike the general notion, cloud computing technology is not only used in information technologies' structure but also used as an important tool in teaching activities to reach innovative teaching applications and methods [16, 38]. Usability of cloud computing based tools independently from time and location and their convenience on reaching information with mobile technologies give possibility for this technology to be used in teaching activities. Popularity of cloud computing services in teaching platforms that are considered under "Software as a Service (SaaS)" category in software classification has increased day by day [21]. Software under SaaS category enables one or more users to reach the same source and them to manage this source in the framework of user authorities. With platforms in this category, more than one author can create the same document, use the same program and manage the same physical hardware. With this specifications, SaaS based applications become ideal platforms for learning processes for collaborative learning activities, and individual and group activities. Individuals who realize these facilities of the platforms focus on using tools in SaaS category (i.e. Google Docs, Dropbox, and Skydrive) in computer assisted collaborative learning and group study activities [30, 36].

In literature, it could be found that, with cloud computing support, collaborative group studies increase in-group communication, facilitate in-group information, idea and perception sharing and study results could be jointly evaluated within groups. It is stated that cloud computing technology can support collaborative, active and individual learning processes with the help of its communication and interaction opportunities [7, 25, 35]. Moreover, it is argued that learners can prefer to choose traditional learning tools due to easy to use characteristics of cloud computing based technological tools [4]. Without hesitation, attention to cloud based teaching tools has increased since convenience that is offered by cloud based platforms to teaching propose material sharing and increase learner-teacher interaction through the documents that are created by learners [25]. In this context, especially with their potential sharing and interaction abilities, remote education platforms are considered from new perceptions and cloud based e-learning platforms that are liked by learners are created [23]. Additionally, it is also found in literature that flexibility of cloud based online collaborative learning platforms is an important factor supporting collaborative learning processes [33].

Today, use of cloud computing based teaching tools in different teaching activities has increased day by day. Especially, in programming teaching in which traditional tools and technics are used, cloud computing technologies, and communication and interaction facilities that are offered by this technology are utilized. Especially, in recent years, emerging of software development platforms, which work based on cloud computing, causes the major popularity of this idea for its possible use in business and academic world. For example, Nordio, Estler, Furia and Meyer [26] compared traditional and cloud based software development platforms in their studies, which they mentioned about their experience of software developing in cloud computing based platforms, and stated that cloud computing based software development platforms offered different flexibilities and conveniences to group members. Levin [22], stated that cloud computing platforms offered major conveniences to software developers in concurrently software development processes. Rajaei and Aldakheel [28] argued that cloud based tools could be used in engineering education however, a research must be conducted for this subject matter in order to be able to declare what kind of advantages could be offered by these tools, compared to traditional learning platforms.

The cloud computing specifications of Microsoft Visual Studio Online platform can be used as an alternative collaborative learning platform for programming teaching. In the view of this platform, this study was conducted for programming learning in terms of perceptions toward making extracurricular group duties in the basis of group studies in cloud computing learning platforms. In this direction, answers were sought for below listed questions under the coverage of this study:

1) What are the perception levels of participations in cloud computing based software development platforms for group studies?
2) Do perception levels of participations in cloud computing based software development platforms for group studies differentiate in terms of gender differences?
3) Do perception levels of participations in cloud computing based software development platforms for group studies differentiate in terms of class differences?
4) Do perception levels of participations for cloud computing based teaching platform differentiate in terms of education time?
5) Do perception levels of participations for cloud computing based teaching platform differentiate in terms of daily computer usage?
6) Do perception levels of participations for cloud computing based teaching platform differentiate in terms of daily internet usage?
7) Do perception levels of participations for cloud computing based teaching platform differentiate in terms of the mostly used type of software?

2 Method

This study aims to analysis the collaborative group studies, which are conducted through cloud computing based programming platform and under the coverage of extracurricular group learning activities, depending on perception levels.

2.1 Analysis technic

In this study, static group comparison technic was preferred. From weak experimental technics, static group comparison technic is a single factor technic which does not use random selection [6].

2.2 Population and sample

Sample of this study was determined using an appropriate sampling strategy. Convenient sampling is to include available, volunteer or occasionally accessible people to the research [18]. Sample of the study was comprised by students who enrolled to Computer Programming II course in University of Ataturk, Faculty of Engineering, and Department of Industrial Engineering.

100 students participated to the study as 34 were male and 66 were female. Age of participants ranged from 17 to 29. All of the students in the study previously had taken Computer Programming course and experienced Visual Studio Online development platform.

2.3 Data collection tools and process

Questionnaire, which was developed by the researchers about student opinions on cloud computing based group studies, was used to analyze participants' perceptions toward group studies. This questionnaire form was consisted of 16 questions. The questionnaire included three factors as group study satisfaction, perception of platform usage easiness, and platform usage satisfaction. Group study satisfaction factor was consisted of 6 questions as focusing on the satisfaction level of the participants for their group studies during learning processes. Perception of ease of use of platform factor focused on determining the participants' perceptions toward easiness of the platform in which cloud computing based group studies were conducted. Platform usage satisfaction focused on satisfaction levels of the participants for the platform in which cloud computing based group studies were conducted. Reliability co-efficiency of the questionnaire was found as .907. Reliability coefficiencies of each factor was found as .864, .887 and .848, respectively. The first factor explained 23.78% of the total variance while the second and third factors explained 22.99% and 21.66% of the total variance, respectively. The total variance that was explained by the questionnaire was 68.4%. Questionnaire that was developed for student opinions on cloud computing based group studies was applied as printed forms.

2.4 Implementation

The study lasted a total of 8 weeks. Participants made their homework in Visual Studio Online (VSO) during the study process. Cloud based software development specifications were added to the new version of Microsoft Visual Studio. Software developers can prepare a common project concurrently, and see and review all the codes that are created by project team with the help of cloud based tools that are offered in the platform, which was released in 2013 and named as "Microsoft Visual Studio Online". More than one software developers can work independently from time and location through VSO with cloud technology and make progresses on project management and create codes with only a web browser. Additionally, the developed codes were stored in servers that were managed by Microsoft. Therefore, the possible data loss cases that were experienced in traditional project management tools were avoided. For all these reasons, VSO was selected as the platform where the education would be delivered and it was targeted for the individuals, who took programming education during the study period, to experience project development processes as creating similar structures with professional developer teams.

Participants were divided into three member groups depending on a volunteer basis for the study. Each of groups made their group studies in VSO. Prior to the study, 2-week pilot study was made to develop the groups' mutual study culture and they were expected to prepare 2 group homework during the pilot application period. After the pilot study, final groups were created as meeting the demands of some members who wanted to change their groups. Duringthe pilot, a presentation was delivered to the participants about VSO platform in which they would prepare their homework. During the presentation process, a presentation including exercises was delivered to the participants that lasted almost 60 minutes. Additionally, various exercise duties were assigned to them for them to get familiar with VSO platform and their success rates in these exercises were observed. As overcoming the deficiencies, the participants ensured to get sufficient level to use the platform. Additionally, questions of the participants about VSO platform were answered and the difficulties that they had using the platform were eliminated.

2.5 Short period group duties (subject based)

Under the concept of this study, participants performed 5 short period group duties. Each of group study period was 1 week. The groups were informed about study evaluation criteria and deadlines. Their homework was evaluated depending on the criteria and necessary feedbacks were given to the students using detailed score tables. Group duties and the related subjects were presented in Table 1.

Table 1. Short period group duties and the related subjects

Homework Name	Subject
Homework 1	Basic Database Applications
Homework 2	Introduction to MS SQL
Homework 3	Web Programming and database development
Homework 4	Desktop Programming and database development (Basic): Dictionary
Homework 5	Desktop Programming and database development (Intermediate): Address book

2.6 Long term group duties (project assignment)

Under the scope of this study, free time group study was performed with project assignment that covered all objectives of the course. Groups chose one of 3 alternative projects. Projects had a basic structure that covered different exercises for both web and desktop programming. In the first of the application, evaluation criteria and deadline were presented to the assigned project. During 8 weeks, the prepared homework was evaluated depending on the criteria and necessary feedbacks were given to the students using detailed score tables.

3 Findings

A total of 100 students, as 34 male and 66 female, participated to this study that aimed to compare the group studies, which were performed through cloud computing platform under the scope of extracurricular learning activities, to the level of participants' perception. In this section of the study, findings were categorized depending on the research questions.

1) What are the perception levels of participations in cloud computing based software development platforms for group studies?

Perception levels of participants were analyzed through factors' average scores. The results were presented in Table 2.

Table 2. Participants' satisfaction scores

Factor	N	$\bar{x}$	Std.
Group study satisfaction	96	3,5868	,86179
Perceived ease of use of platform	89	3,1236	,94299
Platform usage satisfaction	94	3,3378	,96142

According to the factor scores in Table 2, participants' satisfaction levels for group studies was found as "I agree" ($\bar{X}$=3,59). Moreover, perception of ease of use of platform and platform usage satisfaction levels were found as "rarely agree" ($\bar{x}$=3,12; $\bar{x}$=3,34, respectively).

2) Do perception levels of participations in cloud computing based software development platforms for group studies differentiate in terms of gender differences?

Before analyzing participants' opinions related to their perception levels, Shapiro Wilk normality test was applied depending on gender variable (Table 3). According to test results, data is not distributed normally.

Table 3. Results of normality test (gender)

Factor	Male			Female		
	Std.	sd	p	Std.	sd	p
Group study satisfaction	,892	28	,007	,936	54	,007
Perceived ease of use of platform	,906	28	,016	,971	54	,210
Platform usage satisfaction	,883	28	,005	,925	54	,002

Participants' perception levels in terms of gender variable were analyzed with Mann Whitney U test that did not require parametric test assumptions. Test results were presented in Table 4.

Table 4. Mann Whitney u test results (gender)

Factor	Group	N	Mean Rank	Sum of Means	U	p
Group study satisfaction	Male	31	55,18	1710,50	800,500	,104
	Female	65	45,32	2945,50		
Perceived ease of use of platform	Male	31	53,87	1670,00	624,000	,018
	Female	58	40,26	2335,00		
Platform usage satisfaction	Male	32	51,05	1633,50	878,500	,361
	Female	62	45,67	2831,50		

As seen in Table 4, there is not a meaningful difference between male and female participants' group studies satisfaction levels (U=800,500 p>.05). There is a statistically meaningful difference between male and female participants' perception of ease of use of platform (U=624,000 p<.05). Additionally, there is not a statistically meaningful difference between male and female participants' platform usage satisfaction levels. (U=878,500 p>.05).

3) Do perception levels of participations in cloud computing based software development platforms for group studies differentiate in terms of class differences?

Before analyzing participants' opinions related to their perception levels, Shapiro Wilk normality test was applied depending on class differences (Table 5). According to test results, data for group study satisfaction and platform usage satisfaction factors is not distributed normally. On the other hand, data for ease of use of platform perception factor is distributed normally.

Table 5. Results of normality test (class differences)

Factor	1.Grade			2.Grade			3.Grade			4.Grade		
	Std.	sd	P	Std.	sd	p	Std.	sd	p	Std.	sd	p
Group study satisfaction	,955	19	,476	,908	23	,037	,819	23	,001	,836	14	,014
Perceived ease of use of platform	,937	19	,233	,948	23	,263	,934	23	,135	,911	14	,164
Platform usage satisfaction	,879	19	,021	,835	23	,001	,932	23	,122	,912	14	,171

In terms of class differences variable, participants' ease of use of platform perception factor was analyzed with One Way Anova from parametric tests and group studies satisfaction and platform usage satisfaction factors were analyzed with Kruskal Wallis H test that did not require parametric test assumptions. Test results were presented in Table 6 and Table 7.

Table 6. One Way ANOVA test results (perception of ease of use in platform)

Source of Variance	Sum of Squares	Sd	Avarage of Squares	F	p	Significant Difference
Inter-Group	6,303	3	2,101	2,430	.071	Yok
Intra-Group	70,911	82	,865			
Total	77,214	85				

As seen in Table 6, there is not a statistically meaningful difference among groups for ease of use of platform perception factor in terms of class differences (F(3-82=2,43, p>.05).

Table 7. Kruskal Wallis H test results (group studies satisfaction and platform usage satisfaction)

Factor	n	Mean Rank	sd	X^2	p	Significant Difference
Group Studies Satisfaction						
1. Grade	20	39,00	3	4,046	.257	None
2. Grade	29	44,83				
3. Grade	24	47,71				
4. Grade	18	56,00				
Platform Usage Satisfaction						
1. Grade	20	33,55	3	9,332	.025	1.Grade-2.Grade
2. Grade	28	50,11				1. Grade-4.Grade
3. Grade	25	41,72				
4. Grade	17	57,53				3.Grade-4.Grade

As seen in

Table 7, there is not a statistically meaningful difference between scores for group studies satisfaction factor in terms of class differences (X2(sd=3, n=91)=4,046, p>.05). There is a statistically meaningful difference between scores for platform usage satisfaction factor in terms of class differences (X2(sd=3, n=90)=9,332, p<.05). The meaningful difference in terms of class differences was analyzed with Mann Whitney U test. According to test results, there is a meaningful difference between 1st class and 2nd and 4th classes, and between 3th class and 4th class.

4) Do perception levels of participations for cloud computing based teaching platform differentiate in terms of education time?

Before analyzing participants' opinions related to their perception levels, Shapiro Wilk normality test was applied depending on education time (Table 8). According to test results, data for group study satisfaction and platform usage satisfaction factors is not distributed normally. On the other hand, data for ease of use of platform perception factor is distributed normally.

Table 8. Normality Test results (education time)

Factor	Morning			Night		
	Std.	sd	p	Std.	sd	p
Group studies satisfaction	,876	53	,000	,892	29	,006
Perceived Ease of Use of Platform	,966	53	,139	,957	29	,273
Platform usage satisfaction	,910	53	,001	,878	29	,003

In terms of education duration variable, participants' ease of use of platform perception factor was analyzed with Sample T Test from parametric tests and group studies satisfaction and platform usage satisfaction factors were analyzed with Mann Whitney U test that did not require parametric test assumptions. Test results were presented in Table 9 and Table 10.

DOI: 10.1051/shsconf/20173701033

Table 9. Mann Whitney U test results (education time)

Factor	Grup	N	Mean Rank	Sum of Means	U	p
Group studies satisfaction	Morning	60	42,93	2576,00	746,000	,011
	Night	36	57,78	2080,00		
Platform usage satisfaction	Morning	61	42,02	2563,50	672,500	,008
	Night	33	57,62	1901,50		

As seen in

Table 9, there are statistically meaningful differences between perceptions of the participants, who took education in night and morning, for group studies satisfaction and platform usage satisfaction factors ((U=746,000 p<.05; U=672,500 p<.05) respectively).

Table 10. T test results (education time)

Factor	Group	N	$\overline{X}$	S	Sd	t	p
Perceived Ease of Use of Platform	Morning	56	2,9762	,95792	87	1,951	.049
	Night	33	3,3737	,87553			

As seen in Table 10, there is a statistically meaningful difference between perceptions of the participants, who took education in night and morning, for ease of use of platform factor (t(87)=1951, p<.05).

5) Do perception levels of participations for cloud computing based teaching platform differentiate in terms of daily computer usage?

Before analyzing participants' opinions related to their perception levels, Shapiro Wilk normality test was applied depending on daily computer usage (Table 11). According to test results, data is not distributed normally.

Table 11. Normality test results (daily computer usage period)

Factor	0-2 Hours			2-4 Hours			4-6 Hours			Greater than 6 Hours		
	Std.	sd	P	Std.	sd	p	Std.	sd	p	Std.	sd	p
Group studies satisfaction	,920	35	,014	,905	27	,018	,964	10	,830	,899	9	,248
Perceived Ease of Use of Platform	,943	35	,069	,953	27	,249	,979	10	,960	,834	9	,049
Platform usage satisfaction	,906	35	,006	,899	27	,013	,917	10	,335	,708	9	,002

In terms of daily computer usage period variable, participants' perceptions were analyzed with Kruskal Wallis H test that did not require parametric test assumptions. Test results were presented in Table 12.

DOI: 10.1051/shsconf/20173701033

Table 12. Kruskal Wallis H test results (daily computer usage period)

Factor	n	Mean Rank	sd	X^2	p	Significant Difference
		Group studies satisfaction				
0-2 hours	41	50,11	3	5,429	,143	None
2-4 hours	30	53,72				
4-6 hours	14	39,46				
Greater than 6 hours	10	34,15				
		Perceived Ease of Use of Platform				
0-2 hours	37	42,85	3	2,872	,412	None
2-4 hours	28	50,05				
4-6 hours	14	36,61				
Greater than 6 hours	9	46,28				
		Platform usage satisfaction				
0-2 hours	39	47,55	3	3,169	,366	None
2-4 hours	29	51,90				
4-6 hours	16	37,13				
Greater than 6 hours	9	46,39				

As seen in

Table 12, there is not a statistically meaningful difference between scores for group studies satisfaction factor in terms of daily computer usage period (X2(sd=3, n=95)=5,429, p>.05). There is not a statistically meaningful difference between scores for ease of use of platform perception factor in terms of daily computer usage period(X2(sd=3, n=88)=2,872, p>.05). There is not a statistically meaningful difference between scores for platform usage satisfaction factor in terms of daily computer usage period(X2(sd=3, n=88)=3,169, p>.05).

6) Do perception levels of participations for cloud computing based teaching platform differentiate in terms of daily internet usage?

Before analyzing participants' opinions related to their perception levels, Shapiro Wilk normality test was applied depending on daily internet usage (Table 13). According to test results, data is not distributed normally.

Table 13. Normality Test results (daily internet usage period)

Factor	0-2 Hours			2-4 Hours			4-6 Hours			Greater than 6 Hours		
	Std.	sd	P	Std.	sd	p	Std.	sd	p	Std.	sd	p
Group studies satisfaction	,925	39	,012	,938	21	,198	,936	9	,542	,889	11	,134
Perceived Ease of Use of Platform	,930	39	,018	,975	21	,838	,975	21	,838	,934	11	,453

Platform usage satisfaction	,933	39	,023	,798	21	,001	,914	9	,348	,802	11	,010

In terms of daily internet usage period variable, participants' perceptions were analyzed with Kruskal Wallis H test that did not require parametric test assumptions. Test results were presented in Table 14.

Table 14. Kruskal Wallis H test results (daily internet usage period)

Factor	n	Mean Rank	sd	X^2	p	Significant Difference
Group Studies Satisfaction						
0-2 Hours	45	48,44	3	3,440	,329	Yok
2-4 Hours	24	53,52				
4-6 Hours	12	43,21				
Greater than 6 Hours	13	37,08				
Perceived Ease of Use of Platform						
0-2 Hours	41	40,43	3	1,763	,623	Yok
2-4 Hours	24	48,69				
4-6 Hours	10	46,45				
Greater than 6 Hours	12	44,79				
Platform Usage Satisfaction						
0-2 Hours	43	44,15	3	2,987	,394	Yok
2-4 Hours	23	54,59				
4-6 Hours	13	44,92				
Greater than 6 Hours	13	41,54				

As seen in Table 14, there is not a statistically meaningful difference between scores for group studies satisfaction factor in terms of daily internet usage period(X2(sd=3, n=94)=3,440, p>.05). There is not a statistically meaningful difference between scores for ease of use of platform perception factor in terms of daily internet usage period(X2(sd=3, n=87)=1,763, p>.05). There is not a statistically meaningful difference between scores for platform usage satisfaction factor in terms of daily internet usage period(X2(sd=3, n=92)=2,987, p>.05).

7) Do perception levels of participations for cloud computing based teaching platform differentiate in terms of the mostly used type of software?

Before analyzing participants' opinions related to their perception levels, Shapiro Wilk normality test was applied depending on the mostly used type of software (Table 15). According to test results, data is not distributed normally.

Table 15. Normality test results (the mostly used type of software)

Factor	Office Application Internet			Programming			Design		
	Std.	sd	P	Std.	sd	p	Std.	sd	p
Group studies satisfaction	,920	18	,131	,881	43	,000	,793	10	,012
Perceived Ease of Use of Platform	,953	18	,476	,957	43	,109	,831	10	,035

Platform usage satisfaction	,920	18	,132	,880	43	,000	,868	10	,094

In terms of the mostly used type of software variable, participants' perceptions were analyzed with Kruskal Wallis H test that did not require parametric test assumptions. Test results were presented in Table 16.

Table 16. Kruskal Wallis H test results (the mostly used type of software)

Factor	n	Sum of Means	sd	X^2	p	Significant Difference
Group Studies Satisfaction						
Office Applications Internet	22	40,45	2	,123	,940	Yok
Programming	49	41,65				
Design	10	39,00				
Perceived Ease of Use of Platform						
Office Applications Internet	20	35,53	2	2,349	,309	Yok
Programming	47	42,64				
Design	11	33,32				
Platform Usage Satisfaction						
Office Applications Internet	22	38,41	2	1,037	,595	Yok
Programming	46	42,00				
Design	11	34,82				

As seen in Table 16, there is not a statistically meaningful difference between scores for group studies satisfaction factor in terms of the mostly used type of software (X2(sd=2, n=81)=,123, p>.05). There is not a statistically meaningful difference between scores for ease of use of platform perception factor in terms of the mostly used type of software (X2(sd=2, n=88)=2,349, p>.05). There is not a statistically meaningful difference between scores for platform usage satisfaction factor in terms of the mostly used type of software (X2(sd=2, n=77)=1,037, p>.05).

4 Discussion and conclusion

This study aims to compare the group studies that were performed through a cloud computing based development platform in terms of participants' group studies satisfaction, ease of use of platform perception and platform usage satisfaction factors, under the scope of extracurricular learning activities. Group studies satisfaction levels of participants of this study was found high. This condition shows that they are content with group studies for extracurricular learning activities. Additionally, their perceptions toward cloud computing based learning platform usage easiness for group studies was found as "rarely agree". This condition shows that participant do not find usage of cloud computing based learning platforms are very easy and according to them, cloud computing based learning platforms do not provide any convenience compared to traditional learning platforms. Similarly, in their studies that Pike, Pittman, and Hwang [27] compared two different student groups that took web programming training and used either cloud based or one of the traditional tools (i.e. personal computer etc.) reported that usage of cloud based development platforms was considered by students more difficult than traditional development platforms. This condition might be attributed to the facts that participants have more experience on usage of traditional learning platforms and they might not want to change their habits, moreover, cloud computing based platform using participants are not allowed to enter into group studies without making pre-preparation studies although they do not want to make any pre-preparation studies by themselves. Participants' satisfaction levels for cloud computing based learning platform usage were found as "rarely agree". This condition shows that participants partially like cloud computing based learning platforms and they do not find these platforms are entirely superior to traditional learning platforms. Therefore, cloud computing based software development platforms might not entirely meet the needs of traditional based (i.e. desktop, laptop etc.) professional software development tool sets although use of those platforms in educational institutions and activities are beneficial [12]. Moreover, it is observed that according to users' considerations, cloud based software development platforms are not "sufficiently beneficial to change the development platforms" in terms of currently used traditional development platforms. This result is similar to the results of the study that was conducted by Huang, Wang and Liu [17]. In the related study, a cloud based tool (Google Docs) was used in a course in which a web site was designed however a difference on students' learning motivation was not observed between those who used this tool and those who did not use.

There is not a meaningful difference between male and female participants' perceptions for group studies for extracurricular learning activities in terms of gender difference factor. Contrary to those studies that concluded that gender was considered as a factor affecting collaborative and group studies in engineering education [11, 34], this condition shows that both of the groups obtain a similar perception for extracurricular group studies. On the other hand, there is a statistically meaningful difference between male and female participants in terms of cloud computing ease of use of platform perception. In the observations of the related averages, male participants find usage of cloud computing based learning platform is easier than female participants. Male participants' attitudes to software usage process might be attributed to this condition. This finding can be explained with the role of computer concern that was determined in Gender Based Digital Separation model [8]. In the related model, technology usage concern of women was attributed to societal gender classification that have deeply affected individuals' behaviors starting from their early childhood. According to this view of point, boys are considered more competitive than girls by their parents and that they have better abilities in more masculine subjects (i.e. engineering etc.) and they are motivated to those areas during their education [8]. Another reason that female participants find software and internet based tools more difficult might be that majority of these tools have been designed in an industry that has been dominated by men [2, 15]. On the other hand, other reasons giving rise to this result can be listed as teaching strategies do not fit women's learning styles, they have more responsibilities in family duties compared to men, their desire to avoid occupations that are mainly held by men, their hesitation that is aroused from low level of self-sufficiency perceptions, compared to men, in spite of equal levels of performance [3]. Moreover, there is not a statistically meaningful difference between perceptions for cloud computing based learning platforms' usage satisfaction. This condition shows that female participants have similar level of satisfaction for usage of these platforms as male participants do although female participants find using these platforms more difficult than male participants. This conclusion can be interpreted as male participants in collaborative teams have more knowledge about the subject compared to female participants and cloud based platform using female participants have position notions for cloud based learning platforms because of the platforms' benefits although they have difficulties on using these platforms, as also stated in another study in this subject [13].

There is not a statistically meaningful difference between group studies' satisfaction among participants in terms of class differences. This condition shows that group studies satisfaction factor does not differentiate in class levels. Additionally, not having difference between groups can be interpreted as group studies have positive effects on academic success perception. Williams and Kessler [39] stated that students in dual programming teams in programming education demanded less support from instructors and benefited helps from their teammates when they have difficulty on a subject. Moreover, the notion of both of the platforms have similarly positive effects on academic success reveals that effects of learning habits rather than the platform itself is put forward. There is not a statistically meaningful difference between perceptions for cloud computing based learning platforms' usage easiness in terms of class differences. This condition shows that participants have generally similar perceptions for usage easiness. On the other hand, there is a statistically meaningful difference between perceptions for cloud computing based learning platforms' usage satisfaction. Especially, there is a difference between the first graders and 2nd and 4th graders, in favor of upper classes. Additionally, there is a statistically meaningful difference between 3rd and 4th classes. Upper classes' higher level of satisfactions for platform usage can be attributed to their familiarity to development tools and their programming experiences [27].

There is a statistically meaningful difference between perceptions of the students, who take morning and night education, for group studies satisfactions in favor of the students, who take night education, in terms of education time. This condition shows that the students, who take night education, prefers group studies more compared to other group and education time is effective on planning the common study periods. As Layman [20] stated that this condition can be attributed to personal characteristics of participants and their desire to allocate less time for common studies. In other words, studying with group members in a location which is outside of course classroom is more difficult for various reasons (i.e. course Schedule intensity, social activity diversity etc.) for the students, who take morning education, while this kind of activity is more enjoyable and attractive in a similar time frame for the students, who take night education. Similarly, there is a statistically meaningful difference between participants' perceptions for cloud computing based learning platforms usage easiness, in favor of the students, who take night education. This condition might be attributed to that they can find more time to practice these platforms. Additionally, there is a statistically meaningful difference between participants' perceptions for cloud computing based learning platforms usage satisfaction, in favor of the students, who take night education. This condition can be attributed to that these students find the platforms easier to use.

There is not a statistically meaningful difference between participants' perception levels in terms of daily computer usage period. Similarly, there is not a statistically meaningful difference between perception levels of the participants who are categorized in terms of daily internet usage period and the mostly used software types. The results show that computer and internet usage levels are not effective on satisfaction levels toward group studies. This condition can be attributed to the fact that there is communication efficacy in the basis of group studies and technology usage level is not effective for communication. According to [29] there are four types of collaborative study model in software engineering projects, as compulsory, verbal, purpose based and individual. Individual and purpose based study models are the mostly preferred study models [29]. Similarly, study participants preferred generally individual and purpose based study collaborative study model during the application. Therefore, this condition can be the reason of that daily computer and daily internet usage period does not create a difference on participants' perceptions. Additionally, computer and internet usage period have not effects on cloud computing based learning platforms' usage easiness perception. Similarly, there is not a statistically meaningful difference between participants' perceptions for cloud computing based learning platforms usage satisfaction in terms of computer and internet usage period. This condition can be interpreted as computer and internet usage skills are not effective on ease of use of platform and satisfaction. Moreover, participants' general skill levels might have caused this result.

As a result, the individuals, who use cloud computing based learning platforms, are content that group studies are used for extracurricular activities. Additionally, participants do not think that cloud computing based platforms that they performed their group studies are easy to use. Besides, their satisfaction levels for cloud computing based group study platforms are very high. Satisfaction levels of male and female participants for group studies are similar. On the other hand, male participants find cloud computing based platforms easier to use compared to female participants. There is not a difference between male and female participants for usage satisfaction although male participants find cloud computing based platforms easier to use compared to female participants. Perceptions for group studies satisfaction and cloud computing based learning platforms usage easiness are similar in terms of class difference. Additionally, upper classes have higher satisfaction levels for cloud computing based learning platforms compared to primary classes. Night students are more satisfied from extracurricular group studies than morning students. Similarly, an advantageous condition for night students is present for cloud computing based learning ease of use of platform and satisfaction levels. Computer and internet usage period diversities do not have significant effects on satisfaction levels of group studies and cloud computing based learning platforms. A similar condition is also valid in cloud computing based learning platforms' usage easiness.

5 Suggestions

The present study was conducted with students from industrial engineering department. Conducting similar studies with different groups and students from different education level can strengthen the study results. Additionally, conducting similar studies for lessons which have different theoretic and application levels will make contribution to literature. Lastly, increasing cloud based tools usage experience as intensifying the courses which will be delivered through cloud based development platform can affect users' cloud based tools usage easiness perception and their satisfaction levels.

References

1. Açıkgöz Ün, K. (2003). Etkili öğrenme ve öğretme. İzmir: Eğitim Dünyası Yayınları.
2. Ahuja, M. K., (2002). Women in the information technology profession: A literature review, synthesis and research agenda. European Journal of Information Systems, 11(1), 20-34.
3. Aldağ H. ve Tekdal M. (2015). Bilgisayar Kullanımı ve Programlama Öğretiminde Cinsiyet Farklılıkları, 1.Uluslararası Çukurova Kadın Çalışmaları Kongresi, ADANA, TÜRKİYE, 9-11 Nisan 2015, pp.236-243.
4. Behrend, T. S., Wiebe, E. N., London, J. E., and Johnson, E. C. (2011). Cloud computing adoption and usage in community colleges. *Behaviour & Information Technology*, *30*(2), 231-240.
5. Bruner, C., (1991). *Ten questions and answers to help policy makers improve children's services*. Washington, DC: Education and Human Services Consortium.
6. Buyukozturk, S., Kilic Cakmak, E., Akgun, O., Karadeniz, S., ve Demirel, F. (2009). Bilimsel arastirma yontemleri. Ankara: Pegem Akademi.
7. Calvo, R. A., O'Rourke, S. T., Jones, J., Yacef, K., and Reimann, P. (2011). Collaborative writing support tools on the cloud. *IEEE Transactions on Learning Technologies*, *4*(1), 88-97.
8. Cooper, J. (2006). The digital divide: The special case of gender. Journal of Computer Assisted Learning, 22(5), 320-334.

9. Dinh, H. T., Lee, C., Niyato, D., and Wang, P. (2013). A survey of mobile cloud computing: architecture, applications, and approaches. *Wireless communications and mobile computing, 13*(18), 1587-1611
10. Ercan, T. (2010). Effective use of cloud computing in educational institutions. *Procedia-Social and Behavioral Sciences, 2*(2), 938-942.
11. Felder, R. M., Felder, G. N., Mauney, M., Hamrin, C. E., and Dietz, E. J. (1995). A longitudinal study of engineering student performance and retention. III. Gender differences in student performance and attitudes. *Journal Of Engineering Education-Washington*, 84, 151-164.
12. Fylaktopoulos, G., Goumas, G., Skolarikis, M., Sotiropoulos, A., and Maglogiannis, I. (2016). An overview of platforms for cloud based development. SpringerPlus, 5(1), 38.
13. Guzdial, M., Ludovice, P., Realff, M., Morley, T., Carroll, K., and Ladak, A. (2001). The challenge of collaborative learning in engineering and math. In Frontiers in Education Conference, 2001. 31st Annual (Vol. 1, pp. T3B-24). IEEE.
14. Holschuh, D. R., and Caverly, D. C. (2010). Techtalk: Cloud Computing and Developmental Education. *Journal of Developmental Education, 33*(3), 38-39.
15. Huang, W. H. D., Hood, D. W., and Yoo, S. J. (2013). Gender divide and acceptance of collaborative Web 2.0 applications for learning in higher education. The Internet and Higher Education, 16, 57-65.
16. Huang Y.M., Wang C.S., Guo J.Z., Shih HY and Chen Y.S. (2013). Advancing collaborative learning with cloud service. *Lecture Notes in Electrical Engineering,* 253, 717–722.
17. Huang, Y. M., Wang, C. S., and Liu, Y. C. (2015) "A Study of Synchronous vs. Asynchronous Collaborative Design in Students Learning Motivation".*International Journal of Information and Education Technology,5*(5), 354-357.
18. Johnson, B. and Christensen, L. (2014). Educational research: Quantitative, qualitative, and mixed approaches 4th edition, Sage: USA.
19. Johnson, D., Johnson, R. ve Smith, K. (1991). Cooperative learning: Increasing college faculty instructional productivity, *ASHE-ERIC Higher Education Report (4).* Washington, DC: The George Washington University.
20. Layman, L. (2006) "Changing Students' Perceptions: An Analysis of the Supplementary Benefits of Collaborative Software Development," Proc. 19th. IEEE Conf. Software Eng. Education and Training, 159-166.
21. Lawton, G. (2008). Developing software online with platform-as-a-service technology. *Computer, 41*(6), 13-15.
22. Levin, S. (2013), "Synchronized software development," http://www.cs.tau.ac.il/thesis/thesis/Levin.Stas-MSc.pdf adresinden 29.05.2016 tarihinde erişildi.
23. Liao, J., Wang, M., Ran, W., and Yang, S. J. (2014). Collaborative cloud: a new model for e-learning. *Innovations in Education and Teaching International, 51*(3), 338-351
24. Lin, A., and Chen, N.-C. (2012). Cloud computing as an innovation: Percepetion, attitude, and adoption. *International Journal of Information Management, 32*(6), 533-540.
25. Murah, M. Z. (2012). Teaching and learning cloud computing. *Procedia-Social and Behavioral Sciences, 59*, 157-163.
26. Nordio, M., Estler, H., Furia, C. A., and Meyer, B. (2011). *Collaborative software development on the web*. 2011.
27. Pike, R. E., Pittman, J. M., Hwang, D., and Pomona, C. A. (2016). Cloud-based Versus Local-based Web Development Education: An Experimental Study in Learning Experience. In Proceedings of the EDSIG Conference ISSN (Vol. 2473, p. 3857)..

28. Rajaei, H. and Aldakheel, E. A. (2012). Cloud computing in computer science and engineering education, American Society for Engineering Education.
29. Robillard, P. N., and Robillard, M. P. (2000). Types of collaborative work in software engineering. Journal of Systems and Software, 53(3), 219-224.
30. Siegle, D. (2010). Cloud Computing: A Free Technology Option to Promote Collaborative Learning. *Gifted Child Today*, *33*(4), 41-45.
31. Slavin, R. E. (1980). Cooperative Learning. *Review Of Educational Research*. 50(2), 315-342.
32. Slavin, R. E. (1991). Synthesis of research on cooperative learning. *Educational Leadership, 48,* 71-82.
33. Stevenson, M., and Hedberg, J. G. (2013). Learning and design with online real-time collaboration. *Educational Media International*, *50*(2), 120-134.
34. Stump, G. S., Hilpert, J. C., Husman, J., Chung, W. T., and Kim, W. (2011). Collaborative learning in engineering students: Gender and achievement. Journal of Engineering Education, 100(3), 475-497.
35. Sultan, N. (2010). Cloud computing for education: A new dawn?. *International Journal of Information Management*, *30*(2), 109-116.
36. Thomas, P. Y. (2011). Cloud computing: A potential paradigm for practising the scholarship of teaching and learning. *The Electronic Library*, *29*(2), 214-224.
37. Vaquero, L. M. (2011). EduCloud: PaaS versus IaaS cloud usage for an advanced computer science course. *IEEE Transactions on Education*, 54(4), 590-598.
38. Wang, C. S., Huang, Y. M., and Huang, Y. M. (2012). Interactive e-Learning with Cloud Computing Framework. *Lecture Notes in Electrical Engineering*, 182, 311-316.
39. Williams, L. A., and Kessler, R. R. (2000). The effects of" pair-pressure" and" pair-learning" on software engineering education, 13th Conference on Software Engineering Education, 59-65.
40. Wright, J. C. (1996). Authentic learning environment in analytical chemistry using cooperative methods and open-ended laboratories in large lecture courses. *J. Chem. Educ, 73*(9), 827.

The awareness level of the parents about the benefits of the physical education lesson in secondary grade of the primary education schools

Burak Taş[1], Hakan Akdeniz[2,a], Gülşah Sekban[1], and Fatmanur Öztürk[1]

[1] Department of Physical Education and Sport Teaching, Sports Science Faculty, Kocaeli University, Kocaeli, Turkey
[2] Department of Physical Education and Sports Teachership, Institute of Educational Sciences, Sakarya University, Sakarya, Turkey

Abstract. This study is intended to determine the awareness level of the parents on the benefits of the Physical Education Course in the Secondary Grade of the Primary Education Schools. The sample of this study consists of 130 parents whose children studied at Şehit Ümit Balkan Secondary School in the District of İzmit in the Province of Kocaeli in the 2015-2016 academic year. The study is carried out by using the survey method for the purpose of collecting any and all data. The data collected is calculated through package program SPSS 17.0. In respect of the analysis of the data, the frequency (N) and percentage (%) values which are the descriptive statistics for all of the independent variables are determined primarily. Then, T-Test is utilized to determine the difference between the binary variables. The level of significance is considered as $p<0.05$, and any required results have been specified accordingly. In consequence of the study carried out, no significant difference at the level of $P>0,05$ is determined between the awareness level of the parents regarding the variable of gender concerning the benefits of the physical education course in the secondary grade of the primary education schools
Keywords: Secondary Grade of the Primary Education, Physical Education, Awareness

1 Introduction

There is the human at the starting point of the education and also at the heart of the short and long termed targets. In this sense, the sport as a part of the education should be considered so as to contribute to the integrity and the whole personality of the human for social health, rest, and peace [8].

[a] Corresponding author: hakanakdeniz@gmail.com

These merits that the human naturally has and emerges by the sport and improves reflect his/her daily life as well. In this regard, the sport is a significant tool of the values education. Physical education is based on the necessities of the individual. The movement is accepted as the most basic requirement. Physical activity is essential to living. The stable modern life makes the physical education more relevant within this context. The physical education is an inseparable part of the general training [8].

The primary goal of the physical education and the sport that are the significant parts of the general education is to help for the student to maximize movement capacity by training with moves, viz the physical activities. The other purpose is also to contribute to maximizing the physical, mental, social and emotional developments of children. [17] Moreover, the physical training is necessary regarding using the free time actively, influencing the health positively, developing the collaboration abilities and increasing the self-confidence of the individuals.

While the parents encourage their children for the sport to present a good family example and improve the school success, they spent both the money and the time. In other words, the parents positively support the participation of the children to the sport by paying the admission charge, buying pieces of equipment and being all ears for the game and applications of the children. That is to say, the parents create opportunities for children to be comfortable in the sports environment and are untroubled by the family resources spent as well as they organize the family budget so as to support the participation of their children in the sport [13].

In our country, in primary schools, the 1st-2nd-3rd and 4th classes are called as the First Grade, and the 5th-6th-7th and 8th classes are called as the Second Grade. The first social institution that provides individuals to recognize the physical education and the world of sport is the family. This effect of the family on socialization determines whether the child to join in with the physical training and sports activities and in what way she/he does if she/he enters. The attitude of the parents on this subject is almost the most decisive factor concerning the decision of the children on participation [9]. It is important regarding the future of our sport that to improve the basic education skills of the children, find the successful athletes by being determined their abilities and raise them. Therefore, the parents should believe all the benefits of the sport and place importance on the school-family cooperation. In brief, the parents need to have a sports culture for educating their children about this issue. The parents who have enough information will encourage their children to the sport in the healthiest manner and support them as well [4]. Our schools have important missions about being generalized, endeared and promoted the physical education and sport. There can be created a large base for the individual school and mass sport if the sports love is started in the family such as the basic education and reinforced by supporting in school [5].

In the education field, the 'parent' word is defined as the person who follows the works about the student and is responsible for his/her each kind of behavior and attitude. The parents need to be at a certain awareness level for being the physical training lesson in schools beneficial.

The awareness is a learnable skill. The awareness is a competence to be able to look at the happenings and daily events without being prejudiced by our previous experiences, thoughts, and beliefs [11].

This study is conducted to determine the awareness level of the parents on the benefits of the physical training lesson for children in Secondary Grade of the Primary Education School.

2 Material and method

2.1 Research group

The population is composed of the parents of the children who study in Şehit Ümit Balkan Secondary School in the 2015-2016 academic year in İzmit District of Kocaeli Province. The working group of the research consists of the parents joined accidentally. It is reached totally 130 parents that 94 of them are women and 36 of them are the men.

2.2 Data collection tools

The survey that is created by receiving the opinions of Prof. Dr. Semra Ünal is used as the data collection tool. The survey entirely has two parts. The first part consists of 7 questions necessitate the demographic information.

The second part has 33 questions that reveal the awareness level of the parents about the benefits of the physical training lesson for children in Secondary Grade of the Primary Education School. The quartet rating scale is used for the questions asked in the second part. These are the following statements; 'Strongly Agree' 'Partly Agree' 'Barely Agree' and 'Disagree.'

Below intervals are considered when being evaluated the arithmetic means of the opinions obtained under the survey.

Weight Given	Alternatives	Limit	Degree
1	Strongly Agree	4 (107,25-132)	High
2	Partly Agree	3,24 (82,5-106,92)	Middle
3	Barely Agree	2,49 (57,75-82,17)	Enough
4	Disagree	1,74 (33-57,42)	Low

2.3 Collecting the data

The data was collected in Şehit Ümit Balkan Secondary School in 2015-2016 academic year. 280 parents among from 551 ones received the survey, and entirely 130 of these receivers sent the questionnaire back.

2.4 Analyzing the data

SPSS 17.0 packaged software is used to analyze this research reviews the awareness levels of the parents about the benefits of the physical training lesson in Secondary Grade of the Primary Education School.

Firstly the frequency (N) and percentage (%) values that are the descriptor statistics for all independent variables are revealed for being analyzed the data. Later on, the T-Test is used to specify the difference between the binary variables. The significance level is accepted as $p<0.05$, and the required results are stated.

3 Findings

As is seen in Table 1, 72,3%of the parents are the women, 27,7% are the men. 6,2% of the parents are in 20-25 age range, 6,9% of them are in 25-30 age range, 35,4% of them in 30-35 age range and finally 51,5% of them are 36 age and older. 65,4% of the attendees answered the 'Degree' question as a mother, 25,4% of them answered this question as the father, 6,2% of them answered as the brother or sister and 3,1% answered as the others. 0,8% of the parents responded 'Your Education Status' question as the literate, 27,7% of them responded as primary school, 24,6% of them responded as the secondary school, 28,5% of them answered as the high school and equivalents, 8,5% of them graduated from the college, 7,7% of them are bachelors, and 2,3% of the responded as the other. 6,9% of the parents are unemployed, 10% of them are self-employed, 17,7% of them are the employees, 4,6% of them are artisans, 6,2% of them are soldiers, policemen, and officers, 50,8% of them are housewives, and 3,8% of these attendees are retired.

Table 1. The frequency and percentage values of the demographic information of attendees

Variables		f	%
Gender	Female	94	72,3
	Male	36	27,7
	Total	130	100
Age	20 – 25	8	6,2
	25 – 30	9	6,9
	30 – 35	46	35,4
	36 and older	67	51,5
	Total	130	100
Your degree as the parent to the student (Degree)	Mother	85	65,4
	Father	33	25,4
	Brother or Sister	8	6,2
	Other	4	3,1
	Total	130	100
Your Educational Status	Literate	1	0,8
	Primary School	36	27,7
	Secondary School	32	24,6
	High Sch. and Equivalents	37	28,5
	College	11	8,5
	Undergraduate	10	7,7
	Other	3	2,3
	Total	130	100
Your Job	Unemployed	9	6,9
	Self-Employment	13	10
	Employee	23	17,7
	Artisan	6	4,6
	Soldier-Police-Officer	8	6,2
	Housewife	66	50,8
	Retired	5	3,8
	Total	130	100

Table 2. The frequency and percentage values for the variable called 'do you deal with the physical education lesson of your child?'

	f	%
I do, I praise his/her success	97	74,6
I don't care much even if I do	29	22,3
I don't care	4	3,1
Total	130	100

As is seen in Table 2, 74,6% of the parents responded as 'I do, I praise his/her success' 22,3% of the parents answered as 'I don't care even if I do' and 3,1% of them said that 'I don't care.'

Table 3. The frequency and percentage values for the variable called 'if required, do you procure the materials about the physical education lesson of your child.'

	f	%
I procure by thinking that it is required	93	71,5
Not all of them, I procure what I find necessary	35	26,9
I evaluate as a waste	2	1,5
Total	100	100

According to Table 3, 71,5% of the parents answered the question called 'If Required, Do You Procure the Materials About the Physical Education Lesson of Your Child' as 'I procure by thinking that it is required' 26,9% answered this question as 'Not all of them, I procure what I find necessary' and 1,5% of these attendees responded as 'I evaluate as a waste'.

Table 4. Being compared the answers of the question called 'do you deal with the physical education lesson of your child?' regarding the educational status

Educational Status	I do, I praise his/her success	I don'care much even if I do	I don't care
Literate	%0,8	%0	%0
Primary School	%19,2	%6,2	%2,3
Secondary Scholl	%17,7	%6,9	%0
High Sch. and equiv.	%23,1	%5,4	%0
College	%6,9	%1,5	%0
Undergraduate	%5,4	%2,3	%0
Other	%1,5	%0	%0,8
Total	%74,6	%22,3	%3,1

As is seen in Table 4, the question called 'Do you deal with the physical education lesson of your child?' is answered as 'I do, I praise his/her success' by 0,8% of the attendees who are literate, 19,2% of them who graduated from primary school, 17,7% of them graduated from the secondary school, 23,1% graduated from high school and equivalents, 6,9% of them graduated from college, 5,4% of them graduated from the undergraduate and finally 1,5% of them are in the category of others. 2,3% of the participators who answered as 'I don't care' is primary school graduate, 0,8% of them graduated from other. 74,6% of the attendees answered as 'I do, I praise his/her success,' 22,3% of them said 'I don't care much even if I deal with' and 3,1% of them said 'I don't care.'

Table 5. Comparing the answers for the question called 'do you deal with the physical education lesson of your child' in terms of the gender

Gender	I do, I praise his/her success	I don' t care much even if I deal with	I don't care
Male	%20,8	%6,9	%0
Female	%53,8	%15,4	%3,1
Total	%74,6	%22,3	%3,1

According to the Table 5, 20,8% of the participants are the male who answered as 'I do, I praise his/her success, ' and 53,8% of them are female. 6,9% of the attendees are male, and 15,4% of them are the female who responded as 'I don't care much even if I deal with.' While 3,1% of the participants are the male who returned as 'I don't care,' there is not any man answered like that.

Table 6. Being compared the responses to the article called 'the physical education lesson effects the physical development of the students' regarding the gender variable

Gender	Strongly Agree	Partly Agree	Barely Agree	Disagree	Total
Male	%24,6	%3,1	%0	%0	%27,7
Female	%63,1	%6,2	%2,3	%,8	%72,3
Total	%87,7	%9,2	%2,3	%,8	%100

As is seen in Table 6, 24,6% of the attendees are male, and 63,1% of them are the female who responded as 'Strongly agree.' 3,1% of the participants are male, and 6,2% of them are the female who answered as 'Partly agree.' 2,3% of the attendees who answered as 'barely agree' are women. 0,08% of the participants who said 'disagree' are the females. 27,7% of the participants is male, and 72,3% of them are women who responded this article called 'The Physical Education Lesson Effects the Physical Development of the Students'.

Table 7. Being compared the answers for the article called 'The Physical Education Lesson Has Impact on the Students to Stand of the Bad Habits' regarding the gender variable

Gender	Strongly Agree	Partly Agree	Barely Agree	Disagree	Total
Male	%17,7	%6,9	%3,1	%0	%27,7
Female	%51,5	%13,8	%3,1	%3,1	%72,3
Total	%69,2	%20,8	%6,2	%3,1	%100

Based on Table 7, 17,7% of the people who said 'Absolutely agree' for this article is male, and 51,5 of them are the females. 6,9% of the attendees who said 'Partly agree' are males, and 13,8% of them are the females. 3,1% of the attendees are male and 3,1 of them female who responded as 'Barely agree.' 3,1% of the people who said 'Disagree.' Totally, 27,7% of the attendees are male, and 72,3% of the female are females who responded the question.

Table 8. Being compared the Awareness Levels of the Parents About the Benefits of the Physical Education Lesson in the secondary grade of the primary education schools in terms of the gender

	n	X	ss	p
Female	94	123,1101	12,82	
Male	36	122,1017	9,92	,671

As is seen in Table 8, there is not determined any discrepancy at P>0,05 level between the awareness levels of the parents regarding the gender variable of T-Test.

4 Discussion

72,3% of the parents are female, and 27,7 of them are the males who participated in the survey. 6,2% of them are in the age range of 20-25, 6,9% of them are in the age range of 25-30, 35,4% of them are in 30-35 age range, and 51,5% of them are 36 age and older. About the degree of the attendees as the parent to the students, 65,4 of them are mothers, 25,4 of them are fathers, 6,2% of them are brother or sisters, and 3,1% of these participants are the others. 0,8% of the parents are literate, 27,7% of them are primary school graduate, 24,6% of them are secondary school graduate, 28,5% of them graduated from the high school and equivalents, 7,7% of these participants are bachelor's, and finally 2,3% of them are in the category of others. Under these circumstances, the greater part of the attendees is composed of the parents who are 36 age and older. It is seen when the educational status is evaluated that the general run of the parents graduated from the high school and the equivalents. 6,9% of these attendees are unemployed, 10% of them are self-employed, 17,7% of them are the employee, 4,6% of them are artisans, 6,2% of them are soldiers, policemen and officers, 50,8% are the housewives and 3,8% are the retired ones. Regarding the question called 'Do You Deal With the Physical Education Lesson of Your Child'; 74,6% of the parents responded as 'I do, I praise his/her success' 22,3% of them responded as 'I don't care much even if I deal with' and 3,1% of these participants answered as 'I don't care' . The answers for the question called 'If Required, Do You Procure the Materials About the Physical Education Lesson of Your Child' as follows; 71,5% of the parents said 'I procure by thinking that it is required' 26,9% of them said 'Not all of them, I procure what I find necessary' and 1,5% of them answered as 'I evaluate as a waste'.

23,1% of the parents who said that they deal with the physical education lesson constitute the highest rate by mentioning that they graduated from the high school and the equivalents. 53,8% ratio consists of the female parents who said that they deal with the physical education lesson.

The male attendees got $\bar{x}$= 123,11 points concerning the T-Test analysis about the gender variable for the awareness levels of the parents on the benefits of the Physical Education Lesson in the secondary grade of the primary education schools. The female attendees got $\bar{x}$= 122,10 points. There is not determined a significant inequality at $P>0,05$ level between the two gender groups.

24,6 of the parents are male, and 63,1% of them are the females who think that physical education lesson has positive impacts on the physical development of the students. Totally 87,7% of the parents expect that the physical training lesson has positive impacts on the physical development of the students. Thampson et al., found in their study in 2001 that the parents from India and America believe that the sports activities have the positive contribution to the physical development of the children [16]. Similarly, Pehlivan confirmed in his study in 200 that the parents perceive that the sports activities are irrevocable for the physical development of the children [13].

17,7% of the parents are the males, and 51,5%of them are the females who think that the physical education lesson has the impact on the students to stand of the bad habits. Entirely 69,2% of the attendees confirm this positive contribution to sport. Opper et al., mentioned in their research as in the same direction with our results that the rate of smoking and alcohol and substance use are lower of the children who play sport in comparison with the others [10]. Also as it stated in the investigation of Öğel et al. that the parents confirm the positive effect of the sport for keeping the children out of smoking and other harmful substances [12].

Çon et al., mentioned in their study in 1997 that the parents are disposed to be valued the free time by sports activities in the physical education lesson of the secondary grade of the primary education schools [3].

Keskin determined in his investigation in 2006 that the parents who motive their children to the sport are mostly high school graduates by a rate of 33,2%. In our research, the parents who care the physical education lesson are mostly high school graduates as well [6].

According to the scale research [2] about the parents who incredibly attend to the sport of their child that these parents mainly aim the 'physical development' 'athletic skill' and 'competition' [2]. Kılcıgil [7] stated in his research with Turkish families about the family expectation that the first reason for being sent the child to the football club is the desire of the child, the second reason is to provide financial gain and the third one is not to be any traffic risk. According to the study [13], the 'skill development' and 'competition' are placed near the top of the participation motives of the children [14]. It is found in the study of Colchico et al., [1] that the girls who attend to physical activity after the school feel themselves worthwhile and healthy. Moreover, reported that there is an increment in the social skill of children who attend to the physical activity after the school [13, 15].

Since the free times of the children increased since the early of the 1950s, the parents also enhanced the number of the sports activities organized for children. After the Second World War, there occurred a severe increase in the sports programs organized for the children and the Youngs. Before these developments, the girls were being raised to be a good mother in the home environment while the boys were more active in sports. After the 1970s and 1980s, the girls and boys were given the chances by the same ratios in schools and some sections of the society, and the girls became successful as much as the boys.

5 Conclusion and suggestions

The purpose of this study is to reveal the awareness level of the parents about the benefits of the physical education lesson in the secondary grade of the primary education schools. 94 female and 36 male parents from Şehit Ümit Balkan Secondary School attended to the survey.

In terms of the gender variable, there is not determined a significant difference at P>0,05 in between the awareness levels of the parents about the benefits of the physical training lessons.

87,7% of the parents think that the physical education teaching has powerful effects on the physical development of the children. 69,2% of them confirm that this lesson keeps their kids out of the bad habits.

The male participators got $\bar{x}$= 123,11 points as a result of the statistical calculations. The female attendees got $\bar{x}$= 122,10 points. The awareness level of both two groups about the benefits of the physical education lesson is found as high.

The physical education teachers and the school management should provide the children and parents to be more conscious by telling them the benefits of the sport and the physical education lesson.

The physical education and sports activities should be organized in schools, and the support of the families must be provided.

There should be conducted works for raising the awareness of the parents about the integrity of the physical education lesson with the other lessons. The parents should be advised for not to isolate their children from the sport because of the other lessons.

It should be efforted for being encouraged the children for sport in the free times by the parents. Thus, the children can be reintroduced to society by improving physically and socially

References

1. Colchico, K., Zybert, P., & Basch, C. E. (2000). Effects of after-school physical activity on fitness, fatness, and cognitive self-perceptions: a pilot study among urban, minority adolescent girls. *American Journal of Public Health, 90*(6), 977.
2. Çepikkurt, F. (2005). Psychological benefits of extreme familial involvement in children's sports: A scale research. *Mersin University, Department of Physical Education and Sports of Health Sciences Institute, Master Thesis*, (49).
3. Çon, M. (1997). The effect of primary and secondary education institutions on the spore orientations of elite sportsmen. Gazi University Journal of Physical Education and Sports Sciences. 2(1), 41-53.
4. Hergüner, G, Ondokuz Mayıs University Journal of Education Faculty 'The Role and the importance of the Family in motiving the child to sports' , Samsun, 1991.
5. Hergüner, G. (1992). Education-Sport Relationship. *Ondokuz Mayıs University Journal of Education Faculty*, *7*(1), 63-66.
6. Keskin, V. (2006). The expectations of the parents who motives their children to the sport. (Published Graduate Thesis). Afyon: Kocatepe University
7. Kılcıgil, E. (2003). The reasons and expectations of the families when their child play sport and their socio-economic status. *Gazi University High school of Physical Education and Sports, Physical Education and Social Areas Congress in Sports*, 214-221.
8. Kuter, M. (2012).Values Education Through Physical Education and Sports. Uludağ University Journal of Education and Humanities: Theory and Practice (Vol): 3 Sayı (No): 6 (Fall), 75-94
9. Larson, C.A. (1970). Curriculum Foundation and Standarts for Physical Education, Englewood Cliffs, New Jersey.
10. Opper, E., Worth, A., Bös, K. (2005). Kinderfitness-kindergesundheit. Bundesgesundheitsbl Gesundheitsforsch Gesundheitsschutz. 48(1), 854-862.

11. Öğel, K(2005). 'What is Awareness'. http://www.ogelk.net/makale/62-herkes-icin-farkindalik-kabullenme-farkindalik-nedir.html. Access date: 02.05.2016.
12. Ögel, K. Çorapçıoğlu, A., Sır, A., Tamar M., Tot Ş., Doğan O., et al., (2004). Tobacco, alcohol and substance use prevalence in primary and secondary education in 9 Provinces. Journal of Turkish Psychiatry, 15(2), 112-118.
13. Pehlivan Z.(2009) Expectations of families for children participating in sports, Behavioral changes observed in children and obstacles for the participation in sport, Sportmeter Physical Education and Journal of Sports Sciences, VII (2) 69-76
14. Pehlivan, Z. (2009). Expectations of families for children participating in sports, Behavioral changes observed in children and obstacles for the participation in sport. Journal of Physical Education and Sports Sciences. 7(2), 69–76.
15. Shephard, R. J. (1995). Physical activity, health, and well-being at different life stages. *Research quarterly for exercise and sport*, *66*(4), 298-302.
16. Thompson, J. L., Davis, S. M., Gittelsohn, J., Going, S., Becenti, A., Metcalfe, L., Stone, E., Harnack, L., Ring, K. (2001). Patterns of physical activity among American Indian children: An assesment of barriers and support. Journal of Community Health. 26(6), 423-445
17. Yaylacı, F. (1998). Evaluation of primary school physical education course teaching programs. Afyon Kocatepe University Journal of Social Sciences. (1)

The definition of success in education and new approaches

Ülkü Gezer[1a]

Graphic Design Department, Fine Arts Faculty, Fatih Sultan Mehmet Vakıf University, Istanbul, Turkey

Abstract. Do postmodern approaches replace the modern approaches while the classical approach is replaced by modern approaches in education? It seems that the changing needs of the societies lead to the creation of new paradigms. Our paradigms which derived from preexisting knowledge, experiences, and implied conditioning, constitute our 'way to perceive a situation' and manage our perspective which directs our behaviors. Thus, globalization, accelerating the flow of information through the internet network, should change the way we observe a situation and our perspective on education and educators. As a continuation of this, our point of view should change our behavior. Success is a combination of many factors mentioned above, which are related to each other. Hence, the study intends to examine the utmost prominent factors in the education systems that may be taken as an example and after comparing these factors with Turkey's status, the study intends to investigate which lessons could be taken from this knowledge.
Keywords: visual arts education, teacher, new

1 Introduction

There are continuous developments in science and technology. While these developments change the needs of the individuals and their lives, it reveals the necessity of educating the qualified human power that can catch the speed of new technology and the era in every way. In other words, it has become compulsory for countries to make innovation in the education strategies. Do postmodern approaches replace the modern approaches while the classical approach is replaced by modern approaches in education?

Since these approaches should also be contemplated in terms of educational strategies, are these strategies being considered and altered through in physical, principal and methodological context?

It seems that the changing needs of the societies lead to the creation of new paradigms. When thinking that way, we need first to investigate and reveal what are the problems among today's paradigms.

[a] Corresponding author: ulkugezer@gmail.com

Thus, globalization and the acceleration of the flow of information through the internet network should change "the way we observe a situation" and our perspective on education and educators. As a continuation of this, our point of view should change our behavior. "In the third millennium, the countries all around the world are constantly renewing their education systems and are implementing reform practices with the objective of education more people for a longer time. Thanks to the use of new technologies, the 'individual competencies' that were important in the past lose their importance. The fast change observed in every area requires making innovations in the objectives of education, in the learning-teaching process, the period of study, and as well as in the competencies of the educators." [12]

Unfortunately, our current education system does not prepare students for citizen opportunities awaiting them in the 21st century. Using skills such as communication, problem solving and creativity in real life is essential in every area. Young people will need to establish links between various sources of information and their forms of representation in the future. They will need to be able to contemplate deeply and use their judgment about their transactions. They will need to explain others their comments and their judgments. As it is obvious, the PISA results indicate unfortunately that the vast majority of young people in our country do not possess these skills. Thus, this would be challenging entering in the global competition in production, innovation, science, and art.

So, what is the secret of successful countries in PISA? "These are not totally new strategies, a new curriculum, a flexible structure, each school to define its own goal and vision, the education and selection of teacher and school administrators, giving importance to the preschool education." [4]

In this study, we examined the utmost prominent factors in the world after examining various education system that can be taken as examples and after comparing these factors with Turkey's status, this study intends to investigate which lessons could be taken from this knowledge.

The aim of this study is to address only the crucial points since we know that the comprehensive review and the development of proposals are primarily the duty of educational scientists.

We prioritized the immediate approaches that may be applied today like asking the right questions and to make appropriate determinations as an educator.

We may evaluate the development of a country by investigating its education system. In other words, when we analyze various countries in the world, it is possible to say that there is a proportional relationship between the education systems and the development of countries.

Hence, it is accurate that we should examine as an example the education systems of Singapore, Japan, Korea, USA and China and monitor them, apart from European Union countries.

These countries have been chosen according to their results across the world.

1.1 New approaches in education (in terms of structure)

The changes caused by the globalization process are reflected in a developing community like the EU and affect Turkey as well.

"In the progress reports prepared since 1998; it is noted that Turkey's education system is generally in line with the EU education policies, however Turkey provides lower standards in terms of education services, courses, education personnel and general personnel in comparison with the EU. In addition, there were significant differences between Turkey and EU because of the big lack of education among poor people, poor education opportunities and low participation to the life long learning. It is emphasized that the developments observed every years are very limited. " [13]

DOI: 10.1051/shsconf/20173701035

At this point, it is necessary to mention this prominent data network.

Eurydice Network: provides information and analysis on European education systems and policies. It consists of 37 national units located in the 33 countries (EU Member States, EFTA countries, Croatia and Turkey) that are involved in the EU Lifelong Learning program.

Fig. 1. Eurydice Network providing information and analysis on European education systems and policies

EU Education, Audiovisual and Culture Executive Agency, located in Brussels, is responsible for the coordination of this network.

This agency defines the draft of the education practices and provides a series of online resources. All Eurydice publications are available free of charge at http://eacea.ec.europa.eu/education/eurydice/

Turkey should resolve its problems in quality assurance of the educator training programs and the number of students per educator, etc. in accordance with EU standards.

In the majority of European countries, the total proportion of public spending on education appears to be more than 5% of GPD.

The process of transition to the information society in developed countries began in the 1980s and a new global economic structure called as "the information economy" has emerged.

Accordingly, many studies have proven that the "knowledge" is the driving force of economic growth in terms of total factory productivity.

Fig. 2. Examples from EU Eurydice Network sources.

1.2 New approaches in education (in terms of human factor)

As we have mentioned before, the name of the society is now called as the 'information society'. Information is constantly and rapidly increasing and spreading. This requires that we review the concepts of adult education, lifelong education, on-the-job training and continuous education.

In European countries, "adult education" is an important subject.

In order to increase the educational success of the adult population, "second chance" programs are created, and formal education procedures are formulated to fulfill the demand. (Figure:3)

However, there is no alternative way in our country.

Source: Eurydice

Fig. 3. Higher education alternatives for various candidates in Europe, 2009/10

On-the-job training and administrator training are important titles that were highlighted.

In Europe, in addition to professional teaching experience, a separate professional management education is required to be a school administrator in many countries.

"Administrator training" is not compulsory in our country.

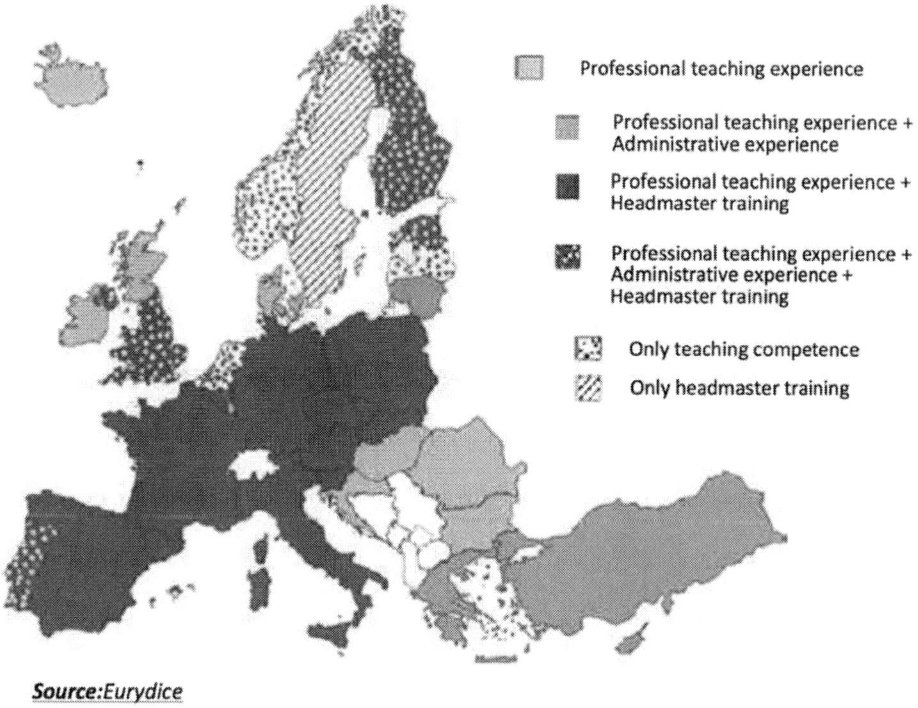

Fig. 4. Professional experience and training required becoming a principal for primary and secondary schools in Europe, 2010/11

Continuing Professional Development is another prominent title for Educators.

According to this research, whose results are presented in Figure 5 and published in Eurydice, 40% of the school administrators in our country stated that the pedagogical lack of educators has a "very negative" effect on the education.

Continuing Professional Development (CPD) came into prominence in recent years. It is accepted as a mandatory occupation in the educational system of 28 EU countries.

It has been ascertained that the schools must have Continuing Professional Development plans.

In Turkey, Continuing Professional Development exists legally but is not imperative. Unfortunately, schools do not have CPD plans, as they are not compulsory.

Since the educators lack of pedagogical formation and their knowledge is not improved by CPD programs, it is very crucial in order to show the correct attitude against student behaviors and use information and communication technologies more effectively.

DOI: 10.1051/shsconf/20173701035

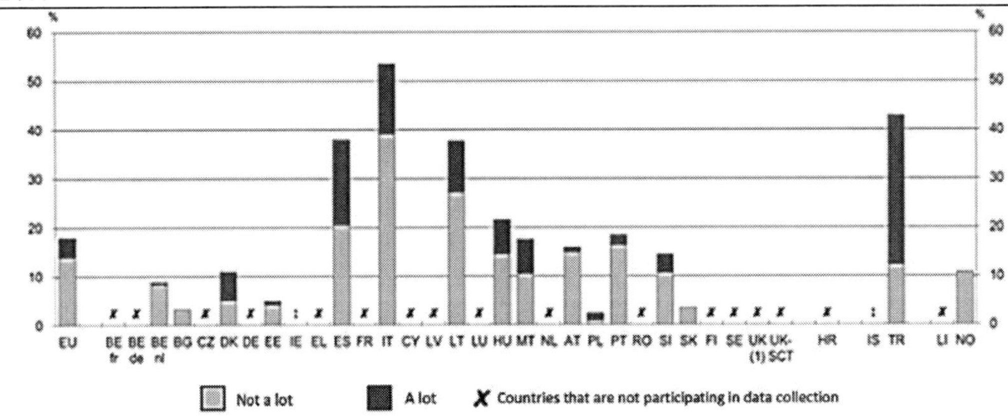

	AB	BE nl	BG	DK	EE	IE	ES	IT	LT	HU	MT	AT	PL	PT	SI	SK	IS	TR	NO
Not a lot	14.0	8.5	3.3	5.1	4.3	:	20.6	39.2	27.2	14.6	10.7	15.0	1.0	16.4	10.7	3.5	:	12.4	10.9
A lot	3.9	0.3	0.0	5.9	0.7	:	17.4	14.3	10.5	7.0	6.9	1.0	1.4	2.1	3.8	0.0	:	30.5	

Source: OECD, TALIS 2008 database

Fig. 5. The percentage (%) of administrators in Turkey who stated that the pedagogical lack of educators has a "very negative" effect on the education, 2008.

The mobility scheme of the educators for foreign education is another important title.

Many European countries have introduced political measures for the EU Lifelong Learning Program (LLP). However, incentive plans to promote the participation of Europe in learning activities of different countries are not very widespread. Unfortunately, Turkey is one of the countries where this plan is not available.

Fig. 6. The existence of foreign education mobility plan for educators, 2011/12

The ratio of Student/Educator is another prominent title.

"In the majority of countries, the ratio of student/educator varies from 10 to 15 students per teacher. Turkey is the only country that exceeds that ratio with 20 students per teacher, equals to 22.1%. The ratio of student/educator is found by dividing the total number of students by the total number of educators, and this should not be confused with the number of students in a single class." [14]

2 Conclusion

Turkey should develop policies to promote the investment of private sector in education in order to approach countries and particularly EU countries that have achieved very goods results in terms of budget spent for education.

The decision should be taken to integrate agriculture, technology, the industry with science and education in our country.

Turkey should increase its investments in developed universities, thus create policies in order to gain a share in the competitive environment in higher education. Accordingly, income sources of higher education should be diversified.

Practices for lifelong learning intended for young population should be increased.

School-recruitment relationship should be prioritized in order to ensure functionality of training programs to be opened for new professions arising based on the technological and scientific developments. In addition, school-industry partnerships should be established in order for vocational and technical education institutions to be able to provide training in accordance with the demands.

New foreign language methods should be developed so that graduates of the primary school may speak at least one foreign language fluently.

Training programs based on occupational standards should be developed so that secondary education may be linked to lifelong education.

We need to ensure that the rate of lifelong learning increases and information and communication technologies become more prevalent in schools.

Particularly the cooperation of primary and secondary schools with families should be ensured.

With the policies that intend to develop entrepreneurial skills of the students, we should encourage the development of entrepreneurial skills of educators and school administrators.

Educators training programs in Turkey should be reviewed in global standards. All teachers (primary-secondary-high school and university) should be given the opportunities to profit from EU's mobility programs for studying abroad.

Researches should be conducted to evaluate the existing policies and programs concerning education supervision and non-formal education in Turkish Education System.

We are aware that all this information and researches are very important. However, it is important to underline this valuable information mentioned as following: "A good system does not guarantee good education output."

That means, we cannot achieve a good result if we fail to achieve our target in a few important parameters of success. Even if the system is good...

As an educator, when we think about our responsibilities, we realize that we need to continuously monitor researches and developments.

When we evaluate successful countries, we realize that their education is based on knowledge and generated other information with new knowledge and that they achieved to reform the educators training.

Despite what has been explained so far, the principal point of this subject is the motivation of educators and their adaptation to the new era where we are living in.

It seems we need to be aware of this critical change as school and educators.

References

1. Turan, S. "Ögrenen Toplumlara Dogru Avrupa Birligi Egitim Politikalarında Yasam Boyu Ögrenme." Ankara Avrupa Çalısmaları Dergisi, 5 (1) 2005, 87-98.
2. Gülcan, M. G. (2010). "Avrupa Birligi ve Egitim." (2. Baskı) Pegem Akademi, Ankara

3. M. Saglam, F. Özüdogru, F. Çıray, "Avrupa Birligi Egitim Politikaları ve Türk Egitim Sistemine Etkileri", Yüzüncü Yıl Üniversitesi, Egitim Fakültesi Dergisi. Aralık (2011), Cilt:VIII, Sayı:I, 87-109 http://efdergi.yyu.edu.tr)
4. Aybat Burcu, "Ögretmen 2.0" kitap, Abakus (2016) İstanbul
5. Demirel Özcan, "Gelecek İçin Egitim.", kitap, Pegem (2012) Ankara
6. Tanrıkulu D. "Yüksekögretime Erisimin Arz ve Giris Kosulları Açısından Degerlendirilmesi ve Türkiye İçin Çözüm Önerileri.", DPT Uzmanlık Tezi, (2009) Ankara
7. Yavuz Mehmet, Kalkınma Bankası Planlama Uzmanı, "Neden Yüksek Ögretim Reformu" Yüksekögretim ve Bilim Dergisi/Journal of Higher Education and Science, (2012)
8. Yavuz M. "Yüksekögretim Yönetiminde Yasanan Dönüsüm ve Türkiye İçin Alternatif Yönetim Modeli Önerisi.", Kalkınma Bakanlıgı Uzmanlık Tezi, (2012) Ankara
9. Tanrıkulu D. "Yüksekögretime Erisimin Arz ve Giris Kosulları Açısından Degerlendirilmesi ve Türkiye Için Çözüm Önerileri.", DPT Uzmanlık Tezi, (2009) Ankara
10. Philippe A., Dewatripont M., Hoxby C., Mas-Colell A., Sapir A. "The Governance and Performance of Universites: Evidence From Europe and the US", Economic Policy, (2010), 7-59.
11. Wissema J.G., "Üçüncü Kusak Üniversitelere Dogru" (çev. Devrim N, Belge T), Özyegin Üniversitesi Yayınları, (2009) İstanbul
12. Erginer Aysun, "Avrupa Birliği egitim Sistemleri" kitap, Pegem, (2006) Istanbul
13. Eurydice Report, 2010b
14. Eurodice, Basic Data on Educators and School Leaders, (2013)
15. OECD, "Education At a Glance" (2010), Paris
16. OECD, "TALIS veritabanı", (2008)
17. Eurodice, "Avrupa'da Ögretmenler ve Okul Liderlerine İliskin Temel Veriler", (201)3
18. http://eacea.ec.europa.eu/education/eurydice/

The relationship between organizational commitment and whistleblowing tendency: An empirical research

Nusret Çiftçi[1a] and Aykut Bedük[1]

[1]Faculty of Economics and Administrative Sciences, Selcuk University, Konya, Turkey

Abstract. The ethical position of organizations is of great importance to both organizations and society in general considering people spend their considerable lifespan in organizations. It is important to sustain the determination on ethics by detecting and revealing the ethical infringements inside the organization. In this context; whistleblowing, which is a concept deriving from the field of organizational psychology is defined as the action that informing the individuals and organizations for the on-going unethical and amoral activities in the organizations, has become important. The courage of individuals to report unethical, immoral or illegal activities to the authorities can be affected by the attitude of individuals towards the organization. One of the attitudes that are considered to affect that courage, which is named as whistleblowing, is organizational commitment. Organizational commitment shows the loyalty of employees to the organization. In this study it has been examined the relationship between employees' organizational commitment and tendency to reporting immoral behaviours. The sample of the study is composed of the employees of Faculty of Economics and Administrative Sciences at Selcuk University. For this empirical study, survey method has been used, and the reached sample chosen by simply random sampling is 88 employees.

1 Introduction

It is important for the stakeholders of both for-profit and non-profit organizations the ethical positions of organizations. People who deposit money in banks for valuation and protection, who buy food to feed healthy his/her kid, who buy a car with high security standards in order to fulfill that experience, and people who trust to international organizations and consider their work valuable to world peace are examples of these stakeholders.

There are some responsibilities to be carried out by some inner actors (top management, administrative board, board of directors, auditing professionals) or external actors (State, legal authorities, international organizations etc.) in order to protect the mentioned stakeholders by auditing the ethical environment of these organizations. However, in order to obtain the control sometimes there may be the need for specific information of the inner

[a] Corresponding author: nusret@selcuk.edu.tr

worlds of the organizations. At this point there can be some situations in which employees reveal unethical behaviors in the organizations to the related authorities by behaving morally. Such behaviors, which are important in raising the ethical level of organizations, started to conceptualize under the concept of "whistleblowing" in the organizational behavior literature. The characteristics of individuals who have a tendency towards whistleblowing started to appear as a topic in the field of organizational psychology. Organizational commitment, job satisfaction, personal characteristics of employees are some of the subjects which are studied as factors affecting people's tendency to whistleblowing in the literature. In this study it has been investigated the relationship of organizational commitment and demographic characteristics of employees between whistleblowing tendency of them.

2 Conceptual framework

According to Robbins, et al. [1] organizational commitment is the identification of employees with the organization and its goals, and their will to continue their membership in the organization. Organizational commitment; is a topic which has been studied for a long time in many researches in the management literature. This study is grounded on the organizational commitment model of Allen and Meyer [2]. According to this model, organizational commitment is divided into three different components that are (1) affective commitment, (2) continuance commitment, (3) normative commitment.

At affective commitment, the employee feels himself/herself as part of the organization and establishes an emotional relation with the organization. Continuance commitment is defined as the low probability of the employee to pass to another organization or in other words due to lack of alternatives the commitment to the current organization. In normative commitment, the employee is grateful to the organization and does not find morally appropriate to leave the organization.

The concept of whistleblowing, which has not been defined with today's meaning even in the dictionaries until 1986, has been defined by Oxford English Dictionary as "to blow the whistle on (a person or thing): to ring an activity to a sharp conclusion, as if by the blast of a whistle; now usually by informing on (a person) or exposing (an irregularity or crime)". In the literature, Near and Miceli [3] defines whistleblowing as "disclosure by organization members (former or current) of illegal, immoral or illegitimate practices under the control of their employers, to persons or organizations that may be able to effect action.". In the same way whistleblower has been defined as the "individual who does the whistleblowing" [4]. Whistleblowing is a concept which derived from the referees who blow a whistle when a foul occurs [5].

Whistleblowing, without any doubt is a civil virtue behavior. Not keeping quiet towards wrong behaviors and acts inside the organization, and fighting against it is a virtue of high personal responsibility. Many times unfortunately, whistleblowers seen as conscientious objectors are object to various blames (treacherous, sneakers, spy, problematic etc.) and have been exposed to several risks (dismissed, exclusion, psychological violence, humiliation, retaliation etc.) [6]. However, what define the distinction between "whistleblowing" and spying is the legal and the ethical status of the action in the organization. This is because in order to consider an act as whistleblowing requires that act to be against the laws or moral.

Whistleblowing is divided into three components; according to the authority where it will be done, whether the whistleblower prefer to maintain privacy, and the procedures to be fulfilled. These distinctions too are divided into two components themselves. Figure 1 provides a clear picture of this distinction [7].

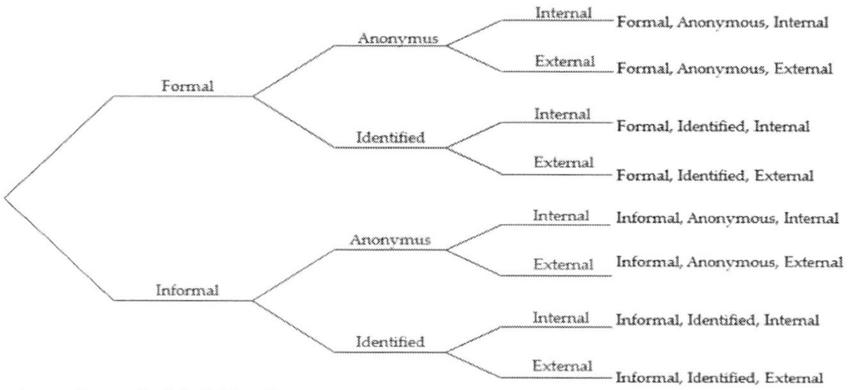

Fig. 1. A typology of whistleblowing

There is no common sense among the works studying the relationship between organizational commitment and whistleblowing. While in the works of Sims and Keenan [8] and Mesmer-Magnus and Viswesvaran [9] there is no relationship between whistleblowing tendency and organizational commitment; Miceli, et al. [10] found a positively significant relationship between whistleblowing tendency and organizational commitment. On the other hand, Somers and Casal [11] in their study found a U shaped reverse correlation between whistleblowing tendency and organizational commitment. In other words; whistleblowing tendency is seen mostly in individuals who are at the middle level of the organizational hierarchy. According to the work of Toker Gökçe [12] there exists a negative sided significant relationship between organizational commitment and normative commitment with whistleblowing tendency. In other words, individuals who are more related to the organization show a low tendency towards whistleblowing. Manjughi and Fasihizadeh [13] in their study on nurses found a strong relationship between organizational commitment and whistleblowing tendency.

3 Method

3.1 Population and sample

The population of the study is composed of the employees at the Faculty of Economics and Administrative Sciences at Selcuk University. The sample of the study is 88 and has been chosen by simply random sampling. The demographic characteristics of the participants in the sample are given at Table 1.

Table 1. Frequency table

		f	%
Gender	Male	62	70.5
	Female	26	29.5
Status	Married	60	68.2
	Single	28	31.8
Education	Elementary School	2	2.4
	High school	4	4.8
	Pre-University	8	9.5
	University	8	9.5
	Master/PhD	62	73.8
Task type	Academic staff	64	72.7
	Administrative Staff	24	26.1
Title	Administrative Staff	24	27.3
	Research Assistant	42	47.7
	Assistant Lecturer	3	3.4
	Assistant Professor	7	8.0
	Associate Professor	5	5.7
	Professor	7	8.0

3.2 Data collection tool and reliability analysis

This study is an empirical research. For this research, survey method was chosen as data collection tool. The questionnaire of the research has been developed by taking advantage of scales whose validity and reliability have already proven. For organizational commitment the three dimension scale developed by Allen and Meyer [2] has been used. On the other hand, for Whistleblowing the six dimension scale developed by Park, et al. [7] and translated to Turkish by Zamantılı Nayır [14] has been used. For both scales Likert scale requiring to rate the items from 1. Totally Disagree … 7. Totally Agree has been used. Cronbach alpha values are as follows. It has been noticed that all the scales were in an acceptable level.

Table 2. Reliability analysis

Scale	Scale Dimension	Number of Items	Cronbach Alpha
Organizational Commitment	Affective	6 (1 item erased)	0.824
	Continuance Commitment	6	0.701
	Normative	6 (1 item erased)	0.815
Whistleblowing	Internal	3	0.904
	External	3	0.905
	Identified	2	0.898
	Anonymous	2	0.700
	Formal	2	0.834
	Informal	2	0.686
	Silence	2	0.898

4 Findings

The differences among whistleblowing tendencies according to gender are seen in Table 3.

Table 3. The differences among whistleblowing tendencies according to gender

	Gender	N	X	SD	t	p
Internal Whistleblowing	Male	62	4.34	1.70	.972	.334
	Female	26	3.96	1.65		
External Whistleblowing	Male	62	2.43	1.48	-.955	.342
	Female	26	2.76	1.42		
Identified Whistleblowing	Male	62	3.02	1.74	.062	.951
	Female	26	3.00	1.48		
Anonymous Whistleblowing	Male	62	2.45	1.38	-.346	.730
	Female	26	2.56	1.14		
Formal Whistleblowing	Male	62	4.10	1.85	-.230	.819
	Female	26	4.19	1.59		
Informal Whistleblowing	Male	62	3.98	1.61	-2.236	.028*
	Female	26	4.79	1.34		
Staying Silent	Male	62	2.77	1.60	.350	.727
	Female	26	2.63	1.63		

*p<,05

According to Table 3, the whistleblowing type that shows difference according to the gender is informal whistleblowing. The tendency for whistleblowing of female participants in the sample is significantly more than the tendency of male participants. In other words, female employees do report the unethical behaviors in the organization without having a tendency to follow specific procedures.

The differences among whistleblowing tendencies according to task type are according to the values in Table 4.

Table 4. The differences among whistleblowing tendencies according to task type

	Task type	N	X	SD	t	P
Internal Whistleblowing	Academic	64	4.24	1.75	-.016	.987
	Administrative	24	4.25	1.54		
External Whistleblowing	Academic	64	2.75	1.48	2.424	.019*
	Administrative	24	1.97	1.26		
Identified Whistleblowing	Academic	64	2.93	1.69	-1.041	.301
	Administrative	24	3.35	1.54		
Anonymous Whistleblowing	Academic	64	2.61	1.34	1.312	.193
	Administrative	24	2.20	1.17		
Formal Whistleblowing	Academic	64	4.01	1.74	-1.144	.256
	Administrative	24	4.50	1.85		
Informal Whistleblowing	Academic	64	4.32	1.59	.833	.404
	Administrative	24	4.00	1.55		
Staying Silent	Academic	64	2.65	1.61	-.842	.405
	Administrative	24	2.98	1.61		

*p<.05

According to Table 4, the whistleblowing type that shows difference according to the task type is external whistleblowing. The tendency for whistleblowing of academic staff participants in the sample is significantly more than the tendency of administrative staff. In other words, academic staff is more likely to report the unethical behaviors witnessing in the organization to external authorities without consulting first internal authorities than administrative staff.

Table 5. The differences among whistleblowing tendencies according to marital status

	Marital Status	N	X	SD	t	p
Internal Whistleblowing	Married	60	4.48	1.71	2.098	.039*
	Single	28	3.69			
External Whistleblowing	Married	60	2.54	1.58	0.116	.908
	Single	28	2.5			
Identified Whistleblowing	Married	60	3.09	1.72	0.616	.540
	Single	28	2.86			
Anonymous Whistleblowing	Married	60	2.33	1.32	-0.627	.109
	Single	28	2.8			
Formal Whistleblowing	Married	60	4.29	1.79	1.3	.197
	Single	28	3.77			
Informal Whistleblowing	Married	60	4.04	1.59	-1.582	.118
	Single	28	4.61			
Staying Silent	Married	60	2.59	1.66	-1.166	.247
	Single	28	3.02			

*p<.05

DOI: 10.1051/shsconf/20173701036

According to findings of the research, the whistleblowing type that shows difference according to the marital status is internal whistleblowing. According to Table 5, married employees have more significant level of tendency towards internal whistleblowing than single employees do. In other words, married employees are more likely to report the unethical behaviors witnessed in the organization to internal authorities rather than to external authorities compared to single employees. The reason for this situation could be the fact that married employees are more family-conscious and for this reason, they trust more individuals in the organization.

In Table 6 the relationship among organizational commitment and its dimensions with whistleblowing types has been analyzed by correlation method. According to this analysis, a negative significant relationship was found among organizational commitment and anonymous whistleblowing ($r=-0.299$, $p<0.01$). Additionally, it was found a negative significant relationship between affective commitment which is one of the dimensions of organizational commitment with anonymous whistleblowing ($r=-0.328$, $p<0.01$). Further, it was found a negative significant relationship between normative commitment which is another dimension of organizational commitment with anonymous whistleblowing ($r=-0.234$, $p<0.05$). Moreover, it was found a negative significant relationship between normative commitment and keep quiet tendency ($r=-0.283$, $p<0.01$). The topic for the found relationships needs to be addressed according to the comment suggested by Kalaycı [15] whether they are very weak (0.00-0.25) or weak (0.26-0.49). When considering the literature and the studies on the relationship among organizational commitment whistleblowing tendency we see that they produce different results compared to each other. That is why there is no common sense on this topic.

Table 6. The correlation table among organizational commitment dimensions and the types of whistleblowing

	1	2	3	4	5	6	7	8	9	10	11
1. Internal WB	1										
2. External WB	.274**	1									
3. Identified WB	.465**	.533**	1								
4. Anonymous WB	.309**	.427**	.185	1							
5. Formal WB	.750**	.335**	.611**	.271*	1						
6. Informal WB	.018	.250*	-.058	.174	.015	1					
7. Staying Silent	-.377**	.029	-.150	.108	-.283**	-.068	1				
8. Affective Commitment	.199	-.204	.079	-.328**	.034	.033	-.223*	1			
9. Continuance Commitment	.204	-.076	.007	-.171	.077	.03	-.009	.419**	1		
10. Normative Commitment	.146	-.173	.017	-.234*	.023	.19	-.283**	.694**	.489**	1	
11. Organizational Commitment	.219*	-.186	.044	-.299**	.051	.102	-.215*	.866**	.738**	.884**	1

*p<.05 **p<.01

5 Results and discussion

Whistleblowing has become an important concept in the field of organizational psychology. Whistleblowing, which means reporting unethical behaviors to the authorities, is being studied increasingly. In the researches conducted, it is frequently examined what personal characteristics and different attitudes and behaviors affect the tendency of individuals to whistleblowing. Among the attitude and behaviors, there are organizational commitment, organizational citizenship, and job satisfaction. In this study, it has been explored the relationship between organizational commitment and the tendency towards different types of whistleblowing. According to findings of the study, a negative relationship between organizational commitment also its two dimensions –affective commitment and normative commitment- and tendency to anonymous whistleblowing Furthermore, there was found a negative significant relationship between normative commitment and staying silent behavior. However, these relationships showed a weak correlation. It is difficult to say whether the results of the study are compatible to the literature or not. Even among the studies exploring the relationship between organizational commitment and whistleblowing there is no single unified view. However the result obtained from this study is that managers who aspire to create an ethical and fearless environment should keep their employees committed to the organization through affective and normative standpoints. Therefore, employees witnessing an unethical behavior can report to the authorities the situation without hiding their identity information instead of being quiet.

References

1. T. L. Robbins, M. D. Crino, L. D. Fredendall. An integrative model of the empowerment process. *Human resource management review* **12**, 419-443 (2002).
2. N. J. Allen, J. P. Meyer. The measurement and antecedents of affective, continuance and normative commitment to the organization. *Journal of occupational psychology* **63**, 1-18 (1990).
3. J. P. Near, M. P. Miceli. Organizational dissidence: The case of whistle-blowing. *Journal of Business Ethics* **4**, 1-16, doi:10.1007/bf00382668 (1985).
4. W. Vandekerckhove. *Whistleblowing And Organizational Social Responsibility.* (2006).
5. F. Qusqas, B. H. Kleiner. The Difficulties Of Whistleblowers Finding Employment. *Management Research News*, 97-100 (2001).
6. C. C. Aktan. Organizasyonlarda Yanlış Uygulamalara Karşı Bir Sivil Erdem, Ahlaki Tepki ve Vijdani Red Davranışı: Whistleblowing. *Mercek Dergisi*, 1-13 (2006).
7. H. Park, J. Blenkinsopp, M. K. Oktem, U. Omurgonulsen. Cultural orientation and attitudes toward different forms of whistleblowing: A comparison of South Korea, Turkey, and the UK. *Journal of Business Ethics* **82**, 929-939 (2008).
8. R. L. Sims, J. P. Keenan. Predictors of external whistleblowing: Organizational and intrapersonal variables. *Journal of Business Ethics* **17**, 411-421 (1998).
9. J. R. Mesmer-Magnus, C. Viswesvaran. Whistleblowing in organizations: An examination of correlates of whistleblowing intentions, actions, and retaliation. *Journal of Business Ethics* **62**, 277-297 (2005).
10. M. P. Miceli, J. P. Near, C. R. Schwenk. Who blows the whistle and why? *Industrial & Labor Relations Review* **45**, 113-130 (1991).
11. M. J. Somers, J. C. Casal. Organizational Commitment and Whistle-Blowing A Test of the Reformer and the Organization Man Hypotheses. *Group & Organization Management* **19**, 270-284 (1994).
12. A. Toker Gökçe. Okullarda bilgi uçurma: İş doyumu ve örgütsel bağlılık ilişkisi. *Dicle Üniversitesi Ziya Gökalp Eğitim Fakültesi Dergisi* **22**, 261-282 (2013).
13. N. Manjughi, N. Fasihizadeh. Simple and multiple relationships between organizational commitment with Whistle-blowing in nursing profession. *Interdisciplinary Journal of Contemporary Research In Business* **4**, 846 (2012).
14. D. Zamantılı Nayır. *Kurumsal Etik ve Whistleblowing.* (2012).
15. Ş. Kalaycı. *SPSS uygulamalı çok değişkenli istatistik teknikleri.* Vol. 6 (2014).

The effects of academic mentoring perceptions of research assistants on their organizational commitment

Nusret Çiftçi[1a], Ebru Ertürk[2], Burcu Doğanalp[1], and Esra Kızıloğlu[1]

[1]Faculty of Economics and Administrative Sciences, Selcuk University, Konya, Turkey
[2]Academy of Applied Sciences, Necmettin Erbakan University, Konya, Turkey

Abstract. Mentoring can be expressed as a supportive relationship in which an experienced person transfers his or her expertise and knowledge to someone else. Universities are one of the most appropriate environments that this process, the samples of which can be seen in many sectors, is experienced. Academicianship is one of the professions in which the mentoring process is the most intense and most-needed. This study was aimed to investigate how research assistants perceive the academic mentor and mentee relationship, how these perceptions are related to the desired working behaviour, performance, and organizational effectiveness, and how these relationships affect "organizational commitment," which has an increasing importance. Thus, both a sample based on the academic mentoring process was obtained and the academic mentoring process, as a factor affecting the organizational commitment, was studied. As a result of the research, it was found that there was a positive relationship between perceived mentoring and organizational commitment, affective commitment from subcategories of commitment. The relationship between normative commitment and organizational commitment were also found to be positive and meaningful. However, no relationship between perceived mentoring and continuance was found, and the established regression model did not make sense either.

1 Introduction

In today's world, it is seen that experienced and intelligent individuals in business life and private life direct younger and inexperienced individuals by positively contributing to their development. Academia is the most appropriate field in which the process is best experienced and considered to be the best example of the mentoring process [1] which is defined as "a process in which an experienced person guides or helps an inexperienced member of the profession to reach a desired level" [2]. The support that experienced faculty members provides to new research assistants and those at post-graduate level is highly significant. This orientation, which is called academic mentoring, provides significant contributions to the teaching faculty candidates both in learning academic research methods and internalizing professional ethics and academic culture.

[a] Corresponding author: nusret@selcuk.edu.tr

DOI: 10.1051/shsconf/20173701037

In addition, it is thought that academic mentoring along with its positive aspects such as research assistants' behaviors, attitudes and positive effects in their relationship that lead to career advancement and motivation [3] would increase organizational commitment. Applying mentoring in an institution indicates that the organization values its employees and attributes its success on its employees' commitment and abilities. The fact that mentoring is practiced in an institution shows that the institution values its employees and indicates that the success of the organization is based on the loyalty and abilities of the employees [2]. The more the individual identifies himself or herself with the organization, the more valuable he feels in the institution he works for; the more he believes and contributes to the organizational goals, the more the individual's sense of belonging increases and the easier it will be for the individual and the organization to achieve their goals.

2 Literature

2.1 Academic mentoring

According In literature, mentoring, which is also conceptualized as counseling and advising, is defined as "the process of helping and assisting a less experienced and knowledgeable individual by an expert with advanced knowledge and experience in order to support professional development [4]", and it was first developed in academic field.

Training of the future faculty members is a product of planned and attentive effort. Within the master-apprentice relationship, the importance of being guided and educated by academic mentors, research assistant's efforts to become a scientist cannot be denied. Mentoring, in an academic sense, is an upbringing process in which a senior lecturer supports the younger faculty member to gain scientific ability, to understand the institution he is working for and to solve the problems he or she faces at work place. This process is precious regarding the quality of the relationship between the consultant and the research assistant, the effectiveness of information exchange, research assistants' personal and academic development and job satisfaction. The academic mentor will enhance the efficiency of the activity by sharing his / her experience with the research assistant, providing moral education, evaluating performance, and being a good source of information, a guide and an academic model for the assistants [5].

In literature, the studies on academic mentoring are as follows. "Training Roles of Faculty Members," [5] found that the thesis advisors of the research assistants at Gazi University utilized the role of 'thesis advisor' more than their roles of 'facilitator' and the role of 'being a model.' The thesis advisors with the title of associate professor performed the role of upbringing at a higher level than the thesis advisors with other titles.

In their study with research assistants working at Graduate School of Social, Science and Health sciences at Anadolu University, Özkalp, et al. [1] have concluded that advisors are a source of information and guidance, shared their experience and knowledge, and maintained the master-apprenticeship relationship to improve personal performance. To establish a mentoring program at nursing college, in their study, Nick, et al. [6] grouped the best practices in academic mentoring under six main themes by analyzing the data obtained from face-to-face interviews: (1) a good mentor and mentee match, (2) the creation of clear goals for the mentoring process, (3) the strengthening of the relationship between the mentor and the mentee, (4) to defend the mentee and guide him or her, (5)to integrate the mentee with academic culture and (6) to mobilize of the academic sources.

2.2 Organizational commitment

In Turkish Language Association dictionary, 'commitment' is defined as individuals' considering themselves as a member of a community, a social group or congregation [7].

Organizational commitment, on the other hand, is the relative strength of the individual's identification with and participation in the organization [8]. Mowday, et al. [9] in their study, defined organizational commitment as "employees' high level belief in organization's aims and values, the desire to make intensive efforts for the purposes of the organization, and a strong desire to stay in the organization and maintain organizational membership"[10]. Organizational commitment begins with acceptance of the employee and his employment with a psychological contract. It improves by acquiring knowledge about goals, objectives and what the job requires. From this point of view, organizational commitment is the unity of power that a person has formed by entering into union identity with an individual organization [11]. Allen and Meyer [12] in their model on organizational commitment mention about three types of commitment. The dimensions of the commitment are "affective," "normative," and "continuance". Employees with strong affective commitment stay in the organization because they want this and remain in the organization with their wish; those with strong normative commitment feel they have to stay. They see it as a moral responsibility and obligation towards the organization, and those with a strong continuing commitment continue to work in the organization because they need it both socially and economically. This commitment, also called rational attachment, triggers the maintenance of the membership of the organization believing that the cost of separation from the organization will be high [10, 13].

In literature, the studies related to organizational commitment are as follows: In her 2007 thesis, "Organizational Commitment in Working Life," which aimed to determine the level of organizational commitment of municipal employees, Sürgevil [8] found that among organizational commitment dimensions affective commitment had the highest score which was followed by continuance commitment, and the normative commitment had the lowest score. In their study they conducted in Balikesir in private enterprise, Örücü and Sezen Kışlalıoğlu [11] found that there was no difference between the levels of affective, continuance and normative commitment according to the age of the employees; there was a difference between levels of affective commitment according to the study period and educational status. There was a difference between levels of affective and normative commitment according to the positions of the employees, but there was no difference between levels of continuing commitment. In their study to determine organizational commitment among the academicians working at Gazi University, according to the results of the correlation analysis of the academicians in general and one's level of commitment to their work, Boylu, et al. [10] found that academicians had a high level of positive and meaningful relationship in all three commitment levels about their university and unit they are working for.

"Mentoring, Organizational Commitment and Intentions to Leave Public Accounting," conducted with the largest accountancy firms registered with the American Institute of Certified Public Accountants, Stallworth [14]found that mentoring relationships have a positive impact on each of the dimensions of organizational commitment and concluded that among these commitments affective was the most influenced one, [5].

3 Method

3.1 The purpose and importance of the study

The aim of this study was to examine how mentoring process, considered as a career development technique, is perceived by research assistants involved in both master's and doctoral stages and to examine its impact on organizational commitment. The research was empirical study and to collect data face to face survey technique was used. Our questionnaire was prepared by using Noe's Mentoring Scale and Mayer and Allen's Organizational Commitment Scale. SPSS 22.0 packet program was used to evaluate the data. The study population of the research is composed of research assistants working at Selçuk University, Konya. 112 questionnaires distributed using face to face survey method have returned. This research was designed to measure the effect of research assistants' perceptions of the academic mentoring process on organizational commitment. Model and hypotheses were prepared considering the related studies.

3.2 Research model and hypotheses

This research was designed to measure the effect of research assistants' perceptions of the academic mentoring process on organizational commitment. Model and hypotheses were prepared considering the related studies.

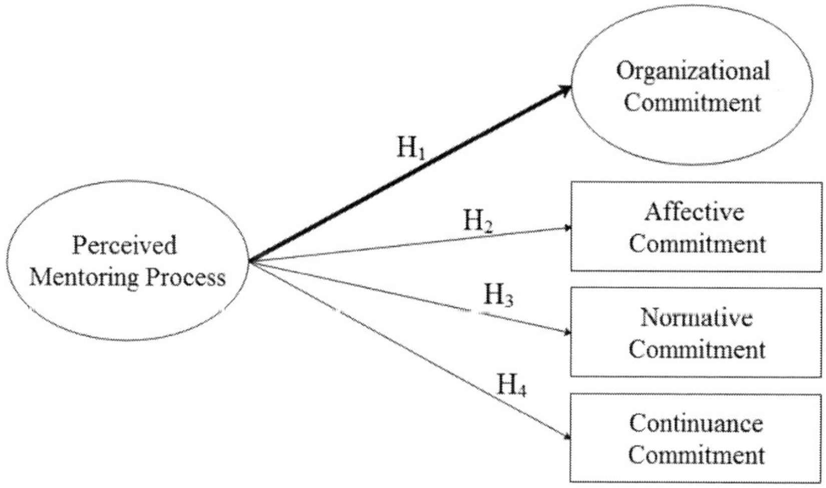

Fig. 1. Theoretical model

H_1: There is a positive and meaningful relationship between research assistants' mentor perceptions on mentor and organizational commitment.
H_2: There is a positive and meaningful positive relationship between research assistants' mentor perceptions and their affective commitment.
H_3: There is a positive and meaningful relationship between research assistants' mentor perceptions and normative commitment.
H_4: There is a positive and meaningful relationship between research assistants' mentor perceptions and continuance commitment.

3.3 Research method and scales

A four-part questionnaire was prepared to obtain the findings of the research. In the first part of the questionnaire, there were demographic questions such as age, gender, marital status, academic career status, affiliated institution, etc. In the second part, organizational commitment, and in the third part, the perceptions about the perceived mentoring process were questioned. In the fourth part, the question "How do you describe your relationship with your advisor?" was asked and the participants were asked to reply to the question using similes such as teacher-apprentice, parent-child, etc.

Organizational Commitment Scale: An authentic 18-item "Organizational Commitment Scale," the reliability of which is tested and very often used in literature, developed by Meyer, et al. [15] and adapted to Turkish by Al [16] used. The scale consists of three sub-dimensions, affective commitment, normative commitment and continuance commitment.

DOI: 10.1051/shsconf/20173701037

The perceived mentoring scale items are the expressions of Noe [17]'s Mentoring Scale. The scale items in Turkish were taken from Özkalp, et al. [1]. It consists of total 30 items.

Questionnaires were prepared by using a 5-point Likert scale. In Likert scale "1", means "never agree"; "5" corresponds to the phrase "I fully agree". The data obtained from questionnaire forms were analyzed by SPSS 22.0 program. Correlation and regression analysis tests were used to determine the relationship and effect between variables. Also, descriptive statistical methods such as frequency, percentage, etc., t-test and ANOVA tests were also used.

4 Findings

The demographic characteristics of the survey participants are shown in Table 1.

Table 1. Demographic characteristics of participants

Demographic Values	Sub-characteristics	Frequency	
		N	%
Gender	Female	50	44.6
	Male	62	55.4
Marital Status	Married	62	55.4
	Single	50	44.6
Age	Between 22-26	33	29.5
	Between 27-31	39	34.9
	Between 32-36	29	25.9
	Between 37-41	8	7.2
	Over 41	3	2.7
Academic Career	Master's Graduate Course	13	11.6
	Master's Thesis Stage	11	9.8
	Intro to PhD	3	2.7
	PhD Graduate Course	21	18.8
	PhD Proficiency	9	8.0
	PhD Dissertation Stage	30	26.8
	Doctor	25	22.3
Institute	Graduate School of Social Sciences	63	56.3
	Graduate School of Sciences	39	34.8
	Graduate School of Sciences	10	8.9
Work Experience	Less than a year	6	5.4
	1-5 years	65	57.9
	6-10 years	23	27.8
	11-15 years	16	14.4
	16 years and over	2	1.8
Advisor's gender	Male	96	85.7
	Female	16	14.3
Advisor's age	Between 30-40	11	9.9
	Between 41-50	51	45.6
	Between 51-60	38	34.1
	Between 61-70	12	10.8
Academic Position of Mentor	Asst. Professor	8	7.1
	Assoc. Professor	24	21.4
	Professor	80	71.4

According to the Table 1, 55.4% of the respondents were male, while 44.6% were female. 62 of the participants were married, while 50 were single. When the age average of the participants was analyzed, it was found that participants aged 22-26 years accounted for 29.5% of the respondents, 34.9% of the participants aged 27-31 and 25.9% of the participants aged 32-36 accounted 25.9%. The vast majority of respondents was in their doctoral dissertation stage (26.8%) and affiliated with the Graduate School of Social Sciences (56.3%). When the characteristics of the advisors of participants were examined; it was seen that 85.7% of the advisors were male and 14.3% were female. The ages of advisors were mainly in the range of 41-50 years (45.6%). Academic positions of the advisors were as follows: 7.1% were assistant professors, 21.4% were associate professors and 71.4% were full professors.

According to **Hata! Başvuru kaynağı bulunamadı.**, 34.8% of surveyed research assistants identified their relationship with their counselors as a professional relationship based on mutual respect. And 17% likened the relationship with the advisor to the master-apprentice relationship.

Reliability analysis and frequency analysis for the scales of the variables under investigation are shown in the Table 2.

Table 2. Reliability and frequency analysis

Scales	Number of Item	Cronbach Alpha	Average	Standard Deviation
Perceived Mentoring Scale	30	0.970	3.53	0.788
Organizational Commitment	18	0.829	3.06	0.562
-Affective Commitment	6	0.840	3.19	0.857
-Normative Commitment	6	0.753	3.02	0.565
-Continuance Commitment	6	0.686	2.92	0.677

According to Table 2, the Cronbach Alpha values of the scales used in the study were high (since $\alpha>0.70$). It is understood here that the scales are reliable and sufficient for the study. When we look at the average, the participation score on the perceived mentoring scale was 3.53 and on the organizational commitment scale it was 3.06. Participants had higher scores on expressions of organizational commitment subscale and affective commitment dimension.

For the study, t-tests and ANOVA tests were used to determine whether the perceived mentoring and organizational commitment differed on the demographic variables. According to the results of the study, there were meaningful differences between the organizational commitment and the affiliated institute in ANOVA test conducted to define only the difference between the institution and variables ($p=0.001<0.05$). According to the averages, the academicians at Graduate School of Health Sciences (N: 3.60), responded more to items on organizational commitment than those at Graduate School of Social Sciences (N: 2.89) and Graduate School of Sciences (N: 3.09).

Correlation analysis was used to investigate the relationship between perceived mentoring scale and organizational commitment and its sub-dimensions. The results of correlation analysis were shown Table 3. According to this, there is a positive relationship between perceived mentoring and organizational commitment ($r=0.473$, $p<0.01$). In addition, there was a positive and significant relationships between perceived mentoring and affective commitment dimension ($r = 0.460$, $p<0.01$) and normative commitment dimension ($r = 0.430$, $p<0.01$). There was no relationship between continuance commitment and mentoring.

Table 3. Correlation analysis

	1	2	*3*	4	5
1. Perceived Mentoring	1				
2. Organizational Commitment	.473**	1			
3. Affective Commitment	.460**	.813**	*1*		
4. Normative Commitment	.430**	.766**	.511**	1	
5. Continuance Commitment	.092	.505**	*.006*	.332**	1

***Correlation is meaning at 0.01 level.*

In the Table 4, simple linear regression models of variables were included. According to the table, it is seen that the rate of explanation of the change in mentality perceived by our independent variable over our dependent variable on organizational commitment was 0.217. It means that 21.7% of organizational commitment dimension can be explained by perceived mentoring. As it is seen in the table, the established regression model was found significant (F: 31.774, p <0.001<0.05).

Table 4. Regression analysis

Independent Variable : Perceived Mentoring	Model Summary					
Dependent Variables	R	R Square	Corrected R Square	SE of Result	F	p
Organizational Commitment	.473	.224	.217	.49758	31.774	.000
Affective Commitment	.460	.211	.204	.76507	29.447	.000
Normative Commitment	.430	.185	.178	.51261	25.004	.000
Continuance Commitment	.092	.009	.000	.67722	.946	.333

According to the table, it is seen that the perceived rate of explanation on the mentor's affective commitment sub-factor was 0.204. That is, 20.4% of the affective commitment sub-dimension can be explained by perceived mentoring. The rate of change of the perceived mentoring on the normative sub-factor was 0.178. According to this result, 17.8% of the normative commitment subscale can be explained by perceived mentoring. It is also seen that the established regression models were significant (F: 29.447, F: 25.004 p <0.001<0.05). The regression model established between perceived mentoring and continuing commitment was not found meaningful. According to the results of the study, the rate of perceived change in mentor perception on the subscale of affective commitment was the highest when compared to the other commitments (Figure 3), which is similar to the results of Stallworth [14]'s study. As the result of the Pearson correlation and simple linear regression analysis, established $\mathbf{H_1}$, $\mathbf{H_2}$, $\mathbf{H_3}$ hypotheses were accepted, while $\mathbf{H_4}$ was rejected.

5 Results

Academic mentors are the greatest supporters and helpers of research assistants during graduate education, who have assumed the role of a lecturer at the beginning of their academic life. During this process, sometimes there was a master-apprentice, sometimes a parent-child, sometimes a brother – sister-sibling, sometimes a superior-officer, and sometimes a teacher-student relationship. Research assistants' perceptions on this process also affect their organizational commitment. In our study it was studied how research assistants' academic perception of mentoring affected their organizational commitment. The results achieved in this context show that there was a positive relationship between perceived mentoring and organizational commitment. The affective commitment from the sub-dimensions of commitment and the relationship between normative commitment and organizational commitment were also positive and significant. However, no relation was found between perceived mentoring and continuance, and the established regression model was not significant. It is not possible to generalize these results for all universities because our research consists of research assistants only at Selcuk University. However, further research may contribute to the literature by conducting a comparative analysis including more than one university and adding a new dimension of how academic mentors perceive the process as well as the research assistant dimension.

References

1. E. Özkalp, Ç. Kırel, Z. Sungur, A. A. Cengiz. Örgütsel Toplumsallaşma Sürecinde Mentorluk ve Mentor'un Yeri ve Önemi: Anadolu Üniversitesi Araştırma Görevlileri Üzerine Bir İnceleme. (2006).
2. N. Anafarta. Bireysel kariyer danışmanı olarak rehber (Mentor). *CÜ İktisadi ve İdari Bilimler Dergisi* **3**, 115-128 (2002).
3. A. Kuzu, M. Kahraman, H. F. Odabaşı. Mentörlükte yeni bir yaklaşım: E-Mentörlük. (2012).
4. K. Özdaşlı, S. Kanten, P. Kanten. Yöneticilerin Kariyer İlerleme Arzusu ile Örgütsel Bağlılıklarının, Akıl Hocalığı Eğilimlerine Etkisini Belirlemeye Yönelik Bir Araştırma. *Süleyman Demirel Üniversitesi İktisadi ve İdari Bilimler Fakültesi Dergisi* **14** (2009).
5. F. Sezgin. Öğretim üyelerinin yetiştiricilik rolleri. *Kuram ve Uygulamada Eğitim Yönetimi* **33**, 132-159 (2003).
6. J. M. Nick,. Best practices in academic mentoring: a model for excellence. *Nursing research and practice* **2012** (2012).
7. TDK. <www.tdk.gov.tr> (2017).
8. O. Sürgevil. *Çalışma yaşamında örgütsel bağlılık* Yüksek Lisans thesis, Ege Üniversitesi, (2007).
9. R. T. Mowday, R. M. Steers, L. W. Porter. The measurement of organizational commitment. *Journal of vocational behavior* **14**, 224-247 (1979).
10. Y. Boylu, E. Pelit, E. Güçer. Akademisyenlerin örgütsel bağlılık düzeyleri üzerine bir araştırma. *Finans Politik & Ekonomik Yorumlar* **44**, 55-74 (2007).
11. E. Örücü, R. Sezen Kışlalıoğlu. Örgütsel bağlılık üzerine bir alan çalışması. *Uluslararası Yönetim İktisat ve İşletme Dergisi* **10**, 45-65 (2014).
12. N. J. Allen, J. P. Meyer. The measurement and antecedents of affective, continuance and normative commitment to the organization. *Journal of occupational psychology* **63**, 1-18 (1990).
13. G. Ülker. Örgütsel Bağlılık, Örgütsel Vatandaşlık ve Örgütte Kalma Niyeti Arasındaki İlişki: Bunların Bazı Değişkenler Açısından İncelenmesi. *Abant İzzet Baysal Üniversitesi Sosyal Bilimler Enstitüsü Dergisi* **14**, 227-248 (2007).
14. H. L. Stallworth. Mentoring, organizational commitment and intentions to leave public accounting. *Managerial Auditing Journal* **18**, 405-418 (2003).
15. J. P. Meyer, N. J. Allen, C. A. Smith. Commitment to organizations and occupations: Extension and test of a three-component conceptualization. *Journal of applied psychology* **78**, 538 (1993).
16. A. Al. *Üniversitelerdeki yabancı diller birimleri yöneticilerinin yönetsel yeterlik düzeyi ile ingilizce öğretim elemanlarının örgütsel bağlılık düzeylerinin araştırılması* Yüksek Lisans thesis, (2007).
17. R. A. Noe. An investigation of the determinants of successful assigned mentoring relationships. *Personnel psychology* **41**, 457-479 (1988).

Misconceptions about the particulate structure of science teacher candidates

Hüseyin Polat[1a] and Fatma Bilge Emre[1,2]

[1]Department of Mathematics and Sciences Education, Faculty of Education, İnönü University, 44280 Malatya, Turkey.
[2]Prof. Dr. HikmetSayılkan Advanced Materials Research an Application Laboratory Scientific and Technological Research Centre, İnönü University, 44280 Malatya, Turkey.

Abstract. The aim of this study is to determine preservice science teachers' misconceptions related particulate nature of matter. For this purpose misconceptions evaluation tool about particulate nature of matter was prepared 118 preservice science teachers who 48 of them first grade and 70 of them fourth grade was applied. The findings show that preservice science teachers' misconceptions about the atomic structure is more than the other concepts. Misconception related to the concept of element is minimum. Also there is no significant differences between the first and fourth grade in the misconceptions measurement tool about particulate nature of matter.

Keywords: Misconceptions, Particulate Nature of the Substance, Misconceptions Evaluation Tool

1 Introduction

Scientific developments, and depending on them, the technologies produced, play important roles in the development of countries. For this reason, the importance of science and its education is growing with each passing day. For this reason, countries want to raise individuals who have the requirements of future ages by providing them with quality education-training services [1].

When the literature is reviewed, it is observed that misconception is defined in different ways. According to Bilgin and Geban[2], it is defined as the thinking method of students on any topic different than the specialists of that specific topic. On the other hand, Tekkaya, Çapa and Yılmaz [3] defined misconception as the concept developed by students as an alternative to the concepts accepted scientifically. Misconceptions are the ones acquired by students as a result of their experiences. These alternative concepts make it difficult to understand new topics and affect meaningful learning in a negative way.

The abstract structure of physical science misconceptions in this field pose a difficult situation for students and teachers. When the reasons of misconceptions are considered, it is

[a]Corresponding author: h.polat44@hotmail.com

seen that they stem from the prejudices, ideas, perceptions, and life experiences of the students when they are at pre-learning stage. For this reason, before the science classes start, the pre-learnt concepts of students must be checked, and if there are any misconceptions, these must be corrected to facilitate future learning [4, 6].

When the literature is reviewed, it is observed that there are many reasons for misconceptions in the science field. In order to determine and eliminate these factors, firstly, it is necessary that science teachers have the scientific process skills and they require knowledge and experience on conceptual change. One of the ways to ensure this is to share the results of studies conducted in this field with teachers and make them acquire some pedagogical skills with in-service trainings [4].

Misconceptions must be resolved within the teaching and learning process. Students need to understand the contents of science classes in order to understand the natural world. Contributions may be made to the understanding of the students about the natural world by eliminating their misconceptions [6].

Obtaining information on misconceptions and their possible causes is extremely important for teaching concepts and to eliminate misconceptions. Because this information makes use of at a maximum level in the stage where the teaching material on concepts are prepared [7].

In the study of Akgün, Gönen and Yılmaz [4] it was reported that science teachers had misconceptions on the structure of the mixtures and their conductivity. Ayas and Özmen[1] conducted a study and reported that there were misconceptions on 5 topics related with to the particulate structure of matter in daily life (vaporization, the change of pressure with temperature in a closed medium, condensation, diffusion and the states of matter). Aydoğan, Güneş and Gülçiçek[5], Kaptan and Korkmaz[8] also conducted studies and showed that students had misconceptions about the topics.

Bilgin and Geban[2] conducted another study on chemical balance and determined that students had misconceptions about the topic. Demircioğlu, Demircioğlu and Yadigaroğlu[9] reported in their study that worksheets were influential in teaching the oxidation and reduction concepts. Erdem, Yılmaz and Morgil[10] conducted another study and determined that students had misconceptions on topics like mol-molecule, atom mass-mass number and oxidizing-oxidized agents. In the study of Sökmen and Bayram[11] which was conducted on eight different concepts, including chemical change and physical change, it was revealed that students could not learn these concepts in a due manner during their educations, and therefore, they were having misconceptions. In their study conducted of the structure of the atom, Tezcan and Salmaz[12] reported that although there were differences between the control group and the study group in terms of academic success levels in favor of the study group, according to the data obtained in the study, misconceptions continued in both groups. Yılmaz, Erdem and Morgil[13] showed in their studies that the question type was influential in the emergence of misconceptions. The purpose of the present study is to determine the existing misconceptions of science teacher candidates on the particulate structure of matter, and to recommend solutions.

2 Method

The literature survey method, which is among quantitative research designs, was used in this study in which the aim was to determine the misconceptions on the particulate structure of matter, and to make recommendations in this context. The survey method is defined as collecting data to determine certain characteristics of a group [14]. The sampling of the study consisted of 118 Science teacher candidates 48 of whom were 1st Graders and 70 of whom were 4th Graders.

In the context of the study, "the Scale to Measure the Misconceptions of the Particulate Structure of Matter" was used to determine the misconceptions of teacher candidates. Six different particulate models were given in the scale to show the particulate structure of matter. Teacher candidates were asked to classify the particle models in terms of being in atomic, molecular, elementary or compound structure by stating the reasons. They were then asked to define the concepts of atomic structure, molecular structure and element and compound. Based on the definitions made by the teacher candidates, their definitions of the concepts in question were examined, and scores were given according to the answers given in the scale by the teacher candidates.

3 Findings

The misconceptions of the science teacher candidates in the particulate structure of matter were examined in the context of their answers given to the questions in the scale, and the definitions of them on atomic structure, molecular structure, element and compound were analyzed. When all the sampling was examined (Table 1), it was observed that teacher candidates, especially have problems in defining the concepts like atomic structure and molecular structure. The rate of answering accurately in atomic structure concept was 10,3%; and the rate of answering accurately in molecular structure concept was 16,2%. On the other hand, the rate of answering accurately in element and compound concept definitions were 76,6%and 65%, respectively.

Table 1. Rates of the answers based on the sampling

Concept	Atomic structure		Molecular structure		Element		Compound	
Definition	N	%	N	%	N	%	N	%
Wrong Answer	105	89,7	98	83,8	27	23,1	41	35,0
True Answer	12	10,3	19	16,2	90	76,9	76	65,0
Total	117	100	117	100,0	117	100,0	117	100,0

Similarly, when the sampling was examined in terms of the grades (Table 2), it was observed that aside from the element concept, the rate of the true answers given by the teacher candidates at the 1st grade in all other concepts was higher than those of the 4th grade teacher candidates.

Table 2. Rates of the answers based on the grades

	Concept	Atomic		Molecular		Element		Compound	
Grade	Definition	N	%	N	%	N	%	N	%
1	Wrong Answer	41	85,4	38	79,2	13	27,1	16	33,3
	True Answer	7	14,6	10	20,8	35	72,9	32	66,7
	Total	48	100,0	48	100,0	48	100,0	48	100,0
4	Wrong Answer	64	92,8	60	87,0	14	20,3	25	36,2
	True Answer	5	7,2	9	13,0	55	79,7	44	63,8
	Total	69	100,0	69	100,0	69	100,0	69	100,0

3.1 Atomic structure concept

When the answers of the science teacher candidates given to the questions in the scale to measure the misconceptions of the particulate structure of matter were examined it was observed that 7 teacher candidates from the 1st grade gave true answers to the question on Atomic Concept (Success $Rate_1$=0,14); and 5 teacher candidates gave true answers at the 4thGrade (Success $Rate_4$=0,07). The Success average comparison (The *z*-Test) was made to determine whether the difference between the success rates was significant or not (Table 3), and no significant differences were detected between the groups (z=1,287, p>0,05).

Table 3. The Z-Test on the atomic structure concept

Grade	n	N	n/N	z	P
1	7	48	0,14	1,287	0,19
4	5	69	0,07		

(p<0,05)

3.2 Molecular structure concept

On the scale to measure the misconceptions of the particulate structure of matter, 10 teacher candidates gave true answers at the 1stGrade on Molecular Concept (Success $Rate_1$=0,208); 9 teacher candidates gave true answers at the 4th Grade (Success $Rate_4$=0,13). The Success average comparison (The *z*-Test) was made to determine whether the difference between the success rates was significant or not (Table 4), no significant difference was detected between the groups (z=1,124, p>0,05).

Table 4. The z-Test on molecular structure concept

Grade	n	N	n/N	z	p
1	10	48	0,208	1,124	0,21
4	9	69	0,13		

(p<0,05)

3.3 Element concept

On the scale to measure the misconceptions of the particulate structure of matter,35 teacher candidates gave true answers on the element concept at the 1stGrade (Success $Rate_1$=0,729); and 5 teacher candidates gave true answers at the 4th Grade (Success $Rate_4$=0,797). The Success average comparison (The *z*-Test) was made to determine whether the difference between the success rates was significant or not (Table 5), no significant difference was detected between the groups (z=0,858, p>0,05).

Table 5. The *z*-Test on element concept

Grade	n	N	n/N	z	p
1	35	48	0,729	0,858	0,39
4	55	69	0,797		

(p<0,05)

3.4 Compound concept

On "the Scale to Measure the Misconceptions of the Particulate Structure of Matter", 32 teacher candidates at the 1st Grade gave true answers on the Compound Concept (Success $Rate_1$=0,667); 9 teacher candidates gave true answers at the 4th Grade (Success $Rate_4$=0,638). The Success average comparison (The *z*-Test) was made to determine whether the difference between the success rates was significant or not (Table 6), no significant difference was detected between the groups (z=0,323, p>0,05).

Table 6. The z-test on compound concept

Grade	n	N	n/N	z	p
1	32	48	0,667	0,323	0,75
4	44	69	0,638		

(p<0,05)

3.5 The t-Test results

When the data obtained as a result of scoring the answers given to the questions in the scale to measure the misconceptions of the particulate structure of matter were analyzed, it was observed that the arithmetic average, median and peak value, which are the central inclination measurements, were close to each other. In the equality of the variances test that was conducted in the dataset, it was observed that the variance between the grades were equal to each other. The *t*-test was also conducted on the dataset.

The results of the independent groups t-test conducted to determine whether there were any significant differences between the grades are given in table 7.

Table 7. The result of the t-test

Groups	N	$\overline{X}$	SS	sd	t	p
1stGrade	48	48,56	16,03	115	,311	,757
4thGrade	69	47,74	12,64			

(p<0,05)

When Table 7 is analyzed, it is observed that the arithmetic averages of both groups were low and close to each other. According to the *t*-test result, it was determined that there was no significant difference between the 1stGrade ($\overline{X}$ =46,56) and 4thGrade ($\overline{X}$ =47,74) [$t_{(115)}$=,311 p>,005].

4 Discussion

The Scale to Measure the Misconceptions of the Particulate Structure of Matter was applied to 118 teacher candidates studying at 1st and 4thGrades of science teachers department in order to determine the misconceptions in the Science Teacher Candidates on the Particulate Structure of Matter subject; and the answers given by the teacher candidates were analyzed. When Table 1 is examined, it is observed that misconceptions exist mostly on the atomic structure concept. The misconceptions were at the lowest level in element concept. Similarly, when the answers of the teacher candidates are examined in terms of the grades (Table 2), it is observed that the true answers given by the teacher candidates except for the element concept are more than the true answers given by the 4th Graders. In addition, when Table 2 is examined, it is also observed that the number of the teacher candidates who gave true answers to the atomic and molecular Concept at both grades was close to each other and at low levels. Based on this situation, it might be claimed that the misconceptions of science teacher candidates on the basic concept that constitute the basic structure of the atom do not change throughout the educational process of the teacher candidates. Among the reasons of this, it is possible to consider the education being performed in a traditional method in the educational process. Parallel to this result, the t-test was conducted between the points received in the scale to measure the misconceptions of the particulate structure of matter to see whether there was significant differences (Table 7) and it was observed that there were no significant differences between the 1stGrade ($\overline{X}$ =48,56) and 4thGrade ($\overline{X}$ =47,74) [$t_{(117)}$=0,311, p<,005].

When the literature is reviewed, it was observed that there were no direct studies on the atom, molecule, element and compound concepts in particulate structure of matter subject. However, in the study conducted by Ayas and Özmen [1], misconceptions were detected in particulate structure of matter subject in the concepts like vaporization, the change of pressure with temperature in a closed medium, condensation, diffusion and the states of matter. Similarly, in the study conducted by Tezcan and Salmaz [12], it was determined those misconceptions continued on subjects like the structure, movement style, size, weight, lifespan and the composition of matter. It is possible to claim that the results reported in the literature are parallel to the ones determined in the present study. The structure of the atom may be considered as one of the basic subjects in science. Without knowing the structure of the atom, it is difficult to learn some other subjects like the structure of the matter, chemical reactions, chemical bonds, etc. For this reason, when the results obtained in this study and the ones reported in the literature are analyzed together, it is possible to claim that the basis of the difficulty in understanding the structure of the matter and the misconceptions in further subjects is the misconceptions that exist in the particulate structure of matter.

5 Result and recommendations

The scale to measure the misconceptions of the particulate structure of matter was applied to 118 teacher candidates studying at 1st and 4thGrades of science teacher's department in order to determine the misconceptions in the science teacher candidates on the particulate structure of matter subject; and the answers given by the teacher candidates were analyzed. When the answers given by the teacher candidates were examined in terms of the sampling (Table 1) it was observed that the rate of the wrong answers given in atomic structure (% 89,7) and molecular structure (% 83,8) concepts were more than those of the element and compound concepts. The concept in which the wrong answer rate was the lowest was the concept element (23,1%). When the analysis results were examined in terms of grades (Table 2) it as observed that the rate of true answers of 1st Grade students was higher than those of the 4th Graders. The *z*-Test was made to determine whether there was a significant difference between the grades according to the true answers given to the concepts, and it was observed that there was no difference in any concept. In addition, the t test was applied again to determine whether there was a significant difference between the points received in the scale and it was observed that there were no significant differences between the 1stGrade ($\overline{X}$ =48,56) and 4thGrade ($\overline{X}$ =47,74) [$t_{(117)}$=0,311, p<,005].

The misconception in the teacher candidates will influence the conceptual development in the students in a negative manner. For this reason, the misconceptions must be determined in teacher candidates and eliminated [4]. Questions with long answers may be asked in order to reveal the misconceptions in students. Because such questions require that students revise and reorganize their knowledge to explain what they understand from the subject. Questions with long answers which enable students to show their reasoning, must be emphasized in homework assignments to help students define misconceptions [6]. Yılmaz, Erdem and Morgil [13] conducted a study and showed that the question type used in the study was influential in detecting misconceptions.

The bilateral communication between the student and the teacher must be increased in order to eliminate misconceptions. By doing so, it may be ensured that students become aware of the concepts they are going to develop. In addition, it must be considered that preparing the course books in such a way that will lead to misconceptions will deteriorate the situation [6].

In order to succeed in science education, student-centered methods must be preferred rather than traditional methods. When the literature is reviewed, it is observed that student-centered methods are replacing traditional methods in science education. According to Yağbasan and Gülçiçek [6], science education is a complex process and hosts may components. In order to have a more influential science education, it has been claimed that methods that are different from the traditional methods should be used such as cooperation-based science education, concept mapping method, asking questions techniques, reflective thoughts skills, and computer-assisted science teaching.

In the study conducted by Polat [15], a positive result was reported in favor of the study group in which argumentation method was applied ad the control group in which traditional method was applied, which shows that argumentation method may also be used as an influential method on the subject the structure of the atom.

References

1. Ayas, A. & Özmen, H. Lise kimya öğrencilerinin maddenin tanecikli yapısı kavramını anlama seviyelerine ilişkin bir çalışma. *Boğaziçi Üniversitesi Eğitim Dergisi***19,** 45–60 (2002).
2. Bilgin, İ. & Geban, Ö. Benzeşim (Analoji) Yöntemi Kullanarak Lise 2. Sınıf Öğrencilerinin Kimyasal Denge Konusundaki Kavram Yanılgılarının Giderilmesi. *Hacettepe Üniversitesi Eğitim Fakültesi Dergisi* 26–32 (2001).
3. Tekkaya, C., Çapa, Y. & Yılmaz, Ö. Genel Bivoloji Ögretmen Adavlarinin Bivoloji Konularındaki Kavram Vanilgiları. *Hacettepe Üniversitesi Eğitim Fakültesi Dergisi***18,** 140–147 (2000).
4. Akgün, A., Gönen, S. & Yilmaz, A. Fen bilgisi öğretmen adaylarının karışımların yapısı ve iletkenliği konusundaki kavram yanılgıları. *Hacettepe üniversitesi eğitim fakültesi dergisi***28,** 1–8 (2005).
5. Aydoğan, S., Güneş, B. & Gülçiçek, Ç. Isı ve sıcaklık konusunda kavram yanılgıları. *Gazi Üniversitesi Gazi Eğitim Fakültesi Dergisi***23,** 111–124 (2003).
6. Yağbasan, R. & Gülçiçek, Ç. Describing the characteristic of misconceptions in science teaching. *Pamukkale Üniversitesi Eğitim Fakütesi Dergisi***13,** 102–120 (2003).
7. Coştu, B., Alipaşa, A. & Ünal, S. Kavram Yanılgıları Ve Olası Nedenleri: Kaynama Kavramı. *Kastamonu Education Journal***15,** 123–136 (2007).
8. Kaptan, F. & Korkmaz, H. İlköğretimde Fen Bilgisi Öğretimi. *Milli Eğitim Bakanlığı İlköğretimde Etkili Öğretme ve Öğrenme Öğretmen El Kitabı, Modül 7.*(2001).
9. Demircioğlu, H., Demircioğlu, G. & Yadigaroğlu, M. Çalışma yapraklarının öğrencilerin yükseltgenme ve indirgenme kavramlarını anlamaları üzerine etkisi. *Journal of Research in Education and Teaching***3,** 243–256 (2014).
10. Yilmaz, A., Erdem, E. & Morgil, İ. Öğrencilerin Elektrokimya Konusundaki Kavram Yanılgıları. *Hacettepe Üniversitesi Eğitim Fakültesi Dergisi***23,** 234–242 (2002).
11. Sökmen, N. & Bayram, H. Lise 1. Sınıf Öğrencilerinin Temel Kimya Kavramlarını Anlama Düzeyleriyle Mantıksal Düşünme Yetenekleri Arasındaki İlişki. *Hacettepe Üniversitesi Eğitim Fakültesi Dergisi***16,** 89–94 (1999).
12. Tezcan, H. & Salmaz, Ç. Atomun Yapısının Kavratılmasında ve Yanlış Kavramaların Giderilmesinde Bütünleştirici ve Geleneksel Öğretim Yöntemlerinin Etkileri. *Gazi Üniversitesi Gazi Eğitim Fakültesi Dergisi***1,** 41–54 (2005).
13. Morgil, İ., Erdem, E. & Yılmaz, A. Kimya eğitiminde kavram yanılgıları. *Hacettepe Üniversitesi Eğitim Fakültesi Dergisi***25,** 246–255 (2003).
14. Büyüköztürk, Ş., Kılıç Çakmak, E., Akgün, Ö. E., Karadeniz, Ş. & Demirel, F. *Bilimsel Araştırma Yöntemleri.* (Pegem Akademi, 2012).
15. Polat, H. Atomun yapısı konusunda argümantasyon yönteminin ilköğretim 7.sınıf öğrencilerinin başarısı üzerine etkisi. (İnönü Üniversitesi Eğitim Fakültesi İlköğretim Anabilim Dalı Başkanlığı, 2014).

Levels of prospective science teachers' ability to structure 5E model

Sibel Demir Kaçan[1a] and Fatma Şahin[2]

Department of Science Education, Faculty of Education, Ondokuz Mayıs University, Samsun, Turkey
Department of Science Education, Faculty of Education, Marmara University, İstanbul, Turkey

Abstract. The research was conducted with 3rd year prospective science students, who study at the science teaching department of a university in Istanbul province. For that purpose, 34 prospective science teachers cooperated and participated in the study. In the study, the prospective teachers were asked to select a certain subject and plan that subject in accordance with the 5E model. Therefore, the objective of the study is to determine the levels of prospective science teachers' ability to structure the 5E model. The data retrieved from the study were analyzed ad compared through content analysis and percentages. The results of the study suggest that some prospective teachers are not sufficient at each phase of the 5E model, thereby the researchers made suggestions for that situation.
Keywords: research and investigation based learning, science education, prospective teacher, 5E model

1 Introduction

Science education has a significant place in the educational cycle of the world and our country. Considering where science education is in countries in the world, the results of certain studies prove that in our country it is our responsibility to provide our children with a more attentive science education. Of course, this change is not something that can be done immediately through magic, but needs to be done through a consistent process. In fact, this change is about enabling students to have experiences that are suitable for them, not about conducting activities that are cliché and against the nature of science. One of the most effective ways to do so is placing the learning based on research and investigation in the center and bringing students to the backstage of the work.

Today's 5E model is accepted as an effective and significant model in learning, which is based on research and investigation. Therefore, the ability to structure and implement 5E model is of importance in terms of education. Especially from the perspective of science education, research and investigation-based learning exists in the nature of science. However, various teaching models and strategies must be applied in order to reveal,

[a] Corresponding author: sibelfe@hotmail.com

implement, and structure that potential. One of these effective teaching methods is, with no doubt, 5E model. 5E model is a learning model that consists of five phases including engaging, exploring, explaining, extending, and evaluation. In the engaging phase of the 5E model, activities that could grab the attention of students are conducted; in the exploring phase, certain experience processes are carried out; in the phase of explaining, students are promoted to define and to infer; in the phase of extending, the students are expected to make new transfers to the existing knowledge; finally in the phase of evaluation, the reflections of the process on the students are evaluated.

In our country, 5E model is a research field that has just started to be studied in the science education field in the recent years [1, 2, 3]. Reviewing the studies carried out in this field, 5E model appears to be an effective teaching model.

Considering all of these facts, the importance of the study is focused on raising efficient prospective science teachers, who will provide a good science education.

2 Method

2.1 Participants

The research was conducted with 3rd year prospective science students, who study at the science teaching department of a university in Istanbul province. For that purpose, 34 prospective science teachers cooperated and participated in the study.

2.2 Procedure

In the study, the prospective teachers were asked to select a certain subject and plan that subject in accordance with the 5E model. Therefore, the objective of the study is to determine the levels of prospective teachers' ability to structure the 5E model after studying science. The engaging, exploring, explaining, extending, and evaluation phases of those plans were examined. The phases of the 5E model were prepared by the researchers, evaluated through evaluation criteria and eventually interpreted. In this study, each phase of the 5E model plans prepared by the prospective teachers was evaluated according to two categories which are sufficient and insufficient.

The pattern of the study is ''case study''. Case study can be defined as a system, in which one or multiple cases, environments, programs, social groups or other interdependent systems are thoroughly examined [4]. The data retrieved from the study were analyzed ad compared through content analysis and percentages. The content analysis is implemented as a technique, in which information can be elaborately examined through codings and categories. The data collected from the open-ended questions were evaluated through content analysis. According to the researchers, content analysis is a systematical and iterable technique, through which certain words of a text can be summarized in smaller content categories via codings [4].

3 Findings

The data obtained from the study are divided into two headings. The first section consists of the evaluation of the plans prepared by the prospective teachers according to 5E model, in sufficient and insufficient categories, whereas; the second section involves the examples created by the prospective teachers on the phases of 5E model.

3.1 Prospective teachers' competency of 5E model

The data obtained from the research are displayed in Table 1. Table 1 displays frequencies in two categories including Sufficient and Insufficient, which are related to prospective science teachers' ability to structure the processes of the 5E model.

Table 1. The prospective science teachers are generally able to structure the 5E model

5E model	Sufficient	Insufficient
Engage	31	3
Exploration	17	17
Explanation	11	23
Elaboration	10	24
Evaluation	18	16

As demonstrated in Table 1, the prospective science teachers are generally able to structure the 5E model, they have difficulty with the explanation and elaboration processes, and they mostly succeed at the engage phase.

3.2 Examples created by prospective teachers on 5E model

The tables in this section demonstrates the examples of the plans created by the prospective teachers on the phases of 5E model.

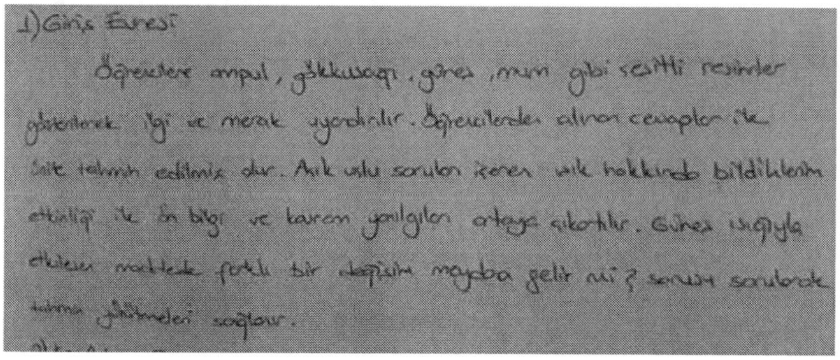
1) Giriş Evresi

Öğrencilere ampul, gökkuşağı, güneş, mum gibi çeşitli resimler göstererek ilgi ve merak uyandırılır. Öğrencilerden alınan cevaplar ile ışık tahmin edilmiş olur. Açık uçlu soruları içeren ışık hakkında bildiklerim etkinliği ile ön bilgi ve kavram yanılgıları ortaya çıkartılır. Güneş ışığıyla etkileşen maddede farklı bir değişim meydana gelir mi? sorusu sorularak tahmin yürütmeleri sağlanır.

Fig. 1. An example on the engage phase

Examining the example displayed in the Figure1, it is observed that the prospective science teacher is quite sufficient at the engage phase.

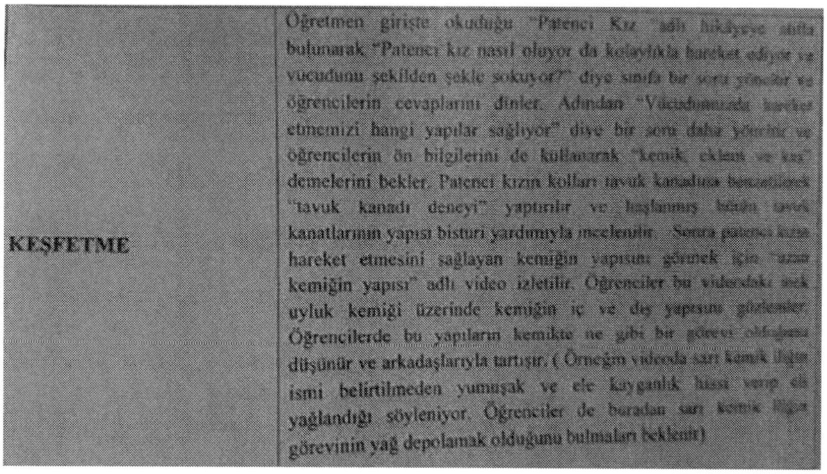

KEŞFETME	Öğretmen girişte okuduğu "Patenci Kız" adlı hikâyeye atıfta bulunarak "Patenci kız nasıl oluyor da kolaylıkla hareket ediyor ve vücudunu şekilden şekle sokuyor?" diye sınıfa bir soru yöneltir ve öğrencilerin cevaplarını dinler. Ardından "Vücudumuzda hareket etmemizi hangi yapılar sağlıyor" diye bir soru daha yöneltir ve öğrencilerin ön bilgilerini de kullanarak "kemik, eklem ve kas" demelerini bekler. Patenci kızın kolları tavuk kanadına benzetilerek "tavuk kanadı deneyi" yaptırılır ve haşlanmış bütün tavuk kanatlarının yapısı bisturi yardımıyla incelenir. Sonra patenci kızın hareket etmesini sağlayan kemiğin yapısını görmek için "uzun kemiğin yapısı" adlı video izletilir. Öğrenciler bu videodaki sığır uyluk kemiği üzerinde kemiğin iç ve dış yapısını gözlemler. Öğrencilerde bu yapıların kemikte ne gibi bir görevi olduğunu düşünür ve arkadaşlarıyla tartışır. (Örneğin videoda sarı kemik iliğinin ismi belirtilmeden yumuşak ve ele kayganlık hissi verip elin yağlandığı söyleniyor. Öğrenciler de buradan sarı kemik iliğinin görevinin yağ depolamak olduğunu bulmaları beklenir)

Fig. 2. An example on the exploration phase

Taking a look at the example demonstrated in the Figure 2, it is observed that the prospective science teacher is sufficient at the exploration phase.

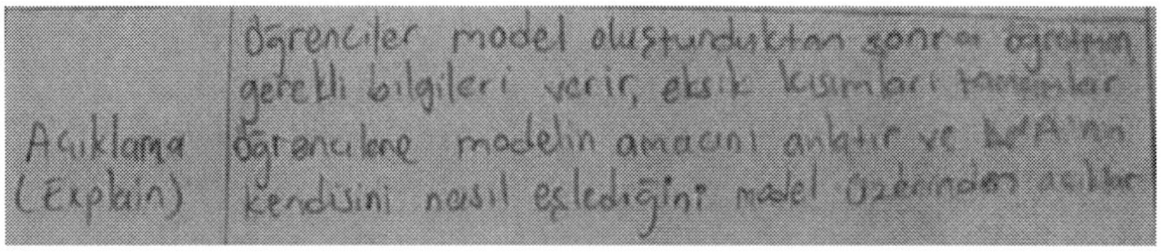

Fig. 3. An example on the explanation phase

Looking at the example displayed in the Figure 3, it is observed that the prospective science teacher is not quite sufficient at the explanation phase.

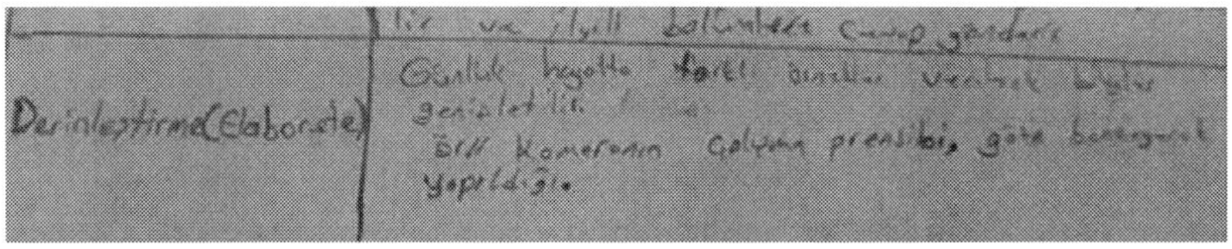

Fig. 4. An example on the elaboration phase

Examining the example shown in the Figure 4, it is observed that the prospective science teacher is not quite sufficient at the elaboration phase.

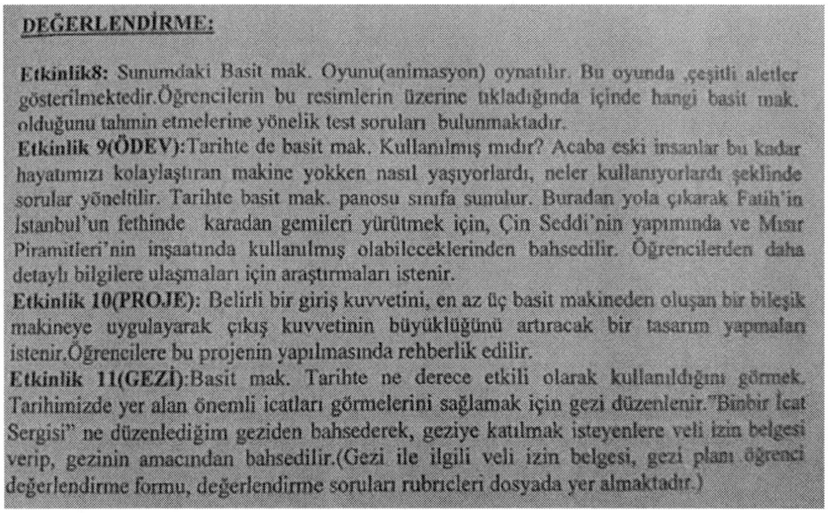

DEĞERLENDİRME:

Etkinlik8: Sunumdaki Basit mak. Oyunu(animasyon) oynatılır. Bu oyunda ,çeşitli aletler gösterilmektedir.Öğrencilerin bu resimlerin üzerine tıkladığında içinde hangi basit mak. olduğunu tahmin etmelerine yönelik test soruları bulunmaktadır.
Etkinlik 9(ÖDEV): Tarihte de basit mak. Kullanılmış mıdır? Acaba eski insanlar bu kadar hayatımızı kolaylaştıran makine yokken nasıl yaşıyorlardı, neler kullanıyorlardı şeklinde sorular yöneltilir. Tarihte basit mak. panosu sınıfa sunulur. Buradan yola çıkarak Fatih'in İstanbul'un fethinde karadan gemileri yürütmek için, Çin Seddi'nin yapımında ve Mısır Piramitleri'nin inşaatında kullanılmış olabileceklerinden bahsedilir. Öğrencilerden daha detaylı bilgilere ulaşmaları için araştırmaları istenir.
Etkinlik 10(PROJE): Belirli bir giriş kuvvetini, en az üç basit makineden oluşan bir bileşik makineye uygulayarak çıkış kuvvetinin büyüklüğünü artıracak bir tasarım yapmaları istenir.Öğrencilere bu projenin yapılmasında rehberlik edilir.
Etkinlik 11(GEZİ):Basit mak. Tarihte ne derece etkili olarak kullanıldığını görmek. Tarihimizde yer alan önemli icatları görmelerini sağlamak için gezi düzenlenir."Binbir İcat Sergisi" ne düzenlediğim geziden bahsederek, geziye katılmak isteyenlere veli izin belgesi verip, gezinin amacından bahsedilir.(Gezi ile ilgili veli izin belgesi, gezi planı öğrenci değerlendirme formu, değerlendirme soruları rubricleri dosyada yer almaktadır.)

Fig. 5. An example on the evaluation phase

Taking a look at the example demonstrated in the Figure 5, it is observed that the prospective science teacher is sufficient at the evaluation phase.

4 Discussion and conclusion

5E learning cycle model was implemented by Robert Karplus at late 1950's and early 1960's for the first time [5] and by Bybee & Landes in the biology program in 1990 [6]. 5E model promotes children to discover, implement, and, structure concepts [7]. With its student-centered approach, 5E model supports children in taking more responsibility for their own learning [8].

The results of the study suggest that the prospective science teachers are generally able to structure the 5E model, however, some of the prospective science teachers are not completely sufficient at each stage of the 5E model. It was detected that the prospective teachers especially had difficulty with elaboration and explanation phases as well as organizing activities related to these phases. The deepening phase is of high importance for the 5E model, since the ability to transfer knowledge into other knowledge is regarded as one of the most significant steps in the science education.

5E model has also a significant place in query-based learning. As a matter of fact, this was revealed in the study carried out by the researchers [9, 11]. It is believed that in order to execute this learning method in an efficient manner, it is important to have a high number of experiences. Therefore, more studies must be conducted on the 5E model both at elementary school and faculty level. Within that context, this study tries to shed light on the importance of the learning process of prospective teachers, especially for science education as well as to take a step towards enabling others to conduct new studies in future.

References

1. Şenel Çoruhlu, T., & Çepni, S. Effects of the enriched 5E model on students' conceptual change: Astronomy sample. Kastamonu Eğitim Dergisi, 24(4), 1785-1802, (2016).
2. Açışlı, S., Turgut, Ü., Altun Yalçın, S., & Gürbüz, F. (2009). Elektrik konusunda 5E öğrenme modeline dayalı öğretimin üniversite öğrencilerinin bilimsel işlem becerilerine ve fizik laboratuvarına karşı tutumlarına etkisi. Bayburt Üniversitesi Eğitim Fakültesi Dergisi 4(I-II), 80-92, (2009).
3. Demir, S. Bilimsel tartışma ve araştırmaya dayalı tasarlanan laboratuvar programının, fen bilgisi öğretmen adaylarının bilimsel yaratıcılıklarına etkisi. Unpublished doctoral thesis, Marmara University, Institute of Education Sciences, İstanbul. (2014).
4. Büyüköztürk, Ş., Kılıç Çakmak, E., Akgün, Ö. E., Karadeniz, Ş. & Demirel, F., Bilimsel araştırma yöntemleri. Ankara: Pegem Akademi, (2008).
5. Liu, T.C., Peng, H., Wu, W., & Lin, M. S. The effects of mobile natural-science learning based on the 5E learning cycle: A case study. Educational Technology & Society, 12(4), 344-358, (2009).
6. Champbell, M. A. The effects of the 5E learning cycle model on students' understanding of force and motion concepts. Unpublished master thesis, B. S. Millersville University, Orlondo, Florida. (2006).
7. Martin, D.J. Elementary science methods, a constructivist approach. Belmont: Thomson Learning Academic Resource Center. 4 Edition. (2006).
8. Köseoğlu, F., & Tümay, H. Bilim eğitiminde yapılandırıcı paradigma teoriden öğretim uygulamalarına. Ankara: Pegem Akademi, (2013).
9. Cheng, P. H., Yang, Y. T. C., Chang, S. H. G., & Kuo, F. R. R. 5E mobile inquiry learning approach for enhancing learning motivation and scientific inquiry ability of university students. IEEE Transactions on Education, 59(2), 147-153, (2016).
10. Demirhan İşcan, C., & Keleşoğlu, S. Practices of prospective teachers based on constructivism. Kastamonu Eğitim Dergisi, 25(3), 1055-1070, (2017).
11. Kırıktaş, H., & Ünal Çoban, G. Effects of multiple intelligence based inquiry practices on critical thinking and academic achievement of preservice teachers. Mehmet Akif Ersoy Üniversitesi Eğitim Fakültesi Dergisi, 37, 69-88, (2016). ISSN:1302-8944

Importance of pre-school science education

Sibel Demir Kaçan[1a], and Dilek Çelikler[1]

[1]Department of Science Education, Faculty of Education, Ondokuz Mayıs University, Samsun, Turkey

Abstract. Considering this aspect of the study, the objective of the study is determining the importance of science education in pre-school period. In this research, two open-ended questions were asked to the prospective teachers. In these questions, the focus was the importance of science education in the pre-school period for children and teachers. These two open-ended questions were developed and presented by two researchers, who are experts in their fields. The research was conducted with 4th year prospective pre-school students, who study at the pre-school teaching department of a university in Karadeniz region. For that purpose, 40 prospective pre-school teachers participated in the study. The data retrieved from the study were analyzed through content analysis. The results of the study provided various answers from the prospective teachers on the importance of science education both for children and themselves.
Keywords: Pre-school education, Science education, Prospective teacher

1 Introduction

Science education is a process that begins when children start to discover their surroundings. Therefore, it is important to provide children with a qualified science education starting from pre-school period. Our perceptions may vary throughout the time spent between our birth and puberty, furthermore; different objects, events, and people may draw our attention. As of the first month, a baby starts to realize and recognize its surroundings while its sense of curiosity increases day by day. This sense of curiosity may continue until the baby becomes an adult. However, due to outer factors, this motive, which is much more intense in the pre-school and early-childhood period, may not regarded as important or may be repressed. Some family members or teachers may behave in a manner that could prevent the development of child's sense of curiosity. Such behaviors may be performed intentionally or unintentionally. Moreover, during this process, children work towards completing their cognitive, affective, and characteristic development. Therefore, the sense of curiosity is a motive that should be developed and is quite significant for the development of children of this age. Children in pre-school age ask many questions about their surroundings and seek for answers to satisfy their curiosity. Especially the children,

[a] Corresponding author: sibelfe@hotmail.com

who ask various questions and receive answers about their science-related surroundings, grow more interest in science and start to ask more questions about such subjects. This situation is of great importance for raising inquisitive and interrogating individuals. Raising individuals, who grow interest in science in pre-school period, ask questions, research, and produce ideas, will increase their motivation in science and enable them to look at events from different perspectives.

Children do not only obtain scientific, technological, and practical knowledge through formal education, but also through informal education. These everyday-life contexts can also be used in developing scientific knowledge at school, by means of extracurricular activities [1]. For that reason, pre-school period is very important for science education and this process should be an effective one. This also highlights the need to raise prospective pre-school teachers in a more precise manner.

In order for an adult to become a competent person, certain types of awareness must be developed at an early age. This awareness sometimes occurs in the routine course of life, whereas; some other types of it occur in a disciplinary learning process. Thus, early childhood and pre-school phase are of significance for this disciplinary approach. During the pre-school phase, children form the basis for their adulthood. The stronger this basis is, the more well-equipped the person will be as they older and integrate into the society. Pre-school era is not only important for the overall development of an individual, but also for the development of different abilities. The education received in the preschool era is important for children to have the perspective of a musician, athlete, actor/actress or scientist. Therefore, this era is of high significance in terms of raising an individual, who is in peace with nature, can live and see science as a part of life. This pre-school era is when the child questions and reflects his/her sense of wonder the most. Indeed, sense of wonder is quite effective for improvement and fundamentals of science. A small sense of wonder is the most significant step for a new and big discovery. For that reason, it is of utmost importance that a child does not lose his/her sense of wonder and keep questioning and seeking answers to certain questions. This young individual, who poses questions to his/her family and teacher, actually executes the most fundamental activity of a scientist. A scientist conducts this questioning in a more disciplinary manner, whereas; a child conducts this randomly. These questions, which may seem "minor, basic, non-sense" to some, are in fact indicators of a questioning and creative approach. That's why these questions of children should not be randomly answered, instead their questions should be valued as much as possible and they should be given logical explanations. Scientists believe that the best way to learn science is learning by doing. During this era children need to ask questions, to research, to examine, and to learn implementing trial and problem solving skills [2].

The quality of the science education delivered at the pre-school era is important. It is believed that children, who already naturally have a sense of wonder during this era, must frequently encounter science-related situations and a certain discipline. Indeed, the way a child is raised during this era reflects the prospective society, therefore, children's perception of a scientist and science, their scientific process skills as well as the development of their creativity skills and scientific creativity skills must be taken into account [3]. In that context, the education of prospective pre-school teachers must be highlighted. Prospective pre-school teachers must be able to transfer science knowledge into children and must structure this processes in a well-equipped manner. For that reason it is believed that prospective pre-school teachers must be well-trained in terms of their science knowledge. Raising prospective pre-school teachers with good science qualifications will significantly affect the interest of children in science and research.

DOI: 10.1051/shsconf/20173701040

Considering this aspect of the study, the objective of the study is determining the importance of science education in pre-school period.

2 Method

2.1 Participants

The research was conducted with 4th year prospective pre-school students, who study at the pre-school teaching department of a university in Karadeniz region. For that purpose, 40 prospective pre-school teachers participated in the study.

2.2 Procedure

In this research, two open-ended questions were asked to the prospective teachers. In these questions, the focus was the importance of science education in the pre-school period for children and teachers. These two open-ended questions were developed and presented by two researchers, who are experts in their fields.

The pattern of the study is ''case study''. Case study can be defined as a system, in which one or multiple cases, environments, programs, social groups or other interdependent systems are thoroughly examined. The data retrieved from the study were analyzed through content analysis. The content analysis is the ability to elaborately examine information through certain codings and categories. The data collected from the open-ended questions were evaluated through content analysis. According to the researchers, content analysis is a systematical and iterable technique, through which certain words of a text can be summarized in smaller content categories via codings [4].

3 Findings

The data obtained from the research are displayed in two tables. Table 1 demonstrates themes related to importance of pre-school science education for children, whereas; Table 2 displays themes relevant to the significance of science education for prospective pre-school teachers.

As demonstrated in Table 1, "mental skills, hand skills, environmental awareness, science-literacy, being a basis for vocational training, problem and observation skills" come to the front for the significance of science education for children.

Examining the themes relevant to the significance of science education for prospective pre-school teachers as displayed in Table 2, concepts such as "environmental awareness, sense of wonder, questioning, everyday-life, teacher-student competency" come to the front.

Table 1. Themes related to importance of pre-school science education for children

Themes	f
Using mental skills	20
Using hand skills	17
Environmental awareness	17
Problem solving skills	12
Being a basis for vocational training	12
Observation skills	10
Being science-literate	10
Sense of wonder	9
Social skills	9
Experiment	9
Questioning skills	7
Research	6
Observation	6
Understanding the world	6
Discovery	6
Interpreting everyday-life	5
Creating cause and effect relationship	5
Examination	4
Having knowledge	4
Being interested in science	4
Promoting to ask questions	4
Enabling success	4
Others…	

Table 2. Themes relevant to the significance of science education for prospective pre-school teachers.

Themes	f
Environmental awareness	17
Sense of wonder	13
Questioning	12
Every day-life	8
Observation	7
Teacher sufficient-student sufficient	6
Learning by doing and experiencing	5
Mental skills	5
Understanding the world	5
Survey	5
Experimental	5
Hand skills	4
Activity	4
Entertainment	4
Being a guide	3
Having knowledge	3
Paying attention to interests and needs	3
In selecting a profession	3
Using a convenient method or technique	3
Knowing how to transfer	3
Motor skills	3
Paying attention to cognitive development	3

4 Discussion and conclusion

Since children are curious and interested in research and asking questioning during the pre-school era, they learn more easily through learning by doing and experiencing. The science education delivered at the pre-school phase must not be based on transferring science knowledge, but on providing environments, where children can satisfy their sense of wonder, be promoted to discover, research, examine, observe, assume, and make conclusions [5].

The results of the study suggest that prospective pre-school teachers attach importance to science education not only for themselves, but also for the children they will raise. Likewise, in a study carried out by a researcher, it is stated that teachers must provide children with convenient learning opportunities and environments, where children can research, satisfy their sense of wonder, see the cause-effect relationship, assert their ideas, and make assumptions by using their senses [6]. The same researcher also argues that pre-school teacher's ability to prepare such environments depends on how well the pre-school teacher knows the nature of science and technology and the relationship between the society and environment.

The prospective teachers evaluated the importance of science education from their own perspective and stated that if they are sufficient enough, so will be the children. Moreover, they stressed on environmental awareness, science-literacy, and problem solving skills from the perspective of children. Indeed, in the study conducted by the researchers, it was found out that the majority of the pre-school teachers were not able to plan and execute science and nature activities at the desired quality, were unable to develop original materials, did not know about the effective teaching methods used in activities and did not use such teaching methods [7].

There exists many studies on the importance of science education in pre-school phase [7, 11]. The results of the study provided various answers from the prospective teachers on the importance of science education both for children and themselves Within that context, this study tries to shed light on the importance of the learning process of prospective pre-school teachers, especially for science education as well as to take a step towards enabling others to conduct new studies in future.

References

1. Şahin, F. Okul öncesinde fen kavramları ve öğretimi. F. Şahin (Ed.) içinde, Okul öncesi dönemde fen eğitimi (p.85-108), Ankara: Hedef CS Yayıncılık, 3.Baskı, (2016).
2. Uyanık Balat, G. Fen nedir ve çocuklar feni nasıl öğrenir? B. Akman, G. Uyanık Balat, & T. Güler Yıldız (Ed.) içinde, Okul öncesi dönemde fen eğitimi (p.1-17). Ankara: Pegem Akademi. 4.Baskı, (2014).
3. Demir, S. Okul öncesi dönemde bilim anlayışı ve düşünme becerilerinin geliştirilmesi. F. Şahin (Ed.) içinde, Okul öncesi dönemde fen eğitimi (p.25-60). Ankara: Hedef CS Yayıncılık, 3.Baskı, (2016).
4. Büyüköztürk, Ş., Kılıç Çakmak, E., Akgün, Ö. E., Karadeniz, Ş. & Demirel, F. Bilimsel araştırma yöntemleri. Ankara: Pegem Akademi, (2008).
5. Ünal, M., & Akman, B. Early childhood teachers' attidutes towards science teaching. H.Ü. Eğitim Fakültesi Dergisi, 30, 251-257, (2006).
6. Çınar, S. Okul öncesi öğretmenlerinin fen-teknoloji-toplum-çevre hakkındaki görüşleri. Journal of Research in Education and Teaching, 2(1), 349-363, (2013), ISSN: 2146-9199.
7. Ayvacı, H. Ş., Devecioğlu, Y. & Yiğit, N. Okul öncesi öğretmenlerinin fen ve doğa etkinliklerindeki yeterliliklerinin belirlenmesi. V. Ulusal Fen Bilimleri ve Matematik

Eğitimi Kongresi, Orta Doğu Teknik University, Ankara. http://www.fedu.metu.edu.tr/ufbmek5/bkitabi/PDF/OgretmenYtistirme/Bildiri/t277d.pdf. (2002).
8. Büyüktaşkapu, S. Montessori yaklaşımı ve okul öncesinde fen eğitimi. Tubav Bilim Dergisi 5(3), 19-25, (2012).
9. Onur, A., Çağlar , A., & Salman, M. Evaluation of waste paper and improvement of environmental awareness for 5 years old preschool children. 24(5), Kastamonu Eğitim Dergisi, 2457-2468, (2016).
10. Ayvacı, H. Ş., & Yurt, Ö. Çocuk ve bilim eğitimi. Çocuk ve Medeniyet, 1, 15-28, (2016).
11. Karamustafaoğlu, S., & Kandaz, U. Using teaching methods in the science activities and difficulties encountered in pre-school education. GÜ, Gazi Eğitim Fakültesi Dergisi, 26(1), 65-81, (2006).

Examination of group cohesiveness levels and goal orientations of basketball players

Can Çavin Ötkan[1a], Gönül Tekkurşun Demir[2], and AlperenHalıcı[3]

[1]Faculty of Sport Science, Gazi University/YüzüncüYıl University, 06000 Ankara, Turkey
[2]Faculty of Sport Science, Gazi University, 06000 Ankara, Turkey

Abstract. This research intends to examine goal orientation and group cohesiveness levels of basketball players. 243 mature players who play in the leagues of Turkish Basketball Federation in 2016-2017 season participated the study. "Task and Ego Orientation in Sports" and "Group Cohesiveness" questionnaires are used in study. While frequency, arithmetic mean and standard deviation is used for the analysis of data, T-Test, One-Way Analysis of Variance (ANOVA) and Post-Hoc test statistics (Tukey HSD) are used for independent samples. Depending on the variables of gender and educational background of players, a significant difference is identified in sub-dimension of Task Attraction of Group and a low-level negatively significant difference is identified between Ego Orientation in terms of age and sportive age. Significant differences are identified between the Perception of Team Success and sub-dimensions of Social Integration of Group and Social Attraction of Group. No statistically significant difference can be found for the variable of time spent in team in terms of group cohesiveness and goal orientation.
Keywords: Group cohesiveness, goal orientations, motivation, basketball.

1 Introduction

There are some major facts to achieve the intended objectives in all team sports. Mental potentials of athletes as well as their physical and technical capacities are critical criteria. Particularly in terms of team sports, the levels of individuals to feel that they belong to the group and orientating themselves, as well as their attitudes

[a]Corresponding author: cancavitotkan@gazi.edu.tr

towards the tasks undertaken in line with intended objectives are requisites of group [12, 17]. In this context, group cohesiveness and task and ego orientation levels of individuals in the group play an important role in the future of organization.

Cohesiveness which represents the sum of factors and strengths providing group members to stay in group is also generally defined as the level of their attraction to each other and to group [5].

When cohesiveness is examined specific to team sports we see that it has two basic dimensions; task cohesiveness and social cohesiveness. Team cohesiveness describes the process where group members attach themselves to each other in order to achieve intended objectives and/or due to emotional interaction between them and sustain this state [4].

It is stated that the pleasure felt due to the long-time togetherness of team members, homogeneity of group, size of group, cooperation in group and successful performance is an important factor to constitute and develop cohesiveness in a sportive group [14].

In relation to goal oriented motivation in sports the concepts of group cohesiveness of team members, goal orientation with regard to task in behavioral sense and goal orientation in sense of ego intersect at many points [7].

It is observed that athletes who are used to goal orientation in sense of task attach more importance to team rapport and cooperation, development of skills, getting specialized in task and learning while athletes who are used to goal orientation in sense of ego take overcoming their competitors, being superior and focusing on result to forefront [18]. Task oriented athletes believe in the necessity of skill development and intense practice to make it possible. They are more inclined to use internal motivation to fight with resistance and obstacles they face on the road to success. Ego oriented athletes, on the other hand, are more inclined to follow the exact opposite road and exhibit unsporting behaviors to succeed when they face with a similar resistance [20].

When these facts are taken into consideration, it is thought that assessment of cohesiveness levels of groups and how relational are the ego-task orientations of individuals would be beneficial. This research intends to examine the said variables specific to basketball to the accompaniment of different demographic information.

2 Method

2.1 Research model

Out of general screening models, the relational screening model is used in this research to descriptively reveal the relation of group cohesiveness of basketball players with their task and ego orientations. Relational screening model is a research model which describes the extents of differences between two or more variables [13].

2.2 Universe and sampling

Universe of research is composed of mature players who play in the leagues of Turkish Basketball Federation in 2016-2017 season. Sample group is composed of 243 individuals, 152 of whom are males and 91 are females.

DOI: 10.1051/shsconf/20173701041

2.3 Data collection tools

"Group Environment Questionnaire", a nine points Likert Questionnaire developed by Carron, Widmayer and Brawley [5] and adapted to Turkish by Öcel [17] is used to measure the group cohesiveness levels of basketball players. In Turkish version of the Questionnaire which is composed of 18 points and 4 sub-dimensions, Cronbach's Alpha Internal Consistency Coefficients are found as .59, .67, .50, .65 and .64 for "Dimension of Task Integration in Group", "Dimension of Social Integration in Group", "Dimension of Social Attraction in Group", "Dimension of Task Attraction in Group" and all of them together respectively. "Task and Ego Orientation in Sports Questionnaire", a five points Likert Questionnaire developed by Duda and Nichols and adapted for Turkish athletes by Toros [19] is used to determine task and ego orientations of athletes. There are 2 sub-dimensions of the 13-point Questionnaire to measure task oriented objectives and ego oriented objectives. Cronbach's Alpha Internal Consistency Coefficients in Turkish version of Questionnaire are found as .87, .85 and .86 for "task oriented objectives", "ego oriented objectives" and general reliability coefficient respectively.

2.4 Analysis of data

Data obtained from participants are statistically analyzed by using SPSS 23 package program. Before determining the statistical methods to be used, skewness and kurtosis values (normal distribution of data) are tested and Levene's test (equality of variances) is conducted. In this context, it is seen in research that Skewness and Kurtosis values of each independent variable range from +1 to -1. If skewness coefficient is between the range of + 1 and -1, it is interpreted as there is no significant deviation from normal distribution of points (9). After testing the homogeneity of variances of normally distributed variables, these variables are tested via parametric test methods. Frequency, arithmetic mean and standard deviation are used to analyze data and T-Test, One-Way Analysis of Variance (ANOVA) and Post-Hoc test statistics (Tukey HSD) are used for independent samples.

3 Findings

This section includes findings obtained in line with various statistical processes applied to data given by participants and interpretations.

Table 1. Independent group t test results to determine whether or not there is differentiation according to gender variable

		Cinsiyet	N	$\bar{x}$	Ss	df	t	p
Goal Orientation	Task Orientation	Male	152	30,6053	3,96868	241	1,375	,171
		Female	91	29,8242	4,77399			
	Ego Orientation	Male	152	20,5855	5,77439	241	,741	,459
		Female	91	20,0440	5,04185			
Group Cohesiveness	Social Integration of Group	Male	152	24,7171	8,57180	241	1,472	,142
		Female	91	23,0879	7,96471			
	Task Attraction of Group	Male	152	21,0789	7,08092	241	2,272	,024*
		Female	91	19,0879	5,74195			
	Social Attraction of Group	Male	152	23,2303	6,74264	241	,427	,670
		Female	91	22,8462	6,85229			
	Task Integration of Group	Male	152	12,3750	4,11235	241	-,554	,580
		Female	91	12,6703	3,85589			

*p< .05

Whether there is a significant difference in level of group cohesiveness and goal orientation of participants in independent groups or not in terms of gender variable is examined via *t*-test in Table 1. Accordingly, a significant difference is identified in dimension of *Task Attraction of Group* in terms of gender variable.

Table 2. Age variable correlation results according to group cohesiveness and goal orientation

	N	$\bar{x}$	ss	r	p
Age Variable	243	2,2181	1,07841	-,034	,593
Task Orientation		30,3128	4,29502		
Age Variable	243	2,2181	1,07841	-,210**	,001*
Ego Orientation		20,3827	5,50710		
Age Variable	243	2,2181	1,07841	-,035	,591
Social Integration of Group		24,1070	8,37036		
Age Variable	243	2,2181	1,07841	,032	,616
Task Attraction of Group		20,3333	6,66928		
Age Variable	243	2,2181	1,07841	-,120	,061
Social Attraction of Group		23,0864	6,77233		
Age Variable	243	2,2181	1,07841	-,013	,839
Task Integration of Group		12,4856	4,01274		

*p< .05; **p<.01

DOI: 10.1051/shsconf/20173701041

Table 2 shows the results of Pearson Moment Correlation Analysis performed to determine if there is a relation between participants' level of group cohesiveness and goal orientation and age variable or not. In this context, it is seen that there is a negative low-level significant difference between *Ego Orientation* of athletes and age variable.

Table 3. Sportive age variable correlation results according to group cohesiveness and goal orientation

Değişken	N	$\bar{x}$	ss	r	P
Sportive Age Variable	243	2,6255	,87415	-,036	,579
Task Orientation		30,3128	4,29502		
Sportive Age Variable	243	2,6255	,87415	-,214**	,001*
Ego Orientation		20,3827	5,50710		
Sportive Age Variable	243	2,6255	,87415	-,043	,591
Social Integration of Group		24,1070	8,37036		
Sportive Age Variable	243	2,6255	,87415	,034	,595
Task Attraction of Group		20,3333	6,66928		
Sportive Age Variable	243	2,6255	,87415	-,026	,688
Social Attraction of Group		23,0864	6,77233		
Sportive Age Variable	243	2,6255	,87415	-,005	,939
Task Integration of Group		12,4856	4,01274		

*$p< .05$; **$p<.01$

Table 3 shows the results of Pearson Moment Correlation Analysis performed to determine if there is a relation between participants' level of group cohesiveness and goal orientation and sportive age variable or not. In this context, it is seen that there is a negative low-level significant difference between *Ego Orientation* of athletes and sportive age variable as in the case of age variable.

Table 4. Anova results according to educational status

		N	$\bar{x}$	Variance Source	Sum of Squares	Avg. of Squares	F	p	Sig. Dif.
Task Orientation	High School	12	28,6667	Inter Groups	34,497	17,249	,935	,394	-
	Undergraduate	210	30,4095						
	Postgraduate	21	30,2857	InGroup	4429,733	18,457			
Ego Orientation	High School	12	18,9167	Inter Groups	28,257	14,129	,464	,629	-
	Undergraduate	210	20,4810						
	Postgraduate	21	20,2381	InGroup	7311,150	30,463			
Social Integration of Group	High School	12	22,1667	Inter Groups	96,6901	48,345	,688	,503	-
	Undergraduate	210	24,0619						
	Postgraduate	21	25,6667	InGroup	6858,529	70,244			
Task Attraction of Group	High School[a]	12	18,8333	Inter Groups	419,095	209,548	4,861	,009*	c>b>a
	Undergraduate[b]	210	20,0000						
	Postgraduate[c]	21	24,5238	InGroup	10344,905	43,104			
Social Attraction of Group	High School	12	23,6667	Inter Groups	5,466	2,733	,059	,943	-
	Undergraduate	210	23,0333						
	Postgraduate	21	23,2857	InGroup	11093,719	46,224			
Task Integration of Group	High School	12	14,7500	Inter Groups	73,211	36,606	1,387	,252	-
	Undergraduate	210	12,4286						
	Postgraduate	21	11,7619	InGroup	3823,488	15,931			

*p< .05

As seen from Table 4, one-way variance analysis applied to points in "Group Cohesiveness Questionnaire" and "Task and Ego Orientation in Sports Questionnaire" in terms of educational backgrounds of participants revealed a significant difference in sub-dimension of *Task Attraction of Group* (F=4,861; p=,009) under "Group Cohesiveness Questionnaire". In order to determine the source of the significant difference appears between groups as a result of this analysis, Post-Hoc test statistics are applied (Tukey HSD). Groups which the score (point) difference is in favor of are stated in table. Accordingly, it is identified that participants with postgraduate education received higher points than the ones with undergraduate and high school education in sub-dimension of *Task Attraction of Group* and showed a significant difference.

Table 5. Anova results according to number of seasons in the team

		N	$\bar{x}$	Variance Source	Sum of Squares	Avg. of Squares	F	p	Sig Dif
Task Orientation	1 and Under	131	29,7786	Inter Groups	82,759	41,379	2,267	,106	-
	2	61	31,0492						
	3 andOver	51	30,8039	InGroup	4381,472	18,256			
Ego Orientation	1 and Under	131	19,7252	Inter Groups	123,877	61,938	2,060	,130	-
	2	61	21,0656						
	3 and Over	51	21,2549	InGroup	7215,531	30,065			
Social Integration of Group	1 and Under	131	23,3817	Inter Groups	234,991	117,495	1,687	,187	-
	2	61	25,7541						
	3 and Over	51	24,0000	InGroup	16720,228	69,668			
Task Attraction of Group	1 and Under	131	20,1145	Inter Groups	130,359	65,179	1,471	,232	-
	2	61	19,6557						
	3 and Over	51	21,7059	InGroup	10633,641	44,307			
Social Attraction of Group	1 and Under	131	22,5649	Inter Groups	158,597	79,299	1,740	,178	-
	2	61	24,4754						
	3 and Over	51	22,7647	In Group	10940,588	45,586			
Task Integration of Group	1 and Under	131	12,3282	Inter Groups	49,027	24,514	1,529	,219	-
	2	61	13,2295						
	3 and Over	51	12,0000	In Group	3847,672	16,032			

*p< .05

As seen from Table 5, no significant difference is identified in one-way variance analysis applied to "Group Cohesiveness Questionnaire" and "Goal and Ego

Orientation in Sports Questionnaire" points received by participants in terms of the number of seasons that participants have been part of their teams.

Table 6. Anova results according toteam's perception of success

		N	$\bar{x}$	Variance Source	Sum of Squares	Avg. of Squares	F	p	Sig. Dif.
Task Orientation	I don'tfindanysuccess	38	30,5263	Inter Groups	50,421	16,807	,910	,437	-
	I find it a bit successful	68	30,6765						
	I find it successful	103	29,7961		4413,810	18,468			
	I find it verysuccessful	34	30,9118	Inter Groups					
Ego Orientation	I don'tfindanysuccess	38	20,3684	Inter Groups	125,713	41,904	1,388	,247	-
	I find it a bit successful	68	20,7353						
	I find it successful	103	19,6893	InGroup	7213,694	30,183			
	I find it verysuccessful	34	21,7941						
Social Integration of Group	I don'tfindanysuccess[a]	38	31,0526	Inter Groups	2216,636	738,879	11,982	,000	a>c> b>d
	I find it a bit successful[b]	68	22,6029		14738,582	61,668			
	I find it successful[c]	103	23.2330	InGroup					
	I find it verysuccessful[d]	34	22,0000						
TaskAttraction of Group	I don'tfindanysuccess	38	22,2368	Inter Groups	180,086	60,029	1,356	,257	-
	I find it a bit successful	68	19,5735		10583,914	44,284			
	I find it successful	103	20,1748	InGroup					
	I find it verysuccessful	34	20,2059						
SocialAttracton of Group	I don'tfindanysuccess[a]	38	22,4211	Inter Groups	395,064	131,688	2,940	,034	d>c> a>b
	I find it a bit successful[b]	68	21,3088		10704,121	44,787			
	I find it successful[c]	103	24, 0194	InGroup					
	I find it verysuccessful[d]	34	24,5588						
Task Integration of Group	I don'tfindanysuccess	38	11,8158	Inter Groups	26,962	8,987	,555	,645	-
	I find it a bit successful	68	12,7206		3869,737	16,191			
	I find it successful	103	12,6699	InGroup					
	I find it verysuccessful	34	12,2059						

*p< .05

Table 6 shows the results of one-way variance analysis applied to "Group Cohesiveness Questionnaire" and Task and Ego Orientation in Sports Questionnaire" points received by participants in terms of team's perception of success. Significant differences are identified in sub-dimension of *Social Integration of Group* (F=2.940; p=.034) and sub-dimension of *Social Attraction of Group* (F=11.982; p=.000) under "Group Cohesiveness Questionnaire". Groups which the score (point) difference is in favor of are stated in table.

4 Discussion and conclusion

It was intended to determine group cohesiveness goal orientation levels of mature basketball players who play in the leagues of Turkish Basketball Federation in 2016-2017 season in the light of different demographic information in this research. At the end of the analyses conducted accordingly, data obtained from "Group Cohesiveness Questionnaire" and "Task and Ego Orientation in Sports Questionnaire" are examined in terms of gender variable. Eys, Evans, Ohlert, Wolf, Martin & Van Bussel [8] aimed to examine cohesiveness of male and female athletes and obtained data from coaches with different demographic characteristics by using semi-structured interview method. The said study suggests that cohesiveness level in teams composed of female athletes is lower because female athletes perceive everything more personally in comparison with male athletes. In this research, on the other hand, a significant difference in favor of male athletes is identified only in sub-dimension of *Task Attraction of Group* under "Group Cohesiveness Questionnaire". Haddera [10]; Gammage, Carron and Estabrooks [9]; Carron, Eys, Bray [4] could not find any difference which would be regarded significant between gender variable and group cohesiveness and Zakaria, Yasim and Taff [23] concluded in their study that group cohesiveness of male individuals is statistically more significant than female individuals. No significant difference is identified between gender variable and sub-dimensions of "Task and Ego Orientation in Sports Questionnaire". Altıntaş [1] identified a significant difference in favor of female athletes with regard to *Task Orientation and Ego Orientation* in his study on athletes from different branches. However White and Duda [22]; Duda [6]; Li, Harmer and Acock [16] concluded in their studies that there is a significant difference between gender and *Ego Orientation* in favor of males. On the other hand, Hanrahan and Cerin [11] and Duda [6] revealed in their studies that there is a significant difference with regard to *Task Orientation* sub-dimension in favor of females.

As a result of Pearson Moment Correlation analysis conducted to see whether there is a significant difference between group cohesiveness levels of participants and their goal orientation and age variable or not, it is observed that there is a low-level and negative significant relation between Ego Orientation of athletes and age variable. Same findings are reached with regard to sportive age variable and a low-level and negative significant relation is identified between sportive age and Ego Orientation. Even if this is a finding in parallel with the perception that athletes grow mature in sportive sense in line with aging and gaining experience and elude their egos and thus behave in a more task-oriented way, Lameiras, Almeida and Garcia-Mas [15] reached a contrariwise conclusion in their study conducted on male athletes and identified a low-level and negative relation between age variable and *Task Orientation*.

Üngür [21] examined goal orientations of participants in terms of age and sportive experience variables while Altıntaş [1] examined the same thing only in terms of sportive experience variable but could not find a significant relation. Haddera [10] examined the relation between age and sportive experience of participants with their group cohesiveness and identified a low-level and negative significant difference between the said variables and *Task Attraction of Group.*

Data obtained from participants are examined in terms of educational background variable and a significant difference is identified in sub-dimension of *Task Attraction of Group.* In this context, the points received from sub-dimension of *Task Attraction of Group* got higher in parallel with the increase in level of education. No statistically significant data could be obtained between educational background variable and none of the sub-dimensions of "Task and Ego Orientation in Sports Questionnaire" and in parallel with this finding, Üngür [21] also couldn't identify a significant relation between level of education and *Goal Orientation* in his study including amateur and professional football players.

When the variable of number of seasons in the same team is analyzed, no statistically significant data could be obtained both in sub-dimensions of "Group Cohesiveness Questionnaire" and "Task and Ego Orientation in Sports Questionnaire". A factor hindering the emergence of a significant difference between the group cohesiveness levels of participants might be the stability of individuals in their group rather than the number of seasons they had in the team.

When the findings regarding perception of team success are examined, significant differences are identified in sub-dimensions of *Social Integration of Group* and *Social Attraction of Group.* In this context, the participants who find their team very successful got highest points in *Social Attraction of Group* sub-dimension. In parallel with this finding, Carron, Colman, Wheeler and Stevens [3] revealed that performance of team and *Social Attraction of Group* are directly associated with each other in their meta-analysis regarding the relation between cohesiveness and performance of team. Öcel [17] identified a significant relation between perception of success and social attraction of group in his study. Participants who don't deem their team successful got highest points in *Social Integration of Group* sub-dimension. This could be assessed as the result of the desire of team members who fail on the field to be freed from the feeling of unsuccessfulness by socially integrating with each other. No finding is obtained regarding the impact of goal orientation on perception of success.

Fundamental characteristics of team members are directly related with performance and success in team sports. Goal orientations and cohesiveness levels of the group composed of athletes are two of these characteristics. In this study, it was intended to examine the said factors in light of different demographic information and identify their extent of impact on the success of teams. Physical capacities of athletes as well as their mental qualities are regarded as important parameters today. Therefore, this research intends to contribute to awareness of sport psychology by executives and trainers who form, design and program the teams and also contribute the future studies on this topic and literature via its findings.

References

1. Altıntaş A. Comparison of Goal Orientations, Motivational Climates and Perceived Physical Competences of Athletes in Terms of Gender and Level of Experience. Postgraduate Thesis, Ankara University. (2010).
2. Büyüköztürk Ş. Data Analysis Handbook for Social Sciences. Ankara: PegemaYayıncılık. (2005)
3. Carron A. V., Colman M. M., Wheeler J., ve Stevens, D. Cohesion and performance in sport: A meta analysis. Journal of Sport and Exercise Psychology, 24 (2), 168-188. (2002).
4. Carron A. V., Eys M., ve Bray, S. Team Cohesion and Team Success in Sport. Journal Of Sports Sciences, 20 (2), 119-126. (2002). doi:10.1080/026404102317200828
5. Carron A.V., Widmeyer W. ve Brawley L. The Development of an Instrument to Assess Cohesion in Sport Teams: The Group Environment Questionnaire. Journal of Sport Psychology, 7, 244-266. (1985). doi: http://dx.doi.org/10.1123/jsp.7.3.244.
6. Duda, J. L. Relationship Between Task and Ego Orientation and the Perceived Purpose of Sport Among High School Athletes. Journal Of Sport & Exercise Psychology, 11(3), 318-335. (1989).
7. Duda, J. L., & White, S. A. Goal Orientations and Beliefs About the Causes of Sport Success Among Elite Skiers. Sport Psychologist, 6 (4), 334-343. (1992). doi: 10.1123/tsp.6.4.334
8. Eys, M., Evans, M. B., Martin, L. J., Ohlert, J., Wolf, S. A., Van Bussel, M., ve Steins, C. Cohesion And Performance For Female And Male Sport Teams. The Sport Psychologist, 29(2), 97-109. (2015).
9. Gammage, K. L., Carron, A. V., &Estabrooks, P. A. Team cohesion and individual productivity: The influence of the norm for productivity and the identifiability of individual effort. Small Group Research, 32(1), 3-18. (2001).
10. Haddera, T. A. Assessing the Relationships between Competitive Trait Anxiety, Self-Efficacy and Task Cohesion in Male and Female University Team Sports. CLEAR International Journal Of Research In Management, Sciences & Technology, 5(10), 1-11. (2015).
11. Hanrahan, S. veCerin, E. Gender, level of participation, and type of sport: Differences in achievement goal orientation and attributional style. Journal Of Science And Medicine In Sport, 12(4), 508-512. (2009). doi:10.1016/j.jsams.2008.01.005
12. Howell, W. C., &Dipboye, R. L. Essentials of Industrial and Organizational Psychology. Chicago: The Dorsey Pr., c1896. (1986).
13. Karasar N. Scientific Research Method: Theories, Principles, Techniques. (23rd Edition) Ankara: Nobel. (2012).
14. Kocaekşi, S. Identification of Relation of Group Cohesiveness and Affecting Variables with Success in Successful and Unsuccessful Handball Teams. Postgraduate Thesis, HacettepeUniversity. (2005).
15. Lameiras J., Almeida P. L. ve Garcia-Mas A. Relationships Between Cooperation And Goal Orientation Among Male Professional And Semi-Professıonal Team Athletes. Perceptual & Motor Skills: Motor Skills & Ergonomics, 119 (3), 851-860. (2014).

16. Li, F., Harmer, P., &Acock, A. The Task And Ego Orientation İn Sport Questionnaire: Construct Equivalence And Mean Differences Across Gender. Research Quarterly For Exercise And Sport, 67(2), 228-238. (1996)
17. Öcel H. Relations of Collective Competence-Self-Efficacy and Cohesiveness with Perception and Expectations of Success. Postgraduate Thesis,Hacettepe University. (2002).
18. Sari İ., Ilic J. veLjubojevic M. The Comparison of Task and Ego Orientation and General Self-Esteem of Turkish and Montenegrın Young Basketball Players. Kinesiology : International Journal of Fundamental and Applied Kinesiology, 45 (2), 203-212. (2013). http://hrcak.srce.hr/112756
19. Toros T. Reliabılity and Validity of "Task and Ego Orientation in Sport Questionnaire -TEOSQ-" For Turkish Athletes. Hacettepe Journal of Sport Sciences, 15 (3), 155-166. (2004).
20. Toros T., Akyüz U., Bayansalduz M. ve Soyer F. Examining the relationship between task-and ego-oriented goals and life satisfaction (A study of people doing mountaineering sports). Journal of Human Sciences, 7 (2), 1039-1050. (2010).
21. Üngür G. Relation between Goal Orientations and Perceived Motivational Climate of Amateur and Professional Football Players. Postgraduate Thesis, Ege University. (2009).
22. White, S. A. ve Duda, J. L. The relationship of gender, level of sport involvement, and participation motivation to task and ego orientation. International Journal of Sport Psychology, 25 (1), 4-18. (1994).
23. Zakaria, J., Yasim, M. M., & Taff, M. M. The Impact of Adventure Based Activity at Malaysian National Service Training Programme on Team Cohesion: A Demographic Analysis. International Journal Of Sport Management, Recreation & Tourism, 10, 64-79. (2012).

Examination of burnout levels and academic procrastination of university students

Gönül Tekkurşun Demir[1], Alperen Halıcı[1a], and Can Çavin Ötkan[2]

[1]Faculty of Sport Science, Gazi University, 06000 Ankara, Turkey
[2]Faculty of Sport Science, Gazi University/YüzüncüYıl University, 06000 Ankara, Turkey

Abstract. In this study, the relationship between the academic procrastination and the students' burnout levels was examined. 406 students from different departments at Gazi University Sports Sciences Faculty participated in the research. In order to collect data, the student version of Maslach's Burnout Inventory and the Academic Procrastination Scale (APS) were used in the study. It was determined that the students at the faculty of sports science did not show any significant difference in terms of gender variable according to MBI-SF and APS. When analyzed in terms of department variable, there was a significant difference in the MBI-SF subscales, while no significance was observed in the total score of APS. Similar results were obtained in the APS total scores among the grades; but there was significance in the subscales of MBI-SF. The analyses indicated that a statistically significant negative relationship at medium level was found between the MBI-SF and APS. The results of the analyses also indicated that there was a statistically significant negative relationship between academic procrastination and student burnout levels.
Keywords: burnout, academic procrastination, sports, students' burnout syndrome

1 Introduction

University life is important both for academic and social development of students. During their university education, students can gain new experiences and opportunities for development, change, maturation and growth while at the same time they can experience some personal and academic problems. In this context, difficulties experienced during university education can affect the functions and performances of the students at different levels [13]. Given the limited ability of students to overcome the difficulties experienced, particularly their academic life can be negatively affected by these difficulties. For this reason, it can be stated that university students have to overcome many personal and environmental difficulties during their academic life [5]. One of the problems that

[a] Corresponding author: alperen_h@hotmail.com

university students have to overcome during their university education is the academic procrastination. Academic procrastination is a problem seen in the fields expected from students at universities such as preparing for the exams, doing homework, meeting with the academic advisor and completing the projects [14, 19]. Another problem that university students have to overcome is the feeling of burnout. Burnout is defined as a physical, emotional, and mental fatigue syndrome which is caused by a long-term relationship in which feelings are intensely experienced [31]. Maslach and Jackson [24] defined burnout as a syndrome with physical and mental dimensions involving physical exhaustion, long-term fatigue, desperation and despair, along with negative attitudes of the individual towards his/her work, life and other people. Studies in the literature indicate that the feeling of burnout is a common problem among students; but it is also clear that the studies about student burnout are not common in our country [22, 26, 35, 36]. It is known that academic procrastination frequently seen in university students increases the level of chronic stress experienced by students. In this context, it can be expected that levels of burnout resulting from stress in students may also have an impact on their academic procrastination. This study aims to examine the burnout levels resulting from stress of university students in sports sciences and the academic procrastination problem which is common in students in terms of various demographic variables.

2 Method

2.1 Research model

Quantitative research model was used in the study. Quantitative research is a type of research that can set forth phenomena and events in a way that they can be observed, measured, and numerically expressed by objectifying them [9]. The purpose of quantitative research is to objectively measure the social behaviors of individuals through similar means such as tests and questionnaires and to explain them numerically. This research is a relational study in the scan pattern which is a descriptive research method.

2.2 Universe and sampling

Students enrolled at the Faculty of Sports Sciences at Gazi University in Ankara in the second semester of the academic year 2016-2017 constitute the universe of this research. It was determined the total number of the students at the departments of coaching education (n = 507), recreation (n = 271), sports management (n = 231) and physical education and sports teaching (n = 291) at Gazi University was 1300. The sample group of the study consisted of a total of 406 students, 150 female and 256 male students, who attended their classes regularly. 128 students of this group were enrolled at the department of coaching education; 92 were enrolled at the department of recreation; 91 were enrolled at the department of sports management and 95 were enrolled at the department of physical education and sports teaching. The research also includes information on the grade level and gender of the students at the faculty of sports science participating in the study.

2.3 Data collection tools

In the research, "Personal Information Form" was used by the researchers to determine the demographic characteristics of the participants. "Maslach Burnout Inventory-Student Form (MBI-SF)", composed of 13 items, developed by Schaufeli et al. [33] and translated into Turkish by Çapri, Gündüz and Gökçakan [10] was used to determine the burnout levels of students. The "Academic Procrastination Scale (APS)" developed by Çakıcı [11] was used as the data collection tool in order to determine the academic procrastination levels of the students.

2.4 Analysis of data

Data collected from the participants in the research was subjected to statistical analysis in the SPSS 23 package program. Before deciding on the statistical methods to be applied, the values of Skewness and Kurtosis (normal distribution of the data) and Levene (equality of variance) tests were performed. In this context, it was determined that the Skewness and Kurtosis values of each independent variable ranged between +-1. According to this; if the skewness coefficient is within the limits of + - 1, it is interpreted that the scores do not show a significant deviation from the normal distribution [8]. After testing the homogeneity of the variances of the variables with normal distribution, these variables were analyzed by parametric test methods. Frequency, arithmetic mean, standard deviation were used in the analysis of data; and t-test, one-way analysis of variance (ANOVA), and Post-Hoc test statistics (Tukey HSD) tests were used for independent samples.

3 Findings

This section includes the findings and interpretations obtained as a result of subjecting the analyses obtained from the participants to various statistical processes.

Table 1. Independent group t test results to determine whether or not there is differentiation according to gender variable

Variable	Gender	N	$\bar{x}$	Ss	df	t	p
Burnout	Female	256	15,5664	5,29108	404	-1,444	,150
	Male	150	16,3267	4,81677			
Depersonalization	Female	256	11,5156	4,53913	404	-,920	,358
	Male	150	11,9267	3,99176			
Competence	Female	256	14,1836	3,38646	404	-,106	,915
	Male	150	14,2200	3,21880			
Academic Procrastination	Female	256	57,8711	13,12664	404	-1,424	,155
	Male	150	59,7133	11,59804			

*p< .05

In Table 1, whether or not the participants' burnout levels in terms of gender variable and academic procrastination showed significant differences was examined by independent samples t-test. Accordingly, the participants' burnout levels and academic procrastination do not show any significant difference in terms of gender (p>,05).

Table 2. Anova results in terms of department variable

Department		N	$\bar{x}$	Variance Source	Sum of squares	Average of Squares	F	p	Significant Difference
Burnout	CE	128	15,94	Inter Groups	542,437 10108,095	180,81 25,145	7,19*	,000	PEST>CE-R-SM
	R	92	14,84						
	SM	91	14,74	In-Group					
	PEST	95	17,73						
Depersonalization	CE	128	11,39	Inter Groups	632,105 7012,006	210,70 17,443	12,08*	,000	PEST>CE-R-SM
	R	92	10,77						
	SM	91	10,67	In-Group					
	PEST	95	13,86						
Competence	CE	128	14,21	Inter Groups	4,604 4463,632	1,535 11,104	,138	,937	-
	R	92	14,08						
	SM	91	14,37	In-Group					
	PEST	95	14,11						
Academic Procrastination	CE	128	60,61		1080,936 63221,47	360,31 157,26	2,291	,078	-
	R	92	57,67						
	SM	91	58,82						
	PEST								

*p< .05

According to Table 2, as a result of the analyzes performed and as a result of the one-way analysis of variance applied for MBI-SF and APS scores according to the participants' departments, a significant difference was observed in the burnout (F=7,19; p=,000) and the depersonalization (F=1,8; p=,000) subscales of the burnout subscale scores. Post-Hoc test statistics (Tukey HSD) were used to determine the source of the significant difference appearing among the groups in the result of the analysis. Groups whom the score difference is in favor of are shown with (*). Accordingly, the averages of burnout and depersonalization scores of PEST students were found to be significantly higher than CE, R and SM students. The scores in the competency sub-dimension are similar and do not show any significant difference. It was also found that the scores for academic procrastination are higher and similar in CE students than SM, R and PEST students.

Table 3. Anova results in terms of grade variable

	Department	N	$\bar{x}$	Variance Source	Sum of squares	Average of Squares	F	p	Significant Difference
Burnout	1st grade	100	14,1500	Inter Groups	648,908	216,303	8,69	,000*	4>3-2-1
	2nd grade	112	15,1786						
	3rd grade	106	17,0094	In-Group	10001,62	24,880			
	4th grade	88	17,2273						
Depersonalization	1st grade	100	9,8100	Inter Groups	699,575	233,192	13,4	,000*	4>3-2-1
	2nd grade	112	11,1429						
	3rd grade	106	12,6698	In-Group	6944,536	17,275			
	4th grade	88	13,2386						
Competence	1st grade	100	14,9800	Inter Groups	159,014	53,005	4,94	,002*	1>4-2-3
	2nd grade	112	13,9196						
	3rd grade	106	13,3774	In-Group	4309,222	10,719			
	4th grade	88	14,6477						
Academic Procrastination	1st grade	100	61,0500	Inter Groups	1606,502	535,501	3,43	,017	-
	2nd grade	112	59,7768						
	3rd grade	106	56,1321	In-Group	62695,91	155,960			
	4th grade	88	57,0682						

*p< .05

As shown in Table 3, as a result of the one-way analysis of variance applied for MBI-SF and APS scores according to participants' grades, there was a significant difference in the burnout (F=8,69; p=,000), depersonalization (F=13,4; p=,000) and competence (F=4,94; p=,000) subscales of MBI-SF. Post-Hoc test statistics (Tukey HSD) were used to determine the source of the significant difference appearing among the groups in the result of the analysis. Groups whom the score difference is in favor of are shown with (*). It was determined that the scores of the 4th graders in the burnout and depersonalization sub-dimensions showed higher and significant difference than those of 3rd, 2nd and 1st graders. It was also determined that the scores of 1st graders in the competence sub-dimension were higher at a significant level than those of 4th, 2nd and 3rd graders. Finally, it was seen that there was not a significant difference in the participants' academic tendencies and that they had similar scores in this regard.

DOI: 10.1051/shsconf/20173701042

Table 4. Burnout and academic procrastination correlation results

Variable	Burnout	Depersonalization	Competence	Total Burnout
Academic Procrastination Total Score	-,466**	-,462**	,265**	-,401**

*p< .05; **p<.01

In Table 4, a Pearson Moment Correlation analysis was performed to determine the relationship between MBI-SF and APS. According to this result, it can be said that both scales are related to each other. The result of the analysis indicates that the total scores of MBI-SF and APS were statistically significant (r=-401, p<,001). There was a negative relationship at a medium level between the total score of APS and burnout and depersonalization sub-dimensions of MBI-SF while there was a positive relationship at a low level between the total score of APS and the competence sub-dimension.

4 Discussion and conclusion

This study aimed to determine the MBI-SF and APS of 1st, 2nd, 3rd and 4th graders at the departments of recreation, coaching education, sports management, physical education and sports teaching at the faculty of sports sciences at Gazi University in 2017. Before starting the analysis of the study, the values of Kurtosis and Skewness (normal distribution of the data) for each independent variable were examined and the result was that the data showed a normal distribution. No significant difference was determined when the scores from MBI-SF were evaluated in terms of gender. In the light of these findings, we can say that male and female participants have a similar burnout level and academic procrastination. This may be interpreted by the fact that female and male participants join in and be tired of everyday life to the same degree. In parallel with the present research, Adoum [2], Kutsal [22], Esteve [15], LaForge [23], Alexander and Onwuegbuzie [23], Onwuegbuzie [25], Kachgal, Hansen and Nuther [20], Watson [39], Hess, Sherman, and Goodman [17] did not also find a significant difference in burnout levels in terms of gender. Unlike the present research, while Yılmaz [42], Gündüz et al., [16] suggested that women showed the feeling of burnout more than men, Tansel [36], on the other hand, stated that male students experienced the feeling of burnout more than female students. According to the result of the analysis, when the scores from APS were evaluated in terms of gender, no significant difference was found between male and female participants. According to these results, in parallel with the research, there are also results that found no significance in terms of gender [3, 17, 20, 23, 25]. Some different results were also found in the literature. The first of these results indicates that female students showed less academic procrastination than male students [4, 28, 29, 34, 38]; while some other studies, on the contrary, pointed out that male students showed less academic procrastination than female students [30, 40]. According to the analyzes made, when MBI-SF scores were evaluated in terms of the participants' departments, there was a significant difference in the sub-dimensions of burnout and depersonalization while there was not a significant difference in the sub-dimension of competence and the total score of APS. In parallel with the results of this research, there are also studies [16, 36] which determined significant difference in terms of departments. When total scores from APS were evaluated in terms of the department variable, no significant difference was found. Accordingly, it can be said that the majority of participants have similar procrastination behavior. When scores from MBI-SF are evaluated in terms of grades, it was determined that there are significant differences in terms of burnout, depersonalization and competence sub-dimensions. It was also found out that the students at higher grades showed the feeling of burnout more than the other students. It is seen that as the grade level increased, so did the level of burnout. In parallel with this result, there are also other similar results in the literature [1, 12, 21, 27]. The higher the grade level at schools in our country, the more difficult and important the lessons get. When the total scores from APS were evaluated in terms of the grade variable, no significant difference was found. Accordingly, it can be said that the majority of the participants have similar procrastination behaviors. There are studies [6, 7, 32, 37] which suggest that as the grade level gets higher, so does the academic procrastination. In the light of the analyses, it was determined in the research that there is a significant relationship between the burnout levels and academic procrastination of the participants. Parallel to this research, Balkıs [5] also obtained similar results. It was determined that students who show academic procrastination do not do their homework on time, do not study for their examinations on time, and start studying for their exams just before the exam [18]. It can also be said that students who tend to show academic procrastination put a lot of effort into studying for their exams in a short time, which, in turn, affects their burnout levels. Accordingly, the level of burnout also increases in parallel with the increase in academic procrastination [41].

This research argues that students' burnout levels and academic procrastination are interrelated. The reason for the academic procrastination of university students can be shown as an increase in their burnout levels.

References

1. Addis, R.S. Burnout among undergraduate athletic training students, Dissertation. California University, U.S.A. (2006).
2. Adoum, Y., S. Determination of Burnout Levels of Turkish and Foreign Students Studying at Süleyman Demirel University, Süleyman Demirel University, Institute of Social Sciences, Department of Business Administration, Master's Thesis, Isparta. (2017).
3. Alexander, S. E. ve Onwuegbuzie, J. A. Academic procrastination and the role of hope as a coping strategy. Personality and Individual Differences, 42, 1301-1310. (2007).
4. Balkıs, M., Buluş, M., Duru, E. and Duru, S. Examination of academic procrastination of University Students in terms of various variables. Ege Journal of Education, 7, 57-73. (2006).
5. Balkıs, M. The relationship between the pre-service teachers' tendency to delay and their ways of thinking and decision making. Unpublished Doctorate Thesis, Dokuz Eylül University Institute of Educational Sciences. İzmir. (2006).
6. Balkıs, M. The Relationship between the pre-service teachers' tendency to delay and their ways of decision making. Pamukkale University Faculty of Education Journal, 1(21), 67-83. (2007).
7. Berber Çelik, Ç. and Odacı, H. Explanation of Academic Procrastination Behavior In Terms of Some Personal and Psychological Variables, H. U. Journal of Education 30(3): 31-47. (2015).
8. Büyüköztürk, Ş. Data Analysis Handbook for Social Sciences. (Edition 16). Ankara: Pegem Akademi. (2012).
9. Creswell, J. W. Research design: Qualitative, quantitative, and mixed methods approaches (2nd ed.). Thousand Oaks: Sage Publications. (2003).
10. Çapri, B., Gündüz, B. and Gökçakan, Z. Adaptation of Maslach Burnout Inventory-Student Form (MBI-SF) into Turkish: Validity and Reliability Study, Cukurova University Faculty of Education Journal. 40 (1), 134-147. (2011).

11. Çakıcı, D.Ç. Examination of General and Academic Procrastination Behavior in High School and University Students. Unpublished Master's Thesis, Ankara University Faculty of Education Sciences, Institute of Educational Sciences, Ankara. (2003).
12. Çapulcuoğlu, U. and Gündüz, B. Examination of burnout in high school students in terms of the variables of gender, grade level, school type and perceived academic achievement. Trakya University Faculty of Education Journal, 3(1). (2013).
13. Duru, E. "The direct and indirect roles of social support and social commitment in the process of interpreting loneliness in university integration process", Journal of Turkish Psychological Counselling and Guidance, 29, 13–22. (2008).
14. Dryden, W. Overcoming Procrastination (Translated by Günhan Günay) Istanbul: Erdemir Publishing House. (2000).
15. Esteve, E. B., Well Being and Performance in Academics Settings: The Predicting Roles of Self Efficacy, Doktora Tezi, University Jaume I de Castello. (2008).
16. Gündüz, B., Çapri, B., and Gökçakan, Z. Examination of Burnout Levels of University Students, Dicle University, Ziya Gökalp Faculty of Education Journal, 19 (2012), 38-55. (2012).
17. Hess, B., Sherman, M. F., Goodman, M. Eveningness predicts academic procrastination: The mediating role of neuroticism. Journal of Social Behavior ve Personality, 15 (5), 61- 75. (2000).
18. Jackson, T., Weiss, E.K., Lundquist, J.L.,& Hooper, D. The Impact of Hope, Procrastination and Social Activity on Academic Performance of Midwestern College Students. Education, 124,(2), pp. 310-320. (2001).
19. Johnson, J. L., & Bloom, A. M. An Analysis Of The Contribution Of The Five Factors Of Personality To Variance In Academic Procrastination. Personality Ve Individual Differences, 18, 127-133. (1995).
20. Kachgal, M. M., Hansen, L. S., ve Nutter, K. J. Academic procrastination prevention/intervention: Strategies and recommendations. Journal of Developmental Education, 25, 14-21. (2001).
21. Kutsal D. and Bilge F. Burnout and social support levels of high school students. Education and Science, 37(164), 283-297. (2012).
22. Kutsal, D., Examination of Burnout of High School Students, Unpublished Master's Thesis, Hacettepe University, Institute of Social Sciences, Ankara. (2009).
23. LaForge, M. C. Applying explanatory style to academic procrastination. Clemson University, South Carolina, USA. (2005).
24. Maslach, C., ve Jackson, S. E. The measurement of experienced burnout, Journal of Occupational Behavior, 2, 99-113. (1981).
25. Onwuegbuzie, A. J. Academic procrastination and statistics anxiety. Assessment ve Evaluation in Higher Education, 29 (1), 3-19. (2004).
26. Ören, N. and Türkoğlu, H. Burnout in Pre-service Teachers, Muğla University Institute of Social Sciences Journal, 16, 30-42. (2006).
27. Öztan, S. Examination of school burnout of secondary school 6th, 7th and 8th graders in terms of their life satisfaction and self-construal perception, Master's Thesis, Istanbul Arel University Institute of Social Sciences, İstanbul. (2014).
28. Özer, A. and Altun, E. Reasons for Academic Procrastination of University Students. Mehmet Akif Ersoy University, Faculty of Education Journal, 21, 45-72. (2011).
29. Prohaska, V., Morrill, P., Atiles, I., ve Perez, A. Academic procrastination by nontraditional students. Journal of Social Behavior and Personality, 15 (5), 125- 135. (2000).
30. Paludi, M.A., ve Frankell-Hauser, J. An idiographic approach to the study of women's achivement striving. Psychology of Women Quarterly, 10, 89-100. (1986).

31. Pines, A. M. The Burnout Measure Short Version (BMS), International Journal of Stress Management, 12(1), 78-88. (2005).
32. Rosario, P., Costa, M., Nunez, J.C., & Gonzales-Pienda, J. Academic procrastination: Associations with personal, school, and family variables. The Spanish Journal of Psychology, 12(1), 118-127. (2009).
33. Schaufeli, W. B., Salanova, M., Gonzalez-Roma, V., ve Bakker, A. The measurement of burnout and engagement: A confirmatory factor analytic approach. Journal of Happiness Studies, 3, 71-92. (2002).
34. Senecal, C., Julien, E., ve Guay, F., Role conflict and academic procrastination: A self-determination perspective. European Journal of Social Psychology, 33,135-145. (2003).
35. Tümkaya, S., Çam, S., & Çavuşoğlu, İ. Adaptation into Turkish, Validity and Reliability Studies of Short Version of Burnout Scale, Çukurova University Institute of Social Sciences Journal, 18 (1), 387–398. (2009).
36. Tansel, B., Examination of Burnout Levels of University Students, Çukurova University Faculty of Education Journal, 44(2), 241-268. (2015).
37. Yeşil, R. & Şahan, E. Reasons why pre-service teachers delay their academic affairs. Abant İzzet Baysal University Faculty of Education Journal, 12(2), 219-236. (2012).
38. Van Eerde, W. Procrastination at work and time management training. Journal of Psychology, 137, 421- 435. (2003).
39. Watson, D. C. Procrastination and the five-factor model: A facet level analysis. Personality and Individual Differences, 30, 149-158. (2001).
40. Washington, J. A. The relationship between procrastination and depression among graduate and professional students across academic programs: Implications for counseling. Unpublished Doctoral Dissertation. Texas Southern University, Texas, USA. (2004).
41. Van Wyk, L. The relationship between procrastination and stress in the life of the high school teacher. Unpublished Master thesis. University of Pretoria. (2004).
42. Yılmaz, T.D. Levels of Burnout of the Students of Specialty in Medicine at the Hospitals of the Faculty of Medicine, Ankara University and Related Factors, Unpublished Master's Thesis, Ankara University, Ankara. (2009).

An analysis of decision making strategies of Kocaeli region football referees

Sabit Selvi[1], and Elif Karagün[2*]

[1]Institute of Health Sciences, Kocaeli University, Kocaeli, Turkey
[2]Recreation Department, Sports Science Faculty, Kocaeli Üniversity, Kocaeli, Turkey

Abstract. In this study, in a football competition, which is one of the most interesting sports encounters today, the state of the decision-making strategies of referees, who play an important role in terms of final scores, is investigated. In line with this aim, efforts have been made to determine the decision-making strategies of Kocaeli football referees. Whether the decision-making strategies determined have changed according to variables such as gender, age, marital status, educational status, economic income, work done outside of refereeing, professional experience and refereeing years. For this purpose, "Decision Strategies Scale and Personal Information Form" developed by Bacanlı and Kuzgun [1], have been applied to a total of 117 football referees, 11 female and 106 male active football referees in Kocaeli. The results obtained from the scale applications were evaluated in the SPSS 21.00 statistical package program. As a result of the analyzes made; Subscales of decision-making strategies of referees are not significant in terms of gender, marital status, education, work experience, work done outside refereering, refereeing years; while it is not meaningful in terms of unstable, logical and dependent decision making sub-scales when compared to the economic level, it has been seen that only internal tepic decision making increases significantly when economic level is lower.
Keywords: Football, referee, decision making, decision strategy.

1 Introduction

Every human being begins to shape his/her life by constantly making decisions until the later periods of his life from the moment his/her mental ability develops. He gets experience and matures with difficulties or conveniences that he/she has encountered in his life after his decisions. Today's technology has an intense flow of information. The individual in this fast flow is constantly faced with changing circumstances, difficulties and sometimes problems and the individual must cope with these problems quickly. In order to cope quickly and healthily with problems, the individual must produce logical and correct

* Corresponding author: elif.karagun@gmail.com

solutions. Decision-making has been described as an orientation that will solve the problem when there is a need and many alternatives that can achieve a goal [2]. It is defined as "a cognitive process" and the selection of the most favorable solution from the existing options for eliminating any need and meeting this need [3]. When any issue or problem is encountered; it is stated that people use different strategies in order to be able to make a decision and it is the process of knowing how people will behave when a situation should be decided [4]. Decision making, considered as a cognitive state and considered as one of the important functions in an individual's life, has been defined as choosing the most appropriate alternative for problem solving or solution when it is deemed necessary in any matter [3, 5, 6]. It has been stated that the individual will be directed to the alternative that is thought to solve the problem considering the fact that there many alternatives when a decision is made, and a decision is also made to adapt and different strategies will be used in these processes [4, 7]. It has also been reported that cognitive processes that are away from the anxiety and comfort are necessary to provide solutions and make the right decisions [8].

It has been reported that the decisions that are seen as one of the basic skills in a person's life will lead to positive changes in order to bring solutions in human life when given in a healthy way that will lead to correct, timely, correct and appropriate solutions, and wrong decisions will adversely affect life in on the contrary [9]. Researchers working on decision making and putting forward ideas on this issue; defined effective decision-making as "a multifaceted process" involving informed decision-making by individuals who discern the contradiction between the current situation and the situation they are aiming at, testing various alternatives to reduce this contradiction and evaluating the results after these tests, storing information processing and feedback on the effectiveness of the tested cases " [10].

It has been reported that people who are actively involved in this process also perform the probability calculations of events and eliminate and select between two or more options [11].

Referees are defined as the officials who are in the field of competition to manage competitions or games in the most equitable manner by observing the rights of the teams competing against each other, applying the rules of the game in an impartial manner [7].

It was stated that while the success in the sports environment was determined during the competition, it was evaluated within the framework of the rules of the game played. It is explained that the referees are responsible for the execution of the competition, considering the suitability of a game with the rules and the rights of the competing teams. We often witness the decisions of the referees are discussed after the competition on the media and press. While the referees, who play an important role in contests in sports environments, play a supervisory role in complying with the rules, on the other hand, when it is considered that the referees have a decision-making role, the definition of the decision-making, and that it is the selection and elimination of an option among many more options, and that we often see commentaries on the press after the competition that the referees have made incorrect decisions in the game, it was wondered how the decision-making strategies of referees are. In this respect, the decision-making strategies of football referees in the football field, which is of particular interest to the masses, were searched and the answers were asked whether these strategies changed according to gender, age, marital status, educational status, economic income, work done outside of refereeing, professional experience and refereeing years.

This research was carried out in order to determine what strategies the football referees followed while deciding and how the decision strategies differ according to the variables.

DOI: 10.1051/shsconf/20173701043

2 Materials and methods

This research is a descriptive study. After receiving permission to conduct a survey for the research in 2016 from the Kocaeli Provincial Arbitration Board and the Central Referee Board, participants were informed about the research during the referee training seminars held at the Kocaeli International Youth Center and scales were distributed to those who voluntarily participated in the research. A total of 117 football referees actively working in Kocaeli province, including 106 males and 11 females, who were regarded valid after the scale applications, were included in the study.

2.1 Data collection tools

In the light of literature information; Likert type "Decision Strategies Scale" (DSS) consisting of 40 items and 4 subscales developed by Bacanlı and Kuzgun [1], was used to determine decision strategies with the "Information Form" formed by the researchers to determine the socio-demographic characteristics of the referees.
Four sub-scales of these decision strategies are:
1.Impulsive behavior: acting extemporaneously without giving proper thought to options,
2.Logical-Systematic Behavior: Rational decision making; Information about options,
3.Dependency: Taking decisions continuously by asking others,
4.Chaging decisions very often

The lowest score that can be taken from each subscale is 10 and the highest score is 40. The increase in scores from the subscales indicates that the participant adopts the decision-making style for that subscale.

2.2 Statistical data analysis

The collected data were analyzed with the SPSS 21.00 package program. The normal distribution of the data was determined by the Kolmogorov Smirnov test. Parametric tests were used because the sample showed normal distribution. T test was performed in binary comparisons and one-way analysis of variance (ANOVA) in multiple groups to determine the source of the difference between the groups. The error level for the significance of the statistics was accepted as $p < 0.05$.

3 Results

In this section, the analysis results of decision making strategies of football referees according to the demographic variables such as gender, marital status, age, economic status, level of education, work outside refereeing, refereeing years, professional experience, and score averages of the sub-dimensions of the decision-making scale were included.

Table 1. Average points taken from decision-making subscales

Decision Making Subscales Score Averages	Impulsive behavior mean±Sd	Indecisive mean±Sd	Dependant decision-making mean±Sd	Logical decision-making mean±Sd
	22.37±3.81	19.95±4.27	21.71±3,08	27.52±4.11

DOI: 10.1051/shsconf/20173701043

The mean of the subscales of decision-making strategies of referees from the findings: the mean of the scores obtained from the logical-systematic decision making subscale is X = 27.52 ± 4.10. The average of the subscale scores of the impulsive decision making strategy is X = 22.37 + 3.81. The dependent decision making strategy subscale point average is X = 23,90 ± 3,21 and the indecisive decision subscale point average is X = 19,95 ± 4,27. Based on the obtained data, it was found that the mean of the subscale scores and standard deviation values were the highest of the mean of the logical / systematic decision subscale and the lowest of the indecisive subscale.

The general decision-making strategies of the referees vary between 78 and 121, with an average of 93.38 points. It was determined that the referees had a decision strategy in the middle level.

Table 2. Percentage values of participants based on socio-demographic characteristics

Variables		N	%
Gender	**Female**	11	9,4
	Male	106	90,6
Age	**15-19**	14	12
	20-24	45	38,4
	25-29	31	26,5
	30-34	22	18,8
	35-39	3	2,6
	39 and over	2	1,7
Educational level	**High school**	33	28,2
	University	75	64,1
	Postgraduate	9	7,7
Marital Status	**Married**	33	28,2
	Single	84	71,8
Income Level	**0-800 TL**	33	28,2
	801-1500 TL	16	13,7
	1501-2500 TL	30	25,6
	2501 Tl and above	38	32,5
Work experience	**0-5 years**	84	71,8
	6-10 years	21	17,9
	11-15 years	8	6,9
	16-20 years	4	3,4
Work	**Private sektor**	90	76,9
	Public sektor	27	23,1
Refereering years	**1-4 years**	64	54,7
	5-8 years	26	22,2
	9-12 years	17	14,5
	13 years and above	10	8,6

When the socio-demographic distributions of the referees included in Table 2 are examined, it is seen that the majority (90.6) of the referees are male, 20-24 years of age (38.4%), the unemployed is 71.8%, the incomes are 32.5% 71.8% of the work experience is between 0-5 years, 76.9% of them are working in the private sector and 54.7% of them have 1-4 years of refereeing experience.

Table 3. Results of variance analysis (ANOVA) of mean values of decision making subscales of the referees participated in the research

Variables		İmpulsive Mean±Ss	Indecisive Mean ±Ss	Dependant decision-making Mean ±Ss	Logical decision-making Mean ±Ss
Age	15-19	23,28±3,49	18,28±3,22	22,21±2,32	27,42±4,92
	20-24	22,97±3,95	20,71±4,52	21,55±3,45	27,22±4,33
	25-29	21,90±3,57	19,93±3,94	21,51±2,71	27,74±4,05
	30-34	21,45±4,11	20,09±4,68	22,18±3,24	28,09±3,55
	35-39	22,66±4,04	17,00±5,56	19,00±1,73	27,33±2,51
	39 years and more	19,50±1,70	18,00±3,56	24,00±4,24	25,50±4,94
P Value		0,44	0,37	0,48	0,94
Educational level	High school	22,93±3,51	18,66±3,89	21,15±2,59	27,24±4,41
	University	22,14±4,04	20,48±4,18	22,01±3,29	27,73±4,06
	Postgraduate	22,22±2,81	20,33±5,74	21,33±2,95	26,77±3,59
P Value		0,60	0,12	0,38	0,72
Work experience	0-5 years	22,77±3,71	20,27±3,98	21,50±3,10	27,64±4,13
	6-10 years	21,38±3,91	19,19±5,24	22,61±3,02	27,04±4,47
	11-15 years	21,62±4,86	19,12±5,19	21,87±2,79	28,00±3,33
	16-20 years	20,75±2,85	19,00±3,46	21,25±3,94	26,50±4,12
P Value		0,34	0,65	0,51	0,87
Economic income	0-800Tl	22,63±3,59	19,84±4,03	21,96±3,36	27,09±3,98
	801-1500Tl	25,37±3,42	20,62±3,55	20,75±2,88	26,62±4,64
	1501-2500Tl	20,63±3,60	19,30±3,59	21,83±3,04	27,63±4,09
	2501 and more	20,26±3,61	20,28±5,23	21,81±2,99	28,18±4,03
P Value		**0,01**	0,72	0,60	0,55
Refereeing years	1-4 years	22,76±3,64	19,96±4,11	21,70±3,11	27,50±4,64
	5-8 years	21,76±3,93	20,30±3,88	21,92±3,17	28,00±2,81
	9-12 years	22,52±3,79	20,00±5,39	22,05±2,96	26,64±4,04
	13 years and more	21,20±4,73	18,90±4,72	20,70±3,16	27,90±3,63
P Value		0,51	0,85	0,70	0,75

Subscales of decision making strategies of the referees participating in the research group; statistical values of the ANOVA test related to variables such as age, educational status, work outside of refereeing, economic income and refereeing years were not found statistically significant as shown in Table 3 (p> 0,05). Only the results of the impulsive decision making subscale were significant according to the economic situation variable (p = **0,01**, p **<0,05**). As income rises, meaningful results are found in connection with the increase in the impulsive decision.

Table 4. Results of the t-test on the mean values of the decision making subscales of the referees participated in the survey

Variables		İmpulsive Mean ±Ss	Indecisive Mean ±Ss	Dependant decision-making Mean ±Ss	Logical decision-making Mean ±Ss
Gender	Female	23,36±2,83	20,45±5,08	22,63±3,44	26,36±4,05
	Male	22,27±3,89	19,90±4,21	21,62±3,05	27,64±4,11
P Value		0,36	0,68	0,30	0,32
Marital Status	Married	21,81±4,10	19,66±4,81	22,51±2,69	27,30±4,17
	Single	22,59±3,69	20,07±4,07	21,40±3,18	27,60±4,10
P Value		0,32	0,32	0,08	0,72
Work	Private Sector	22,30±3,11	19,96±3,66	21,77±3,11	27,33±3,98
	Public Sector	22,62±3,69	19,92±5,97	21,51±3,03	28,14±4,53
P Value		0,69	0,64	0,70	0,36

When Table 4 is examined, no significant difference was found in any of the subscales of logical-systematic decision making, impulsive decision making, dependent decision making, and indecisive decision making according to the variables gender, marital status and and work done outside refereeing in public or private sector ($p > 0,05$) .

4 Discussion

When we evaluate the results of our work in terms of gender; Internal impulsive, logical, dependent and indecisive decision making subscale scores did not show a significant difference even though they were high in favor of women. In our study, the reason why there is no gender difference in decision-making strategies in male and female referees is that judges should only make judgments on the basis of rules, not on their own emotional states and it is thought that decision-making scale results do not make a difference in terms of gender, as referees make decisions on basis of the rules of the sport branch they arbitrate. When other studies in the literature are examined, there are studies reporting that there is no difference in terms of gender in support of our work [12, 13], and there are also studies that suggest that girls use logic-systematic and dependant and decision-making strategies more than men, and that men use the impulsive decision strategy more than girls [2]. Likewise, some studies have found that girls use impulsive [14], some use logical [15], and others use dependent decision making strategy [16] more than men. Even if a generalization can not be made from the outcomes, it can be said that there is a need for further research to analyze the difference between the decision strategies and the gender and the situation regarding this difference in detail.

It has been seen that decision-making styles are independent of each other but not completely different from one another, and that individuals do not use a single style when making important decisions, instead they use all these styles [17]. In a study, it was seen that although there was no significant difference according to gender, women were more likely to use rational decision-making style than men and males used more dependent decision-making styles compared to females [18].

According to the marital status of the referees in our research, there was no significant difference in the logical-systematic decision making, the impulsive decision making, the dependent decision making, and the indecisive decision making subscales. There is no study in the literature on the variable of marital status.

There was no significant difference in decision making subscales according to age variable (P> 0.05). According to other research results comparing adult and adolescent decision making processes, age and gender have not been effective in making final decisions [13, 18, 19]. This finding is also parallel to the results of our research. While in some studies, it was found that only dependent decision making style showed significant difference according to age [20]. Some studies have shown that managers in the age range of 36-40 years compared those in the 25-30 age range, and managers in the age range of 41-45 compared to those 20-25 are more rationally examining options in the decision making process [13, 18, 21]. Considering these results, it can be considered that as the age progresses, there is an increase in the experience and logical evaluation, and a healthier decision is made.

There was no significant difference in decision-making subscales, if we were to interpret our findings according to educational status variable. When we look at the literature, while some of the studies support our findings [18, 22], some studies have also found that the rational, spontaneous-momentary, dependant, and avoidance decision style averages do not vary significantly relative to their level of education, but that the heuristic decision averages are significantly different as education level increases but there is no difference in other areas [7].

In the study we conducted, there was no significant difference in all the subscales related to decision making based on the work done outside refereeing, and the year of refereeing, ie work experience. It has been stated that being experienced at work is not effective in decisions [7, 22]. In addition to the literature findings supporting our research results [7], it has been stated that managers who have 21-25 years of compared to those who have 20 years of experience have evaluated the options more carefully and evaluated pluses and minuses considering every possibility [21].

There was no significant difference in decision making subscales according to economic income variable. However, there was a significant difference in favor of those who had low incomes only in the impulsive decision making subscale. In a study conducted in the light of literature; It has been determined that the instant decision making strategy is different according to income level, the instant decision making style of low income individuals is higher than other income groups, and the other decision making styles do not show any difference [7].

References

1. Y. Kuzgun, F. Bacanli, *PDR'de Kullanılan Ölçekler*. Ankara, Nobel Yayın Dağıtım, (2005)
2. Y. Kuzgun, Karar Stratejileri Ölçeği: Geliştirilmesi ve Standardizasyonu. VII. Ulusal Psikoloji Kongresi Bilimsel Çalışmaları. Ankara, Türk Psikologlar Derneği, 161-170. (1992)
3. S.S. Güçray, Bazı Kişisel Değişkenler, Algılanan Sosyal Destek ve Atılganlığın Karar Verme Sitilleri İle İlişkisi. Türk Psikolojik Danışma ve Rehberlik Dergisi, **2.9,** 7-16. (1998)
4. H. Ö. Ersever, Karar Verme Becerileri Kazandırma Programının ve Etkileşim Grubu Deneyiminin Üniversite Öğrencilerinin Karar Verme Stilleri Üzerindeki Etkileri. Unpublished doctoral thesis, Ankara Üniversitesi, Ankara Üniversitesi Sosyal Bilimler Enstitüsü, Ankara, (1996)
5. A. Dağlı, Problem çözme ve karar verme. Elektronik Sosyal Bilimler Dergisi, **3(7)**, 41-49, (2004)

6. J. Noone, Concept Analysis of Decision Making. Nursing Forum, 37 (3), 21 – 32. (2002)
7. Ö. A. Tekin, Yönetimde karar verme: Batı Antalya bölgesinde bulunan beş yıldızlı otel işletmelerindeki çeşitli departman yöneticilerinin karar verme stillerini tespit etmeye yönelik uygulamalı bir araştırma, Unpublished master's thesis, Akdeniz Üniversitesi Sosyal Bilimler Enstitüsü Turizm İşletmeciliği ve Otelcilik Anabilim Dalı, Antalya. (2009)
8. J. Eldeleklioğlu, Karar Stratejileri ile Ana Baba Tutumları Arasındaki İliski. Unpublished doctoral thesis, Gazi Üniversitesi, Sosyal Bilimler Enstitüsü, Ankara. (1996)
9. K. Tatlılıoğlu, Üniversite Öğrencilerinin Karar Vermede Öz-Saygı Düzeyleri ile Karar Verme Stilleri Arasındaki İlişkinin Bazı Değişkenlere Göre İncelenmesi.", Akademik Sosyal Araştırmalar Dergisi, **2 (1),** 150-170. (2014)
10. F. Korkut, "Lise Öğrencilerinin Problem Çözme Becerileri", Hacettepe Üniversitesi Eğitim Fakültesi Dergisi, **22,** 177 – 184. (2002)
11. S. Budak, *Psikoloji Sözlüğü*, Ankara, Bilim ve Sanat Yayınları. (2000)
12. O. Çolakkadioğlu, Çatişma kuramina dayali olarak geliştirilen karar verme beceri eğitimi grup uygulamalarinin ergenlerin karar verme stillerine etkisi, Unpublished master's thesis, Çukurova Üniversitesi, Sosyal Bilimler Enstitüsü, Eğitim Bilimleri Anabilim Dalı, Adana. (2010)
13. A. M. Hulderman, Decision-Making Styles and Learning Strategies of Police Officers: Implications for Community Policing. Doctorate Thesis, Oklahoma State University, Faculty of the Graduate College of the Oklahoma State University, Oklahoma. (2003)
14. M. G. Tiryaki, Üniversite öğrencilerinin karar verme davranışlarının bazı değişkenler açısından incelenmesi. Unpublished master's thesis, Hacettepe Üniversitesi Sosyal Bilimler Enstitüsü. (1997)
15. S. Kesici, Üniversite öğrencilerinin karar verme stratejilerinin psikolojik ihtiyaç örüntüleri ve özlük niteliklerine göre karşılaştırmalı olarak incelenmesi. Unpublished doctoral thesis, Konya: Selçuk Üniversitesi Sosyal Bilimler Enstitüsü. (2002)
16. W. Mau, Cultural differences in career decision-making styles and self efficacy. Journal of Vocational Behavior, **57**, 365–378. (2000)
17. P. Thunholm, Decision-Making Scale: Habit, Style or Both?, Personality and Individual Differences, **36,** 931 – 944. (2004)
18. R. P. Sanders, The Decision-Making Styles, Ways of Knowing, and Learnıng Strategy Preferences of Clients At a One-Stop Career Center. Doctorate Thesis, Southern Oklahoma State University, Faculty of the Graduate College of the Oklahoma State University, Stillwater, Oklahoma. (2008)
19. A.K. Ganzel, Adolescent decision making: The influence of mood, age, and gender on the consideration of information [Electronic version]. Journal of Adolescent Research, **14,** 289-318 (1999)
20. A. Arın, Lise yöneticilerinin öğretim liderliği davranışları ile kullandıkları karar verme stratejileri ve problem çözme becerileri arasındaki ilişki düzeyi. Unpublished master's thesis, Eskişehir Osmangazi Üniversitesi, Sosyal Bilimler Enstitüsü, Eğitim Bilimleri Anabilim Dalı, Eskişehir. (2006)
21. K. Özcan, Yöneticilerde Karar Verme ile Kaygı İlişkileri. Unpublished master's thesis, Marmara Üniversitesi, Sosyal Bilimler Enstitüsü, Teknoloji Eğitimi Anabilim Dalı, İstanbul, (1999)
22. H. P. Kao, Taiwanese Executive's Leadership Styles and Their Preffered Decision-Making Models Used in Mainland China. Doctorate Thesis, The University of the Incarnate Word, The School of the Graduate Studies of The University of the Incarnate Word, Texas. (2005)

Effect of learning approaches of pre-service science teachers on the argument create skills

Nilay Aydogan[1a], Huseyin Polat[1], Ozlem Cankaya[1], and Fatma Bilge Emre[1,2]

[1]Department of Mathematics and Sciences Education, Faculty of Education, İnönü University, 44280 Malatya, Turkey
[2]Prof. Dr. Hikmet SAYILKAN Advanced Materials Research an Application Laboratory Scientific and Technological Research Centre, İnönü University, 44280 Malatya, Turkey

Abstract. The aim of this study is to investigate the relationship between science teacher candidates' ability to construct an argument and learning approaches. For this purpose, the "Learning Approach Scale" was applied to Inonu University Educational Faculty Science teachers 'first grade students', and the results were compared with the arguments which were created by the same students. The findings shows that there is a significant relationship between their argument create skills and learning approaches.
Keywords: Argument Create Skills, Learning Approach, Science Education, Pre-Service Science Teachers

1 Introduction

In recent years, student-centered teaching theories in which students research and find or create more systematic information by processing raw information, have been attracting attention as an alternative to the teaching methods currently available in science teaching [1]. One of these methods that serve this purpose is the method of argumentation. Argumentation is defined as scientific discussions aimed at defending or refuting a thought [2].

According to Toulmin [3], the argumentation concept is defined as a coordination of the theories and evidence to support or refute an explanatory result, model or prediction. Argumentation can be expressed as the process of put out claims to solve a problem situation and proving the rightness of ideas to the other side by putting more reasons supporting those claims [4].

It was observed that, the argumentation method, which is mentioned more frequently in science education in the world and in Turkey than in other fields, has developed

[a]Corresponding author: nilay.aydogan@inonu.edu.tr

students' academic achievement, critical thinking, problem solving and decision making skills, and the argumentation process is affected by peer education [5, 6, 7, 8, 9].

The development of scientific literacy levels is one of the goals of science education. It is expected that the individuals with high scientific literacy levels also have high ability to create an argument [10]. In this light, the level of argument create ability of the teachers is very important in science education.

Concepts of superficial and deep learning approaches have been put forward in studies on how students perceive a particular reading part and how they engage in learning [11].

Deep learning approach has been defined as willingness to learn, , intense and critical interaction with content, linking previous knowledge with new learnings, associating concepts with daily experiences, establishing a relationship between events and outcomes and review the logic of the subject and the superficial learning approach also defined as the tendency to complete the tasks required by the job, to memorize the necessary information in the exams, not to distinguish the principles from the examples, to view the learning work as external loading, to focus on individual items without integrity and tendency to do not explore goals and strategies [12].

Learning habits are related to the use of learning strategies and appropriate strategies by students. Motivation points to why the students want to learn, and strategy is how to learn [13].

2 Method

The universe of the research is constituted by 1st grade students of İnönü University, Faculty of Education Science Teacher Education. In the sample, there are pre-service teachers participating in classes to represent the class level. 48 students attending the first grade of the Science Teacher Training Program participated in the research.

2.1 Data collection tool

In order to determine the learning approaches of the pre-service teachers, "Learning Approach Scale (LAS)" developed by Ellez and Sezgin [14] were used. 5-Likert-type scale with 30 items, have "I totally agree", "I agree", "Undecided", "I do not agree", "I do not fully agree" options. The Cronbach Alpha reliability coefficient of the scale is 0.81 and the items in the measure are in two dimensions. These dimensions are called the "Deep Approach (DA)" and "Superficial Approach (SA)". There are 19 items in the dimension of deep approach and 11 items in the aspect of the superficial approach. The items in the scale were scored as 5, 4, 3, 2, 1 starting from the "I totally agree" option. The reliability coefficients of the subscales of the scale are 0.82 and 0.76. Subscale definitions are given in Table 1 [15].

Table 1. Subscale definitions of LAS

Subscales	Definition
Deep Approach (DA)	Actively participating in the lesson, asking questions actively during learning, trying to understand learning materials, linking previous knowledge with new ones, linking what they learn with everyday life, learning to learn, not satisfied with what they learn in the lesson, researching knowledge from different sources, actively participating in the lesson
Superficial Approach (SA)	Acceptance and memorize what teachers say without thinking, to copy information, to memorize the necessary knowledge in examinations, to aim at more lessons from learning, to view the teacher as a single and reliable source of information,

An argument-based science learning report which was developed by using rubrics used by Choi [16] was used to determine pre-service teachers' argument create skills. The arguments they made were evaluated by 8 teaching staff and PhD students as the quality of the arguments and descriptions they used in the reports and the total writing scores.

3 Findings

In this work, where the pre-service teachers' argument skills were evaluated, it was aimed to evaluate the existing arguments about acid-bases, to create arguments and to form counter arguments against existing arguments.

3.1 Activity 1

It was asked to pre-service teachers to evaluate an existing claim about global warming and support this claim with data. They were asked to score between 1 and 3 according to whether they participated in the evaluation or not. The following scale was used when this activity was scored.

Table 2. Activity evaluation scale

Criterion	Score
Only Estimation	1
Using Data	2
Data and Justification	3

The highest score is 15 because there are 5 expressions in total. The average of the first event is 6.91. It is seen that pre-service teachers are able to evaluate the claims of the prospective teachers and support them at least in some cases.

3.2 Activity 2

In this activity, they were asked to evaluate and indicate the cause of an existing claim about the effects of acids on human health. The following scale was used when this activity was scored.

Table 3. Activity evaluation scale

Criterion	Score
Only Estimation	1
Using Data	2
Data and Justification	3

The highest score is 9 because there are 3 expressions in total. The average of the first event is 2.87. This indicates that teachers are in the evaluation stage.

3.3 Activity 3

In this activity, it is requested to create claims about the effects of acids on human health and to support these claims with data. The difference between this activity and the other activities is that the pre-service teachers need to create and justify their own claims in the given issue. The following scale was used when this activity was scored.

Table 4. Activity evaluation scale

Criterion	Score
No Specific Claim	1
Specific Claim	2
Claim + Data	3
Claim + Data + Justification	4
Claim + Data + Justification + Supporting	5

The highest score is 5 in this activity. The average of the first event is 1.12. This indicates that pre-service teachers can only create claims in a particular context, but cannot pass on the data phase.

3.4 Activity 4

In this activity there are 5 different expressions for evaluating the claims about acid-bases. When one of these statements is evaluating, it is necessary to make a counter argument. The following scale was used when this activity was scored.

Table 5. Activity evaluation scale

Criterion	Score
Using Only Data	1
Data + Justification	2
Data + Justification + Supporting	3
Counter Claim + Data	4
Counter Claim + Data + Supporting	5

The highest score to be awarded in the event is 17. The average of this activity is 7.62. This suggests that the pre-service teachers can often use data to support their existing claims.

3.5 The learning approaches of pre-service science teachers

In order to determine the learning approaches of pre-service science teachers, the averages and standard deviations of the scores of the LAS' subscales were calculated. A t-test was conducted to determine whether the difference between the averages was significant. The results of the analysis are given in Table 6.

Table 6. The arithmetic mean, standard deviation results of LAS subscale scores of pre-service science teachers

Subscales	n	A	SD
Superficial Approach	48	3,14	0,47
Deep Approach	48	3,64	0,41

When Table 6 is examined, it is seen that the average of the pre-service science teacher for the deep approach dimension (O = 3.64) is higher than the mean of the superficial approach dimension (O = 3.14). The difference between the averages of the two dimensions was significant, in favor of the deeper approach, according to the t-test results for the purpose of controlling ($p<0,05$).

 DOI: 10.1051/shsconf/20173701044

Table 7. Relationship between argument create skills and learning approaches

	Argument Create Skills (ACS)	Superficial Approach (SA)	Deep Approach (DA)
ACS - Pearson Correlation Coefficient	1,00	-0,239	0,462
Level of Significance	-	0,30	0,20
n	48	48	48
SA - Pearson Correlation Coefficient	-0,239	1,00	-0,36
Level of Significance	0,30	-	0,00
n	48	48	48
DA - Pearson Correlation Coefficient	0,462	-0,36	1,00
Level of Significance	0,20	0,00	-
n	48	48	48

As shown in Table 7, the relationship between pre-service science teachers' deep learning approach and their ability to create an argument is positive and the correlation coefficient is $r = 0.462$. The calculated correlation coefficient was found to be significant at $\alpha = 0{,}20$ level. Negative weak correlation was found between the superficial approach and the ability to create arguments.

4 Discussion and conclusion

Research and inquiry-based approaches include a range of purposes that serve scientific literacy, such as critical thinking, communication and linguistic skills development, and the gaining of scientific process skills. For this reason, argumentation which is one of the methods of inquiry and research based education, is considered as an effective tool in science education [17].

It is expected that a student who has started in university will have a high level of basic language usage skills such as reading, understanding, listening and speaking. The fact that the basic language skills are not at the desired level affects the learning of the students in the negative way and causes the behavior that is expected to occur in the students after higher education to not be realized at the desired level [18].

It has been shown that the learning approach influences the output of education, the superficial learning with the low level of learning output of and the deep learning are related to the high level of learning outcomes [19, 20, 21, 22], academic performance [23] and level of knowledge [12, 24].

One of the most challenged section for the students when they are creating their arguments is counter claim. It was observed that they were forced to find a claim against the claim they created. It is thought to have originated from the fact that they could not understand enough the claims they made.

It was also observed that students were having difficulty in generating data. It may be that they may not be able to fully remember the preliminary information about the cause or they may begin to write without using them. Moreover, it can be said that university students do not understand the importance and role of generating data when making a discussion [25].

Students with a deep learning approach have actively participate in the lesson, asking questions actively during learning, trying to understand learning materials, linking previous knowledge with new ones, linking what they have learned with everyday life, learning to learn, not satisfied with what they learn in the lesson, researching knowledge from different sources, actively participating in the lesson, properties. The results of our study show that students with a deeper learning approach have the ability to build higher arguments. These students can present data about the arguments they have formed and justify these data. They can reasonably support their claims about their arguments. However, they are not fully qualified to form a counter claim.

The learning approach of the students is not fixed and students can change their approach depending on the perception of the subject [26]. Students can be pushed to superficial learning when certain teaching and assessment strategies are used. However, it is not so easy to be guided to deep learning [27]. We think that by using various teaching methods, students will be able to improve their argument creating skills by directing them to deep learning. It is expected that the level of scientific literacy of the students who have the ability to set up arguments will also develop [28]. Thus, it is thought that the learning level of the future students of these pre-service teachers can be positively affected.

References

1. D. Karışan, Fen Bilgisi Öğretmen Adaylarının İklim Değişiminin Dünyamıza Etkileri Konusundaki Yazılı Argümantasyon Yeteneklerinin İncelenmesi (Yüksek Lisans Tezi).Yüzüncü Yıl Üniversitesi Fen Bilimleri Enstitüsü, Van (2011)
2. H. Polat, Atomun Yapısı Konusunda Argümantasyon Yönteminin İlköğretim 7. sınıf Öğrencileirinin Başarısı Üzerine Etkisi (Yüksek Lisans Tezi). İnönü Üniversitesi Eğitim Bilimleri Enstitüsü, Malatya (2014)
3. S. E. Toulmin, *The Uses Of Argument,* Oxford University Press, New York
4. S. Okumuş, 'Maddenin Halleri ve Isı' Ünitesinin Bilimsel Tartışma (argümantasyon) Modeli İle Öğretiminin Öğrenci Başarısına Ve Anlama Düzeylerine Etkisi (Yüksek Lisans Tezi). Karadeniz Teknik Üniversitesi Eğitim Bilimleri Enstitüsü, Trabzon (2012)
5. M. Felton, D. Kuhn, The development of argumentive discourse skills. Discourse Processes, **32**, 135-153 (2001)
6. R. M. Gillies, A. Khan, Promoting reasoned argumentation, problem-solving and learning during small-group work. Cambridge Journal of Education, **39(1),** 7-27 (2009)
7. E. M. Nussbaum, Argumentation, dialogue theory, and probability modeling: Alternative frameworks for argumentation research in education. Educational Psychologist, **46(2),** 84-106 (2011)
8. C. H. Chen, H. C. She, The impact of recurrent on-line synchronous scientific argumentation on students' argumentation and conceptual change. Educational Technology & Society, **15(1),** 197-210 (2012)
9. F. Torun, S. Şahin. Argümantasyon temelli Sosyal Bilgiler Dersinde Öğrencilerin Argüman Düzeylerinin Belirlenmesi. Eğitim ve Bilim. **41**, 186, 233-251 (2016)
10. H. Aktamış, Fen Eğitiminde Kullanılan Argümantasyon Modellerinin Değerlendirilmesi. Mehmet Akif Ersoy Üniversitesi Eğitim Fakültesi Dergisi, **35,** 136 -172 (2015)
11. F. Marton, R. Saljö, On qualitative differences in learning I: -Outcome & process. British Journal of Educational Psychology, **46,** 4-11 (1976)
12. Ş. Beşoluk, İ. Önder, Öğretmen adaylarının öğrenme yaklaşımları, öğrenme stilleri ve eleştirel düşünme eğilimlerinin incelenmesi. Elementary Education Online, **9(2),** 679–693 (2010)
13. L. Zhang, University Students' Learning Approaches in Three Cultures: An Investigation of Bigg's 3P Model. The Journal of Psychology, **134**, 1, 37–55 (2000)

14. A. M. Ellez, G. S. Sezgin, Öğretmen Adaylarının Öğrenme Yaklaşımları. V. Ulusal Fen Bilimleri ve Matematik Eğitimi Kongresi. (16-18 Eylül). Ankara:Orta Doğu Teknik Üniversitesi (2002)
15. G. Selcuk, S. Calıskan, M. Erol, Evaluation of Learning Approaches for Prospective Physics Teachers. The Journal Of Gazi Educational Faculty, **27**, 2, 25-41 (2007)
16. A. Choi, A study of student written argument using the Science Writing Heuristic approach in inquiry-based freshman general chemistry laboratory classes. Unpublished doctoral dissertation. University of Iowa, Iowa City, IA. (2008)
17. N. Duban, İlköğretim fen öğretiminde niçin sorgulamaya dayalı öğrenme? *In 8th International Educational Technology Conference (IETC 2008)* Proceedings (pp. 802-805) (2008)
18. E. Köse, A. Şahin, Yükseköğrenime yeni başlayan öğrencilerin düşüncelerini yazılı olarak ifade edebilme becerilerinin değerlendirilmesi. Milli Eğitim Dergisi, **180**, 227-237 (2008)
19. N. J. Entwistle, P. Ramsden, Understanding student learning. London: Croom-Helm
20. Prosser, M. & Millar, R. The how and what of learning physics. European Journal of Psychology of Education, **4,** 513-528 (1983)
21. K. Trigwell, M. Prosser, Relating approaches to study and the quality of learning outcomes at the course level. British Journal of Educational Psychology, 61, 265-275 (1991)
22. E.J. van Rossum, S. M. Schenk, The relationship between learning conception, study strategy and learning outcome. British Journal of Educational Psychology, **54,** 73-83 (1984)
23. S. Mayya, A.K. Rao, K. Ramnarayan, Learning approaches, learning difficulties and academic performance of undergraduate students of physiotherapy. The Internet Journal of Allied Health Sciences and Practice, 2(4), 1-6 (2004)
24. P.K. Murphy, P.A. Alexander, What counts? The predictive power of subject-matter knowledge, strategic processing and interest in domain-specific performance. The Journal of Experimental Education, 70(3), 197-214 (2002)
25. E. Coskun, E.N. Tiryaki, Writing Skills of University Students on Argumentative Text. H. U. Journal of Education, **28(2),** 102-115 (2013)
26. G. Ünal, Ö. Ergin, Buluş yoluyla fen öğretiminin öğrencilerin akademik başarılarına, öğrenme yaklaşımlarına ve tutumlarına etkisi. Türk Fen Eğitimi Dergisi, **3(1),** 36-52 (2006)
27. P. Ramsden, D. Beswick, J. Bowden, Effects of learning skills interventions on first year university students' learning. Human Learning, **5**, 151-164 (1986)
28. S. P. Norris, L. M. Phillips, How literacy in its fundamental sense is central to scientific literacy. Science Education, **87(2),** 224-240 (2003)

In Turkey, factors which urge physically handicapped sporters to start badminton sport and their expectations

Ersin Arslan[1a], Mustafa Atlı[1], Zekiye Özkan[1], and Şeyhmus Kaplan[2]

[1]School of Physical Education and Sports, Yuzuncu Yil University, 65040 Van, Turkey
[2]Department of Sports Medicine, Medical Faculty, Yuzuncu Yil University, 65040 Van, Turkey

Abstract. The purpose of the study is to determine factors, which lead physically handicapped badminton players in Turkey to tend towards badminton sport, and expectations of sporters. 45 (Male: 29 Female: 16) physically handicapped sporters, who participated in Turkey Bandminton Championship for Physically Handicapped, which was arranged in Antalya on 24-26 February, 2017, from different cities, attended the study voluntarily. Developed by Sunay and his colluages [13], tendency to sports and expectation survey was used in badminton branch after expert opinions, firstly, were received and necessary regulations were made for using it in our study. In order to determine whether the difference between opinions of sporters, attending the study, according to their genders, their ages, their best sport degrees, their sport years, their parents' educational backgrounds and jobs, is important or not, one-way analysis of variance was used. To identify resource of the difference, Duncan's multiple range test was used. Kruskal Wallis H test was used when normality and homogeneity of variances were not provided. Value of p for comparisons was taken as 0,05. Consequently, it was determined that, in Turkey, effects of environment, friend-peer group and trainer on sporters playing at elite level as physically handicapped are high in starting badminton firstly while effects of sport complex, parents and siblings, mass media such as television and media organs on tendency to badminton are quite low. It was ascertained that liking badminton sport and delighting in earning success were effective as the reasons of physically handicappeds' playing badminton sport and their expectations were, firstly, to be chosen for national team and to be national team sporters.
Keywords: Physically Handicapped, badminton, sport

[a] Corresponding author: ersinarslan70@hotmail.com

1 Introduction

Sport activities have become important for the handicapped recently. In our country, an important increase was seen in tendencies of individuals with special necessity to sport thanks to growth of sensitiveness towards the handicapped at government policy and provided facilities.

Physically disability is identified as any physical situation which includes obstacles coming to light from birth or as result of a disease and affects child's educational performance [9]. Education chance of handicapped individual can be increased by removing environmental obstacles and increasing capableness and rehabilitating in the way that he/she can optimise his/her present potential. The physically handicapped people, who have no difference from other children in terms of learning capacity, have been dispossessed of education chances most often due to transportation problems and architectural obstacles at home and schools and their coalescing with society has been precluded. Tending of the physically handicapped people to sport is important in terms of life quality like the individuals who make normal progress [12].

Sport is asserted as competitive, solidarist and cultural notion improving socializer soul and physics and abilities, which individual obtains while he/she turns nature environment into humane environment, and a notion that individual does by making it profession in such a way that the sport will take his/her al lor leisure time individually or with group and with tool or without tool under certain rules [2]. Badminton sport has begun to take place among the sport branches that physically handicapped people interested in.

Among the reasons of being preferred of badminton, its elegant feature and its not requiring special area or track is effective. It is played out of town, at picnic and street and in water and even on ice. Because of this feature, badminton play meets societies' health and need for movement. And also, in terms of charactertistic of the play, badminton sport maintains its characteristic of being one of kind of the activities developing physical capacity ideally and generally as aerob. This feature of badminton brings it in ability in which people of all ages can perform an application according to their own performance [20]. Tending to sport begins at young ages. In physically handicapped people, tending to sport is realised in the fields that individual feels he/she is qualified.

Among the factors which influence a young competitor's attending sport, encouragement and incentive factors, proving himself/herself, aggression, selectness, independance, power, stres and success are influential [19]. Sport has an important role in personality development [21].

2 Method

2.1 The purpose of the study

The purpose of the study is to determine factors, which lead physically handicapped badminton players in Turkey to tend towards badminton sport, and expectations of sporters.

2.2 Problem of the study

Problem of the study is to research whether factors, which lead physically handicapped badminton players in Turkey to tend towards badminton sport, and expectations of sporers show difference according to demographic characteristics or not.

2.3 Data collection tool

The survey, which was used in the study (Tendig to sport and expectations) was developed by Sunay and his colluages and was applied to other branches. Validity and dependability of the survey was accepted [13]. Survey was used in badminton branch by receiving expert opinions and making necessary regulations for using it in our study. In the first part of the survey, there are personal informations of sporters who attended the study, and then in the second part of the survey, there are factors which urge to badminton sport and reasons for playing, lastly, in the third part of the survey, there are opinions about expectations from badminton sport.

2.4 Participants

45 (Male: 29 Female: 16) physically handicapped sporters, who participated in Turkey Bandminton Championship for Physically Handicapped, which was arranged in Antalya on 24-26 February, 2017, from different cities, attended the study voluntarily.

2.5 Statistical analysis

Data obtained from the survey were clarified and commented with frequencies and percentages. Moreover, in order to determine whether the difference between criterions related to genders, ages, best sport degrees, sport years, educational backgrounds and jobs of the parents of sporters attending the study is important or not, one-way analysis of variance was done. To identify resource of the difference, Duncan's multiple range test was used. Kruskal Wallis H test was used when normality and homogeneity of variances were not provided. Value of p for comparisons was taken as 0,05. and significance level was taken as %5 for comparisons.

3 Findings and comment

In this study, determination of the factors which urge male and female (Male: 29 Female: 16) physically handicapped sporters, who participated in Turkey Bandminton Championship for Physically Handicapped, which was arranged in Antalya on 24-26 February, 2017, from different cities, to badminton sport and of expectations was aimed. Many factors are effective in tending of individuals to sport. In the factors which determine the tending, sufficiency of person, family factor, environmental factors, media, social environment, economic factors are effective.

Table 1. Singificance Levels of the factors which urge physically handicapped people to badminton sport

the Factors which urge physically handicapped people to badminton sport	$\bar{X}$	SS	Significance Level
1. Effect of parents and sibling in tending to sport	5,7333	1,87568	7
2. Effect of environment in which you live in tending to sport	3,5111	2,41795	3
3. Effect of friend and peer group in tending to sport	3,2444	1,72093	2
4. Effect of physical education teacher in tending to sport	4,9111	2,15134	5
5. Effect of media organs in tending to sport	4,6889	2,05407	4
6. Effect of television channels in tending to sport	5,1111	1,99114	6
7. Effect of school complex and materials in tending to sport	6,1111	1,84911	8
8.Effect of the trainer in close environment in tending to sport	2,6889	1,90481	1

When examining singificance levels of the factors which urge physically handicapped people to badminton sport, it was seen that in the first level, there is fffect of the trainer in close environment in tending to sport, then in the second level, there is effect of friend and peer group in tending to sport, lastly, in the third level, there is effect of environment in which you live in tending to sport

Table 2. Significance Levels of the reasons of physically handicapped people's playing badminton

Reason For Playing Badminton	$\bar{X}$	SS	Significance Level
9. To increase revenue	6,4667	3,04213	8
10. To like badminton sport	2,1111	1,96818	1
11. To be aware of positive contributions of sport	5,8444	7,93140	7
12. To attend a friend group easily	7,4318	1,82231	9
13. To value leisure time by doing sport	5,8444	1,94183	6
14. To be healthy by playing badminton	4,4444	2,11655	3
15. To be known, loved and respected by friends as a sporter	5,2667	1,83897	5
16. To delight in earning success	3,7556	2,101147	2
17.To move with friends in a team spirit	4,9333	2,28035	4

When examining significance levels of the reasons of physically handicapped people's playing badminton, it has been seen that in the first level, there is to love badminton, and then in the second level, there is to delight in earning success, lastly, in the third level, there is to be healty by playing badminton.

Table 3. Expectations of physically handicapped sporters from badminton sport

Expectations from Badminton Sport	$\bar{X}$	SS	Significance Level
18. To be and keep healthy	4,4667	3,00454	2
19.To have a good physical appearence	6,4000	2,799935	8
20. To maintain relationship with his/her environment as a popular person doing sport	7,5111	2,31224	10
21. To be a good sporter and to earn living through sports	4,8182	2,65253	3
22. To be trained for sport at university level in the future	5,7333	2,35874	5
23. To be trainer	5,0444	2,37368	4
24. To be referee	6,6889	2,66988	9
25. To be physical education teacher	6,2444	2,59506	7
26. To obtain financial potential	5,7333	2,79935	6
27. To be chosen for national team and to be national sporter	2,3556	1,92065	1

When examining significance levels of expectations of physically handicapped sporters from badminton sport, it has been seen that in the first level, there is expectation for being chosen for national team and being national sporter, and then in the second level, there is expectation for being and keeping healthy, lastly, in the third level, there is expectation for being a good sporter and earning living through sport.

Table 4. Variance analysis of factors urging to badminton sport according to sports year of the physically handicapped

Factors Urging to Badminton Sport	Sport Year	N	$\bar{X}$	SS	F	Sig.
Press Factor (media organs, television channels)	<5 year	20	11,5500	3,41012	4,786	**0,013***
	5-10 year	13	8,0769	3,72965		
	≥10 year	12	8,7500	3,13702		
Environmental Factors (environment in which he/she live,friends, parents,siblings)	<5 year	20	12,5500	2,87411	0,345	0,710
	5-10 year	13	13,0000	4,06202		
	≥10 year	12	11,8333	3,92737		
Other Factors(Physical education teacher, school sport complex and matearials, trainer)	<5 year	20	11,9000	3,49285	5,348	**0,009***
	5-10 year	13	14,9231	2,92864		
	≥10 year	12	15,4167	3,50216		

A significant difference of press factor in urgin to badminton sport according to sporters' sports year was seen ($p<0.05$). A significan difference of environmental factors in urginto badminton sport according to sporters' sports year was not seen ($p>0.05$).

Table 5. Results of Kruskal Wallis H test of factors urging to badminton sport according to educational backgrounds of sporters' mother

Factors Urging to Badminton Sport	Education	N	$\bar{X}$	SS	Sig.
Press Factor (media organs, television channels)	Illiterate	10	7.4000	3.77712	**0.038***
	Literate	9	8.8889	2.84800	
	Primary	15	11.4667	3.97971	
	High School	11	10.4545	2.87623	
Environmental Factors (environment in which he/she live,friends, parents,siblings)	Illiterate	10	12.6000	3.83551	0.937
	Literate	9	12.4444	2.60342	
	Primary	15	12.4667	3.60291	
	High School	11	12.4545	4.05866	
Other Factors(Physical education teacher, school sport complex and matearials, trainer)	Illiterate	10	16.0000	3.23179	**0.035***
	Literate	9	14.6667	2.00000	
	Primary	15	12.0667	3.84460	
	High School	11	13.0909	3.88470	

A significant differecen was found among education level of mother in terms of pres factor ($p<0.05$). Difference was seen in primary and illiterate according to multiple range test which was done to determine resource of the differance (chi square=7.19). A significant differecen was observed among education level of mother in terms of school sport complex and materials and trainer factors ($p<0.05$). Similarly, difference was found in primary and illiterate according to results of multiple range test which was done to determine resource of the difference (chi square=8.12). A significant difference among fathers' education levels was not found in terms of press, environment and other factors.

Table 6. Variance analysis of the reasons of physically handicapped people's playing badminton according to sports degree of the physically handicapped

Reasons for playing badminton	Sport Degree	N	X̄	SS	F	Sig.
To move with friends in a team spirit To be known, loved and respected by friends as a sporter To attend a friend group easily	Turkey	31	18.0645	3.82043	3.433	**0.042***
	Wold	8	19.0000	4.34248		
	Province	6	13.6000	3.045981		
To increase revenue To like badminton sport To be aware of positive contributions of sport To value leisure time by doing sport . To be healthy by playing badminton To delight in earning success	Turkey	31	26.8387	3.55993	7.004	**0.002***
	World	8	26.0000	4.34248		
	Province	6	40.1667	21.64640		

A significant difference between variables, forming a circle of friends and providing moral and material benefits, and sports degree was determined ($p<0.05$).

4 Discussion and conclusion

In this study, determination of the factors which urge male and female (Male: 29 Female: 16) physically handicapped sporters, who participated in Turkey Bandminton Championship for Physically Handicapped, which was arranged in Antalya on 24-26 February, 2017, from different cities, to badminton sport and of expectations was aimed. Many factors are effective in tending of individuals to sport. In the factors which determine the tending, sufficiency of person, family factor, environmental factors, media, social environment, economic factors are effective.

In our study, when examining divisions of views related to factors which urge the physically handicapped sporters to badminton sport, it was seen that the trainer in close environment was effective in the first level. Alibaz and his colluages determined in their study that the tranier was effective highly in starting of taekwondo, karate and kick-box sporters to this sport, and it supports our study. But in the studies which were done with different sample groups in literature, the most effective factor in urging to sport was mother, it is seen that the results contrary to our study revealed [4,5,6,8,13,16,18,22]. It is thought that this is because parents, who have physically handicapped individual, behave extremely protector and do not have essential confidence and information for urging their child to sport.

In our study, it was seen that effects of friend, peer group and environment in which he/she lives in tending to sport are important. While Salman and Sunay [18] has found effects of friend and environment high as result of the study they did, it is claimed that while effect of the trainer in close environment is at second rank in the study Sunay and Saraçoğlu [13] did, friend and peer group is third order of importance. And also, in our study, it was determined that effects of parents, sibling and pyscial education teachers in urging to badminton sport were at low level. Results of the study Bavlı [17] and Akçay [15] did supports our study.

In our study, it was seen that effect of media organs in starting to sport was not much. Result of the study which Salman and Sunay [18], Bayraktar and Sunay [4], Sunay and Saracoglu [13] did with different sample groups supports our study. It is known that in mass media, badminton and other sports branches, except for futbol and a few sports branches, are not taken on interests adequately. Inadequancies are seen in social lifes of the physically handicapped compared to individuals showing normal development. That's why, it is thought that press factor can provide important contributions for tending of the physically handicapped to sport.

As a result of our study, physical education teacher was not seen to be much effective in starting of sporters to badminton sport. Based on this result, it was concluded that introduction of the physically handicapped with badminton sport did not occur during school education. However, Bayraktar and Sunay [4] claim that in the first level, physical education teacher has effect in urging to sport in volleyball branch at elite level, and Şimşek and Gokdemir [10] suggest that in the first level in tending of high school students to athleticism, physical education teacher has effect in urging to sport. Based on these results, it can be said that in different sports branches, effects of physical education teacher are different in urgint to sport and this is due to information and experiences of physical education teacher.

In our study, when examining divisions of the reasons for playing badminton sport, it was seen that to love badminton sport was so effective. The studies in literature also supports our study [1,4,5,18,22]. It can be said that the sport done by loving brings continuity and success with itself. It was observed that to delight in earning success was quite effective in being interest in badminton sport. That every success is a big resource of motivation for sporters and is known by society reinforces competitor identity of sporters. Furthermore, in our study, it was seen that effect of being healthy by playing badminton sport in being interested in badminton sport also was so effective. And it is supported with the study Bayraktar and Sunay [4] did. Sporters' being healthy by doing sport, their keeping fit, their having a durable body and their making philosophy of lifelong sport a unchangable activity of life increase life quality of physically handicapped individuals.

In our study, when examining divisions of opinions related to expectations of sporters from badminton sport, it was seen that being a national team player had important role and most of sporters wanted to be a national team player and represent the country by wearing national team uniform. This result is supported with the studies done in different branches [14,18].

In our study, a significant difference between press(media organs, television channels) and other factors(physical education teacher, school sport complex and materials, trainer) in urging sporters to badminton sport was seen ($p<0.05$). And also, significant difference between press and other factors and mother education level was found ($p<0.05$).

Kılınç and Kumartaşli [11] claim that education level of family is influential in handicapped individuals' doing sport. In the study Kotan and his colluages [7] did with primary school children, it is suggested that education level of family has effect on doing sport of child. In the study Yucel and his colluages [13] did, it is stated that some factors such as place, parents education, level of income, diet habits etc. are effective in preferring sports branches. These studies support our study. All of literature studies that we examined includes sporters showing normal development. However, because our study includes physically handicapped sporters, inadequancies of the studies related to this field limited our comparison chance.

As a result of our study, it was seen that effects of the trainer in close environment, friend, peer group and environment where he/she lives in tending to sport were important in urging physically handicapped in Turkey to badminton sport. effects of parents, siblings and physical education teacher in urging to badminton sport was seen to be at low level. When examinin reasons for playing the sport, to like badminton sport, to delight in earning success, to healthy by playing badminton sport were seen to be important. When examining expectations from badminton sport, in the first degree, there were to be chosen for national team, to be a national sporter, to be healthy, to keep healthy, to be a good sporter and to earn living through sports. It is thought that raising awareness of society will influnce sports life of individuals with special necessity in a positive way and families having individual with special necessity will be effective in urging to sport.

References

1. A. Alibaz, N. Gündüz, M. Şentunay, Spormetre Physical Education and Sport Sciences Journal, **4**, 3 (2006)
2. A. N. İnal, *Phscical Education and Sport Science.* (Nobel Publishing) (2003).
3. A. S. Yücel, B. Kılıç, M. Korkmaz, K. Göral, International Refereed, Academic, Sport, Health and Medicine Sciences Journal, **5**, 14 (2015).
4. B. Bayraktar, H. Sunay, Spormetre Physical Education and Sport Sciences Journal, **5**, 2 (2007)
5. B. Ölçücü, G. Erdil, Ö. Bostancı, A. Canikli, A. Aybek, Journal of Sports and Performance Researches, **3**, 2 (2012)
6. B. Ölçüçü, Ş. Özen, M. Altınkök, International Turkish Sciences Journal, October (2014)
7. C. Kotan, G. Hergüner, C. Yaman, Nigde University Journal of Physical Education and Sport Sciences ,**3**, 1 (2009)
8. D. K. Arpa, Master's Thesis at Graduate School of Health Sciences, Haliç University, (2014)
9. D. S. Özer, *Engelliler için beden eğitimi ve spor.* (Nobel, 4th press) (2013)
10. D. Şimşek, K. Gökdemir, Spormetre Physical Education and Sport Sciences Journal, **4**, 3 (2006)
11. F. Kılınç, M. Kumartaşlı, 1st International Congress on Physical Education and Sport at Physically Handicapped, (2011)
12. H. Kayihan. *Fiziksel Engellilerde rehabilitasyon eğitim ve toplumsal katılım.* N. Baykoç Dönmez (Ed.), *Özel Gereksinimli Çocuklar ve Özel Eğitim içinde.* (p. 244 Eğiten Kitap) (2011)
13. H. Sunay, A. S. Saraçoğlu, Spormetre Physical Education and Sport Sciences Journal, **1**, 1 (2003)
14. M. Binboga, İ. Kılıç, K. Gökdemir, Journal of Sport and Performance Researches, **4**, 2 (2013)
15. N. Ş. Akca, Graduate School of Health Sciences (2012)
16. O. Özbek, E. Şanli, Nigde University Journal of Physical Education and Sport Sciences, 5, 3 (2011)
17. Ö. Bavlı, Nigde University Journal of Physical Education and Sport Sciences, **3**, 3 (2009)
18. Ö. Salman, H. Sunay, Spormetre Physical Education and Sport Sciences Journal, **10**, 1 (2012)
19. R. Kale, E. Erşan, *Beden eğitimi ve spor bilimlerine giriş.* (Printing of Karadeniz Technical University). (2003)
20. R.C. Memedov, R. Kale, *Uçan Tüytop Badminton*, (1994)
21. Ü. Tazegül, 2nt International Congress on Physical Education and Sport at Physically Handicapped, (2014)
22. Y. Yıldırım, H. Sunay, Spormetre Physical Education and Sport Sciences Journal, **7**, 3 (2009)

Evaluation of attitudes of university students for handicapped individuals

Zekiye Özkan[1a] , Mustafa Atlı[1], and Ersin Arslan[1]

[1]School of Physical Education and Sports, Yuzuncu Yil University, 65040 Van, Turkey

Abstract. Education has an important role in humans' behaviours. Undergraduate education has headed among factors that influence maturation period before vocational lifes of individuals. The purpose of this study is to determine whether attitudes of university students for handicapped individuals differ according to some variables. This study which was carried out in screening model was done with 1167 people including 646 females 521 males who maintain their education at faculties taking initial teacher training in 2016 spring term at Yuzuncu Yil University. As data collection tool, Attitude Scale for Being Educated of Handicapped Individuals and Personal Information Form, which was developed by Kosterilioglu [12], was used. As statistical method, Duncan's multiple range test was used in determining different groups following one-wat analysis of variance. Among these variables, pearson coefficients of correlation were calculated separately in groups in determining relation. In determining relationship between groups and categorical variables , chi square test was used. In calculations, value of p was taken as 0,05 and SPSS statistic program was used for calculations. While point average of attitudes of male students , who maintain their educations at Yuzuncu Yil University, for handicapped people was ascertained as 54.27±23.54, point average of attitudes of female students was determined as 55.86±26.34. A significant difference between male and female students according to gender variable was not seen in attitudes for being educated of handicapped individuals (P>0,05). It was observed that attitudes for being educated of handicapped individuals in starting and end of undergraduate term were higher than intermediate classes (P<0,01). Although a significant difference in kind of high schools from which students graduated was not seen, attitudes of graduates from science and sport high schools were found higher than graduates from other high schools. Those of students who has low and intermediate academic success were found more significant and different than those of students who has high success. (P<0,01). Whereas a significant difference between students, who took lessons related to education of handicappeds and the students who did not take those lessons during education period was not seen, attitudes of those who took the lesson were found higher. A significant difference was found in attitudes of those who took Handicapped and Sport lecture among

[a] Corresponding author: zekiyeozkan06@hotmail.com

lessons learned in comparison to those who took other lectures (P<0,01). Attitudes of those who do not use social media were found more significant and higher (P<0,05). It is thought that addition of practice along with theoretical lectures for individuals with special needs during university education and including public service ads related to handicappeds in social media will make a significant contribution to vocational experiences of teacher candidates.
Keywords: Attitudes for Handicapped, Sport, Academic Success

1 Introduction

Training activities carried out for handicapped have become important in recent years. They have become quite effective in educations of individuals with special needs thanks to growth of sensitiveness towards the handicapped at government policy and provided facilities. Accumulations gained during university education have become effective in Professional competency.

Educations of handicapped children in Turkey have been secured with laws especially Constitution [18]. Students with special needs need to have an intense training by starting from early childhood and being suited for their needs. Education and training services offered to individuals with special needs in our country are becoming different day-by-day, and in the direction of this differentiation, they are flourishing. Individuals with special needs have participated in training activities at special training classes, at business college and in inclusive environment with their peers showing normal development [20]. When field definition is examined at the Ministry of Education's regulations for special training services, special training is defined as the education which is maintained suitable environments resting on personnels trained peculiarly for meeting education and social needs of individuals with special needs, features of individuals with special needs in all areas of development with enhanced training programmes and methods and sufficiencies of individuals with special needs in the academic disciplinary fields [17]. According to definitions of World Health Organisation, disability is a status in which roles expected from person are restricted or are not performed due to a defect or handicap based on age, gender, social and cultural factors [2]. Individuals who have needs in terms of education experiences are in need of individualized education programs for maximisation of their education performances [19]. In the environment in which we live, the most fundamental and permanent barriers in front of handicapped and disability are attitudes created and lived in social extent.

Attitude functions as protector of self like a defence mechanism. In other words, It has structure that protects personality of individual and is supposed to prevent any threats against his/her basic values. Therefore, naturally, individual tends to develop the attitudes protecting his/her personality. Individual can develop the attitudes providing for expressing himsef/herself in terms of self-values and perceiving as he/she wants to see. Attitudes doing this duty complete self identity of individual and can strengthen it [11]. In undergraduate education period, development of our attitudes healthily and positively has an important position in terms of professional competency. Acquirements that teacher candidates gain during education not only contribute to professional competency and also increase education quality of disadvantageous groups.

One of the occupational groups having an important position in formation of these attitudes is teachership. Attitudes of teachers have effects on handicapped individuals attitudes that occur between childhood and maturity of individuals and then they carry to work lifen [14]. Attitudes of individuals working at educational institutions are seen important in this point.

2 Method

2.1 The purpose of the study

The purpose of this study is to research attitudes of teacher candidates, who took lessons related to education of handicappeds and who did not take those lessons during education period, for education of handicapped individuals

2.2 The problem of the study

The purpose of this study is to determine whether attitudes of teacher candidates, who took lessons related to education of handicappeds and who did not take those lessons during education period, for education of handicapped individuals change according to some demographical variables or not.

2.3 Data collection tool

As data collection tool, Attitude Scale for Being Educated of Handicapped Individuals and Personal Information Form, which was developed by Kosterilioglu [12], was used.

2.4 Participants

This study which was carried out in screening model was done with 1167 people including 646 females 521 males who maintain their education at faculties taking initial teacher training in 2016 spring term at Yuzuncu Yil University.

2.5 Statistical analysis

As statistical method, Duncan's multiple range test was used in determining different groups following one-way analysis of variance. Among these variables, pearson coefficients of correlation were calculated separately in groups in determining relation. In determining relationship between groups and categorical variables, chi square test was used. In calculations, value of p was taken as 0,05 and SPSS statistic program was used for calculations.

3 Findings and interpretation

The purpose of this study is to try to determine attitudes of teacher candidates, who took lessons related to education of handicappeds and who did not take those lessons during education period, for education of handicapped individuals according to some demographical variables

Table 1. Gender

Gender of Variables	X±SD	P
Male	54.27± 23.54	0,282
Female	55.86 ± 26.34	

A significant difference between male and female students according to gender variable was not seen in attitudes for being educated of handicapped individuals (P>0,05).

Table 2. Academic success and attitude points for being educated of handicapped individuals

Academic Success	X±SD	P
Low	57.34 ± 22.75a	**0.001***
Intermediate	57.01 ± 22.75a	
High	50.71 ± 25.13b	

Those of students who has low and intermediate academic success were found more significant and different that those of students who has high success. (P<0,01).

Table 3. Grades

Grades	X±SD	P
1st Grade	58.76 ± 25.91	**0.001***
2nd Grade	46.48 ± 22.95	
3rd Grade	55.59 ± 24.57	
Grade(4th Grade)	58.03 ± 25.13	

It was found that attitudes for being educated of handicapped individuals in starting and end of undergraduate term were more significant and different intermediate classes (P<0,01).

Table 4. Name of lecture

Name of lecture	X±SD	P
Handicapped and Sport	71.11 ± 18.86a	**0.001***
Special Training	52.62± 24.93b	
Others	48.15 ± 26.05b	
Not taken	54.37 ± 25.17b	

Whereas a significant difference between students, who took lessons related to education of handicappeds and the students who did not take those lessons during education period was not seen, attitudes of those who took the Handicapped and Sport lesson were found more significant and different. (P<0,01).

Table 5. Reading habit

Reading Habit	X±SD	P
Yes	55.34 ± 25.83	0.300
No	57.05 ± 22.50	
Sometimes	53.79 ± 25.47	

Significant difference was not seen statistically (P>0,05).

Table 6. Following social media

Following social media	X±SD	P
Yes	55.44 ± 25.60ab	**0.36***
No	59.48 ± 20.96a	
Sometimes	52.71 ± 25.36b	

Attitudes of those who do not use social media were found more significant and higher(P<0,05).

4 Results and discussion

Education of individuals with special needs is among the important issues that developing societies have dwelled on recently.

Special Training lecture is critical for teacher candidates who have undergraduate training at faculties of educations' departments that train teachers out of special training field. Teacher candidates will definitely come across with special students during teaching professions.

Along with increasing of importance given education and training activities, special training gains importance. Students with special needs need to have an intense training by starting from early childhood and being suited for their needs [20].

In our study, whereas a significant difference between students, who took lessons related to education of handicappeds and the students who did not take those lessons during education period was not seen, attitudes of those who took the lesson were found higher. Average of those who took lesson was determined as 56.03±24 and average of those who did not take lessons was ascertained as 54.47±25.28. It supports our result that we found at literature research [22]. Contrary to our study, there are literature studies which state that attitudes of participants were found positive [1, 5, 7, 8, 9, 11]. Alptekin and Batık [16] determined that Special Training lecture affected attitudes of 1st grade students at Deaf or Hard of Hearing Teaching for individuals, who were affected from inadequacy, in a positive way. Melekoglu [13] stated that as result of the study, teacher candidates' acquisition positive attitudes for individuals with special needs and their awareness was positive. Sarı and Bozgeyik [11] point out that generally, teacher candidates who do not take special training lecture have rather negative opinions for handicapped children.

İzci [6] suggests that information and abilities of class teacher candidates about special training and inclusive education are not enough.

Durdukoca [21] points out that teacher candidates who have enough practicums will make important contributions to successfully implementation of programs, which will be prepared for students needing special training, in their work lifes. Tortop et. al. [10] assert that there are differences and mistakes in teacher candidates perception related to "mentally handicapped individual" term due to lack of information of teacher candidates about mentally handicapped individuals and education of mentally handicapped individuals.

It is stated that detailed traineeship of teachers, who change and develop society positively, about disability, being hired of people who are expert about this issue and being performed of regularly information sharing for students about disability can influence attitudes for disability positively [14].

In our study, while point average of males was ascertained as 54.27±23.54, point average of females was found 55.86±26.34. A significant difference between male and female students according to gender variable was not seen in attitudes for being educated of handicapped individuals ($P>0,05$). In the studies which were carried out with different sample groups within the scope of special training in literature, it is seen that gender variable is not influential in attitude points [3, 4, 5, 9, 11, 14, 15].

In our study, although a significant difference in kind of high schools from which students graduated was not seen, attitudes of graduates from science and sport high schools were found higher than graduates from other high schools. In the study done in this field, it is pointed out that difference in attitudes of participants for handicapped individuals according to kind of high school from which they graduated was not seen [8, 14].

In our study, it was determined that reading habit did not affect attitude points ($P>0,05$). Attitudes of students against handicapped individuals according to following publication state that there is no significant difference in scale extents [8].

Attitude points of students who has low and intermediate academic success were found more significant and different than those of students who has high success (P<0,01). In another study that was done in literature, it is asserted that a significant difference in attitudes for inclusive education according to academic success variables was not found [15].

In our study, it was observed that there was no significant difference between those who have handicapped individual in their family and those who do not. While supporting our study [3, 4, 11, 22], a different study states that a significant difference was seen on behalf of teachers candidates who do not have handicapped individual in their environment [15].

Colak and Cetin [14] point out that sense of disability of those who have handicapped individual in their family is higher.

In our study, it was observed that attitudes for being educated of handicapped individuals in starting and end of undergraduate term were higher than intermediate classes (P<0,01). Attitudes of students who do not follow social media were found more significant and higher (P<0,05).

In consequence of the study, that attitude points of those who do not follow social media are high was examined as thought-provoking. Experience and practice is an important issue in teaching profession. It can be said that being taught of lessons related to special training during undergraduate education theoretically is not enough to increase awareness. Evaluation of lessons with practice and theoretical extent during undergraduate education will ease orientating of teacher candidates to the profession, and also will make positive contributions to education of individuals showing normal development as well as individuals with special needs.

References

1. A. Örel, G. Toret, Z. Zerey, Ankara University Faculty of Educational Sciences Journal of Special Education , 5, 1 (2004)
2. D. S. Özer, *Engelliler için beden eğitimi ve spor*. Nobel.4th press. (2013)
3. D. Yaralı, Erzincan University Journal of Faculty of Educational Sciences, **17**, 2 (2015).
4. D. Yaralı, Pamukkale University Journal of Institute of Social Sciences, **24**, (2016).
5. E. Altıntaş, S. Şengül, e-Kafkas Educational Research Journal, **1**, 3 (2014)
6. E. İzci, Electronic Journal of Social Sciences, **4**, 14 (2005).
7. F. Gürsel, Hacettepe University Journal of Faculty of Education, 31(2006)
8. F. Şahin, B. Güldenoğlu, Amasya University Journal of Faculty of Education, **2**; 1 **(2013)**
9. H. Bek, H. Gülveren, A. Başer, Uşak University Journal of Social Sciences, **2**, 2 (2009)
10. H. S. Tortop, B. Kandemir, Ö. E. Kaya, F. Demir, Abant İzzet Baysal University Journal of Faculty of Education, 15, (2015)
11. H. Sarı, H. Bozgeyik, Selçuk University Journal of Institute of Social Sciences, **9**, 183-204 (2003).
12. İ. Kösterelioglu, Ahi Evran University Journal of Faculty of Education, **14**, 3 (2013)
13. M. A. Melekoglu, Theory and Educational Sciences, **13**, 2 (2013)
14. M. Çolak, C. Çetin, C. Dokuz Eylül Univeristy Journal of Faculty of Economics and Administrative Sciences, **29**, 1 (2014).
15. N. Göçmen. M. Bozkurt, M.Ç Aydın. e-Kafkas Educational Research Journal, **4**, 1 (2017).
16. S. Alptekin, M. V. Batık, International Journal of Educational Research, **4**, 4 (2013)

DOI: 10.1051/shsconf/20173701046

17. S. Çuhadar, *Özel Eğitim Süreci.* S. Vuran (Ed.), Özel Eğitim içinde (p 7). Ankara: Maya Academy. (2013).
18. S. Eripek, Ankara University Faculty of Educational Sciences Journal of Special Education, **5**, 2 (2004)
19. S. Şahin, H. Yaban, E. Acar, B. Dönmez (Ed.), *Özel Gereksinimli Çocuklar ve Özel Eğitim içinde* (p.71). Ankara: Eğiten Kitap. (2011).
20. S. Talas, F. Kaya, N. Yıldırım, L. Yazıcı, H. Nural et. al. Journal of European Education, **6**, 3, 31-42. (2016).
21. Ş. F. Durdukoca, International Periodical for the Languages, Literature and History of Turkish or Turkic, **10**, 11 (2015)
22. Z. F. Temel, Hacettepe University Journal of Faculty of Education, **18**, (2000)

Effects of in-water and dryland warm-ups on 50-meter freestyle performance in child swimmer

Fatih Kaya[1a], Mustafa Said Erzeybek[2], Bilal Biçer[3], and Tuncay Meral[4]

[1]Faculty of Education, Department of Physical Education and Sports, Erzincan University, Turkey
[2]School of Physical Education and Sports, Dumlupınar University, Turkey
[3]School of Physical Education and Sports, Mustafa Kemal University, Turkey
[4]Erzincan Municipality Sports Club, Erzincan, Turkey

Abstract. In this study, effectiveness of 3 warm-up (WU) modes on 50m free style on child swimmers has been evaluated. In repeated-measures counterbalanced design, 10 male swimmers of a local sports club (10-12 ages) have tried out 50m freestyle after each WU on different days. Each WU took 15 minutes and the intensity of WU has been checked over by Borg's rating of perceived exertion (RPE) 15-point scale. a) no warm-up (NWU): the swimmers sat or laid down for 15 minutes, b) dryland warm-up (DWU): continuous rope-jumping at RPE 12 for 5 minutes, 2 sets 10x15s calisthenics with 15s breathing spaces and continuous rope-jumping at RPE 14 for 5 minutes, c) in-water warm up (SWU): continuous freestyle swimming at RPE 12 for 5 minutes, freestyle swimming with 8x15m maximum performance with 30s breathing spaces and continuous freestyle swimming at RPE 14 for 5 minutes. RPE, stroke count and heart rate (HR) have been evaluated together with the best time in swimming performance. Compared with NWU swimming time post DWU was faster, however the fastest swimming time was achieved post SWU. After NWU swimming RPE was significantly higher. Significant difference could not be found in terms of HR and stroke count. Consequently, SWU is better for swimming performance and DWU can be used when swimming pool is not available.
Keywords: 50-m freestyle, warm-up, child swimmer

1 Introduction

Muscle and inner body temperature are needed to be increased before competition at sportive performance. Increase at body temperature prepares the body before serious competitions. A 1-2 degrees increase on body temperature is important in terms of mechanic and bioenergic efficiency and for this significant temperature increase, at %5-70 of maximum heart rate minimum 10-15 minutes exercise is known to be needed [7]. By

[a] Corresponding author: fkaya@erzincan.edu.tr

means of these thermal effects of warm up (WU), disintegration of oxygen from hemoglobin and myoglobin increases [7, 15], energy generation increases through accelerating enzyme kinetics and substrate use [2, 16], viscosity of running muscles decreases [15, 16], speed of neural transmission and neural receptor sensitivity increases [8, 15], blood flow on active skeletal muscles increases [10, 11, 16] and lipid metabolism increases [2, 9].

Swimming is a branch of sports requiring muscular force and endurance and the winner is determined with only seconds even with split seconds. A good swimming performance is affected not only from exercise, genetic or physical fitness but also from WU which is also agreed as a key element on sportive performance [5]. Swimmers resort to increase their performances via WU just before competition. Even though it is possible to increase body temperature (active and passive) in different activities, in-water WU will probably be much more effective for swimming competition. Specific WU has been indicated to be much more superior than warm ups that are not specific to the branch. This situation enables the competitor's special motor units to work much more efficiently as well as it provides practice effect [14, 15]. By this means, the swimmers get used to dive blocks, strips, return flags and wall surfaces for return. Besides this, dryland WU exercises to warm up, when swimming pool is not available, will make the swimmer much more prepared relatively to no warm up due to the increase at body temperature.

Even though there are studies researching different WU protocols' effects on swimming performance [3, 14, 17] this situation have not been researched enough on child swimmers at competition level.

In this study, activity of three WU modes – in-water warm-up (SWU), dryland warm-up (DWU), and no warm-up (NWU) – on 50 meter (50m) free style swimming performance on child swimmers has been evaluated.

2 Method

In repeated-measures counterbalanced design, 10 child swimmers of a local sports club had 50m freestyle trials after each 3 different WU modes on different days. The reason why 50m swimming performance was chosen, it is the shortest event in a swimming competition. Because, at longer swimming events, the swimmers perform multi-returns during competition and longer swimming durations and longer swimming distances can decrease the effect of WU. In addition to 50m swimming performance, effects of WU have been evaluated on variables such as stroke count, heart rates (HR) and rating of perceived exertion (RPE).

2.1 Subject

10 male athletes between the ages 10-12 having at least 2 years swimming experience and having swimming experiences at official competitions participated in this study voluntarily. The participants and each of their legal representatives read "informed consent forms" and signed them. During the study, the participants were at season-end period and had 3 workouts a week.

In order to provide coherent conditions at trials, the subjects were requested to 1) avoid physical activities every test morning, 2) come to the pool by a vehicle rather than walking or cycling, 3) continue usual diet and sleeping patterns and 4) perform the highest performance at each test.

Besides, they were requested to avoid caffeine and physical activities (not related to swimming practices) at least 24 hours before each session, to avoid heavy food at least 3 hours before each session and not to consume energy drink.

The participants having one of the following factors were excluded from the study: (a) if had a shoulder mutilation in the last 6 months; (b) if had a cardiovascular or respirator problem; (c) if had other chronic diseases restricting to participate in exercises; (d) if had a physical injury or surgical operation which makes the participation to exercise risky.

In order to minimize the errors that can arise in experiment period, one of the researchers got involved in the workouts of the children as their trainer before tests for one week. In this period, the children were comprehended the motions that will be performed in WU protocols and they were provided to be able to comment RPE cards. Also, they were taught to find and count pulse from neck or wrist. At this phase, the children were not informed about the research in detail to prevent practice effects arise at experiment period.

When it came to experiment period, the study design and procedure were explained to the children in detail before test sessions. By showing RPE charts, the RPE numbers were reminded verbally and visually.

Ages, heights and weights of the participants were recorded. Simbo SBS4432 bascule was used for body weight and 1/100s scaled EPSAN electronic chronometer (Multistar EP-69052) for swimming times.

2.2 Experimental procedure

2.2.1 Warm-up modes

The WU protocols, which were previously used by Romney and Nethery [14] were used by remodifying. At counterbalanced design, each subject performed a 50m freestyle trial at maximum effort after each WU protocol. Between each trial period, 48 hours relaxation was given. All testing was done at 8 A.M.

Swimming performance started 3 minutes after the WU completed. 15 minutes WU protocols are as following: 1) No warm-up (NWU): the subjects sat or laid down on an exercise mat for 15 minutes. 2) Dryland warm-up (DWU) : a) RPE= at 12 (fairly light-somewhat hard) continuous rope-jumping for 5 minutes; b) at 5 minutes periods pushups, sit-ups, lunge jump, back hyperextensions, surgical tubing butterfly pulls (2 sets, each exercise 15s, 15s rest in between); c) RPE=at 14 (somewhat hard) continuous rope-jumping for 5 minutes; 3) In-water warm-up (SWU): a) RPE=at 12, 5 minutes continuous freestyle swimming b) 8x15m freestyle sprints for 5 minutes (each at 30s rest intervals and each run at 50m competition speed); and c) RPE=at 14, continuous freestyle swimming for 5 minutes.

In order to determine the intensity of the WU, RPE assessment was carried out at first and last 5 min. sessions of the each WU activity. The intensity of the WU was prescribed with RPE relatively to heart rate and monitored because of the reasons like; high-conductivity of the water effects the signals coming from heart rate monitor, maximum heart rates are 10-13 pulses lower in a minute relatively to exercises like rope jump, maximum heart rates often change by 20 pulses a minute on age mates [12].

2.2.2 50m maximal performance trial

The subjects were allowed to use bonnets and goggles, to sit, to stand, to walk, or to talk as might be done preceding a competitive event. Any motions including warm-up were not allowed behind block. The same lane was assigned to each subject at trials.

Standard starting procedure was used for swimmers climbing dive block: the researcher's voice command (take your mark) after electronic bip sound time was started. The time was stopped when the participant touched swimming wall. During swimming, 2 persons followed each swimmer and 2 chronometers were used for their swimming times. Average of the two chronometers was recorded as the best swimming time.

2.2.3 Rating of perceived exertion

The participants were requested to scale their warm-ups and 50m swimming performances by using Borg's 15 point scale [6]. RPE was determined after warm-up and after 50m swimming performance.

2.2.4 Heart rate

Heart rate was measured by manual palpation method at the wrist or neck. All the participants were familiar with this procedure because they used this method in regular swimming training. The heart rate was measured 30 seconds before the swim trial and immediately after the 50m maximal performance trial. The participants counted their own HR for 15 seconds. Heart rate was reported as beats per minute.

2.2.5 Stroke count

During the 50m maximal performance trial, strokes were counted. However, to minimize error, stroke count was counted in cycles. One cycle was equal to 2 strokes. The cycle started when the first arm of the participant entered the water and it ended when it recovered.

Outdoor environment temperature: 24 C^0
Water Temperature: 26.5 C^0
Ph: 7.4 (ideally 7.2)
Moisture: %20 (rises till %50, adjusted to 20-25 by air-conditioners)
Chlorine: 1.4 (between 1-1.5)
Relative chlorine: 0.02 (between 0.02-0.04)

2.2.6 Statistical analysis

One-way repeated-measures ANOVA was used to analyze the difference in 50m freestyle time trial performance, stroke count, RPE, and HR between the three different WU protocols. Significant was accepted at an $p < 0.05$ level. When a significant F ratio was obtained, a post hoc multiple comparison test was used to determine the location of the significant differences. All data reported as the mean ± SE.

3 Findings

Basic characteristics of the subjects are demonstrated at Table 1.

Table 1. Participants' age, weight, swimming experience, best 50m time, and weekly training distance. Mean (SE)

Characteristic N=10	
Age (yrs)	11.00 (0.21)
Height (cm)	146.20 (2.59)
Weight (kg)	37.75 (2.28)
HR rest (b.min^{-1})	68.80 (2.52)
Yrs. Swimming	2.50 (0.22)
Weekly training (km)	10.70 (1.05)
Best 50m time (s)	41.38 (1.66)

Table 2. Effects of three different warm-ups on variables. Mean (SE)

	NWU	DWU	SWU
50m time (s)	42.78 (1.97)a	41.67 (1.66)b	40.47 (1.62)bc
HR pre 50 ($b.min^{-1}$)	82.40 (2.33)a	113.60 (5.85)b	110.40 (6.65)bc
HR post 50 ($b.min^{-1}$)	134.80 (8.83)	140.00 (9.02)	133.60 (7.30)
WU RPE	7.20 (0.20)a	10.80 (0.77)b	12.00 (0.49)bc
50m RPE	14.90 (0.35)a	14.20 (0.42)b	13.90 (0.31)bc
Stroke count	31.25 (0.92)	31.55 (1.16)	31.50 (0.89)

Means sharing the same subscript are not significantly different from each other

Findings obtained show that there is significant difference among three WU protocols for 50m swimming performance, $F(2,18)=8.547$, $p=0.00$ (Table 2). When post hoc comparisons were compared with NWU (42.78s), it revealed that average 50m swimming time (41.67s) after DWU is significantly better ($p=0.03$), however the best swimming time was revealed to be achieved after SWU (40.47s), ($p=0.01$, Figure 1).

Furthermore, RPE scores after WU and after swimming were significantly different [respectively $F(2,18)=24.850$, $p=0.00$; $F(2,18)=5.427$, $p=0.01$, Table 2]. Post hoc comparisons showed that after warm-up RPE scores are higher at DWU (10.80=60% near to effort) and at SWU (12.00=65% effort), (respectively $p=0.01$; $p=0.00$). In addition to this, RPE scores after NWU (14.90=80% near to effort) are significantly higher respectively to both WU protocols (respectively $p=0.03$; $p=0.03$).

There was significant difference at HR before swimming, $F(2, 18) = 11.258$, $p=0.00$. Compared with NWU, while being higher at DWU ($p=0.01$) and SWU ($p=0.02$), significant difference could not be found for after swimming HR and stroke counts [respectively $F(2,18)=0.717$, $p=0.50$; $F(2,18)=0.199$, $p=0.82$, Table 2].

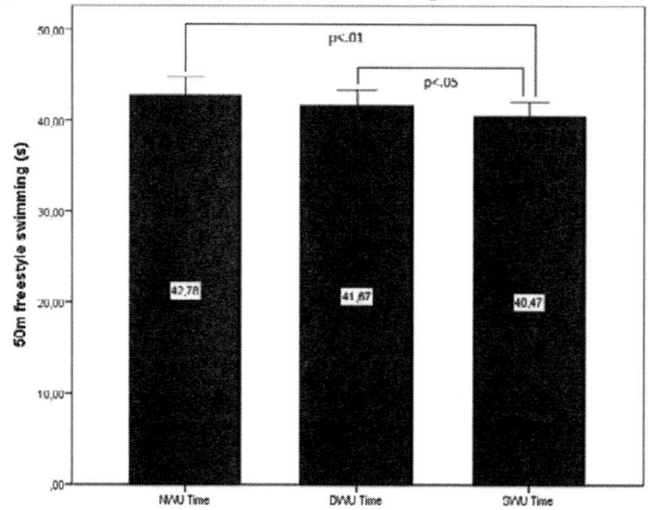

Fig. 1. Mean performance times for 50m freestyle following no warm-up, dryland warm up, and in-water warm up (+/-1 SE).

4 Discussion

The outcomes obtained in this study show that the best 50m swimming time has been achieved after in-water WU. Besides this, when compared with NWU, after DWU 50m swimming performance showed significantly better result. These findings have showed the activity of WU's ergogenic value both theoretically and practically again. With WU; body temperature, blood flow, respiratory rate, heart rate and flexibility of the needed muscles increase [10]. Moderate and not lesser than 5 minutes WU has also been reported to increase muscle and body temperature [1, 4, 18]. Intensity and duration of the in-water and dryland WU protocols used in this study mean to be sufficient to increase muscle and body temperature (despite the body temperature wasn't measured directly). As we have already stated, maximum %65-70 MUSCLE and at least 10-15 minutes exercise are necessary in order to increase significant body temperature [7]

Similar results were achieved in Romney et al. [14] study, we used their WU protocols by remodifying, and they explained this with a number of physiological alterations: decrease of tissue resistance with the systemic increase and increase in tissue heat, facilitation in transportation and distribution of oxygen, increase of usability and energy generation of substrate, getting ready of cardiorespiratory system. However in the above-mentioned study, increase in swimming performance after dryland WU was accepted significant by researchers although it wasn't and they stated dryland WU can be sufficient too for physiological preparation when swimming pool is not available. A significant point here is; the participants were in average 20 age group and evaluated swimming distance is 100 yard (91.44m).

The fact that in-water WU is much more effective can be explained with a few reasons. First of all, in-water WU protocol is well-designed to increase body temperature. Secondly, in-water WU revealed the practice effect of specific WU. Environmental adaptation and neuromuscular facilitation are stated to positively effected by specific to skill WU [10]. By this means, the athletes get used to dive blocks, strips, return flags and wall surfaces during returns. Also in this study, the participants regularly practiced in the swimming pool in which the tests were carried out and they were accustomed to environmental conditions.

Besides, in limited availability of studies that research swimming performance by using different WU protocols, mostly WU activities based upon short/long distance or low/high intensity swimming have been investigated and the outcomes in these studies have been found contradictory to the evidences on usefulness of WU [5, 10, 13]. Reasons like sample structures and wide age variable have been demonstrated as the basis of contradiction. Moreover, low intensity WU have been stated not to increase body temperature sufficiently and high intensity WU to cause fatigue [3].

Another finding achieved is RPE after NWU is significantly higher. This finding shows that the participants much more slog when they perform swimming performance without WU. 14.90 RPE score means the participants make about %80 effort. This condition is normal and it is accepted as an ordinary condition likely to be encountered when the body is not ready for performance. Thusly RPE scores are slightly lower in both WU protocols and the scores show that they feel the effort almost %70-75.

An interesting finding achieved from this study that there wasn't a difference between swimming protocols in terms of HR. Eventhough the participants felt the swimming trial after NWU compelling in terms of RPE, there wasn't a difference in terms of HR. This finding is contradictory with the previous study results. In previous studies, rising HR results were achieved when after swimming performance compared with no WU. Bishop [4] stated that a rise can happen at HR based upon after WU muscle and core temperature and rising VO2 [4]. In addition to this, after low and high intensity swimming WU protocols, high HR and high VO2 were stated [13]. However, when after swimming RPE scores analyzed, RPE score felt at NWU was close to %80 effort while the difficulty level felt after two WU protocols was about %70/75 effort. Although RPE scores differentiate significantly after swimming, difficulty level felt indeed is almost similar at every three protocols. From this point, the fact that rising HR scores are similar, can be taken normally.

Similarly, there wasn't a significant difference at stroke counts between WU protocols. This finding promotes the study results by Balilionis et al. [3] who didn't find difference at stroke counts between 50m and 200-m swimming performances [3-18]. In this study, it's seen that the swimmers swim the same distance with similar stroke counts. In addition to this, it is possible to achieve difference at trials in which swimming distance is longer.

Consequently; in water warm-up has come up with a better result at achieving the best 50m freestyle swimming performance. On the other hand, it can be said that dryland warm-ups can be used for physiological preparation when swimming pool is not available.

References

1. Arnett, MG. Effects of prolonged and reduced warm-ups on diurnal variation in body temperature and swim performance. J Strength Cond Res **16**, 256-261, (2002).
2. Åstrand, P.O., and K. Rodahl. *Textbook of work physiology*: New York: McGraw-Hill, (1986).
3. Balilionis, G., Nepocatych, S., Ellis, C. M., Richardson, M. T., Neggers, Y. H., & Bishop, P. A. Effects of different types of warm-up on swimming performance, reaction time, and dive distance. J Strength Cond Res, **26**(12), 3297-3303, (2012).
4. Bishop, D. Warm-up II. Performance changes following active warm-up and how to structure the warm up. Sports Med **33**,483-498, (2003).
5. Bobo, M. The effect of selected types of warm-up on swimming performance. Int Sports J., **3**, 37-43, (1999).
6. Borg, G. Perceived exertion: A note bon ''history'' and methods. Med Sci Sports **5**, 90-93, (1972).
7. DeVries, H.A. *Physiology of exercise for physical education and athletics*, Wm.C.Brown Company, (1974).
8. Franks, D. *Physical warm-up. In: Ergogenic Aids in Sport.* Melvin H. Williams (Ed.), Human Kinetics, Champaign, 340-375, (1980.),
9. Hetzler, Ronald K., et al. "Effect of warm-up on plasma free fatty acid responses and substrate utilization during submaximal exercise." Research Quarterly for Exercise and Sport **57**(3), 223-228, (1986).
10. King, A. The relative effects of various warm-up procedures on 50 meter times of trained, competitive swimmers. J Phys Educ **7**, 22-24, (1979).
11. Martin, BRUCE J., et al. "Effect of warm-up on metabolic responses to strenuous exercise." Medicine and science in sports 7(2), 146-149, (1974).
12. McArdle, W. D., Katch, F. I., & Katch, V. L. *Exercise physiology: nutrition, energy, and human performance*. Lippincott Williams & Wilkins, (2010).
13. Mitchell, JB and Huston, JS. The effect of high- and low-intensity warm-up on the physiological responses to a standardized swim and tethered swimming performance. J Sports Sci **11**, 159-165, (1993).
14. Romney, Neil Conrad, and V. M. Nethery. "The effects of swimming and dryland warm-ups on 100-yard freestyle performance in collegiate swimmers." J Swim Res **9**: 5-9, (1993).
15. Shellock, F.G. Physiological benefits of warm-up, Phys. And Sports Med. Oct., 135-139, (1983).
16. Watson, A. W. S. *Physical fitness and athletic performance. A guide for students, Athletes, and Coaches*. London: Longman, (1983).
17. Wilson, E. E., McKeever, T. M., Lobb, C., Sherriff, T., Gupta, L., Hearson, G., & Shaw, D. E. Respiratory muscle specific warm-up and elite swimming performance. Br J Sports Med, bjsports, (2013).
18. Zochowski, T, Johnson, E, and Sleivert, GG. Effects of varying post warm-up recovery time on 200-m time-trial swim performance. Int J Sports Physiol Perform **2**, 201-211, (2007).

The effect of awareness raising about using cognitive strategies in foreign language teaching on students' development of reading comprehension skills

Gülper Güvenç[1a]

[1]TOBB University of Economics and Technology, Ankara, 06560, Turkey

Abstract. The purpose of this study is to analyze the development of students' reading comprehension skills about using cognitive strategies in foreign language teaching by means of awareness raising activities. To this end, the research was conducted for 11 weeks with 77 students studying in an English preparatory school program. The experimental group was exposed to a training which is based on awareness raising activities about using cognitive strategies. A pre-test and a post-test were designed for 2 experimental and 2 control groups with random sampling, and then the statistical differences were tested based on the scores of the both groups in terms of significance. Moreover, the study aims to determine the views of the participants about the strategy training. The results show that there was a significant difference between the pre-test and post-test scores of the experimental group in terms of their achievement in reading skill, and the post-test scores of the both experimental group and control group were in favor of the experimental group. Also, it has also found that the experiment had a positive impact on the participants.
Keywords: reading comprehension; reading strategies, cognitive strategies, language learning strategies

1 Introduction

Language teaching is based on four skills which are reading, writing, listening and speaking, and structure. Among these four skills, reading is one of the most significant communication and perception skills. Demirel [5] defines reading as the inference from written symbols through the collaborative activity of cognitive behavior with psychomotor skills. In particular, one focus of research in the area of EFL is concerned with applying language learning strategies which is considered to have an influence on the process of improving reading skill. In this context, it is fundamental to know and apply various strategies, techniques and methods to enable students to improve their progress in

[a] Corresponding author: gulperguvenc@hotmail.com

DOI: 10.1051/shsconf/20173701048

acquiring, storing, retaining, and using information in reading skill. Thus, the current study has been conducted within the scope of language strategy research in reading contexts.

According to Oxford [11], one of the first to carry out research in this area, "learning strategies are specific actions taken by the learner to make learning easier, faster, more enjoyable, more self-directed, more effective, and more transferrable to new situations". What turns a reading activity into a learning strategy is practicing it consciously. Although there are a number of studies about improving reading comprehension skill [1, 6, 7, 8, 9, 13, 16, 17 and 19] the potential strategies to be used in reading lessons are generally neglected or are not applied in a proper way. The term language strategy has been emphasized by various researchers. Rubin [15] state that learning strategies are "... any sets of operations, steps, plans, routines used by the learner to facilitate the obtaining, storage, retrieval, and use of information." Richards and Platt [14] define learning strategies as "intentional behavior and thoughts used by learners during learning to better help them understand, learn, or remember new information."

While language learning strategies were categorized in several ways by various researchers [10,15], Oxford [11] took this process a step further. In her Strategies Inventory for Language Learning (SILL) she highlighted six categories namely: Memory strategies (e.g., grouping, representing sounds in memory), cognitive strategies (e.g., repeating, analyzing, getting the idea quickly and taking notes), compensation strategies (e.g., switching to the mother tongue, using other clues), metacognitive strategies (e.g., linking new information with already known one, self-monitoring), affective strategies (lowering anxiety by use of music, encouraging oneself and discussing feelings with others) and social strategies (asking for clarification, cooperating with others and developing cultural understanding). The present study has been conducted based on Oxford's taxonomy since it is comprehensive, detailed and systematic [18]. Besides, it links with each of the four language skills of listening, reading, speaking and writing, and it is reliability and validity is remarkable across many cultural groups [12].

It is anticipated that the higher the students' awareness about strategy usage, the better they choose strategies that fit their learning style. Therefore, these strategies become a useful instrument for active, conscious and purposeful self-regulation of learning. As all universities have a different level and program of English preparatory class education, it is especially compelling for the students who are supposed to take a test like TOEFL, which necessitates a higher level of knowledge in English, and who have difficulty in concentrating on quite long reading passages at the end of preparatory school. Therefore, cognitive strategies are like a tactic for students especially in reading passages having multiple choice questions. It is remarkable that there are many studies about foreign language education, reading comprehension skill, teaching methods together with learning strategies, yet very few researches are held about reading comprehension and strategy usage, especially the cognitive strategy group. As Oxford [11] states "Cognitive strategies are typically found to be the most popular strategies with language learners". They are based on mental processes about acquiring and processing data.

Based on the research discussed above, language learning strategies, especially cognitive strategies, appear to be a significant issue related to ELT learners' reading skill. Hence, the purpose of this study is to analyze the development of students' reading comprehension skills about using cognitive strategies in the area of EFL by means of awareness raising activities. In this sense, this study can be beneficial for contributing to the foreign language teaching methods as well as for the English instructors. For this purpose, the following questions were addressed in the current research:

1. Is there a significant difference between the comparison of pretest and posttest scores of both experimental and control groups?

DOI: 10.1051/shsconf/20173701048

2. Is there a significant difference between posttest scores of both experimental and control groups?
3. What is the overall opinion of the experimental group about the cognitive strategy training program?

2 Method

In this study, both qualitative and quantitative methods, in other words mixed methods, were used. The randomized pre-test and post-test control group model was designed for the experimental research. The pre-test and post-test were used for 2 experimental and 2 control groups, and then after the training, the statistical differences were tested based on the test scores of the both groups. Before the main study, a pre-study was conducted in order to justify the problem with the same research questions and method, but with some limitations in terms of the materials and the schedule.

2.1 Data collection procedure

In order to collect information, an Individual Background Questionnaire (IBQ) and "Strategy Inventory for Language Learning (SILL)", which was developed by Oxford [11] and adopted to Turkish by Cesur and Fer [2], were used to identify the frequency of use of language strategies of the attendants and to prepare the training program accordingly. As the focus was cognitive strategies, 14 items of this group were chosen as an instrument. It appears that SILL is the 'most often used strategy scale around the world', and the only language learning strategy instrument that has been checked for reliability and validity in multiple ways [12]. After the 20-multiple-choice-question pre-test was applied, a presentation of the strategies was made by the researcher in order to inform the experimental group about learning strategies in general. The cognitive strategies training program was carried out during students' regular Reading & Writing classes for 11 weeks, 1 or 2 lessons for each, according to the flow of the weekly program with readily-prepared materials for activities. Its purpose is to raise awareness with reading texts and activities. After the post-test, the feedback of the participants about the training of cognitive strategies were also collected and the responses were investigated.

As to the students' some sample answers to SILL, which was applied before the strategy program, it has been found that experimental group does not tend to skim first before reading the whole text. The highest rate to this item was "somewhat true" (35%). The item which has the highest rate (39%) for "always or almost always true" is "I watch English language TV shows spoken in English or go to movies spoken in English", which indicates that students like real life settings. This item has a similar and the highest percentage (44%) in the control group, as well. In the control group the item that follows this one with the percentage of 28% is "I look for words in my own language that are similar to new words in English". That is to say, students are prone to learning a word with a Turkish definition instead of an English definition or synonym.

2.2 Participants

The research group was composed of 77 students (CEFR B1-B2) attending the preparatory class in Department of Foreign Languages at TOBB Economics and Technology University (TOBB ETU DFL) in Ankara in 2015-2016 Academic Year. There were 41 females and 36 males. When the demographical information in the Individual Background Questionnaire (IBQ) was analyzed, it was found out that most of the students graduated from Anatolian

High Schools both in the experimental and control groups. All students were between 18-25 ages. Besides, most of the students stated that they have been learning English for 6-10 years (experimental group 66%, control group 50%). The subjects were also asked to report on their staying in a foreign country, and they expressed that only 7 (17%) out of 41 students in the experimental group and 8 (22%) out of 36 students in the control group answered "yes" to this question. Neither the students in the experimental group nor in the control group studied in a preparatory school in a different university before. As a measure to language self-efficacy, the students were asked to rate themselves on a scale as poor, fair and good to indicate how successful they perceived themselves to be in English. Most of them reported that their level is average (fair, experimental group 85%; fair, control group 69%).

2.3 Data analysis

Data elicited from the pre-test and post-test scores were analyzed using SPSS 20. The statistical analysis between the achievement scores of experimental and control groups was carried out through paired t-test technique in order to find out if there is a significant difference. P-value of <0.05 was considered statistically significant.

3 Results and discussion

Results of the first question: Is there a significant difference between the comparison of pretest and posttest scores of both experimental and control groups?

On the basis of the pre-test and post-test scores of both experimental and control groups, Table 1 presents statistical analysis of paired samples t-test results.

Table 1. Paired sample t-test results of the pretest and posttest scores

		N	Mean	Std. Dev.	df	t	P
Experimental Group	B17 pretest-posttest	21	2,523	2,112	20	5,475	0,000
	B18 pretest-posttest	20	1,550	1,538	19	4,507	0,000
Control Group	B12 pretest-posttest	15	1,400	1,882	14	2,881	0,012
	B15 pretest-posttest	21	1,571	4,272	20	1,685	0,107

$p<.05$

According to the results, the experimental group (B17 and B18) resulted in a significant increase after the training program. On the other hand, p score for the control group B12 is 0.012, which means this is a significant increase, too. However, its mean score is 1,400 which means it is still lower than the experimental groups. Also, p score for other control group is 0,107 and there isn't any significant increase. When the means are compared, more specifically, the emerging picture is that there were significant differences between in favor of the students in the experimental group.

Results of the second question: Is there a significant difference between posttest scores of both experimental and control groups?

As to the second question of the study, paired sample t-test was used to compare the post-test scores of the experimental and control groups.

Table 2. Paired sample t-test results of the posttest scores

	S	M	Std. Dev.	df	t	P
Post test scores of experimental and control group	42	2,000	3,781	20	2,424	0,025

$p<.05$

Two experimental and two control groups were analyzed together within themselves. The results indicated that p score is 0,025 as is seen and according to Cohen's standard, this is a large effect. Apart from this, experimental group's posttest mean score is 16 out of 20, yet control group's posttest mean score is 14 out of 20.

Results of the third question: What is the overall opinion of the experimental group about the cognitive strategy training program?

When the students' feedback was evaluated, it was concluded that the training about cognitive strategies had a positive impact on the participants and overall, the students were pleased with the strategy training program. Based on the comments, we can deduce that they mostly benefited from skimming, scanning analyzing expressions. They stated that these strategies were useful not only in developing their reading skill, but also in exams. Actually, taking into account that most reading passages include questions regarding main idea and details, the students who answer these questions make use of skimming and scanning. However, the experimental group's advantage is being aware of the strategy usage and therefore, making out more easily and quickly. Some samples from students' comments are as follows (The statements in the quotation marks are direct translations of the students' comments):

"Thanks to these techniques, my reading scores have increased considerably." (P1)

"Dividing the word into pieces, finding its root and part of speech help me to understand sentences more easily. I learned to guess the meaning of a word without looking up a dictionary." (P2)

"We used to read texts just like reading a book, but when we learned the strategies this term, we made a difference." (P3)

"I can get the meaning more easily now. I wish I could practice more and improve my reading." (P4)

4 Conclusions and suggestions

The results of this study reveal that awareness raising activities about cognitive strategies have an impact on TOBB ETU DFL students' development of reading comprehension skills in foreign language teaching. The results regarding the first research question indicate that there is a significant difference in the comparison of the pretest and posttest scores of the group which raised awareness about cognitive strategies in reading skill as opposed to the group which was not exposed to any training. As might be expected, the findings obtained from this study are consistent with the general results of previous language learning strategy studies. A previous research conducted by Çetinkaya [4] presents that repeating strategy is the third out of 20 strategies in terms of frequency of the usage by the participants. Apart from that, guessing the meaning, which is similar to analyzing expressions, rank eight in the experiment.

Regarding the second research question, it is seen that there is a large effect on behalf of the experimental group, as well. Based upon these findings we can deduce the strategy training program has affected the students positively. In another research where cognitive strategies were studied, Chun Ou [3] searched for the effect of summarizing strategy on Taiwanese students who just started learning English. It was concluded that summarizing has an effect on improving reading comprehension. Apart from answering detail questions, it also developed students' getting the main idea and inference skills. Therefore, these findings are in concordance with our claim, too.

Finally, according to the third question of the study, the participants' viewpoints were positive regarding the experiment. Their feedback includes getting more efficiency in the reading process, saving on time and following the text more easily. Taking these points into consideration, it can be concluded that incentive and efficient reading activities, getting some tactics to analyze the texts and enjoying their own learning affected the students' reading comprehension skills constructively.

The most significant suggestion regarding the findings of the study is the need to incorporate the strategies into the curriculum and explicitly teaching students how to make use of the strategies for meeting their individual language needs. In doing so, these results may be used for pedagogical purposes with respect to English language learning in Turkey. As strategy usage affects students' participation, interest and learning processes positively, it could be beneficial to encourage them to use the same strategy in a variety of texts. Alternatively, it is worth mentioning that focusing on other skills (listening, writing etc.) by using the same strategy group could be another study area. I can also be advisable to analyze the students' mistakes in detail and focus on the strategies where most errors are targeted.

References

1. Alyas, A. Metacognitive Strategies to Foster Learner Autonomy in EFL Reading. (Master's Thesis, Hacettepe University/Institute of Educational Sciences, Ankara)., (2011).
2. Cesur, M. O. & Fer, S. Dil Öğrenme Stratejileri Envanterinin Geçerlik ve Güvenirlik Çalışması Nedir? Yüzüncü Yıl Üniversitesi, Eğitim Fakültesi Dergisi, **IV**, II, 49-74., (2007).
3. Chun Ou, F. The Effects of the Summarization Strategy on Reading Comprehension of non-Proficient Taiwanese University EFL Learners. (Phd Thesis, The University of Kansas)., (2006). http://sunzi.lib.hku.hk/ER/detail/hkul/5000363.
4. Çetinkaya, G. Anadilinde ve Yabancı Dilde Okuma Sürecine Yönelik Gözlemler: Okuma-Anlama Stratejileri Üzerine Uygulamalı Bir Çalışma. (Master's Thesis, Ankara University/Institute of Social Sciences)., (2004).
5. Demirel, Ö. *Yabancı Dil Öğretimi.* Ankara: Pegem Yayıncılık. (2012).
6. Ghasemi, Y. Cognitive and Metacognitive Strategies Employed by Iranian and Turkish EFL Learners. (Phd Thesis, Hacettepe University/Institute of Social Sciences, Ankara)., (2010).
7. Hong-Nam, K. & Leavell, A. G. Language learning strategy use of ESL students in an intensive English learning context. System **34**, 3, 399-415., (2006). https://doi.org/10.1016/j.system.2006.02.002
8. Karapınar, A. The Relationship between Reading Strategies of English Language Teaching Freshman Students and their Achievement. (Master's Thesis, Hacettepe University/Institute of Educational Sciences, Ankara)., (2014).

DOI: 10.1051/shsconf/20173701048

9. Mendi, H. B. The Relationship between Reading Strategies, Motivation and Reading Test Performance in Foreign Language Learning. (Master's Thesis, Marmara University/Institute of Educational Sciences, İstanbul)., (2009).
10. O'Malley, J. M. et al. Learning strategy applications with students of English as a second language. TESOL Quarterly **19**, 3, 557-584., (1985).
11. Oxford, R. *Language Learning Strategies: What Every Teacher Should Know*. Boston: Heinle & Heinle., (1990).
12. Oxford, R., & Burry-Stock, J. A. Assessing the use of language learning strategies worldwide with the ESL/EFL version of the strategy inventory for language learning (SILL). System **23**, 1, 1-23., (1995). https://doi.org/10.1016/0346-251X(94)00047-A
13. Özçaylak, S. The Development of Students' Use of Reading Comprehension Strategies in English Texts. (Master's Thesis, Çağ University/Institute of Social Sciences, Mersin)., (2013).
14. Richards, J., & Platt, H. *Longman Dictionary of Applied Linguistics*. (2nd ed.). London: Longman Group Ltd., (1992).
15. Rubin, J. *Learner Strategies: Theoretical Assumptions, Research History and Typology*. Englewoods Cliffs, NJ: Prentice Hall, (Chapter 1)., (1987).
16. Sadık, S. Effects of Strategy Instruction Focus Activities on Students' Reading Strategy Use. (Master's Thesis, Bilkent University/Institute of Social Sciences and Economics, Ankara)., (2005).
17. Tuncel, F. An Integration of Metacognitive Reading Strategies in English Lessons. (Master Thesis, Çağ University/Institute of Social Sciences, Mersin)., (2014).
18. Vidal, R. J. Is there a correlation between reported language learning strategy use, actual strategy use and achievement? Linguagem & Ensino **5**, 1, 43-73., (2002).
19. Wilkes, J. C. A Case Study on Primary School Student's Perceptions about their Use of Language Learning and Reading Strategies and Strategy Training. (Master's Thesis, Bilkent University/Institute of Educational Sciences, Ankara)., (2011).

The effects of one day wrestling tournament on muscle damage and delayed onset muscle soreness of male wrestlers

Ismail Kaya[1a]

[1]Dumlupinar University School of Physical Education and Sport, Kutahya, Turkey

Abstract. The aim of this study was to investigate muscle damage and following delayed onset muscle soreness of elite wrestlers after one-day wrestling tournament. The study sample consists of 20 male wrestlers from Dumlupinar University School of Physical Education and Sports who are the contestant and have national degrees. The wrestlers voluntarily participated in the study. Measurements of the sampling group's features such as height and weight etc. were made after 12 weeks of preparation and 3 days of rest before the one-day competition. Venous blood samples were taken from the wrestlers before the first competition and after the fifth competition and serum, Creatine Kinase values were measured. In the evaluation of pre and post tournament measurement results, dependent samples t-test was applied at %99 significance value and Likert-type pain scale was used in order to determine muscle pain of the wrestlers. The wrestlers were asked to specify their muscle pain from 0 (no pain) to 10 (the most severe pain) and pain values of the wrestlers were determined before the competition, after the 1st, 3rd, 5th competitions and after 24 and 48 hours. Analyze results revealed that creatine kinase level of the wrestlers was (155.35 ± 44.89) before the tournament and (644.50 ± 216.73) after the tournament and both creatine kinase level and muscle pain values significantly increased after the tournament. As a result, this study showed that after one day wrestling tournament muscle damage occurs in wrestlers and even after 48 hours following muscle pain continues.
Keywords: Wrestling, Muscle Damage, Creatine Kinase, Delayed onset Muscle Soreness

1 Introduction

Wrestling is one of the most common individual sports in the world [19] and among bilateral fighting sports, wrestling was an important part of the Ancient Olympics and it is still one of the most popular contests in the Modern Olympic Games [8]. Wrestling is a kind of sport in which the anaerobic energy system predominantly used and, factors such as speed, flexibility, balance, muscular and cardiovascular durability and coordination effects

[a] Corresponding author: ismail.kaya@dpu.edu.tr

the performance, requires a great deal of power and energy during training and competition [3]. Sportsmen aim to maximize their performances with training [18]. And in wrestling, anaerobic power and capacity are both important because of the short-term and high-intensity performance requirements. Anaerobic metabolisms, especially glycolytic changes, are fundamentals in the energy distribution to the muscles [14]. Conscious exercises are effective in the fall of the blood pressure, reducing the loss of muscle and the bone mass [15].

Damage to muscles after exercise causes muscle-specific components to migrate from membrane ruptures into the bloodstream. In such cases, the most common component seen in the blood is the creatine kinase (CK). Besides, another indicator of muscle damage is elevated serum lactate dehydrogenase (LDH) level [17].

Wrestling is one of the most demanding sports of skeletal, muscular and cardio-vascular systems [7]. As a result of intense exercises performed in a short time, it is possible that some damages and aches occur in the muscles. Since all the systems of the organism work at the maximal level of a wrestling competition or in heavy training sessions, this condition is explained as muscle damage.

In the studies which aimed to investigate both skeleton and myocardium damage, commonly looked through the creatine kinase and its' sub isomorphs; myoglobin, aspartate aminotransferase (AST), lactate dehydrogenase (LDH), brain natriuretic peptide (BNP), atrial natriuretic peptide (ANP), carbonic anhydrase, lactate dehydrogenase, troponin and muscle building proteins. Among these enzymes creatine kinase is perhaps the most important and most commonly used enzyme. Because creatine kinase is the enzyme which regenerates the ATP in the contraction and transportation systems. Creatine kinase becomes physiologically functional in the muscle cell and as a result, ATP is formed using creatine phosphate in each contraction cycle of the muscle. This result keeps muscle ATP level steady and in this returning reaction, creatine kinase acts as a catalyst [10]. When examined the studies, investigating the relationship of strength training and its damage in the skeleton muscle and the muscle pain in sedentary individuals, it can be said that creatine kinase as an indicator of muscle damage and pain values increases after training. It was also found that it peaked 24 hours after the training, started falling at 48 hours, and at the 72nd hour, it reached a parallel level to the level just after exercise [11].

Three types of muscle damage are known to be present in the long-running period, continuing or intermittent severe contractions. The first and most commonly observed of the three types of muscle damage is known as delayed onset muscle soreness and according to this type of muscle soreness individuals complain of feeling weakness, tiredness and tenderness starting from the muscles after 12-48 hours of exercise [2].

In order to be successful in a fighting sport such as wrestling, it is necessary to maintain very heavy training for a long time. But it is observed that sudden decreases in the performance of wrestlers who have been exposed to long and high-intensity exercises. These decreases, which causes swelling in the sportsmen, is a condition that causes muscle exhaustion, loss of function, weakness, and pain after severe exercises ([5], [13]). Part of the responses to the situations mentioned above such as muscle exhaustion etc. is the process of filtering macrophages into damaged tissue. As a result these macrophages result in free radicals causing greater damage. But increased antioxidant content can theoretically neutralize these radicals and thus reduce muscle damage and muscle pain [1].

2 Material and method

2.1. Study sample

20 male wrestlers, who are the contestant and have degrees at the national level from various departments of Dumlupinar University School of Physical Education and Sports voluntarily, participated in the study. The mean age of sampling group is 21.55±1.61 years and means height is 175.81±8.97 cm, mean body height 77.75±11.25 kg and mean age of training is 7.45±2.06 years. Measurements of the sampling group's features such as height and weight etc. were made after 12 weeks of preparation and 3 days of rest before the tournament.

2.2 Procedure

Venous blood samples were taken from the subjects before the first competition and after the fifth competition. Creatine Kinase level of the serums obtained from centrifuging blood was assessed with using Hitachi 912 biochemical device with Roche Diagnostic kit. In order to evaluate the subjects' muscle pain, Likert-type pain scale was used. The subjects were asked to specify their muscle pain from 0 (no pain) to 10 (the most severe pain) and pain values of the subjects were determined before the first competition, after the 1st, 3rd, 5th competitions and after 24 and 48 hours.

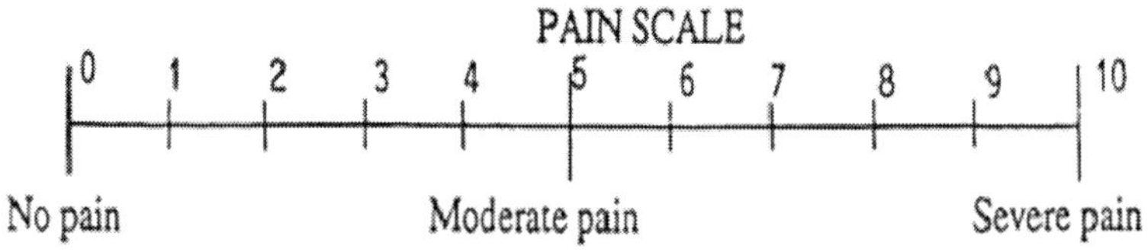

Figure 1. Likert-Type Pain Scale (Source: [9]).

One day wrestling tournament, suitable for the international wrestling rules and international tournament guidelines was designed for the wrestlers. All the participants participated in all five competitions regardless of whether they won or not. The rest periods between competitions are shown in Figure 2.

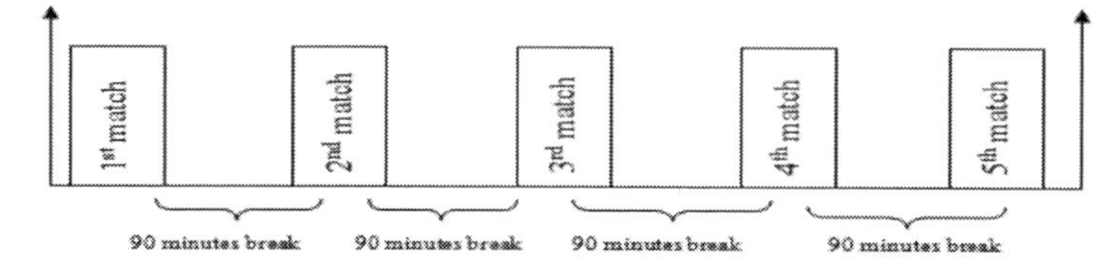

Figure 2. Tournament Chart

2.3 Statistical analyze

The obtained data was evaluated with SPSS version 20.0 Package Program. In order to evaluate the homogeneity of the data normality tests were done and in order to evaluate creatine kinase level before and after the competitions paired samples t-test was done. Also in order to evaluate demographic features and pain values of the wrestlers' descriptive statistics were used.

3 Findings

Graph 1. Creatine Kinase levels

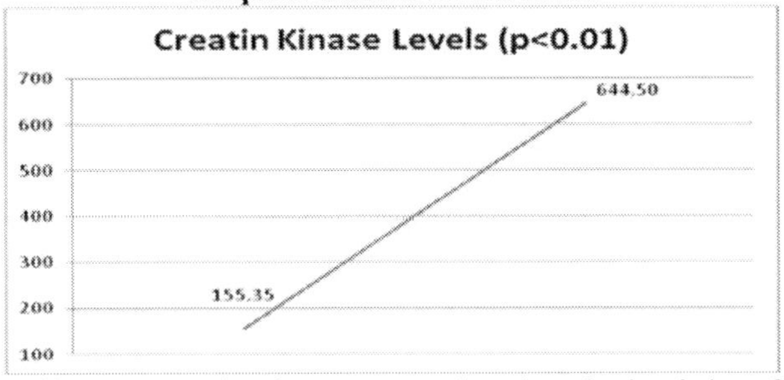

According to normality test results, it was seen that the obtained data for creatine kinase level was normally distributed and in order to evaluate significant differences between creatine kinase levels for the participants' dependent samples t-test was used at %99 significance level. Analyze results revealed that the increase of the creatine kinase levels between the pre (155.35 ± 44.89) and post (644.50 ± 216.73) measurements was significant (p<0,01).

Table 1. Delayed onset muscle soreness values

	N	Mean	Std Dev
After 1st competition	20	5.05	2.31
After 3rd competition	20	5.20	2.33
After 5th competition	20	6.25	2.15
After 24 hours	20	6.30	2.92
After 48 hours	20	5.80	3.05

Delayed onset muscle soreness values of the participants were evaluated before the first competition and after the 1st, 2nd, 5th competitions and after 24 and 48 hours, using Likert-type pain scale. And according to descriptive analyze results onset muscle soreness of the participants were found 5.05 after the 1st competition, 5.20 after the 3rd competition, 6.25 after the 5th competition, and 6.30 after 24 hours and 5.80 after 48 hours.

4 Discussion

This paper aimed to investigate muscle damage and following delayed onset muscle soreness for the wrestlers after one-day wrestling tournament consisted of 5 competitions. Analyze results revealed that creatine kinase levels of the wrestlers' significantly increased after the tournament (p<0.01). And according to descriptive analyze results it was seen that delayed onset muscle soreness of the wrestlers increased after all competitions, peaked after 24 hours and, after 48 hours it started to decrease. In his study Kayhan [12] indicated that when exposed to eccentric training creatine kinase level of the individuals' increases. According to his findings, a statistically significant increase in creatine kinase levels before and after exercise consisted of 10 cycles and 15 sets with their maxima. Besides delayed onset muscle soreness values significantly increased. Present findings are parallel to the findings of Kayhan [12].

In the study conducted by Barbas and colleagues, the investigated the effects of one-day wrestling tournament on physiological and performance adaptation of Greco-Roman wrestlers and similar to present findings they stated a significant increase in creatine kinase levels and delayed onset muscle soreness [4]. In their study, Ojala and Hakkinen specified similar findings to present findings and according to Ojala and Hakkinen [16] delayed onset muscle soreness for the athletes especially peaks after 24 hours of physical activity.

5 Conclusion

As a result of this study, it was found that one-day wrestling tournament causes muscle damage and delayed onset muscle soreness in elite wrestlers. It is thought that similar studies, conducted in wider and different groups, will be useful in order to minimize the reasons that cause muscle damage and delayed onset muscle soreness and maximize competition performance.

References

1. Atabek Çakır. H., Özdemir. F., C Vitamini İlavesinin Egzersiz Performansına Ve Kas Hasarına Etkisi. Celal Bayar Üniversitesi Beden Eğitimi Ve Spor Bilimleri Dergisi, 5(2) (2010).
2. Atalay Güzel, N., Effects of different resistance exercise protocols on nitric oxide, lipid peroxidation and creatine kinase activity in sedentary males, Journal of Sports Science and Medicine, 6, (2007).
3. Aydos. L., Taş. M., Akyüz. M., Ahmet Uzun, A., Genç Elit Güreşçilerde Kuvvetle Bazı Antropometrik Parametrelerin İlişkisinin İncelenmesi, Gazü Üniversitesi Beden Eğitimi Ve Spor Bilimleri Dergisi, Cilt.11, Sayı. 4, (2009).
4. Barbas. İ., ve ark., Physiological and performance adaptations Of Elite Greco-Roman Wrestlers During A One-Day Tournament, Eur. Apple Physiol 111, (2011).
5. Çoban. O., Güreşçilere uygulanan koenzim Q 10 Takviyesinin Kas Hasarı İle Eser Elementler Üzerine Etkisinin İncelenmesi, Erciyes Üniversitesi Sağlık Bilimleri Enstitüsü Beden Eğitimi Ve Spor Bilimleri Anabilim Dalı,Yüksek Lisans Tezi, Kayseri, (2011).
6. Erdoğan. M., Farklı Isı Koşullarında Uygulanan Maksimal Aerobik Yüklenmenin Kas Hasarı ve Performans Üzerine Etkileri, Gazi Üniversitesi Sağlık Bilimleri Enstitüsü Beden Eğitimi Ve Spor Anabilim Dalı Doktora Tezi,Ankara, (2009).
7. Filiz. K., Gazi Üniversitesi Güreş Takımı İle Kara Harp Okulunda Güreşen Azeri Öğrencilerin Bazı Test Ölçüm Sonuçlarının Karşılaştırılması, Kastamonu Eğitim Dergisi, Cilt.II,No.3, (2003).
8. Garcıa-Pallares. J., ve ark., Physical fitness factors to predict male Olympic wrestlingperformance, Eur J Appl Physiol, 111:1747–1758DOI 10.1007/s00421-010-1809-8 (2011).
9. Harbili, S., Sıcak Stresin Ekzentrik Egzersizin Neden Olduğu Kas Hasarına Etkisi. Hacettepe Üniversitesi Sağlık Bilimleri Enstitüsü Spor Bilimleri ve Teknolojisi Programı Doktora Tezi, Ankara, (2007).
10. Hazar. S., Egzersize Bağlı İskelet Ve Kalp Kası Hasarı, Spormetre Beden Eğitimi ve Spor Bilimleri Dergisi, 2 (3) (2004).
11. Hazar. S., Erol. E., Gökdemir. K., Kuvvet Antrenmanı Sonrası Oluşan Kas Ağrısının Kas Hasarıyla İlişkisi, Gazü Üniversitesi Beden Eğitimi Ve Spor Bilimleri Dergisi, 6(3) (2006).
12. Kayhan. M., Basketbolcularda Eksantrik Egzersiz Sonrası Oluşan Gecikmiş Kas Ağrısının Bazı Biyokimyasal Parametrelere Ve Şut Yüzdesine Etkisinin İncelenmesi Dumlupınar Üniversitesi Sağlık Bilimleri Enstitüsü Beden Eğitimi Ve Spor Anabilim Dalı Yüksek Lisans Tezi, Kütahya, (2014).

13. Kılıç. T., Basketbol Turnuvasının Kas Hasarı Ve Toparlanma Süresine Etkileri, Gazi Üniversitesi Sağlık Bilimleri Enstitüsü Beden Eğitimi Ve Spor Anabilim Dalı Doktora Tezi, Ankara, (2010).
14. Koç. H., Effect Of Anaerobik Power On The Reaction Times Of Junior National Team Wrestlers, İnternational Journel Of Academic Research, Vol.5,No.1. (2013).
15. Ocak. Y., Tortop Y., Kadınlarda Halk Oyunları Çalışmalarının Bazı Fiziksel Uygunluk Parametreleri Üzerine Etkisinin İncelenmesi, Spor ve Performans Araştırmaları Dergisi,Cilt.4, Sayı.1, (2013).
16. Ojala. T., Hakkinen. K., Effect Of Tennis Tournament On Players Physical Performance, Hormonel responses,Muscla Damage And Recovery, Sports Sci. Med. Jun. 1; 12(2) (2013).
17. Şendil. A., Dehidrate Olmuş Bireylerde Step Machine Aletinde Yapılan Egzersize Bağlı Olarak Oluşan, Gecikmiş Kas Ağrısı (Doms) Üzerine İzotonik Spor İçeceklerinin Etkisi, Hacettepe Üniversitesi Sağlık Bilimleri Enstitüsü Spor Bilimleri Ve Teknolojisi Doktora Tezi, Ankara, (2008).
18. Şentürk. A., Kılınç. F., Şiktar. E., Şiktar. E., Hentbolcülere Uygulanan Aerobik Dayanıklılık ve Kuvvet Antrenmanlarının Deri Altı Yağ Ölçüm Değerleri Üzerine Etkisinin Araştırılması, Atatürk Journal Of Physicial Education And Sport Science, Cilt..10, Sayı.1,S.29-36.Erzurum, (2008).
19. Zaccakni.L., Antropometrics And Body Composition Of Italian National Wrestlers, Europen Journal Of Sport Science,12, (2012).

Examination the pre-service physics teachers' cognitive structure about the concept of "torque"

Özgür Özcan[1a]

[1]Hacettepe University, Faculty of Education, 06800, Beytepe, Ankara, Turkey

Abstract. In order to realize the exact learning, it is important to know that how the individuals learn and how they construct the knowledge in their minds. If the prior knowledge that existed already in the mind of the individuals overlaps with the newly learned knowledge so the exact learning takes place in the mind of the individuals. In this context, according to the constructivism, it can be said that the individuals constructed the new knowledge by linking the prior knowledge to the existing one in their minds. This study aims to investigate the cognitive structures of 32 pre-service physics teachers related to the concept of torque by using the qualitative research methods. The data collected through the word association test (WAT) and it was analyzed by using content analysis method. The cognitive structures of the pre-service physics students were determined by different categories at the end of the content analyses process.
Keywords: Cognitive structure, pre-service physics teachers, torque, word association test

1 Introduction

Cognition is an umbrella term containing such concepts as thinking, learning and recalling in its body. In other words, it is the general name given to all of these processes. Individuals' understanding or learning a concept is directly related with the development of their mental activities. Structure is a structure exhibiting the mutual relations of concepts recorded in the long-term memory. Development in individuals' cognitive structure in terms of concepts is a process beginning with recording information about the relevant concept in the long-term memory [1, 2]. Learning a concept should not be considered as learning only the name of the concept or only its definition. On the contrary, it should be considered as the ability to set up associations between the concept and other related concepts. That is to say, knowledge elements forming in individuals' mind are associated with structures arising in consequence of their later learning. This means that individuals

[a] Corresponding author: ozcano@hacettepe.edu.tr

set up close associations between their previous learning and what they acquire later. If the association is set up correctly, meaningful learning can occur to a great extent. To put it in other words, if correct connections are set up between the newly learnt knowledge and previous knowledge, cognitive structure related with the learnt concept is formed [3]. Thus, when the above mentioned activity happens, meaningful learning occurs [4]. A number of studies have been conducted by using word association tests in science education [5, 6, 7, 8, 9, 10, 11 and 12]. When considered in this context, word association test is a very effective method in uncovering students' cognitive structures and in teaching concepts.

Within the scope of the study, pre-service physics teachers' conceptual framework about the concept of "toque" was examined by using the word association test, and the following research questions were tried to be answered:

1. How is the cognitive structure of the pre-service physics teachers in relation to the concept of "toque"?
2. How do the pre-service physics teachers configure the concept of "torque" in their mind?

2 Method

The current study was designed according to the qualitative research methods and it was conducted with pre-service physics teachers during the 2016-2017 academic year. The word association test (WAT) was used as a data collection tool and the collected data were analyzed by using the content analysis method.

2.1 Participants

This study was performed so as to determine 32 pre-service physics teachers' cognitive structures about the concept of torque. All of the participants were the third and fourth year students who had taken and passed Mechanics I course. They were in the 20-22 age range and took part in the research on the basis of volunteering.

2.2 Data collection tool

Word association test was used in the research as the tool of data collection. In addition, the drawings made by students related to the concept of "torque" have been used to identify the conceptual framework of the participants. Prior to the application, the participants were informed of word association tests. They were given a key concept and were asked to write the words coming into their mind related with the key concept in 40 seconds. The participants were also allowed 20 seconds to write sentences about the key concept. The key words were written repeatedly one under another as a list. The reason for this was to minimize the likelihood of chain answers and to prevent the students' previous word from influencing their next word. Even though writing the key word only once makes everything easier, it is also possible that participants can get away from the key word with each word they write [9].

2.3 Data analysis

The data collected through word association test were analyzed in this study by using the number of words, the number of answers and semantic relations technique. The data having semantic connections were grouped under the same category. Besides, the words which seemed not to be related, having nothing to do with the key word and used only once were removed from analyses. The initial results of the analysis were discussed with other physics education researcher and the inter coder reliability coefficient was archived to be 0.86.

After discussing the incompatibility between the researchers, the full agreement was reached finally. At the end of the study, pre-service physics teachers' cognitive structure in relation to the concept of torque was exhibited. Discussions as to the accuracy of the concepts pre-service physics teachers associated torque with and of their examples for torque were also offered in this study. The extent to which pre-service physics teachers' associations were scientific was also discussed in the study.

3 Findings

The findings obtained are presented on the basis of the analysis results of Word association test and students' drawings. The concepts determined through Word association test were primarily divided into categories by sequencing them according to their similarities and differences. After data collection by means of WAT, the findings were divided into four categories by taking semantic proximity into consideration. Table 1 shows the words and the categories the words are divided into. As is clear from Table 1, the categories are labelled as "Torque definition", "Torque – Lesson Relationship", "Direction of Torque", and "Torque in Daily Life". In addition to that, the words in each category are also listed.

Table 1. The Distribution of Pre-service Physics Teachers' Cognitive Structure related to the Concept of "Torque"

Categories	Concepts and Frequencies in Categories	Total Frequencies
Torque definition	Axis (3) Rotation effect (11) Moment (19) Force – Effort arm (18) Rotation (3)	54
Torque – Lesson Relationship	Physics (20) Difficult questions (7) Exam (5) Mechanics (4)	36
Direction of Torque	Direction (5) Right-hand rule (3) Balance (3)	11
Torque in Daily Life	Ferris wheel (5) Door handle (10) Pulley (3) Seesaw (3) Trolley (3) Nippers (3) Weighing machine (3)	30
Total	**19 words**	**131 words**

The pre-service physics teachers used five different concepts in the category of "Torque definition" 54 times in total. The concept most frequently used in this category was the concept of "moment"- which was followed by the concept of "Force – Effort arm". In the category of Torque-Lesson Relationship, four concepts were used in total. The concept most frequently used in this category was the concept of "Physics". Pre-service teachers set up direct associations between the concept and the lesson. Because the students had encountered the concept of Torque in mechanics course for the first time, some of them also associated the concept with the course. The pre-service physics teachers used three concepts in total in the category of "Direction of Torque". It was interesting that they associated the concept with the concepts of right hand rule and equilibrium, and it was an expected result. One of the most important findings was the findings in relation t the category of "Torque in Daily Life". In this category, prospective physics teachers set up direct associations between the concept of torque and daily life and offered explanations. The most frequently used word was "door handle". This might be because it was the most frequently given example in course books.

A model reflecting pre-service physics teachers' cognitive structures about the concept of torque was created (see Figure 1). As is clear from the model, the pre-service teachers' cognitive structures about the concept of torque are composed of the four categories distinguished with the analysis of WAT. An examination of Figure 1 shows that the category having the biggest number of concepts is the category of "Torque Definition". Besides, it is also remarkable that there are scientific concepts in the concepts students use. In other words, it may be said that some students' knowledge about the concept of torque is at comprehension level. The pre-service physics teachers explained the concept of torque by giving examples from daily life in the category of "Torque in Daily Life". They explained the concept by using the incidents in their life and the materials they used in daily life as examples.

The majority of the students included in this category also made scientific sentences about torque. The following are some of the examples for their sentences:

St 14: *When force is applied to a substance fixed on a point, the substance rotates. This situation shows that force has rotating effect.*

St 21: *Thanks to the force we apply to the door handle, we open the door. This is an example for torque.*

St 8: *Car mechanics apply torque to screws while tightening screws, but they are not aware of this.*

On examining the examples above, we can say that the students' words and examples about the concept of torque are scientific. That is to say, it may be stated that the students' definitions about the concept of torque are operational definitions.

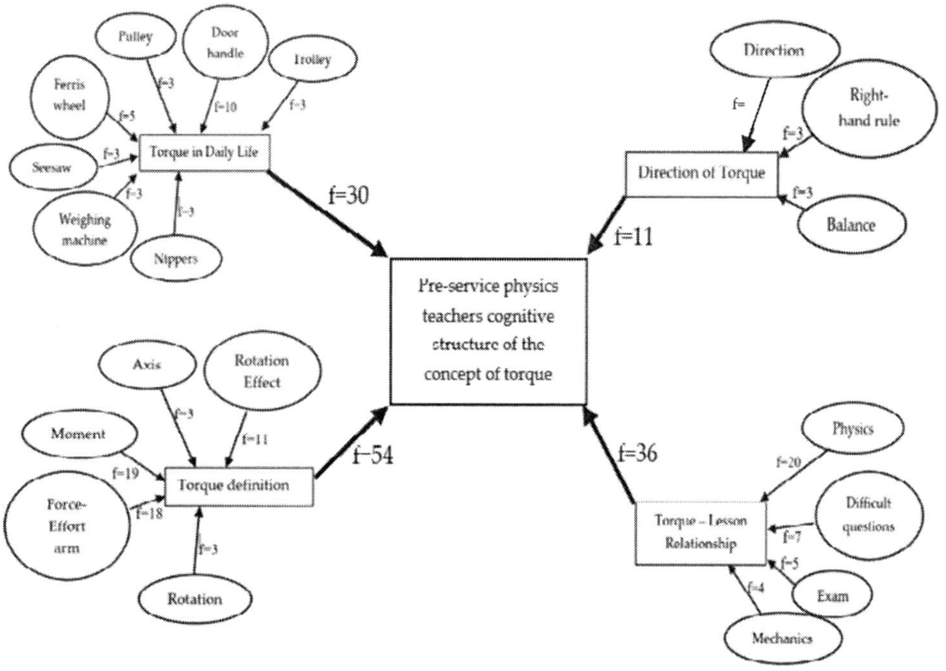

Fig. 1. The Model of Pre-Service Physics Teachers' Cognitive Structures of Torque Concept.

Another property of WAT is that it determines students' alternative conceptions and misconceptions. It was found in this study that pre-service physics teachers had some

DOI: 10.1051/shsconf/20173701050

alternative conceptions. Most important of them was that some of the pre-service teachers used the concepts of "torque" and "force" interchangeably. An example for this is given below:

St 5: *In Mechanics course, the force we apply to a substance to rotate is called torque.*

As in this example, a pre-service teacher states that torque- which arises in consequence of force- is identical with force. That is to say, the student means that force and torque are the same things. To exemplify this:

St29: *Torque is the force of rotation.*

In this example also the concepts of torque and force are used interchangeably. Pre-service teachers have not fully understood that there should be force in order for torque to occur. On the other hand, drawings made by pre-service teachers were found to be related with typical question samples available in course books. The fact that students' drawings were restricted in scope in contrast to the categories indicated that they had superficial knowledge about the concept of torque. That is to say, it may be stated that variation in pre-service teachers' cognitive structures about the concept is at minimum level. As supportive of this finding, it may be said that only 12 out of 32 pre-service teachers made drawings in addition to their answers to word association test.

4 Discussion and conclusion

The concept of Torque is one of the fundamental concepts included in mechanics course basically and in many physics subjects in general, and it is an important concept. In this context, teaching this concept will influence the teaching of other concepts connected with it. In other words, pre-service physics teachers' having sound knowledge about the concept of torque will pave the way for complete understanding/learning in other subjects. This study distinguished four distinct categories about the concept of torque by using WAT. The categories were labelled as "Torque definition" (54), "Torque – Lesson Relationship" (36), "Direction of Torque" (11), and "Torque in Daily Life" (30) following content analysis. The examples pre-service physics teachers gave for the category of "Torque in Daily Life" were quite interesting. The category provides important information about structures arising in their minds about the concept of torque. In those examples given in relation to daily life, pre-service teachers heavily preferred actions in which there is the movement of "rotation". Additionally, examples related with seesaw or simple machines (such as nippers, pulley, etc.) were also remarkable. Indeed, students' use of scientific knowledge that they have learnt in daily life is an example indicating that complete learning has occurred. Yet, research has found that students have difficulty in setting up associations between what they have learnt in physical sciences and daily life or that they are inadequate in using scientific knowledge in appropriate scientific statements [13, 14, 15 and 16].

References

1. J. Gilbert, M. Watts, Concepts, Misconceptions and Alternative Conceptions: Changing Perspectives in Science Education, *Studies in Science Education*, **10**, (1983)
2. E.L. Smith, T.D. Blakeslee, C.W. Anderson, Teaching strategies associated with conceptual change learning in science, *J. of Res. in Sci. Tech.*, **30**, 2, (1993)
3. R. R. Skemp, *The psychology of learning mathematics* (Penguin Books, Middlesex, England, 1971).
4. D.P. Ausubel, *Educational Psychology: A Cognitive View* (New York: Holt, Rinehart & Winston, 1968).

5. H. Kurt, G. Ekici, Ö. Aksu, M. Aktaş, Determining cognitive structures and alternative conceptions on the concept of reproduction: The case of pre-service biology teachers, *Creat. Educ.*, **4**, 9, (2013a)
6. H. Kurt, G. Ekici, M. Aktaş, Ö. Aksu, Determining biology student teachers' cognitive structure on the concept of "diffusion" through the free word-association test and the drawing-writing technique, *Int. Educ. Stud.*, **6**, 9, (2013b)
7. H. Kurt, Biology student teachers' cognitive structure about "Living thing", *Educational Research and Reviews*, **8**, 12, (2013)
8. F. Ercan, A. Taşdere, N. Ercan, Kelime ilişkilendirme testi aracılığıyla bilişsel yapının ve kavramsal değişimin gözlenmesi [Observation of cognitive structure and conceptual changes through word associations tests], *Türk Fen Eğit. Derg.* **7**, 2, (2010)
9. M. Bahar, S. Özatlı, Kelime İletişim Testi Yöntemi ile Lise 1. Sınıf Öğrencilerinin Canlıların Temel Bileşenleri Konusundaki Bilişsel Yapılarının Araştırılması [Investigating the high school students' cognitive structures about the main components of living beings via word association test], *Bal. Üni. Fen Bil. Ens. Derg.*, **5**, (2003)
10. F. Köseoğlu, E. Bayır, Examining cognitive structures of chemistry teacher candidates about gravimetric analysis through word association test method, *Trakya Üniv. Eğit. Fak. Derg.*, **1**, 1, (2011)
11. H. Gökbaş, A. Erdoğan, Matematik Öğretmen Adaylarının Fonksiyon Hakkındaki Kavramsal Yapıları, *J. of Res. in Educ. and Teach.*, **5**, 3, (2016)
12. H. G. Y. Hastürk, *Investigating and assessing the changes in the teacher candidates' cognitive structures about some environmental topics in authentic learning environments*, (Unpublished PhD Thesis, Gazi University, Ankara, 2013).
13. H. Kurt, B. Kaya, A. Ateş, S. Kılıç, Biyoloji öğretmen adaylarının biyolojik okuryazarlığı, *Sel. Üniv. Ahmet Keleşoğlu Eğit. Fak. Derg.*, **27**, (2009)
14. H. Özmen, Kimya öğretmen adaylarının asit ve baz kavramlarıyla ilgili bilgilerini günlük olaylarla ilişkilendirebilme düzeyleri [Pre-service chemistry teachers' correlation level about the knowledge of everyday life event relating to acid and base topics], *Kast. Eğit. Derg.*, **11**, 2, (2003)
15. D. H. Palmer, Exploring the link between students' scientific and nonscientific conceptions, *Sci. Educ.*, **83**, (1999)
16. A. Taşdemir, M. Demirbaş, İlköğretim öğrencilerinin fen ve teknoloji dersinde gördükleri konulardaki kavramları günlük yaşamla ilişkilendirebilme düzeyleri [The level of correlation of concepts that primary students seen topics in science and technology class with daily life], *Uluslararası İnsan Bil. Derg.*, **7**, 1, (2010)

An analysis of students' cognitive structures in relation to their environmental sensitivity

Cem Gercek[1a]

[1]Faculty of Education, Department of Mathematics and Science Education, Hacettepe University, Ankara, Turkey

Abstract. One of the basic aims of environment-related subjects included in the biology curriculum is to raise environmental awareness. Yet, the fact that the concepts taught especially in the context of environmental issues are abstract influences meaningful learning. This, in turn, influences behaviours displayed. Exhibiting students' cognitive structures in assuring effective and meaningful concept teaching increases the importance of studies conducted. Unavailability of studies in the literature analysing students' cognitive structures in relation to their sensitivity to the environment demonstrates the importance of this current study. This study aims to analyse students' cognitive structures in relation to their environmental sensitivity. The study employs survey model- one of the qualitative research designs. The study group was composed of 56 high school students in the 2016-2017 academic year. The study group was formed through purposeful sampling. Word Association Test (WAT) was prepared in order to uncover students' cognitive structures in relation to their environmental sensitivity. Having transcribed the data obtained, they were put to content analysis and were transferred to the medium of computer. The results showed that students' cognitive structure concerning their environmental sensitivity was divided into categories.
Keywords: Student, cognitive structure, environmental sensitivity.

1 Introduction

High school biology curriculum is heavily loaded. Therefore, the course students have difficulty with is primarily biology [1]. Students tend to memorise the concepts presented in biology course, which influences meaningful learning and causes misconceptions and alternative concepts. Posner et al (1982) point out that students' misconceptions hinder their understanding and interpreting science subjects.

An examination of biology curriculum demonstrates that the curriculum contains abstract subjects and concepts. Teaching the abstract concepts in biology and shaping them in students' mind can be difficult for teachers [2]. Here, constructivist approach occupies an

[a] Corresponding author: cgercek@hacettepe.edu.tr

important place. Constructivist approach is based on two basic principles. The first is that knowledge is not received passively by individuals. The second is that making sense of knowledge assures adjustment and life organisation [2, 3]. It is pointed out in various studies that students have problems in understanding biological concepts, activities and processes [4, 5]. Pendley, Bretz and Novak attribute those problems to memorising the subjects and to education's failure to set up associations between key concepts and concepts [6]. Considering these problems, it becomes evident that students' knowledge structures should be determined and accurate knowledge structures should be developed. In other words, forming a well organised conceptual framework will assure that students will prefer meaningful learning instead of rote learning [7]. The reason for this is that meaningful learning necessitates students' setting up conceptual associations between students' current knowledge and new knowledge presented to them. If they have incomplete conceptual ties, they have difficulty in learning the new material.

It is clear from studies conducted that cognitive structures are determined through various techniques [1, 5]. The most established technique in this respect is the technique of word association. The technique has been applied for over 20 years. The purpose of word association technique is to understand the associations students set up between concepts and to correct the misconceptions. Studies conducted in this respect are not restricted to primary and secondary school levels but they were also applied to high school students [8]. Application has two forms: prior to transfer of knowledge to students and after transfer of knowledge. In consequence of the applications, significant data were reached in determining students' cognitive structures [4, 9]. Therefore, this method is also helpful to constructivist educational system. It provides the opportunity to measure and monitor the knowledge transferred to students. Word association technique, which is also commonly used today, can be applied to all students. Although word association technique is frequently used in traditional system of education, it is used very much in contemporary educational system- that is to say, in constructivist approach.

Studies on conceptual change are based on Piaget's assimilation and accommodation processes in the field of education. Assimilation is the process of including new knowledge in existing cognitive structure. For instance, a child's thinking that he/she should throw the bottle into dustbin after drinking water in it because he/she knows that it is now garbage. The concept of accommodation, on the other hand, is the process of re-shaping the existing cognitive structure according to new incidents [5, 6]. According to the above given example, with learning that recycling water bottles is important both for nature and for assuring materialistic gain, re-arranging the behaviour by throwing the bottles into recycling bins instead of dustbins exemplifies the concept of accommodation. Although biology education is a discipline interacting with the environment, students cannot associate concepts with the environment and unfortunately they form misconceptions and alternative concepts [10]. This situation, in turn, leads to gaining undesired behaviours. Studies concerning environmental education aim to instil in students desired behaviours in relation to the environment [11, 12]. Yet, several studies report that individuals do not display environment-related behaviours [11, 12, 13]. Researching the reasons and exhibiting the relevant students' cognitive structures are considered important. Absence of a similar study concerning students' environmental sensitivity and word association test shows the importance of this study.

1.1 Purpose of the study

This study seeks answers to the following questions since it aims to analyse high school students' cognitive structures about their environmental sensitivity.

1. How are students' cognitive structures about their sensitivity to the environment?

2. What are students' views about their sensitivity to the environment?
3. What place does environmental sensitivity occupy in high school biology curriculum?

2. Method

The study employs survey model- one of the qualitative research designs. Survey models are the models aiming to describe a current situation [14].

2.1 Research group

The study group was composed of 56 (27 male, 29 female) high school students in the 2016-2017 academic year. The study group was formed through purposeful sampling. The selected research group were the high school students at 17 (8 male, 14 female), 18 (13 male, 12 female) and 19 years old (6 male, 3 female) and they took part in the research on the basis of volunteering.

2.2. Data collection tools

Word association test was used in this research as the tool of data collection. The test contained two parts. In part one, key phrase "Environmental Sensitivity" was written 10 times one under another, and the participants were asked to write a related word opposite each. The participants were allowed 35 seconds for this part. In part two, the students were asked to write a sentence related with "Environmental Sensitivity" in 15 seconds. The overall test lasted 50 seconds.

2.3 Data analysis

The data obtained from word association test were put to content analysis and were thus analysed. The concepts were divided into categories by consulting expert opinion according to their relevance. The frequencies of the words in the categories were determined.

2.4 Validity and reliability

It is important to perform validity and reliability analyses in studies. For validity, the process of data analysis was described in this study. For reliability, whether or not the concepts represented the categories to which they belonged was evaluated by two experts of the field. The concepts obtained were divided into categories by two experts. The agreement and disagreement between the two experts in terms of coding were determined, and agreement between the coders was found to be 86%.

3 Findings

This section presents the findings obtained following the analyses. In relation to the first research problem, students' answers to the word association test about environmental sensitivity are shown in Table 1. According to the Table, 443 concepts concerning students' cognitive structures about environmental sensitivity are divided into 4 categories. Because 10 concepts were meaningless, they were excluded from analysis. 30 students reported fewer than 10 concepts. As is clear from the Table, the biggest number of concepts (15 concepts) was reported in the category of current environmental problems whereas the smallest number of concepts (6 concepts) was reported in the category of recycling.

Table 1. Categories for students' cognitive structures about environmental sensitivity.

Categories	Concepts	Frequencies of the concepts	Total frequencies
Current environmental problems	Environmental pollution	(51)	176
	Cutting down-planting trees	(32)	
	Air pollution	(20)	
	Water pollution	(12)	
	Factories	(11)	
	Carbon release	(8)	
	Cigarettes	(8)	
	Global warming	(8)	
	Noise pollution	(7)	
	Soil pollution	(5)	
	Atmospheric layer	(4)	
	Fossil fuels	(4)	
	Cosmetic products	(2)	
	Holes dug by municipality	(2)	
	Germs	(2)	
Environmental effects	Ecological balance	(48)	148
	vegetation	(32)	
	Natural life	(24)	
	Deforestation	(15)	
	Died organisms	(19)	
	Producing substances harmful to nature	(6)	
	Natural disasters	(4)	
Social values	Morals	(49)	80
	Consciousness	(12)	
	Street animals	(7)	
	Selfishness	(6)	
	Work on nature	(4)	
	Health	(2)	
Recycling	Recycle bin	(9)	39
	Waste	(9)	
	Rarity of recycling	(9)	
	Organisations	(6)	
	Paper	(4)	
	Saprophyte bacteria	(2)	

In relation to the second research problem, some of the statements made by students about environmental sensitivity are as in the following. 2 of the students did not state their views on environmental sensitivity.

"Environmental sensitivity in general is the respect we should have for living and non-living things in the area we live."

"Setting up new industrial plants, restricting living creatures' habitat and poisoning them with wastes... this is unfair."

"People throw cigarette ends, food and drinks around thoughtlessly."

"Think of clean environment. For example, you lie on the grass with no litter around and you read your book with bird calls and clean air. How

nice it would be! If only we were sensitive and conscious and protected our environment and left a good world to the next generation".
"Sensitivity in our environment is related with every living thing's respect for each other. If they do not respect each other and obey environmental rules, it is harmful in every respect."
"I think man's gradually ruining the order of biomes in the world is making our end approach."
"An individual who is respectful to the operation routine of the ecosystem he is in, who performs activities (such as planting trees) without disrupting the routine and by contributing to oxygen recycle and who does not put an end to the life of living things in the environment according to his evaluation is a model individual."
"Environmental sensitivity means balancing our consumption and production without depleting nature."
"One's cultural level is directly proportional to his adopting the world in which he lives and keeping it clean".

In relation to the third problem, on examining the subjects about the environment included in high school biology programme, it is found that a subject called "Current Environmental Problems" is available in Unit 3 of the 9th grade [15]. No subjects were found for the other grade levels. An examination of 9th grade high school biology curriculum makes it clear that the purpose in this unit is to make students aware of the negative effects of human activities on the environment and to make them suggest solutions to relevant problems, to assure that they understand the effects of environmental problems on human health, and to assure that they gain skills, attitudes, values and understanding necessary for biology literacy around the key word "the environment". The unit aims to enable students to have 7 gains in 18 class hours. This unit contains such headings as:

The causes and effects of environmental problems (air, water, soil, radioactive, food and noise pollution, erosion, forest fire, destruction of natural habitats and ecological footprint),

Natural resources (biological diversity, biological diversity in our country and preserving diversity).

And the gains in the unit are as in the following:

- He/she questions the causes and probable effects of current environmental problems.
- He/she questions his/her individual role in the emergence of current environmental problems.
- He/she demonstrates the effects of current environmental problems on human health with examples.
- He/she analyses the social, economic and biological importance of the sustainability of natural resources.
- He/she becomes aware of the importance of biological diversity.
- He/she questions the factors making Turkey rich in biological diversity.
- He/she makes suggestions for solution in preserving biological diversity and shapes his/her suggestions.

4 Results and discussion

On examining the categories formed in accordance with the first research problem, it may be said that students are knowledgeable about the subject but that they have incomplete knowledge. An analysis of the concepts in all three categories demonstrates that the categories of social values and of recycling contain the smallest number of concepts. Although concepts such as morals, awareness, separating or evaluating the wastes were written, the frequencies of them were high- which was important for sensitivity to the environment (see Figure 1) because gains in this category are reflective of behaviours and attitudes about environmental sensitivity [11, 12, 16]. It is already expected that students forget what they learn in classes over time. Yet, it was found that diminishing in students' knowledge about current environmental problems in the unit was quite high [8].

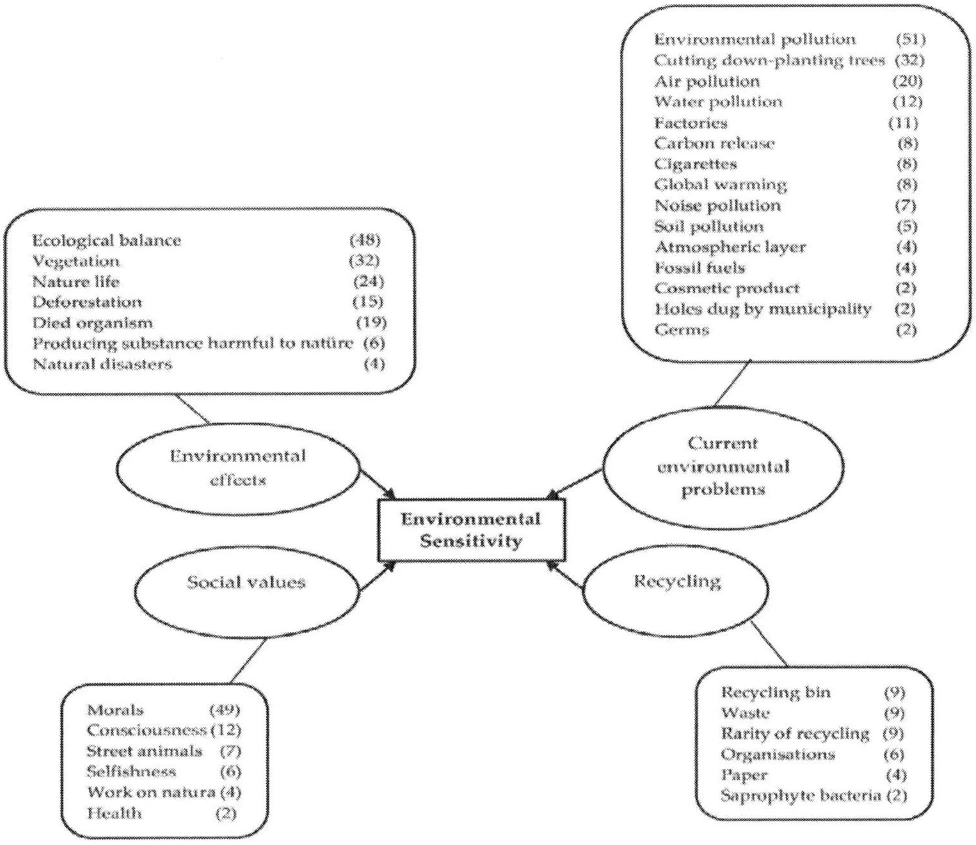

Fig. 1. Model for Students' Cognitive Structure about Environmental Sensitivity.

It was found in relation to the second research problem that students' views of environmental sensitivity were not adequate in providing attitudes and behaviours towards environmental sensitivity. The gains in Unit 3 of 9th grade curriculum [15] are the gains in questioning individuals effects on current environmental problems, demonstrating the impacts on human health with examples, factors assuring biological diversity, and their importance and preserving them. It was remarkable that those gains were not directly about environmental sensitivity. This might have stemmed from the fact that efforts had been made to instil is students the existing gains in a short time.

The formation of environmental sensitivity is the acquisition of determined gains about environmental issues- that is to say, reflection into behaviours. On examining high school biology subjects concerning environmental sensitivity in accordance with the third research problem, we find that the subject of "Current Environmental Problems" is available in Unit three of the 9th grade textbook. No subjects about the environment were available in the units of 10th, 11th and 12th grades [15]. On examining the unit of Current Environmental

Problems in the 9th grade biology course book, it was found that concepts such as acid rains, erosion, electromagnetic contamination, radioactive contamination, food pollution and ecological foot print were also included as different from the concepts presented by students [15]. This situation may be considered as that students could not learn some concepts and subjects or that they have forgotten them. Failure to have complete learning in environmental sensitivity may cause students' failure to reach the determined gains in relation to the subject.

5 Implications

Environmental sensitivity is important for the protection of the environment and of biological diversity and for recycling. When we look around, it is not difficult to see that our sensitivity to the environment is insufficient. It is important that students be taught subjects about the environment and sensitivity to the environment beginning with early ages and to provide them with gains about environmental sensitivity. Misconceptions and alternative concepts they have should be determined prior to and after classes, and they should be eliminated in appropriate methods and techniques. Doing all these and thus gaining sensitivity to the environment at early ages in different grade levels is considered important.

References

1. M. Bahar, M. H., Hansell, The relationship between some psychological factors and their effect on the performance of grid questions and word association tests, Educational Psychology: An Int. J. of Experimental Educational Psychology, **20**, 3, 346 – 364 (2000).
2. J. R., Savery, T. M., Duffy, Problem based learning: an instructional model and its construtivist framework. Educational Technology, September-October, 31-38 (1995)
3. J., Piaget, Cognitive development in children: development and learning, J. Research in Science Teaching, **2**, 176–186 (1964)
4. M. C. P. J., Knippels, A. J., Waarlo, K.T., Boersma, Design criteria for learning and teaching genetics. J. of Biological Education, **39**, 3, 108-112 (2005)
5. H. S., Lee, O. L., Liu, Assessing learning progression of energy concepts across middle school grades: the knowledge integration perspective, Science Education, **94**, 4, 665–688 (2010)
6. B. D., Pendley, R. L. Bretz, J. D., Novak, Concept maps as a tool to assess learning in chemistry. J. of Chemical Education, **71**, 9-17 (1994)
7. R., Maskill, A. F., Cachapuz, V., Koulaidis, Young pupils' ideas about the microscopic nature of matter in three different European countries, Int. J. of Science Education, **19**, 6, 631-645 (1997)
8. G., Polat, Determination of the cognitive structures of year secondary school students through word association test techniques, Necatibey Faculty of Education Electronic J. of Science and Mathematics Education, **7**, 1, 97-120 (2013)
9. W., Wagner, J., Valencia, F., Elejabarrieta, Relevance, discourse and the hot stable core of social representation-A structural analysis of word association, British J. of Social Psychology, **35**, 331-351 (1996)
10. Z., Kostova, B., Radoynovska, Word association test for studying conceptual structures of teachers and students, Bulgarian J. of Science and Education Policy, **2**, 2, 209-231 (2008)

11. M., Daskolia, A., Dimos, P. G., Kampylis, Secondary teachers' conceptions of creative thinking within the context of environmental education. Int. J. of Environmental and Science Education, **7**, 2, 269–290 (2012)
12. G. H., Erol, K., Gezer, Prospective of elementary school teachers' attitudes toward environment and environmental problems. Int. J. of Environmental and Science Education. **1**, 1, 65-77 (2006)
13. V.N., Kırtak-Ad, N., Demirci, Prospective teachers' levels of associating environmental problems with science fields and thermodynamics laws, Ahi Evran University Journal of Kirsehir Educatioan Faculty, **13**, 3, 19-46 (2012)
14. H., Şimşek A., Yıldırım, *Qualitative research methods in the social sciences*, Ankara: Seçkin Puplishing (2013)
15. Ministry of National Education of Turkey [MONE] Biyoloji Dersi (9, 10, 11 ve 12. Sınıflar) Öğretim Programı [Secondary Education, Curriculum of Biology Course (Grades 9th-12th)], Retrieved from http://ttkb.meb.gov.tr/program2.aspx., (2013)
16. Z. F., Pluhar, B. F., Piko, S., Kovacs, A., Uzzoli, Air pollution is bad for my health: hungarian children's knowledge of the role of environment in health and disease, Health & Place, **15**, 239-246 (2009)

DOI: 10.1051/shsconf/20173701052

The relationship between critical thinking disposition, problem solving and empathetic tendency in counsellor candidates*

Cengiz Şahin[1a], and Hatice Kumcağız[2]

[1]Ahi Evran University, Department Psychological Counseling and Guidance, Kırşehir, Turkey
[2]Ondokuz Mayis University, Department Psychological Counseling and Guidance, Samsun, Turkey

Abstract. The aim of this research was to examine the relationship between the level of critical thinking disposition, problem solving and empathetic tendencies of the candidate counsellors. Data were collected from a total of 406 counsellors (207 females, 199 males; 103 freshman year, 101 second grade, 98 third grade and 104 senior class) for this purpose. The Turkish Version of California Critical Thinking Disposition Inventory, The Turkish Version of Problem Solving Inventory and Empathetic Tendency Scale were used to collect data. In the data analysis process, descriptive statistics, t tests for independent groups and Pearson Product-Moment Correlation analysis tests were used. According to the first finding, there was no significant difference in the levels of critical thinking, problem solving and empathetic tendency according to gender. Secondly, positive relationships between critical thinking, problem solving, and empathetic tendency levels were achieved.
Keywords: Critical thinking, problem solving, empathetic tendency.

1 Introduction

In contemporary education understanding, the aim of education is not to load students with information, but to facilitate them to become individuals who are aware of their own interests and values, who can analyze, think critically and solve problems. Ideally, they will become individuals who possess elegant identities, who are rational, creative, constructive, sceptical, emotionally and rationally stable, warm-hearted, tolerant, emphatic and respectful to universal norms [1]. In this sense, it is necessity to determine the critical thinking,

[a]Corresponding author: csahim40@gmail.com

* This work was supported by the Ahi Evran University Scientific Research Projects Coordination Unit. Project Number: EGT.E2.17.023

problem solving and empathy levels of psychological counsellors and related trainings are to be organized during their education.

People are bombarded with unlimited sources of information today and have difficulty in selecting and understanding which information is true. It is a necessity of living in society to possess the skills of questioning, searching and decision-making. The adaptation to a developing society is possible therefore with bringing up critically thinking individuals [2]. Paul, who is known for his studies on critical thinking, defines critical thinking as thinking when the person is achieving the act of thinking in order to develop his/her self-thinking [3].

Critical thinking skills are necessary in every field of life. The significance of these skills increases especially in social professions. Finkelman indicates that, in addition to the individuals who work in the health care sector, other individuals such as psychological counsellors, psychologists, teachers etc. who have a direct role in contribution to human life, are expected to possess critical thinking skills [4]. A psychological counsellor should have the skills of looking at a problem from different angles, seeking profound evidence for a subject of belief, making right decisions, problem-solving, being unbiased, behaving flexibly, and making empathy [5].

One receives, processes and uses information while solving a problem [6]. Problem solving is defined as a conscious, demanding and goal-oriented activity [7]. Individuals with high levels of problem-solving skills are open to change and creative with critical thinking skills [8]. Problem solving involves critical thinking, decision making, questioning and empathetic thinking [9]. Therefore, it is important for psychological counsellors to listen to their counselees and try to understand what the real problem is. According to Dökmen, empathy is one's putting himself into another one's shoes, looking from another one's perspective, truly understanding another one's thoughts and feelings as well as conveying this situation. Candidates of psychological counselling should acquire these skills during their education [27].

In the related literature, there are various researches addressing critical thinking [10, 11, 12, 5, 13, 14, 15, 16], problem solving [17] and empathetic tendencies [18, 19, 20] among different professions both in Turkey and different countries. Yet, there is no specific research dealing with the interaction of these three concepts in the field of psychological counselling. Hence, conducting a study in this context is thought to be beneficial and to bring light to the future studies in this issue.

It is expected that the findings of this study will put forth the relationship between critical thinking, problem solving and empathetic tendency, which is to clarify the importance of some concepts associated with psychological counselling and shed light on further research.

Within the related literature, the aim of the study is to compare the critical thinking, problem solving and empathetic tendencies of psychological counsellor candidates based on gender as well as to examine the relations between these concepts.

1.1 Objective of the study

General objective of this study is to examine the relationship between critical thinking, problem solving and empathetic tendency levels of students studying guidance and psychological counselling as per gender level. In direction with the general objective of the study, answers have been sought for following questions:

1. How are students' critical thinking, problem solving and empathetic tendency levels?
2. Do students' critical thinking, problem solving and empathetic tendency levels differ as per gender level?

3. Is there a significant relationship between students' critical thinking, problem solving and empathetic tendency levels?

2 Method

The study was designed as a relational scanning model [21] and made use of the survey technique, which is a commonly applied technique in this model [22].

2.1 Study group

The sample of the study consisted of 406 psychological counselling candidates who were studying at the Psychological Counselling and Guidance department in a public university during the 2016-2017 academic year. Among the participant students, 207 were females and 199 were males. 103 were 1st year, 101 were 2nd year, 98 were 3rd year and 104 were 4th year.

2.2 Data collection tools

The Turkish Version of the California Critical Thinking Disposition Inventory [23, 24], The Turkish Version of the Problem Solving Inventory [25, 26] and the Empathetic Tendency Scale [27] were used as data collection instruments in the study.

2.2.1.Turkish version of the California Critical Thinking Disposition Inventory (CCTDI-T):

The original English version of The California Critical Thinking Disposition Inventory CCTDI [23] measures a student's propensity to think critically. Kökdemir, has been administered to identify preservice teachers' attitudes. The index is comprised of 75 questions that represent 7 categories or scales. The Turkish version of the original scale contains 51 items and has 6 factors, Analyticity Open-mindedness, Inquisitiveness, Self-confidence, Truth-seeking, Systematicity [24]. The internal consistency of the scale was ,85.

2.2.2.Turkish version of the Problem Solving Inventory (PSI-T):

Rather than assessing actual problem solving capabilities, the PSI [25] was designed to assess an individual's perceptions or awareness of one's own problem solving behaviors and attitudes. The inventory's reliability and validity for the Turkish culture has been tested by Taylan [28], by Şahin, Şahin, & Heppner [26], and by Çam [29]. Statistical tests of the instrument's validity indicated that the measurement model was highly valid. Taylan [28] and Çam [29] found a high relation among subscales which resulted in a factor loading different than that of the original form. For this reason, they strongly suggested that the total score of the PSI must be used instead of using subscale scores separately. The internal consistency of the scale was ,88.

Empathetic Tendency Scale (ETS): Prepared by Dökmen in order to determine the potentials of individuals to develop empathy in daily life [27]. Nearly half (eight items) of the items in the emphatic tendency scale (ETS) which was developed as a 5-point likert scale and consisting of 20 items was written as negative in order to balance the tendencies of participants to answer positively. The internal consistency of the scale was ,72 [27].

DOI: 10.1051/shsconf/20173701052

2.3 Data analysis

In the data analysis process, descriptive statistics, t tests for independent groups and Pearson Product-Moment Correlation analysis tests were used. For significant test, level of p<.05 is accepted. Analysis with the help of the SPSS 20 package software.

3 Results

This section includes the results on whether critical thinking, problem solving and empathetic tendencies differed among the candidates of psychological counsellor in terms of their numbers and genders as well as the relationship between the scores of critical thinking, problem solving and empathetic tendencies.

The participants included 336 students 207 (50,9%) females, 199 (49,1%) males at different class levels in psychological counseling and guidance departments. Distributions of participants as per their class levels have been examined. In this context of students 103 (25,3%) were 1st year, 101 (24,8%) were 2nd year, 98 (24,2%) were 3rd year and 104 (25,7%) were 4th year.

3.1 Students' critical thinking, problem solving and empathetic tendency levels

Findings related to students' critical thinking, problem solving and empathetic tendency levels in psychological counselors candidate have been specified in Table 1.

Tablo 1. Descriptive statistics

Variable	N	Minimum	Maximum	M	SD
Critical thinking	406	51,00	306,00	209,16	20,62
Problem solving	406	32,00	192,00	91,02	3,72
Empathetic tendency	406	20,00	100,00	71,69	7,90

Table 1 shows that students' critical thinking (209,34±20,62), problem solving (91,02±3,72) and empathetic tendency (71,69±7,90) levels is middle.

3.2 Examination of students' critical thinking, problem solving and empathetic tendency levels as per gender

The fact whether critical thinking, problem solving and empathetic tendency vary or not as per gender at significant levels has been analyzed by t-test technique for independent groups. Points obtained from the scales by participants basing on result of the examination have been shown in Table 2.

Tablo 2. Statistics related to scale point averages of students as per gender.

Variable	Gender	N	M	SD	t	df	p
Critical thinking	Female	207	210,34	18,63	.80	404	.491
	Male	199	208,12	23,14			
Problem solving	Female	207	91,90	4,18	.43	404	.538
	Male	199	90,51	3,47			
Empathetic tendency	Female	207	72,28	8,16	1,22	404	.262
	Male	199	71,56	7,68			

It is seen in Table 2 that critical thinking (210,34±18,63), problem solving (91,90±4,18) and empathetic tendency (72,28±8,16) point of male students is higher than critical thinking (208,12±23,14), problem solving (90,51±3,47) and empathetic tendency (71,56±7,68) point of female students (35,03±15,02). The results indicated no meaningful average score differences among female and male psychological counsellors' critical thinking (t(404)=.80), problem solving (t(404)=.43) and emphatic tendencies (t(404)=1.22) in terms of gender (p>.05). In other explanations, critical thinking, problem solving and empathetic tendencies in psychological counselors do not differ according to gender.

3.3 Relationship between students' critical thinking, problem solving and empathetic tendencies levels

Relationship between students' critical thinking, problem solving and empathetic tendencies points was calculated as per Pearson correlation technique and results have been presented in Table 3.

Table 3. Correlation between students' critical thinking, problem solving and empathetic tendencies levels

Değişkenler	M	SD	(1)	(2)	(3)
(1) Critical thinking	209,16	20,62	1		
(2) Problem solving	91,02	3,72	,52**	1	
(3) Empathetic tendency	71,69	7,90	,48**	,44**	1

**p<0.01

As seen in Table 4, a statistically low but positive relationship was determined between critical thinking and problem solving (r=.52; p<.01), and emphatic tendency scores (r=.48; p<.01), and between problem solving and empathetic tendency scores (r=.44; p<.01). This result may indicate that critical thinking, problem solving and empathetic tendency are positive covariants.

4 Discussion and conclusion

General objective of this study is to examine the relationship between critical thinking, problem solving and empathetic tendency levels of students studying guidance and psychological counselling as per gender level. According to research findings, critical thinking, problem solving and empathetic tendency levels of psychological counsellor candidates are moderate. Secondly, there was no significant difference in the levels of critical thinking, problem solving and empathetic tendency based on gender. Thirdly, positive relationships were found between critical thinking, problem solving, and empathetic tendency levels. These results are in agreement with those of Deniz and Ekinci [30, 31].

It is concluded that there is not significant difference between critical thinking levels of psychological counsellor candidates in terms of gender. This finding is in parallel with those of [11, 24, 32, 33, 31, 34]. Özelçi and Aktaş & Ünlü detected a difference in terms of gender in favour of male participants [35, 36]. Yıldırım, Gurleyuk and Kızıltaş found a significant difference in favour of female participants [37, 9, 38].

Another finding of the research is the lack of significant difference between problem solving levels of psychological counsellor candidates in terms of gender. This result is in line with the previous research in which gender was also an insignificant variable in terms of students' problem solving skills [39, 40].

It is concluded in the same way that there is not significant difference between empathetic tendency levels of psychological counsellor candidates in terms of gender. This finding is in parallel with several research [41, 42, 20]. When the literature is viewed, it is seen that there are different findings on the effect of gender on empathetic tendency [43, 31, 44]. Some researchers find significant difference in favour of female participants [45, 19].

The research results indicate the existence of significant relationships between critical thinking, problem solving and empathetic tendency. According to this, an increase in one variable affects the other positively. These results are supported by those of Korur and Ekinci [16, 31].

In light of these findings, additional courses which include critical thinking problem solving and empathetic tendency contents can be delivered to psychological counseling and guidance department students. Specific different topics and challenging concepts can be discussed with students in classroom. Students can benefit from reading related literature, making use of library and internet resources and following popular publications.

References

1. Şahin, C. Bireyi Tanıma. C. Şahin, (Ed.). Bireyi tanıma teknikleri (s.1-44). Ankara: Pegem Akademi (2016)
2. Ekinci, Ö., Aybek, B. Öğretmen adaylarının empatik ve eleştirel düşünme eğilimlerinin incelenmesi. İlköğretim Online, **9**, 2, 816-827 (2010)
3. Paul, R. Critical Thinking. Retrieved From http://outopia.org/teach/resources/ critthink1.pdfrohner, (1993)
4. Finkelman, A. W. Problem solving, decision making, and critical thinking: how do they mix and why bother? Home care provider, **12**, 194–198 (2001)
5. Eldeleklioğlu, J., Özkılıç, R. Eleştirel düşünme eğitiminin PDR öğrencilerinin eleştirel düşünme becerilerine etkisi. Türk Psikolojik Danışma ve Rehberlik Dergisi, **3**, 29, 25-36 (2008)
6. Myrick, F., Yonge, O. Preceptor behaviors ıntegral to the promotion of student critical thinking. Journal For Nurses in Staff Development, **18**, 131-132 (2002)
7. Erzincanlı, S. & Zaybek, A. Hemşirelerde eleştirel düşünme eğilimi ve problem çözme becerileri arasındaki ilişki. Uluslararası Hakemli Hemşirelik Araştırmaları Dergisi, **2**, 3, 26-38 (2015)
8. Günüşen, N.P., Üstün, B. Hemşirelik öğrencilerinin problem çözme beceri düzeyleri ile kontrol odağı arasındaki ilişki. Dokuz Eylül Üniversitesi Hemşirelik Yüksekokulu Elektronik Dergisi, **4**, 72-77 (2011)
9. Gürleyük, G. C. Sınıf Öğretmeni adaylarının çeşitli değişkenler açısından eleştirel düşünme eğilimleri, problem çözme becerileri ve akademik başarı düzeylerinin incelenmesi, Yüksek Lisans Tezi (Basılmamış), Karaelmas Üniv., Zonguldak (2008)
10. Hager, P. & Kaye, M. Critical thinking ability and teacher effectiveness. Higher Education Research and Development, **10**, 2, 177-186 (1991)
11. Mcdonough, M. An Assessment of Critical Thinking at The Community College Level. Unpublished Doctoral Thesis, Columbia University (1997)
12. Akbıyık, C. Eleştirel düşünme eğilimleri ve akademik başarı. Yüksek Lisans Tezi (Basılmamış), Hacettepe Üniversitesi, Ankara (2002)
13. Tufan, D. Öğretmen adaylarının eleştirel düşünme becerileri: Orta doğu teknik üniversitesi yabancı dil öğretmenliği örneği. Yüksek Lisans Tezi (Basılmamış), Orta Doğu Teknik Üniversitesi, Ankara (2008)
14. Yeşilpınar, M. Sınıf Öğretmenlerinin ve Öğretmen Adaylarının Eleştirel Düşünmenin Öğretimine Yönelik Yeterliklerine İlişkin Görüşleri. Yüksek Lisans Tezi (Basılmamış),

Çukurova Üniversitesi, Adana (2011)
15. Göbel, D. Ş. Sınıf Öğretmenlerinin Eleştirel Düşünme Becerisi Öğretimi Yeterlilikleri ve Uygulamaları. Yüksek Lisans Tezi (Basılmamış), Sakarya Üniv., Sakarya (2013)
16. Korur, E. N., Öncü, E., Küçük Kılıç, S. Eleştirel düşünme ve empatik eğitim ilişkisi: beden eğitimi öğretmeni adayları örneği. Journal of Computer and Education Research, **4**, 8, 179-204 (2016)
17. Kesicioğlu, O. S., Güven, G. Okul Öncesi Öğretmen Adaylarinin Özyeterlik Düzeyleri ile Problem Çözme, Empati ve İletişim Becerileri Arasindaki İlişkinin İncelenmesi. Turkish Studies, **9**, 5, 1371-1383 (2014)
18. Sargın, N. Rehber Öğretmenlerin Empati Düzeylerinin Geliştirilmesine İlişkin Bir Model Önerisi. Doktora Tezi (Basılmamış), Dokuz Eylül Üniversitesi, İzmir (1993)
19. Myyry, L., & Helkama, K. University Students Value Priorities and Emotional Empathy. Educational Psychology, **21**, 1, 25-40 (2001)
20. Balcı, E. Sınıf öğretmenlerinin empatik eğilim düzeyleri (Beşiktaş İlçesi Örneği). Yüksek Lisans Tezi (Basılmamış), Yeditepe Üniversitesi, İstanbul (2012)
21. Karasar, N. Bilimsel Araştırma Yöntemi. Ankara: Nobel Akademi (2013)
22. Nachmias, C. F. & Nachmias D. Research Methods in The Social Sciences. (5th Edition), New York: St. Martin's Press (1996)
23. Facione, P. A., Facione. N. C. & Giancarlo, C. A. The Disposition toward Critical Thinking: Its Character, Measurement, and Relationship to Critical Thinking Skill. California Academic Press, **20**, 1, 91-84 (2000)
24. Kökdemir, D. Belirsizlik Durumlarında Karar Verme ve Problem Çözme. Doktora Tezi (Basılmamış), Ankara Üniversitesi, Ankara (2003)
25. Heppner, P. P. & Petersen, C. H. The Development and Implications of a Personal Problem Solving Inventory. Journal of Counseling Psychology, **29**, 1, 66-75 (1982)
26. Şahin, N., Şahin, N. H. & Heppner, P. P. The Psychometric Pro-Perties of the Problem Solving Inventory. Cognitive Therapy and Research, **17**, 4, 379-396 (1993)
27. Dökmen, Ü. Empatinin Yeni Bir Modele Dayanılarak Ölçülmesi ve Psikodrama ile Geliştirilmesi. Ankara Üniv. Eğitim Bilimleri Fakültesi Dergisi, **21**, 1, 156-190 (1988)
28. Çam O. Hemşirelik Yüksekokulu Öğrencilerinde Psikodramanın Empatik Eğilim ve Empatik Beceri Üzerine Etkisi. Ege Üniversitesi Hemşirelik Yüksekokulu Dergisi, **11**, 55-63 (1995)
29. Deniz, E. Öğretmen Adaylarının Eleştirel Düşünme Beceri Düzeyleri Üzerine Bir İnceleme. Yüksek Lisans Tezi (Basılmamış), Hacettepe Üniversitesi, Ankara (2009)
30. Ekinci, Ö. Öğretmen Adaylarının Empatik ve Eleştirel Düşünme Eğilimlerinin İncelenmesi. Yüksek Lisans Tezi (Basılmamış), Çukurova Üniversitesi, Adana (2009)
31. Loken, M. L. Critical Thinking Abilities of Undergraduate Entry-Level Athletic Training Students. Unpublished Doctoral Thesis, The University Of South Dakota, USA (2005)
32. Akar, C. İlköğretim öğrencilerinde eleştirel düşünme becerileri. Doktora Tezi (Basılmamış), Gazi Üniversitesi, Ankara (2007)
33. Erdoğan, İ. İlköğretim din kültürü ve ahlak bilgisi öğretmen adaylarının eleştirel düşünme eğilim düzeyleri üzerine bir inceleme. Yüksek Lisans Tezi (Basılmamış), Necmettin Erbakan Üniversitesi, Konya (2012)
34. Özelçi, S. Y. Eleştirel düşünme tutumunu etkileyen faktörler: Sınıf öğretmeni adayları üzerine bir çalışma. Doktora Tezi (Basılmamış), Adnan Menderes Üniversitesi, Aydın (2012)
35. Aktaş, G.S., Ünlü, M. Critical Thinking Skills of Teacher Candidates of Elementary Mathematics. Procedia-Social And Behavioral Sciences, **93**, 831-835 (2013)
36. Yıldırım, A. Empati ve Çatışmalar. Ankara: Yargı (2005)
37. Kızıltaş, Y. Sınıf Öğretmeni Adaylarının ve Sınıf Öğretmenlerinin Eleştirel Düşünme

Eğilimlerinin Çeşitli Değişkenler Açısından İncelenmesi (Van İli Örneği). Yüksek Lisans Tezi (Basılmamış), Yüzüncü Yıl Üniversitesi, Van (2011)

38. Taylan, S. Heppner'in problem çözme envanteri'nin uyarlama, geçerlik ve güvenirlik çalışmaları. Doktora Tezi (Basılmamış), Ankara Üniv., Ankara (1990)
39. Tümkaya, S., İflazoğlu, A. Ç.Ü. Sınıf öğretmenliği öğrencilerinin otomatik düşünce ve problem çözme düzeylerinin bazı sosyo-demografik değişkenlere göre incelenmesi. Ç.Ü. Sosyal Bilimler Dergisi, **6**, 6, 143-158 (2000)
40. Tanrıdağ, Ş. R. Ankara'daki Ruh Sağlığı Hizmetlerinde Çalışan Personelin Empatik Eğilim ve Empatik Beceri Düzeylerinin Çeşitli Değişkenler Açısından İncelenmesi. Doktora Tezi (Basılmamış), Hacettepe Üniversitesi, Ankara (1992)
41. Ercoşkun, H. M. Sınıf Öğretmenliği Öğrencilerinin Empatik Eğilimlerinin Çeşitli Değişkenler Açısından İncelenmesi. Yüksek Lisans Tezi (Basılmamış), Atatürk Üniversitesi, Erzurum (2005)
42. Genç, S. Z., Kalafat, T. Öğretmen adaylarının demokratik tutumları ile problem çözme becerilerinin çeşitli değişkenler açısından incelenmesi, Pamukkale Üniversitesi Eğitim Fakültesi Dergisi, **22**, 10-22 (2007)
43. Arslanoğlu, C. Farklı Bölümlerde Öğrenim Gören Beden Eğitimi ve Spor Yüksekokulu Öğrencilerinin Empatik Eğilim Düzeyleri ve Saldırganlık İlişkisinin İncelenmesi. Doktora Tezi (Basılmamış), Gazi Üniversitesi, Eğitim Bilimleri Enstitüsü (2012)
44. Schieman S., Van Gundy K. The Personal and Social Links between Age and Self-Reported Empathy. Social Psychology Quarterly, **63**, 152–174 (2000)

The relationship between quality of life and social support among adolescents

Hatice Kumcağız[1a], and Cengiz Şahin[2]

[1] Ondokuz Mayis University, Department Psychological Counseling and Guidance, Samsun, Turkey
[2] Ahi Evran University, Department Psychological Counseling and Guidance, Kırşehir, Turkey

Abstract. Social support plays an important role in quality of life. The social support given to adolescents is thought to positively affect identity development and life quality as well as physical and psychosocial health. In this context, this study aims to examine the relationship between adolescents' quality of life and social support levels. Designed as a relational screening model, the study was conducted at 5 secondary schools with 436 voluntarily participating students in Dulkadiroğlu, Kahraman Maraş during the 2016-2017 academic year. Within the study, the "Life Quality Scale for Children" and the "Social Relationship Principles Scale for Adolescents" was implemented. In the data analysis process, descriptive statistics, multiple regression analysis and Pearson Product-Moment Correlation analysis tests were used. According to the study results, a positive relationship was found between friends and family support and physical health, psychosocial health and quality of life.
Keywords: Social support, quality of life, adolescent.

1 Introduction

Adolescence is one of the critical stages in human's developmental process. Especially in adolescence, unhealthy behaviors such as substance abuse, sexually risky behaviors and anti-social attitudes or life styles are observed [1], which negatively affect the life quality of adolescents.

Quality of life is described by the World Health Organization as an individual's expectations, anxieties and standards s/he possess for both the past and future within the context of his/her values and culture [2]. In recent years, the number of researches for improving the life quality of adolescences through providing them with guidance has increased [3]. In the related literature, there are specific studies examining the effects of life

[a] Corresponding author: haticek@omu.edu.tr

quality on health during adolescence [4, 5, 6]. Life quality is thought to be associated with social support.

Social support refers to support systems in which an individual receives emotional, financial, social and cognitive help from his surroundings [7]. Social support systems play an important role in an individual's well-being being high. Social support systems are especially of significance during adolescence. Social support possesses a intervention role in both preventing risky situations and plays a facilitating role in attaining targets [8]. In the related literature, studies show that family support enhances the well-being of adolescents [9, 10].

Inadequacies in social support among adolescents can result in specific problems such as loneliness, low self-respect etc. [11]. Quality of life is one of the basic goals of humankind. It is pointed out that adolescents who have a high quality of life experience less physical and psychological problems [12]. Covering many sides of an individual's life, quality of life is defined as an individual's self-perceptions concerning his own life. Certain indicators such as physical and psycho-social well-being, participation in social life, and satisfactory relationships with family and friends are among the essential factors of life quality [13]. An adolescent of which physical and emotional needs are met by his parents can adapt to the changes in his surrounding environment more easily [14]. In this study, the relationships between quality of life and social support among adolescents were examined. The study findings are significant in terms of revealing the effects of social support on life quality.

2 Method

2.1 Research design

This is a descriptive study. The study makes use of a relational screening model so as to examine the relationships between life quality and social relations of adolescents.

2.2 Study sample

The study was conducted at 5 different secondary grade schools in Dulkadiroğlu, Kahraman Maraş during the 2016-2017 education year. The study sample consists of 436 voluntarily participating students. Among the participant students, 242 were girls (55.5%) and 194 were boys (44.5%); 148 were in 6th grade (33.9%), 146 were in 7th grade (33.5%), 142 were in 8th grade (32.6%). In terms of the participants' mothers' educational backgrounds, it was revealed that 55 mothers (12.6%) were illiterate; 257 had graduated from primary school (58.6%); 85 had graduated from secondary school (19.5%); 24 from high school (5.5%) and 15 from university (3.4%). Regarding their fathers' educational background, it was seen that 16 fathers were illiterate (3.7%); 216 had graduated from primary school (49.5%); 55 from high school (12.6%) and 29 from university (6.7%). Upon reviewing the mothers' occupations, the results indicated that 381 were housewives (87.4%); 36 were workers (8.3%); 9 were officers (2.1%); 9 were self-employed (2.1%) and 1 was retired (2%). As for the fathers, 18 were unemployed (4.1%); 174 were workers (39.9%); 54 were officers (12.4%); 165 were self-employed (37.8%) and 25 were retired (5.7%).

2.3 Data collection instruments

The study data was collected using the "Life Quality Scale for Children (LQSFC)" and the "Social Relationship Principles Scale for Adolescents."

The Life Quality Scale for Children (LQSFC) – The LQSFC was developed by Varni et al. (1999) to measure the life quality of children ages 2-18 and adolescents in terms of health, and adapted into Turkish by Memik et al. (2008) [15, 16]. The LQSFC consists of 23 items questioning the physical functioning, emotional functioning, social functioning and school functioning domains of children. The scoring is applied on three domains. The Psycho-Social Health Total Score (PSHTS) is measured by calculating firstly the total scale score, secondly the physical health total score (PHTS), and thirdly calculating the items assessing the emotional, social and educational/school functioning. The instrument indicates that the higher the total score is, the better the participants' perceptions are towards what a healthy life quality entails [16].

Social Relationship Principles Scale: The Social Relationship Principle Scale was developed by Turner, Frankel and Levin (1983) in order to measure individuals' social support perceptions, and the instrument was adapted into Turkish by Duyan et al. (2013) [17, 18]. It has two sub-dimensions labelled Family support and Friends support. The Cronbach Alpha value was measured as .81 and the test-retest reliability was found to be .85. Regarding the sub dimensions of the scale, the Cronbach Alpha was measured as .74 for Family support and .75 for Friend support. There are 15 items in the scale measuring the social relationship principles of individuals. The scores that can be obtained from the scale ranges between 15 and 75. High scores from the scale indicates that an individual thinks that s/he receives high social support from his/her environment [18].

2.4 Data analysis

In the data analysis process, descriptive statistics, multiple regression analysis and Pearson Product-Moment Correlation analysis tests were used, all of which were parametric tests, and the significance level was accepted as .05.

3 Findings

The findings obtained from this study are listed below:

1. Do the sub dimensions of the Social Relationship Principles Scale for Adolescents' Family and Friend Support predict the physical and psycho-social health and life satisfaction levels of the children, which are the components of the Life Quality Scale for Children?

A multiple regression analysis was conducted to determine whether the sub dimensions of the Social Relationship Principles Scale for Adolescents' Family and Friend Support predict the physical and psycho-social health and life satisfaction levels of the children, which were obtained from the Life Quality Scale for Children. The analysis results are presented in Table 1 below.

Table 1. Multiple regression analysis results related to predicting adolescents' physical and psycho-social health, and life satisfaction

Multiple Regression Analysis Results In Predicting Adolescents' Physical Health					
Variable	B	Std Error	Beta	T	p
Constant	393.790	45.796	-	8.713	.000
Friend support	2.210	1.237	.095	1.787	.075
Family support	5.700	1.750	.173	3.257	,001
R=0.233 R^2= 0.054, F(2,433)=12.470 p= .000					
Multiple Regression Analysis Results In Predicting Adolescents' Psycho-social Health					
Variable	B	Std Error	Beta	T	p
Constant	545.771	74.966		7.280	.000
Friend support	7.404	2.051	.185	3.610	.000
Family support	11.726	2.903	.208	4.040	.000
R= 0.338, R^2= 0.114, F(2,433)=27.863 p= .000					
Multiple Regression Analysis Results In Predicting Adolescents' Life Satisfaction					
Variable	B	Std Error	Beta	T	p
Constant	939,562	104,743		8,970	,000
Friend support	9,614	2,866	,172	3,355	,001
Family support	17,426	4,056	,221	4,297	,000
R= 0.338, R^2= 0.115, F(2,433)=27.997 p= .001					

Table 1 displays a meaningful relationship between the scores of friend and family support, and physical health (R= .233 , R^2= .054, p< .01), and that friend and family support scores explained the .05% of the total variance of physical health values. Similarly, a statistically significant relationship was seen between the scores of friend and family support, and psycho-social health (R= .338; R^2= .114, p<.01). Family and friends support scores explained the .11% of the total variance of psycho-social health values. Additionally, there was a meaningful relationship between the scores of friends and family support, and life quality (R= .338; R^2= .115, p< .01), and family and friends support scores explained about .11% of the total variance of life quality values.

2. Is there a meaningful relationship between the sub dimensions of the Social Relationship Principles Scale for Adolescents' Family and Friend Support and the components of the Life Quality Scale for Children -physical and psycho-social health scores, and life satisfaction?

Pearson Product-Moment Correlation analysis was applied to determine the relationships between the sub dimensions of the Social Relationship Principles Scale for Adolescents-Family and Friend support- and the components of the Life Quality Scale for Children -physical and psycho-social health scores, and life satisfaction. The analysis results are given in Table 2 below.

DOI: 10.1051/shsconf/20173701053

Table 2. Pearson product-moment correlation analysis results fostering the relationships among the scores obtained from "social relationship principles scale for adolescents" and "life quality scale for children"

	Correlation coefficients related to the relationship between family and friend supports, and physical health			
		n	r	p
Social Relationship Principles	Family support	436	.218	.000**
	Friend support	436	.177	.000**
	Correlation coefficients related to the relationship between family and friend supports, and psycho-social health			
		n	r	p
Social Relationship Principles	Family support	436	.296	.000**
	Friend support	436	.284	.000**
	Correlation coefficients related to the relationship between family and friend supports, and life quality			
		n	r	p
Social Relationship Principles	Family support	436	.302	.000**
	Friend support	436	.277	.000**

**p<0.01

Table 2 demonstrates that there is statistically weak but positive relations between family support and physical health (r=.218; p<.01), friend support and physical health (r=.177; p<.01), family support and psycho-social health (r=.296; p<.01),), friend support and psycho-social health (r=.284; p<.01), family support and life quality (r=.302; p<.01),), and friend support and life quality (r=.277; p<.01).

4 Discussion

The study results found meaningful relationships between family and friends support, and physical and psycho-social health and life quality. To the multiple regression analysis results, friends and family support explained .05% of the physical health, and .11% of the life quality and psycho-social health. In this sense, family and friends support can be said to predict the life quality of adolescents.

Another finding of the study is that there was a positive relationship between family and friends support and physical and psycho-social health and life quality. Thus, the adolescents who receive high family and friend support can also be said to possess high levels of psycho-social and physical health, and life quality.

In the related literature there are studies showing that students who do not receive support from their friends and families tend to experience specific problems such as anxiety, introversion, identity confusion etc. [19, 20, 21]. Similarly, research findings indicate low levels of life quality among those adolescents who receive insufficient social support [22]. In this sense, the study findings can be claimed to be supported by the findings in the literature. It can be inferred that receiving support from family and friends is influential on adolescents' physical, psycho-social health and life quality. The reason for this might be that adolescents who receive sufficient support from family and friends tend to develop positive attitudes and behaviors, and to improve social skills, which in turn have a positive effect on their life quality.

The study findings suggest that organizing seminars for families and students and psycho-educational group guidance programs for students with low life quality will be helpful in raising awareness about the importance of social support.

References

1. Ramos, P., Moreno, C., Rivera, F. & Pérez P.J. Integrated Analysis of The Health and Social İnequalities of Spanish Adolescents. International Journal of Clinical Health Psychology, **10**, 3, 477-98 (2010)
2. Whoqol Group. The World Health Organization Quality of Life Assessment (Whoqol): Position Paper From The World Health Organization. Social Science & Medicine, **10**, 1403-1409 (1995)
3. Barker, G. Adolescents, social support and helpseeking behavior: an international literature review and program consultation with recommendations for action. Department of child and adolescent health and development, World Health Organization: WHO Discussion Papers on Adolescence (2007)
4. Edwards, T.C., Huebner, C.E., Connell, F.A.,& Patrick, D.L. Adolescent quality of life, part I: Conceptual and measurement model. Journal of Adolescence, **25**, 275-286 (2002)
5. Drukker, M., Kaplan, C., Schneiders, J., Feron, F.J.M., Van, Os, J. The wider social environment and changes in self-reported quality of life in the transition from late childhood to early adolescence: A Cohort Study. BMC Public Health, **6**, 133 (2006)
6. Polinder, S., Haagsma, J.A., Belt, E., Lyons, R.A., Erasmus, V., Lund, J., et al. A systematic review of studies measuring health-related quality of life of general injury populations. BMC Public Health, **10**, 783 (2010).
7. Cohen, S. Social Relationships and Health. American Psychologist, 676-684(2004).
8. Traş Z., Arslan, E. An Investigation of Perceived Social Support and Social Self-Efficacy in Adolescents. Elementary Educational Online, **12**, 4, 1133-1140 (2013).
9. Sarkova, M., Bacikova - Sleskova, M., Orosova, O., Greckova, A.M., Katreniakova, Z., & Jitse, W. The Associations Between Assertiveness, Psychological Well-Being and Self-Esteem İn Adolescents. Journal Of Applied Social Psychology, **43**, 1, 147-154 (2013)
10. Leme, V.B.R., Del Prette Z.A.P., & Coimbra, S. Social Skills, Social Support and Well-Being in Adolescents Of Different Family Configurations. Paidéia , **25**, 60, 9-18 (2015)
11. Çivitci, N., Çivitci A. Self-esteem as mediator and moderator of the relationship between loneliness and life satisfaction in adolescents. Personality and Individual Differences, **47**, 954-8 (2009)
12. Gilman, R., Huebner, E.S. Characteristics of adolescents who report very high life satisfaction. Journal of youth and adolescence, **35**, 311-9 (2006)
13. Ateş, F. B. & Akbaş, T. Ergenlerde Görülen Kural Dışı Davranışların Aile İşlevselliği Ve Yaşam Kalitesi Açısından İncelenmesi. Ç.Ü. Sosyal Bilimler Enstitüsü Dergisi, **21**, 2, 337-352 (2012)
14. Buehler, C., Gerard, J.M. Marital Conflict, Ineffective Parenting, and Clidren's and Adolescents' Maladjustment. Journal of Marriage and Family, **64**, 78-92 (2002)
15. Varni, J.W., Seid, M.,& Rode, C.A. The Pedsql: Measurement Model for the Pediatric Quality of Life Inventory. Med Care, **37**,126-139 (1999)
16. Memik, Ç.N., Ağaoğlu, B., Coşkun, A. & Karakaya, I. Çocuklar İçin Yaşam Kalitesi Ölçeğinin 8-12 Yaş Çocuk Formunun Geçerlik Ve Güvenirliği. Çocuk ve Gençlik Ruh Sağlığı, **15**, 2, 87-98 (2008)
17. Turner, R. J., Frankel, B. G., Levin, D. M. Social Support: Conceptualization, Measurement, and Implications for Mental Health. In J. R. Greeley (Ed.), Research İn

DOI: 10.1051/shsconf/20173701053

Community And Mental Health (67-111). Greenvich, CT: JAI Press (1983)

18. Duyan, V., Gelbal, S. & Çalık V.E. Sosyal İlişki Unsurları Ölçeği'nin Türkçeye Uyarlama Çalışması. Hacettepe Üniversitesi Eğitim Fakültesi Dergisi, **44**, 159-169 (2013)
19. Açıkgöz, Ö. 11. Sınıf Öğrencilerinin Algıladıkları Sosyal Destek Düzeyleri İle Sosyal Beceri Düzeyleri Arasındaki İlişkinin Bazı Değişkenler Açısından İncelenmesi, Yüksek Lisans Tezi (Basılmamış), Gaziantep Üniversitesi, Eğitim Bilimleri Enstitüsü, Gaziantep (2013)
20. Ermiş, B.B. Bir Sosyal Destek Kaynağı Olarak Aile. 5. Aile Şurası Aile Destek Hizmetleri Bildirileri. Ankara: T.C. Başbakanlık Aile Ve Sosyal Araştırmalar Genel Müdürlüğü Yayınları, 11-19 (2008)
21. Demaray, M.K., & Malecki, C. Critical Levels of Perceived Social Support Associated With Student Adjustment. School Psychology Quarterly, **17**, 213–241 (2002)
22. Yount, M.A. Loneliness lack of perceived social support and the development of anger in adolescent. Unpublished Master's Thesis. California State University, Fullerton (2000)

Research on the achievement motivation levels of the amateur football players

İlimdar Yalçın[1a], Fehmi Çalık[2], Fikret Ramazanoğlu[1], and Ömer Faruk Tutar[3]

[1]Department of Physical Education and Sport Teaching, Faculty of Sport Sciences, Sakarya University, Turkey
[2]Department of Recreation, Faculty of Sport Sciences, Sakarya University, Turkey
[3]Department of Physical Education and Sport Teaching, Institute of Educational Sciences Sakarya University, Turkey

Abstract. This study was conducted to determine the achievement motivation levels of the amateur football players based upon the importance of motivation on the athletes' successes. The research group comprises 243 voluntary amateur football players who actively participated in the competitions during 2016-2017 season in Elazig. In the study, "Sports-Specific Achievement Motivation Scale" that was developed by Willis (1982) and adapted to Turkish by Tiryaki and Godelek (1997) was used. The collected data were analyzed through SPSS 22 programme. The margin of error was accepted as $p<0.05$. The cronbach alpha value was found as ,78. Consequently; when the subscales of achievement motivation of the amateur soccer players participating in the study were analyzed with some variables, it was found that there was a statistically significant difference between those aged 22-24 years and those aged 25-27 years in approach success. In the team playing year variable, the statistical significance was found between the ones who have 1 year football history in the team and those who are 5 years or more in the approach success. It was observed the approach to achievement motivation increased as the experience of playing for a team increased. As for the year of working with a trainer variable, it was found that there was a statistically significant difference between those who had 1 year past with coach and those who had 2 years past with the motivation to avoid failure.
Keywords: Amateur, football, achievement, motivation

1 Introduction

Athletes generally want to keep their performance levels at the highest level, whether they are participating in training or participating. At this stage, the athlete sometimes faces both physical and psychological factors. Physical skills may be at the highest level in

[a] Corresponding author: ilimdaryalcin@gmail.com

sports, however; if the athlete is psychologically inadequate, performance can not be successful. One of the most important factors affecting physical and psychological performance is motivation.

Motivation is to drive a person to work, to act and to inspire. Motivation can also be defined as "people behave with their own desires to achieve a specific purpose" [5].

The simplest way to understand motivation is to accept it as a process and divide it into the basic parts (needs, motivations, goals) that make up it [8]. Motivation can also be defined as the name of the process, which is influenced by one's motive and leads to sport activities depending on the current situations [4]. Motivation is also directly related to learning experiences, different personality traits, environmental factors, and physical well-being [2].

One of the most misunderstood areas of motivation is the sports. The reasons for this can be listed as follows:

-Motivation is often confused by the coaches with the concept of arousal or activation. Before the match or training, it is wrong to consider that talking to the team at the meeting, talking about the game etc. are motivated athletes.

-A second concept mixed with motivation is positive thinking. Expressing the long working hours of the team may provide a positive impression of being a team based on talented athletes, but it does not provide motivation [9].

The relationship between the power of motivation and success is very important, especially in the sports environment. If the motive power is low, it is sure to result in a low success. Every individual tends to being in peaceful situations and avoiding in disturbing situations. Orientation and avoidance situations are present in the structure of the instigators. If which tendency is more severe, motives belong to it is emerge. According to this, while success is driven by success or avoidance of failure, friendship motivation occurs in the search for reputation or avoiding rejection [8].

Motivation in sport is gathered under two different themes. First of them are the orientation of the purpose of fulfilling a certain task and improving the talent and competence of the person; the second is the ego orientation, which demands motivation to perform better and be better than other factors [3].

In sports achievement motivation, the immediate vicinity of the athlete usually plays a decisive role in his or her expectation level. The athlete, who can pass on to the athletes who are shown competitors to him/her, would not be satisfied if he could not choose the standards for his/her success and could not put them because she/he can not develop a feeling beyond whose vicinity wants. Every athlete who wants to be successful develops a qualification scale for himself. When the athlete passes or reaches the limits of his superior achievement, he may not make much efforts to achieve it. The athlete balances himself / herself with the fear of failure and the achievement prospect [7].

The studies on the concept of motivation for success from the psychological factors which are important influences on the performance situation in the sports environment are frequently discussed both our country and the international arena. It is thought that the investigation of this concept will contribute to both the psychological and physical qualities of the coaches and the athletes in the contest or competition environment in the positive direction. In this respect, the aim of this study is to examine the motivation level of success of the athletes playing football in amateur leagues.

2 Method

The research is a descriptive model for determining the motivation level of amateur soccer players and is in the relational screening model.

2.1 Research group

The research group consists of 248 volunteer athletes who are actively play football in amateur clubs in Elazig during the 2016-2017 season. The 248 data obtained were not processed because 5 data did not show normal distribution. Therefore, the research group based on the study was designated as 243.

2.2 Data collection tools

In the research, "Sports Specific Achievement Motivation Scale" developed by Willis (1982) was used [12]. The scale consists of a total of 40 items and the items are of the five-point likert type, expressed as "never", "very little", "sometimes", "pretty much" and "always". The scale consists of three sub-dimensions. These; 12 items (1,3,5,7,9,10,11,13,21,29,30,35) related to power motive, 17 items (4,6,8,12,16,18,19,20,23,24,26,31,32,33,36,38,39) related to motive to approach success and 11 items (2,14,15,17,22,25,27,28,34,37,40) related to motive to avoid failure. The validity and reliability studies of your scale were made on 996 university and high school students. For three subscales, the alpha reliability coefficient was between $r = 0.76$ and 0.78, and the test repeatability reliability coefficient was between $r = 0.69$ and 0.75. The scale adapted to Turkish athletes by Tiryaki and Gödelek (1997). As a result of the reliability analyzes conducted by Tiryaki and Gödelek (1997), alpha reliability coefficients were found as $r = 0,81$ for the power motive subscale, $r = 0,82$ motive to approach success subscale and $r = 0,80$ for the motive to avoid failure [9].

2.3 Analysis of the data

The data obtained in the study were taken from the SPSS 22 package program and the frequency (f) and percent (%) distributions of the variables were calculated. The histograms were checked by evaluating skewness and kurtosis to ensure normal distribution of the data. Therefore, the t-test and variance analysis (Anova) test was used. Tukey test results were used to determine which groups differed in meaningful differences. The margin of error in the study was taken as $p<0.05$. The cronbach alpha value of the study was found as 0,78.

3 Findings

In this section, findings about variables of study are included. The findings showing the distribution of amateur football players according to their personal qualities were analyzed and interpreted.

Table 1. Sports specific achievement motivation according to age variation of amateur footballers statistical distribution values related to the level of sub-dimensions

	Age	N	$\overline{X}$	Sd	F	p
Power Motive	16 - 18	23	45.21	6.47	1.41	0.23
	19 - 21	95	43.30	5.23		
	22 - 24	35	42.60	5.48		
	25 - 27	34	44.32	5.46		
	28 and over	56	44.83	6.63		
	Total	243	43.88	5.79		
Approach Success	16 - 18	23	68.26	5.20	3.05	0.01*
	19 - 21	95	68.64	5.90		
	22 - 24*	35	66.51	6.98		
	25 - 27*	34	71.11	3.55		
	28 and over	56	68.78	4.83		
	Total	243	68.67	5.60		
Avoid to Failure	16 - 18	23	38.95	5.13	0.09	0.98
	19 - 21	95	39.57	6.75		
	22 - 24	35	39.45	6.38		
	25 - 27	34	39.50	6.76		
	28 and over	56	39.98	8.29		
	Total	243	39.58	6.91		

*Level of meaningful difference determined as $p<0.05$.

When the analysis results of the level of success motivation sub-dimensions specific to the age of the amateur football players participating in the study in table-1 are examined, a statistically significant difference was found between those in the age range of 22-24 years and those in the range of 25-27 years in the success approach motivation sub-dimension ($p<0.05$).

Table 2. Statistical distribution values related to the level of sports specific achievement sub-dimensions according to the yearly variable of amateur football players playing in the team

	Year of the Play Football in Team	N	$\overline{X}$	Sd	F	p
Power Motive	1 year	62	42.59	5.58	1.22	0.30
	2 years	52	43.78	5.10		
	3 years	40	44.30	7.07		
	4 years	30	44.40	5.59		
	5 and over	59	44.76	5.66		
	Total	243	43.88	5.79		
Approach Success	1 year*	62	66.82	6.64	2.65	0.03*
	2 years	52	68.67	4.84		
	3 years	40	69.22	5.64		
	4 years	30	69.56	4.99		
	5 and over*	59	69.81	4.94		
	Total	243	68.67	5.60		
Avoid to Failure	1 year	62	37.95	7.13	1.61	0.17
	2 years	52	40.48	6.47		
	3 years	40	41.15	6.87		
	4 years	30	39.60	5.56		
	5 and over	59	39.44	7.50		
	Total	243	39.58	6.91		

*Level of meaningful difference determined as $p<0.05$.

When the analysis results of the level of the sport-specific success motivation sub-dimensions according to the variable year of playing in team amateur football players participating in the study in table-2 are examined, it was found that there was a statistically significant difference between the playing 1 year and 5 years and over in approach success ($p<0.05$).

Table 3. Statistical distribution values regarding sports-specific achievement motivation sub-dimension levels by amateur footballer's yearly variable of coaching work

	Years of Woking with Coach	N	$\bar{X}$	Sd	F	p
Power Motive	1 year	86	43.73	5.94	1.09	0.35
	2 years	41	43.24	4.50		
	3 years	54	43.14	4.92		
	4 years	30	45.06	4.98		
	5 years and over	32	45.21	8.30		
	Total	243	43.88	5.79		
Approach Success	1 year	86	67.61	6.16	1.28	0.27
	2 years	41	68.90	5.20		
	3 years	54	69.20	5.58		
	4 years	30	69.50	3.86		
	5 years and over	32	69.59	5.81		
	Total	243	68.67	5.60		
Avoid to Failure	1 year*	86	37.93	7.11	3.48	0.00*
	2 years*	41	42.12	5.82		
	3 years	54	39.48	6.58		
	4 years	30	41.66	4.79		
	5 years and over	32	39.00	8.60		
	Total	243	39.58	6.91		

*Level of meaningful difference determined as $p<0.05$.

When the results of analysis of the level of success motivation subspecific according to the variation of year of coach working with amateur soccer players participating in the study in table- 3 were examined, It was observed that there was a statistically significant difference between the ones who worked 1 year and those who worked for 2 years.with the coach in the failure avoidance motivation subscale ($p<0.05$).

4 Discussion and conclusion

In this section, the findings about whether the sub-dimensions of the sport-specific success motivation of 243 amateur soccer players participating in this study differ according to some variables are discussed and interpreted.

When the results of amateur soccer players' age variable and sport - specific success motivation sub - dimensions were examined, a statistically significant difference was found between those in the 22-24 age range and those in the 25-27 age range in the success approach motivation subscale ($p<0.05$). It was found to be a favorable difference between age 25-27. It has been observed that older footballers have a higher level of approaching success than younger ones. This confirms that the age factor is directly related to experience. When different studies are examined; it is observed that there is a statistically significant relation between age and power motive in a study on sport-specific success motivation made to the sportsmen participating in the summer school sports made by Ustun et al. . Although there is no significant difference in approach to achievement subscale, we found that older adults had higher levels of motivation to approach success than younger ones [11]. It has been determined by Mladenovic et al. hat there is a statistically significant difference in age level between young athletes and non-athletes in relation to their ability to show individual strength and achievement motivation, and to show a decisive effect [6].

When the results of amateur soccer players' variation of current team playing years and sport-specific success motivation sub-dimensions are examined, it is determined that there is a statistically significant difference between the ones who played in the current team and those who played 5 years in the approach motivation sub-dimension ($p<0.05$). It has been observed that there is a meaningful difference in favor of soccer players who played in the current team for more than 5 years. It has been found that as the number of years of team play increases, it also steadily increases at the level of approaching success. It can be said that the approach of the athletes to the success and the increase of their performance are related to the duration of the team and get to know team well. When a different study result is examined, there is no statistically difference between the duration of playing in the team and the sport-specific success motivation sub-dimensions in a study on motivational factors affecting team performance by Ural [10]. However, although there is no difference, as the number of years of playing in the current team increases, it has been observed that there is an impetus to approach success and an impetus to avoid failure [10]. In this respect, Ural's work shows smilarity with our study [10].

When the results of amateur soccer's woking years with current coach and sport-specific success motivation sub-dimensions are examined, it was observed that there was a statistically significant difference between the ones who worked 1 year and those who worked for 2 years.with the coach in the failure avoidance motivation subscale ($p<0.05$). The difference was found to be favorable to the current coach who has been working for 2 years. It has been observed that the level of motivation for avoiding unsuccessful athletes who have started to work with the current coach is very low. This indicates that the athletes who started to work with a new coach are related to the period of adaptation team and coach. When different studies are examined; in a study conducted by Yalcin in order to examine the motivations of success of hearing-impaired futsal athletes, it was determined that there is a statistically significant relationship between the current coach working year variant and the approach to success. As the number of years of work with the current coach increased, the level of approach to success increased [13]. Similarly, in a study conducted by Abakay on the relation of footballer and coach communication with success motivation of footballers of different statutes, it was determined that there is no statistically difference between the subscales of success motivation specific to sport and the current coach working year variable. However, it was observed that the level of motivation for avoidance of unsuccessful athletes with low working years with current coach was low. Although it did not differ, it was observed that the level of motivation for avoidance of failure athletes with low working years with current coach was low [1].

As a result; Statistically significant results were found between the age variable of amateur soccer players participating in the study and the level of motivation to approach success. It has been observed that older athletes tend to approach success more than young athletes. It has been determined that there is a statistically significant difference between playing in the current team year variance and the approach to success. As the number of years of playing in the current team increased, it was observed that the level of approach to success increased proportionally. When we look at the variation of yearly work with current coach, It was observed that there was a statistically significant difference between the motive to avoid failure and the current coach and working years.

Regarding the results of the study the following recommendations are made:

-As playing time of amateur football players increase their approach to success also increase in a proportional way. That is why it is reccomended to coaches and club menagers to make long-time period aggrements with football players.

-As working time increase between amateur football players and coaches while their approach to success increase, their avoid to failure reduce. So it is suggested that a coach has to be employed in a club for a long-term period.

References

1. Abakay, U. Futbolcu-antrenör iletişiminin farklı statülerdeki futbolcuların başarı motivasyonuyla ilişkisi. Gazi Üniversitesi, Sağlık Bilimleri Enstitüsü, Beden Eğitimi ve Spor Anabilim Dalı, Doktora Tezi, Gaziantep, 76, (2010)
2. Barrett, D.W., Patock-Peckham, J.A., Hutchinson, G.T. & Nagoshi, C.T. Cognitive 19. motivation and religious orientation. Personality and Individual Differences, **38**, 461–74 (2005)
3. Hutzler, Y., Oz, M., Barak S. Goal perspectives and sport participation motivation of special olympians and typically developing athletes. Research in Developmental Disabilities, **34**, 2149–2160 (2013)
4. İkizler, C. Sporda başarıyı etkileyen psikolojik faktörler. Alfa Basım Yayım Dağıtım, İstanbul, 47, (1994)
5. Koçel, T. İşletme Yöneticiliği. Beta Yayınları, İstanbul, 633-653, (2003)
6. Mladenovic, M., Lazarevic, P., Trunic N., Bogavac, D. & Zivkovic, M. Differences in personality features and achievement motivation in child athletes and non-athletes. Facta Universitatis, Series: Physical Education and Sport, **14**, 3, 415 – 425 (2016)
7. Mungan, S. Sporda motivasyon faktörü olarak ödül ve ceza. Marmara Üniversitesi, Sağlık Bilimleri Enstitüsü, Beden Eğitimi ve Spor Anabilim Dalı, Yüksek Lisans Tezi, İstanbul, p.75, (1995)
8. Soyer, F., Can, Y., Güven, H., Hergüner, G., Bayansalduz, M. & Tetik, B. Sporculardaki başarı motivasyonu ile takım birlikteliği arasındaki ilişkinin incelenmesi. Uluslararası İnsan Bilimleri Dergisi, **7**, 1, 225-239 (2010)
9. Tiryaki, Ş. & Gödelek, E. Spora özgü başarı motivasyonu ölçeğinin türk sporcuları için uyarlanması çalışması. I. Uluslararası Spor Psikolojisi Sempozyumu Bildiri Kitapçığı, Bağırgan Yayınevi, Ankara, pp.128-141 (1997)
10. Ural, O. Futbolda takım performansına etki eden motivasyonel faktörlerin belirlenmesine yönelik bir uygulama (Gençlerbirliği spor kulübü örneği). Gazi Üniversitesi, Sağlık Bilimleri Enstitüsü, Beden Eğitimi ve Spor Anabilim Dalı, Yüksek Lisans Tezi, Gaziantep, p.59 (2008)
11. Üstün, Ü.D., Acet, M. & Ersoy, A. Sporcular için spora özgü başarı motivasyonu. Yaz Spor Okulundan Bir Örnek. Sosyal Bilimler Dergisi, **49**, 114-123 (2016)
12. Willis, J.D. Three Scales to Measure Competition-related Motives in Sports. Jaurnal of Sport Psychology, 338-353 (1982)
13. Yalçın, İ. İşitme engelli futsal sporcularının başarı motivasyon düzeylerinin incelenmesi. Fırat Üniversitesi, Sağlık Bilimleri Enstitüsü, Beden Eğitimi ve Spor Anabilim Dalı, Yüksek Lisans Tezi, Elazığ, p.71 (2015)

Knowledge and opinions of parents of children hospitalized in hematology/ oncology units regarding complementary and alternative medicine

Gülzade Uysal[1a], Duygu Sönmez Düzkaya[2], and Ayşe Karakoç[3]

[1] Faculty of Health Science, Department of Nursing, Okan University, Turkey
[2] Istanbul Faculty of Medicine, Directorate of Nursing Services, Istanbul University, Turkey
[3] School of Health Science, Department of Midwifery, Marmara University, Turkey

Abstract. The current study aimed to determine the knowledge and opinions of parents who had children with cancer regarding complementary and alternative medicine. This descriptive study was performed with 145 parents. Data collection was implemented by means of a literature-based questionnaire. Of the parents who were enrolled into the study, 42.1% were aged 36 years or older and 57.2% had primary school education only. A total of 86.9% of the information was gathered from the mothers of the children. All parents preferred CAM therapies for their children's treatment; more than half used herbs as CAM, and 81.4% of the parents who used CAM with held this information from healthcare professionals. All parents had insufficient knowledge about complementary and alternative treatments, including those who had opted out of conventional medicine, but wanted to learn more about them. Therefore, healthcare professionals should improve their knowledge of CAM methods and be able to appropriately enlighten parents while providing an environment in which families can freely discuss information.
Keywords: Child, cancer, parent, complementary and alternative practices.

1 Introduction

Complementary and alternative medicine (CAM) therapies are frequently used to support modern medical treatments in adult and pediatric patients. They are used often, especially for diseases that prove difficult to cure, such as cancer, and repetitive and chronic diseases, such as asthma. Families turn towards CAM therapies due to the fact that childhood cancers have increased in number and threaten life. Studies have shown that the use of CAM in treating childhood cancers and reducing symptoms have gradually increased [1-5].

[a] Corresponding author: gulzade.uysal@okan.edu.tr

The frequency of CAM therapy use for childhood cancers is between 24% and 90% [6]. The reported reasons for choosing CAM therapies among parents that have children with cancer are preventing/reducing the adverse effects of medical treatment; wanting to do everything they can for their children; slowing the progression of cancer; and strengthening the immune system [2, 3, 5, 7-11]. However, when studies regarding CAM therapies and their use are analyzed, it can be observed that there are few studies about pediatric patients and their parents. The aim of this study was to determine the knowledge and opinions regarding CAM therapies of parents with children who were hospitalized in hematology/oncology units because of cancer.

2 Method

The current study aimed to determine the knowledge and opinions of parents who had children with cancer regarding complementary and alternative medicine.

2.1 Participants

This is a descriptive cross-sectional study performed with parents of children who had been diagnosed as having cancer, aged 0-18 years, in a hematology/oncology unit of a training research hospital between February 2015, and June 2015. The samples consisted of 145 parents whose children were hospitalized between the set dates and volunteered to participate in the study.

2.2. Procedure

The data collection tools were prepared by the researchers in view of the literature and comprised 20 questions regarding the socio-demographic and condition-related characteristics of the patients and parents, and semi-structured forms that included 3-point Likert-type (Agree, Not sure, Disagree) questions regarding the parents' knowledge and opinions of CAM.

This study was organized in accordance with the Declaration of Helsinki and was given written approval by the University Research Committee. Oral and written consents were taken from all the parents that participated in the study.

The collected data in the study were analyzed through descriptive statistical calculations using the SPSS version 17.0 program.

3 Findings

Of the children who participated in the study, 42.1% were aged between 6 and 10 years, 50.3% were female, and 77.2% were hospitalized with the diagnosis of ALL. Some 59.3% were attending school and 47.6% had had their disease for less than a year. The mothers of 86.9% of the patients were informed and involved in discussions. Of the parents, 42.1% were aged 36 years or older, 88.3% were married, and more than half (57.2%) had primary school education only (Table 1).

Table 1. Descriptive Characteristics of Children and Parents (n=145)

		n	%
Age	1-5 years	38	26.2
	6-10 years	61	42.1
	11 years and above	46	31.7
Sex	Female	73	50.3
	Male	72	49.7
Diagnosis	ALL	111	77.2
	Other*	33	22.8
Attending school	Yes	86	59.3
	No	59	40.7
Year of illness	Under 1 year	69	47.6
	1-3 years	50	34.5
	More than 4 years	26	17.9
Interviewed parents	Mother	126	86.9
	Father	19	13.1
Parent age	17-27 years	34	23.4
	28-35 years	50	34.5
	36 years and over	61	42.1
Marital status	Married	128	88.3
	Single	17	11.7
Graduation	Elementary school	83	57.2
	High school	42	29.0
	University	20	13.8
Total		145	100

* XLPS, Hemolytic anemia, Ewing's sarcoma, osteosarcoma

It was determined that all parents had used CAM therapies during their child's treatment. After analyzing the methods that were used, it was discovered that 53.8% of the parents used herbs, 22.7% spiritual/physical practices, 15.2% aromatherapy, and 8.3% manipulative and body-based treatments. At the end of CAM therapies, 38.5% of the parents stated that it had had a positive effect on the treatment, 30.8% said it had had a negative effect, whereas 26.9% expressed that it had had no impact on the treatment process (Table 2).

Of the entire parent population, 76.6% thought that CAM therapies were used to reduce adverse effects, 50% to support treatment, and 34.6% to provide treatment. Additionally, 19.2% declared that they used the methods as "a last resort" (Table 2).

Some 40.7% of the parents stated they had information about CAM therapies and their sources were relatives/friends (37.2%), media (22.8%), plant scientists/herbalists (15.9%), and 9.7% said they received information through other oncology patients and patient's relatives. Furthermore, 95.2% of the parents also stated they wanted information on CAM therapies (Table 3).

Table 2. Status of parents using CAM methods (n=145)

	n	%
The methods used		
*Herb	78	53.8
Spiritual/physical practices	33	22.7
Aromatherapy	22	15.2
Manipulative and body-based treatments	12	8.3
****The reason for using CAM**		
Reducing adverse effects	111	76.5
Supporting the treatment	73	50.3
Providing treatment/Treating	50	34.4
As a last resort	27	18.6
Changes after CAM use		
It had a positive effect on the treatment	55	38.0
It had a negative effect on the treatment	45	31.0
There were no changes	39	26.8
It reduced the adverse effects of the treatment	6	4.2

*Stinging nettle, cumin, reishi mushroom, turmeric, herbal tea…
**Parents who use CAM gave multiple answers.

The knowledge and opinions of parents regarding CAM therapies are shown in Table 4. Some 81.4% of the parents agreed with the statement "I hide the fact that I use CAM therapies from healthcare professionals"; 44.8% agreed with "I shy away from asking healthcare professionals questions about CAM therapies"; and 36.6% agreed with "I think healthcare professionals will judge me for using CAM therapies." In contrast, statements of "Using CAM therapies alone is more effective"; "CAM therapies may affect treatment negatively"; and "CAM therapies can be used throughout the duration of the disease" were answered with "not sure" by nearly half of the parents (Table 4).

Table 3. Knowledge of parents regarding CAM methods (n=145)

		n	%
Receiving information about CAM	Yes	59	40.7
	No	74	51.0
	I do not remember	12	8.3
Source of information*	Relatives/friends	54	37.2
	Through media	33	22.8
	Plant scientists/herbalists	23	15.9
	Oncology patients/patient relatives	14	9.7
	Healthcare professionals (eg doctors, nurses)	5	3.4
Willingness to get information on CAM methods	Yes	138	95.2
	No	7	4.8

*There were multiple answers.

The knowledge and opinions of parents regarding CAM therapies are shown in Table 4. Some 81.4% of the parents agreed with the statement "I hide the fact that I use CAM therapies from healthcare professionals"; 44.8% agreed with "I shy away from asking healthcare professionals questions about CAM therapies"; and 36.6% agreed with "I think healthcare professionals will judge me for using CAM therapies." In contrast, statements of "Using CAM therapies alone is more effective"; "CAM therapies may affect treatment negatively"; and "CAM therapies can be used throughout the duration of the disease" were answered with "not sure" by nearly half of the parents (Table 4).

Table 4. Knowledge and Opinions of Parents Regarding Complementary and Alternative Medicine (n=145) (Agree:**A**, Not Sure:**NS**, Disagree:**D**)

	A	NS	D
1. I hide the fact that I use CAM methods.	**81.4**	11.0	7.6
2. I believe CAM methods are effective while applied with the medical treatment.	31.0	40.7	28.3
3. Using CAM therapies alone is also effective.	38.0	**49.0**	13.0
4. CAM therapies can be applied throughout the duration of the disease.	24.1	**52.5**	23.4
5. I shy away from asking healthcare professionals questions about CAM therapies.	**44.8**	38.6	16.6
6. CAM practices can be applied by a non-healthcare professional (Lokman physicians, herbalists etc.).	24.5	**41.4**	24.2
7. CAM practices should be carried out under the supervision of only healthcare professionals (nurses, physicians etc.).	31.7	**47.6**	20.7
8. I believe CAM methods could have positive effects on the patient.	22.1	**45.5**	32.4
9. I think important responsibilities fall on parents with CAM practices.	17.3	36.6	**46.2**
10. I think healthcare staff will judge me because I use CAM methods.	36.6	**45.5**	19.9
11. I believe CAM methods also have adverse effects.	26.2	**43.4**	30.4
12. Healthcare professionals should provide information about CAM practices to parents and patients.	18.6	26.9	**54.5**
13. The adverse effects of CAM methods can affect the medical treatment in a negative way.	26.9	**42.8**	30.3
14. Parents and children have the right to demand information about CAM.	20.0	33.1	**46.9**
15. I would like to get information on CAM therapies from healthcare professionals (eg doctors, nurses).	17.9	27.6	**53.5**
16. Parents and children have the right to use CAM methods, if they wish to do so.	17.2	37.9	**44.9**
17. Parents who use CAM methods should inform healthcare professionals.	19.3	29.7	**51.0**
18. Using CAM methods alongside with medical treatment shortens the treatment process.	29.7	**46.9**	23.4

4 Discussion

The incidence of childhood cancer has gradually increased, and is among the most life-threatening diseases in Turkey, as well as in the world. Pediatric patients with cancer who receive conventional treatment are often given CAM therapies to reduce or remove symptoms that appear in the course of treatment.

In our study, all parents had used CAM therapies during their child's treatment. Kilicarslan Toruner et al. [9] reviewed 14 studies published between 1998–2008 and reported that the frequency of CAM therapy use among pediatric oncology patients was high (49.8%), and similarly in other studies, the frequency of CAM therapy use for pediatric patients with cancer was reported to be between 31-84% [5, 12-15]. The frequency of CAM therapy use was lower in our study than in other studies. This result can be explained with the insufficiency in parents' educational backgrounds and therefore the difficulty they may have had in obtaining information.

The primary reasons for choosing CAM therapies reported among families' were stopping/treating the progression of cancer, and reducing the adverse effects of medical treatment [2, 8, 11, 14]. Gottscling et. al. [5] found that CAM therapies had been used physical stabilization (29%), to streghten the immune system (24%). Gomez-Martinez et al. [16] discovered that CAM therapies had been used to reduce adverse effects (53%) and fight cancer (32%) in their study. Similarly, most of the parents in our study declared that they used CAM therapies to reduce adverse effects and support the treatment.

In a literature review by Kilicarslan Toruner et al.[9], the most frequently used CAM method by parents was determined as biologically based treatments such as plants, vitamins, and minerals. Accordingly, in a study by Yeter [17], it was found that herbal CAM methods were frequently used. This method was followed by spiritual/physical practices such as praying and dreaming, aromatherapy, and manipulative body-based treatments such as massage. In our study, 53.8% of the parents who had used CAM stated that they had used herbs, and 23.1% used spiritual/physical practices.

In the literature, parents have explained that they received information about CAM methods from their friends and relatives [2, 3, 5, 12, 16, 18]. Molassiotis and Cubbin [8] found that 69.4% of the parents in their study received information through the media and 66.7% through healthcare professionals, whereas Yeter [17] reported that families had stated that they received their related information from other patients' relatives. In our study, similar to other studies, it was found out that the parents received information about CAM through relatives/friends (37.2%), media (22.8%), and other patients/patients' relatives (9.7%). The fact that most families reach information regarding CAM methods through other family members and friends shows the importance of providing reliable information that would allow for informed use of CAM.

Many studies have drawn attention to the fact that most families that use CAM therapies do not inform healthcare professionals [2, 10, 14, 19, 20]. In our study, we discovered that 81.4% of the parents withheld the CAM therapy use from healthcare professionals; 44.8% were hesitant to ask healthcare professionals questions about CAM therapies; and 36.6% thought they would be judged by healthcare professionals because they were using CAM methods. The fact that parents withheld CAM therapy use from healthcare professionals indicates that healthcare team members need to openly discuss the advantages and disadvantages of the use of these methods with the families of pediatric patients and without being judgmental. In order for children and families to adapt themselves to the disease and treatment and improve their coping skills, families should feel like they are included in the treatment process.

In our study, the parents answered with "Not sure" to "Using CAM therapies alone is also effective"; "The adverse effects of CAM therapies may affect the treatment negatively"; and "CAM therapies can be used throughout the duration of the disease" to statements that measured knowledge and opinions of parents regarding CAM (Table 4). This shows that parents need information on CAM methods.

The diagnosis and treatment processes of cancer deeply affect the child and parents. Parents strive to get information from sources such as relatives, healthcare professionals, media, and the internet to treat the disease and to reduce symptoms. In this period, they come across information and suggestions about CAM methods [16, 21]. These information and suggestions tend to increase the parents' questions and worries. Nurses should evaluate opinions, values, and information requirements of the child and parents regarding CAM methods and plan healthcare accordingly while they collect data. During this process, it makes children and parents feel more at ease about consulting healthcare professionals for information about the CAM method they are using/planning to use and expressing their thoughts and actions; it also increases nursing quality when nurses inform patients and parents without judging them in any way.

5 Conclusion and suggestions

After analyzing the findings, we conclude that the parents' knowledge regarding CAM methods is insufficient/ limited, and they feel the need withhold details about the use of CAM from healthcare professionals for fear of their opinion of its use. Concordantly, environments where families can discuss and get information on CAM methods should be created and training sessions should be planned by healthcare professionals.

Acknowledgment

The authors wish to thank Esra Ozpitir, Sabriye Celik, Zeynep Cetin and Merve Pasayigit for their assistance to this study. Regarding the research and/or authorship of this article, the authors didn't receive any financial

References

1. Bauer-Wu, S. Critique 1: Complementary and alternative medicine in pediatric oncology. Seminars in Oncology Nursing, **21**,115-118 (2005)
2. Karadeniz, C., Pınarlı, G., Oğuz, A., Gürsel, T. & Canter, B. CAM medicine use in a pediatric oncology unit in Turkey. Pediatric Blood Cancer, **48**, 540-543 (2007)
3. Gozum, S., Arikan, B., Büyükavci, M. Complementary and alternative medicine use in pediatric oncology patients in Eastern Turkey. Cancer Nursing, **30**, 38-44 (2007)
4. Quimby, E.L. The Use of Herbal Therapies in Pediatric Oncology Patients: Treating Symptoms of Cancer and Side Effects of Standard Therapies. Journal of Pediatric Oncology Nursing, **24**, 35-40 (2007)
5. Gottscling, S., Meyer, S., Langler, A., Ebinger, F., Bialas P., Gronwald, B. Use of complementary and alternative medicine in diblings of pediatric cancer patients in Germany. A population- based survey. Open Journal of Pediatrics, **4**, 93-101 (2014)
6. National Center of Complementary and Alternative Medicine-NCCAM (2007). Retrived from http://nccam.nih.gov/health/whatiscam/ Accessed: 05.02.2016
7. Mc Curdy, E., Spangler, J., Wofford, M., Chauvenet, A.R., McLean, T.W. Religiosity is associated with the use of complementary medical therapies by pediatric oncology patients. Journal of Pediatric Hematolog and Oncology, **25**, 125-129 (2003)
8. Molassiotis, A., Cubbin, D. Thinking outside the box: complementary and alternative therapies use in paediatric oncology patients. European Journal of Oncology Nursing, **8**, 50-60 (2004)
9. Kilicarslan, Toruner, E., Uysal, G., Hanoglu, Z., Algier, L. Pediatrik Onkoloji Hastalarında Tamamlayıcı ve Alternatif Tedavi Yöntemlerinin Kullanımı: Bir Literatür Taraması. DEUHYO ED, **2**, 102-109 (2009)
10. Laengler, A., Spix, C., Seifert, G., Goottschling, S., Graf, N., Kaathsch, P. Complementary and alternative treatment methods in children with cancer: A

population-based retrospective survey on the prevalence of use in Germany. European Journal of Cancer, **44**, 2233-2240 (2008)
11. Naja, F., Alameddine, M., Abboud, M., Bustami, D., Halaby, R.A. Complementary and alternative medicine use among pediatric patients with leukemia: the case of Lebanon. Integrative Cancer Therapies, **10**, 38-46., (2011)
12. Fernandez, C.V., Stutzer, C.A., Macwilliam, L., Fryer, C. Alternative and complementary therapy use in pediatric oncology patients in British Columbia: Prevalence and reasons for use and nonuse. Journal of Clinical Oncology, **16**, 1279-1286 (1998)
13. Kelly, K.M., Jacobson, J.B., Kennedy, D.D., Braudt, S.M., Mallick, M., Weiner, M.A. Use of Unconventional Therapies by Children with Cancer at an Urban Medical Center. Journal of Pediatric Hematology and Oncology, **22**, 412-416 (2000)
14. Martel, D., Bussières, J.F., Théorêt, Y., Lebel, D., MoghrABİ, A., Laurier, C. Use of alternative and complementary therapies in children with cancer, Pediatric Blood & Cancer, **44**, 660-668 (2005)
15. Hamidah, A., Rustam, Z.A., Tamil, A.M., Zarina, L.A., Zulkifli, Z.S., & Jamal R. Prevalence and Parental Perceptions of Complementary and Alternative Medicine Use by Children with Cancer in a Multi-Ethnic Southeast Asian Population. Pediatric Blood Cancer, **52**, 70-74 (2009)
16. Gomez-Martinez, R., Tlacuilo-Parra, A., Garibaldi-Covarrubias, R. Use of complementary and alternative medicine in children with cancer in Occidental, Mexico. Pediatric Blood and Cancer, **49**, 820-823 (2006)
17. Yeter G. Çocuk kanser hastalarında semptomlara yönelik tamamlayıcı ve alternatif tedavi kullanımı. (Yükseklisans Tezi, Mersin Üniversitesi, Sağlık Bilimleri Enstitüsü, Hemşirelik Anabilim Dalı) (2012)
18. Araz, N., Bülbül, S. Use of complementary and alternative medicine in a pediatric population in southern Turkey. Clinical Invest Medicine, **34**, 21-29 (2011)
19. Yeh, C.H., Tsai, J.L., Li, W., Chen, H.M., Lee, S.C., Lin, C.F., Yang, C.P. Alternative therapy in pediatric patients in Taiwan. Journal of Pediatric Hematology and Oncology, **17**, 55- 65 (2000)
20. June, B., Anne, L. Unconventional therapy use among children with cancer in Saskatchewan. Journal of Pediatric Oncology Nursing, **18**, 16-25 (2001)
21. Genc, R.E., Senol, S., Turgay, A.S., Kantar, M. Complementary and alternative medicine used by pediatric patients with cancer in western Turkey. Oncology Nursing Forum, **36**, 159-164 (2009)

The impact of spiritual leadership on empowerment and work procrastination

Arif Damar [1a], and Ersin Eskiler[2]

[1]School of Applied Sciences, Department of Accounting and Auditing, Bilecik Seyh Edebali University, 11300 Bilecik, Turkey
[2] Faculty of Sport Sciences, Department of Sport Management, Sakarya University, 54050 Sakarya, Turkey

Abstract. How will employees who get away from society because of factors such as increasing work intensity with globalization, rapid consumption by impact of capitalism, mechanized organizational structure due to technological development and momentary satisfaction through easy access to information, ensure that organizations maintain their existence, protect their level of competitive and make profits on the average? In this context, the aim of the present study was to investigate the effects of spiritual leadership on employee empowerment and work procrastination in organizations. A questionnaire was applied face-to-face to the employees of the private sports-fitness center operating in Sakarya by using judicial sampling method within the scope of the study. As a result of the analysis of the obtained data; it was determined that there was low and positive relationship between "meaning/call" which was the sub-dimension of spiritual leadership, discretion and responsiveness which was the sub dimensions of empowerment. Adoption of work by employee, sense of belonging to work and meaning of the work can produce solutions without the approval of the managers and meet the requests and needs. A negative relationship was determined between altruistic love which was the sub-dimension of spiritual leadership and work procrastination. The managers who are honest, consistent, courteous and look after employees' rights provide them not to delay their works. One of the important findings of the research is that individuals who have the control in their works will develop their self-confidence however they could delay their work.
Keywords: Empowerment, spiritual leadership, procrastination.

1 Introduction

The human is one of the indispensable elements of production resources, which will increase the competitiveness of enterprises and provide competitive advantage. Actually, to attach importance to people means to care about enterprise. The value, authority and

[a] Corresponding author: arifdamar@yandex.com

responsibility given to employees, and participation in decisions will be facilitated objectives predetermined. However, it will not be possible for employees to increase their productivity and efficiency levels alone under changing environmental conditions. It will ensure that employees find their jobs meaningful, thanks to the leaders who create the values, attitudes and behaviors and who motivate themselves and their employees in the direction of the objectives of the enterprises. Employees who are given authority and responsibility by their managers, who see that they make a difference, will adopt their works and try to do their best for their own purposes and goals. Therefore, the employees will be able to fulfill their work on time with pleasure and without delay and getting bored. Managers will improve employees' productivity, and efficiency by giving confidence and valuing their employees.

The employees really believe that managers are fair and they respect their courtesy and ideas, will enable employees to adopt the work they do, feel themselves belong to organization, increase their belief in the organization's mission and vision, and move comfortably without the approval and idea of the manager. In addition, they will continue their competitive superiority with their beliefs, comfort and creative ideas.

2 Conceptual framework

2.1 Spiritual leadership

Today, it is getting harder day by day to adapt to rapidly changing resources and conditions. For this reason, leaders are needed, who are not afraid of making decision, who can take risks, who care about not only themselves but also group as a whole. In this context leadership is to increase the degree of harmony with environment and people you work with.

Despite the development of various leadership definitions in the studies, it is possible to say that it has not been reached a consensus on the subject. The concept of leadership thought to be derived from the word "lira", which means furrow in Latin, is the creation of conditions under which self-organizing or self-learning can take place [41]. The concept that has not lost its significance throughout history and has an Anglo-Saxon origin, has entered the academic literature in the 14th century. It is a phenomenon that is seen in every developed and underdeveloped human community [4], especially in the 1950s, where in-depth studies have been made about the concept that has become a current [23]. There is a merit at the core of leadership. Namely, it is to be worthy, to benefit, and to be able to perform a task successfully [7]. In this context, leadership is the ability to make others accept its will and requests by earning their respect, trust, obedience and commitment [38]. In recent years, the concept of spiritualism has become so popular because of many factors such as the rapid consumption of capitalism by the widespread use of the internet, momentary satisfaction through easy access to information and loneliness felt by the individual and isolation from society, stress and so on [6]. Industry revolution that reduces dependency on nature has made it difficult to explain the concept of spirit and spirituality by making organizations more uncontrolled and incomprehensible with traditional, decentralized, standardized, formal bureaucracy-based and fear-based insights [1]. The concept of spirituality has not been considered in the organizational sense, and psychology discipline has been more concerned with it [19].

Soul is expressed as the essence, the life bird that religions and religious philosophies regard as a separate entity from the human body (tdk.gov.tr). It comes from the Latin word "spiritus" which means breath [22], and is defined as the power necessary for survival [6]. The spirit, which is an invisible power that gives us life, energy and inspiration, is hidden in individuals and organizations [1]. In this regard, spirituality represents an inseparable part of the identity of the person who is influential everywhere, including the workplace and a part of the center of the individual's worldview [44].

In the most general sense, spiritual leadership is "the process of touching the basic needs of both himself and his followers for spiritual prosperity, defining the values, attitudes and behaviors necessary to motivate them, creating a shared vision and value by creating a strengthened team spirit, and ultimately increasing productivity and loyal commitment through belonging" [13, 15].

Spiritual leadership consists of 5 dimensions: vision, altruistic love, hope/faith, meaning/calling, membership [13, 28]. The altruistic love is expressed as favour, harmony and integrity that arise through interest and anxiety and as care for themselves and others. Hope is the desire to perform the work while faith is more than desirable. Assurance of hope is to believe in invisible [13]. Vision is a photo that reflects the goals and objectives of organizations desired to perform in the future [7]. Hence, a vision is needed to encourage and challenge employees to do their best [14]. Employees' work and life are meaningful when they are motivated and feel to be useful at work [32]. Membership is stated as the feeling of being a member of the organization who are understood and appreciated by the managers [19].

2.2 Empowerment

Today, in the face of changing competition conditions, customer expectancies, consumer needs and demands, organization are no longer interested only in maintaining their presence, they want to make a profit on the average, and even to gain a competitive advantage in the market. Therefore, organization help the worker to improve the quality of their work and to adopt their work as their own by educating, developing, increasing their authority and responsibilities, enabling them to participate in decisions and to take the initiative in what they do, on the basis of human resource management. In fact, the power is defined as "a motion that causes an event and ability to resist" according to Turkish Language Association but is described as affecting the behavior of others in the direction of their own goals and objectives [38]. The concept of empowerment in the context of management is asserted to have firstly emerged in the writings and philosophies of American political scientist Follet at beginning of 19th century [20, 40].

Researches on the concept of empowerment defined as the basic component of organizational and managerial effectiveness; began with Founder of Scientific Management, Taylor's motion and time study in the 1920s [24] and are considered as a cognitive situation and a managerial approach [25]. Later, Elton Mayo against Taylorism, revealed that employees' morale can be improved by ensuring employee participation in decisions and work, and suggest that employees can do a good job on their own accord without close supervision [5].

The concept of empowerment is defined and expressed in various forms in the fields of organizational behavior, human resources, management and psychology. These are "authorization", "employee empowerment", "personnel empowerment", "psychological empowerment", "structural empowerment" and "organizational empowerment" [40]. Empowerment is defined as the attainment of personal success through the restructuring of attitudes and the redistribution or transfer of decision-making authority to those who do not have that authority [9].

In general, empowerment is expressed as employees have more authority to carry out their tasks and take initiative in solving all problems related to their work [47]. In essence, empowerment refers to the transfer of authority and responsibility to subordinate by the superiors [2].

Several researchers have created dimensions of empowerment from different perspectives. These are payment systems that link a worker's self-control, self-mastery, diversity of teamwork, and wages and performance [21]. In addition, Spreitzer created four dimensions (meaning, competence, autonomy, and influence) that reflect the active state, not the work-oriented passive orientation of employee empowerment [25].

The success or failure and implementation of empowerment cultures at organizational level depends on organizational factors such as structure, culture and size. Here, changes at the organizational level are needed to be considered holistically not as micro or macro factors alone but as rewarding, training, giving new responsibilities, ensuring participation in decisions, work structure, organizational culture and so on. It is a complicated process to evaluate willingness and desire of employees to be empowered and whether they accept the responsibility for them or not. As such, managers directly encourage their employees to be empowered and take great responsibility for the successful implementation and long-term adoption of empowerment [3].

2.3 Procrastination

Procrastination is occurred due to reasons such as increased work intensity, failure in standard business planning, not being able to use time well, difficulty in decision making, personality traits, to postpone the works for the last minute, not to have business-related control, to be afraid of taking responsibility.

This concept, origin in Latin, is based on "pro" which means forward, forth, or in favor of," and “crastinus” which means “tomorrow” [35], is expressed as postponement, delay of a decision or task, conceptualized similarly to researchers. Procrastination is defined as delaying a task that is under an individual’s control, where the delay is under the control of the individual, and task that must be completed [43]. Procrastination is an unreasonable delay that we have voluntarily delayed our tasks, even though it is thought or known that it will lead to bad results [36]. In general, it can be expressed as preferring a task with a lower priority instead of a task with a higher priority [42]. In fact, postponement is sometimes used in positive meanings as functional delay or avoidance from rush [35].. Postponing is the act of postponing the execution of a task, usually postponing a task that feels discomfort [8]. Those who see themselves as those who postpone work try to complete their work on time by setting realistic goals and deadlines in order to complete their tasks within a reasonable amount of time [17]. However, this creates stress on them and therefore, has negative consequences, such as poor performance and low productivity at work [37, 39 and 43].

Procrastination is associated with poor academic performance, low self-esteem, high stress, and high levels of anxiety [26]. Ferrari [11] argues that postponement can be seen as a time delay in task performance and that emotional, behavioral and cognitive elements play a role in procrastination. Researchers have associated the procrastination of tasks for the protection of defenseless self-esteem with the behavioral dimension, deliberately delaying the related task with the cognisitive dimension, and worrying about the anxiety and physical symptoms with the emotional dimension [12, 33].

2.4 Relations between spiritual leadership, empowerment and work procrastination

Organizations today are made up of very complicated, ambiguous structures, rules created by the internal and external environment. Accordingly, organizations operating in such an environment should give the value the employees deserve to them. Employees want to feel important and valuable and to be understood by their managers. In this context, spiritual leaders are needed as motivators who understand employees. Seaborne [34] emphasizes in his work, that flexible leadership style enhances employees' ability, motivation, and commitment and so empowered employees will do their work in a quality, effective and productive way. Besides Yaghoubi, Moloudi and Banihashemi [45] has found that spiritual leadership has a positive influence on personnel empowerment but that leader-performance feedback is more important than other dimensions of spiritual leadership. That is, the high performance at the workplace can be explained as the employees are satisfied with the organizational environment.

Moradi and Shayestehpour [30] shows that his spiritual leadership has a positive influence on personnel empowerment. However, organizational efficiency and productivity are negatively affected by personnel who do not perform their jobs on time, constantly delay their works and postpone their works for the last minute [46]. However, the managers who understand the employee, make them valuable, give authority and responsibility and increase the motivation will help the employees to adopt their work. According to the results of the study, Yavari [46] has find that the increase in the activities and responsibilities of the employees at work reduces the work-related procrastination behavior of the employees.

3 Method

In this study, quantitative methodology was used to answer the question "Does spiritual leadership affect empowerment and work procrastination?". In this context, research hypotheses and theoretical model are created as follows.

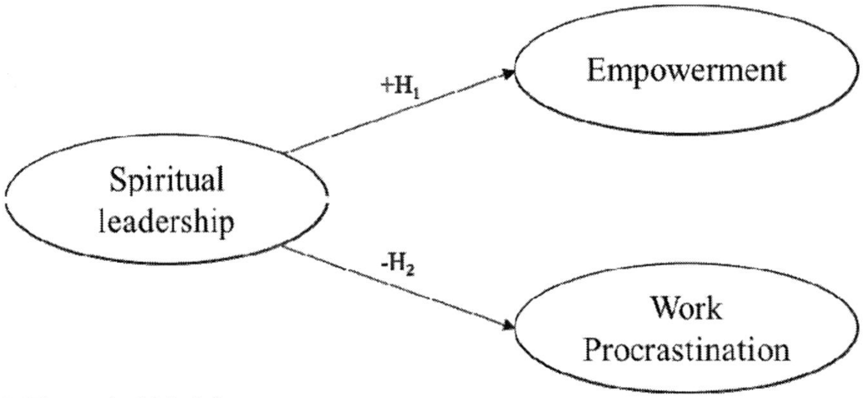

Fig. 1. Theoretical Model

H_1: Spiritual leadership has positive effect on empowerment
H_2: Spiritual leadership has negative effect on procrastination

3.1 Data collection and sample

The private sports and fitness center operating in the province of Sakarya constitute the universe of the research. The questionnaire was distributed voluntarily by judgment sampling technique to total of 200 volunteer employees from such organizations as the sample of the research and 113 questionnaire forms were evaluated. The questionnaire was conducted as face to face way.

DOI: 10.1051/shsconf/20173701056

3.2 Data collection tool and scales

The questionnaire created within the scope of the study consists of four parts. First three parts contain items to determine spiritual leadership, empowerment and procrastination, while the last part contains the items to determine the demographic characteristics of the participants. Information about the measurement tools used in the research is as follows:

Spirituality Leadership Scale; developed by Fry et al. [16] and adapted to Turkish by Kurtar [27] was used, and it consisted of 21 items and 5 sub-dimensions. The sub-dimensions were vision, hope/faith, altruistic love, meaning/call, membership.

Empowerment Scale; developed by Melhem [29] and adapted to Turkish by Özbek and Gözde [31] was used, and it consisted of 12 items and 3 sub-dimensions. The sub-dimensions were discretion, control and responsiveness.

Work Procrastination Scale; developed by Dutschmann [10] and adapted to Turkish by Gül [18] was used, and it consisted of 22 items and a sub-dimension.

A five-point scales that ranges from 1- Strongly disagree to 5-Strongly agree was used and the reliability (cronbach alpha) of it was over 0.70. In the last part of the questionnaire, there were questions about the socio-demographic characteristics of the participants.

4 Findings

The findings of the employees' demographic characteristics such as gender, marital status, age, education, work period in the organization in the research are all shown in Table 1 below;

Table 1. Demographic findings (n = 113)

		Frekans(n)	Oran (%)
Gender	Male	69	61,1
	Female	44	38,9
Marital Status	Married	53	46,9
	Single	55	48,7
	Unanswered	5	4,4
Age	18 years and below	7	6,2
	Between 18-24 years	19	16,8
	Between 25-29 years	37	32,7
	Between 30-39 years	23	20,4
	Between 40-49 years	21	18,6
	Between 50-65 years	2	1,8
	Unanswered	4	3,5
Education	Primary School and Secondary School	9	8
	High School	28	24,8
	Vocational High School	23	20,4
	Bachelor Degree	39	34,5
	Master Degree	6	5,3
	Unanswered	8	7,1
Work period	Less than 1 year	14	12,4
	1-3 years	28	24,8
	4-6 years	31	27,4
	7-9 years	17	15
	10 years and over	21	18,6
	Unanswered	2	1,8

A total of 113 people participated in this research, 69 males and 44 females, and 48.7% of them were single and 46.9% were married. A significant number of participants are in the range of 25-29 age (32,7%). According to the educational status, 34.5% of the participants have a bachelor's degree, 24.8% have a high school and 20.4% have a vocational high school degree. In addition, 27.4% of the participants are employees for 4-6 years.

As a result of the explanatory factor analysis, it was determined that the data set was suitable for the factor analysis by the fact that the value of the Kaiser-Meyer-Olkin (KMO) sample adequacy exceeded 0.50 and the tail probability of the Bartlett test was significant at 0.05 significance level.

Table 2. KMO and reliability

Spirituality Leadership Scale	KMO=0.750 Cronbach Alpha (α=0,704)	X^2Bartlett: 655,268 Sd: 210 tail probability test p: 0,00
Empowerment Scale	KMO=0,801 Cronbach Alpha (α=0,702)	X^2Bartlett: 287,855 Sd: 45 tail probability test p: 0,00
Work Procrastination Scale	KMO=0,608 Cronbach Alpha (α=0,765)	X^2Bartlett: 568,981 Sd: 231 tail probability test p: 0,00

In this context, sub-dimensions in our study have been defined in the literature, where validity and reliability have been proven before. Spiritual leadership sub-dimensions are defined in literature as vision, hope/faith, altruistic love, meaning/call and membership. Empowerment sub-dimensions are defined as discretion, control, and responsiveness. However, it is deemed necessary to item 4. and 11. from the analysis because of reliability reduction. Procrastination was made up of a dimension and no item was subtracted from the analysis. The means, standard deviations, and correlation values between the data obtained for the study variables are summarized in Table 3.

Table 3. Means, standard deviations, correlation values of research variables

	Mean	Sd.	1	2	3	4	5	6	7	8
Vision	3,95	1,140	1							
Hope/faith	3,92	,670	0,224*	1						
Altruistic Love	3,85	,598	,275**	,480**	1					
Meaning/Call	3,91	,668	,125	,582**	,475*	1				
Membership	3,98	,613	,232*	,521**	,629**	,606**	1			
Control	3,16	,856	-,007	,084	-,054	,167	,065	1		
Discretion	3,29	,995	-,049	,143	,142	,330**	,265**	,640**	1	
Responsiveness	3,23	,577	,015	,099	,008	,255*	,098	,335**	,177	1
Procrastination	2,64	,487	-,179	-,043	-,246	-,075	-,135	,388**	,093	,095

**p<,01; *p<,05

According to Table 3, it is possible to say that the mean values of these variables vary between 2,64 and 3,98 and statistically significant relationships between the variables. As a result of the analysis of the obtained data; It was determined that there was a low and positive relationship between "meaning/call" which was the sub-dimension of spiritual leadership and discretion (r=.330; p<.01) and responsiveness (r=.255; p<.05) which are the sub dimensions of empowerment. There was a positive and low level relationship between membership and discretion (r=.265; p<.01). There was a negative relationship between procrastination and altruistic love (r=-.246; p<.05), and positive relationship between procrastination and control (r=.388; p<.01).

Three regression analyzes were conducted to test the effect of spiritual leadership on empowerment (Table 4). Stepwise method is used in regression analysis.

Table 4. Regression analysis

Independent Variable	Dependent Variable (Empowerment)								
Spiritual Leadership	Control			Discretion			Responsiveness		
	β	t	p	β	t	P	β	t	p
Vision	-	-	-	-	-	-	-	-	-
Hope/Faith	-	-	-	-	-	-	-	-	-
AltruisticLove	-	-	-	,540	4,137	0,000	-	-	-
Meaning/call	,217	2,034	,045	-	-	-	,278	2,689	,009
Membership	-	-	-	-,319	-2,443	,017	-	-	-
Anova	F: 4,138 Sig.α: ,045			F: 8,607 Sig.α: ,000			F: 7,230 Sig.α: ,009		
Adjusted R^2	0,036			0,150			0,067		

It appears that the spiritual leadership has significantly predicted the control dimension (3,6%), which is the empowerment sub-dimension (F:4,138; p:,045). The meaning/call dimension affects the control dimension in the positive direction (β:,217; p:,045). In addition, the spiritual leadership subdimension, alturistic love and membership has significantly predicted the discretion dimension (15%), which is the empowerment sub-dimension (F:8,617; p:,000). Also, the spiritual leadership subdimension, meaning/call has significantly predicted the responsiveness dimension (6,7%), which is the empowerment sub-dimension (F:7,230; p:,009).

Finally; altruistic love has negative effect on procrastination (β:-,269, p:,026), discretion affects the procrastination negatively (β:-,291, p: ,040) and control has positive effect on procrastination (β:,579; p:,000).

5 Discussion and conclusion

This research was conducted to evaluate spiritual leadership, empowerment and work procrastination and to determine the structural relationships among the variables.in private sports and fitness centers operating in Sakarya. As a result of the analysis, business becomes meaningful with the feeling of being pleased with the task or job, feeling that they make a difference and being motivated. Therefore, this increases the control over the work (β:,217; p:,045). Yaghoubi et al. [45] has reached the conclusion that empowerment is moderately related to meaning. Employees have all kinds of information about their work and the level of control over their work increases when they make sense of their work. The fact that managers take care of their employees with reward and appreciation ensure that they are spiritually good. Thus, they help the employees in their spiritual existence in the organization. In other words, employees become a part of the organization. Employees who have proven themselves in the spiritual context will be more comfortable in taking initiative, making decisions and finding solutions in the organization, and therefore will increase efficiency and productive levels. In this case, employees will not hesitate to reveal their potential (β:,540, p:,000). However, those who feel themselves belong to the organization have difficulty in deciding alone within the organization because they take care of the group's common interests and well-being. There is a negative relationship between membership and discretion (β:-,319, p:,017). The study of Moradi and

Shayestehpour [30] support the results we had. Vision, altruistic love, membership, meaning and hope / faith dimensions have a positive effect on empowerment. Managers allow employees to perform more than what is defined in their work with reward and appreciation. So they do not postpone their work and carry out their business in the most sincere and pleasant way. So, in our study, it is concluded that the self-employed who use the initiative to make decisions about their jobs will perform their jobs on time. As a matter of fact, it should not be understood at this point that all the authorization will be delivered to employees. Employees must be given authorization and also responsibility as a result of their decisions. At the same time, it can be stated that employees should be inspected through various audit mechanisms. It is important to pay attention to the consequence that the worker will have an increased control over work behavior, and strategic decisions should be made in this context.

Managers in organizations keep employees under constant control and the inability of employees to make decisions without consulting their senior manager for all decisions hinder the work within the increasing workload, and even those who do not have a connection with their work will escape the responsibility of coming to work late, absenteeism or not finishing their work on time. Therefore, managers who understand their employees, establish emotional ties and deep relationships with them will strengthen their commitment of the work by knowing where, how, when, and in what jobs they will trust their talents.

Thus, the individual who makes sense of work will completely avoid the postponement and procrastination by developing his sense of responsibility as a worker who sees himself as valuable and contributes to the organization's goals.

According to the results obtained from the research; the leaders and managers in organization must ensure that their employees were valued as members of a group that achieve their goals, not as those who work or do business by taking into account the principles of equality and fairness.

In addition, it can be stated that the authority and responsibility are given to the employees together, taking into consideration feedback of the employees in taking the decisions, will increase the motivation of the employees and strengthen them and thus increase the efficiency of the employees.

References

1. A. C. Akar, *Ruhsal liderlik ve ruhsal liderliğin eğitim örgütlerinde uygulanabilirliği hakkında teorik bir çalışma,* (Yüksek Lisans), Yeditepe Üniversitesi, İstanbul (2010)
2. S. H. Appelbaum, R. Karasek, F. Lapointe, K. Quelch, Employee empowerment: factors affecting the consequent success or failure-Part I. Industrial and Commercial Training, **46,** 7, 379-386 (2014)
3. S. H. Appelbaum, R. Karasek, F. Lapointe, K. Quelch, Employee empowerment: factors affecting the consequent success or failure (Part II). Industrial and Commercial Training, **47**, 1, 23-30 (2015)
4. Ş. Arslanoğlu, *Lise müdürlerinde liderlik, liderlik düzeylerinin öğretmenlerin motivasyonuna etkisi (konya ili örneği),* (Master), Karatay Üniversitesi, Konya (2016)
5. H. Asgarsani, O. Duostdar, A. Rostami, Empowerment and its impact on the organization productivity. Interdisciplinary Journal of Contemporary Research In Business, **1**, 11, 25-32 (2013)
6. N. Baloğlu, E. Karadağ, Ruhsal liderlik üzerine teorik bir çözümleme. Kuram ve Uygulamada Eğitim Yönetimi, **58** ,58, 165-190 (2009)
7. A. Bedük, *Karşılaştırmalı işletme-yönetim terimleri sözlüğü* (3. Basım ed.). Konya: Nobel Yayın (2012)

8. N. H. Bui, Effect of evaluation threat on procrastination behavior. The Journal of social psychology, **147,** 3, 197-209 (2007)
9. I. Cunningham, J. Hyman, C. Baldry, Empowerment: the power to do what? Industrial Relations Journal, **27,** 2, 143-154 (1996)
10. S. L. Dutschmann, *Procrastination as a predictor of job performance,* (Air Force University, Ohio, USA (1996)
11. J. R. Ferrari, Compulsiveprocrastination: Some self-reported characteristics. Psychological reports, **68,** 2, 455-458 (1991)
12. J. R. Ferrari, Dysfunctional procrastination and its relationship with self-esteem, interpersonal dependency, and self-defeating behaviors. Personality and Individual Differences, **17**, 5, 673-679 (1994)
13. L. W. Fry, Toward a theory of spiritual leadership. The leadership quarterly, **14**, 6, 693-727 (2003)
14. L. W. Fry, Introduction to the leadership quarterly special issue: Toward a paradigm of spiritual leadership. The leadership quarterly, **16,** 5, 619-622 (2005)
15. L. W. Fry, M. P. Cohen, Spiritual leadership as a paradigm for organizational transformation and recovery from extended work hours cultures. Journal of business ethics, **84**, 265-278 (2009)
16. L. W. Fry, M. Nisiewicz, S. Vitucci, M. Cedillo. *Transforming city government through spiritual leadership: measurement and establishing a baseline.* Paper presented at the National Meeting of the Academy of Management, Philadelphia, Pennsylvania (2007)
17. R. Gupta, D. A. Hershey, J. Gaur, Time perspective and procrastination in the workplace: An empirical investigation. Current Psychology, **31,** 2, 195-211 (2012)
18. A. Y. Gül, *İş yaşamında iş erteleme davranışı ve nedenleri,* (Yüksek Lisans Tezi), Dokuz Eylül Üniversitesi, İzmir (2015)
19. Ş. Gündüz, *Ruhsal liderlik ile örgütsel sinizm arasındaki ilişki: Duygusal zekânin araci etkisi,* (Doktora Tezi), Marmara Üniversitesi, İstanbul (2014)
20. A.-M. Hede, *A research agenda for the study of empowerment in hospitality organisations,* (Victoria University of Technology (1999)
21. L. Honold, A review of the literature on employee empowerment. Empowerment in organizations, **5,** 4, 202-212 (1997)
22. S. Howard, A spiritual perspective on learning in the workplace. Journal of managerial psychology, **17**, 3, 230-242 (2002)
23. N. Işık, *Liderlik yaklaşımları ve hizmetkâr liderliğin işgörenlerin organizasyonel bağlılıklarına etkileri,* (Bahçeşehir Üniversitesi, İstanbul (2014)
24. G. Kerse, C. N. Karabey, Personel güçlendirme ile bireyin yaratıcılık algısı arasındaki ilişki: Bankacılık sektöründe bir uygulama. Akdeniz University Faculty of Economics & Administrative Sciences Faculty Journal/Akdeniz Universitesi Iktisadi ve Idari Bilimler Fakultesi Dergisi, **14**, 29, 22-41 (2014)
25. S. Y. Kim, S. Fernandez, Employee empowerment and turnover intention in the US federal bureaucracy. The American Review of Public Administration, **47**, 1, 4-22 (2017)
26. K. B. Klingsieck, Procrastination in different life-domains: is procrastination domain specific? Current Psychology, **32**, 2, 175-185 (2013)
27. Ş. Kurtar, *Ruhsal Liderlik Ölçeği: Türkçe Dilsel Eşdeğerlik, Geçerlik ve Güvenirlik Çalışması,* (Yüksek Lisans Tezi), Yeditepe Üniversitesi, İstanbul (2009)
28. P. Malone, L. W. Fry, Transforming schools through spiritual leadership: A field experiment. Academy of Management, Seattle, WA(2003)
29. Y. Melhem, The antecedents of customer-contact employees' empowerment. Employee Relations, **26**, 1, 72-93 (2004)

30. M. Moradi, J. Shayestehpour, Studying the relation between the spiritual leadership and empowerment of the staff in the organization of research and educational planning. Journal of Applied Environmental and Biological Sciences, **5**, 11, 322-331 (2015)
31. M. F. Özbek, K. Gözde, Duygusal Bağlılık, Örgütsel Destek, Üst Yönetim Desteği ve Personel Güçlendirmenin Hizmet Kalitesi Üzerindeki Etkisi: Kırgızistan'da Banka İşgörenleri Üzerinde Bir Uygulama. Erciyes Üniversitesi İktisadi ve İdari Bilimler Fakültesi Dergisi, **34**, 189-212 (2009)
32. S. Polat, T. Tülübaş, Üniversite hazırlık sınıfı öğrencilerine göre öğretim elemanlarının ruhsal liderlik davranışlarını gösterme düzeyleri. Eğitim ve bilim, **38**, 170, 32-47 (2013)
33. E. D. Rothblum, L. J. Solomon, J. Murakami, Affective, cognitive, and behavioral differences between high and low procrastinators. Journal of counseling psychology, **33**(4), 387 (1986)
34. W. Seaborne, An examination of the relationship between leadership style and empowerment. PhD, Regent university (2003)
35. P. Steel, *The nature of procrastination: a meta-analytic and theoretical review of quintessential self-regulatory failure*: American Psychological Association (2007)
36. P. Steel, *The procrastination equation: How to stop putting stuff off and start getting things done*: Murdoch Books (2011)
37. P. Steel, T. Brothen, C. Wambach, Procrastination and personality, performance, and mood. Personality and Individual Differences, **30**, 1, 95-106 (2001)
38. M. Ş. Şimşek, A. Çelik, *Yönetim ve organizasyon* (16. Baskı ed.). Konya: Eğitim Kitabevi (2014)
39. A. Thatcher, G. Wretschko, P. Fridjhon, Online flow experiences, problematic Internet use and Internet procrastination. Computers in Human Behavior, **24**, 5, 2236-2254 (2008)
40. Y. Torun, *Personel güçlendirme ve işten ayrılma niyeti ilişkisinde örgütsel sinizmin aracılık rolü: Örgütsel sinizm ölçeği geliştirmeye yönelik bir araştırma,* (Doktora), Marmara Üniversitesi, İstanbul (2016)
41. P. Tunçer, Örgütsel değişim ve liderlik. Sayıştay Dergisi, **80**, 57-83 (2011)
42. B. Uzun, A. Demir, Erteleme: Türleri, bileşenleri, demografik etkenler ve kültürel farklılıklar. Ege Eğitim Dergisi, **16**, 1, 106-121 (2015)
43. H. C. Wan, L. A. Downey, C. Stough, Understanding non-work presenteeism: Relationships between emotional intelligence, boredom, procrastination and job stress. Personality and Individual Differences, **65**, 86-90 (2014)
44. B. G. Whitaker, J. W. Westerman, Linking spirituality and values to personal initiative through psychological empowerment. Journal of Management, Spirituality & Religion, **11**, 3, 269-291 (2014)
45. N.-M. Yaghoubi, J. Moloudi, S. A. Banihashemi, The relationship between spirituality leadership and empowerment. American Journal of Scientific Research, **12**, 180-186 (2010)
46. Y. Yavari, Procrastination and psychological empowerment in sports sciences faculty members. Sport Science-International Scientific Journal of Kinesiology, **9**, 2, 54-60 (2016)
47. D. Zeglat, M. Aljaber, W. Alrawabdeh, Understating the impact of employee empowerment on customer-oriented behavior. Journal of Business Studies Quarterly, **6**, 1, 55-67 (2014)

Predictions of academic achievements of vocational and technical high school students with artificial neural networks in science courses (physics, chemistry and biology) in Turkey and measures to be taken for their failures

Ali Yağcı[1a], and Mustafa Çevik[2]

[1] Karamanoğlu Mehmetbey University, Institute of Science, Karaman, 70100, Turkey
[2] Karamanoğlu Mehmetbey University, Education Faculty, Department of Primary Education, Karaman, 70100, Turkey

Abstract. The aim of this study is to predict academic achievements of vocational and technical high school (VTHS) students with artificial neural networks (ANN) in physics, chemistry and biology courses in Turkey and reveal measures to be taken for their failures. The study group consisted of 922 students studying in 10th and 11th grade in VTHS. This study was conducted with the survey method and a 34-item demographic questionnaire was developed in order to collect the data. The parameters in the questionnaire were identified as the items that were considered to influence academic achievements of the students. Opinions of 3 field specialist, 1 measurement and evaluation specialist and 2 technical teachers were taken and it was supported by the literature for the content validity and the KR20 reliability coefficient was found as .90 using SPSS 16.0 package program. The items in the questionnaire that are considered to influence academic achievements of the students were approved as independent variables/input and academic achievement mean scores of the students in physics, chemistry and biology courses in the previous year were approved as dependent variables/output. Academic achievements of the student were predicted with ANN in Matlap R2016a program using these parameters and a model was created. A successful academic achievement prediction system with an average sensitivity of %98 was developed over 922 data and the measures to be taken to prevent the failures of the students were determined at the end of the study.
Keywords: Vocational and technical high schools, artificial neural networks, and science courses academic achievement prediction

[a] Corresponding author: ayagci89@gmail.com

1 Introduction

Vocational and technical education institutions, which play an important role in the development of the country, require increasing productivity in education to raise the number and quality of human power that the society needs [1]. The question to be raised in order to increase productivity in education is firstly the relevance of the instructional programs with the personality traits of individuals, job specifications and institutional strategies and to what extent these factors are taken into account when preparing the program. Therefore the need analysis/assessment is a prerequisite for an effective instructional program. Thus, one of the most important issues in research related to education is whether the need analysis/assessment was made before the teaching [2]. It is vital for the vocational schools to carry out the need analysis/assessment. This is because vocational students are expected not only to complete their education that supports their cultural and personal development, but also to complete their vocational training at the best level to ensure their future [3]. Vocational high schools are educational institutions aiming at students to gain work experience at an early age and get involved in business life, meeting the need for intermediate staff in the working segment of the society with lessons that mostly require skills and practice. In this respect, vocational high school graduates need to cultivate themselves in every sense. These characteristics of students ought to be considered when preparing especially instructional programs of science courses besides vocational courses [4]. From this point of view, the success of vocational education, an area that can be regarded as the benchmark of the society, is one of the factors that directly affect the socioeconomic structure of the country. In this context, what need to be done for qualified student training in VTHS and what measures should be taken to avoid failures are the main objectives of educational researches. This situation was statistically determined in the university entrance exam conducted by the Measuring, Selection and Placement Center (MSPC) in Turkey. For instance, the achievement average score of MS (mathematics-science) courses of vocational high schools is below the country average score in 2016. In recent years, the Ministry of National Education (MNE), which has undertaken a task to ensure that young people who have been classified according to vocational skills such as wood technologies, metal, electricity, computer and automotive have the opportunity to study in the direction of their interests and abilities, is far from satisfying needs of the students in verbal and numerical lessons [5-7]. Science courses (physics, chemistry and biology) are among the numerical courses and considered to be very important for vocational high school students to be better prepared for the profession, to increase their working life achievements and to grow in the quality that contemporary technologies desire. It is vital to prevent possible failures in these courses. Regression based methods are techniques used generally in the literature to determine variables that are considered to influence achievements of the students and the effect of these variables. Nevertheless, one of the methods used successfully in every field where data mining is carried out, no matter it is science, health sciences or social sciences, is "Artificial Neural Networks [8]. ANN method aims clustering of given examples and classifying them into specific classes as well as deciding the classes that the following samples would join [9]. ANN's modeling of the human brain emerged with the desire to create machines that function like human brain, which also exists in the modeling of digital computers [10]. ANN is computer systems that perform the learning function, which is the most basic feature of the human brain. A model is created by ANN in the direction of inputs and outputs. Inputs are information received from outside or other nerve cells for an artificial neural cell. These inputs consist of the samples for which learning of the nerve cell is desired [11, 12]. Learning in artificial neural networks takes place by changing the weights between the nerves. Accordingly, nerves whose weights on the inter-nervous links are changeable dynamically with a specific method can be trained. Networks that can learn may recognize new forms or decide the class the given entry belongs to. Although there is a limited number of applications in the field of education regarding ANN today, this method is successfully used in areas such as manufacturing, control, transportation and aviation, medicine, engineering, meteorology, biomedical and pharmaceutical industry, finance, stock market and credit card applications. It is seen that ANN and regression analyzes are used together in the education field especially in the academic achievement estimations. One of the earliest studies in the field of education in which ANN was used in predicting the academic achievements of the students was the work of Gorr, Nagin and Szcypula [13] that compares multi-linear regression and stochastic linear regression analyses with artificial neural network analysis in predicting students' weighted grade averages. Subbanarasimha, Arinzeb & Anandarajanb [14] used two different sets of data to compare artificial neural networks and regression techniques in predicting the academic performance of the students. As a result of the study, it is revealed that the accuracy of the analysis using artificial neural networks is higher. Several researches compared artificial neural networks, decision trees and linear regression methods in predicting students' achievements. As a result of the research, ANN indicated better results than the others. Oladokun, Adebanjo and Charles-Owaba [15] aimed to determine the variables that influenced students' achievements and to test the analysis of artificial neural networks in predicting students' performances. At the end of the study, it was concluded that ANN is highly predictive and effective in determining variables that affect the students' achievements. Çırak and Çokluk [16] found in their study in which ANN and logistic regression methods were used in classifying students' achievements in the higher education that the total correct classification rate is 66.10% with the logistic regression analysis and 70.10% with ANN analysis for the proposed model. As seen in the literature, there is a rapid increase in the studies in which ANN is used, especially in the academic achievement predictions in recent years.

1.1 The rationale and aim of the study

When the literature is viewed, it is seen that many methods and techniques were used in predicting academic achievements of students and teacher candidates who are studying at different educational institutions. However there seems to be no study indicating prospective academic achievement prediction of science course of students in VTHS using the ANN analysis, which is the most reliable prediction mechanism of information age and the program with the closest functional feature to the human brain. Furthermore, there seems to be no study determining the factors affecting the academic achievements of these students and necessary measures to prevent their failures. In this context, the research questions of this research are:

1. To what extent does the model emerged with the ANN analysis in the direction of parameters that are considered to affect the academic achievements of VTHS students in physics courses classify students with their achievements?

2. To what extent does the model emerged with the ANN analysis in the direction of parameters that are considered to affect the academic achievements of VTHS students in chemistry courses classify students with their achievements?

3. To what extent does the model emerged with the ANN analysis in the direction of parameters that are considered to affect the academic achievements of VTHS students in biology courses classify students with their achievements?

4. What are the most important factors affecting the academic achievements of VTHS students in science (physics, chemistry and biology) courses and the measures to be taken in order to prevent their failures?

2 Methodology

2.1 The design and study group of the study

The study was structured in the survey model based on the quantitative research model. Survey models are research approaches that aim to describe the past or present instance as it exists. The event, the individual or object that is the subject of the investigation is tried to be defined within their own circumstances [17]. The study group of the research consisted of 922 students studying in 10th and 11th grades at VTHS in Turkey. Face-to-face meetings were held with the students.

2.2 The data collection instrument

A pool of questions was formed in this study conducted in the survey model for the collection of data. A questionnaire consisting of 40 items selected by the researchers from this pool was developed. While the questionnaire used in the study was being developed, 6 items removed as they were not appropriate with language and measurement criteria according to opinions of 3 science field specialists, 1 measurement and assessment specialist and 2 technical education experts. Eventually, a 34-item questionnaire was created. The content validity of the questionnaire was provided in this way. To perform item factor analysis of the data obtained with the pilot study (250 participants) in the construct validity phase of the questionnaire, the KMO value was calculated as .86, the barlett test value was calculated as .00 and chi-square value was calculated as 2.183, indicating item analysis can be carried out. Item 9, 29, 33 and 34, whose item loads are below .30, were removed from the questionnaire for the item factor analysis. The KR20 reliability coefficient was calculated as .90 in order to determine the reliability. The final questionnaire consisted of 30 items and 3 sub-dimensions. The parameters that are considered to affect academic achievement were grouped under the following headings: 1. Student Features, 2. Teacher-School Features, 3. Parent

2.3 Data analysis

ANN analysis was used in the statistical analysis process. Grade point averages of the students at the end of the academic year were determined as output variables for ANN in the research. A discrete variable with two categories that are unsuccessful (0) for students with a grade average (0-2) and successful (1) for students with a grade average (3-5) was formed. The items in the questionnaire that are considered to affect academic achievement were approved as inputs. The prediction of the academic achievements of the students was realized with ANN in the Matlab R2016a program using the inputs and outputs and a model was created. Bayesian Regularization (trainbr) algorithm was used in training the feed-forward back-propagation network. A three-layer feed-forward network that is input, hidden, and output layer was used in the study. There are 70 neurons in the input layer, 30 neurons in the hidden layer, and 1 neuron in the output layer in the academic achievement prediction model of each course.

3 Result

In this section, the findings and interpretations obtained by analyzing the data for the purpose of the data are discussed.

3.1. Findings on the prediction of students' achievements in science course with the ANN analysis

80% (738 items) of the data set was used in training, 5% (46 items) of the data set was used in validation, and 15% (138 items) of the data set was used in testing. The ANN used in the study has 70 inputs and 1 output with 30 layers. Findings obtained by analysis of artificial neural network to classify students according to their academic achievements are presented in Table 1.

Table 1. Classification Table obtained with ANN Model for Physics Course

ANN Steps	Actual Situation	Estimated		Accurate Estimation Percentage (%)
		Successful	Unsuccessful	
Training	Successful	363	1	99.7
	Unsuccessful	367	2	99.5
	Total	%49	%51	99.6
Validation	Successful	16	1	94.1
	Unsuccessful	29	0	100
	Total	%37	%63	97.8
Test	Successful	47	16	74.6
	Unsuccessful	64	10	86.5
	Total	%43	%47	81

As seen in Table 1, 363 successful students were correctly classified, 1 was misclassified into 364 from 738 individuals participating in total for physics course and the accurate classification rate is 99.7%. 367 students were correctly classified, 2 were misclassified into 369 unsuccessful students and the accurate classification rate is 99.5%. The total accurate classification rate is 99.6%. 16 of the 17 successful students of 46 individuals who participated in the validation analysis were correctly classified, 1 was misclassified and the accurate classification rate is 94.1 %. 29 of the 29 unsuccessful students were correctly classified, 0 was misclassified and the accurate classification rate is 100%. The total accurate classification rate is %97.8. 47 of the 63 successful students of 138 individuals participating in the test were correctly classified, 16 were misclassified and the accurate classification rate is %74.6. 64 of the 74 unsuccessful students were correctly classified, 10 were misclassified and the accurate classification rate is 86.5%. The total accurate classification rate is 81%.

3.2. Findings on the prediction of students' achievements in chemistry course with the ANN analysis

Findings obtained by analysis of artificial neural network to classify students according to their academic achievements in the chemistry course are presented in Table 2.

Table 2. Classification Table obtained with ANN Model for Chemistry Course

ANN Steps	Actual Situation	Estimated		Accurate Estimation Percentage (%)
		Successful	Unsuccessful	
Training	Successful	423	0	100
	Unsuccessful	309	0	100
	Total	%58	%42	100
Validation	Successful	27	0	100
	Unsuccessful	19	0	100
	Total	%59	%41	100
Test	Successful	83	5	94.3
	Unsuccessful	45	5	90
	Total	%60	%32.8	92.8

As seen in Table 2, 423 of the 423 successful students of 738 individuals participating in total in the chemistry course were correctly classified, 0 was misclassified and the accurate classification rate is 100%. 309 of the 309 unsuccessful students were correctly classified, 0 was misclassified and the accurate classification rate is 100%. The total accurate classification rate is 100%. 19 of the 19 successful students of 46 individuals participating in the validation analysis were correctly classified, 0 was misclassified and the accurate classification rate is 100%. The total accurate classification rate is 100%. 83 of the 88 successful students of 138 individuals participating in the test analysis were correctly classified, 5 were misclassified and the accurate classification rate is 94.3%. 45 of the 50 unsuccessful students were correctly classified and 5 were misclassified and the accurate classification rate 90%. The total accurate classification rate is %92.8

3.3. Findings on the prediction of students achievements in biology course with the ANN analysis

Findings obtained by analysis of artificial neural network to classify students according to their academic achievements in the biology course are presented in Table 3.

Table 3. Classification Table obtained with ANN Model for Biology Course

ANN Steps	Actual Situation	Estimated		Accurate Estimation Percentage (%)
		Successful	Unsuccessful	
Training	Successful	425	3	99.3
	Unsuccessful	305	1	99.7
	Total	%58	%42	99.5
Validation	Successful	30	1	96.8
	Unsuccessful	15	0	100
	Total	%67	%33	97.8
Test	Successful	82	0	100
	Unsuccessful	51	3	94.4
	Total	%62	%38	97.8

As seen it Table 3, 425 of the 428 successful students of 738 individuals participating in total in the biology course were correctly classified, 3 were misclassified and the accurate classification rate is 99.3%. 305 of the 306 unsuccessful students were correctly classified, 1 was misclassified and the accurate classification rate is 99.7%. The total accurate classification rate is 99.5%. 30 of the 31 successful students of 46 individuals participating in the validation analysis were correctly classified, 1 was misclassified and the accurate classification rate is 96.8%. 15 of the 15 unsuccessful students were correctly classified, 0 was misclassified and the accurate classification rate is 97.8%. 82 of the 82 successful students of 138 individuals participating in the test analysis were correctly classified, 0 was misclassified and the accurate classification rate is 100%. 51 of the 54 unsuccessful students were correctly classified, 3 were misclassified and the accurate classification rate is 94.4%. The total accurate classification rate is 97.8%.

Table 4. Classification Table obtained with ANN Model for Study-wide

Courses	Actual Situation	Estimated	Accurate Estimation Percentage (%)
Physics	Successful	426	95.9
	Unsuccessful	460	97.5
	Total		96
Chemistry	Successful	533	99.1
	Unsuccessful	373	98.7
	Total		98.9
Biology	Successful	437	99.3
	Unsuccessful	371	98.9
	Total		99.1

As seen in Table 4, the total accurate estimation percentage is 96% for physics, 98.9% for chemistry and 99.1% for biology in the study-wide.

3.4. The most important factors affecting the academic achievements of VTHS students in science (physics, chemistry and biology) courses and the measure to be taken in order to prevent their failures

The most important factors with significance at p<. 01 affecting the academic achievements of VTHS students in physics, chemistry and biology courses are given in Table 5.

Table 5. The Most Significant Factors of Academic Achievement with ANN

Courses	Order of Importance	Factors	Significance	Normalized Significance Percentage (%)
Physics	1	Class size	.030	98.2
	2	Use of different method in the course	.029	95.2
	3	Participating in activities	.029	95
	4	Having a study room	.024	79.7
	5	The economic situation of the family	.023	74.2
Chemistry	1	Class size	.032	100
	2	The father being literate	.028	88.9
	3	The father having an occupation	.026	82.3
	4	Regular studying situation	.024	74.5
Biology	1	Enthusiasm for Biology	.032	100
	2	Regular preparation for exams	.029	92.4
	3	Coexistence of parents	.026	83.3
	4	Liking the biology teacher	.026	82.9
	5	Class size	.026	82.1

As seen in Table 5, class size (%98.2) is forefront in the affecting factors in academic achievements in the physics course. This is followed by different teaching methods (95.2%), participating in activities (%95%), having a study room (79.7%) and the economic situation of the family (74.2%), respectively. One of the most important factors affecting academic achievements in the chemistry course is class size (100%). In addition, factors such as father's literacy status (88.9%), father's occupation status (82.3%) and regular studying (74.5%) are among the most important factors affecting academic achievements in the chemistry course. The most important factors affecting the academic achievements of the students in the biology course are: enthusiasm for the biology course (100%), regular preparation for exams (92.4%), coexistence of parents (83.3%), liking biology teacher (82.9%), and class size (82.1%). It can be considered that eliminating the negative impacts of these factors can increase academic achievements of the students.

4 Conclusion and discussion

As a result of the study, a model that can predict the academic achievements of the students with ANN was created. When it is desired to predict the future academic achievements of a new student included in the model, with the emerged ANN model in science courses, the probability of being predicted correctly is 96% for physics, 98.9% for chemistry and 99.1% for biology. The multilayered model created by ANN correctly classifies 95.9% of the successful students and 97.5% of the unsuccessful students for the physics course. This suggests that the performance of predicting students who failed in physics is higher than the performance of predicting successful students in this course and therefore the model created by ANN can indicate better results especially in predicting unsuccessful students. The multilayered model created by ANN correctly classifies 99.1% of the successful students and 98.7% of the unsuccessful students in the chemistry course. In this context, this suggests that the performance of predicting successful students in the chemistry course is higher than the performance of predicting the students who failed in this course and therefore the model created by ANN can indicate better results especially in predicting successful students. For the biology course, the multilayered model created by ANN correctly classifies 99.3% of the successful students and 98.9% of the unsuccessful students. According to this finding, the performance of predicting the students who succeeded in the biology course is higher than the performance of predicting the students who failed in this course and therefore the model created by ANN can indicate better results in predicting successful students. It is possible to pay attention to factors such as setting the class size in the pedagogical sense, delivering the lesson with different teaching methods and techniques, increasing participation in activities, the fact that the student has a study room and the fact that the economic situation of the family is well in order to influence academic achievements of the students in physics positively. When considering the factors that affect the academic achievements of the students in the chemistry course, it is possible to interpret that appropriate class size, the father being literate and having an occupation, and regular studying situation of the student affect the academic achievement positively. Furthermore, it is possible to consider that having enthusiasm for the biology courses, regular preparation for exams, coexistence of parents, liking the biology teacher, and appropriate class size are influential on the positive direction of the academic achievements in the biology course. One of the strengths of the model created by ANN is high accuracy of the prediction of academic achievements of the students. However, this research is a specific implementation since the study was carried out with a certain number of data obtained from VTHS students. For this reason, it is useful to evaluate the results obtained from the study, taking into account the limitations. It is considered that comparing predictions by using logistic regression analysis or other techniques together with the ANN technique carried out in the study can be beneficial to reach more accurate predictions.

This study forms a part of a thesis study titled « Prediction of Academic Achievements of Vocational and Technical High School Students with Artificial Neural Networks in Science Courses (Physics – Chemistry – Biology) and Measures to be Taken for Failure (Turkey- Malaysia Comparison) » conducted by Ali YAĞCI.

References

1. Erol, N. Mesleki Ortaöğretimde Yeni Müfredat Doğrultusunda Öğretmenlerin Eğitim İhtiyaçlarının Belirlenmesi. Yayınlanmamış Yüksek Lisans Tezi. Gazi Üniversitesi Eğitim Bilimleri Enstitüsü, Ankara (2010)
2. Aycan, Z. Balcı, H. Hizmet İçi Eğitimin Etkililiğini Yordayan Bireysel ve Kurumsal Faktörler. Türk Psikolojisi Dergisi, **16,** 48, 15 (2001)
3. Eker, G. Endüstri Meslek Lisesi Öğrencilerinin Tükenmişlik Düzeyi. Yüksek Lisans Tezi. İstanbul: Marmara Üniversitesi Fen Bilimleri Enstitüsü (2007)
4. Çevik, M. (2014). Mevcut Biyoloji Öğretim Programının Mesleki ve Teknik Liselerde Görevli Yönetici, Öğretmen ve Öğrenci Görüşlerine Göre Değerlendirilmesi ve Yeni Bir Taslak Program Önerisi (Fotosentez Konusu Örneği). Yayınlanmış Doktora Tezi. Gazi Üniversitesi Eğitim Bilimleri Enstitüsü, Ankara.
5. Binici, H., Arı, N. Mesleki ve teknik eğitimde arayışlar. Gazi Üniversitesi Eğitim Fakültesi Dergisi, **24,** 3, (2004)
6. Şahin, İ. Fındık, T. Türkiye'de mesleki ve teknik eğitim: Mevcut durum, sorunlar ve çözüm önerileri. *TSA*/Yıl:12, **3**, 65-86 (2008)

7. Yörük, S. Dikici, A., Uysal, A. Bilgi toplumu ve Türkiye'de mesleki eğitim. *Fırat Üniversitesi Sosyal Bilimler Dergisi,* **24**, 3, 229-312 (2002)
8. Han, J., Kamber, M. Data Mining, Southeast Asia Edition: Concepts and Techniques. Morgan Kaufmann, **81** (2006)
9. Öztemel, E. *Yapay sinir ağları.* (1.Basım). İstanbul: Papatya Yayıncılık (2003)
10. Tosun, Ö. Sınıflandırmada yapay sinir ağları ve karar ağaçları karşılaştırması: öğrenci başarıları üzerine bir uygulama, Yüksek Lisans Tezi, İstanbul teknik Üniversitesi Fen Bilimleri Enstitüsü, İstanbul (2007)
11. Yurtoğlu, H. Yapay sinir ağları metodolojisi ile öngörü modellemesi: bazı makroekonomik değişkenler için türkiye örneği, Doktora Tezi, Ankara (2005)
12. Baş, N. Yapay Sinir ağları Yaklaşımı ve Bir Uygulama. Yayınlanmamış Yüksek Lisans Tezi. Mimar Sinan Güzel Sanatlar Üniversitesi Fen Bilimleri Enstitüsü. İstanbul (2006)
13. Gorr, W. L., Nagin, D., Szczypula, J. Comparative study of Artificial Neural Network and Statistical Models for Predicting Student Grade Point Averages. Interntional Journal of Forecasting, **10,** 17-34 (1994).
14. Subbanarasimha, P. N., Arinzeb, B., Anandarajanb, M. The Predictive Accuracy of Artificial Neural Networks and Multiple Regression in the Case of Skewed Data. Exploration of Some Issues Expert Systems with Applications, **19,** 117-123 (2000)
15. Oladokun, V. O., Adebanjo, A. T., Charles-Owaba, O. E. Predicting Students' Academic Performance using Artificial Neural Network: A Case Study of an Engineering Course. The Pacific Journal of Science and Technology, **9,** 1 (2008)
16. Çırak, G., Çokluk Ö. Yükseköğretimde öğrenci başarılarının sınıflandırılmasında yapay sinir ağları ve lojistik regresyon yöntemlerinin kullanılması. Mediterranean Journal of Humanities, **3**, 2, 71-79 (2013)
17. Karasar, N. Bilimsel araştırma yöntemi. Ankara: Nobel Yayın Dağıtım (2005)
18. Güneri, N., Apaydın, A. Öğrenci Başarılarının Sınıflandırılmasında Lojistik Regresyon Analizi ve Sinir Ağları Yaklaşımı. Ticaret ve Turizm Eğitim Fakültesi Dergisi, **1**, 170-188 (2004)
19. Ibrahim, Z., Rusli, D. "Predicting Students' Academic Performance: Comparıng Artificial Neural Network, Decision Tree and Linear Regression. *21st Annual SAS Malaysia Forum*, Shangri- La Hotel, Kuala Lumpur, September, 5 (2007)
20. MEB. Matematik ve meslek matematiği dersi öğretim programı. Milli Eğitim Bakanlığı Çıraklık ve Yaygın Eğitim Genel Müdürlüğü, Ankara (2005)

Effects of different strength training methods on dynamic balance in basketball players

Adnan Ersoy[1a], Oğuzhan Yüksel[1], Mustafa Erzeybek[1], Halit Harmancı[1], and M. Barış Karavelioğlu[1]

[1]School of Physical Education and Sport, Dumlupınar University, Kütahya, Turkey

Abstract. You should leave 8 mm of space above the abstract and 10 mm after the abstract. The heading Abstract should be typed in bold 9-point Arial. The body of the abstract should be typed in normal 9-point Times in a single paragraph, immediately following the heading. The text should be set to 1 line spacing. The abstract should be centred across the page, indented 17 mm from the left and right page margins and justified.
Keywords: Strength training methods, dynamic balance, basketball players.

1 Introduction

Muscle power required for get high sport performance levels in basketball [16]. At the same time, balance and speed are important factors for the success of basketball players [3]. The good balance in basketball provides controlled body for players, minimize their errors, protect against the drop when change their directions, quick moves and effective technical skills [19]. Not only preseason but also season training plan contain some coordinative and balance workout for devolop biomotor abilities in basketball. Some training programs provide to increase muscular function and neuromuscular control at the same time develops balance and joint proprioception [2]. Neuromuscular training protocols include plyometric, biomechanics and technique, power, balance and core stability for provide neuromuscular changes and protect against possible injuries [13, 22]. Functional training is defined as an exercise process that best teaches that an athlete manages body weight on all planes of motion. It's make a movement economically [9]. Hypertrophy and general power exercises can improve performance but specific exercise programs must be choice for the optimal transfer of the training [34]. Functional exercise programs are effective in preventing the recurrence of painless function and injuries of athletes. In general, four factors are targeted. A) Exercises to improve the stability of the spine during movement B) Works to improve equilibrium and proprioception. C) Win back to range of motion in a muscle. D) Exercises for functional strength development [33] Variable resistance has gained popularity in the last decade. Use of chain and elastic bands in resistance exercise cause the change speed

[a] Corresponding author: adnan.ersoy@dpu.edu.tr

and strength directions [29] Behm and Anderson examined the resistance training and instability effect may have a role force output, body and extremity muscle activation, co-contractions, coordination and rehabilitation applications [8] Strength exercises using the Bandbell earthquake bar are preferred to increase the balance and joint proprioception interaction. All functions to a normal classic bar it can be by bandbell earthquake bar. Strength training forms can be applied to the end portions of the 5-pound bamboo stick with weights placed with elastic bands [4] Anderson, Sforzo and Sigg tried to determine different power and power adaptations according to free weight resistance training, elastic resistance and free-weight resistance training on 44 college-aged athletes [1]. The results of this study indicate that the athletes applying combined elastic and free-weight resistance alone have greater strength development in the upper and lower extremity than the traditional free weight [1]. Hess et al. They found that there was a strong relationship between lower extremity strength and postural control ability [12] Paterno et al. [26] and Young et al. [34] strength training results in a significant increase in static and dynamic stability. In this study, it was aimed to investigate the dynamic balance effect of the strength training program which is formed by using traditional bar with bandbell earthquake bar as functional training.

2 Materials and methods

33 male basketball players (13 control, 10 classic strength training, 10 earthquake strength bar training) whom at least 18 years old participated voluntarily in the study. The participants mean of body height measured (n=33) 187,9 ± 9,82 cm, mean of body weight measured 84,5 ± 10,7 kg, mean of age recorded 21,7 ± 1,62 years. One day before the measurements the participants were informed about the test and information was provided that there was no drawbacks to the health of the tests.

The body weights of the athletes have been measured when they were standing upright in the standard sports clothing (shorts and tank-top) bare foot on the scale (Tanita TBF 401 A Japan) with ± 100 gr error. Length: The length has been measured using a Holtain Limited branded tool, when the participants were standing upright bare foot with minimum clothing, the soles being adjacent, heads being high and eyes looking straight ahead. The sliding caliper on the scale has been adjusted as to be right on the top of the participant's head, read and recorded. Participants of experiment group divided into two group and traditional strength training (Figure 2) was applied for eight weeks. While participants who in-group one was practice with normal weight bar in their training program, participants who in-group two was practice with bandbell earthquake bar in their training program.

Bandbell Earthquake Bar: Bandbell earthquake bar made from Bamboo wood. Bar's weight is 2,5 kg, lenght 2,03 cm, diameter 3,81 cm, maximal carrying capacity 150 kg and distance between collars 137 cm. Bandbell earthquake bar actually made from hardened ash wood with a composite resin center section scientifically engineered for maximum flexibility and durability. There are two channels for the wood parts to prevent super loop bands from slipping. Bar was designed oscillating kinetic energy principle. Weight plates with 4 red flexible band (cherry super loop medium sanctband) was placed bandbell earthquake bar (figure1)(http://www.fitnessshop.com.tr/urunler/fonksiyonel-egzersiz-kipmanlari/bandbell-earthquake-bar/#aciklama) (http://www.ardsport.com/?uid=176).

Fig. 1. Bandbell Earthquake Bar and Normal Traditional Bar

Dynamic Balance: When measuring the stability level, the authors used a Libra seesaw balancing board manufactured by EasyTech (length: 43 cm; width: 42 cm; height: 65 cm). The testing stand was comprised of two components: a balance board with USB interface, controlled by EasyTech 2.2001-2.0 computer software developed by the device's manufacturer, and a computer set. The stabilometer allowed for measurements in the frontal plane (FP) and sagittal plane (SP) within the range of angular inclination of ±15°, with a maximum measurement error of 0.1°. Electrical signals obtained from a potentiometer in the measurement circuit were converted by means of an analog-to-digital converter card. EasyTech 2.2001-2.0 software interface compute 4 parameters of balance (Figure 4)
Total Area (TA) - the area contained between the line of a movement pathway recorded for a subject and the model line.External Area (EA) - the area contained between the line of a movement path recorded for a subject and the line of a pre-set level of difficulty.

External Time (ET) - total time when a subject remains outside the area of a pre-set level of difficulty.

Recovery Time (RT) - the longest individual time when the subject remained outside the area of a pre-set level of difficulty [31].

Libra hardness level adjustable from the board's surface (10 cm, 25 cm ve 40 cm). The level of our test was 10 cm. At the beginning every participants put each foot center (transvers plane). Three trial were given and the best one was recorded. Libra balance plate was placed a box (50 cm x 50 cm x 50 cm) for the participants sit (Feet and hands without touching any place). When sitting the box feet and hands without touching any place, attempted to maintain the balance line on the Libra seesaw balancing board with the right-left lateral flexion of the torso. Balance scores were recorded at the end of 3 trials (Figure 3) [32].

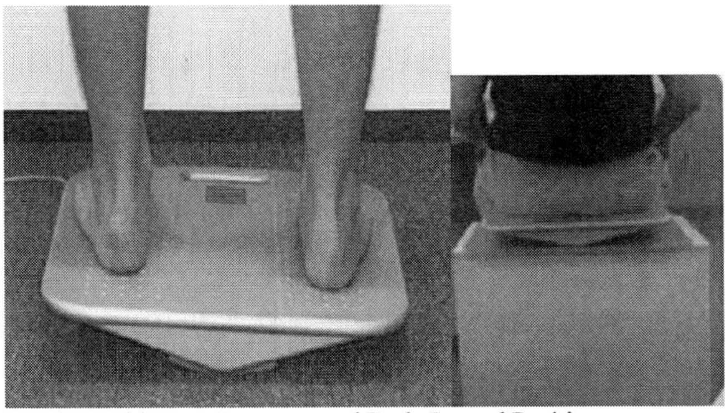

Fig. 3. Double Leg Transvers and Body Lateral Position

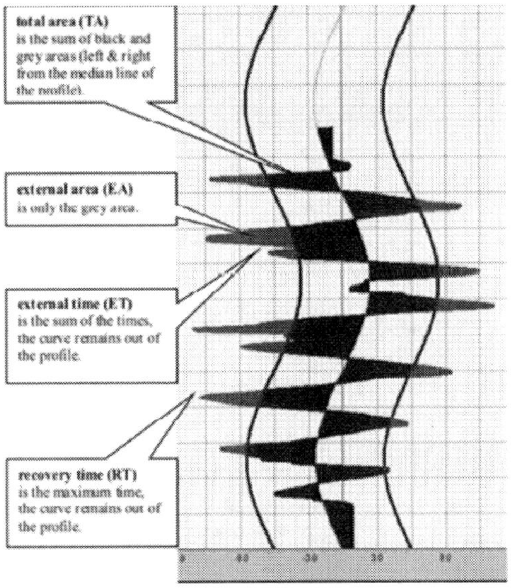

Fig. 4. EasyTech Libra Screenshot [31].

2.1 Training program

One repeat maximum of participants between 60-80%, 3 set, and 8-10 repeat was chose both strength training group. When they reach the 80% density, repetition was drop 8 and set was increased 4. Participants were practice half squat, military press, calf raise and bench press for eight weeks, three day in a week. Load densities for the first three weeks are one, 60% of maximum repetition, 4-6. 70% between weeks and 80% over the last two weeks. In the bandbell earthquake bar group, the set numbers were modified as 5 when reaching 145-150 kg at 80% load at half squat station. Bandbell earthquake bar's capacity is limited to 150 kg by the manufacturer [1].

Dynamic balance (Libra) values from participants; Two-way repeated measures of ANOVA were performed by determining the balance values at the lateral position and the transverse position of the two feet.

3 Results

Three different group (Classic Strength Training Group, Bandbell Earthquake Bar Group and Control Group) Body Balance at Lateral Position and Double Foot Transverse Balance first test and last test values shown on Table 1. According to results, there was a significant difference between Body Balance at Lateral Position (F= 24.86, p<0.05) and Double Foot Transverse Balance (F=14.571, p<0.05) scores.

Table 1. Athletes Balance Values ANOVA Results

Variables		Pre-*test* Mean ± SD	Post-test Mean ± SD	Group X Time F
Body Balance at Lateral Position	Classic Strength Training Group	37.23 ± 5.49	26.45 ± 6.52	24.86*
	Bandbell Earthquake Bar Group	41.66 ± 5,24	31.49 ± 8.16	
	Control Group	39.38 ± 5.33	37.74 ± 5.64	
Double Foot Transvers e Balance	Classic Strength Training Group	33.85 ± 4.34	27.94 ± 4.38	14.571*
	Bandbell Earthquake Bar Group	34.26 ± 2.99	29.32 ± 3.52	
	Control Group	28.12 ± 3.36	27.6 ± 3.64	

* p < 0.05

4 Discussion and conclusion

The results of the study showed significant reductions in equilibrium values in participants' practice of traditional bar and bandbell Earthquake bar strength training. The decline in equilibrium scores indicates that equilibrium is affected positively. It was seen that muscle activation produced by unbalanced loads at reduced loads compared to conventional equipment is higher in the literature McBride et al., [20], Park & Yoo, [25]; Pinto et al., [27]. Azar's assessment of the effect of the Bandbell Earthquake Bar on the shoulder muscle activation of the traditional bar suggests that the quake bar increased muscle activation more than the traditional bar [4]. While the conventional bench press is generating linear force with a fixed line the bench press performs action with a high degree of freedom, which the participant's movement direction cannot easily predict by Bandbell Earthquake Bar [8, 11, 15, 23]. Ostrowski et al. defined all hanging load with elastic bands fast and securely press to a flexible bar [24].

In bandbell earthquake bar excessive muscular activation in strength training depending interaction is expected to increase load density and repetition. During the eight weeks training process it is likely that there will be an increase in strength values depending on resistance. It is thought that the change in participants' equilibrium values depends on the resistance gain of the lower extremity and upper extremity muscles. Furthermore, it was expected that the muscular activation of the Bandbell Earthquake bar would be more effective in balance values. When balance scores are taken into account the effect of the Bandbell Earthquake bar appears to be in parallel with the results of training with the traditional bar. Muehlbauer et al. in their study of 27 healthy adults, they found no significant relationship between dynamic-static equilibrium and isometric strength upper, lower and body strength. (Static-dynamic balance and isometric strength; r=+0.041 to

+0.0387, p>0.05) [21]. Lee and Park's study indicates that increase in lower extremity strength positively affects balance in older adults aged 65-82 [17]. Filipa et al. found to have a significant effect star excursion balance test young women athletes neuromuscular strength training program [12]. General strength trainings increases body mass reduces risk of injury and contributes to the development of core stability [34]. In particular, where the players active branches leading to effective results application of functional training to the core region. Strengthening muscle groups that are effective on balance is important since balance will provide technical advantage to athlete.

As a result, it has been found that both methods contribute to the balance in this study where the balance scores are evaluated in the traditional bar and bandbell Earthquake bar strength training practices. Bandbell earthquake bar strength training practice should consider the upper limit of resistance of the bamboo bar.

References

1. Anderson, C. E., Sforzo, G. A., Sigg, J. A. The effects of combining elastic and free weight resistance on strength and power in athletes. Journal of Strength and Conditioning Research, **22**, 2, 567–574 (2008)
2. Ashton-Miller JA, Wojtys EM, Huston LJ, et al. Can proprioception really be improved by exercises? Knee Surg Sports Traumatol Arthrosc (2001)
3. Arazi H, Coetzee B, Asadi A Comparative effect of land and aquatic based plyometric training on the jumping ability and agility of young basketball players. S Afr J Res Sport Phys Edu Rec **34**, 1–1, (2012)
4. Azar, J. A. Effects of Unstable Versus Stable Free Weights on Surface EMG of Shoulder Musculature in Males (Doctoral dissertation, Ohio University (2016)
5. http://www.fitnessshop.com.tr/urunler/fonksiyonel-egzersiz-ekipmanlari/bandbell-earthquake-bar/#aciklama) Access date:14.06.2017
6. http://www.ardsport.com/?uid=176_Access date:14.06.2017
7. D. G., Anderson, K. G. (2006). The role of instability with resistance training. Journal of Strength and Conditioning Research, **20**, 3, 716–722.
8. Behm, D. G., Leonard, A. M., Young, W. B., Bonsey, A. C., & MacKinnon, S. N. Trunk muscle electromyographic activity with unstable and unilateral exercises. Journal of Strength and Conditioning, **19**, 1, 193–201, (2005)
9. Boyle, M. Advances in functional training: training techniques for coaches, personal trainers and athletes. On Target Publications. (2012)
10. Dasteridis, Giorgos., Piliandis, T., Mantzouranis, Nikos. The effect of different strength training programmes on young athletes' sprint performance. Stud Phys Cult Tourism, **18**, 2, 141-147 (2011)
11. Dunnick, D. D., Brown, L. E., Coburn, J. W., Lynn, S. K., Barillas, S. R. Bench press upper-body muscle activation between stable and unstable loads. Journal of Strength and Conditioning Research, **29**, 12, 3279–3283 (2015)
12. Filipa, A., Byrnes, R., Paterno, M. V., Myer, G. D., Hewett, T. E. Neuromuscular training improves performance on the star excursion balance test in young female athletes. Journal of orthopaedic & sports physical therapy, **40**, 9, 551-558 (2010)
13. Hewett Te, Stroupe Al, Nance Ta, Noyes Fr. Plyometric training in female athletes. American Journal of Sports Medicine, **24**, 765-773 (1996)
14. Hess, J. A., Woollacott, M. Effect of high-intensity strength-training on functional measures of balance ability in balance-impaired older adults. Journal of manipulative and physiological therapeutics, **28,** 8, 582-590, (2005)

15. Kellis, E., Arabatzi, F., Papadopoulos, C. Muscle co-activation around the knee in drop jumping using the co-contraction index. Journal of Electromyography and Kinesiology, **13**, 3, 229–238 (2003)
16. Klinzing, J.E. Training for improved jumping ability of basketball players. Nat Strength Cond Asso J, **13**, 27-32 (1991)
17. Lee, I. H., Park, S. Y. Balance improvement by strength training for the elderly. Journal of physical therapy science, **25**, 12, 1591-1593 (2013)
18. Lehnert, M., Hůlka, K., Malý, T., Fohler, J., Zahálka, F. The effects of a 6 week plyometric training programme on explosive strength and agility in professional basketball players. Acta Gymnica, **43**, 4, 7-15 (2013)
19. Mahmoud H. Mahmoud Balance Exercises as the Basis for Developing the Level of Physical and Skill Performance in Basketball Young Players .World Journal of Sport Sciences **4**, 2 172-178 (2011)
20. McBride, J. M., Larkin, T. R., Dayne, A. M., Haines, T. L., Kirby, T. J. Effect of absolute and relative loading on muscle activity during stable and unstable squatting. International Journal of Sports Physiology and Performance, **5**, 2, 177– 183 (2010)
21. Muehlbauer, T., Gollhofer, A., Granacher, U. Association of balance, strength, and power measures in young adults. The Journal of Strength & Conditioning Research, **27**, 3, 582-589 (2013)
22. Myklebust G, Engebretsen L, Braekken Ih, Skjolberg A, Olsen Oe, Bahr R. (2003) Prevention of anterior cruciate ligament injuries in female team handball players: A prospective intervention study over three seasons. Clinical Journal of Sports Medicine. 13:71-78.
23. Nairn, B. C., Sutherland, C. A., Drake, J. D. M. Location of instability during a bench press alters movement patterns and electromyographical activity. Journal of Strength and Conditioning Research, **29**, 11, 3162–3170 (2015)
24. Ostrowski, S, Carlson, LA, and Lawrence, MA. Effect of an unstable load on primary and stabilizing muscles during the bench press. J Strength Cond Res **31**, 430–434 (2017)
25. Park, S. Y., & Yoo, W. G. Differential activation of parts of the serratus anterior muscle during push-up variations on stable and unstable bases of support. Journal of Electromyography Kinesiology, **21**, 5, 861–867 (2011)
26. Paterno mv.myer g. Jun.Neuro muscular training improves single-limb stability in young female athletes. J Orthop Sports Phys Ther, **34**, 6, 305-16 (2004)
27. Pinto, R., Cadore, E., Correa, C., Gonçalves Cordeiro da Silva, B., Alberton, C., Lima, C., & de Moraes, A. Relationship between workload and neuromuscular activity in the bench press exercise. Medicina Sportiva, **17**, 1, 1–6. (2013)
28. Randa, et al. Effect of physical activity and sporting activities on balance control in elderly people.British journal of sportsmedicine, **33**, 2 (2001)
29. Soria-Gila, M. A., Chirosa, I. J., Bautista, I. J., Baena, S., & Chirosa, L. J. Effectsof variable resistance training on maximal strength: A meta-analysis. Journal of Strength and Conditioning Research, **29**, 11, 3260–3270 (2015)
30. Tchórzewski, D., Bujas, P., Jankowicz-Szymańska, A. Body posture stability in ski boots under conditions of unstable supporting surface. Journal of human kinetics, **38,** 33-44 (2013)
31. Tchórzewski, D., Jaworski, J., Bujas, P. Influence of long-lasting balancing on unstable surface on changes in balance. Human Movement, **11**, 2, 144-152 (2010)
32. Thompson, C. J., Cobb, K. M., Blackwell, J. Functional training improves club head speed and functional fitness in older golfers. The Journal of Strength & Conditioning Research, **21**, 1, 131-137 (2007)

33. Young, M.D.,Jordan D. Metzl, MAY. Strength Training for the Young Athlete Warren K. Mdpedıatrıc Annals **39**, 5 (2010)
34. Young, W. B. Transfer of strength and power training to sports performance. International journal of sports physiology and performance, **1**, 2, 74 (2006)

Studying attention levels of the university students from various sport branches

Baybars Recep Eynur[1a], Aytul Eynur[1], and Mustafa Said Erzeybek[1]

[1]Dumlupınar University, Department of Physical Education and Sport, 43020 Kütahya, Turkey

Abstract. The objective of this study is to examine the attention skills of the university student athletes from various sport branches. A total of 174 university students have been participated into the study of which 46.6% were female and 53.4% were male. The neurofeedback method has been used in the study. With regard to the research statistics, the independent variable t-test and ANOVA have been used; and in order to evaluate the diversity of the subgroups, Bonferroni and Tamhane (α=0.05) have been used. The study has revealed that female athletes are significantly more succeful in terms of attention consistency, staying focused against time, controlling attention, hand-eye-brain coordination, and concentration compared to male athletes ($p<0.05$). It has been seen that the number of years spent doing sports (years of sports) is not an active variable with regard to the attention skills ($p>0.05$). It has also been seen that on the basis of the branches, the spatial memory skills of the wrestlers are significantly higher than the soccer players ($p<0.05$); that the attention consistency, visual follow-up and staying focused despite the distractors skills of the national athletes are significantly higher than others ($p<0.05$). The reseach has revealed that attention is instantaneous and definitely an important factor for the sportive success; and besides its unique efficiency for experience and success, also similarly with the sportive success, it exists with "You can succeed only if you do it" understanding.
Keywords: Attention skills, university students, sport branches.

1 Introduction and objective

Many studies have already revealed that a lot of factors affect the success in performance sports and the trainings should cover a wide range of purposes as is widely accepted around the world [1]. The current situation shows that what is underlying the sportive competition and what is perceived as a set of psycho-motor movements may be something more than psycho-motor acitivities of that sport; something that also comprises a mental process [2]. The studies conducted have revealed that any skill can be manifested only and only if all of the appropriate mental processes are passed through [3, 4].

[a] Corresponding author: baybars.eynur@dpu.edu.tr

This fact has caused the thought "no sportive competition can be succesful without reaching the required mental concentration" to be spread widely. Accordingly, in order to reach the appropriate performance level, one should take part in competition with an appropriate mental state. This study has been regarded significant since it targets to determine the attention levels shown by the athletes from the different branches in different situations as defined with certain measurements upon reaching the required brain frequencies levels; as well as to reveal the sport lives of the athletes and their present efficiencies/inadequacies.

The attention deficit that we encounter more and more nowadays is a disorder that is not much cared by individuals, however it reduces the quality of life significantly, if not treated [5, 6]. This situation is defined as bad mood in the life span [5]. Since the recent studies have reported that the elite athletes show an increasing tendency toward the attention deficit, a more careful and analytical examination is necessary [7]. It is seen that the studies regarding the attention deficit have been conducted from 1980's to date [8].

Examining the literature shows that most of the studies regarding the attention deficit are based on the individuals with the attention deficit disorder, but certain studies involving the sports have also been encountered [9-12]. These studies have reported that the sports can be an auxilliary element in order to eliminate the attention deficit. However, there was no written descriptive study that concerns the determination of the attention levels of the athletes or the attention level required for the appropriate performance level in the literature. This study targets to analyse the sportive attention in terms of the branch, gender, being national or non-national athlete variables and the individual or team characteristic of the concerned sport.

It is considered that the present study would enable the performance awareness of the athletes as well as help to increase their mental skill levels.

1.1 Attention

More than a century ago, William JAMES wrote "everybody knows what is attention" and expressed this as "Embracement of any instantaneously emerged object or thought by the mind clearly and explicitly [13]. The fundemental elements of attention are focusing, concentration and consciousness. Attention means to give up certain things in order to deal efficiently with others."[14].

The first scientific reference about attention was from Descartes as seen by tracing back his etymology to Rome. Descartes has associated attention with the reactions of the pineal body active in the animal soul [15]. Again, the same study claims that attention is a prerequisite for the perception [15].

In another statement, attention is defined in more general terms as the "concentration of the mental efforts on sensual or mental events" [13]. Within this process, attention is also included together with several other mental activities and its importance is highlighted [16]. In addition, the influence of attention in terms of directing and sustaining the learning efforts is emphasized [17-19].

The psychological studies regarding attention describe it with at least six definitions and emphasize the effectiveness of three dimensions in the description process. These are awareness, ability to select information and attention sense that is the product of limited information processing capacity [20].

At this point, attention is defined as a mental process carried out by focusing. Also, the maintainability of attention is defined as the ability to draw away oneself from the environmental events [21].

The general definition of attention that was read as how we perceive the truth underlying a certain act, has been changed when focused attention allowed the individual to accept mentally the influences of the observed subject by the individual. Attention that is segmented properly, reunite at certain point that represent the truth as a whole without focusing on any part specifically and at this point the individual selects his/her orientation using all of the senses. Studying attention is closely related with what happens now, but equally away from what could be happened. This situation can be maintained mentally upon determining new ways of thinking and what may come out. The concept of attention also concerns the success capacity with the experience of the unknown, as much as that of the known. Those listed under the term and expression of attention refer to a significant depth and richness as well as both active and passive words. An improved attention capacity allows us to know what happens now, rather than what has been done. Bion's approach goes a little beyond this idea; he reports that the quality of the complete attention enables us to know not only what happens now or what we do, but also what others do. The idea of attention that defines the ability of our minds to get opened to the space, has been used as to focus on a certain point despite all other things around. Bion claims that what underlies the poor quality of attention are observation errors and reasonably, observations' focus on the inconsistency. Attention means maintaining our thoughts with a strong thinking support; the thoughts except those we have abandoned, vain and not consistent with our purposes. Accordingly, attention is a deep awareness, beyond focusing. Consequently, attention is an effect that explore the exact solution of the problems through development, learning, openness for change and continous renewal [22].

The only central part of a new approach for the description of attention (may be the most important part coming from a psychological point of view) is that it changes the responsibilities of our comprehension mechanisms for the selectivity of attention. As from Broadbent's inspiring works, this perceived opinion is that the selectivity of attention arises from the limitations of the brain capacity for processing information. At this point, attention selects the subdimension of the information that is obtained somehow and processed by a part of our perception system, until it passes to the next part of the system. Briefly, it is attention that selects the information to overcome bottlenecks of the limited capacity [14].

It is emphasized that the practice of paying attention is a requirement for coding, verifying and then recalling the information by the brain [21].

With regard to the sensual dimension of attention, it has been stated that the sense organs may cooperate to create a new pattern, but cannot sense two different patterns at the same time. However, it has been added that for the same pattern, several sense organs can cooperate [15].

Also, the efficiency of attention in the learning process has been defined strategically, for fulfilling the cognitive management strategies during the language learning [23].

Attention is defined as a meaningful activity that can be internalized, interested in and a mental activity that can cause to sustain the productivity and willingness. Also, it has been emphasized that attention can be controlled deliberately, however same does not apply for its intensity [24].

Attention is perceived as an activity of the organism and it is thought that it benefits from the nerve energy generated by the attention organ; it is also defined as an activity that enables the use of the energy required by the mechanism to perform the requested function [25]. In this context, attention should also be accepted as the foundation of the perceiving/sensing system.

When the concept is examined in this context, it has been seen that there is a development in terms of the definition of attention. Previously, attention being only on the individual basis and relevant for the interested objects and patterns, currently it is emphasized that the selectivity of attention should be focused on both individual and environment.

1.2 Attention in sports

An important characteristic of those showing learned performance is their attention efficiency. The succesful performers do not only preserve their attention for long time, but they also note the descriptive and remarkable clues required for success [26].

A study has been conducted among cricketers in order to see if there is a correlation between their attention levels and performance levels, by describing the relation between their way to pay attention and sportive performances [27].

Upon examination of the results obtained from the on-going measurements of the attention studies carried out with four university student who were soccer players, it has been seen that these four players who had been subjected to attention training, have significantly improved their accuracy in terms of manifesting their soccer skills [28].

A study regarding the effect of the exercise stimulation on processing the visual information by children and adults has been conducted. The study has revealed that the selected children who are over 8 years old and adults show lower performance, and also their rank and characteristics are influenced by the age [29].

It has been reported that attention is particularly important in sports for figuring out the sportive process and that it has an important role in the development of performance as well as at the dissociation point where the mind deviates to other subjects outside the interest of the individual [30, 31]. Also, there exist the studies targeting to emphasize the importance of attention at the point of conversion of the sportive performance into the score as well as a literature that shows that the shot performance and attention of the basketball players are significantly correlated ($r=0.67$) [32].

In a study conducted to evaluate the efficiency of attention in sports according to this very approach, the researchers have tried to analyse the expectations of the players in Greek national basketball, volleyball and water-polo teams with the help of the field expert trainers; and it has been reported that the basketball players are significantly different from others in terms of estimation and selective attention; the volleyball players are significantly different from others in terms of perceptual speed, focused attention, estimation as well as speed estimation and movement direction estimation and the water-polo players are significantly different in terms of perceiving the inexperienced players, visual reaction time and plane-based orientation ($p<0.5$) [33].

The literature supports the fact that different methods are used to evaluate attention in sports. However, it has been reported that none of these methods were completely sufficient in the process [34].

It has been indicated that the socio-economical status of the athletes is efficient to enable early physical relaxing and that the athletes at higher socio-economical level recover oxygen faster than other athletes. Whereas, it has been reported that the attention level is not related with the socio-economical level [35].

When attention is under threat, performance supervisor and motivational systems warn in combination, unproficiently and audibly. This effort process that requires attention continues until the individual regulates and control him/herself [24].

There is literature showing that attention can also be increased by using drugs [36]. Even the existence of this study shows the importance of attention in terms of performance.

The literature shows that attention is directly effective on several subdimensions of performance; formation of movement accuracy; controlling; describing the energy level required for the skill as well as the parameters that directly influence the performance.

The literature shows that the formula described to enable the required level of skill is very simple.

Skill = Speed x Accuracy x Form x Adaptability [37]. When the formula is examined, it is seen that the adaptability skill that describe the mental and psychological preparation, also defines attention as the most important element enabling the manisfestation of performance; and even this reason alone shows that attention is necessary not only for the manisfestation of the skill, but also for its manifestation at the required level.

2 Material and method

The study has been conducted according to the screening model. The screening model is a reasearch approach that targets to describe a past or present situtation as it is. The approach tries to describe any event, individual or object which is subject to the research as it is, under its own conditions. No effort is made to change or to affect them in any way. There is something to find out and it is out there. What is important is to "observe" properly and specify it [38].

2.1 Study group

A total of 174 persons studying at Dumlupınar University (DPU), Department of Physical Education and Sport (DPES) from different branches have been participated into the study group. The distribution of the participating students/athletes is as follows.

Table 1. Descriptive statistics of the participants

			Branch						Total
			Soccer	Basketball	Volleyball	Handball	Athletics	Wrestling	
Gender	F	Count	18	16	16	19	12	0	81
		% of Total	10,3%	9,2%	9,2%	10,9%	6,9%	0,0%	46,6%
	M	Count	19	13	15	18	12	16	93
		% of Total	10,9%	7,5%	8,6%	10,3%	6,9%	9,2%	53,4%
Total		Count	37	29	31	37	24	16	174
		% of Total	21,3%	16,7%	17,8%	21,3%	13,8%	9,2%	100,0%

Table 1 shows the 46,6% of the participating students are female and 53,4% of them are male. Also, according to the female participants' proportion to all athletes, 10,3% are soccer players; 9,2% are basketball players; 9,2% are volleyball players; 10,9% are handball players and 6,9% do athletics. According to the male participants' proportion to all athletes 10,9% are soccer players, 7,5% basketball players, 8,6% volleyball players, 10,3% hanball players, 6,9% do athletics and 9,2% are wrestlers.

A total of 174 persons with various ages, studying at Dumlupınar University, Department of Physical Education and Sport performing in different sport branches have been participated into the study group. The sport lives of the participants were still active at the time and 46,6% of them were female and 53,4% of them were male.

The system used in the research is a neurofeedback system that does not comprise any subcutaneous tool. The device registered in the name of Freer Logic, LLC measures the individual attention level using various sub-tests, on the basis of the individual's reactions to the content provided in the computer environment. The reactions are measured through instant data transfer between computer and the student.

The system is recalibrated for each individual. Accordingly, when the system is open using it for another individual requires recalibration by the authorized persons. The sub-tests used in the system are Attention Consistency, Staying Focused Against Time, Visual

Follow-Up, Short Term Memory, Staying Focused Despite the Stimulators and Distractors, Controlling Attention, Hand-Eye-Brain Coordination, and Concentration.

2.2 Evaluation of data and statistics

The data obtained from the measurements carried out within the scope of the research have been evaluated using SPSS 22 software. The attention obtained by the participants have been evaluated considering also the characteristics of data, on the basis of the independent variables. In this context, for the groups having two different independent variables t-test with independent sample and for the groups having 3 or more independent variables ONE-WAY ANOVA test have been used. Furthermore, in order to determine the differences between the groups, Bonferroni and Tamhane tests have been used. The significance level has been set as $\alpha=0,05$.

3 Results (Findings)

The data obtained in the research have been evaluated on the basis of the sub dimensions included in the Active Participation (AE) neurofeedback measurements and analysed in terms of the independent variables. Thus, the results have been indicated under five sub titles.

3.1 Attention levels of the athletes according to gender variable

The attention levels of the participating athletes according to the gender variable is as follows.

Table 2. The independent sample t-test results regarding the attention consistency of the participating athletes by gender

	Gender	N	Mean	Std. Deviation	T	P
Attention Consistency	Female	81	82,40	7,713	**3,424**	**0,001**
	Male	93	78,22	8,299		

Table 2 shows that the attention consistency skills of the participating female athletes (N=81) was = 82,4 + 7,713 and for the male participants (N=93), this value was =78,22 + 8,299. Table 2 also shows that on the basis of the gender variable, there is a significant difference favouring the female athletes ($t_{.05}=3,424$; $p<0.05$) with regard to the attention consistency.

Table 3. The independent sample t-test results regarding the visual follow-up sub tests of the participating athletes by gender

	Gender	N	Mean	Std. Deviation	T	P
Visual Follow-Up	Female	81	82,78	6,387	1,698	,091
	Male	93	80,97	7,670		

Table 3 shows that no significant difference has been identified between the groups in the visual follow-up sub test by gender ($t_{.05}=1,698$; $p>0.05$).

Table 4. The independent sample t-test results regarding the staying focused sub tests of the participating athletes by gender

	Gender	N	Mean	Std. Deviation	T	P
Staying Focused Against Time	Female	81	83,46	5,727	**3,974**	**0,000**
	Male	93	79,08	8,684		

Table 4 shows that the staying focused against time skills of the participating female athletes (N=81) was = 83,46 + 5,727 and for the male participants (N=93) this value was =79,08 + 8,684. Table 4 also shows that on the basis of the gender variable, there is a significant difference favouring the female athletes in terms of staying focused against time (t.05=3,974; $p<0.05$).

Table 5. The independent sample t-test results regarding the short term memory sub tests of the participating athletes by gender

	Gender	N	Mean	Std. Deviation	T	P
Short Term Memory	Female	81	82,23	7,263	1,952	0,53
	Male	93	79,71	9,465		

Table 5 shows that no significant difference has been identified between the groups in the short term memory sub test by gender (t.05=1,952; $p>0.05$).

Table 6. The independent sample t-test results regarding the staying focused despite stimulators and distractors sub tests of the participating athletes by gender

	Gender	N	Mean	Std. Deviation	T	P
Staying Focused Despite Stimulators and Distractors	Female	81	81,84	8,433	0,936	0,351
	Male	93	80,60	8,930		

Table 6 shows that no significant difference has been identified between the groups in the staying focused despite stimulators and distractors sub test by gender (t.05=0,936; $p>0.05$).

Table 7. The independent sample t-test results regarding the attention control sub tests of the participating athletes by gender

	Gender	N	Mean	Std. Deviation	T	P
Controlling Attention	Female	81	84,26	8,128	2,474	0,014
	Male	93	80,60	10,925		

Table 7 shows that the attention control skills of the participating female athletes (N=81) was = 84,26 + 8,128 and for the male participants (N=93) this value was =80,60 + 10,925. Table 7 also shows that on the basis of the gender variable, there is a significant difference favouring the female athletes in terms of attention control skills (t.05=2,474; p<0.05).

Table 8. The independent sample t-test results regarding the hand-eye-brain coordination sub tests of the participating athletes by gender

	Gender	N	Mean	Std. Deviation	T	p
Hand-Eye-Brain Coordination	Female	81	84,40	5,781	3,498	0,001
	Male	93	80,92	7,113		

Table 8 shows that the hand-eye-brain of the participating female athletes (N=81) was = 84,40 + 5,781 and for the male participants (N=93), this value was =80,92 + 7,113. Table 8 also shows that on the basis of the gender variable, there is a significant difference favouring the female athletes in terms of hand-eye-brain coordination (t.05=3,498; p<0.05).

Table 9. The independent sample t-test results regarding the spatial memory sub tests of the participating athletes by gender

	Gender	N	Mean	Std. Deviation	T	P
Spatial Memory	Female	81	80,49	7,849	0,359	0,720
	Male	93	80,01	9,898		

Table 9 shows that no significant difference has been identified between the groups in the spatial memory sub test by gender (t.05=0,359; p>0.05).

Table 10. The Independent Sample T-Test Results Regarding the Concentration Sub tests of the Participating Athletes by Gender

	Gender	N	Mean	Std. Deviation	T	p
Concentration	Female	81	83,31	7,361	3,942	,000
	Male	93	78,23	9,614		

Table 10 shows that the concentration skills of the participating female athletes (N=81) was = 83,31 + 7,361 and for the male participants (N=93) this value was =78,23 + 9,614. Table 10 also shows that on the basis of the gender variable, there is a significant difference favouring the female athletes in terms of concentration (t.05=3,942; p<0.05).

3.2 Attention levels of the athletes according to sports years

The attention levels of the participating athletes according to the sports years variable is as follows.

Table 11. The sub test regarding the attention consistency skills of the participating athletes by sports years

	Sports Years	N	Mean	Std. Deviation	F	p
Attention Consistency	5	12	79,83	7,030	0,637	0,746
	6	12	79,08	9,737		
	7	12	78,17	8,167		
	8	28	81,14	7,012		
	10	26	81,23	7,163		
	11	33	80,73	9,362		
	12	15	82,60	7,059		
	13	17	78,18	10,327		
	15	19	78,26	8,685		
	Total	174	80,16	8,277		

Upon comparison between the sports years groups, no significant difference has been found in terms of the attention consistency scores of the participating athletes ($F_{8,165}=0,637$; $p>0,05$).

Table 12. The sub test regarding the visual follow-up skills of the participating athletes by sports years

Sports Years		N	Mean	Std. Deviation	F	p
Visual Follow-Up	5	12	83,25	6,690	0,492	0,861
	6	12	79,42	10,247		
	7	12	82,17	5,766		
	8	28	82,57	5,872		
	10	26	82,31	7,336		
	11	33	81,00	7,215		
	12	15	83,53	5,817		
	13	17	81,35	8,717		
	15	19	80,84	7,335		
	Total	174	81,81	7,140		

Upon comparison between the sports years groups, no significant difference has been found in terms of the visual follow-up scores of the participating athletes ($F_{8,165}=0,492$; $p>0,05$).

Table 13. The sub test regarding staying focused against time skills of the participating athletes by sports years

Sports Years		N	Mean	Std. Deviation	F	p
Staying Focused Against Time	5	12	83,25	6,635	0,539	0,826
	6	12	80,58	8,795		
	7	12	82,67	5,176		
	8	28	80,93	6,503		
	10	26	80,62	10,016		
	11	33	81,39	6,910		
	12	15	82,00	4,408		
	13	17	81,76	7,250		
	15	19	78,32	11,076		
	Total	174	81,11	7,751		

Upon comparison between the sports years groups, no significant difference has been found in terms of the staying focused against time scores of the participating athletes ($F8,165=0,539$; $p>0,05$).

Table 14. The sub test regarding short term memory of the participating athletes by sports years

Sports Years		N	Mean	Std. Deviation	F	p
Short Term Memory	5	12	80,00	7,769	,263	,977
	6	12	80,42	8,939		
	7	12	79,58	5,089		
	8	28	81,21	7,608		
	10	26	79,62	11,997		
	11	33	81,55	8,537		
	12	15	82,87	6,390		
	13	17	81,53	8,804		
	15	19	80,53	8,959		
	Total	174	80,89	8,581		

Upon comparison between the sports years groups, no significant difference has been found in terms of the short term memory scores of the participating athletes ($F8,165=0,263$; $p>0,05$).

Table 15. The sub test regarding staying focused despite stimulators and distractors skills of the participating athletes by sports years

Sports Years		N	Mean	Std. Deviation	F	p
Staying Focused Despite Stimulators and Distractors	5	12	82,33	5,774	0,492	0,861
	6	12	81,42	7,982		
	7	12	83,75	7,533		
	8	28	80,82	9,113		
	10	26	81,69	7,176		
	11	33	78,97	9,548		
	12	15	82,73	5,824		
	13	17	80,94	12,153		
	15	19	81,32	10,028		
	Total	174	81,18	8,699		

Upon comparison between the sports years groups, no significant difference has been found in terms of the staying focused against stimulators and distractors scores of the participating athletes (F8,165=0,492; p>0,05).

Table 16. The sub test regarding attention control skills of the participating athletes by sports years

Sports Years		N	Mean	Std. Deviation	F	p
Controlling Attention	5	12	84,00	8,146	0,798	0,605
	6	12	83,92	5,282		
	7	12	84,58	5,384		
	8	28	82,86	6,473		
	10	26	80,77	11,459		
	11	33	82,48	9,843		
	12	15	84,00	7,464		
	13	17	82,94	8,743		
	15	19	77,84	17,231		
	Total	174	82,30	9,868		

Upon comparison between the sports years groups, no significant difference has been found in terms of the attention control scores of the participating athletes (F8,165=0,798; p>0,05).

Table 17. The sub test regarding hand-eye-brain coordination of the participating athletes by sports years

Sports Years		N	Mean	Std. Deviation	F	p
Hand-Eye-Brain Coordination	5	12	83,75	5,707	0,672	0,715
	6	12	83,50	4,964		
	7	12	83,83	7,334		
	8	28	83,29	5,530		
	10	26	81,42	7,834		
	11	33	81,36	7,557		
	12	15	83,87	7,772		
	13	17	83,65	3,481		
	15	19	80,79	8,004		
	Total	174	82,54	6,736		

Upon comparison between the sports years groups, no significant difference has been found in terms of the hand-eye-brain coordination scores of the participating athletes (F8,165=0,672; p>0,05).

Table 18. The sub test regarding spatial memory of the participating athletes by sports years

Sports Years		N	Mean	Std. Deviation	F	p
Spatial Memory	5	12	76,42	9,549	0,585	0,789
	6	12	81,08	6,403		
	7	12	77,75	7,412		
	8	28	80,46	10,269		
	10	26	80,50	10,481		
	11	33	79,82	8,579		
	12	15	80,80	8,970		
	13	17	82,65	8,631		
	15	19	81,11	8,306		
	Total	174	80,24	8,980		

Upon comparison between the sports years groups, no significant difference has been found in terms of the spatial memory scores of the participating athletes (F8,165=0,585; p>0,05).

Table 19. The sub test regarding concentration skills of the participating athletes by sports years

Sports Years		N	Mean	Std. Deviation	F	p
Concentration	5	12	81,42	7,868	0,653	0,732
	6	12	82,08	6,501		
	7	12	81,50	9,765		
	8	28	79,89	7,455		
	10	26	80,54	10,693		
	11	33	81,64	8,930		
	12	15	82,13	4,422		
	13	17	80,59	9,042		
	15	19	76,63	12,566		
	Total	174	80,59	8,982		

Upon comparison between the sports years groups, no significant difference has been found in terms of the concentration skills scores of the participating athletes (F8,165=0,653; p>0,05).

3.3 Attention levels of the athletes according to branches

The attention levels of the participating athletes according to the sports branch variable is as follows.

Table 20. The sub test regarding the attention consistency skills of the participating athletes by sports branch

Branch		N	Mean	Std. Deviation	F	p
Attention Consistency	Soccer	37	79,86	9,861	1,764	0,123
	Basketball	29	79,41	7,204		
	Volleyball	31	80,10	7,049		
	Handball	37	82,68	6,770		
	Athletics	24	80,75	9,237		
	Wrestling	16	75,63	8,958		
	Total	174	80,16	8,277		

Upon comparison between the sports branch groups, no significant difference has been found in terms of the attention consistency scores of the participating athletes (F5,165=1,764; p>0,05).

Table 21. The sub test regarding the follow-up skills of the participating athletes by sports branch

Branch		N	Mean	Std. Deviation	F	p
Visual Follow-Up	Soccer	37	81,32	7,696	1,107	0,358
	Basketball	29	82,79	5,759		
	Volleyball	31	80,87	8,310		
	Handball	37	83,70	5,661		
	Athletics	24	81,08	7,021		
	Wrestling	16	79,69	8,631		
	Total	174	81,81	7,140		

Upon comparison between the sports branch groups, no significant difference has been found in terms of the visual follow-up scores of the participating athletes (F5,165=1,107; p>0,05).

Table 22. The sub test regarding the staying focused against time skills of the participating athletes by sports branch

Branch		N	Mean	Std. Deviation	F	p
Staying Focused Against Time	Soccer	37	80,73	8,928	1,342	0,249
	Basketball	29	82,55	6,015		
	Volleyball	31	79,39	11,053		
	Handball	37	82,81	4,364		
	Athletics	24	81,50	6,750		
	Wrestling	16	78,25	6,894		
	Total	174	81,11	7,751		

Upon comparison between the sports branch groups, no significant difference has been found in terms of the staying focused against time scores of the participating athletes (F5,165=1,342; p>0,05).

Table 23. The sub test regarding the short term memory of the participating athletes by sports branch

Branch		N	Mean	Std. Deviation	F	p
Short Term Memory	Soccer	37	79,73	9,500	1,082	0,372
	Basketball	29	82,59	6,395		
	Volleyball	31	80,06	12,514		
	Handball	37	82,89	5,087		
	Athletics	24	78,96	8,805		
	Wrestling	16	80,31	5,963		
	Total	174	80,89	8,581		

Upon comparison between the sports branch groups, no significant difference has been found in terms of the short term memory scores of the participating athletes (F5,165=1,082; p>0,05).

Table 24. The sub test regarding the staying focused despite stimulators and distractors skills of the participating athletes by sports branch

Branch		N	Mean	Std. Deviation	F	p
Staying Focused Despite Stimulators and Distractors	Soccer	37	80,00	8,293	2,466	0,035
	Basketball	29	83,66	7,654		
	Volleyball	31	80,26	9,381		
	Handball	37	84,16	5,781		
	Athletics	24	78,08	11,021		
	Wrestling	16	78,94	9,808		
	Total	174	81,18	8,699		

The comparison between the branch groups have revealed a significant difference in terms of the staying focused despite stimulators and distractors skills (F5,165=2,466; p<0,05). In order to specify the groups showing the significant difference, Tamhane test has been applied as a second level test, since the variances were not homogen. However, no significant difference has been observed between the sub groups (p>0,05).

DOI: 10.1051/shsconf/20173701059

Table 25. The sub test regarding the attention control skills of the participating athletes by sports branch

Branch		N	Mean	Std. Deviation	F	P
Controlling Attention	Soccer	37	81,49	8,704	1,514	0,188
	Basketball	29	84,41	6,489		
	Volleyball	31	78,81	15,041		
	Handball	37	83,89	8,027		
	Athletics	24	81,54	9,869		
	Wrestling	16	84,63	7,597		
	Total	174	82,30	9,868		

Upon comparison between the sports branch groups, no significant difference has been found in terms of the attention control scores of the participating athletes ($F_{5,165}=1,514$; $p>0,05$).

Table 26. The sub test regarding the hand-eye-brain coordination of the participating athletes by sports branch

Branch		N	Mean	Std. Deviation	F	P
Hand-Eye-Brain Coordination	Soccer	37	81,57	7,855	1,548	0,178
	Basketball	29	83,45	5,262		
	Volleyball	31	82,35	9,506		
	Handball	37	83,73	4,011		
	Athletics	24	83,71	6,403		
	Wrestling	16	79,00	4,274		
	Total	174	82,54	6,736		

Upon comparison between the sports branch groups, no significant difference has been found in terms of the hand-eye-brain coordination scores of the participating athletes ($F_{5,165}=1,548$; $p>0,05$).

Table 27. The sub test regarding the spatial memory of the participating athletes by sports branch

Branch		N	Mean	Std. Deviation	F	P	Groups
Spatial Memory	Soccer	37	77,49	9,648	2,546	0,030	Soccer-Wrestling
	Basketball	29	81,69	8,528			
	Volleyball	31	79,48	10,484			
	Handball	37	81,86	6,588			
	Athletics	24	77,88	9,373			
	Wrestling	16	85,19	6,833			
	Total	174	80,24	8,980			

The comparison between the branch groups have revealed a significant difference in terms of the spatial memory skills ($F_{5,165}=2,466$; $p<0,05$). In order to specify the groups showing the significant difference, Tamhane test has been applied as a second level test, since the variances were not homogen. The test results have revealed a significant difference in favour of wrestlers, between the soccer and wrestling groups ($p>0,05$).

Table 28. The sub test regarding the concentration skills of the participating athletes by sports branch

Branch		N	Mean	Std. Deviation	F	P
Concentration	Soccer	37	79,51	8,846	0,891	0,488
	Basketball	29	82,66	6,773		
	Volleyball	31	80,26	13,117		
	Handball	37	80,89	6,288		
	Athletics	24	81,79	9,325		
	Wrestling	16	77,50	7,789		
	Total	174	80,59	8,982		

Upon comparison between the sports branch groups, no significant difference has been found in terms of the concentration scores of the participating athletes (F5,165=0,891; p>0,05).

3.4 Attention levels of the athletes according to branch type variable

The attention levels of the participating athletes according to the sports branch type variable is as follows.

Table 29. The sub test regarding the attention consistency skills of the participating athletes by branch type

	B. Type	N	Mean	Std. Deviation	T	P
Attention Consistency	Individual	41	78,76	9,251	-1,245	0,215
	Team	133	80,59	7,940		

Table 29 shows that the attention consistency skills of the participating individual athletes (N=41) was = 78,76 + 9,251 and for the team member athletes (N=133) this value was =80,59 + 7,940. Table 29 shows that there is no significant difference in terms of the attention consistency skills of the participating athletes, on the basis of the branch type variable (t.05=-1,245; p>0.05).

Table 30. The sub test regarding the visual follo-up skills of the participating athletes by branch type

	B. Type	N	Mean	Std. Deviation	T	P
Visual Follow-Up	Individual	41	80,34	7,624	-1,512	0,132
	Team	133	82,26	6,951		

Table 30 shows that the visual follow-up skills of the participating individual athletes (N=41) was = 80,34 + 7,624 and for the team member athletes (N=133) this value was =82,26 + 6,951. Table 30 shows that there is no significant difference in terms of the visual follow-up skills of the participating athletes, on the basis of the branch type variable (t.05=-1,245; p>0.05).

Table 31. The sub test regarding the staying focused against time skills of the participating athletes by branch type

	B. Type	N	Mean	Std. Deviation	t	P
Staying Focused Against Time	Individual	41	80,22	6,825	-,845	,399
	Team	133	81,39	8,019		

Table 31 shows that the staying focused against time skills of the participating individual athletes (N=41) was = 80,22 + 6,825 and for the team member athletes (N=133) this value was =81,39 + 8,019. Table 31 shows that there is no significant difference in terms of the staying focused against time skills of the participating athletes, on the basis of the branch type variable (t.05=-0,845; p>0.05).

Table 32. The sub test regarding the short term memory of the participating athletes by branch type

	B. Type	N	Mean	Std. Deviation	t	P
Short Term Memory	Individual	41	79,71	7,753	-1,005	0,316
	Team	133	81,25	8,816		

Table 32 shows that the short term memory of the participating individual athletes (N=41) was = 79,71 + 7,753 and for the team member athletes (N=133) this value was =81,25 + 8,816. Table 32 shows that there is no significant difference in terms of short term memory skills of the participating athletes, on the basis of the branch type variable (t.05=-1,005; p>0.05).

Table 33. The sub test regarding the staying focused despite stimulators and distractors skills of the participating athletes by branch type

	B. Type	N	Mean	Std. Deviation	T	P
Staying Focused Despite Stimulators and Distractors	Individual	41	78,41	10,300	-2,064	,044
	Team	133	82,03	7,995		

Table 33 shows that the staying focused despite stimulators and distractors skills of the participating individual athletes (N=41) was = 78,41 + 10,300 and for the team member athletes (N=133) this value was =82,03 + 7,995. Table 33 shows that there is a significant difference in terms of the staying focused despite stimulators and distractors skills of the participating athletes, on the basis of the branch type variable (t.05=-2,064; p<0.05).

Table 34. The sub test regarding the attention control of the participating athletes by branch type

	B. Type	N	Mean	Std. Deviation	T	P
Controlling Attention	Individual	41	82,73	8,944	,316	,752
	Team	133	82,17	10,163		

Table 34 shows that the attention control skills of the participating individual athletes (N=41) was = 82,73 + 8,944 and for the team member athletes (N=133) this value was

=82,17 + 10,163. Table 34 shows no significant difference in terms of the attention control skills of the participating athletes, on the basis of the branch type variable (t.05=0,316; p>0.05).

Table 35. The sub test regarding the hand-eye-brain coordination of the participating athletes by branch type

	B. Type	N	Mean	Std. Deviation	T	P
Hand-Eye-Brain Coordination	Individual	41	81,76	5,995	-0,852	,395
	Team	133	82,78	6,951		

Table 35 shows that the hand-eye-brain coordination of the participating individual athletes (N=41) was = 81,76 + 5,995 and for the team member athletes (N=133) this value was =82,78 + 6,951. Table 35 shows no significant difference in terms of the hand-eye-brain coordination of the participating athletes, on the basis of the branch type variable (t.05=-0,852; p>0.05).

Table 36. The sub test regarding the spatial memory of the participating athletes by branch type

	B. Type	N	Mean	Std. Deviation	t	P
Spatial Memory	Individual	41	81,12	9,225	,722	,471
	Team	133	79,96	8,921		

Table 36 shows that the spatial memory of the participating individual athletes (N=41) was = 81,12 + 9,225 and for the team member athletes (N=133) this value was =79,96 + 8,921. Table 36 shows no significant difference in terms of the spatial memory of the participating athletes, on the basis of the branch type variable (t.05=0,722; p>0.05).

Table 37. The sub test regarding the concentration of the participating athletes by branch type

	B. Type	N	Mean	Std. Deviation	T	P
Concentration	Individual	41	79,88	8,875	-,581	,562
	Team	133	80,81	9,037		

Table 37 shows that the concentration of the participating individual athletes (N=41) dikkati yoğunlaştırabilme alt testinde = 79,88 + 8,875 and for the team member athletes (N=133) this value was =80,81 + 9,037. Table 37 shows no significant difference in terms of the concentration of the participating athletes, on the basis of the branch type variable (t.05=-0,581; p>0.05).

3.5 Attention levels of the athletes according to membership in national teams

The attention levels of the participating athletes according to the membership to the national teams is as follows.

The attention consistency results of the participating athletes in terms of the national team membership are indicated in the below table (Table 38).

Table 38. The sub test regarding the attention consistency skills of the participating athletes by branch type

	National Team Membership	N	Mean	Std. Deviation	t	P
Attention Consistency	Yes	38	84,11	6,517	3,568	,001
	No	136	79,56	8,293		

Table 38 shows that the attention consistency of the national athletes (N=38) was = 84,11 + 6,517 and for those athletes who were not members of the national teams (N=136) this value was =79,56 + 8,293. Table 38 shows that there is a significant difference in terms of attention skills between the athletes who are member of the national teams and those who are not, on the basis of the national team membership variable (t.05=3,568; $p<0.05$).

Table 39. The sub test regarding the visual follow-up skills of the participating athletes by branch type

	National Team Membership	N	Mean	Std. Deviation	t	P
Visual Follow-Up	Yes	38	84,16	5,587	2,313	,024
	No	136	81,63	7,171		

Table 39 shows that the visual follow-up of the national athletes (N=38) was $\overline{X}$ = 84,16 $\pm$ 5,587 and for those athletes who were not members of the national teams (N=136) this value was $\overline{X}$ =81,63 $\pm$ 7,171. Table 39 shows that there is a significant difference in terms of visual follow-up skills between the athletes who are member of the national teams and those who are not, on the basis of the national team membership variable (t_{05}=2,313; $p<0.05$).

Table 40. The sub test regarding the staying focused against time skills of the participating athletes by branch type

	National Team Membership	N	Mean	Std. Deviation	T	p
Staying Focused Against Time	Yes	38	82,45	6,272	1,106	,270
	No	136	80,89	8,014		

Table 40 shows that the staying focused against time skills of the national athletes (N=38) was = 82,45 + 6,272 and for those athletes who were not members of the national teams (N=136) this value was =80,89 + 8,014. Table 40 shows that there is no significant difference in terms of staying focused against time skills between the athletes who are member of the national teams and those who are not, on the basis of the national team membership variable (t.05=1,106; $p>0.05$).

Table 41. The sub test regarding the short time memory skills of the participating athletes by branch type

	National Team Membership	N	Mean	Std. Deviation	T	p
Short Term Memory	Yes	38	82,11	6,370	,805	,422
	No	136	80,85	9,030		

Table 41 shows that short term memory skills of the national athletes (N=38) was = 82,11 + 6,370 and for those athletes who were not members of the national teams (N=136) this value was =80,85 + 9,030. Table 41 shows that there is no significant difference in terms of short time memory skills between the athletes who are member of the national teams and those who are not, on the basis of the national team membership variable ($t_{.05}$=0,805; $p>0.05$).

Table 42. The sub test regarding the staying focused despite stimulators and distractors skills of the participating athletes by branch type

	National Team Membership	N	Mean	Std. Deviation	T	p
Staying Focused Despite Stimulators and Distractors	Yes	38	84,53	5,129	2,563	,012
	No	136	81,70	8,449		

Table 42 shows that the staying focused despite stimulators and distractors skills of the national athletes (N=38) was = 84,53 + 5,129 and for those athletes who were not members of the national teams (N=136) this value is =81,70 + 8,449. Table 42 shows that there is a significant difference in terms of staying focused despite stimulators and distractors skills in favour of the national athletes, between the athletes who are member of the national teams and those who are not, on the basis of the national team membership variable ($t_{.05}$=2,563; $p<0.05$).

Table 43. The sub test regarding the attention control skills of the participating athletes by branch type

	National Team Membership	N	Mean	Std. Deviation	t	P
Controlling Attention	Yes	38	84,47	5,954	1,773	,079
	No	136	82,15	10,365		

Table 43 shows that the attention control skills of the national athletes (N=38) was = 84,47 + 5,954 and for those athletes who were not members of the national teams (N=136) this value was =82,15 + 10,365. Table 43 shows that there is a significant difference in terms of attention contrl skills in favour of the national athletes, between the athletes who are member of the national teams and those who are not, on the basis of the national team membership variable ($t_{.05}$=2,563; $p<0.05$).

Table 44. The sub test regarding the hand-eye-brain coordination of the participating athletes by branch type

	National Team Membership	N	Mean	Std. Deviation	T	P
Hand-Eye-Brain Coordination	Yes	38	84,00	5,261	1,390	,166
	No	136	82,29	7,029		

Table 44 shows that the hand-eye-brain coordination of the national athletes (N=38) was = 84,00 + 5,261 and for those athletes who were not members of the national teams (N=136) this value was =82,29 + 7,029. Table 44 shows that there is no significant difference in terms of hand-eye-brain coordination between the athletes who are member of the national teams and those who are not, on the basis of the national team membership variable (t.05=1,390; p>0.05).

Table 45. The sub test regarding the spatial memory skills of the participating athletes by branch type

	National Team Membership	N	Mean	Std. Deviation	T	P
Spatial Memory	Yes	38	80,53	9,209	,136	,892
	No	136	80,30	8,916		

Table 45 shows that the spatial memory skills of the national athletes (N=38) was = 80,53 + 9,209 and for those athletes who were not members of the national teams (N=136) this value was =80,30 + 8,916. Table 45 shows that there is no significant difference in terms of spatial memory skills between the athletes who are member of the national teams and those who are not, on the basis of the national team membership variable (t.05=0,136; p>0.05).

Table 46. The sub test regarding the concentration skills of the participating athletes by branch type

	National Team Membership	N	Mean	Std. Deviation	T	P
Concentration	Yes	38	81,47	8,526	,493	,623
	No	136	80,66	9,104		

Table 46 shows that the concentration skills of the national athletes (N=38) was = 81,47 + 8,526 and for those athletes who were not members of the national teams (N=136) this value was =80,66 + 9,104. Table 46 shows that there is no significant difference in terms of concentration skills between the athletes who are member of the national teams and those who are not, on the basis of the national team membership variable (t.05=0,493; p>0.05).

4 Conclusion (Discussion)

The results of the research have revealed that there is a significant difference in favour of female participants with regard to the attention consistency, staying focused against time, controlling attention, hand-eye-brain coordination and concentration skills when compared to the male participants (See Table 2,4,7,8,10). This result showing once again the above mentioned gender based characteristics of females, or in other words, males' lower performance in these skills implies that the infrastructure establishment efforts are not based on an efficient planning.

The analysis by the sports years variable has showed that the variations observed between the groups in terms of attention are not influenced by latter (See Table 11,12,13,14,15,16,17,18,19). Considering that the sports years variable influences the performance in several aspects except attention ($p>0,05$), it has been concluded that although certain level of experience is required for attention, the real determinant is the instant performance. Accordingly, there is no past in terms of performance in the sports, there is only today and if you win today, you are the champion. In the next competition, your competitors would see you only as the winner of the previous competition and you can still lose. Another result that can be analysed concordantly with this, seems to be the comparisons in terms of membership of the national team. The significant differences ($p<0,05$; See Table 38,39,42) observed between the athletes who are members of the national teams and those who are not in terms of attention consistency, visual follow-up and staying focused despite the stimulators and distractors skills have revealed that attention is an efficient factor in every aspect for the participating athletes and they hold it as a characteritics. However, they underperform when it comes to use attention for the success. According to the research results, we can conclude that in order to be a national athlete, high level of attention consistency, visual follow-up and staying focused despite the stimulators and distractors skills are required. The existence of other studies that show the significant correlation between high level performance and concentration in the literature, supports the results of the present research [1]. Also indicated in the literature is that independently from the sports branch, the staying focused despite stimulators and distractors skill is efficient for showing the required performance [39]. Another finding of the present research, higher attention level in focusing on the target despite external factors, is also supported by the literature [40]. In addition, there are certain studies that show that internal focalization influence the performance negatively [41]. In the studies conducted among the 3rd grade students with the visual and audible attention stimulators for the on going motor skills, it has been observed that the skill level significantly increases for those who do it[42]. Furthermore, certain studies show that it is possible to increase the performance by keeping attention alerted through medication [36].

The research conducted by Olsen among top level athletes, normal level athletes and non-athletes has revealed that the top level athletes are significantly ($p<0,05$) better in terms of reaction time, understanding and anxiety process compared to other groups. Also, it has been seen that the normal level athletes are significantly ($p<0,05$) more successful in terms of the subdimensions, compared to those do not do any sports [43].

In a study carried out in 1988, it has been concluded that among the university students, the attention level of the female students were higher after the recreational running activities, compared to the male students and the attention level of the recreational runners was higher than those who do not run [44].

Furthermore, with regard to the spatial memory dimension, the researches have revealed that the training based on focusing on the factors in the close neighborhood affects the performance positively compared to the training based on internal focalization [45]. With regard to the spatial memory dimension, the research has revealed that the wrestlers' spatial memory skills are significantly different than soccer players. This implies that the competition area that is specific to branch is also influential.

The research results show that attention is an efficient factor for high performance; from the gender point of view, the attention skills of the female athletes are better than those of the males; the athletes should consider attention as a factor in the way to be accepted into national sports teams and establish their programs accordingly; and finally, the sports years is not an efficient variable in terms of attention.

DOI: 10.1051/shsconf/20173701059

In this context, on the basis of the research results;

Attention should be included in the training programs as a situational variable. More detailed studies should be conducted in terms of the efficiency of the mental trainings. Attention should be systematically analysed and the working areas should be enriched according to the different environments and athletes.

Acknowledgment

This study has been generated under a project carried out by Dumlupınar University Scientific Researcj Projects Commission (Proje No: 2015-61).

References

1. Vast, Young, and Thomas, Emotions in sport: Perceived effects on attention, concentration, and performance. Aust Psychol, **45**, 2,132-140 (2010)
2. Vuijk, et al., Motor performance of children with mild intellectual disability and borderline intellectual functioning. J Intell Disabil Res, **54**, 955-965 (2010)
3. Yan, Cognitive styles affect choice response time and accuracy. Personality and Individual Differences, **48**, 6, 747-751, (2010)
4. Gutierrez Diaz del Campo, et al., Differences in Decision-Making Development between Expert and Novice Invasion Game Players. Percept Motor Skill, **112**, 3, 871-888 (2011)
5. Hickey, Fricker, Attention deficit hyperactivity disorder, CNS stimulants and sport. Sports Med, **27**, 1, 11-21 (1999)
6. Parr, Attention-Deficit Hyperactivity Disorder and the Athlete: New Advances and Understanding. Clinics in Sports Medicine, **30,** 3, 591-+ (2011)
7. Conant-Norville and Tofler, Attention deficit/hyperactivity disorder and psychopharmacologic treatments in the athlete. Clinics in Sports Medicine, **24** ,4, 829-+ (2005)
8. Corrigan, Attention deficit hyperactivity disorder in sport: A review. Int J Sports Med, **24**,7, 535-540 (2003)
9. Saemi, et al., Adopting an external focus of attention facilitates motor learning in children with attention deficit hyperactivity disorder. Kinesiology, **45**, 2, 179-185 (2013)
10. Lee, Dunn,Holt, Youth Sport Experiences of Individuals With Attention Deficit/Hyperactivity Disorder. Adapt Phys Act Q, **31**, 4, 343-361 (2014)
11. Putukian, et al., Attention Deficit Hyperactivity Disorder and the Athlete: An American Medical Society for Sports Medicine Position Statement (vol 21, pg 392, 2011). Clin J Sport Med, **22**, 1, 79-79 (2012)
12. Putukian, et al., Attention Deficit Hyperactivity Disorder and the Athlete: An American Medical Society for Sports Medicine Position Statement. Clin J Sport Med, **21**, 5, 392-401 (2011)
13. Solso, Maclin, and Maclin, Cognitive Psychology. İstanbul: Kitabevi (2013)
14. Wu, Smithies, and Mole, Attention : Philosophical and Psychological Essays. Oxford [England]: Oxford University Press. (2011)
15. Tsotsos, A Computational Perspective on Visual Attention. Cambridge, Mass: The MIT Press. (2011)
16. Nikolajeva, Reading for Learning : Cognitive Approaches to Children's Literature. Children's Literature, Culture, and Cognition. Amsterdam: John Benjamins Publishing Company. (2014)

17. Carré and Hiemstra, A Feast of Learning : International Perspectives on Adult Learning and Change. Adult Education Special Topics: Theory, Research, and Practice in Lifelong Learning, Charlotte, N.C.: Information Age Publishing (2013)
18. Lim and Tay, Creating Holistic Technology-enhanced Learning Experiences : Tales From a Future School in Singapore. Rotterdam: Sense Publishers (2013)
19. Webster and Stewart, Problematizing Service-learning : Critical Reflections for Development and Action. Charlotte, N.C.: Information Age Publishing (2011)
20. Posner and Bodies, Components of Attention Psychol Rev, **78**, 5, 391-408 (1971)
21. Steinmetz and Kensinger, Emotion's Effects on Attention and Memory : Relevance to Posttraumatic Stress Disorder. Psychology of Emotions, Motivations and Actions. Hauppauge, N.Y.: Nova Science Publishers, Inc. (2010)
22. French and Simpson, Attention, Cooperation, Purpose : An Approach to Groups Using Insights From the Work of Bion. London: Karnac Books (2014)
23. Thoma, Strategic Attention in Language Testing : Metacognition in a Yes/no Business English Vocabulary Test. European University Studies. Reihe XXI, Linguistik. Frankfurt am Main: Peter Lang AG. (2011)
24. Bruya, Effortless Attention : A New Perspective in the Cognitive Science of Attention and Action. Cambridge, Mass: A Bradford Book (2010)
25. Marchetti, Consciousness, Attention and Meaning. Psychology Research Progress. New York: Nova Science Publishers, Inc. (2010)
26. Schmidt and Wrisberg, Motor Learning and Performance A Situation - Based Learning Approach. Ankara: Anı Yayıncılık (2012)
27. Summers and Maddocks, Attentional Profiles of Cricket Players. Journal of Sport Psychology, **9**, 3, 199-199 (1987)
28. Ziegler, The effects of attentional shift training on the execution of soccer skills: a preliminary investigation. Journal of Applied Behavior Analysis, **27**, 545-552 (1994)
29. Deakin, Starkes, and Elliott, Feature integration of children during exercise. J Sport Exercise Psy, **10**, 248-261 (1988)
30. Hill, Pay attention! JOPERD: The Journal of Physical Education, Recreation & Dance, **62**, 18-20 (1991).
31. Sargent, Developing a mental skills training program. Sports Coach, **20**, 1 (1997)
32. Wilson and Kerr, Attentional style and basketball shooting. Perceptual & Motor Skills, **73**, 1025-1026 (1991)
33. Kioumourtzoglou, Kourtessis, and Michalopoulou, Differences in several perceptual abilities between experts and novices in basketball, volleyball and water-polo. Perceptual & Motor Skills, **86**, 3, 899-912 (1998)
34. Summers, Miller, Ford, Attentional style and basketball performance. J Sport Exercise Psy, **13**, 239-253 (1991)
35. Smith, Gill, Crews, Attentional strategy use by experienced distance runners: physiological and psychological effects. Research Quarterly for Exercise & Sport, **66**, 142-150 (1995)
36. Biological Aids to Improve Performance. Journal of Sport Psychology, **7**, 4, 330-330 (1985)
37. Johnson, Skill=SpeedXAccuracyXFormXAdaptability. Philadelphia: Lea & Febiger (1972)
38. Karasar, Bilimsel Araştırma Yöntemi. 15. ed. Ankara: Nobel Yayın Dağıtım (2005)
39. Lawrence, et al., Internal and External Focus of Attention in a Novice Form Sport. Research Quarterly for Exercise & Sport, **82**, 3, 431-441 (2011)
40. Shafizadeh, McMorris, Sproule, Effect of different external attention of focus instruction on learning of golf putting skilL. Perceptual & Motor Skills, **113**, 2, 622-670 (2011)

41. Weiss, The Effects of Reinvestment of Conscious Processing on Switching Focus of Attention. Research Quarterly for Exercise & Sport, **82**, 1, 28-36 (2011)
42. Mortimer, et al., Sport stacking in auditory and visual attention of grade 3 learners. Perceptual & Motor Skills, **112**, 4, 98-112 (2011)
43. Olsen, Relationship between psychological capacities and success in college athletics. Research Quarterly of the American Association for Health, Physical Education & Recreation, **27**, 79-89 (1956)
44. Wrisberg, Pein, Past running experience as a mediator of the attentional focus of male and female recreational runners. Perceptual & Motor Skills, **70**, 427-432 (1990)
45. Merchant, et al., Instructions to Adopt an External Focus Enhance Muscular Endurance. Research Quarterly for Exercise & Sport, **82**, 3, 466-473 (2011)

Studying the intended uses of the social networks by the students of the department of physical education and sport

Baybars Recep Eynur [1a], and Aytul Eynur[1]

[1]Dumlupınar University, Department of Physical Education and Sport, 43020 Kütahya, Turkey

Abstract. The objective of this research is to study the intended uses of the social networks by the students of the Department of Physical Education and Sport (DPES). A total of 407 DPES students have been participated into the research; 25,6% of them were women and 74.4% were men. The data collection tool used for the study was the Scale for the Intended Uses of the Social Networks. With regard to the research statistics, the independent variable t-test and ANOVA have been used; and in order to evaluate the diversity of the subgroups, Bonferroni and Tamhane (α=0,05) have been used. The analysis has revealed that on the basis of the social networking sites for which the males show a higher usage tendency according to the gender variable ($p<0,05$); there is no difference in terms of intended uses between those who use Facebook, Snapchat and those who do not ($p>0,05$). It has been seen that the Twitter users show a higher tendency in terms of the research and content sub-dimensions ($p<0,05$); and that the Instagram and other social network users show a higher tendency in terms of keeping in touch and content sharing ($p<0,05$). The research has revealed that the intended social network uses by the students arises mostly from the social network services, besides certain cultural influence.
Keywords: University, student, social network, intended use, sport

1 Introduction and objective

An important sphere of influence that has been introduced to the current daily life by the technological developments as an efficient element is the social networking. The social networking sites are the internet based technologies that help people to establish communication with other people and to interact. It is remarkable that in the recent years, the social networking sites are also used as academical education tools [1]. The previous studies indicate that the new generation is defined as digital native; however, it is emphasized that the digital native status of the individuals shall be differentiated not only in terms of their births, but also in terms of their characteristics. It has been stated that the

[a] Corresponding author: baybars.eynur@dpu.edu.tr

efficiency of the social network use is one of these characteristics [2]. Currently, the availability of the studies revealing similarities between the internet usage of the individuals as well as the efficient use of the internet for sharing also indicate how efficient the sharing-based social networking [3]. The internet based social networking that covers different applications also influences the teaching efforts [4-6]. Also, it has been indicated that the zone of proximal development of the social networks may render the teaching media more meaningful [7, 8].

However, although the social networking is qualified as a supportive element for the education basically, it is considered that the social networks may restrict the efficiency of the teaching activity due to the problems arisen at the application level [9-11]. Currently, with the increasing number of the smart phones, the use of the social networks has become a global phenomenon, reaching addiction levels [12]. Also similarly, it has been observed that the hours spent for the internet and other technologies due to the overuse of the social networks triggers problems for the young people in various development areas [13, 14].

The new developments, i.e. the most significant evidences of the developing world, are also an activity area for any nation, state and individual who wants to survive in this world. Mostly, this situation renders the social networking an obligation for the individuals, public establishments and legal entities. In general, the institutions' informing the public through the social networks rather than the local communication channels is not found strange, even appreciated by the citizens.

In this context, considering that the DPES students will serve for the sports, a need for reviewing the use of the social networks by these students has arisen as a dimension of their reactions to the developing world, besides the efficiency of the education provided. Also, it is thought that the significance of the present study increases since it provides a foresight about the expectations of the participant students with regard to the development of the university's own social network application.

2 Material and method

The study has been conducted according to the screening model. The screening model is a reasearch approach that targets to describe a past or present situtation as it is. The approach tries to describe any event, individual or object which is subject to the research as it is, under its own conditions. No effort is made to change or to affect them in any way. There is something to find out and it is out there. What is important is to "observe" properly and specify it [15].

A total of 407 Dumlupınar University, Department of Physical Education and Sport (DPES) students have been participated into the research; 25,6% of them were women and 74.4% were men. The distribution of the participating students by divisions is as follows.

The Scale for the Intended Uses of the Social Networks has been used in this research in order to specify the intended uses of the social networks by the participant students [16]. The scale consists of the research, cooperation, initiating communication, keeping in touch, content sharing and entertainment subdimensions; however, it does not provide a total score on the basis of the scores obtained from these subdimensions. In this research, the coefficient of consistence for the scale has been calculated as α=0.897.

DOI: 10.1051/shsconf/20173701060

Table 1. Distribution of the participating students by divisions.

			Gender		Total
			Female	Male	
Division	Physical Education Teacher	Count	28	58	86
		% of Total	6,9%	14,3%	21,1%
	Coaching Education	Count	23	69	92
		% of Total	5,7%	17,0%	22,6%
	Sport Management	Count	27	73	100
		% of Total	6,6%	17,9%	24,6%
	Recreation	Count	26	103	129
		% of Total	6,4%	25,3%	31,7%
Total		Count	104	303	407
		% of Total	25,6%	74,4%	100,0%

During the analysis process, the univariate normal distribution degree of the materials has been determined by calculating the trendline and flatness coefficients. The analysis results have not revealed any trendline value higher than 3 and any flatness value higher than 10. Kline (1998), on the basis of the Monte Carlo simulation studies where the forecasting methods are used in the structural models, has indicated that the variables show normal distribution when the trendline index is higher than 3 and the flatness index is higher than 10 [17].

With regard to the research statistics, the t-test for the independent samples and ANOVA have been used, and in order to evaluate the diversity of the subgroups, Bonferroni and Tamhane (α=0,05) have been used. Also, the significance level has been set as (α=0,05).

3 Result (Findings)

The results obtained from the research have been evaluated in accordance with the subdimensions indicated in the research scale used in the research and studied on the basis of the variables accepted as independent variables. However, only the subdimension results showing significant differences have been included in the table.

Table 2. The independent samples t-test result of the attention stability sub-test of the participating athletes on the basis of the gender variable

	Gender	N	Average	Std. Deviation	t	p
Attention Stability	Female	104	9.1058	4.86900	2.936	.004
	Male	303	10.7822	5.07546		

The table 2 shows that the intention for initiating communication of the female participants (N=104) was = 9.1058 + 4.869 whereas for the male participants (N=303), this was =10.7822 + 5.07546. The examination of the table 2 reveals that on the basis of the gender variable, there is a significant difference in favour of the male students with regard to the use of the social networks for initiating communication ($t_{.05}$=2.936; $p<0.05$). In this study, no significant difference has been determined with regard to the branch, having own computer, fixed internet payment, division and grade variables ($p>0,05$). However, the differences observed on the basis of the used social networks have been listed in the below table respectively.

Table 3. The independent samples t-test result of the participants on the basis of the use of the twitter social network

	Gender	N	Average	Std. Deviation	T	p
Research	No	204	14.6373	4.74220	2.497	.013
	Yes	169	15.7988	4.12250		
Content Sharing	No	204	19.3088	6.84362	3.161	.002
	Yes	169	21.7278	7.93556		

The table 3 shows that the research intention of the participating Twitter user students (N=169) was = 15.988 + 4.1225 whereas it was =14.6373 + 4.7422 for the non-Twitter user students (N=303). Also, with regard to the Twitter user students participating in the research, the intention of use for content sharing has been determined as = 21.7278 + 7.93556 and for the non-Twitter user students, this intention was = 19.3088 + 6.84362. The research has revealed any significant difference between the Twitter user and non-Twitter user students ($t_{.05}$=2.497; $p<0.05$). Similarly, a significant difference has been revealed in favour of the Twitter users while comparing the Twitter users with non Twitter users ($t_{.05}$=3.161; $p<0.05$).

Table 4. The independent samples t-test result of the participants on the basis of the use of the instagram social network

	Gender	N	Average	Std. Deviation	T	p
Keeping in Touch	No	137	18.4672	6.09128	2.412	.016
	Yes	236	20.0381	6.04756		
Content Sharing	No	137	19.3139	7.33821	2.166	.031
	Yes	236	21.0381	7.45102		

The table 4 shows that the keeping in touch intention of the Instagram user students who have participated in the research (N=236) was = 20.0381 + 6.04756 whereas the non-Instagram user students' (N=137) keeping in touch intention was =18.4672 + 6.09128. Also, the content sharing intention of the Instagram user students who have participated in the research has been calculated as = 21.0381 + 7.45102 whereas the non-Instagram user students' content sharing intention was = 19.3139 + 7.33821. The analysis has revealed a significant difference between the Instagram user and non-Instagram user students in terms of the keeping in touch intention ($t_{.05}$=2.412; $p<0.05$). Similarly, a significant difference in favour of the Instagram users has been observed with regard to the content sharing intention while comparing the Instagram users with non-Instagram users ($t_{.05}=2.166$; $p<0.05$).

Table 5. The independent samples t-test result of the participants on the basis of the use of other social networks

	Gender	N	Average	Std. Deviation	t	p
Keeping in Touch	No	278	19.0612	6.06879	2.176	.030
	Yes	95	20.6316	6.08285		
Content Sharing	No	278	19.8345	7.17406	2.549	.011
	Yes	95	22.0737	8.00032		

The table 5 shows that the keeping in touch intention of other social network user students who have participated in the research (N=95) was = 20.6316 + 6.08285 whereas the keeping in touch intention of non-other social network user students (N=278) was =19.0612 + 6.06879. Also, it has been observed that the content sharing intention of other social network user students who have participated in the research was = 22.0737 + 8.00032 and that the content sharing intention of non-other social network user students was = 19.8345 + 7.17406. The analysis has revealed a significant difference between other social network user students and non-other social network user students in terms of the keeping in touch intention in favour of other social network user students ($t_{.05}=2.176$; $p<0.05$). Similarly, a significant difference has been observed between other social network user students and non-other social network user students in terms of the content sharing intention in favour of other social network user students ($t_{.05}=2.549$; $p<0.05$).

4 Discussion (Conclusion)

According to the research; among the gender, branch, having own computer, fixed payment for internet, division and grade variables, only the gender variable has caused a significant difference with regard to the initiating communication intention subdimension. It has been observed that the male students show significantly higher tendency to use the social networks for initiating communication than the females ($p<0.05$). This result seems similar with the patriarchal nature of the Turkish family structure. It has been seen that the female students avoid to initiate communication through the social networks with an overall social attitude.

As another dimension of the research, the evaluations based on the social networking sites used have not revealed any difference between the participating students in terms of the Facebook and Snapchat usage; however, it has been observed that the Twitter using students show higher tendency in terms of the research and content sharing intentions compared to the non-Twitter users. The students using Instagram and other social networks have shown higher tendency in terms of keeping in touch and content sharing intentions ($p<0.05$). Recent studies have revealed that the use of Facebook by the students for academical purposes is limited [18]. Also, in other studies, it has been stated that the Facebook addiction affects negatively the body image of the people and the ability to communicate with others in the actual environments [12]. Furthermore, it has been seen that the university students prefer those social networks that are related with their academical field and that provide more services. In a study conducted in Kenya, it has been seen that the students of the faculty of pharmacy mostly use Youtube which is a social network that covers mainly video content; that they do not benefit from the social networks academically and that they chat with the actual persons through applications such as "WhatsApp" rather than Facebook [10]. The obtained results support the research. However, it has been emphasized that any research involving the social network usage should also cover the specific name of the social network used [19]. Because, many current researches support that a lot of students use the social networks for educational purposes today [1]. The obtained results have also revealed that the social networks are also efficiently used to establish graduate relations and to help the concerned university afterwards [20]. This situation supports the creation of the social identities of the universities as well as the research results obtained with regard to the content sharing and keeping in touch subdimensions. The fact that the individuals using certain social networks show tendency to benefit from different social networks for keeping in touch purposes may be interpreted as a wish to create a specific social group [6, 21, 22]. Also, the conducted studies show that the social networks affect the educational motivation; these networks are accepted as an auxilliary element in programming and they help to create motivation with regard to the education [7, 8, 11, 23]. Todays having social network is important many different needs [24].

Consequently; it has been concluded that the underlying factor for the social network usage intentions is the socio-cultural behavior as is the case with all social events taking place in all actual or virtual environments; that the individuals are affected by the social dynamics all along the line; that the social networks affect the social dynamics and that the general variables (division, grade, having own computer, gender and branch, etc.) do not have an active role with regard to the social network usage intentions, on the contrary, the preferences are formed on the basis of the services and contents provided by the social network. In this regard, it should be useful for the universities to carry out a needs analysis and support/use the social networks accordingly.

References

1. G. Akcayir, Why do faculty members use or not use social networking sites for education? Comput Hum Behav, **71**, 378-385 (2017)
2. V. Wagner, D. Acier, Factor Structure Evaluation of the French Version of the Digital Natives Assessment Scale. Cyberpsych Beh Soc N, **20**, 3, 195-201 (2017)
3. J. Son, The impact of initial experience and user attachment on application downloads Information-seeking and - sharing applications. Internet Res, **27**, 2, 256-276 (2017)
4. A. Nogales, M. A. Sicilia-Urban, and E. Garcia-Barriocanal, Measuring vocabulary use in the Linked Data Cloud. Online Inform Rev, **41,** 2, 252-271 (2017)
5. L. H. Wong, et al., Seamlessly learning Chinese: contextual meaning making and vocabulary growth in a seamless Chinese as a second language learning environment. Instr Sci, **44**, 5, 399-422 (2016)
6. P. Tsatsou, Digital technologies in the research process: Lessons from the digital research community in the UK. Comput Hum Behav, **61**, 597-608 (2016)
7. S. K. Sharma, A. Joshi, and H. Sharma, A multi-analytical approach to predict the Facebook usage in higher education. Comput Hum Behav, **55**, 340-353 (2016)
8. S. A. Pradia, Understanding College Students' Readiness to Use Web 2.0 Technologies in Online Education, Walden University: Ann Arbor. 137 (2016)
9. M. G. Sanmamed, P. C. M. Carril, I. D. A. de Sotomayor, Factors which motivate the use of social networks by students. Psicothema, **29**, 2, 204-210 (2017)
10. I. J. Ogaji, et al., Pattern of use of social media networking by Pharmacy students of Kenyatta university, Nairobi, Kenya. Comput Hum Behav, **66,** 211-216 (2017)

11. A. Luqman, et al., Empirical investigation of Facebook discontinues usage intentions based on SOR paradigm. Comput Hum Behav, **70**, 544-555 (2017)
12. J. H. Tang, et al., Personality traits, interpersonal relationships, online social support, and Facebook addiction. Telemat Inform, **33**, 1, 102-108 (2016)
13. M. Foerster, M. Roosli, A latent class analysis on adolescents media use and associations with health related quality of life. Comput Hum Behav, **71**, 266-274 (2017)
14. J. D. Elhai, et al., Non-social features of smartphone use are most related to depression, anxiety and problematic smartphone use. Comput Hum Behav, **69**, 75-82 (2017)
15. N. Karasar, Bilimsel Araştırma Yöntemi. 15. ed. 2005, Ankara: Nobel Yayın Dağıtım.
16. Y. K. Usluel, Ö. Demir, and M. Çınar, Sosyal Ağların Kullanım Amaçları Ölçeği. Eğitim Teknolojileri Araştırma Dergisi, **5**, 2 (2014)
17. R. B. Kline, Principles and Practice of Structural Equation Modeling, New York: The Guilford Press (1998)
18. D. Olson, The relationship between community college student engagement and student usage of online social networking., Northern Illinois University: Ann Arbor. p. 165 (2011)
19. K. Weller, Trying to understand social media users and usage The forgotten features of social media platforms. Online Inform Rev, **40**, 2, 256-264 (2016)
20. E. J. Varney, Macro and micro levels of university identification: Using social network sites to reactivate latent social identities within college alumni., Illinois State University: Ann Arbor. p. 71. (2016)
21. Y. Jordaan, G. Van Heerden, Online privacy-related predictors of Facebook usage intensity. Comput Hum Behav, 2017. 70: p. 90-96.
22. H. Y. Huang, P. L. Chen, Y. C. Kuo, Understanding the facilitators and inhibitors of individuals' social network site usage. Online Inform Rev, **41**, 1, 85-101 (2017)
23. O. Ozyurt, H. Ozyurt, Using Facebook to enhance learning experiences of students in computer programming at Introduction to Programming and Algorithm course. Comput Appl Eng Educ, **24**, 4, 546-554 (2016)
24. S. Ayan, Evaluation of the Reasons behind the City Of Istanbul's Failure to Win The Right to Hold The Olympic Games by Students Studying at Higher Education of Physical Education and Sports. Selçuk University Journal of Physical Education and Sport Science, **11**, 1, 24-31 (2009)

 DOI: 10.1051/shsconf/20173701061

Evaluation of Low Back and Neck Pain and Disability of Interns at Physiotherapy and Rehabilitation Department of Afyon Kocatepe University

Emel Taşvuran Horata[1a] and Suat Erel[2]

[1]Afyon Health School, Department of Physiotherapy and Rehabilitation, Afyon Kocatepe University, Afyonkarahisar 03100, Turkey
[2]School of Physical Therapy and Rehabilitation, Pamukkale University, Denizli 20160, Turkey

Abstract. Repetitive tasks, high force, direct pressure, and awkward joint and prolonged constrained posture are cited as prime risk factors, making particularly younger adult physiotherapists vulnerable to musculoskeletal injury. Fourth-grade students (interns) perform clinical practice at Afyon Kocatepe University Hospital. They apply hydrotherapy, electrotherapy, robotic therapy, virtual reality therapy and exercise therapy to patients (inpatient and outpatient) at both orthopaedic and neurology units approximately twelve months. Because we think they are under the risk of low back and neck disorders therefore aim of the present study is to evaluate recent low back and neck pain and disability of them. 50.6% participants had recent low back pain; 52.9% participants reported mild and moderate low back disability. 21.8% participants had recent neck pain; 16% participants showed mild, moderate and severe neck disability. The difference between units related to low back and neck pain or disability wasn't significant statistically ($p>0.05$). Most participants announced that they used the body biomechanics correctly (84.1%) and took care of ergonomic conditions (91.5%). In conclusion, it is vital to identify prevalence of low back and neck pain among physiotherapy students and take necessary precautions to prevent further problems.
Keywords: Low back pain; neck pain; disability; physiotherapist; intern

1 Introduction

Musculoskeletal disorders is abnormalities in the soft tissues associated with the bones and joints in the upper limbs, lower limbs, and spine that have been described as 'the most notorious and common causes of severe long-term pain and physical disability, affecting hundreds of millions of people across the world [1, 2]. Low back and neck pain are the most common musculoskeletal disorders. About half of the individuals have experienced low back and neck pain at least once in their lifetime [3]. In young adults between the ages

[a] Corresponding author: ethorata@gmail.com

of 18-25, low back pain is reported 51.1% and this body site is the most common area of pain [4]. Within this context that musculoskeletal disorders are considered to be one of the most significant health problems encountering contemporary workforces [2].

The World Health Organization (WHO) defines 'work-related disorders' have multiple causes that are significantly associated with physical, psychosocial, and sociological factors present at the workplace. According to WHO, certain professional risks such as injuries, noise, carcinogenic agents, airborne particles and ergonomic risks lead chronic disorders: 37% of all cases of back pain, 16% of hearing loss, 13% of chronic obstructive pulmonary disease, 11% of asthma, 8% of injuries, 9% of lung cancer, 2% of leukaemia and 8% of depression [4]. The term work-related musculoskeletal disorders (WMSDs) are defined by WHO as "describes a wide range of inflammatory and degenerative diseases and disorders that result in pain and functional impairment. They arise when individuals are exposed to work activities and conditions that significantly contribute to their development or exacerbation, but which may not be their sole cause". In developed countries, work-related musculoskeletal disorders cause economic impacts in the society by reducing productivity by reasons such as taking off from work and early retirement [5].

Majority of physiotherapists (91%) undergo WMSDs. Low back and neck most susceptible body area to injury with the highest prevalence of WMSDs is the 63% low back, followed by 48% neck. [6]. Lifting, handling and transferring of dependent patients, repetitive movements, awkward and static postures, physical load, treating a large number of patients in a single day and working while injured are the major factor to lead low back pain [4, 7]. According to [4], "...among health professionals; 33.8% of physiotherapists seldom worked with dependent patients, 39.1% often and 27.1% exclusively."

Younger therapists announce a higher prevalence of injury; approximately more than 50% experienced an injury in their first episode as a student or in their first five years of practice [8]. Below the age of 30, particularly during the first four or five years of practice, lifting or transferring patients, lack of take rest breaks, inadequate staffing levels and a heavy caseload, repetitive tasks, high force, direct pressure, and awkward joint and prolonged constrained posture are cited as prime risk factors among younger adult physiotherapists vulnerable to musculoskeletal injury [2, 8].

Özünlü and collages [9] searched the differences and effects of these differences between neck, back and low back pain of physiotherapy students according to education years. According to this study, education years did not affect neck, back and low back pain among physiotherapy students. Taşpınar and collages [10] assessed the musculoskeletal discomforts in physiotherapy and rehabilitation students at Dumlupınar University. They claimed that third and fourth-grade students had more musculoskeletal discomforts.

At the Department of Physiotherapy and Rehabilitation of Afyon Kocatepe University, the first grade students are given theoretical, the second and third grade students are given practical vocational lessons. Fourth grade students (intern) perform clinical practice at Afyon Kocatepe University Hospital. They apply hydrotherapy, electrotherapy, robotic therapy, virtual reality therapy and exercise therapy to patients (inpatient and outpatient) at both orthopaedic and neurology units approximately twelve months. Because we think they are under the risk of low back and neck disorders therefore the main aim of the present study is to evaluate recent low back and neck pain and disability of them and investigate low back and neck pain and disability regarding with their units. Seconder aim of this study is to evaluate them according to using the body biomechanics correctly and taking care of ergonomic conditions. For this purpose, we hypotheses that:

(1) Interns have a higher prevalence of low back and neck pain and disability.

(2) Interns who study at the neurology unit have higher prevalence of low back and neck pain and disability than at the orthopaedic unit.

(3) Prevalence of interns who utilize biomechanical advantages and ergonomic conditions is high.

2 Method

The present study is a descriptive study that evaluates low back and neck pain and disability of interns at the Department of Physiotherapy and Rehabilitation of Afyon Kocatepe University. The Afyon Kocatepe University Health Sciences Scientific Research and Publication Ethics Committee gave approval for the present study and informed consent was obtained from each participant at the beginning of the study.

2.1 Participants

The fourth-grade students of the Department of Physiotherapy and Rehabilitation were included the study. Participants with pain more than 12 month were excluded from the study because onset of pain occurred before intern period.

2.2 Procedure

In our study, we practiced to the participants Visual Analogue Scale (VAS), Oswestry Disability Index (ODI) and Neck Pain and Disability Index (NPDI) and asked questions about utilizing biomechanical advantages and ergonomic conditions.

For the statistical analysis of the study, 22.0 version of the Windows-based SPSS program was used. We summarised the prevalence recent (current) low back pain and neck pain of participants as percentages. Because we think that the patients at the neurology unit need more physical aid than the patients at the orthopaedic unit, the frequencies of the low back and neck pain and disability of the participants may vary according to units. Therefore we analyse low back and neck pain and disability regarding with their units by using Chi-square test.

2.1.1 Visual Analogue Scale

VAS is a simple and commonly used method for the assessment of variations in intensity of pain. The patient is asked to mark the severity of the recent pain on a 10-cm length linear horizontal or vertical line. There are zero-value at the beginning of the line, and ten-value at the end. Zero-value means ‘no pain, ten-value means ‘unbearable pain’ [11, 12].

2.1.2 Oswestry Disability Index

It is a questionnaire that assesses how much pain affects an individual's daily activities. The development of the ODI was initiated by John O’Brien in 1976 and revised in 1989 by a chiropractic study group in the United Kingdom. It consists of 10 subgroups and each section contains 6 questions. Subgroups are pain severity, self-care, lifting-carrying, walking, sitting, standing, sleeping, degree of pain change, travel and social life [12, 13].

2.1.3 Neck Pain and Disability Index

It is a commonly used measure to assess pain and disability in individuals with neck pain. It consists of 10 subgroups related to pain severity, headache, concentration, sleep, personal care, lifting, reading, work life, driving and leisure activities [12].

3 Findings

In this study, 93 subjects participate in the study. However five participants with low back and one participant with neck pain excluded from the study because of their durations of pain onset were more than 12 months. The average age of participants was 22.48±1.10 years. Also 56 (64.4%) participants were women and 31 (35.6%) were men.

Table 1. The prevalence of the low back pain and disability of the participants

		Units		p
		Orthopaedic n (%)	Neurology n (%)	
Recent pain	No Pain	22 (50%)	22 (50%)	0,229
	Painful	27 (62.8%)	16 (37.2%)	
Disability	No disability	26 (63.4%)	15 (36.6%)	0,453
	Mild	12 (50%)	12 (50%)	
	Moderate	11 (50%)	11 (50%)	

50.6% participants had recent low back pain; 52.9% participants reported mild and moderate low back disability. There was no differences between units (Table 1) and neither pain nor disability ($p>0.05$). 21.8% participants had recent neck pain; 16% participants showed mild, moderate and severe neck disability. Similarly the differences between units (Table 2) and either neck pain or disability wasn't significant statistically ($p>0.05$). Most participants announced that they used the body biomechanics correctly (84.1%) and took care of ergonomic conditions (91.5%).

Table 2. The prevalence of the neck pain and disability of the participants

		Units		p
		Orthopaedic n (%)	Neurology n (%)	
Recent pain	No Pain	27 (55.1%)	22 (44.9%)	0,403
	Painful	28 (63.6%)	16 (36.4%)	
Disability	No disability	41 (42%)	32 (31%)	0,573
	Mild, moderate and severe	9 (64.3%)	5 (35.7%)	

4 Discussion and Conclusion

In the present study, we searched recent low back and neck pain and disability of interns and investigate low back and neck pain and disability regarding with their units at the Department of Physiotherapy and Rehabilitation of Afyon Kocatepe University. Also we evaluated them whether using the body biomechanics correctly and taking care of ergonomic conditions. We recruited 87 participants who practiced at the Afyon Kocatepe University Hospital.

Younger therapists experienced a higher prevalence of injury; approximately more than 50% experienced an injury in their first episode as a student or in their first five years of practice [8]. According to Glover and colleagues [2], low back pain is the most common musculoskeletal condition in health-working populations, with a lifetime prevalence of 48%. West and Gardner [14] claimed that 35% of physiotherapist suffered from low back pain, dramatically. According to findings of one research that is practiced by Cromie and colleagues [15], the prevalence of low back disorders 63%. In our study we analysed 50.6% of interns, this results are similar to researches in the literature.

Neck is seconder common suffered area of the body from WMSDs among the physiotherapists and affects 48% of them [15]. West and Gardner determined that 24% of physiotherapists experienced neck pain [14]. According to Glover and colleagues showed that 33% health-working populations have neck disorders [2]. In the present study, we found neck pain influence 21.8% of the participants. Results from our study prevalence of neck pain less than the others. WMSDs can be reduced by improving intrinsic and extrinsic factors such as designing of the physical environment, elimination of extreme postures and force, or prolonged static postures that cause them [6]. Therefore, we believed that good ergonomic conditions may reduce neck pain prevalence.

WMSDs can lead to limitations in physiotherapist's activities of daily life and leisure activities [16]. In the present study we pointed that 52.9% of participants' activities of daily living are limited with mild and moderate due to low back pain. Likely, Shehab and colleagues [17] reported that 50% physiotherapists reported low back pain affected their regular activities, 28.6% reported limitation due to pain and 11.4% changed their work settings because of low back pain. Neck disorders are a common problem in physiotherapists and rise from by physical workloads, poor ergonomic work design and certain psychosocial factors. These problems, if ignored can prove debilitating and can cause crippling injury forcing one to change one's profession [18]. Also 16% of participants have difficulty in daily life activities with mild, moderate and severe because of neck pain. According to the findings of a study conducted in 2500 office workers in Sri Lanka by Ranasinghe and colleagues, 36% of the participants were found to have complaints of current neck pain, 15% of them described functional limitations due to neck pain, and 9% reported instances when they could not go to work due to neck pain [19]. We believe that more research is needed to investigate the prevalence of low back and neck disability in physiotherapists.

In the present study, there was no difference between prevalence of the low back and neck pain and disabilities of the interns that practice at orthopaedics and neurology units. In a research conducted by Shehab and colleagues [17] the most common areas of specialty with work-related low back pain were orthopaedics (34%) and neurology (24%). We could not reach any studies that compare low back and neck pain and disability according to units among physiotherapist. Therefore we think more research should be conducted about these issues. Also many factors such as environmental conditions, number of patients, individual professional awareness etc. can cause work-related musculoskeletal disorders. Therefore, the prevalence of pain and disability among the units may vary in their conditions.

Majority of factors involved in WMSDs such as physical exposure, sustained static and/or awkward posture, prolonged sitting and standing, forward bending of trunk, excessive neck flexion and extension, wrong lifting, pulling or pushing at work, repetitive and/or forceful work, repetitive upper arm elevation above 90°, demanding work schedule can be prevented with simple measures like ergonomic design of the work environment, postural re-education and regular exercises [20]. According to Glover and colleagues [2] "The most commonly applied preventive strategies, adopted in response to sustaining a musculoskeletal injury at work, were for the therapist to adjust the plinth/bed height (86% of physiotherapists almost always did this after their injury), modify their position or the position of their patient (79% almost always did this), and obtain assistance when handling heavy patients (66% almost always did this)." In the present study, interns reported that they used the body biomechanics correctly (84.1%) and took care of ergonomic conditions (91.5%). We achieved higher prevalence of utilizing body biomechanics and ergonomic conditions. The 'Professional Orientation' course that is given in the first year for the purpose of professional awareness may have influenced this outcome.

As a conclusion, lower back pain and neck pain is the most common work-related disorders among young physiotherapist. Also they can cause having difficulty in activities of daily living in varying degrees. It is important to identify prevalence of low back pain and neck pain among physiotherapy students and take necessary precautions to prevent further problems. Information on patients' weight, adoption of a minimal lifting, approach as a core principle, utilizing body biomechanics and ergonomic conditions, using of other technical aids, having rest breaks, encouragement and monitoring of reporting procedures to promote early detection of injury and assess the effectiveness of preventive action is vital to reduce risk of WMSDs [8]. Finally, more research is needed to investigate activity limitation and participation restrictions about low back and neck pain among physiotherapists.

References

1. M. Aptel, A. Aublet-Cuvelier, J. C. Cnockaert. Work-Related musculoskeletal disorders of the upper limb. Joint Bone Spine, **69,** 6 (2002).
2. W. Glover, A. McGregor, C. Sullivan, J. Haguea. Work-related musculoskeletal disorders affecting members of the Chartered Society of Physiotherapy. Physiotherapy, **91**, 138–147 (2005).
3. S. Uz Tunçay, İ. Yeldan. Is physical inactivity associated with musculoskeletal disorders? Ağrı, **25,** 4 (2013).
4. D. Rugelj. Low back pain and other work-related musculoskeletal problems among physiotherapists. Ergonomics, **34,** 635–639 (2003).
5. World Health Organization. *Protecting workers' health* (Fact sheet No 389, 2014) http://www.who.int/mediacentre/factsheets/fs389/en/
6. J. E. Cromie, V. J. Robertson, M. O. Best. Occupational health and safety in physiotherapy: Guidelines for practice. Aust J Physiother, **47,** 43-51 (2001).
7. M. Milhem, L. kalichman, D. Ezra, D. Alperovitch-Najenson. Work-related musculoskeletal disorders among physical therapists: A comprehensive narrative review. Int J Occup Med Environ Health, **29,** 5 (2016).
8. W. Glover. Work-related strain injuries in physiotherapists: Prevalence and prevention of musculoskeletal disorders. Physiotherapy, **88,** 6 (2002).
9. N. Özünlü, A. Akyüz, G. Baltacı. Evaluation of the difference between neck, back and low back pain of physiotherapy students related to education years. Turkiye Klinikleri J Sports Sci, **1,** 1 (2009).
10. F. Taşpinar, B. Taşpinar, C. C. Aksoy. Investigation of musculoskeletal discomforts in physiotherapy and rehabilitation students. J Exerc Ther Rehabil, **2,** 1 (2014).
11. A. M. Carlsson. Assessment of chronic pain. I. Aspects of the reliability and validity of the Visual Analogue Scale. Pain, **16,** 87-101 (1983).
12. U. Cavlak, U. Baş Aslan, N. Yağcı, F. Altuğ. Chronic musculoskeletal pain management with physiotherapy and rehabilitation. Türkiye Klinikleri J Physiother Rehabil Special Topics, **1,** 1 (2015).
13. J. C. T. Fairbank, P. B. Pynsent. The Oswestry Disability Index. Spine, **25,** 22 (2000).
14. D. J West, D. Gardner. Occupational injuries of physiotherapists in North and Central Queensland. Aust J Physiother, **47,** 179-186 (2001).
15. J. E. Cromie, V. J. Robertson, M. O. Best. Work-related musculoskeletal disorders in physical therapists: Prevalence, severity, risks and responses. Physical Therapy **80,** 336-351 (2000).
16. S. Dsouza, A. Mathew, D. Kumar K.U. Work related musculoskeletal disorders in physiotherapist; prevalence and associated factors: A review of literature. Int J Health Sci Educ, **6,** 6 (2016).
17. D. Shehab, K. Al-Jarallah, M.A. Moussa, N. Adham. Prevalence of low back pain among physical therapists in Kuwait. Med Princ Pract, **12,** 4 (2003).
18. A. Bansode, D. Hande. Effectiveness of isometric neck exercises, stretching and ergonomics over ergonomic alone for neck pain in physiotherapists. IJIR, **2,** 10 (2016).
19. P. Ranasinghe, Y.S. Perera, D.A. Lamabadusuriya, S. Kulatunga, N. Jayawardana, S. Rajapakse, P. Katulanda. Work related complaints of neck, shoulder and arm among computer office workers: a cross-sectional evaluation of prevalence and risk factors in a developing country. Environmental Health, **10,** 70-79 (2011).
20. N. Ganer. Work related musculoskeletal disorders among healthcare professional and their preventive measure : A report. IJSRSET, **2,** 4 (2016).

 DOI: 10.1051/shsconf/20173701062

Evaluation of professional awareness in physiotherapy and rehabilitation students of Afyon Kocatepe University

Emel Taşvuran Horata[1a] and Suat Erel[2]

[1]Afyon Health School, Department of Physiotherapy and Rehabilitation, Afyon Kocatepe University, Afyonkarahisar 03100, Turkey
[2]School of Physical Therapy and Rehabilitation, Pamukkale University, Denizli 20160, Turkey

Abstract. In latest years, physiotherapists have been progressively interested in defining their professional identity. For this purpose, Physiotherapy and Rehabilitation Departments of universities in Turkey lecture courses about this profession. The students have the opportunity to improve their professional awareness in these courses. The aim of this research is to determine the professional awareness of the students of the Department of Physiotherapy and Rehabilitation at Afyon Kocatepe University. In the present study, "Professional Awareness Questionnaire" was applied to 227 students who is the first, second, third and fourth grade students at Afyon Kocatepe University. According to this study, the most correctly answered question was related to type of grade point for placement the department (95.2%). İnterns respond more questions correctly ($p<0.01$). Prevalence of students who prefer the physiotherapy due to their interest is 40.5%. There were no differences between the students who choose physiotherapy for their interest and the other reasons ($p>0.05$). In conclusion, the findings from this study show that professional awareness can be influenced by individual differences. However, the level of professional awareness and the interest in the profession of the student can be increased by professional courses.
Keywords: Professional awareness; physiotherapy; student

1 Introduction

Profession can be defined as a set of activities those rules are determined by society and based on knowledge, skills as a result of certain education. It provides individuals to earn their lives. Also it is most important factor that enables the individuals to establish their identity and a reciprocal relationship with the society and gain prestige. Therefore, the choice of profession is great importance for both individuals and society [1]. The suitable

[a] Corresponding author: ethorata@gmail.com

choice of profession makes the individuals successful, happy and productive. Factors such as talent, interest, value and belief system, family culture and environment influence the individual's career choice [2].

A Profession is valuable because it serves humanity. Nowadays, rapid social change contributes to the formation of different professions, which leads to the reduction of the social status and economic possibilities of some professions. This creates problems for students in their professional preferences [3]. It is ideal to choose a profession based on the specific interests and skills of the individual. But most students consider the opportunity to find a job and the high-income levels when choosing a profession [1]. The most common reason for the preference of professions in the field of health sciences is also the opportunity to finding a job and the high-income level. Çiftçi and colleagues showed that only 78.9% of the students at the Department of Physiotherapy and Rehabilitation had detailed knowledge about the department before their preference. In addition, 24% of students in physiotherapy and rehabilitation department (if they had a chance to choose again) reported that they would prefer this department again [4].

Professional awareness requires knowledge of the competencies of the profession, occupational laws and regulations, duties and responsibilities, the individual's psychological and physical suitability to the profession, and professional sensitivity. In the society, it is vital to ensure professional awareness in the area of health that is necessary for individual happiness, economic efficiency and prosperity. With the increase in the quality of health services, it is possible to increase the level of economic efficiency and prosperity by improving the health condition in the groups with social problems. [5]

According to World Confederation for Physical Therapy (WCPT), physiotherapists provide services that develop, maintain and restore people's maximum movement and functional ability. They can help people at any stage of life, when movement and function are threatened by ageing, injury, diseases, disorders, conditions or environmental factors [6]. WCPT has arranged own ethical principles to make recommendation about this profession. These ethical principles include equality, obedience to the law, patient responsibility, professional health care and community health issues [7, 8]. Educational results for professions are obtained through the socialization of students to the values, attitudes and beliefs of their choosing profession and a commitment to a professional career [9, 10].

The first school of Physical Therapy and Rehabilitation is established at Hacettepe University in Turkey in 1961. Today, including private universities, there are a total of 52 departments of physiotherapy at the universities in Turkey and about 7900 physiotherapists graduated from these schools [8]. The Physiotherapy and Rehabilitation Department of Afyon Health School which was established at Afyon Kocatepe University in 2008 consists of 4-year undergraduate program. "Professional Orientation" course is included in the curriculum of the first-year students that has detailed information about the department and occupational subjects such as Physiotherapist Professional Law, World Physical Therapy Day, and Turkish Physiotherapy Association. The aim of this course is to provide the students to adaptation for school and improvement of their professional awareness.

Therefore, the main purpose of this study is to determine the professional awareness of students of the Department of Physiotherapy and Rehabilitation at Afyon Kocatepe University and investigate any differences between professional awareness of the students according to grades. And seconder purpose of this study is to search any differences between professional awareness of the students who prefer physiotherapy due to their interest and the others. For this purpose we hypotheses that:

(a) The students of in this study ratio of correct answer to questions which are about professional awareness are high

(b) Fourth-grade (intern) students answer more correctly to questions about professional awareness.

(c) The students who prefer physiotherapy due to their interest answer more correctly to questions about professional awareness.

2 Method

The present study is a descriptive study that evaluates the professional awareness of the students of the Department of Physiotherapy and Rehabilitation at Afyon Kocatepe University. The Afyon Kocatepe University Health Sciences Scientific Research and Publication Ethics Committee gave approval for the present study and informed consent was obtained from each participant at the beginning of the study.

2.1 Participants

The first, second, third and fourth-grade students of the Department of Physiotherapy and Rehabilitation were included the study.

2.2 Procedure

In the previous study, Razak Özdinçler and colleagues [12] applied the professional awareness questionnaire to the students of Department of Physiotherapy and Rehabilitation of the Faculty of Health Sciences at Istanbul University. In our study, we arranged the previous questions according to our department. The questionnaire consists of 15 questions about Physiotherapist Professional Law, World Physical Therapy Day, Turkish Physiotherapy Association, the Department of Physiotherapy and Rehabilitation and postgraduate education. Also, we added a question about the reasons for choosing this department.

Approximately 10 minutes were given to students to complete the questionnaire. In addition, the questionnaire was applied in the classrooms and supervisor-guided.

For the statistical analysis of the study, 22.0 version of the Windows-based SPSS program was used. We summarized the descriptive analysis of correct answers. Also we analysed the difference in correct answers among the grades by using ANOVA and between the students who prefer physiotherapy due to their interest and the others by using t-test. Values of p less than 0.05 were considered statistically significant.

2 Findings

In the present study, "Professional Awareness Questionnaire" was applied to 227 students who is the first, second, third and fourth-grade students at Afyon Kocatepe University. We recruited 64 (28.2%) students of first grade, 56 (24.7%) of second grade, 70 (30.8%) of third grade, 37 (16.3%) of fourth-grade students participated. The average age of participants was 20.58±1.53 years and 152 (67.0%) participants were women and 75 (33.0%) were men.

According to this study, more correctly answered questions were; 95.2% of the participants respond correctly the question about type of grade point for placement the department, 84.6% the conditions required for master and 82.4% World Physical Therapy Day, respectively. Also less correctly answered questions were; 30.4% of the participants respond correctly the question about Physiotherapist Professional Law formation and 38.8% the minor at the department (Table 1). Post hoc comparisons using Tukey's honest significant difference test indicated that interns answer more questions correctly between groups ($p<0.01$). There were no differences between first-grade and second-grade students, first-grade and third-grade students and second-grade and third-grade students ($p>0.05$).

Table 1. Level of the participant's professional awareness

Questions	Correct answers		Wrong answers	
	n	%	n	%
When was the Physiotherapist Professional Law made?	69	30.4	158	69.4
When is the World Physical Therapy Day celebrated?	187	82.4	40	17.6
Which is Turkish Physiotherapy Association a member of international organization?	127	55.9	100	44.1
Which year was the first physiotherapy department at the universities in Turkey established?	133	58.6	94	41.4
How many credits are required to graduate from Department of Physiotherapy and Rehabilitation at Afyon Kocatepe University?	141	62.1	86	37.9
How many credits does students of Department of Physiotherapy and Rehabilitation at Afyon Kocatepe University have each semester?	120	52.9	107	47.1
Which is type of grade point for getting into Department of Physiotherapy and Rehabilitation at Afyon Kocatepe University?	216	95.2	11	4.8
Which branch do you have an opportunity to do minor at Department of Physiotherapy and Rehabilitation at Afyon Kocatepe University?	88	38.8	139	61.2
What are the conditions for master in Department of Physiotherapy and Rehabilitation at the universities in Turkey?	192	84.6	35	15.4
According to the latest adopted resolution by the Ministry of Health, which physicians do orient the physiotherapists for patients' physiotherapy program?	113	49.8	114	50.2
Who is the president of the Turkish Physiotherapist Association?	109	48.0	118	52.0

Reasons for choosing this profession were; 40.5% of students chose because of their interests, 17.6% job opportunities, 17.2% friend or teacher referral, 9.7% family pressure and 13.2% others. There were no differences between the students who prefer physiotherapy due to their interest and the others in terms of correct answers ($p>0.05$).

3 Discussion and Conclusion

In the present study, we searched professional awareness of the students at the Department of Physiotherapy and Rehabilitation at Afyon Kocatepe University. For this purpose we conducted Professional Awareness Questionnaire to 227 students who is the first, second, third and fourth-grade students at Afyon Kocatepe University.

According to results of our study, we showed that participants answer more correctly questions about the Department of Physiotherapy and Rehabilitation except the question about minor. The question about type of grade point for placement the department is the most correctly answered (95.2%). Also the question about Physiotherapist Professional Law formation is the least correctly answered. Razak Özdinçler and collages [12] applied Professional Awareness Questionnaire to 201 students of Department of Physiotherapy and Rehabilitation of the Faculty of Health Sciences at Istanbul University. In the previous study participants' ratio of correct answer to questions which were about Physiotherapist Professional Law was higher (73.63%). We are surprised that different results between two universities. These results are thought this question might be relevant for individual concern. The correct answer rates of the questions related to the department and the master are similar. In this study we adapted the questions about department and master for participants; this was effective in obtaining similar results.

We showed that there were significant differences between interns and first, second and third-grade students. Interns answered questions more correctly than other grades. In fact we expected the increasing of awareness in progressive grades, no significant differences between grades. The previous study supports our findings; they claimed that there were no differences between grades but also they found that fourth-grade students had a higher percentage of responding to questions related to master conditions [12]. Similarly, Kunduracılar and collages conducted with the first-grade students of questionnaire about their professional awareness in the physiotherapy and rehabilitation, [5]. Based on the findings of their studies on the evaluation stated that level of "awareness of qualifications in physiotherapy" and "professional sensitivity" were high, even though did not even take basic professional courses. However they did not include first, second and fourth-grade students in their research [5]. At the Department of Physiotherapy and Rehabilitation of Afyon Kocatepe University, interns practise in the hospital differently than other grades and thus spend more time with the patients and the physiotherapists working there. This may have increased their level of professional awareness. In addition, interns may be anxious to find a job after graduation and they may want to study for master degree. Therefore, they may have more knowledge about professional law, department, graduate and Turkish Physiotherapy Association related questions than others.

Based on results of the present research; 40.5% of the participants preferred this department due to their interest, 17.6% job opportunities, 17.2% friend or teacher referral, 9.7% family pressure and 13.2% others. In the previous research, Kunduracılar and collages [5] obtained similar results. They found that the percentage of participants who preferred this department due to their interest and job opportunities was higher than the participants who preferred it for other reasons [5]. Öhman and collages [13] asked to the Canadian students who study in physiotherapy, the reasons for the career choice and professional preferences. According to their study "Six factors influenced the students' choice of career." Job opportunity and the potential to earn a good salary were the most frequently chosen reasons (25.5%). Other reasons are a positive exposure to the profession, the interesting aspects of the profession, a desire to be able to help other people and interest in sports and athletic injuries [13]. Gotlib and collages [14] investigated that the attitudes of European physiotherapy students towards their chosen career. An interest in physiotherapy was the main reason why students decided to study physiotherapy, with more than 79% of students indicating that this was the most important factor in their decision, according to their studies [14]. Different living conditions in communities also change the status within the profession [3, 4]. We believe that this affects the reasons for the preferences of the profession in the future.

In our study, there were no differences between the students who prefer physiotherapy due to their interest and the others in terms of correct answers ($p>0.05$). We expected that the participants who prefer due to their interest have more correctly answered questions. Kunduracılar and collages [5] claimed that the students who prefer physiotherapy due to their interest have higher levels of awareness for competences in physiotherapy and professional awareness. However, according to Razak Özdinçler and collages "Professional success and satisfaction are related to the individual's awareness of individual characteristics and capabilities." [12]. Also we believed that because each of the students has taken "Professional Orientation" course increases the level of professional awareness of the non-interested students.

In conclusion, the findings from this study show that professional awareness can be influenced by individual differences. However, the level of professional awareness and the interest in the profession of the student can be increased by professional courses at the beginning of undergraduate education. Therefore professional courses should consist of contemporary knowledge about professional law, post graduate education and department. Also these courses should be guidance to student on plans of career in the future.

References

1. T. Sarıkaya, L. Khorshid. Üniversite öğrencilerinin meslek seçimini etkileyen etmenlerin incelenmesi: Üniversite öğrencilerinin meslek seçimi. Türk Eğitim Bilimleri Dergisi, **7,** 2 (2009)
2. Y. Kuzgun, *Meslek Danışmanlığı* (Doğuş Matbaacılık, Ankara, 2000)
3. A. Karakuş, N. Karadağ, F. Bilgili, Ç. Işıkay, G. Çadır, D. Çeker. Lise son sınıf kız öğrencilerinin hemşirelik mesleğine bakış açıları ile mesleği tercih etme durumları. Hemşirelik Forumu Dergisi, **5,** 1 (2005).
4. G. E. Çiftçi, S. F. Bülbül, N. Bayar Muluk, G. Çamur Duyan, A. Yılmaz. Factors in selecting a university and career among students studying in the Faculty of Health Sciences (Kirikkale University). J Kartal TR, **22,** 3 (2011).
5. Z. Kunduracılar, E. Akbaş, Ç. Büyükuysal, D. Biçki, E. U. Erdam. Assessment of job awareness in Department of Physical Therapy and Rehabilitation students. J High Educ Science **2,** 3 (2012).
6. World Confederation for Physical Therapy (WCPT). Policy statement: Description of physical therapy. (WCPT, London, UK, 2017). http://www.wcpt.org/policy/ps-descriptionPT
7. World Confederation for Physical Therapy (WCPT). Ethical principles. (WCPT, London, UK, 2017). www.wcpt.org/ethical-principles
8. World Confederation for Physical Therapy (WCPT). Policy statement: Ethical responsibilities of physical therapists and WCPT members. (WCPT, London, UK, 2017). http://www.wcpt.org/policy/ps-ethical-responsibilities
9. I. Lindquist, M. Engardt, L. Garnham, F. Poland, B. Richardson. Physiotherapy students' professional identity on edge of working life. Medical Teacher, **28,** 3 (2006).
10. H.M. Vollmer, D.L. Mills. *Professionalisation* (Prentice Hall, Englewood Cliffs, NJ, 1966).
11. F. Can. Professional development history of physical therapy and rehabilitation. İKÇÜSBFD, **1,** 3 (2016).
12. A. Razak Özdinçler, E. Tarakci, Y. Aslan. Investigation of professional awareness of students in Physiotherapy and Rehabilitation Division. HSP, **2,** 2 (2015).
13. A. Öhman, P. Solomon, E. Finch. Career choice and professional preferences in a group of Canadian Physiotherapy Students. Advances in Physiotherapy, **4,** 16 –22 (2002).
14. J. Gotlib, D. Białoszewski, J. Opavsky, R. Garrod, N. E. Fuertes, L. P. Gallardo, B. P. Lourido, S. Monterde, C. S. Serrano, M. Sacco, I. Kunicka. Attitudes of European physiotherapy students towards their chosen career in the context of different educational systems and legal regulations pertaining to the practice of physiotherapy: implications for university curricula. Physiotherapy **98,** 76–85 (2012).

An innovative approach study "Health students example"

Nuran Akyurt[1a]

[1]Vocational School of Health Services, Department of Medical Imaging Techniques, Marmara University, Istanbul, Turkey

Abstract. Globalization; A process of international integration arising from the exchange of products, ideas, cultures and worldviews. Globalization is an economic as well as political, technological and cultural process. As in other areas, technological developments have brought innovations into the training of health care workers, as well as access to information and the use of this information. These developments necessitated new orientations in the education systems of health students. In this study, the effects of computer assisted instructions involving the topics of medical and vocational terminology course on the attitudes and academic achievement levels of students' use of medical and vocational terms were investigated. Marmara University Health Services Vocational School Medical Imaging students constitute the sample of the research. In the experimental group, medical and vocational terminology topics were processed and tested by computer aided instruction method for 12 weeks.
Keywords: Computer aided teaching, Terms related to human anatomy, Cardiovascular system and endocrine system, Attitudes towards the use of medical and occupational terms, Academic achievement

1 Introduction

The technological innovations and the continuous development of the technology show its effect in all areas as well as in the education. In parallel with these developments, researchers, educators and managers are exploring ways of integrating technology into education in order to increase learning capacity and improve the quality of teaching.

In the world, rapid developments in health education require that the terminology to be used in this area be common. Just as it is important and natural in a country to communicate in its own language, it is also important that the staff working in scientific areas around the world communicate with a common language. Medicine, one of the earliest professions in human history, needed a common language for its international character. Words used as medical terminology are usually of Latin origin. However, the words of Greek and other languages are also used. As the terms used in the health area of preventive, diagnostic and treatment methods and in health education are common, it is an advantage for the

[a] Corresponding author: nakyurt@hotmail.com

communication of those working in these scientific fields. For this reason, it is important in health institutions to learn the technical, managerial and health terms as a common language and to use them in the field.

2 Terminology Definition and History

The term; It is used to express special words which are used in different fields of science and arts and occupation, have a special usage area and have a long working memory. Terminology is a scientific discipline dealing with terms.

Medical terms originate from Latin and Greek. Scientific anatomy has been the first science of medical terms. After the alphabet revolution, the Turkish alphabet, based on the Latin alphabet, was accepted and in particular the Latin and Greek terms started to be used more actively in our language.

3 Computer Aided Learning

Computer-assisted learning (BDI) with its audiovisual elements is a method used in the teaching of abstract concepts where the students have difficulties describing it by other methods, difficulties understanding it, and difficulties visualizing it in their minds.

4 Aim

In the literature, there are studies using computer-aided learning methods. For effective use of BDI methods there are studies with content of contribution of students to academic achievement, the great convenience it provides in research in the field of health, the differentiation of anatomical structures, and the effective use of medical and Latin terms in health education. The following statements can be taken for computer-aided learning: concepts and processes can be better understood [1], the themes are easier to learn through visualization [2], self-confidence can be built, the information process can be supported, critical thinking can be stimulated and the ability to solve problems can be improved [3 -20].

The main purpose of the study is to facilitate the learning process and to ensure the permanence of the learning process by experimenting with different teaching methods in order to ensure that the students in health field learn the medical terms effectively and easily.

In order to reach this aim, the following questions were tried to be answered:

1. Medical imaging techniques; What are the opinions and perceptions about the places of use of medical and professional terms, their purpose of use, methods of computer assisted learning?
2. What are the thoughts about "computer technology", "computer games", "smart phone applications" used in medical terminology and vocational courses?

5 Methods

The research started with literature search in October 2016. Electronic database PubMed, ScienceDirect and various Publisher databases are used. As a keyword to search engines; "Motion System", "The circulatory system", "Respiratory system", "Digestive System", "Uriner System", "Uregenital System", "Endocrine System", "Sense Organs", "Professional Terms", "Medical Terms", "Education", "Undergraduate Medical Education", "Teaching", "Learning", "Anatomy", "Cross-Sectional Anatomy", "Radiology", "Medical Imaging", "Diagnostic Imaging", "X-Rays", "3-D Imaging", "Magnetic Resonance Imaging", "Ultrasound Imaging", "Ultrasonography", "Computed Tomography Scanner", "X-Ray", "Four- Dimensional Computed Tomography", "4D Computed Tomography", "Multidetector

Computed Tomography", "Internet", "Online systems" and "PACS (Radiology)" were given. In the obtained literature, it was aimed to reveal the medical imaging techniques program students' ability to use the terms and the items in the terms with "Computer Assisted Instructional Method".

In the study, relevant to control group pretest-posttest model, a semi-experimental study was conducted in order to investigate the effect of computer-aided processing of medical and vocational terminology course on the attitude and academic achievement of first-year students of medical imaging techniques program. In the questionnaire prepared in the light of the literature, socio-demographic characteristics of the students and expressions about computer usage are given.

In the study; computer, internet use, computer-assisted teaching method and traditional teaching methods are the independent variables. Dependent variables are the level of academic achievement in medical and vocational terminology course and attitudes towards medical and vocational terminology. When the research was completed, the same tests were carried out as a final test, and the data collected was taken as the basis.

Table 1. Research figures

Groups	Pre-test	Practice	Post-test
Control	Medical and Professional Terminology	Traditional Teaching Methods (10 Weeks)	Medical and Professional Terminology
Experimental	Medical and Professional Terminology	Computer Aided Teaching Methods (10 Weeks)	Medical and Professional Terminology

5.1 Universe and Sampling

The sample of the study is composed of 2nd grade students who are educated in medical imaging techniques program in 2016-2017 academic year. In the sample, there are two groups as "Control Group" and "Experimental Group". The total number of students participating in the pretest-posttest was 89 (female = 55, male = 34), the number of students in the control group was 36 (40.4%), and 53 in the experimental group (59.6%).

5.2 Data Collection Tools

In order to measure the medical terminology knowledge of the first year students, a questionnaire consisting of multiple-choice questions of Motion System, Joints and Bones, The Circulatory System, Respiratory System, Digestive System, Urinary System, Uregenital System, Endocrine System, Sense Organs, Professional Terms and Medical Terms was created. Created question bank is presented to experts. In line with the opinions, 12 multiple-choice tests suitable for "Medical and Professional Terminology" topics were developed. The prepared tests were applied as a pilot project to the 2nd grade students of the medical imaging techniques program. The reason for the application of the pilot application to the 2nd grade class is that the medical imaging program students should have learned the medical and vocational terminology the previous year. The test was then applied as pre-test and post-test to the first-year students. Points were scored with "1" points for each correct answer and "0" for false and blank answers. On the tables in the results, identification information (name and surname) of the students voluntarily participating in the survey was kept confidential. The identity information was coded by the researcher in the form of a sequence number.

5.3 Application of the research

In the experimental group, a session was created by computer assisted teaching methods (by using smart phone applications). From the teacher applications, "username and password" was received in order to get the software ready for use. By preparing slides covering all curriculum topics of terminology, with animations, subject tests, puzzles and short experimental videos the course content has been enriched. In the control groups, the same lessons were carried out with traditional teaching methods such as lecture, question-answer, discussion.

5.4 Analysis of Data

Analysis of the data was made using the SPSS 17.0 package program. In the analysis, groups (experimental and control) were used as independent variables, and pre-post test scores of the students who took the course with computer-assisted teaching method were taken as dependent variables. Frequency distributions are given in table form.

6. Results

6.1 Demographic Characteristics

When the genders of the participating students were examined, it was seen that 38.2% (n = 34) of the participants were male and 61.8% (n = 55) were female students. The total number of students is n = 89. According to educational status 59.6% (n = 53) are 1st class, 40.4% (n=36) are 2. class students. The tables showing the socio-demographic characteristics of the students of medical imaging techniques are given below.

Table 1a: Socio-demographic characteristics

What grade

1st year	53	59,6%
2nd year	36	40,4%
Total	89	100,0%

Gender

Male	34	38,2%
Female	55	61,8%
Total	89	100,0%

Age range

between 15 - 18	14	15,7%
between 19 - 22	69	77,5%
between 23 - 27	6	6,7%
Total	89	100,0%

The economic situation of the family

Well done	17	19,1%
Mediocre	69	77,5%
Poor	3	3,4%
Total	89	100,0%

Who are you living with at school time?

with family	76	85,4%
with relatives	2	2,2%
People sharing an apartment	3	3,4%
Dormitory	8	9,0%
Total	89	100,0%

When we examined the age range of the students who participated in the research, we see that the age range of 19-22 years constituted the majority with 77.5% (n = 69); The economic situation of their families gave 19.1% (n = 17) as well treated, 77.5% (n = 69) as mediocre and 3.4% as poor (Table 1a).

DOI: 10.1051/shsconf/20173701063

Table 1b: Socio-demographic characteristics

The number of computer in your family?

1	45	50.6%
2	25	28,1%
3	4	4,5%
None	15	16,9%
Total	89	100%

Connection to the Internet?

From the family's computer / mobile phone	5	5.6%
From friends computer	3	3,4%
From own mobile phone	61	68,5%
No possibility to connect	2	2,2%
From own computer	17	19,1%
From tablet	1	1,1%
Total	89	100%

What social media applications do you use?

Facebook	70	78.7%
Whatsapp	89	100%
Twitter	59	66,3%
Snapchat	34	38,2%
Instagram	69	77,5%
Youtube	35	39,3%
Others	34	38,2%

Do you believe in the power of social media?

Yes	88	98,9%
No	1	1,1%
Total	89	100%

Can you connect to internet from your mobile phone?

Yes	88	98,9%
No	1	1,1%
Total	89	100%

Are you playing computer games?

Yes	52	58,4%
No	37	41,6%
Total	89	100%

How many hours a day do you spend with computer/phone??

0-1 hour	10	11,2%
2-5 hours	62	69,7%
6-8 hours	13	14,6%
9+ hours	4	4,5%
Total	89	100%

Do you want your university courses to be supported By computer technology?

Yes	82	92,1%
No	7	7,9%
Total	89	100%

Do you have an e-mail account?

Yes	89	100%
No	0	0%
Total	89	100%

For what purpose do you use Internet the most?

For research	32	36%
For course follow-up	30	33,7%
To track social media	27	30,3%
Total	89	100%

Do you follow the activities of friends and other People you have on your follow up list on social media?

Yes	73	82%
No	16	18%
Total	89	100%

Do you have a smartphone?

Yes	88	98,9%
No	1	1,1%
Total	89	100%

Who has mobile phones in your family??

Mother	61	68,5%
Father	79	88,8%
Sister	54	60,7%
Brother	54	60,7%

Are you playing games?

Yes	62	69,7%
No	27	30,3%
Total	89	100%

Does the university have computer facilities?

Yes	11	12,4%
No	78	87,6%
Total	89	100%

Dou you think that computer technology is necessary in vocational courses like medical terminology?

Yes	78	87,6%
No	7	7,9%
Undecided	4	4,5%
Total	89	100%

Dou you think that Wi-fi services in university are Adequate and convenient?

Unideaed	6	6,7%
Sufficient	23	25,8%
Insufficient	60	67,4%
Total	89	100%

 DOI: 10.1051/shsconf/20173701063

The question, in vocational courses such as medical terminology whether computer technology is necessary has answered 87.6% (n = 78) with yes, 7.9% (n = 7) with no and 4.5% (n = 4) answers with undecided.

6.2 Medical Terminology "Control Group" and "Experimental Group"

Table 2. Medical Terms Pre-Post Test

Unit	Number of Questions	Total Correct	Total Incorrect Answers	Average Score (points)
The Circulatory system	20 of 20 questions	77,46%	22,54%	17261,910156
Sense Organs	30 of 30 questions	69,70%	30,30%	21321,837891
Joints and Bones	25 of 25 questions	76,31%	23,69%	20598,623047
Endocrine System	25 of 25 questions	69,83%	30,17%	17579,082031
Motion System	25 of 25 questions	35,21%	64,79%	11485,217773
Professional Terms	25 of 25 questions	69,70%	30,30%	21321,837891
Digestive system	20 of 20 questions	79,45%	20,55%	17602,699219
Respiratory system	21 of 21 questions	78,57%	21,43%	17903,216797
Medical Terms	25 of 25 questions	67,24%	32,06%	17252,589844
Uregenital System	25 of 25 questions	65,94%	34,06%	17076,882813
Uriner system	20 of 20 questions	71,66%	28,34%	13913,317383

When we evaluate some results in the table; **Motion System:** Understanding, correct response rate 35.21%, post test scores 11485.2777; **Joints and Bones:** Understanding, correct answer rate 76.31%, post test scores 20598.62305; **The Circulatory System:** Understanding, correct answer rate 77.46%, post test scores 17261.91; **Respiratory System:** Understanding, correct response rate 78.57%, post test scores 17903.216; **Digestive System:** Understanding, correct answer rate 79.45%, post test scores 17602.69922 (Table 2).

7 Discussion

When the answers to the questions about socio-demographic characteristics are examined; 87,6% of respondents answered yes to the question of whether they need computer technology in vocational courses such as medical terminology, 79.8% think that it is necessary to make vocational courses with smartphone, 98.9% have smart phone, 87.6% of the respondents answered that there is no computer opportunities in the university, 69.7% play mobile games, 69.7% of those who spend their time with computer / phone between 2 and 5 hours a day, the proportion of those who want to support their university courses with computer technology is 92.1% (Table 1a and 1b).

When studying exams made to the control group and experimental groups related to all terms; the total score of the control group is 118; the total score of the experimental group (pre-test) was 200, and the total score of the experimental group (post-test) was 388. In our study, the total scores of students who learned and used medical terminology by classical method were low. The final test scores of the study conducted with computer aided teaching methods are high with 30704 (correct: 24, false: 1).

Uriner System: Nutrients and oxygen are needed for the cells that make up the human body to survive. Some of the metabolic products resulting from reactions within the cell are transported through the blood to the kidneys to be discarded. Understanding, the correct answer rate is 71.66% and the post test score is 13913.31738.

Uregenital System: It is through reproductive function that human beings can survive their generation. A collection of organs that differs in structure, shape and location, which fulfills the reproductive function in men and women and allows for the shaping of sex specific characters, constitutes the genital system. Understanding, correct response rate is 65.94% and the post test score is 17076.88281.

Endocrine System: Inner secretion glands are defined as endocrine glands (glandulae endocrinae). The system that these glands form is called Endocrine System. Understanding, correct answer rate is 69.83% and the post test score is 17579.08203.

Sense Organs: It is through sense organs that they perceive and evaluate events that occur in the environment of living things. Understanding, correct response rate is 69.70% and the post test score is 21321.84.

Professional terms: It is a branch of medical science dealing with the treatment of these diseases by radiotherapy and other ionizing radiation methods such as diagnosis of diseases of internal organs of the body and X-ray gamma. Understanding, correct response rate is 69.70% and the post test score is 21321.84.

Medical Terms: The term is used to refer to specific words that are used in different fields of science and arts and have a long history of employment, which have been found to be of special use. Terminology is the science branch dealing with terms. Understanding, correct response rate is 67.24% and post test score is 17252.58984 (Table 2).

The dizzying progress in the health field results in a large number of terms and concepts emerging. This fast information and term loading also brings with it important problems. These new medical terms entering the language used can lead to confusion and problems in the use of the language. Today, in many academic curricula, the imaging anatomy is integrated as part of anatomical education according to a variety of strategies. [21, 22, 23, 24, 25, 26, 27,].

8 Conclusion

It is very important to use medical terms effectively and correctly in every area of health. More extensive work is needed to achieve this. In this context, our work is a study that can be used in the health field, which can easily use medical terms for the students, and the writers will rise. In connection with globalization, universities need to offer cost-effective training to students using information technology.

References

1. Klopfer, E., Squire, K. Environmental Detectives - The Development Of An Augmented Reality Platform For Environmental Simulations. Educational Technology Research and Development. April 2008, Volume 56, Issue 2, pp 203–228.
2. Kaufmann, H., Schmalstieg, D. Mathematics and geometry education with collaborative augmented reality. Computers & Graphics. Volume 27, Issue 3, June 2003, Pages 339–345.
3. Kaufmann, H., Schmalstieg, D., Wagner, M. Construct 3D: A Virtual Reality Application for Mathematics and Geometry Education. Education and Information Technologies. December 2000, Volume 5, Issue 4, pp 263–276.
4. Abersek, B., Abersek, M. K., Technologia Vzdelavania "Role Of Teacher and/or Technology In The Education Process" ; Nitra 20.6 (2012): 1-11.
5. Bassett, L. W., Squire, L. F. (1985). Anatomy instruction by radiologists. Invest Radiol 20:1008–1010.

6. Benninger, B., Matsler, N., Delamarter, T. (2014). Classic versus millennial medical lab anatomy. Clin Anat 27:988–993.
7. Craig, S., Tait, N., Boer, D., McAndrew, D. (2010). Review of anatomy education in Australian and New Zealand medical schools. ANZ J Surg 80:212–216.
8. Drake, R. L., Pawlina, W. (2014). Multimodal education in anatomy: the perfect opportunity. Anat Sci Ed 7:1–2.
9. Grignon, B., Oldrini, G., Walter, F. Teaching medical anatomy: what is the role of imaging today? Surg Radiol Anat (2016) 38:253–260 DOI 10.1007/s00276-015-1548-y.
10. Ganske, I., Su, T., Loukas, M., Shaffer, K. (2006). Teaching methods in anatomy courses in North American medical schools: the role of radiology. Acad Radiol 13:1038–1046.
11. Granger NA, Calleson DC, Henson OW, Juliano E, Wineski L, McDaniel MD, Burgoon JM (2006) Use of web-based materials to enhance anatomy instruction in the health sciences. Anat Rec B New Anat 289:121–127.
12. Mena, G., Llupià, A., García-Basteiro, A. L., Sequera, V. G., Aldea, M., Bayas, J. M. and Trilla, A. Educating on professional habits: attitudes of medical students towards diverse strategies for promoting influenza vaccination and factors associated with the intention to get vaccinated" BMC Medical Education. 2013 13:99. 18 July 2013. DOI: 10.1186/1472-6920-13-99.
13. Hege, I., Radon, K., Dugas, M., Scharrer, E., Nowak, D. "Web-based training in occupational medicine. International Archives of Occupational and Environmental Health; Heidelberg 76.1 (Jan 2003): 50-4.
14. Jack, A., Burbridge, B. (2012). The Utilisation of radiology for the teaching of anatomy in Canadian medical schools. Can Assoc Radiol J 63:160–164.
15. Aoki, K., Downes, E. J. An analysis of young peoples use of and attitudes toward cell phones. Telematics and Informatics 20 (2003) 349–364. http://www.angelfire.com/ego2/lostboyrahul/work/cellphoneuse.pdf 27.05.2017 tarihinde ulaşılmıştır.
16. Aydoğdu Karaaslan, İ., Budak, L. Üniversite Öğrencilerinin Cep Telefonu Özelliklerini Kullanımlarının ve Gündelik İletişimlerine Etkisinin Araştırılması. Journal of Yasar University 2012 26(7) 4548 – 4525.
17. Kuronen, R., Jallinoja, P., Airola, R., Patja, K. Educational implementation programme of guidelines on cardiovascular risk factors: an analysis of changes in familiarity, use and attitudes. Primary Health Care Research & Development; Cambridge 11.3 (Jul 2010): 241-249.
18. Maleck, M., Fischer, M., Kammer, B., Zeiler, C., Mangel, E., Schenk, F., Pfeifer, K. J. (2001). Do computers teach better? A media comparison study for case-based teaching in radiology. Radiographics 21:1025–1032.
19. Kish, G., Cook, S. A., Kis, G. (2013). Computer-assisted learning in anatomy at the international medical school in Debrecen, Hungary: a preliminary report. Anat Sci Educ 6:42–47.
20. Korner, N. (1973). Diagnostic radiology in the medical curriculum. Med J Aust 24:605–611.
21. Mitchell, B. S., William, J. E. (2002). Trends in radiological anatomy teaching in the U.K. and Ireland. Clin Radiol 57:1070–1072.
22. Rakel, D. P., Hedgecock, J. Healing the healer: a tool to encourage student reflection towards health. Med Teach 2008, 30:633–635.
23. Phillips, A. W., Smit, S., Straus, C. M. (2013). The role of radiology in preclinical anatomy: a critical review of the past, present, and future. Acad Radiol 20:297–304.

DOI: 10.1051/shsconf/20173701063

24. Shaffer, K., Small, J. E. (2004). Blended learning in medical education: use of an integrated approach with web-based small group modules and didactic instruction for teaching radiologic anatomy. Acad Radiol 11:1059–1070.
25. McNulty, J. A., Halama, J., Espiritu, B. (2004). Evaluation of computer-aided instruction in the medical gross anatomy curriculum. Clin Anat 17:73–78.
26. Phillips, G. S., LoGerfo, S. E., Richardson, M. L., Anzai, Y. (2012). Interactive web-based learning module on CT of the temporal bone: anatomy and pathology. Radiographics 32:E85–E105.
27. Tam, M. D., Hart, A. R., Williams, S. M., Holland, R., Heylings, D., Leinster, S. (2010). Evaluation of a computer program ('disect') to consolidate anatomy knowledge: a randomised-controlled trial. Med Teach 32:e138–e142.
28. Johnson Jr, T. H. (1969). Medical school radiology teaching and examination methods. Radiology 93:443–446.
29. Dunleavy, M., Dede, C., Mitchell, R. Affordances and Limitations of Immersive Participatory Augmented Reality Simulations for Teaching and Learning. Journal of Science Education and Technology. February 2009, Volume 18, Issue 1, pp 7–22.

Smoking of health students "State and Foundation University Example"

Nuran Akyurt[1a]

[1]Vocational School of Health Services, Department of Medical Imaging Techniques, Marmara University, Istanbul, Turkey

Abstract: The purpose of the study is to take a look at the smoking habits of the undergraduate students studying in the health programs of state and private universities, and to determine their opinion about the smoking ban. The research is a descriptive type study. The survey was conducted in February 2017. The participation rate in the survey is 75.5%. A questionnaire consisting of 23 questions was applied to the students. In the questionnaire, students were asked about their socio-demographic characteristics, the age at which they started smoking, in which situations they resort to cigarette, their opinion about addiction and on the implementation of the law "Prevention and control of the harmful effects of tobacco products".

Keywords: Cigarettes, Smoking, Health Students, Law, Habit

1 Introduction

Tobacco use is currently responsible for the death around the world which considers a public health problem worldwide. Tobacco smoking is a direct cause of high morbidity all over the world, which could be prevented. Substantial and sustained efforts are required to further reduce smoking prevalence and the associated morbidity and mortality [1]. Smoking causes different diseases such as cancer; about 90 % of all lung cancer deaths in men and 80 % of all lung cancer deaths in women [2, 3]. Smoking is a behavior that generally starts in adolescents. An early exposure or initiation of smoking is associated with lower cessation rates, longer duration of smoking, and higher nicotine dependence in adulthood [4]. About 70 % of adolescent smokers are likely to become adult smokers because some adolescent may believe that can quit smoking at any time [5, 13]. Strong relationship exists between cigarette smoking and premature death [6]. According to WHO 10 million deaths annually will be attributed to cigarette smoking by 2030 [7]. Tobacco is the biggest cause of adult death in developed countries [8] while smoking is the single most preventable cause of death among the greatest risk factors for mortality. According to WHO, there are about 1 billion smokers in the world and annually 6 million people succumb to death from cigarette smoking

[a] Corresponding author: nakyurt@hotmail.com

[9]. If a person quits smoking by age 30, his life expectancy is almost same as that of non-smoker [10]. According to WHO, there are about 1 billion smokers in the world and annually 6 million people succumb to death from cigarette smoking [11]. Worldwide China has the highest tobacco consumers and this is attributed to sharing and gifting tobacco products [12]. Smoking is widespread in the developing countries, the spread is growing at a high rate especially among young people.

Numerous studies show that medical students and health professionals themselves smoke cigarettes despite knowing its adverse effect on health. In the literature, there are studies on the smoking habits of the students [13, 24]. The effect of this result may not only effect on the health of individuals, but also an economic burden which includes direct medical care for tobacco-induced illnesses and loss of life from early death [25]. The effect of this result may not only effect on the health of individuals, but also an economic burden which includes direct medical care for tobacco-induced illnesses and loss of life from early death [26].

2 Objective

As in the whole world, even in our country smoking is an important health problem which is one of the social problems and which can be addictive in a short period of time brings an economically additive load to the person who smokes and also affects his health negatively. Smoking is a harmful and widespread habit in terms of community health. Smoking is a problem all over the world as well as waiting for an urgent solution in our country.

It is shown as risk factor for six out of the eight death causes in the world. The purpose of the study is to take a look at the smoking habits of the undergraduate students studying in the health programs of state and private universities, and to determine their opinion about the smoking ban.

The purpose of this study was to determine the smoking status of the undergraduate students studying at the state and foundation universities in the health field and to evaluate the points of view of the "Law on the Prevention and Control of Hazards of Tobacco Products" which took place in 2008. In accordance with this purpose, the sociodemographic characteristics of the students (gender, age, university) as well as the position on smoking, smoking cessation and the laws on smoking bans are to be assessed to show whether there is a significant difference.

3 Materials and Methods

Studies that examine the prevalence and factors that initiate smoking were identified through online literature using the following database: Science Direct, Web of Science, Google Scholar and Pubmed.

The research is a descriptive type study. The survey was conducted in February 2017. The participation rate in the survey is 75.5%. Selection sampling technique was not used in the research. All students who wanted to fill out the questionnaire were included in the sampling. The data were collected in a form developed in line with the literatüre. A questionnaire consisting of 23 questions was applied to the students. In the questionnaire, students were asked about their socio-demographic characteristics, the age at which they started smoking, in which situations they resort to cigarette, their opinion about addiction and on the implementation of the law "Prevention and control of the harmful effects of tobacco products". The obtained data were evaluated by transferring them to SPSS 17.0 program. The data shows arithmetic mean, standard deviation values, percent and number values. T testi ve Anova yapılmıştır. Statistical significance was accepted as $p<0.05$.

DOI: 10.1051/shsconf/20173701064

4 Results

The total number of students participating in the survey is 867. The questionnaire included questions about students 'sociodemographic characteristics, smoking status, relatives and friends' smoking status, smoking cessation considerations, and smoking prohibition at closed places. The distribution of the answers to the questions is given in Tables 1 - 6.

Table 1. Sociodemographic characteristics of the students

Gender

Female	546	63,0%
Male	321	37,0%
Total	867	100,0%

Age range

between 18 - 23	738	85,1%
between 24-28	104	12,0%
between 29 - 34	17	2,0%
35+	8	0,9%
Total	867	100,0%

Studying at

State university	511	58,9%
Foundation university	356	41,1%
Total	867	100,0%

Field of study

Medical Imaging	618	71,3%
Anesthesia	33	3,8%
Pathology Laboratory	106	12,2%
First and Emergench Help	53	6,1%
Nursing	42	4,8%
Physical Therapy and Rehabilitation	3	0,3%
Orthopedic Prosthetic Orthosis	12	1,4%
Total	867	100,0%

Of the students who participated in the survey, 63% were female, 37% were male; 85.1% are in the age range between 18-23. 58.9% of the students are studying at state universities, 41.1% at foundation universities in associate degree programs; Most of them, 71.3% studying in medical imaging techniques associate degree program.

Table 2. Sociodemographic characteristics of the students

The economic situation of the family

Poor	3	0,3%
Bad	50	5,8%
Mediocre	599	69,1%
Good	215	24,8%
Total	867	100,0%

Who are you living with at school time?

State Dormitory Institution	636	73,4%
Priate dormitory	91	10,5%
People sharing an apartment	33	3,8%
with family	36	4,2%
with relatives	71	8,2%
Total	867	100,0%

As can be seen in the table, the students indicated that their families' economic situation was moderate with 69.1%. The proportion of students staying in state dormitories during education is 73.4%.

Table 3. Smoking status of the students

Smoking status		
Never smoked	340	39,2%
Once tried	195	22,5%
Previously smoked	49	5,7%
Social smoker	131	15,1%
Smoking regularly	152	17,5%
Total	867	100,0%
Age to start smoking		
Never tried	330	38,1%
Under 13 years	39	4,5%
Between 13 - 18	345	39,8%
Between 19 – 22	143	16,5%
22+	10	1,2%
Total	867	100,0%
Causes of starting smoking		
Smokers in the family	18	2,1%
Friend circles	242	27,9%
Role models like teacher etc.	6	0,7%
Cinema / Sports Stars	3	0,3%
Stress / Troubles	157	18,1%
No answer	441	50,9%
Total	867	100,0%
Do you smoke in the presence of maily elders?		
Yes	77	8,9%
No	790	91,1%
Total	867	100,0%
Smoking status dring exam period		
It is increasing	241	27,8%
It does not change, same level	626	72,2%
Total	867	100,0%

It is seen that the number of non-smokers (n=340, 39,2%) is higher than that of smokers (n=152, 17,5%). 39.8% (n=345) who stated that they started smoking between 13 and 18 years of age. Friendship circumstance (n=242, 27.9%) and stress/distress (n=157, 18.1%) were shown as the reasons for starting. 72.2% would not and do not smoke in the presence of elders, 27.8% of the students said that smoking increased at special times like the exam period, and 72.2% of them did not.

Table 4. Smoking status of the relatives

Smoking status of mother / father		
None of both	378	43,6%
Mother smokes	68	7,8%
Father smokes	270	31,1%
Both of them smokes	151	17,4%
Total	867	100,0%
Do your three closest friends smoke?		
None of them	294	33,9%
Only one them	203	23,4%
Two of them	183	21,1%
Three of them	187	21,6%
Total	867	100,0%

When we consider the smoking situation of relatives and friends, in the families the mother (n=68, 7.8%), father (n=270, 31.1%) or both (n=151, 17.4%) are smokers. As can be seen from the table, the majority of friends (n = 573, 66.1%) are also smokers.

Table 5. Smoking cessation of the students

Doyou want to quit smoking?		
Want to quit	369	42,6%
undecided	460	53,1%
Want to continue to smoke	38	4,4%
Total	867	100,0%
Doyou resolve to give up smoking in the last 12 month?		
Yes	225	26,0%
No	295	34,0%
No answer	347	40,0%
Total	867	100,0%

The number of students who want to quit smoking (n = 369, 42.6%) is high. The number of people who thought in the last 12 month to quit smoking (n=225, 26%) and those who did not (n=295, 34%) are close to each other.

Table 6. Students' thoughts on smoking ban

What is your opinion about the ban on cigarette advertising?		
Necessary	605	69,8%
Unnecessary	262	30,2%
Total	867	100,0%
What do you thing about smoking ban in restaurants, cafes, cafeterias, etc.?		
Necessary	786	90,7%
Unnecessary	81	9,3%
Total	867	100,0%
What do you think about smoking ban on public transportation?		
Necessary	844	97,3%
Unnecessary	23	2,7%
Total	867	100,0%
Prohibition of the sale of cigarettes to children younger than 18 years		
Necessary	821	94,7%
Unnecessary	46	5,3%
Total	867	100,0%

The ban on cigarette advertising is appropriate find 69.8% of respondents, 90.7% of them think that it is necessary to prohibit smoking in restaurants, cafes and cafeterias, 97.3% of them think that it is correct to prohibit smoking in public transportation vehicles. The sale of cigarettes to adolescents under 18 years of age should be prohibited find 94.7% of the students.

5 Analysis of the research questions

T-test (Independent Samples Test) and One-way ANOVA (Analysis of Variance) were used to test the hypotheses of our research. Independent samples T-test is a statistical technique used to test whether the difference between the averages is significant at a certain confidence level (95%, 99%, etc.), by comparing two groups that are independent of each other or a sample with a dependent variable [27].

5. 1 T-test results

Independent samples T-test were used to measure the level of quitting smoking by gender.

Table 7. Measuring the level of quitting smoking by gender

Dimension	Gender	n	Mean X	Std. Deviation SS	F	p
To quit smoking	Male	546	1,5311	1,04922	17,068	,000*
	Female	321	1,7196	1,13574		

*p<0,05

If we compare the level of quitting smoking by gender, X for female students is 1,5311 and for male students 1,7196. As a result of the analysis, a significant difference was found according to the level of quitting smoking by gender. It was found that the level of quitting smoking by female students was significantly higher.

Table 8. Measuring the level of quitting smoking by university

Dimension	University	n	Mean X	Std. Deviation SS	F	p
To quit smoking	State	511	1,7006	0,5589	7,001	0,008
	Foundation	356	1,5	0,56419		

If we compare the level of quitting smoking by university, X for state universities is 1,7006 and for foundation universities 1,5000. As a result of the analysis, no significant difference was found according to the level of quitting smoking by university.

Table 9. Age to start smoking by university

Dimension	University	n	Mean X	Std. Deviation SS	F	p
Age to start smoking	State	511	1,4501	0,97264	80,202	0,000*
	Foundation	356	1,8174	1,19757		

*p<0,05

If we compare the age to start smoking by university, X for state universities is 1,4501 and for foundation universities 1,8174. As a result of the analysis, a significant difference was found according to the age to start smoking by university. It was found that the age to start smoking by foundation universities was significantly higher.

5.2 One-way Anova results

One-Way ANOVA test was used for the research hypothesis. One way ANOVA is performed to test whether the difference between three independent or more sample averages is significantly different from zero.

Table 10. Levels of quitting smoking according to age ranges

Dimension	Agerange	n	X	SS	F	p	Significance
Wants to quit smoking	18-23	738	1,6301	0,577	2,317	0,074	
	24-28	104	1,5769	0,515			
	29-34	17	1,5882	0,507			
	35+	8	1,125	0,353			
	Total	867	1,6182	0,569			

If we compare the level of quitting smoking by age range of the students, X for age range 18-23 is 1.6301 and for age range 24-28 it is 1.5769. One-way analysis of variance, a parametric test of statistical tests, was used to test whether university students significantly differentiated their desire to quit smoking. As a result of the variance analysis, a statistically significant difference was calculated for F = 2,317, (p <0,05). The Tukey test was used as a post-hoc test to test the source of the difference. The direction of the difference is the age range of 18-23 and 24-28 years.

6 Discussion

This study summarized and provides insight into the prevalence of smoking among students and factors of early intention of smoking among students in different ages. The prevalence of current smoking found in this review study among students was alarming especially among adolescents [29, 30]. The rate of those who stated that they tried smoking cigarettes when they were under 13 years old was 4,5%; the age range of starting smoking regularly is 13-18 with rate of 39.8%.

As the reason for the start of smoking, health students have indicated the friends (27.9%) and stress/distress (18.1%) in the first place. 17.5% of the students are still smoking regularly.

Adolescence is very important because it will determine what kind of adult the child will be in the future. This period is also important in terms of the habits of the child. If you look at smoking, 300 thousand adolescents die each year due to cigarette and tobacco-related diseases. 70% of premature deaths in adulthood and 1/3 of diseases are due to habits acquired in adolescents [28].

The study show that the influence of friends is the main reason for smoking among adolescents and university students followed by the stress, curiosity and imitation of others. Other recent studies done in other countries, peer pressure was also the reason, initiating from smoking [31, 32]. As a result of the analyzes made, the desire to quit smoking in female students was found significantly higher than male students. Compared to age, the level of wanting to quit smoking was found to be significantly higher for students who were between the ages of 18-23 and 24-28.

Health students said that parents played very important role in cigarette smoking. Most students think that the prohibition of smoking in public and closed places diminishes the use of cigarettes [33 - 36].

From the students who will work in health care institutions after graduation and will play a good role model in case of smoking we are awaiting in our research, that they will have a low tendency to smoke, knows the harm of smoking and will act accordingly.

If we look at studies about smoking in developed countries we see that non-health educated people who do not receive health education have a significantly higher rate of knowledge of non-smoking and cigarette harm.

7. Conclusion

In order to have lower smoking rates of the health care workers in our country, education is not the only factor in the fight against smoking. A strict smoking policy should be implemented and early counseling among adolescents and awareness campaigns to the health effects of smoking and the prevailing beliefs that smoking habit can easily quit. As they become the future professionals of the society. Smoking control programs should be considered in this group.

Medical personnels should be given regular lectures and video trainings on the hazardous effects of tobacco especially smoking so that not only they refrain from them, but also advise others to refrain from them.

Because restrictive legislation is in effect, cigarette use of the students is reduced even it is low, nevertheless universities must absolutely develop supportive strategies so that their students quit smoking and re-think their quit smoking trainings in their curricula.

References

1. Almutairi, Khalid M. "Smoking Among Saudi Students: A Review of Risk Factors and Early Intentions of Smoking". J Community Health (2014) 39:901–907. Published online: 2 July 2014 DOI 10.1007/s10900-014-9909-8.

2. U.S. Department of Health and Human Services. (2004). The health consequences of smoking: A report of the surgeon general. Atlanta: U.S. Department of Health and Human Services, Centers for Disease Control and Prevention, National Center for Chronic Disease Prevention and Health Promotion, Office on Smoking and Health.
3. U.S. Department of Health and Human Services (2010) How tobacco smoke causes disease: What it means to you. Atlanta: U.S. Department of Health and Human Services, Centers for Disease Control and Prevention, National Center for Chronic Disease Prevention and Health Promotion, Office on Smoking and Health.
4. Abdalla, A. M., Al-Kaabba, A. F., Saeed, A. A., Abdulrahman, B. M., Raat, H. (2007). Gender differences in smoking behavior among adolescents in Saudi Arabia. Saudi Medical Journal, 28(7), 1102–1108.
5. Center for Disease and Control (CDC). (1994). Preventing tobacco use among young people: A report of the surgeon general. MMWR, 43(RR-4), 1–10.
6. Dhala, A., Pinsker, K., Prezant, D. J. Respiratory heath consequences of environmental tobacco smoke. Med Clin North Am 2004; 88:1535-5.
7. Al-Kaabba, A. F., Saeed, A. A., Abdalla, A. M., Hassan, H. A., Mustafa, A. A. Prevalence and associated factors of cigarette smoking among medical students of King Fahad Medical City in Riyadh of Saudi Arabia. J Family Community Med 2011;18(1):8-12.
8. Boyle, P. Cancer, cigarette smoking and premature death in Europe: a review including the Recommendations of European Cancer Experts Consensus Meeting, Helsinki, October 1996. Lung Cancer 1997;17(1):1-60.
9. WHO. Tobacco free initiative (TFI). 2009. (Accessed on 3rd May, 2017). Health Organization, Media Centre. Tobacco, Fact Sheet N 339. Available from URL: http://www.who.int/tobacco/health priority/en/.
10. Doll, R., Peto, R., Boreham, J. Mortality in relation to smoking: 50 years' observations on Male British doctors. BMJ 2004; 328: 1519.
11. World Health Organization, Media Centre. Tobacco, Fact Sheet N 339. (Accessed on 3rd May, 2017). Available from URL: http://www.who.int/mediacentre/factsheets/fs339/en/
12. Ding, D., Hovell, M. F. Cigarettes, social reinforcement, and culture: a commentary on "Tobacco as a social currency: cigarette gifting and sharing in China". Nikotine Tob Res. 2012 Mar;14(3):255-7. doi: 10.1093/ntr/ntr277. Epub 2011 Dec 16. PMID: 22180592.
13. Wetter, D. W., Kenford, S. L., Welsch, S. K., Smith, S. S., Fouladi, R. T., Fiore, M. C., et al. Prevalence and predictors of transitions in smoking behavior among college students. Health Psychol. 2004 Mar;23(2):168-77. PMID: 15008662 DOI: 10.1037/0278-6133.23.2.168
14. Jradi, H., Wewers, M. E., Pirie, P. R., Binkley, P. F., Ferketich, K. Cigarette and waterpipe smoking associated knowledge and behaviour among medical students in Lebanon. East Mediterr Health J. 2013 Oct;19(10):861-8.
15. Öztürk, C., Bektaş, M., Yılmaz, E., Salman, F., Şahin, T., İlmek, M., et al. Smoking status of Turkish nursing students and factors affecting their behavior. Pac J Cancer Prev. 2011;12(7):1687-92.
16. Ulus, T., Yurtseven, E., Donuk, B. Prevalence of smoking and related risk factors among Physical Education and Sports School students at Istanbul University. Int J Environ Res Public Health. 2012 Mar;9(3):674-84.
17. Askarian, M., Kouchak, F., Youssef, M., Romito, L. M. Comparing tobacco use knowledge, attitudes and practices between engineering students at a public and Islamic Azad university in Shiraz, Iran 2011. Int J Prev Med. 2013 Oct;4(10):1154-61.

18. Sabahy, A. R., Divsalar, K., Bahreinifar, S., Marzban, M., Nakhaee, N. Waterpipe tobacco use among Iranian university students: correlates and perceived reasons for use. Int J Tuberc Lung Dis. 2011 Jun;15(6):844-7.
19. Maziak, W., Fouad, F. M., Asfar, T., Hammal, F., Bachir, E. M., Rastam, S., et al. Prevalence and characteristics of narghile smoking among university students in Syria. Int J Tuberc Lung Dis. 2004 Jul;8(7):882-9.
20. Al-Kubaisy W, Abdullah NN, Al-Nuaimy H, Halawany G, Kurdy S. Epidemiological study on tobacco smoking among university students in Damascus, Syrian Arab Republic. East Mediterr Health J. 2012 Jul;18(7):723-7.
21. Khabour OF, Alzoubi KH, Eissenberg T, Mehrotra P, Azab M, Carroll MV, et al. Waterpipe tobacco and cigarette smoking among university students in Jordan. Int J Tuberc Lung Dis. 2012 Jul;16(7):986-92.
22. Waheedi, M, Al-Tmimy, A. M., Enlund, H. Preparedness for the smoking cessation role among health sciences students in Kuwait. Med Princ Pract. 2011;20(3):237-43.
23. Taha, A. Z., Sabra, A. A., Al-Mustafa, Z. Z., Al-Awami, H. R., Al-Khalaf, M. A., Al-Momen, M. M. Water pipe (shisha) smoking among Male students of medical colleges in the eastern region of Saudi Arabia. Ann Saudi Med. 2010 May-Jun;30(3):222-6.
24. El-Ansari, W., Labeeb, S., Kotb, S., Yousafzai, M. T., El-Houfey, A., Stock, C. Correlates of smoking, quit attempts and attitudes towards total smoking bans at university: findings from eleven faculties in Egypt. Asian Pac J Cancer Prev. 2012;13(6):2547-56.
25. U.S. Department of Health and Human Services. (2004) The health consequences of smoking: A report of the surgeon general. Atlanta: U.S. Department of Health and Human Services, Centers for Disease Control and Prevention, National Center for Chronic Disease Prevention and Health Promotion, Office on Smoking and Health. (Accessed on 3rd May, 2017). Available from: https://www.cdc.gov/tobacco/data_statistics/sgr/2004/index.htm
26. Rothman, K. J., Greenland, S. Causation and causal inference in epidemiology. J. Inf. 2005, 95(Suppl. S1), S144–S150.
27. Ural, A., ve Kılıç, İ. (2005). Bilimsel Araştırma Süreci ve SPSS le Veri Analizi, Detay Yayıncılık, Ankara.
28. World Health Organization, The second decade: Improving adolescent health and development. WHO/FRH/ADH/98.18 Rev.1 (Accessed on 3rd May, 2017). http://www.who.int/maternal_child_adolescent/documents/frh_adh_98_18/en/
29. Âmin, T. T., Amr, M. A., Zaza, B. O. (2011). Psychosocial predictors of smoking among secondary school students in Al- Hassa, Saudi Arabia. Journal of Behavioral Medicine, 34(5), 339–350. Doi:10.1007/s10865-011-9319-7.
30. Agaku, I. T., Ayo-Yusuf, O. A., Vardavas, C. I., Connolly, G. (2014). Predictors and patterns of cigarette and smokeless tobacco use among adolescents in 32 countries, 2007–2011. Journal of Adolescent Health, 54(1), 47–53.
31. Oh, D. L., Heck, J. E., Dresler, C., Allwright, S., Haglund, M., Del Mazo, S. S., et al. (2010). Determinants of smoking initiation among women in five European countries: a cross-sectional survey. BMC Public Health, 10, 74.
32. Rudatsikira, E., Muula, A. S., Siziya, S. (2009). Current cigarette smoking among in-school American youth: results from the 2004 National Youth Tobacco Survey. International Journal for Equity in Health, 8, 10. doi:10.1186/1475-9276-8-1.
33. Gilman, S. E., Rende, R., Boergers, J., Abrams, D. B., Buka, S. L., Clark, M. A., et al. (2009). Parental smoking and adolescent smoking initiation: An intergenerational perspective on tobacco control. Pediatrics, 123(2), e274–e281. Doi:10.1542/peds.2008-2251.

34. Exter Blokland, E. A., Engels, R. C., Hale, W. W. 3rd, Meeus, W., Willemsen, M.C. (2004) Lifetime parental smoking history and cessation and early adolescent smoking behavior. Preventive Medicine 38(3):359–368. [PubMed: 14766120].
35. Gilman et al., Parental smoking and adolescent smoking initiation: an intergenerational perspective on tobacco control. Published in final edited form as: Pediatrics. 2009 February; 123(2): e274–e281. Doi:10.1542/peds.2008-2251
36. Hardy, J. B. (2003). The collaborative perinatal project: Lessons and legacy. Annals of Epidemiology, 13(5), 303–311.

The Factors Effect the Venue Selection and Joining to Physical Activity of the Users Visit 'Özgürlük Park and Recreation' area for Physical Activity

Onur Kavi[1a], Hakan Akdeniz[2], and Fatma Yeşim Körmükçü [3]

[1] Kocaeli University, Health Sciences Institute, Department of Physical Education and Sports Teacher Training, Kocaeli, Turkey
[2]Sakarya University, Institute of Educational Department of Physical Education and Sports Teacher Training, Sakarya, Turkey
[3]Kocaeli University, Sport Sciences Faculty, Academician of the Department of Recreation, Kocaeli, Turkiye

Abstract. The aim of this study is to examine the influencing factors of people to choose the place and participate in physical activities for parks and recreational sites. The participants of this study are the people who live in İstanbul, Kadıköy, 15 years or older people and regular users of Özgürlük Park and Recreational field. 232 people volunteered for this study. When we look at the data, we have gathered from these people we decided some participant's answers are invalid thus we decided to study on 200 valid answers we have. 50,5% percent of the participants are male, 49,5% percent of participants are female. As data gathering tool we used FAMDÖ which adopted to Turkey, and its correspondence and trustworthiness are proven. FAMDO consists 33 questions and two sub-categories (choosing physical activity place and factors which prevent people from participating physical activities). It is five scale Likert-type questionnaire. It evaluates the reason of participants picking a park and recreational site for physical activity and the reasons that prevent people from participating physical activities. For data analysis, we used descriptive statistics and single variable variance analysis (ANOVA) and Independent Samples T-Test. The data we have obtained from the field (Özgürlük Park and Recreation site) showed us, as place choosing Scale points is statistically significant($p>0,05$) gender wise. At the end of the study, we found the factors that influence people choosing parks and recreational places for physical activity. We also found the reasons that prevent people from participating physical activities and came up with solutions that minimize the reasons. We shared our finding with local administrators.

[a] Corresponding author: onurkavi92@gmail.com

1 Introduction

The general run of the healthcare staff has observed throughout history that the people become sick more than the individuals sport, [17]. Many years ago, the investigators believed a significant connection between the physical fitness and health care need. This belief became respected further in the modern cultures. Today, the moves to reach the physical fitness are made to withstand to the business climate and the stress environment created by this climate, [28]. Need for the health care and to protect the health care need has always been one of the primary purposes of the humanity. In fact, it is not possible in our society to think a television channel without the health-related program, a newspaper or a magazine without a health page. It needs to define the 'health' word and introduce its historical development for explaining how our health changed as a result of regular sports exercises, [29].

The World Health Organization defined the health as follows: The health is the state of affair that the person has the full-blooded welfare regarding his/her soul and social aspects besides not to be sick or disabled, [30]. Turkish Language Association explained this word as the healthy condition of the body, body wellness, welfare, livingness, [20].

There are several ways to protect and promote the health. One of the common ground where these differences meet is the sport undoubtfully, [8]. The various authors and scientists identify the 'sport' concept as the biological, pedagogic and a social work cures the health of the person regarding physiological and psychological needs, provides him to get social, brings the development of mental and motoric skill to a certain level, [27]. Being positively affected of societies in terms of either health and social or cultural and economic aspects by the sport caused to be shown this concept as a lifestyle in developed countries. Because the physical education and sports activities contribute to being raised the children as the mentally and spiritually healthy generation by keeping them out of each kind of bad habits, establish and sustain the bilateral relations between both interpersonal and inter-societal by increasing the life quality, [14].

The sports policies and the economic conditions of the governments are the most decisive factors to raise healthy individuals. The perspectives of educated administrators to the game and their conscious level about healthy quality life are the main ones of the reasons determine the importance, qualifications of school or office activities and the participation levels as well, [26]. Using the free times by physical exercises and sports activities have importance to avoid the tension of the technology and country life on the people and cure the stress created, [21]. The World Health Organization announced the 'Move for World Health Day' slogan in 7th April 2002. According to the data of World Health Organization that approximately over 2 million people die due to not to sport and do physical activity, [30]. At present, there are government policies exist to regain the moving life, likewise, protecting the health care need of exercise is a scientific truth. At the same time, the necessity of announcing the importance of sport for all ages caused to born the 'life-long sport' principle. In the 1980s, the activities such as folk run started to be popular in most of the villages in our country. In our day, become conscious of the universities and local administrations on this issue led the sport to spread everywhere and address to everyone, [29].

There are too many terms about 'leisure' and 'free time' which have a direct or indirect connection with the name of 'sport.' Several concepts may match with the term of 'free time.' The free time is mostly known as the opposite of working, but the work of a person may be the free time activity of another person. Many activities may include the characteristics of both the free time and work occupation. To be able to get rid of the imperatives and obligations is generally the key feature of the free time, [23]. According to Miller and Robinson, the free time training is an education for the individual to make use of his/her free time well. The goal of this education is to gain the ability to tell oneself creatively and choosing a free time activity to improve personality. Such an education can be formal and informal as well, [22].

The free time is a process spent by the individual to understand oneself, free-time, own lifestyle and social formation. The purpose of this process is to enhance the comfort and welfare of the life, [1]. It is reported in researches that the individuals who have an extensive welfare perception are the people who actively join the activities, [12]

One of the principal factors of sustaining the healthy life is the physical activity. However, people have started to spend time as inactive in houses and offices in comparison with the old periods; this caused to be adopted a lifestyle without sport, [10]. Since the lipidosis ratio in the body of the person who does not sport will increase in the long run, these individuals are at risk of being overweight and obese; therefore it is confirmed that a lot diseases such as diabetes, tension, high cholesterol, and asthma can occur in the body, [25].

The physical activity is a bodily movement keeps and strengthens being healthy and fit. These bodily movements are actualized because of several reasons such as strengthening the cardiovascular system and muscles, improving the sports skills, weighting loss or physical compatibility. The physical activities did frequently and methodical empower the immune system and helps to avoid the diseases such as heart conditions, cardiovascular diseases, type 2 diabetes, and obesity, [19]. The physical activity has positive effects on the public health. The exercises provide a muscular force of all ages, elasticity, joint mobility, coordination and the weight control. Moreover, the practices ensure the development of personal power, to increase the social relations and also to enhance the life quality and lifetime, [3].

All the people need for the educations of physical fitness, health, life-long sport and recreation to raise healthy and lively individuals, [15]. While many countries invest to encourage for lifelong physical activity, they also guide different societies to apply these for programs, [13]. These programs emphasize the fun besides the benefits of sport and physical activity. The recreation that is important to encourage physical activity provides to change the ordinary flow of life; while it ensures refreshing and renewing as is seen by the word meaning, also establishes the physical, mental and emotional stability, [14].

The concept of 'have fun and rest' that becomes more important day by day in the social life of countries can be stated as the components of the free times made by kinds of sport and activities with the art and cultural services. The recreation that means refreshing by joyful activities or exercises also infers that the experiences of the person joins to have fun and get pleasure voluntarily, [26]. In brief, the recreation is the activity selected by individuals to exercise in their free time. This activity may be the physical, social and emotional thematic or all together, [9].

The population density, crowded society and urbanizing facts in metropolises cause positive changings in the expectations of people. Each individual in metropolises desires a greener city environment besides growing demands such as high technology, developed architecture, etc. People want to live the life more healthy by resting and actualizing activities in picnic areas, walking and running paths, park and recreation areas, green spaces, game areas for children, theater buildings, amusement centers, motion picture theaters, shopping malls in almost all city centers. People want to reach these centers and regions for recreative activities in a short time, not via trips for long hours. They also ask to be close to where they work or live. They pine to catch fish, air oneself, blow off steam and relax by visiting a park and recreation area or a picnic site even for a short time. People want to see these areas as close to their houses, schools or kindergarten of their children. While the social activity areas improve in metropolises, the big park and recreation areas are also created to give the citizens these chances.

DOI: 10.1051/shsconf/20173701065

In this context, the goal of this study is to analyze the preventing factors for joining the physical activities and reveal how the parks and recreation areas used as physical activity places. Also, this research will make tremendous contributions to our country about the recreation services and be a lodestar for the local administrators for planning such areas. Moving away from nature by fast-growing cities and becoming of life more inactive by getting easy via technology canalized to people to city parks for physical activity or fun. The local administrations start to build park and recreation areas by the incentive of governments based on the principle of being protected the community health that is one of the prior missions of the state. I believe that this study will remark to these parks. In this study, it is aimed to review the expectation and demands of the users of city parks by contributing to planning the new recreation areas and looking for a solution for how the people play sports comfy. It is thought that this research contributes to the planning process of new park and recreation areas.

2 Method

The investigators conducted the surveys in 'Özgürlük Park and Recreation' area in İstanbul. Before being carried out the questionnaires on the users visit Özgürlük Park and Recreation area in weekday and weekend, it is informed about why this survey is conducted and how they should be answered. It is requested that no names and surnames are written in the questionnaires. It is explained to the investigators that each question must be read one by one and answered.

The wrongly filled questionnaires and the forms have more than one answer to each issue are excluded (50 questionnaires) when the data obtained from 250 people attended to the survey voluntarily. Finally, 200 attendees are taken into the scope of the investigation.

2.1 Research Group

The population of the validity and reliability study of the data collection tools used in research is composed of the users of 'Özgürlük Park and Recreation' area who are 15 and older and living in Kadıköy. 250 people who live in Kadıköy district of İstanbul Province and visit 'Özgürlük Park and Recreation' area joined in this survey. 200 of attendees are taken into the scope of validity and reliability by excluding the wrongly filled forms. The age range of these 200 people is between 15 and 80. Educational statuses of these attendees are the primary school, secondary school, High school, University and Post Graduate. The income levels are limited between 1300 Turkish lira and 10.000 Turkish liras.

2.2. Data Collection Tools

The surveys used in this research have entirely 2 papers. There are 6 questions on the first page about the demographic features of the users visit the recreation park area. On the second page, there are the survey with 15 questions about the reasons for selecting the place as the physical activity area that they go to and another questionnaire consisting of 18 questions about the factors prevent to join the physical activity. In this study, while the first page has demographic questions, on the second page, there is the Two-Factor Physical Activity Area Assessment Scale (PAAAS) asks the reasons of being selected for any place as the physical activity area. This Two-Factor Physical Activity Area Assessment Scale was conducted in literature about this issue, [5].

The sub-dimension of the venue selection for the physical activity measures the factors push the people who visit the park and recreation area for physical activity to choose

DOI: 10.1051/shsconf/20173701065

there as the physical activity place. The scale that consisting of 15 articles is 5 point Likert-type (1: Crucial, 2: Important, 3: It doesn't matter, 4: Unimportant, 5: Very Unimportant/Picayune). The sub-dimension of the factors prevent the joining to the physical activity measures the factors impede the attendance of people to the park and recreation areas. The scale that consisting of 18 articles is also 5 point Likert-type (1: Absolutely Disagree, 2: Disagree, 3: Barely Agree, 4: Agree, 5: Absolutely Agree), [5].
Within the period of being adapted the assessment instruments used in research to Turkey, firstly, Kaiser-Meyer-Olkin (KMO) test is applied to understand whether the date obtained from both two surveys are comply with factorability and Bartlett test is conducted to examine whether the number of sample obtained from the population (universe) is enough for factor analysis. After the face validity process for the scales, Principal Component Factor Analysis is conducted to test the structure validity and reliability of both two scales. The Cronbach Alpha value is considered to determine the internal consistency, reliability of the dimensions in scales and how correct both the two scales measure the feature targeted, [5].

2.3 Analysis of the Data

SPSS 17 packaged software is used to solve the data obtained at the end of the data collection process. The descriptive statistics methods (frequency, percentage) are utilized for the personal details. Independent Samples T-Test technique is utilized to understand if any significant difference exists or not in terms of the gender and marital status of the attendees when they choose these places as the Physical Activity areas. One-Way ANOVA method helped to test whether there is a meaningful difference in terms of the educational status of the attendees when they choose these places (Park and Recreation areas) as the physical activity area. It is tested about if there is a significant difference or not in terms of the gender and marital status between the reasons prevent the participants of the survey to attend the physical activity. One-Way ANOVA is also used to learn whether there is a meaningful difference in terms of the educational status between the reasons prevent the attendees to participate in these areas for physical activity.

3 Findings

Table 1. Demographic Information Table of People Visit the Park and Recreation Areas

Variables		n	%	Total
Gender	Male	99	49,5	200
	Female	101	50,5	
Marital status	Married	70	35,5	200
	Single	130	65,5	
Educational Status	Primary Education	22	11,0	200
	Secondary Education	9	4,5	
	High School	37	18,5	
	University	124	62,5	
	Post Graduate	8	4,0	
Monthly Income	1300-2000	105	52,5	200

DOI: 10.1051/shsconf/20173701065

	2000-3000	52	26,0	
	3000-5000	26	13,0	
	5000-10000	17	8,5	
Job	Student	81	40,5	200
	Nurse	6	3,0	
	Unemployed	3	1,5	
	Self-employed	44	22,0	
	Engineer	9	4,5	
	Teacher	18	9,0	
	House wife	15	7,5	
	Retired	6	3,0	
	Pharmacist	1	,5	
	Doctor	9	4,5	
	Coach	1	,5	
	R&D	1	,5	
	Footballer	3	1,5	
	Lawyer	3	1,5	
Age	15-20	50	25,0	200
	21-26	64	32,0	
	27-32	26	13,0	
	33-38	17	8,5	
	39-44	21	10,5	
	45-50	8	4,0	
	51-56	4	2,0	
	57-62	3	1,5	
	63-68	3	1,5	
	69-74	2	1,0	
	75-80	2	1,0	

There are 101 (50,5%) male and 99 female (49,5%) participants in this research. It is seen when the table is evaluated that 130 (65,5%) of the attendees are single and 70 (35,5%) of them are married. The educational status of 124 (62,5%) of them is University. About the monthly income, 105 of them are in the interval of 1300-2000 Turkish liras. It is also observed from the table that 81 (40,5%) of them are students and 44 (22,0%) of them are self-employed. About the age groups, 32% of them is in 21-26 age range, and 25% of them is in the 15-20 age range.

Table-2. T-Test Results of the Scale Points of Factors Prevent the Participation to Venue Selection and Activity regarding the Gender

	Gender	n	X	ss	t	p
Physical Activity Venue Selection	Female	99	18,07	5,65	-,726	,469
	Male	101	18,78	7,97		
Factors Prevent the Participation to Physical Activity	Female	99	28,93	9,91	-1,260	,209
	Male	101	30,86	11,57		

There is not a significant difference relating to the gender in the scale points of the attendees visit Özgürlük Park, and Recreation for physical activity [t=-,726, p>.05]. This result can be commented as the venue selections for physical activity don't differentiate with regard to the gender.

Table-3: T-Test Results of the Scale Points of the Factors Prevent to Attend to Physical activity and Venue Selection

	Marital Status	n	X	ss	t	p
Physical Activity Venue Selection	Married	70	15,92	5,24	-3,88	,000
	Single	130	19,77	7,34		
Factors Prevent the Participation to Physical Activity	Married	70	27,47	10,34	-2,37	,019
	Single	130	31,22	10,85		

Concerning this finding, the H1-1 Hypothesis called 'Is there a meaningful difference regarding the gender between the scale points of people visit Özgürlük Park and Recreation are for physical activity?' is denied, there is not a significant differentness.
Besides, there is also not a substantial discrepancy in terms of the gender in scale points of people about the reasons of not to attend to physical activities in those areas [t=-1,260, p>.05]. The level point averages of women (x=28,93) about the reasons of not to attend to physical activities in those areas are higher than the scores of male attendees (x=30,86).
This finding can be interpreted as the scale points about the reasons of not to attend to physical activities in those areas don't differentiate regarding the gender. Based on this conclusion, the H1-4 Hypothesis called 'Is there a significant difference in terms of the gender in scale points of people about the reasons of not to attend to physical activities in those areas?' is rejected, there is not a significant discrepancy.

There is an important difference in terms of the marital status in the scale points of people visit Özgürlük Park and recreation area for physical activity. [t=-3,88, p<.05]. This finding can be commented as the venue selections differentiate in terms of the marital status. According to this finding, the H1-2 Hypothesis called 'Is there a meaningful differentness regarding the marital status in scale points of venue selection of people visit Özgürlük Park and recreation area for physical activity?' is accepted, the significant discrepancy exists.

There is also a meaningful difference concerning marital status in scale points about the reasons of not to attend to physical activities in those areas. [t=-2,37, p>,05]. This conclusion can be interpreted as the venue selections differentiate concerning the marital status. Based on this finding, the H1-5 Hypothesis called 'Is there a significant difference in terms of the marital status in scale points of reasons of not to attend to activities in those areas by people visit Özgürlük park and recreation are for physical activity?' is accepted, the meaningful difference exists.

Table-4: Results of ANOVA for Educational Status and Results of Post Hoc Test TUKEY for Educational Status of Scale Points of Factors Prevent to Attend to Physical Activity and Venue Selection

	Educational Status	n	X	ss	f	p	TUKEY
Physical activity Venue selection	Primary School	22	14,36	3,83	2,90	,023	1-4
	Secondary School	9	19,33	6,61			
	High School	37	17,40	5,65			
	University	124	19,24	7,56			
	Post Graduate	8	20,75	4,52			
	Total	200	18,43	6,91			
Factors prevent to attend to the physical activity	Primary School	22	26,31	10,86	2,65	,034	1-5
	Secondary School	9	28,55	7,264			
	High School	37	27,45	11,30			
	University	124	30,83	10,37			
	Post Graduate	8	38,37	13,44			
	Total	200	29,91	10,80			

There is not a significant difference in terms of the educational status in venue selection scale points of people visit Özgürlük park and recreation are for physical activity. [f=2,90, p>.05]. This finding can be interpreted as the venue selections for Özgürlük park recreation areas don't differentiate concerning the educational status.

Based on this conclusion, the H1-3 Hypothesis called 'Is there a meaningful discrepancy in terms of the educational status in venue selection scale points of people visit those areas?' is rejected, there is not a significant difference.

There is also not an important difference regarding the educational status in scale points for the reasons of not to attend to physical activities in Özgürlük park and recreation areas for physical activity. [f=2,65, p>.05]. This outcome can be commented as the scale points for the reasons of not to attend to physical activities in those areas don't differentiate regarding the educational status.

According to this outcome, the H1-6 Hypothesis called 'Is there a notable discrepancy regarding the educational status in scale points for the reasons of not to attend to physical

DOI: 10.1051/shsconf/20173701065

activities in Özgürlük park and recreation area?' is denied, a significant difference could not be found.

According to the results of Tukey test, there is not a meaningful difference for the venue selection scale points between primary and secondary education [f=2,68, p>.05]. A significant difference could not be found between elementary and High school as well. [f=1,82, p>.05]. There is not an important discrepancy between primary education and post graduate [f=2,80, p>.05], but a remarkable difference is found when the primary school graduates and bachelors are compared. [f=1,57, p<.05]. It can be said under these data that there is only one meaningful difference between the scale points of people from primary school and university categories.

4 Discussion and Conclusion

The projects about being used the park and recreation areas as the physical activity places have importance in regard to the determination of the factors prevent the participation or increase or decrease the attendance of the visitors for physical activity. In line with the observations obtained from these findings, it is possible to provide more visitors to benefit from these areas for physical activity with the help of planning and management decisions. It is aimed in my this study that to specify the factors affect the participation, venue selection for physical activity in terms of the variables of gender, age, educational status, marital status, the monthly net income of the users in Kadıköy in İstanbul.

It is found that the reasons of not to attend to the physical activities in these recreation areas don't differentiate with regard to the gender. In other words, the reasons of not to join to the physical activity in those areas don't change in terms of being male or female. It is pointed out in this research that the restrictive causations to attend to physical activity are almost the same for both women and men. Salguero, Gonzalez-Boto, Tuero, Marquez determined in their study about the motivation reasons of young swimmers to sport that there is not a substantial difference based on the gender, [18].

In contrast with these findings, Johnson et al., determined in their research that there are gender-based different perceptions in the participations of female and male attendees to the physical activity, [7]. According to Johnson and his team, this difference mostly results from the security perception. Therefore, the low safety perception may reduce the participation of females to join to the physical activity in those areas. The users of Özgürlük Park and recreation areas feel themselves secure in contrast with the indication of Jonhson et al. (Table-2). On the other side, it is determined in the research of Tsai with 246 male and 415 female attendees that the motivation levels of the individuals for joining to the exercise don't differentiate in terms of the marital status and sub-dimensions, [24]. On the other hand, it can be said through our research that there is a difference in terms of the marital status for attending to physical activities. In line with this result, the marital status of the people has a positive or adverse effects on participation of people to physical activity in those areas. In male-dominated societies, since the women adapt the mission of raising children and dealing with the house works, they may not spare time for physical activity; we can say via our project that the factor of being married can negatively effect the participation to join in the physical activity (Table-3). There is found a significant difference in venue selection scale points for physical activity. This may be derived from being considered the damages from outside due to be single or married. We can point out that the married individuals evaluate the place both for oneself and the family.

It is confirmed when the findings obtained are analyzed that there is determined the difference between the attendees who graduated from the university and post graduate. The points of the participators whose educational status is high school and below are lower than the participants who graduated from university and post graduate (Table-4 ANOVA). This result can be commented on the level of education increases; the individual acquires a healthy living awareness. Similarly, Droomers, Schrijvers, and Mackenbach found that the undereducated people attend to the physical activities with a lower ratio in comparison with the bachelors, [4]. In parallel with these approaches, the study of Aşıkkutlu can be shown as the example. Aşıkkutlu pointed out that the motivation and restrictors differentiate regarding the educational status, [2].

There is not found an important discrepancy with regard to the age, occupational groups and monthly income in scale points about not to attend to the physical activities in park and recreation areas. In other words, these reasons don't differentiate based on the age, gender, job or the monthly income status. But, James found in his research that the appearance of the women may limit the participation to the activities in public, [6]. Moreover, according to the statement of Kunz and Graham, the gender is a major factor effect the attendance to the physical activity and the young individuals are in the tendency to attend to the physical activity more than the older ones, [11].

The results and recommendations below are obtained by this research that determines the factors prevent the attendance of the individual from joining in the physical activities and the venue selection and analyzes the demographic features based on the variables of gender, educational status, marital status, income level, job, and age.

It is determined at the end of the research that the factors that are useful for venue selection don't differentiate regarding the variables of gender, income level, job and age variables. In other words, being female or male, single or married, high or low income don't effect to choose the park and recreation areas as the physical activity area.

There is not found a difference based on the gender when the factors prevent the attendance are analyzed. The gender ratios are close to each other. In another finding, a significant difference is determined regarding the marital status. There is a large discrepancy in the venue selection of married individuals in comparison with the single ones. It is stated that the families have children want playgrounds and places such as kindergartens and also the animal shelters for our animal friends. Since the households with the child are scared of an attack of the animals, they mentioned that they don't feel at ease. It is suggested to the local administrations that more playgrounds and the animal shelters are the necessities for families with child and our animal friends.

130 of the attendees are bachelors and above, 70 of them graduated from the University and below. Based on this finding, the high-school graduate people who prefer the park and recreation areas are in the minority. The theatrical activities, reading activities, Pilates and Zumba, are recommended to increase this minority ratio. I think that the engaging activities may positively affect the venue selection. We should catch the fancies of people from each age group and the educational status. About the venue selection, there is not a significant difference between the primary and secondary education, primary education and the high school. But a meaningful difference exists between the individuals graduated from the primary level and the university. This situation can be explained by this issue that I've just mentioned; the activities and interests of each age and the educational group should be developed and introduced to avoid the differences in the venue selection.

References

1. Ağaoğlu, YS., Taşmaktepligil, MY., Albay, F., Bayrak, M., Paktaş, Y. (2006). Leisure Time Education and its Importance. Journal of National Education; (170): 313.
2. Aşıkkutlu, HS.(2008). Recreational Motivation and Constraints; Example of Ankara Göksu Park ve Harikalar Diyarı Park. Post Graduate. Düzce: Düzce University.

3. Daley, AJ.(2002). School-Based Physical Activity in the United Kingdom: Can It Create Physically Active Quest. (54): 21-33.
4. Droomers, M., Schrijvers, CTM., Mackenbach, JP. (2001). Educational Level and Decreases in Leisure Time Physical Activity: Predictors from the Longitudinal GLOBE Study. Journal of Epidemical Community Health.55(8): 562-568.
5. Gümüş, H.(2012). The Factors Affect the Venue Selection, and Attendance to Physical Activity of the Users Visit the Park and Recreation Areas.
6. James, K.(1995). Ownership of Space: Its Impact on Recreational Participation of Young Women. Perth, Western Australia: Edith Cowan University, Department of Leisure Sciences.
7. Johnson, CY., Bowker, JM., Cordell, K. (2001).Outdoor recreation constraints: Au examination of race, gender, and rural dwelling. Southern rural sociology. 12: 111-113.
8. Kanbir O. (2001). Health Conscious in Sport and First aid. 2nd Edition. Bursa: Ekin Bookstore
9. Karaküçük, S. (2008). Recreation and Use of Free Time. 6th Edition. Ankara: Gazi Bookstore.
10. Kozanoğlu, ME.(2004). Adolescents and Exercise. 111-117
11. Kunz, JL., Graham, K. (1996). Life Course Changes in Alcohol Consumption in Leisure Activities of Men and Women. Journal of Drug Issues,26: 805-827.
12. Lustyk, BKM., Widman, L., Paschane, AE., Olson KC.(2004). Physical Activity and Quality of Life: Assessing the Influence of Activity Frequency, Intensity, Volume, and Motives. Behavioral Medicine. Fall (30), 124-131.
13. MacPhail, A., Lyons, D., Quinn, S., Hughes, AM., Keane, S., A.(2010). Framework for Lifelong Involvement in Sport and Physical Activity: the Irish Perspective. Leisure Studies. 29 (1): 85-100.
14. Mengütay, S., Demir, A, and Çoşan F.(2002). Sportsman's Source Project for the Olympics, Application Model for Guiding Children in Sports in Turkey, Basic Sports Training. 1st edition. İstanbul Olympic Games Preparation and Regulation Board, Eğitim Publishing No:2.
15. O'Connel, M., Lieberman, L., Petersen, S.(2006). The use textile modeling and real guidance as instructional strategies in physical activity for children who are blind. Practice Report. Journal of Visual Impairment & Blindness, August, 471-478.
16. Özbey, S., Çelebi, M.(2011). The basis of Recreation. In: Mirzeoğlu, N. Edt., Introduction to Sports Sciences. Ankara: Spor Publishing House. 241-270.
17. Özer, K.(2010). Physical Fitness. 3rd Edition Ankara: Nobel Publishing and Distribution.
18. Salguero, A., Gonzalez-Boto, R., Tuero, C., Marquez, S.(2004). Relationship Between Perceived Physical Ability and Sport Participation Motives in Young Competitive Swimmers. Journal of Sports Medicine and Physical Fitness. 44(3): 294-299.
19. Stampfer, MJ., Hu, FB., Manson, JE., Rimm, EB., Willett, WC.(2000). Primary Prevention of Coronary Heart Disease in Women through Diet and Lifestyle. New England Journal of Medicine; 343 (1): 16-22.
20. Türk Dil Kurumu (2005). Türkçe Sözlük. 10. Baskı. Ankara: Türk Dil Kurumu Yayınları.
21. Tekin, A., Ramazanoğlu, F., ve Tekin, G.(2004). Social Areas in Sport, Featured Topics 1. Ankara: Bıçaklar Bookstore.
22. Tezcan, M.(1994). Sociology of Using the Leisure Time. 4. Edition. Ankara: Atilla Bookstore.

DOI: 10.1051/shsconf/20173701065

23. Torkildsen, G.(2005). Leisure and Recreation Management. 5th Edition. London: Routledge.
24. Tsai, EH.(2005). Cross-Cultural Study of Influence of Perceived Positive Outcome on Participation in Regular Active Recreation: Hong Kong and Australian University Students. Leisure Sciences. 27(5): 385-404.
25. Vaizoğlu, SA., Akça, O., Akdağ, A., Aykut, A., Omar, AH., Coşkun, O., Güler, Ç. (2004). Determination of Physical Activity Level in Young Adults.
26. Veal, AJ.(1992). Definitions of Leisure and Recreation. Reproduced from: Australian Journal of Leisure and Recreation. 2(4): 44-48,52.
27. Yetim A.(2011). Sociology and Sports. Ankara: Berikan Publishing House.
28. Zorba, E.(2001). Physical Fitness. 2nd Edition. Ankara: Gazi Bookstore.
29. Zorba, E., İkizler, HC., Tekin, A., Miçoğullar, O., Zorba, E.(2006). Sports for All. İstanbul: Morpa Culture Publishings.
30. World Health Organization.(2010).World Health Report. http://www.who.int/whr/2010/en/index.html

Health education in the Spanish education system

Encarnación Pedrero-García[1a]

[1]Facultad de Ciencias Sociales, Universidad Pablo de Olavide, Crta. De Utrera, Km.1 Seville, ES-41013, Spain

Abstract. Health education is an instrument of Health Promotion that seeks to influence the development of healthy lifestyles by eliminating risk factors and thus influencing in a positive way the health of the population. One of the objectives of the educational system is to educate for the development of the integral health of the students as well as to provide the appropriate formation so that they have a healthy vital development from a physical perspective like psychological. To this end, the Ministry of Education, Culture and Sport and in collaboration with the Ministry of Health, Social Services and Equality work on the development of actions and the implementation of stable programs of education and health promotion in the school environment With the purpose of fomenting and supporting an educational model directed to the development of the integral health of the whole educative community.
Keywords: healty, education, spanish

1 Introduction

Education for Health, understood as part of Health Promotion, is an important segment of education in general and a means of promoting health. That is why the educational system is consolidating as one of the most appropriate places to implement Health Education programs in the community.

The need for Health Education to be present in school curricula became clear from the LOGSE [6]. The Educational Policy, which is reflected in the General Organic Law of the Educational System [6], emphasized the importance of giving it a cross-curricular treatment, thus constituting a wake-up call for educators regarding new curricular approaches in terms of Health and enabling in turn the adequacy of the educational system to the needs that a modern society has to generate health. The subsequent educational laws that followed LOPEG [9], LOCE [7] and LOE [8] are implicitly or explicitly implicit in the idea of maintaining this educational need.

Being aware that the educational system as a whole does not constitute the community, but it is part of it and it is in him that the habits and attitudes with which the students will

[a] Corresponding author: epedgar@upo.es

live their life later as adults. It is important, therefore, that the socializing process be given in coordinates that facilitate the appearance of all those skills that help the subject to live in fullness, encouraging the development of healthy habits that contribute to their personal and social development, ultimately their integral development.

Health education must be concretized in the school at the level of objectives, contents, activities, methodology and evaluation. In short, it should be formally considered within the status that the educational project of the centers contributes. Health Education understood as health promotion is an important part of education in general and a means of promoting health.

2 Methodology

The followed methodology is qualitative by using data analysis with the software Atlas.ti to review hundreds of documents on the subject and responds to the objectives that we propose with this investigation:

- Define health promoting schools.
- Determine their characteristics
- Analyze Health education in the Spanish educational curriculum

2.1 Definition of health promoting schools

The development of Health Education within the educational framework is endorsed by a number of well-known institutions such as WHO, UNESCO, UNICEF, the Council of Europe and the European Commission, as well as the Organization for Economic Co-operation and Development (OECD). All of these institutions consider it to be the most effective way of promoting the long-term adoption of healthy lifestyles and the only way for health education to reach the younger population (childhood, adolescence and early life) Youth), regardless of factors such as social class, gender, or the level of education achieved by parents.

This type of school is defined as "a human community that cares about the health of all its members: students, teachers and non-teaching staff as well as all those who relate to the school community" [15] and not only as efficient systems in producing education. On the other hand, for WHO [13] "A health promoting school is defined as one that constantly strengthens the characteristics that make it a healthy environment for living, learning and working.

The origin of this network is in the works carried out in the eighties of the last century within the Pilot Project on health education that had its continuity in the recommendations in the Conference on "Promotion of Education for Health", held in Strasbourg in September these proposals and guidelines are in line with the priorities set by WHO in the field of health promotion, as well as with the conclusions of the Dublin Conference on "Prevention and Health Education in Schools "sponsored by the European Economic Community [6]. According to its organization chart, in each country there is a network coordinator (who in Spain, member of the network since March 1993, is located in the CIDE).

2.2 Characteristics of health promoting schools

With respect to health promoting schools, we find that they have to meet a series of characteristics in order to be able to define them as such. Castillo Lemee [1, p.43] points out the following:

a) The health promotion school considers health education through all aspects of school life and its relationships with the community and not only in classroom activities.

b) It is based on a comprehensive health model that includes the interactions between the physical, mental, social and environmental aspects.
c) It focuses on the active participation of students through a wide variety of methods that contribute to developing skills.
d) Recognize that the health of students is subject to multiple influences and takes into account pre-existing beliefs, values and attitudes.
e) Recognize that there are skills and processes that form the basis of all health improvement and include them as objectives of the school curriculum.
f) It tends to develop in the student a positive image of himself, and to increase his capacity for self-control, as basic elements of the promotion of good health.
g) Recognize the importance of the physical environment and its physiological and effective effects on students and school personnel.
h) See the promotion of health in the school related to the welfare of the school staff and recognize the role of example that plays with the child.
i) It considers the parents of the students as an indispensable support for the school in the promotion of health.
j) Engages school medical services to participate in the educational program and to help students make better use of the resources they can offer.

2.3 Health education in the Spanish educational curriculum

In Spain, regarding the teaching of Health Education for teachers and secondary school teachers, part of the approval of the General Organic Law of the LOGSE Educational System in 1990 [6]. From this moment we start To advance in the implementation of this subject in the curriculum of the Diploma of Teaching, and in the Degree in Education Sciences, today what would be the different degrees in Education and Pedagogy, constituted the subject in most cases as optional .

Health education is included in the curriculum as a transverse matter, that is, as a teaching that does not belong to a particular area of curriculum development, but must be present across the different areas. Through the different regional norms of development of curricula of the stages of infantile, primary, secondary education, Baccalaureate, adult education is based on the need for Health Education.

In secondary and upper secondary education, cross-curricularity is reflected in a holistic sense, emphasizing the need to implement an education in values and attitudes, taking into account the principle of integration of LOGSE [6], but without specifying what capacities of the different transversal themes , And especially the one of Education for the Health, must acquire the students at the end of this educational stage.

After the LOGSE [6] and some attempts at new unapproved educational laws, a new educational law appears, Organic Law 2/2006, of May 3, Education [8]. This law retains part of the LOGSE [6], some extremes of the Law of Quality [7].

The LOE [8] establishes, at all levels of compulsory education, objectives that aim to develop the affective and psychosocial capacities of students, to value and respect the gender aspects and the equality of rights and opportunities between men and women, to strengthen the habits of corporal care and health and to critically evaluate the social habits related to health, consumption, care of living beings and the environment.

In addition, all stages of the LOE [8] deal with important aspects of Health Education in the areas of: Knowledge of the environment, Natural Sciences, Physical Education and Citizenship Education. The school therefore has the responsibility of integrating health education in its projects, and this means above all promoting the value of health among all the groups that make up the school community, throughout the training period, so that healthy behaviors are facilitated, and the decision-making and personal choice of healthy lifestyles is promoted from the autonomy and the establishment of lasting positive attitudes towards health care.

3 Research result

The European Network of Health Promoting Schools aims to facilitate the adoption of healthy lifestyles in a health-friendly environment to the educational community by agreeing that a health promotion school is one that responds to the following objectives [10, p.65]:

a) To promote healthy lifestyles and to offer students and teachers options that are both realistic and attractive in terms of health.
b) Define clear goals of health promotion and safety for the whole school community.
c) Provide a framework and study aimed at health promotion, taking into account: the conditions of the school building, sports and recreational spaces, school canteens, security aspects of access, etc. .
d) Develop the sense of individual, family and social responsibility in relation to health.
e) Enable the full physical, psychic, and social development, and the acquisition of a positive image of itself in all students.
f) Promote good relations between all members of the educational community and the community with its environment.
g) Integrate health education in the Curriculum Project consistently, using methodologies that encourage the participation of students in the educational process.
h) To provide students with the knowledge and skills necessary to make responsible decisions regarding their personal health and to contribute to the development of the health and safety of their environment.
i) Identify and use existing resources in the community to develop actions in favor of health promotion.
j) Expand the concept of school health services to make them an educational resource that helps the community to properly use the health system.

These objectives respond to a precise conception of the educational function, which refers to the school institution must support its students so that, based on a formed and critical opinion, they can make their own decisions in a conscious and responsible manner, at the same time Who acquire the conceptual, procedural resources and skills that allow them to act with autonomy in the resolution of the problems that affect them in the field of health.

Therefore, the acquisition of skills, self-determination and community-oriented action are common concepts to health promotion and education when they are interpreted as a support to be socially critical, reflexive and questioning in the framework of a transformative educational culture. Such an orientation encourages many actors, in a school inserted in their community, to share their points of view and their experiences and to play their role in developing knowledge about their reality and how to modify it in the direction of increase their quality of life. In this way, the development of the concept School health promoter has become a fundamental principle in the orientation of the movements of Health Education [13].

Red SHE (Schools for Health in Europe network) aims to support organizations and professionals in the field of development and maintenance of health promotion in school, providing a European platform whose main objective is Support organizations and professionals in the development and maintenance of health promotion in schools in all countries. The network of Schools for Health in Europe focuses on making schools that promote health and school health a more integrated part of the policies that are developed between the education and health sectors in Europe.

Autonomic Networks of Health Promoting Schools: The participation of the different Autonomous Communities in networks promoting health is developed in two different ways. On the one hand, there are Communities that have created their own networks of health promoting schools, as in Aragon, the Canaries, Cantabria and Extremadura. Other Communities, however, are integrated into the European Network of Health Promoting Schools, through different calls. Such is the case of Asturias, Valencia and Navarre.

Specifically, in Spain, results show that 400-450 health promoting schools are currently part of this network, and the most active Spanish regions are Aragón, Canarias, Cantabria and Navarra.

Most centers belonging to this network include Health Education in the school curriculum, and school teachers and management teams are the ones who suggest the activities. It is then clear the training needs of these teachers on different intervention areas. Moreover, schools face obstacles that hinder development on Health Education programmes, namely lack of material, economic and staff resources. Hence the need of external professionals to support their programme developments. In short, the health promotion school is open to the community, integrates with its processes and uses the resources it can offer by associating it with its programs. The European Network of Health Promoting Schools aims to facilitate the adoption of healthy lifestyles in a health-friendly environment for the educational community.

4 Conclusion

There is increasing evidence that approaches are most effective when Include health education within a comprehensive school approach. These approaches create an environment of physical, social and learning support, which Students, families, communities and organizations. Teaching /Learning about any health issue, such as healthy eating or mental and emotional health, will require linking with broader initiatives on school life in general and the community, if they are to have an impact on behavior related to Health or the situation of the same in the long term.

The international literature review [4], [5] supports the effectiveness of schools approach to health, in terms of the results it can generate. West et al. [12] investigated the effects of school as a whole on student health behaviors. Their results also served to support the approach of health promoting schools. Stewart-Brown [11] concluded that school programs that were effective in changing youth health or health-related behaviors were those that involved activities in more than one area.

Specifically in the case of Spain, Garcia-Vazquez's research [3] concludes that there is sufficient evidence that a proper incorporation of the health education in the educative centres, following the criteria and recommendations of The European Network of Health Promoting Schools, produce positive effects on the students including health improvement.

The United Nations has recognized the potential of schools to influence not only the Educational situation of the youth, but also in their health and economic development. This is evident in the importance given to primary education Universal and the elimination of gender disparity in primary education as secondary, within the Millennium Development Goals. There is a link between good health, educational outcomes and the studies. There is also a well-established relationship between school the improvement of health [2]. These relationships imply that the improvement in efficiency in one sector can potentially benefit another sector, so that the Schools are an important place for both education and health.

References

1. Castillo Lemee, F. *La escuela promotora de salud.* En A. García, (Coord.). Claves de Educación para la Salud. Murcia: DM, (1998).
2. Cohen, S. Social Relationships and Health. American Psychologist, **59**(8), 676–684, (2004). https://doi.org/10.1037/0003-066X.59.8.676
3. García-Vázquez, J. Effects of the School for Health network on students' behaviour in Asturias (Spain). Health Promotion International, **32**(2), 271–279, (2017). https://doi.org/10.1093/heapro/dau076
4. Leger, L.S. & Nutbeam, D. A Model for Mapping Linkages Between Health and Education Agencies to Improve School Health. Journal of School Health. **70**, 2, 45–50, (2000). http://doi.org/10.1111/j.1746-1561.2000.tb07239.x
5. Leger, L. S., Kolbe, L., Lee, A., McCall, D. and Young, I. School health promotion: achievements, challenges and priorities. In McQueen, D. and Jones, C. (eds), *Global Perspectives on Health Promotion Effectiveness.* Springer ScienceþBusiness Media, LLC, New York, (2007).
6. Ley Orgánica 1/1990, de 3 de octubre, de Ordenación General del Sistema Educativo (BOE Nº. 238, 4 de octubre de 1990).
7. Ley Orgánica 10/2002, de 23 de diciembre, de Calidad de la Educación (BOE Nº. 307, de 24 de diciembre de 2002).
8. Ley Orgánica 2/2006, de 3 de mayo, de Educación (BOE Nº. 106, de 4 de mayo de 2006).
9. Ley Orgánica 9/1995, de 20 de noviembre, de Participación, Evaluación y Gobierno de Centros Docentes (BOE Nº. 278, 21 de noviembre de 1995).
10. Pedrero García, E. Educación para la Salud y Pedagogía de la Muerte. Tesis Doctoral. Sevilla: Universidad Pablo de Olavide, (2012).
11. Stewart-Brown, S. What is the evidence on school health promotion in improving health or preventing disease and, specifically, what is the effectiveness of the health promoting schools approach? Copenhagen, WHO Regional Office for Europe (Health Evidence Network report, (2006) http://www.euro.who.int/document/e88185.pdf
12. West, P., Sweeting, H., & Leyland, A. School effects on pupils' health behaviours: evidence in support of the health promoting school. Research Papers in Education - Policy and Practice, **19**(3), 261–29, (2004). https://doi.org/http://dx.doi.org/10.1080/02671522.2004.10058645
13. Williams, M. y Young, I. (Eds.). Promotiong the health of Young people in Europe. Health Education in Schools: a trainign manual of teachers and others working with Young people. Edimburgo: WHO/HEBS, (1993).
14. World Health Organization. Health-Promoting Schools: a healthy setting for living, learning and working. Geneva: WHO, (1997).
15. Young, I. (Coord.). La educación para la Salud en el ámbito educativo. Madrid: Comisión Europea/MEC. Policopia, (1995).

Teaching vocational subjects in a foreign language

Eva Ticha[1a]

[1]University of Hradec Kralove, Rokitanskeho 62,500 02 Hradec Kralove, Czech Republic

Abstract. The article deals with the main aspects and problems of teaching vocational subjects in a foreign language (English) at various degrees of education focusing mainly on secondary and concisely on tertiary learning. The main principles and methods have been outlined, supported by longstanding experience in teaching under the CLIL mode. The answers to both language-related and subject-related questions are sought.
Keywords: CLIL methods; language related subjects; knowledge related subjects

1 Introduction

More than two decades, methods of Content and Language Integrated Learning (hereinafter CLIL) have been used, they have been gradually implemented in all levels of educational systems all over the world and intensively developed and legitimized in most countries in Europe. The CLIL acronym was preceded by various similar terms as described in "CLIL—A Pedagogical Approach from the European Perspective" [1] or "History of CLIL" [2]. CLIL theoretical framework has been built [3] and numerous definitions formed. However, some calls for their clarification have appeared [4]. Concurrently, interest in implementing CLIL has been growing and has become "a breeding (nutritive) ground" for demanded (and sometimes policy-driven) research. The most frequent fields of study is language (L2), followed by attitudes and motivation of learners. The question whether "CLIL leads to better subject matter knowledge than traditional learning"[3] has not brought clear answers yet, and therefore "more research is needed to entangle the considerable number of context variables and their influence on older pupils' knowledge acquisition" [3]

The paper firstly describes the background and context of researched objects, particularly some practices in implementing CLIL in observed schools and finally focuses mainly on post-teaching (learning) self-evaluation, motivation and preferences of / pupils / students of a particular secondary comprehensive school and only marginally compares some results with a smaller sample of university students. The objective of the research is to obtain students opinion of their learning subjects in English and to verify the initial

[a] Corresponding author: eva.ticha@uhk.cz

hypothesis based on observations that (some) students appreciate their study and benefit from getting higher knowledge in lexis, in particular. However, the prime purpose and still the most meaningful reason is to get a feedback and a sort of "fuel" for further teachers' development and appropriate activities while teaching in a CLIL mode.

2 History and background

One of the first results dealing with CLIL practicing in the Czech Republic were published in 2008 (processing the EU document "Promoting language learning and linguistic diversity: An action plan 2004—06") [5]. In the same year the first project of National Institute for Further Education on implementation of CLIL methods started. Both institutions provided the identical data (6%) about the number of schools using CLIL in 2008. For the year 2011, the National Institute published the percentage (19 %) of CLIL inclusion in Czech elementary and secondary school educational plans and even 30 % as its implementation according to headteachers' estimates. The percentage has not changed significantly so far.

The research sample school belongs to the system of secondary comprehensive schools. The particular school integrates business, economics, social studies and languages (intended mainly for the public). The curriculum has usually included a vocational subject – business correspondence - since this type of schools was established. From today's perspective, the subject was based on CBI method (Content-based Instruction) with traditional translations from L1 to L2 (and vice versa) and memorising business letter phrases. Since 2007 it has been included in CLIL subjects (L2 is only English, unlike almost a hundred years ago when French and German were taught) together with economics. In 2013 CLIL biology classes started in cooperating (team teaching) as the only CLIL item based on a Project. As well as in Slovakia a foreign language is used up to maximum 50 % of the lesson time in this country. Therefore all subjects are taught independently both in Czech (L1) or in English (mainly L2), in 45-minute classes (in ratio L1: L2 – 1 : 1, 2 : 2 or 2 : 1) and moreover only in classes of Enhanced Language Teaching, Although CLIL is not confined to higher-achieving students and it should not be an approach for the elite [6] in other classes CBI method has been used only as a part of general language (L2) so far.

Before implementing the first CLIL subjects (business correspondence and economics in English) in 2008 two involved teachers (both language and content qualified) decided to follow the basic principles of CLIL [7] – the topic shall be at least as important as the language, the theme and task should be the driving forces, teachers are supposed to be more facilitators than instructors, making mistakes is a natural process – fluency should be over accuracy (but CLIL is not language teaching without grammar) [8] and teachers should encourage students for their life-long learning. Classes planning was designed (in spite of different content focused and offered subject) according to Brinton and Holton [9] three traditional stages: into – including introduction, initial knowledge and motivation; through – as the main part developing both skills, opening new content, using necessary grammar and processing relevant vocabulary; beyond – stage of consolidation and application, resulting in individual presentations.

Naturally, the essential question was how to present a new subject content using a foreign language, how to explain to students a large number of new words they are exposed to and particularly the words they do not know in their mother tongue (L1) or how to minimize using the L1 [8].

Business correspondence is a subject with a long tradition and sufficient number of various sources less or more convenient for school purposes. Also presenting this subject while giving instructions does not seem to be an obstacle to learning, but yet students' attitudes and final results are usually not much satisfying. One of the CLIL principles –

language does not have to be accurate to be communicative – is modified. Implementing of the other two courses has been a typical example of pioneering and searching own ways in CLIL story. The first experiments were translations of Czech textbooks to English, which failed from many reasons not only because of rather different conceptions of the books. To use (mostly UK) sources helped to tackle the issue considerably but the main problem was to find an appropriate textbook. The conditions have changed dramatically recently as the first CLIL school books in Biology appeared in the Czech market. Economics is based on an English content textbook completed with ESP textbooks and inspired by those books, in particular, supported by own sources. Approximately one third of the content of CLIL subject is almost the same as in Czech version (for example Marketing), one third is quite similar (Human Resources) and one third is different (Businesses).

Vocabulary development which is arguably central to language acquisition and use [10] was a part of the inquiry and is mentioned later.

As described above a foreign language is used up to maximum 50%, this regulation helps in some way to minimize the use of L1 and all CLIL teachers take it seriously trying to keep the character of an English lesson as much as possible. Naturally, there are some unpredictable situations but many times more advanced and trained students can help solve the problem in L2.

Apart a sample secondary school the research also included just a quick preview done at the Faculty of Management (University of Hradec Kralove) which offers 62 content-based classes (2016) with 15 content-based involved teachers (from assistants to professors). All of the teachers′ level of L2 is mostly B2 of CEFRL except for the members of the Department of Management of Tourism where all linguistics tutors teach professional L2 and have also some experience with CLIL elements.

3 Methodology and data

In the paper two analyses have been used: the quantitative analysis based on questionnaire with both closed and open questions and a qualitative one focused on opening questions and observation. Time-lapse questionnaire was designed to search three basic aspects in 15 questions: 1) students′ motivation attitude to CLIL subject, 2) effects on their level of L2, 3) students′ preferable strategies in their studies.

In a 5-year continuous observation and evaluation 270 16-year-old students of the secondary school and 135 18-year-olds participated in the questionnaire, 35 students of third grade of Management of Tourism were interested in filling out a survey form and also 63 Erasmus students of the Faculty of Management were addressed to join the survey.

3 Results

3. 1 Attitudes and motivation

CLIL subjects have become a part of curriculum in the focus secondary school and they are compulsory. The school management like many headteachers in other schools have decided about a possible choice of CLIL subject according to existing appropriate teachers′ qualifications or have motivated willing colleagues to expanded their competence or degree.

At first younger pupils were asked about their attitudes to English, biology and biology in English. Students prefer English because they can communicate much more easily about everyday life, events, hobbies, etc. The percentage was very high – 92% but not surprising. Foreign language does not seem as boring as one of the principles claims – "... they (students) are not asked to discuss "vox-pop" content as in standard learning books... but because the content is important in itself" [11]. To speak in detail of viruses or bacteria seems not to be as attractive as that "vox-pop" content. Nevertheless, there was not a significant difference in students' interests between biology in L1 and L2.

Even though economics is one of the most important subjects for the students' future jobs, the results of older pupils attitudes differ only slightly (85 % of preferences were for English). About 5 % did not like all three subjects but on the other hand 18 percent appreciated the unique chance to take part in the CLIL course. In 2012 there was an experiment - students could take final exams in economics partly in English, in other words, CLIL subject was a part of their leaving exams. Students' preferences of CLIL subject went up dramatically, in fact, they considered economics in English equal to any other subject. The different result from this year is included in the total 5-year score of the focus group of older pupils.

As CLIL subjects are obligatory, students have no other choice, they were asked which other subject(s) after their one or more year experience with biology or economics in L2 they would choose. The results partly correspond to existing CLIL subjects in this country. Most frequently indicated are civics, history and geography (72 %) followed by all possible subjects. Sciences and mathematics, in particular, were reported only rarely. Students could also mention that they would not select any and could report the reasons. Not only one answer was like this: It is better to know the contents in L1 thoroughly than in two languages not so properly. A large number of content subject teachers share the same idea. They usually feel responsible for preparing their students for demanding final exams and cannot appreciate the CLIL duality.

Finally, students were inquired about their motivation of learning CLIL. (In order to get more colourful picture about participants' motivation, the question was open.) There were three strongest motivations – marks, jobs and studying at universities. The higher the class the lower importance of marks – younger students (52 %), older ones (33%). Surprisingly a high number of students (total 46 %) even in the first grade (38 %) reported the importance of CLIL for their future jobs. 61 % of older students consider economics in L2 to be an advantage for studies at universities, which was naturally higher evaluation than in the classes of younger participants (38 %). The last more significant motivation was interest in CLIL subjects, which appeared in 8 % of interviewed students. For the first time (2017) self-education has occurred twice. Among the other possible incentives there was a humorous one: "My parents are proud of me."

3.2 Effects on students' language 2 and content subject / knowledge

After finishing courses 92 % of students reported improvement mainly in vocabulary expansion (94 %), 55 % feel that they speak more fluently, 40 % think that they got better at reading comprehension and only 7 % of interviewees suppose some positive effects on their knowledge of grammar, listening or writing comprehensions. Differences in focused CLIL subjects (biology and economics) were not significant (up to 5 %).

Students' opinions reflect the fact that most of the training time is devoted to vocabulary from the first step - getting familiar with new words to the last stages – testing the knowledge and continuous and never-ending consolidation. All possible techniques, methods and strategies are used not avoiding translation from L1 to L2, which however mainly serves as a support tool or background and is mainly employed by less advanced students or those who are just used to working with it.

Three years ago students were asked for the first time whether they feel some effects of CLIL subject on content subject / knowledge. Younger students' answers were rather evasive (don't know), or negative, if positive (from 30 participants about 2 – 3 every year), they were not able to specify how. Up to 12 students of economics admitted they could have improved. They wrote about better overlook, broadening horizons, different point of views... Almost 30 % feel that CLIL helped them in some way but they were not able to define how.

3.3 Preferable methods, techniques, strategies

Students were asked to choose any teaching / learning method, technique, strategy, activity etc. which they prefer during CLIL classes while getting familiar with new words. This year data changed the position of preferences in this time-lapse research. For the first time the most popular is reading the word in the context – 62 % (more times and try to remember it), 43 % go for an explanation in other words and form a definition, 40 % like examples, 25 % need translation from L2 to L1 and vice versa, less than 10 % mention listening and only 4 % use monolingual (paper) dictionary. One student thinks that mobile application is convenient, in fact, everybody uses it.

3.4 Tertiary education

Although only a part of questionnaire was convenient for a simple comparison of the two levels of education, the essential answers were obtained. Subject content classes at the faculty are also compulsory, there is no other choice. But 62 % expressed their positive attitude to the courses, (even 12 % were interested in some more) and 32 % would prefer different opportunities. The difference between preferences at the secondary and tertiary level are significant. Random sample of the interviewed Erasmus students revealed that about 80 % have some experience with CLIL from their studies in their home countries and that more than 50 % would prefer classes more relevant to their specialisation.

Some elements of CLIL have been implemented in teaching professional English of tourism and finance in the Department of Applied Languages [10].

4 Conclusion

During years of the time-lapse research at a focused secondary school, not many changes appeared in students´ preferences, only a slight movement towards CLIL subjects. Based on continuous observation in surveyed classes, enthusiasm of highly qualified, experienced and committed staff and also the first relatively high percentage of positive attitudes to a CLIL method when CLIL subject was experimentally implemented in a leaving exam programme (which still rather distorts the total results) higher students´ appreciation has been expected. The outcomes of questionnaire revealed quite low interest in all CLIL subjects.

Since 2007 when the first CLIL subjects were implemented, the intention has been to reach approximately the same position of CLIL subjects in preferences as the other ones, to get good reputation inside the school among other colleagues as well as outside in the public and to settle CLIL subjects in curriculum.

The second part of the initial hypothesis has proven to be true.The vast majority of students confirmed that they improved particularly in enhancing their vocabulary and also their speaking in L2 became more fluent.

As mentioned above there is "a significant number of context variables and their influence on older pupils'[3]. They occur in any other subject - such as various students´ levels of a foreign language, teachers´ experience, personality, quality or qualifications. But in CLIL there is not only one but two subjects that have slowly merged and something similar have changed in students´ preferences or teachers´ attitudes, which certainly increases the number of the variables.

The simple questionnaire in the research has not been designed and has not aspired to unknit this issue. However the answer for the question whether CLIL leads to better subject matter knowledge than traditional learning is rather interesting. Almost one third of older pupils feel they were influenced by CLIL in their content subject in some way but were not able to state some details.

The above mentioned findings should be taken into account in further CLIL procedures and following questionnaires focused more on some students′ suggestions for improvements as the part of higher students′ involvement in CLIL courses.

Although the research analyses data of only one particular comprehensive school, some of the identified results may contribute to general discussion about teaching based on CLIL method.

Acknowledgement

The paper was supported by the IGA Project 2017run at the Faculty of Informatics and Management, University of Hradec Kralove No: 1903/1190/024302017.

References

1. Coyle D., *CLIL—A Pedagogical Approach from the European Perspective*, https://www.google.cz/?gws_rd=ssl#q=%E2%80%9CCLIL%E2%80%94A+Pedagogical+Approach+from+the+European+Perspective%E2%80%9D+(Coyle,+2008)&spf=1497537628479, (2008)
2. Hanesová D., Pokrivčáková, S. et al., *History in CLIL, CLIL in Foreign Language Education: e-textbook for foreign language teachers*, ISBN 978-80-558-0889-5, pages 8 16, (2015)
3. Van de Craen P., Mondt K., Allain L., Gao Y., *Why and How CLIL Works.* An Outline for a CLIL Theory, **16** (3) CLIL SPECIAL ISSUE 2 , pg 70, (2007)
4. Cenoz J., Genesee F., Gorter D., *Critical Analysis of CLIL*: Taking Stock and Looking Forward, Applied L Linguistics, Vol Volume **35**, Issue 3, ISSN 0142-6001, EISSN 1477-450X, (2014)
5. *Promoting language learning and linguistic diversity An action plan 2004—06*, Luxembourg: Office for Official Publications of the European Communities, ISBN 92-894-6626-X, (2004)
6. D. Graddol, *English Next*, British Council Publications, (2006)
7. Deller S., Price C., *Teaching Other Subjects Through English (CLIL)* (Resource Books for Teachers) , OUP Oxford; 01 edition, ISBN-10: 0194425789, , (2007)
8. *DEVELOPING TEACHERS.COM NEWSLETTER*, The Mackenzie School of English, issue 7/08, (2008)
9. Brinton D. M. , Holten C., *Into, Through, and Beyond, A Framework to Develop Content-Based Material,* **35**, No 4, http://dosfan.lib.uic.edu/usia/E-USIA/forum/vols/vol35/no4/p10.htm, (1997)
10. Zimmerman C., B., *Historical trends in second language vocabulary instruction,* Second Language Vocabulary Acquisition, pg 5 19, (1997)
11. Bal P., *What is CLIL?*, One-stop English, on-line www.onestopclil.com, (2008)
12. KLÍMOVÁ, B., *CLIL and the teaching of foreign languages.* Cyprus international conference on educational research (CY-ICER) 2012. Procedia of social and behavioural sciences, **47**, 572-576, (2012)

Extension activities of Kazan Imperial University in the 19th century

Evgenia Zhuravleva[1], Rimma Mardanshina[1a], Marina Kudryavtseva[1], and Anisa Khusainova[1]

[1]Kazan Federal University, Institute of Management, Economics and Finance, Russia

Abstract. Based primarily on archival documents, this article explores the development of additional education in Kazan province, Russia, in the 19th century. Its genesis is found in the varying order of Kazan Imperial University extension activities which take the form of foreign academic and scientific mobility; individual mentoring practice of recognised scholars; masters' advancement at Pedagogical Institute; creation of the Pedagogical Society in the framework of University Extension Movement. The historiography shows that in the course of its development additional education in Kazan Imperial University largely relied on the international experience and enthusiasm of its teaching staff.
Keywords: Additional education, Kazan Imperial University, University extension movement, historiography

1 Introduction

Nowadays, according to the Russian legislation, additional education is considered to be a constituent part of the Russian educational system. Therefore, the importance of historiography of education in Kazan province, Russia, in the late 19th and early 20th centuries is determined by the necessity to study the prerequisites for the formation of additional education system and to identify the underlying trends of this process. The subject of this study is extension activities of Kazan Imperial University in the context of additional education formation (the term *additional* is used to refer to education received in addition to formal instruction). Research methods cover the analysis of archival documents (Kazan Imperial University professors' speeches, reports and monographs, University Charter, the Pedagogical Society Charter, and Circular Letters of Ministry of Education etc.) and generalization of the data obtained. This made it possible to identify University widening activities as the foundation for additional education formation in the 19th and early 20th centuries.

[a] Corresponding author: rimylja@mail.ru

DOI: 10.1051/shsconf/20173701068

2 University widening activities

Additional education genesis is found in the varying order of Kazan Imperial University extension activities which take the form of foreign academic and scientific mobility of University professors and lecturers; individual mentoring practice of recognised scholars; masters' advancement at Pedagogical Institute; creation of the Pedagogical Society in the framework of University Extension Movement.

2.1 Academic and scientific mobility

In the course of its development additional education in Kazan Imperial University largely relied on the international experience and enthusiasm of the teaching staff. Practice of foreign academic trips for scientific and educational purposes vividly illustrates it.

Provision of all possible assistance to lifelong education of lecturers and professors was in the best tradition of the University. Thus, the University Council applied to the Minister of Education to provide opportunities for further improvement and introduction of supernumerary habilitation to masters and doctors of medicine who did not have a full-time chair. Paragraph 5 of the University Council Regulations states: "It is necessary that the faculties are provided with sufficient amounts of money for the maintenance of young people if they continue their education at the University, in Russia or abroad to advance in sciences and prepare for professorship" (p. 11).

2.1.1 Evgeny F. Budde

Foreign internships were provided on the results of final exams leading to Master's Degree or Doctor of Medicine and proven scientific research. Academic trips, during which post graduate students developed their professional and scientific potential, could take up to two years. Thus, in summer 1899, Russian Professor of Kazan University, slavist and linguist Evgeny F. Budde (1859-1931) studied old Czech and Polish manuscripts in the libraries and museums in Prague, Vienna, Krakow and Lviv for the purposes of historical dialectology of these languages. While studying the Czech dialects, he was accompanied by the Czech guide. In the Krakow Academy of Sciences Evgeny F. Budde familiarized with the case of publication the Historical Dictionary of Polish Language under the guidance of Professor Baudouin de Courtenay [2].

2.1.2 Nikolai N. Bulich

Academic trips abroad "were expected to expand the horizon of scientific knowledge, to elaborate the critical thinking, to familiarize with the level of philosophical sciences and humanities in the West" [3, p. 6]. Overseas internships were often an important step towards the formation of professors of Kazan University. For instance, the future professor of Russian literature Nikolai N. Bulich (1824-1889) went to Berlin in July 1857, where he spent almost two years of 'seething intellectual life'. On his return, he spent some time in St. Petersburg, where he made acquaintances with such prominent figures of science and culture of the time as F.I. Buslaev, the Korsch brothers, Y.K. Grot, I.I. Sreznevsky, I.S. Turgenev, A.V. Druzhinin. As Professor of Literature N.N. Bulich gave public lectures in Philosophy in favor of Sunday private schools in St. Petersburg and later in Kazan. His lectures titled 'Movement of European thought during the renaissance of sciences in Europe in the 15th and 16th centuries' received a flattering assessment in the newspapers of the time.

2.1.3 Nikolai A. Osokin

Another future Professor of Kazan University, Russian writer, medievalist, genealogist, State Councilor Nikolai A. Osokin (1843-1895) held an internship in Paris collecting material for writings about the First Inquisition. He later defended the Doctorate Degree in General History and in 1889 published three bulky volumes of university readings in medieval European history which "attracted flattering attention of scientists and quickly went on sale" (p. 10).

2.1.4 Alexander M. Butlerov

The world-renowned chemist, a native of Kazan, Alexander M. Butlerov (1828-1886) upon the receiving the Doctorate Degree in Chemistry and Physics and the title of Professor of Kazan University in 1857 was seconded abroad for scientific purposes. Although he 'became a chemist not in foreign lands but in Kazan,' his secondment abroad played a beneficial role in the creation and development of independent chemical school which later received his name. The Kazan University Council identified the main purpose of Butlerov's trip as 'studying the current state of chemistry in Europe and establishing personal acquaintances with famous chemists'. To achieve this goal, Council recommended: "(1) to visit famous chemical laboratories and learn the latest techniques commonly used in chemical works; (2) to attend famous chemists lectures in order to explore teaching methods; (3) not to miss an opportunity to establish personal relationships with scientists enjoying European glory and to get acquainted with different views on the current state of chemistry; (4) to purchase advanced chemical equipment for Kazan University lab and chemicals according to his own choice, and (5) on his return from abroad to submit a report to the University Council" (p. 15).

Having arrived to Germany two weeks before the end of the term, Butlerov managed to visit some laboratories and became acquainted with a number of scientists there, and then he went on the mission journey across Switzerland and Italy, and at the beginning of the winter term came to France. At that time, Paris represented an attractive destination for chemists where the most interesting lectures were held, numerous chemical laboratories worked, and the most famous chemists lived. This prompted Butlerov to dedicate most of his time to studying in Paris. In early May 1858 he went to the University of Heidelberg, which, in his opinion, ranked first in Germany in terms of the chemical science development. Butlerov's report on the academic trip was published in the University Scientific Notes, Volume III, in 1859. The report provided detailed and interesting descriptions of universities, laboratories, the review of the progress and nature of teaching chemistry in Western Europe, and the impressions made by chemists' lectures. On his return, A.M. Butlerov was immediately selected as an ordinary Professor of Kazan University, and shortly was appointed as Rector. After the first trip abroad, A.M. Butlerov went there two more times in 1861 and 1867.

2.1.5 Nikolai I. Ilminsky

The prevalence in the 19th century of such form of additional education as trips with scientific or educational purposes raises no doubt. We found a lot of evidence that not only university professors, but promising graduates from other higher education institutions were often seconded abroad. For instance, Nikolai I. Ilminsky (1822-1892), a known inspirer and creator of the educational system for foreigners in Kazan province, after graduation from the seminary and receiving bachelor's post in the class of the Arab-Turkish language, went to Damascus, Constantinople and Cairo for two and a half years "for collecting fundamental information about Mohammedan doctrine and for improvements in Arabic,

Turkish and Persian languages" (p. 21). His friend and colleague Alexey A. Bobrovnikov also spent a long time in the Kalmyk steppes studying the locals' life and their national languages.

2.1.6 A.Y. Vasiliev

Although academic trips objectives varied, the ultimate goal was to update scientists' professional activity in terms of their research or teaching methodology. In summer 1882, Associate Professor A.Y. Vasiliev visited Berlin and Leipzig Universities. He was interested in methods of teaching pure Mathematics in these educational institutions, and on his return home, he reported the results to the Physics and Mathematics Section of the Naturalists' Society of Kazan Imperial University. The report testified that prominent scientists and mathematicians of Berlin University attracted students and young promising scientists from different universities of Europe. A.Y. Vasiliev was impressed by the Mathematics 'seminary' and the activities of the Students Society of Mathematics that existed in Berlin since 1861, and which contributed to "the awakening of love for self-study among students" [4, p. 9]. Only students of Berlin University and those young Doctors who completed the University courses belonged to this community. The Society members leaving Berlin were chosen as 'alte Herren', and they regularly received term reports on the Society's activities and courses delivered at University of Berlin. The number of 'alte Herren' reached 300 people. Among them were also those who came from Russia. Society meetings took place weekly. Meeting agenda usually included reports delivered by the Society members, reviewing the content of the latest issues of scientific journals, and audience debates. The Students Society had 800-volume library and the catalog. A.Y. Vasiliev noted in his report that such societies existed in all universities and higher technical schools in Germany. Since 1883, it had been decided to publish all Student Societies reports in one book to make it possible to follow the events of teaching mathematics in universities and the scientific life of young mathematicians in Germany. On more than one occasion Russian Associate Professor A.Y. Vasiliev was surprised by the depth of special knowledge and proficiency of his German colleagues, and he used foreign experience to organise the activities of Students' Mathematics Club in his alma mater [4].

2.2 Individual mentoring practice for Nikolai I. Lobachevsky

Alongside with academic and scientific mobility, individual classes may also be viewed as one of the most important forms of additional education. This kind of learning activity was quite common university practice.

2.2.1 Johann Ch. M. Bartels

The publications on the history of Kazan University mention an excellent mathematician Johann Christian Martin Bartels (1769-1836). His works feature prominently in the German mathematical literature 'differing in rigor and clarity of presentation and evidence' [5]. Prof. A. Vasiliev thought highly of this talented teacher who played a significant role in the scientific formation of Nikolai Ivanovich Lobachevsky (1792-1856). "Thanks Bartels, teaching of pure Mathematics at Kazan University was on a par with teaching at the top universities in Germany ... Bartels lectured in the History of Mathematics on his own notes, unfolding the majestic picture of human spirit" [5, p. 4].

N.I. Lobachevsky, having received on July 10th, 1811, Master's Degree for extraordinary achievements and talent in Mathematics and Physics, and for reasoning 'the theory of elliptic motion of celestial bodies', studied Mathematics with Bartels at home for four hours a week. Under the guidance of his talented teacher, he explored The

Disquisitiones Arithmeticae and the first volume of Laplace's celestial mechanics [5]. One of the results of these classes was the argument about the resolution of algebraic equations, represented by N. Lobachevsky in 1813.

2.2.2 Franz Ksavery Bronner

Another Lobachevsky's mentor was Franz Ksavery Bronner (1758-1850), Professor of Physics, first Director of Kazan University Pedagogical Institute, where young masters were supposed to enhance their knowledge. "Bronner's talents, who acted at one time or another as a Catholic monk, an illuminee, the writer of Idylls, a mechanic, a physicist, a historian…, who was carried away by Rousseau and the French Revolution ideas, and Immanuel Kant's Critique of Pure Reason – all these could not but bewitchingly influence his students. His broad philosophical education undoubtedly contributed to the intellectual development of Lobachevsky and his companions" (p. 7).

2.3 Additional education institutions

The creation of Pedagogical Institute at Kazan University was aimed at masters' advancement and can be viewed as a prototype of additional education institution; it was academic and tutorial in nature, and its successful activities were mainly determined by brightness of the University professors and lecturers. Among them were such outstanding scientists and teachers as a great mathematician and Latin scholar, a former Assistant Professor of the University of Gottingen Caspar Friedrich Renner (1692-1772), and a famous astronomer Joseph Johann von Littrow (1781-1840), a highly educated man who followed the Schelling's philosophy. Both of them were mentors of young Lobachevsky and his companions, many of whom later became well-known scientists.

As it was mentioned above, the development of additional education in Kazan Imperial University was largely dependent on teachers' enthusiasm and their personality traits. According to contemporaries, N.I. Lobachevsky was characterized by amazing versatility and interests in areas of knowledge rather distant from each other. Holding Rector's position, he simultaneously "studied architecture with tireless diligence in order to successfully observe the construction of university buildings" [6, p. 4].

Outside the University Lobachevsky did all he could to combat ignorance. Thus, he took an active part in the activities of the Kazan Imperial Economic Society established in 1940s. He was also engaged in organising classes in plotting, accounting and commercial science for merchants' children; besides this, he developed the educational institution project for children of the lower classes, and designed craft school for boys.

Lobachevsky strongly believed in University mission to disseminate knowledge as widely as possible. He always found time to read popular lectures titled 'Folk Physics'. It was no coincidence that in Russia, lectures arranged according to the university extension system (movement developed in Europe by the end of the 19th century), were first delivered in Kazan University on the initiative of Lobachevsky, who was inspired by the idea of nationwide education involving universities [6].

2.4 Pedagogical societies

At the turn of the 19th and 20th centuries pedagogical societies attached to universities started to appear. The basis of this new phenomenon was "the idea of cooperation between universities and all educational environment of the country, the idea of harmonious and balanced national education" [7, p. 3]. Initially, an important task assigned to the university was "supervision and tireless care of teaching and education in all district provinces, so that high schools, county and parish schools were provided with ... honest and knowledgeable teachers and teaching aids" (p. 4). It was spelled out in the Charter of Russian universities 1804, Section 160. To fulfill this obligation, the School's Special Committee was established. Under Rector's chairmanship it included six ordinary professors elected by the University Board. The School's Committee exercised administrative management of the district colleges in all respects. However, over time the universities intervention in the case of middle and lower level education was considered ambiguous.

2.4.1 Kazan University Pedagogical Society as a tribute to university extension movement

The need to restore universities impact on the national education was reflected in the opening pedagogical societies. This trend was realized in Kazan University December 9, 1900, when the Pedagogical Society was created there. This was a tribute to the European trend of widening university education (University Extension), opportunities and challenges of which were actively discussed at international conferences on education, e.g. Congress on Higher Education in Paris in August 1900. Professors of Kazan University participated in such international forums and tried enthusiastically to bring fresh ideas into the university life of Kazan. In major cities of Europe and America people's universities began to appear, which were the real embodiment of the goals 'to distribute higher education'. Many educational leaders viewed their ideal model in the following way: "In its centre there is a small number of individuals, teachers and students devoted to research which requires high intellectual culture; then, a much larger number of young people studying the application of scientific technology to the arts and industry; and, finally, a huge number of curious people dedicated to education and University, which embodies science, literature and art" (p. 12).

All University faculties participated in the spread of university education – Law, Medicine, Physics and Mathematics, History and Philology. Last two faculties were given the main responsibility to train teachers for secondary schools of various types, including teachers' seminary graduates of which worked in folk schools. That is why great importance was given to the issues of upbringing the students. While many universities in Germany and France had special departments of Pedagogy and Experimental Psychology aimed at both receiving the scientific culture, and being prepared for teaching, Kazan University implemented this important idea through establishing the Pedagogical Society.

It was planned to train future teachers in accordance with all advances in this field. In this regard, the international experience of Psychology and Pedagogy departments was studied seriously and deeply. Along with experimental Pedagogy, well set in the western universities at the time, it was supposed to introduce the courses of historical orientation to familiarize future teachers with the history of pedagogical ideas embodied in the works of such prominent thinkers as the Comenius, Locke, Rousseau, Herbart, Pestalozzi, K.D. Ushinsky, L.N. Tolstoy. The need to introduce courses in History of Science was also specified. History of Mathematics was supposed 'to shed more light on the methods of presentation of elementary mathematics', as it was very important for future teachers of Mathematics.

In summer 1899, Russian newspapers published the Ministry of Education Circular addressed to trustees of school districts. It outlined numerous shortcomings of gymnasiums and non-classical secondary schools. Among them, "school alienation from family and its bureaucratic nature resulting in dry formalism and deadness in the living pedagogical practice" was declared as the most serious one [8, p. 9]. Shortcomings, identified in the circular, covered all school practice: the overall system, plans, curriculum, methods and techniques, and final results. The document evoked strong public response. Periodicals, boards of trustees of school districts, teacher and parent circles actively helped society "to understand the reasons for such joyless events when school produces half-educated persons without any curiosity and desire to continue education and without the ability to work" (p. 12). Secondary schools meetings with participation of university professors worked hard in Moscow, St. Petersburg and Kazan, releasing proceedings on the matters of people's school organisation.

The idea of creation of the Pedagogical Society was realised by professors of Kazan University immediately after visiting Paris Exhibition in 1900. Exhibition Congresses were dedicated to education in general, special education (commercial, technical, etc.), and the issues of teaching social sciences. It stated an overall interest in education, and the necessity to move to a higher level. Developing technique required education that would meet the life demands. The spread of education and "the ideals of humanity among lower and upper classes" were seen as a means to mitigate the class struggle. Congresses noted universities beneficial effects on the entire public education system (p. 15).

The University set the goal "to support students' scientific aspirations laid at the university, and not to give them fade away in those provincial and county-level towns of little culture, where young teachers were in most cases sent to work" (p. 20). This can be seen as an attempt to provide opportunities for additional education for teachers. They covered: the activities of central pedagogical libraries in the university towns and school districts; summer courses for teachers of secondary schools to familiarise with the latest discoveries in the field of science or methodology; participation in Teachers' Congresses. Kazan Pedagogical Society set the task of organising and directing these activities. Among its founders were professors of Kazan University A.I. Aleksandrov, A.S. Arkhangelsk, E.O. Budde, A.V. Vasilyev, L.O. Darkshevich, G.O. Dermidontov, N.P. Zagoskin, O.G. Mishchenko, D. Naguevsky, G.O. Shershenevich, and A.A. Shtukenberg. Family-Teacher Circle, a kind of organisation facilitating robust pedagogical views among families and society, cooperated successfully with Kazan Pedagogical Society.

2.4.2 Pedagogical society charter

The Charter of the Pedagogical Society at Kazan Imperial University, which was approved May 17, 1900, defined its main objective as follows: firstly, scientific development of systematic approach to the issues of Pedagogy, Didactics and Methodology, their application and history; secondly, assistance to those who profess teaching activities and their preparation for this activity. The Society was granted the right:

- to organise open and closed meetings;
- to deliver public readings in Kazan and other cities of the Kazan School District according to the programs approved by the Society Board;
- to organize congresses and exhibitions;
- to publish works and translations relevant to the Society objectives in the form of collections, books and brochures;
- to issue special periodical editions;
- to establish scholarships, grant monetary awards and medals;
- to promote pedagogical excursions;
- to establish museums and libraries for educational purposes etc. [9].

It was planned to open Society's special departments: National Language and Literature, History and Geography, Classical Philology, Physics and Mathematics, Natural History, and others.

The funds derived primarily from its members' contributions, distribution of publications, public lectures fees, and donations, were used by the Society to update its library and museum, to organise educational courses, congresses and publishing activities.

3 Conclusion

International experience and enthusiasm of Kazan University teaching staff had a profound influence on the development of additional education in Kazan Province in the late 19th and early 20th centuries. The varying order of extension activities of Kazan Imperial University covered: foreign missions of University professors with research and educational purposes; individual mentoring classes of recognised scholars; widening University activities through creation of additional education institutions in accordance with University Extension Movement. These extension activities can be regarded as the foundation for additional education formation in the 19th and early 20th centuries.

References

1. *Otvety Soveta Imperatorskogo Kazanskogo Universiteta na predlozhennye g. Ministrom Narodnogo Prosveshcheniia voprosy, kasaiushchiesia ustroistva universitetov.* [The answers of the Council of Kazan Imperial University to the questions concerning the organization of universities proposed by Minister of Public Education]. Kazan, Imperial University Tipolitography, (1901), (in Russian).
2. *Kratkii otchet o zagranichnoi komandirovke.* [Short report on business trip abroad]. Imperial University Tipolitography, (1900), (in Russian).
3. *Byloe iz universitetskoi zhizni. Literaturnyi sbornik k 100-letiiu Imperatorskogo Kazanskogo Universiteta.* [The Past of University Life. Literary Collection to the 100th Anniversary of Kazan Imperial University]. Kazan, Imperial University Tipolitography, (1904), (in Russian).
4. *Prepodavanie chistoi matematiki v Berlinskom i Leiptsigskom universitetakh. (Iz otcheta o puteshestvii za granitsu letom 1882 g.) (Soobshchenie, sdelannoe v zasedanii 25-go sentiabria 1882 g. fiziko-matematicheskoi sektsii Obshchestva Estestvoispytatelei pri Imperatorskom Kazanskom Universitete Dotsentom A.V.Vasil'evym).* [Teaching Pure Mathematics in Berlin and Leipzig Universities. (From the Report on Trip Abroad in summer 1882) (Speech made by Associate Professor A.V. Vasiliev at Physical and Mathematical Section of Naturalists' Society of Kazan Imperial University, September 25, 1882], Kazan, Imperial University Tipolitography, (1882), (in Russian).
5. *Nikolai Ivanovich Lobachevskii. Rech', proiznesennaia v torzhestvennom sobranii Imperatorskogo Kazanskogo Universiteta 22 oktiabria 1893 g. professorom A.Vasil'evym.* [Nikolai Ivanovich Lobachevsky. Speech made by Professor A. Vasiliev in the solemn meeting of Kazan Imperial University on October 22, 1893]. Kazan, Imperial University Tipolitography, (1894), (in Russian).
6. *Znachenie N.I. Lobachevskogo dlia Imperatorskogo Kazanskogo Universiteta. Rech', proiznesennaia v den' otkrytiia pamiatnika N.I. Lobachevskomu, 1 sentiabria 1896 goda professorom A. Vasil'evym.* [The Significance of N.I. Lobachevsky for Kazan Imperial University. Speech made by Professor A. Vasiliev on the opening day of the monument to N.I. Lobachevsky, September 1, 1896]. Kazan, Imperial University Tipolitography, (1896), (in Russian).
7. A. Vasiliev, *Universitet i natsional'noe vospitanie. Pedagogicheskoe obshchestvo, sostoiashchee pri Imperatorskom Kazanskom Universitete.* [University and National Education. Pedagogical Society at Kazan Imperial University]. Kazan, Imperial University Tipolitography, (1901), (in Russian).
8. O. Mishchenko, *O zadachakh pedagogicheskogo obshchestva pri Kazanskom Imperatorskom universitete.* [About the Tasks of the Pedagogical Society at Kazan Imperial University]. Kazan, Imperial University Tipolitography (1901) (in Russian)

9. *Ustav Pedagogicheskogo obshchestva, sostoiashchego pri Imperatorskom Kazanskom Universitete.* [The Charter of the Pedagogical Society at Kazan Imperial University]. Kazan, Imperial University Tipolitography, (1912), (in Russian).

A brief history of the Tatar language teaching in universities in the 1920s and 1930s

Gulnara Kalganova[1a], Zoya Kirillova[2]

[1]Department of Foreign Languages, IME&F, Kazan Federal University, Russia
[2]Department of General Linguistics and Turkish Studies, IP&IC, Kazan Federal University Russia

Abstract. This paper investigates the history of the Tatar language functioning in the Tatar Republic which was created in 1920 as the Tatar Autonomous Soviet Socialist Republic. Since 1921, the republic began to grant Tatar the status of the state language which was used in almost all spheres of public life. In our article the main attention is paid to functioning of the Tatar language in the higher educational institutions of the Tatar republic in the 1920s and 1930s. To this end, archival documents and published materials were analyzed; main universities of the republic were reviewed; statistics on the number of Tatar students were given; use the Tatar language in these universities and main teaching methods implemented were explored; the textbooks on the Tatar language were described; some difficulties in the Tatar language teaching in the period under review were pointed out.
Keywords: the Tatar language, higher educational establishments, language teaching, the Tatar Republic, state language, 1920s and 1930s.

1 Introduction

In the 1920s, the process of declaring the language of a titular nation as a state language was widespread in all the republics and regions of Russia, and the Tatar republic did not stay on the sidelines. A year after the formation of the Tatar Autonomous Soviet Socialist Republic, the Tatar language was declared a state language along with Russian. As a result, in the 20-30s of the XX century, the Tatar republic actively pursued the process of implementing the Tatar language as a state language. This process was started on June 25, 1921, i.e. The Decree proclaiming the Tatar language for the first time in history the official state language on a par with Russian [18, p.5-6] was signed by the first anniversary of the formation of the TASSR. It is a fact that the Tatar language, rich in ancient literary traditions, played the role of the second state language in the XVII-XVIII centuries and in the first half of the XIX century in Russia's domestic policy and in diplomatic relations with the countries of the East. It was taught not only in Kazan, but also in the educational institutions of many Russian cities.

[a] Corresponding author: gkalganova@yandex.ru

DOI: 10.1051/shsconf/20173701069

2 Methods

In our work we used the methods as follows: the method of document analysis, the descriptive method, the method of observation, the comparative method, etc. The materials of the National Archives of the Republic of Tatarstan (NA RT), published scientific and periodical literature, and the decrees of the period under review were studied.

3 Findings

3.1 Realization of the Tatar language in Education

In the first years after the proclamation of the Tatar language as a state one the work was going through great difficulties. The implementation of the Decree's resolutions was hampered by the shortage of qualified Tatars who knew Tatar and Russian languages equally well, the small number of Tatar employees working in state institutions, the small number of Tatar teachers with higher education, the shortage of textbooks, teaching aids and programs for teaching the Tatar language, the terrible famine of 1921 and its consequences. However, from the middle of 1922 decrees and resolutions on the Realization of the Tatar Language (RTL) not only in state institutions, but also in cooperatives, trade unions, cantons, volosts and village councils began to be issued. After that, a big campaign to introduce the Tatar language into all spheres of public life in the republic was launched [6, p.996], [3, p.337].

In the first document of 1921 on the implementation of the Tatar language as a state language the teaching of the national language of the indigenous population was determined only for those who wished. However, on the basis of the instruction adopted on December 21, 1922, for all students at all second-level schools (seven- or nine-year-old ones), vocational schools, party schools, workers' faculties and universities, and also in the last grades of the first-level schools in cities the Tatar language studying became compulsory [2, p.6,13].

Work of vocational and technical educational institutions, courses, schools of FZU (factory apprenticeship), technical schools, workers' faculties and universities was supervised by the General Directorate of Vocational Education, abbreviated as Glavprofobr.

In the 1920s, the Tatar republic had only five universities and lagged far behind the center of Russia, for example, by the mid-1920s 28 universities operated in Moscow and 24 universities in Leningrad (now St. Petersburg) [10, p.107]. From the universities of the Tatar republic, which were all located in the capital of Kazan, only the Kazan State University and the Kazan Veterinary Institute were old educational institutions; KSU was opened in 1804, and the Veterinary Institute has been working since 1874. The Eastern Pedagogical Institute, the Kazan Institute of Agriculture and Forestry, and the Tatar Communist University were formed only after the revolution, mainly in 1922 [10, p.111-112].

During the 1920s there was a noticeable shift in attracting Tatars to these educational institutions. For example, in the period of 1922-1931 the number of Tatars studied in universities increased by 18.8%. This was confirmed by some statistical data on the number of Tatar students in the republic: 1922/1923 – 5.17%; 1923/1924 – 9.7%; 1924/1925 - 11.7%; 1925/1926 – 14% [26, p.146-147]; 1926/1927 – 8.2%; 1927/1928 – 9.8% [16, p.15-16]; 1929/1930 – 20.1%; 1930/1931 – 24% [17, p.280]. Among the universities, a small number of Tatar students studied at the Kazan Veterinary Institute and Kazan State University. For example, in 1925-1927 in the Veterinary institute Tatars made 3.7-3.8%, and at the Kazan University – 6.7-7.03% [26, p.147]. To facilitate the entry of Tatars into educational institutions some preparatory courses and groups were formed. But, unfortunately, those years, even in those educational institutions where the majority of students were Tatars, the training was conducted in Russian.

It might be noted that, based on numerous decrees of the Tatar Republic, instruction in the Tatar language in higher educational institutions became compulsory. It is clear from documents that students were required to pass examinations in Tatar, otherwise they did not receive diplomas. There was a postscript as follows: if in exceptional cases graduation diplomas were still awarded, there the absence of a test in the Tatar language was indicated [13, p.229].

But in fact, this instruction was fully realized only in the Eastern Pedagogical Institute [11, p.38], while in other educational institutions instruction in the Tatar language was not either introduced at all or the Tatar language was taught only for those who wished. There wasn't a special program for teaching the Tatar language to Russian-speaking students that complicated the matter as well. Considering that it was still too early to create a special program for universities, the members of the Methodological and Pedagogical Commissions at the Academic Center offered temporarily to take the programs written for the 2nd level (nine years) Russian schools as a basis for higher schools [12, p.12-13].

Since 1919, the State Worker's Faculty at KSU expanded its activities, and a special working department at the Eastern Pedagogical Institute made the same since 1923. To be admitted to the State Worker's Faculty, the Tatars had to go through preparatory groups, because their knowledge was not enough not only for studying at universities, where the training was conducted in Russian, but also for admission to the working faculties [5, p.90].

As can be seen from the archival sources, the General Directorate of Vocational Education did not pay adequate attention to the problems of the Tatar language teaching in its subordinate educational institutions. Except for one document, which stated that within two years the Tatar language was studied 2 hours a week, and there were no other regulations [15, p.8].

In 1925, a resolution on the training of teachers for non-Russian schools was adopted by the Council of People's Commissars of the RSFSR, and, in accordance with it, several universities and pedagogical institutes organized national divisions (for example, the Mari, Udmurt, and Chuvash ones were opened at the Kazan Pedagogical Institute). Creation of the textbooks in national languages was launched. Since 1921, in the Tatar Republic this work, which was done by more than a hundred educators-scientists, linguists, teachers, textbook authors, began to be supervised by the Academic Center under the People's Commissariat of Education of the Republic of Tatarstan [4, p.310].

In the 1920-30s, much attention was paid to textbooks on the Tatar language and literature and school textbooks on the Russian language for Tatar schools. During these years, famous teachers M. Kurbangaliev, R. Gazizov, H. Badigi, Z. Badigullin, Z. Badamshin, M. Galeev, and others worked on the creation of the Tatar language textbooks for Russians. Compilation of the Tatar language minimums for Tatar and non-Tartar students began by the universities' Tatar language departments which were opened up until the 1930s [1, p.148]. Textbooks for different specialties as well as numerous terminological dictionaries for various areas were written. For example, prior to 1927, 15 thousand Tatar terms which formed the basis for terminological dictionaries were created [4, p.310].

During these years, two main methods in teaching the Tatar language to other nationalities were identified: translation-grammatical and natural methods. When teaching by the first method, the words of the native language were the necessary means to study a new language. And the starting point of the natural method was a real object, in the absence of which it was proposed to use pictures or models of these objects, in other words, apply some visual means of teaching. The author of numerous textbooks and programs, a prominent teacher and methodologist M.Kh. Kurbangaliev did not recommend using purely grammatical or only natural methods in teaching. "Taking as a basis the natural method," he wrote, "it is necessary to apply the method of translation and grammar" [9, p.3-4].

In 1934, M.Kh. Kurbangaliev published a special textbook on the Tatar language for non-Tartar students studying in technical and workers' schools, at universities and technical colleges. The author paid special attention to the comparative study of the common elements of both the Tatar and Russian languages, as well as the features of the Tatar language in comparison with the forms and phrases of Russian speech [8]. To the above, we should add that M.Kh. Kurbangaliev and R.S. Gazizov published a special textbook on the comparative grammar of the Tatar and Russian languages which was actively used in the Tatar language classes [7].

3.2 The Tatar language teaching at HEIs

From the history of the Tatar language teaching at HEIs, we would like to consider Kazan Financial and Economic Institute (KFEI) as an example. It was founded in 1930 on the basis of the economic faculty of Kazan State University, so the main academic teaching staff was formed from the university's professors. The teaching of the Tatar language was conducted since the founding of the Institute. The department which was responsible for the language training in different years was called in various ways: in 1931 – the Department of the Tatar language and literature; from January 1932 to 1935 – the Department of Languages; from 1935 to 1946 – Methodical Bureau and language cabinet; from 1946 to 2012 – the Department of Foreign Languages.

In the 1930s, according to "indigenization" (or "korenization") (this term defined the policy of the Tatar language specialists' training and using of local languages in the official structures) the institute put forward the following positions:

1) organization of the indigenous groups with teaching in Tatar;
2) scientific staff training from the "nationals" (i.e. Tatars or other nationalities);
3) organization of a commission for terminology development, as well as the compilation and translation of textbooks on various specialties into the Tatar language;
4) teaching the Tatar language for non-Tatars;
5) reorientation of the Tatar language study into financial and economic field.

According to archival documents, in 1931, several indigenous groups were created (i.e., homogeneous in national composition): 4 – at the full-time department, 3 – at the workers' faculty and one group for Chuvashes. In subsequent years the numbers of groups varied. In these indigenous groups the teaching of all disciplines was envisaged in the Tatar language. By the end of 1931, textbooks on statistics, financial science and accounting were already prepared in the Tatar language [13, p.40].

Moreover, in the same year, a terminological commission headed by professor M.Kh. Kurbangaliev was created that, in turn, included the departments' brigades and worked on the development of Tatar terms for various specialties. In particular, in 1932, more than 500 and 700 terms in dialectical materialism and political economy were developed accordingly [24, p.14-16]. Archival documents testify to the work of the terminological commission for the Chuvash language, but that work was not completed [21]. The following textbooks on various subjects that were compiled or translated into Tatar can be identified: "USSR Finance", "Statistics", "Economic Geography of the USSR", "Political Economic Geography of the Capitalist World", "Accounting"; "Economics and Finance of Industry", "Mathematics" were read in Tatar [25, p.37]. Since there was a shortage of relevant literature and lecturers who knew the Tatar language, the system of instruction in indigenous groups looked as follows: lectures were read in Russian with reference to literature in Russian, but consultations were conducted in Tatar with translation of assignments into Tatar; maps and visual aids were also drawn in the Tatar language. By the 3rd semester the training was planned to be fully translated into Russian [24, p.14].

At that time the professionalising of the Tatar language study had a practical application. Due to predominance of the Tatar population in rural areas, the business and every day communication in the regions distant from Kazan was in Tatar. Therefore, during the students' practice it was recommended to include in their work some elements of Tatar speech activity, namely, practice in live speech, collection of terms, familiarity with samples of business papers, etc.

The Methodological bureau of languages was engaged in promoting various languages. For example, the plans on extracurricular activities for the 1936-1937 academic year included the following activities:

- issuing posters in any foreign language;
- arranging literary circles on Russian and Tatar literature;
- arranging literary evenings in foreign languages;
- setting up groups of German and English studying for the Institute's scientists;
- providing a series of lectures on literature in Russian and Tatar;
- setting up of advisory board in German, English, French, Russian and Tatar languages [19, p.3].

The language cabinet received literature in 13 languages: in foreign languages, Russian, Tatar, Bashkir, Chuvash, Mari, Crimean-Tatar and other languages [20, p.35].

Concerning methods of languages teaching there is quite interesting information. In relation to native languages, a brigade-laboratory method that was popular in the 1930s was used, and in comparison to non-native (foreign) languages – combined one that conjoining elements of brigade-laboratory and classroom methods (speaking, reading aloud, translating, "continuous" exercises in grammar and syntax). The brigade form of training included initially individual work and afterwards working out the material in brigades for 5-6 people [24, p.35].

In the archival documents, since 1939, the Tatar language teaching in the KFEI was not mentioned. In the same year, as it is known, the Tatar language was translated into Cyrillic, and the policy of "korenization" and "tatarization" was curtailed.

In the 1930s, in other Kazan universities the similar situation was observed: providing the "indigenous" policy of the university to any extent, the development of scientific terminology, and the lack of educational literature. For example, at the Kazan State University, the Tatar language for Tatars was taught at the following faculties: geography, physics and mathematics, biology, and chemistry [22]. Until 1939, in the Kazan Institute of Chemical Technology named after S.M. Kirov the Tatar language was taught optionally only for Tatar students. In particular, the report of the Department of Languages for the academic year of 1934-1935 drew attention to the activities of various circles: for the elimination of illiteracy, literary, and translation ones [23].

4. Conclusion

Despite the numerous difficulties, by the end of the 1930s, full-fledged functioning of the Tatar language could already be provided by staff of Tatars trained at the universities of the Tatar republic for working in different fields. For example, in 1936, the number of Tatars working in central organizations and commissariats amounted to 38.5%, and among the leaders the number of Tatars reached even 47.4% [6, p.998].

Summing up the given research, it is possible to come to conclusion that in the Tatar republic during the 1920s-1930s a lot of work on the application of the Tatar language in various fields was done, including attracting Tatars to higher educational institutions and the Tatar language teaching at the republic's HEIs.

DOI: 10.1051/shsconf/20173701069

References

1. Bayramova L.K. Tatarstan: language symmetry and asymmetry. Kazan: Kazan University Publishing House, 267 (2001).
2. Collection of the decisions, regulations, most important circulars and other important materials in the field of the implementation of the Tatar Autonomous Soviet Socialist Republic. Kazan: Publishing center of the Commission for the implementation of the Tatar language under the central executive committee of the Tatar Autonomous Soviet Socialist Republic, 88 (1925).
3. Kirillova Z.N., Kalganova G.F. Activities of the Tatar Studies' Scientific Society. *International Multidisciplinary Scientific Conferences on Social Sciences and Arts SGEM*, **2**, Albena (Bulgaria), 335-340 (2016).
4. Kirillova Z.N. Tatar Education from 1920-1930. *The European Proceedings of Social & Behavioral Sciences EpSBS, IFTE*, 12. Kazan: The Future Academy, 307-312 (2016).
5. Kirillova Z.N. The Tatar language as a state language (20-30 years). Kazan: Master Line, 208 (2000).
6. Kirillova Z.N. The Tatar language realization as the official (20s-30s of the XXth century). *International Multidisciplinary Scientific Conferences on Social Sciences and Arts, SGEM,* **3**, Albena (Bulgaria), 995-1001 (2014).
7. Korbangaliev M., Gazizov R. Systematic grammar of the Tatar language in comparison with Russian grammar. Kazan: Tatizdat, 171 (1932).
8. Korbangaliev M. The Tatar language textbook for non-Tatars. Kazan: Tatgosizdat, 252 (1934).
9. Korbangaliev M., Gazizov R. The Tatar language textbook for the Russians. For the 5th grade of the 2nd level schools, 177 (1930).
10. Over 5 years. For the 5th anniversary of the proclamation of the Tatar Soviet Socialist Republic. Kazan, 208 (1925).
11. Report of the Central Commission on the implementation of the Tatar language under the CEC Tat.ASSR "On the situation of the RTL and perspectives" at the 3rd Session of the Central Executive Committee of the Tatar SSR on 12-13 March 1927 (Transcript). The debate and the report's resolution. Kazan: Central Committee of the RTL under the TCEC, 68 (1927).
12. The Tatar language programme for the 2nd level (9 years) of Russian schools and higher education establishments. Kazan: The People's Commissariat edition, 33 (1927).
13. Documents of the Kazan financial and economic institution's establishing, 1931. NA RT. F.R-7351. Op.1. D.1, 42 (in Russian, unpublished).
14. Materials on activity of the Central Committee on RTL (1 October 1925 – 30 September 1926). NA RT. F. R-732. Op.1. D.768, 297 (in Russian, unpublished).
15. Materials on activity of the Central Committee on RTL (1 – 30 October 1926). NA RT. F. R-732. Op.1. D.769, 235 (in Russian, unpublished).
16. Materials on indigenization of the soviet administration and RTL in the republic in 1927 (1 January – 1 December 1927). NA RT. F. R-732. Op.1. D. 1138, 126 (in Russian, unpublished).
17. Materials on republic's agriculture state, administration's indigenization and RTL, etc. (6 June 1929 – 5 November 1930). NA RT. F.R-732. Op.1. D.1307, 429 (in Russian, unpublished).
18. Minutes of the CEC of the TSSR's general committee (1 October – 6 December 1921). NA RT. F.R-732. Op.1. D.49, 103 (in Russian, unpublished), (1921)
19. Minutes of the meetings, annual and semestrial plans and reports of the institute's language bureau. NA RT. F. R-351. Op.1. D.54, 56 (in Russian, unpublished).

20. Minutes of the meetings, semestrial and language bureau reports of the first semester of the 1937-1938 academic year. NA RT. F. R-7351. Op.1. D.135, 35 (in Russian, unpublished).
21. Minutes of the terminology commission's meetings, 1933. NA RT. F. R-7351. Op.1. D. 26, 45 (in Russian, unpublished).
22. Reports of the department and observatory's activity for the 1932-1933 academic year. NA RT. F. R-1337. Op.32. D.57, 30 (in Russian, unpublished).
23. Report of the language department for the 2nd semester of the 1934-1935 academic year. NA RT. F. R-2647. Op.2. D.35, 5 (in Russian, unpublished).
24. Reports on the state of the Institute's teaching methods during the 1931-32 academic year. NA RT. F. R-7351. Op.1. D.13, 64 (in Russian, unpublished).
25. Semestrial plans and reports on departments' activity for the 1931-1932 academic year. NA RT. F. R-7351. Op.1. D.12, 60 (in Russian, unpublished).
26. Statistics data on ethnic composition of the republic's central and jurisdictional organizations. List of cantons commissions' members on RTL (1 October 1925 – 30 September 1926). NA RT. F. R-732. Op.1. D. 766, 204 (in Russian, unpublished).

The importance of motion games in the psychomotor development of pre-schoolers during the physical education class

Iconomescu Teodora-Mihaela[1a], Mindrescu Veronica[2] and Talaghir Laurentiu-Gabriel[1]

[1]"Dunarea de Jos" University, Faculty of Physical Education and Sport, Garii Street, No. 63-65, Galati, Romania
[2]"Transilvania" University, Faculty of Physical Education and Sport, Universitatii Street, No.1, Galati, Romania

Abstract. The class of physical education is of the essence for the physical, motor and social development of children. Psychomotricity, motor skills and motor qualities can be developed with the methods applied in the physical education class. In the case of preschool age, a primary objective of the physical education class is the development of psychomotricity. This is the reason why the present undertaking targets the development of several psychomotricity components through motion games during the physical education class. During a semester, we applied a syllabus based on the method of motion games. The subjects in the research were assessed with the help of Ozeretski - Guillmain prior and after testing. After the application of the proposed syllabus, an improvement in the test indices has been observed, a significant percentage of subjects advancing towards slight psychomotor inability.
Keywords: Motion games; physical education; preschool

1 Introduction

The study of motor behaviour in the physical education and sport activities is very important because the motor aspect is predominant in the body activities. It is, therefore, natural that psychomotor skills have a significant role in the instructional-educational process. Thus, one of the major specific objectives of physical education is represented by psychomotor education.

It is well-known that certain behaviours of the human subject depend, both structurally and as manifestation, on nature and on the characteristics of the stimuli which trigger them, but also on the particularities of the respective person. It is, then, important that the entire effect of the instructional-educational process depend on the dynamics of the subject's personality, in whose structure, the psychomotor skills play an important role [1, 3].

[a] Corresponding author: teodora.iconomescu@ugal.ro

While in the past, the studies would tackle psychomotricity from the perspective of motor development and its relation with intelligence, the more recent studies consider the motor structures and their relation with the body schema, ideomotricity, laterality and the spatial-temporal structure, as well as the means of learning and adapting of the individual in society. The study of psychomotricity plays an essential role in the organisation of the instructional-educational process. It is not restricted to motor activity, but it also involves the presence of the manifestations of perceptive and intellectual functions. These psychomotor habits of each individual evolve according to their innate skills, to their degree of physical and intellectual development and to the educational environments in which they have been educated during childhood [2, 5, 9].

The aim of this paper is drafting and applying an educational programme for a few selected psychomotor components – spatial orientation, laterality and acknowledgement of the body schema – for small school-age children, during the physical education class, based on the game method (motion games). In what concerns the pupils' age, it will constitute a positive factor in accomplishing the proposed objective, namely in educating the psychomotor components. We have set out from the premise that this would favour all the aspects related to motricity in primary school. The education of psychomotricity in primary school is extremely important because of the age of the pupils. It is a propitious time in the life of an individual, the optimal stage to posit the matter of psychomotor education at the highest parameters.

2 Research methods

2.1 Procedure

The research focused on the educational valences of the motion games, aiming at the education of psychomotor skills. Special attention was granted to motion games, as they provide favourable conditions for the simultaneous development of motor qualities and basic or specific motor skills and of their relation with the psychic processes through its contents, manifestations and effects.

Due to the multiple variants which can be encountered in a motion game and to its instructional-educational forms, it has been included among the learning contents of any lesson as a means for physical education. It is well-known that some teachers of physical education use this method intensively, while others prefer attaining their objectives by using simpler, less thought-of methods which require less preparation, or use the motion game erroneously. We infer from this that the motion game is not granted the importance it deserves, and we aim to underline its educational value and to identify the most effective motion games in view of educating the selected psychomotor components for the small-age school student.

In order to obtain some optimistic results with regard to the use of this method, a long period, covering more curricular cycles, is not necessary, as the effects of this method are almost instant, becoming apparent in less than a semester. The students are receptive; they take an active part in any activity of this type, they think, they interact and relate with their opponents, partners, classmates, creating and looking for solutions.

2.2 Subjects

The pilot-test was carried out during the school year 2016-2017, on a sample of 32 subjects, 11 boys and 20 girls, four-grade students in a rural school in Galati County. The mean age was of 10.4 years.

2.3 Methods

Psychomotricity was tested using the Ozeretski-Guillmain test, an adaptation from P. Vayer and L. Picq [7]. The test is intended to identify the main motor components, with its four aspects: speed, coordination, strength, resistance, on the following coordinates: hands dynamic coordination, general dynamic coordination, balance, rapidity, spatial orientation. The results obtained reveal the students' coefficient of psychomotor delay and their degree of psychomotor inability.

The students in the research were evaluated at the beginning of the research; having applied the test, we clarified the aspects where intervention was required and established the means (motion games) of operation during research. The syllabus was applied during the second semester (16 weeks x 2 hours = 32 hours) during the physical education classes, with objectives pertaining to psychomotricity, by implementing a motion games programme, in view of improving the education level of each student's psychomotricity.

3 Results and discussions

Psychomotricity is one of the basic components of the school curriculum for primary education; however, its specific means and objectives towards its development are not clearly specified. Because of the limited number of physical education classes, some teachers choose to expedite the lessons containing psychomotricity objectives. In Romania, 100 minutes of physical education are allocated weekly for the primary school education. However, in order to develop the psychomotor qualities and the motor skills provided by the curriculum, more classes of physical education and a superior endowment of the schools with sports materials seem extremely necessary.

Our research is intended to underline the fact that the psychomotor components can also be developed in rural schools, even with means which do not require a large number of sport materials.

Because of the small number of students, their differences in age in a class (which is made of up to 20 pupils), and the parents' mentality, these children are particularly difficult to work with. The schools in the rural environment are disadvantaged because of school drop-out rate and the parents' mentality.

In view of outlining the degree of psychomotor development, we used the Ozeretski-Guillmain test, which points to the essential behaviours of motor life, under its four aspects: speed, coordination, strength and resistance, with its specific coordinates: hands dynamic coordination, general dynamic coordination, balance, rapidity, spatial orientation

After applying the proposed syllabus with motion games for the improvement of psychomotor components, a significant percentage of students improved their psychomotor qualities, advancing from one status to the next. Out of the 21 pupils, 38% were 10 years old, and 62% were 11 years old.

Figure 1 shows that, for the research subjects aged 10, the indices of the Ozeretski-Guillmain test point to the decrease of psychomotor inability by 37.5%, a value equally divided in the case of slight psychomotor retardation. The normal psychomotor status remained constant after the final testing. These results are owed to the proposed programme, which aimed at developing the psychomotor components through motion games. Motion games proved the ability to improve the psychomotor components, provided that they are conducted in accordance with the subjects' age and in view of acquiring the proposed objective.

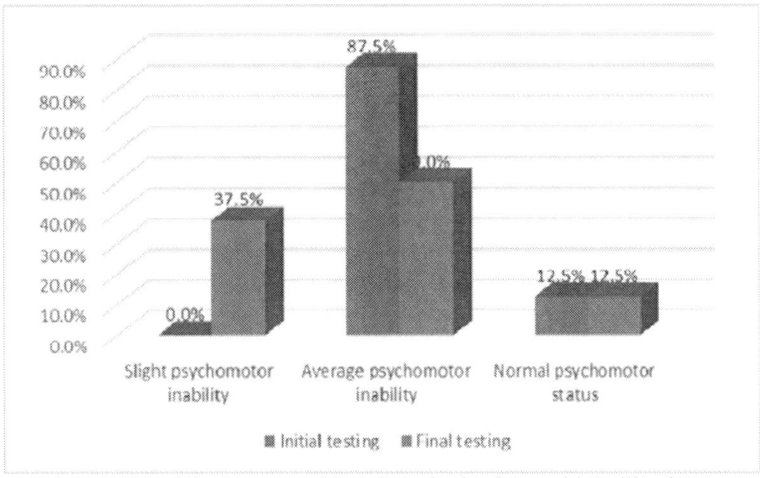

Fig. 1. Comparative results of the 10 years old students in the Ozeretski-Guillmain test

In the case of the 11 years old students, it can be observed that slight motor retardation has remained constant, at 38%, the average psychomotor inability decreased by 23.07%, while 23.08% of the students have reached the normal psychomotor stage at the end of the study. The results of these students were better than the ones obtained by the 10 years old students due to their age and to the skills already formed at this age. Some authors consider that 11 years is the age when the development of psychomotor components reaches its final stage. These improvements of the 11 years old students are owed to the motion games focused on the development of psychomotor components, applied during the physical education class.

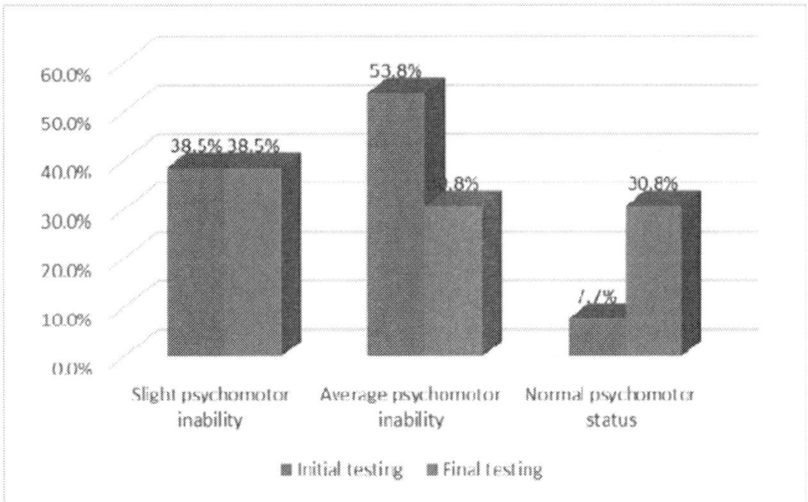

Fig. 2. Comparative results of the 11 years old students in the Ozeretski-Guillmain test

The test indicators have emphasised various motor manifestations of the research subjects. The results of the indices of the Ozeretski-Guillmain test are presented in Figure 3, which depicts the differences obtained by the students in the initial and final testing. The percentage differences range between 0.06% for movements simultaneity, the smallest progress, the 1.3% for general dynamic coordination, the best progress. These small differences prove that, at this age, not all subjects have good static or dynamic coordination or a good hand or leg adroitness. These results are the consequence of the lack of an imposed curriculum providing a number of lessons containing objectives from the domain of psychomotricity.

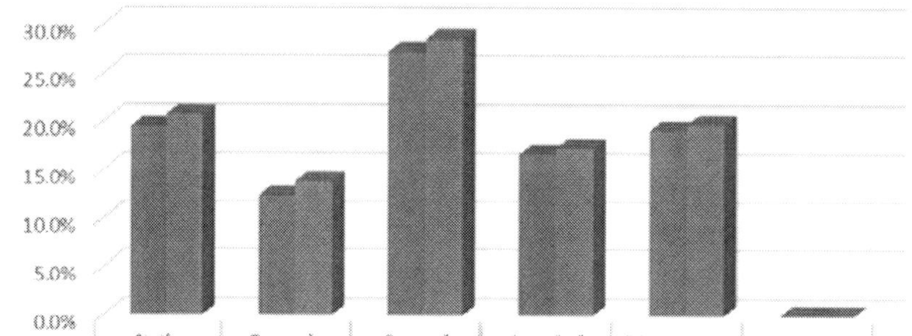

	Static coordination	Dynamic hand coordination	General dynamics coordination	Speed of movement	Movements simultaneity	Sincinezii
■ Initial testing	19.4%	12.3%	27.2%	16.6%	19.1%	0.0%
■ Final testing	20.7%	13.8%	28.5%	17.3%	19.7%	0.0%

Fig. 3. Comparative results of the indices of the Ozeretski-Guillmain test obtained by the research subjects

The programme of motion games we elaborated is based on the Zimmer [8] method described as concerning children's psychomotor development. The motion games applied were fun and ensured the children's enthusiasm. The activities promotes group games and, therefore, social relations between children. The games had simple rules and group tasks, a condition which requires cooperation. The rules were clear and easy to understand, so that they could be interiorised and applied by all children. Some games also contributed in the development of creativity, as they were based on problem-solving, the children being sometimes assisted by their teachers in solving the problem.

A real contribution to the understanding of psychomotricity is to be found in the studies related to psychomotor education and re-education. In the case of psychomotor disorders, Guilmain recommends a complex therapy which points to three aspects: the re-education of the tonic activity through attitude and balance exercises; the re-education of the relationship activities through exercises of synkinesis and development of motor coordination; and the re-education of the intellectual control over the affective functions.

Other researchers consider that children learn about the world and about themselves through physical activity. Through motions, children acquire experience, skills and knowledge in many fields. The contact they have with other children often starts with body language and body activities. This is important for the development of social component. The active use of the environment in open space offers many opportunities [6].

Some authors, such is the case of Camargos and Maciel [4], have reached the conclusion that motion games should be understood as practices which promote the learning and development of various aspects of the human being, from motor, psychological, social and affective points of view. During the physical education classes, the teacher must give up the repetition of movements and the mechanics of the activities which do not develop the body and the brain. The game is a direct channel which the children use to express their wishes and feelings, a very powerful instrument during the initial period, when children enter in a relationship with society [4].

The main components of psychomotricity (the body schema, laterality, ideomotricity, motor intelligence) deem possible:

•pragmatic adaptation (learning the professional, manual or intellectual techniques);

•social adaptation (means of interpersonal communication);

•aesthetic adaptation (body expression techniques); and,

•educational adaptation (physical education, sport training, etc.).

Not only do the motion games and physical activity develop the children from a motor perspective, but also in what concerns their cognitive, social, affective and creative skills and abilities.

4 Conclusions

Psychomotricity, as a primary objective of the physical education lesson, may be developed through various means for pre-schoolers. The means with the highest applicability in psychomotor development is the motion game, because:

- it creates positive emotional states;
- it contributes to the harmonious development of the body and to maintaining an optimal state of health;
- it contributes to the development of the motor qualities, to the formation of basic motor skills, applicative skills and skills specific to some sport branches;
- it stimulates the cooperation with the game partners, it harmonizes the personal interests, motives, actions and efforts with the ones of the group;
- it facilitates the integration into the collective and responsibility;
- it contributes to the education of moral and will qualities;
- it contributes to the education of attentiveness, perception and motor reaction;
- it helps in the development of thinking, initiative, creativity, the decisional and anticipation ability.

Thus, the game has many roles in development, and daily activity should be carried out accordingly. In order to attain maximum effectiveness, it necessary that the games be judiciously selected, organised, carried out and led. The teachers should know their students, their age and gender particularities, their general physical preparation level, the working material (spaces, fields, apparatuses, materials, etc.). All these determine, to a great extent, the quality, the contents and the level of the physical education activities.

References

1. C. Albu, Psihomotricitate. Institutul European Publishing (2006).
2. C. Strujan, D. Bădău, A. Bădău – Physical education. Teacher guide, Publishing House Ria of Botosani, (2009).
3. D. Bădău, F. Dusa, A. Bădău, Physical education and sport.., Publishing University Press, Tirgu Mures, (2015).
4. E.K. Camargos, R.M. Maciel, *The importance of psychomotricity in children education*, In Multidisciplinary Core scientific journal of knowledge. 1 (9). p. 254-275, (2016).
5. G. Barbu, Petruţ Copilul şi motricitatea. Nomina Publishing (2012).
6. H. Zoglowek, M. Aleksandrovich, *Development through Movement – Psychopedagogical Analysis and Psychomotor Approaches*, Revija za Elementarno Izobraževanje. 2016; 9(1-2):151-17, (2016).
7. I. Lozincă, V. Marcu, Psihologia şi activităţile motrice, Oradea University Press pp. 125-136, (2005).
8. R. Zimmer, Bewegung, Körpererfahrung & Gesundheit. Berlin: Cornelsen Scriptor. (2010).
9. T.M. Iconomescu, L.G. Talaghir, Teaching Approach to Enhance Motor Skills for Students in Primary School, ERPA International Congress on Education, ERPA Congress, Published by Proceedia - Social and Behavioral Sciences, Volume 152, pp 746-751, (2014).

The development of spatial orientation and laterality in physical education classes from the countryside - pilot test

Iconomescu Teodora-Mihaela[1a] and Ciapa Mihaela[2]

[1]"Dunarea de Jos" University, Faculty of Physical Education and Sport, Garii Street, No. 63-65, Galati, Romania
[2]National College "Alexandru Ioan Cuza", Saturn Street, No. 26, Galati, Romania

Abstract. The article aims to present a pilot test on the development of space orientation and laterality in pupils in primary education in the physical education lesson. Testing of psychomotricity components was performed by the Piaget Head and Harris test. The differences between the two initial and final tests have shown that through the physical movement of the physical education we have improved the two components of psychomotricity.
Keywords: physical education, spatial orientation, laterality

1. Introduction

Psychomotricity is a complex function, which integrates and connects the motor elements with the mental ones, determining individual behaviour adjustment and including the participation of different mental processes, thus ensuring the proper execution of response actions to different situations and stimuli.

The study of the motor behaviour during physical education activities and sports is extremely important because, in physical activities, the motor component is prevalent. Motor reactions represent elaborate responses to certain stimuli. It is, therefore, natural for psychomotor abilities to hold an important place in the educational process. This is the reason why the main specific objective of physical education is represented by psychomotor education. [1, 4]

In Enciclopedia Universalis – France (1990), we find "The connection between mental and motor and its development within interdisciplinary sciences was named psychomotricity, which may be defined as the result of the integration of motor and mental functions, under the effect of the nervous system maturation, which targets the connection between the subject, his/her body and the environment" [5, p.212]. Horghidan (2000), asserts that "psychomotricity is a primary function, which comprises mental phenomena in

[a] Corresponding author: Teodora.Iconomescu@ugal.ro

its structure, generated by body movements and expressed by means of voluntary movements, whose use is conditioned within actions" [8, p.32].

At the beginning, studies approached psychomotricity from the point of view of motor development and of its relationship with intelligence. Nowadays, studies take into account both the motor structures and their connection with the body scheme, ideomotricity, laterality, with the spatial and temporal structure and the ways of learning and adaptation of the individual within society. The study of psychomotricity occupies an important place in the organization of the educational process. This doesn't only engage the motor activity, but it also involves the presence of the intellectual and perceptive functions. Each individual's psychomotor habits evolve depending on the abilities he/she possesses, on the degree of physical and intellectual development and on the educational environments in which he/she was educated during childhood. [2, 3, 7]

For these reasons, we believe that the education of psychomotricity from an early age must be one of the constant concerns for parents and teachers alike and it must also be focused on during the other stages of human existence, too.

It is well-known that certain behaviours of the human subject depend, in point of structure and of their manifestation, on nature and on the characteristics of the stimuli that cause them, but they also depend on the idiosyncrasies that characterize each and every person. It is therefore important that the entire effect of the educational process also depend on the subject's personality dynamics, within which psychomotor abilities play an extremely important part.

2. Methods

The research was realised through a pilot test over during the school year 2015-2016, we tested and assessed a number of 32 fourth grade students, with ages ranging from 10 to 11 years, from Primary School, Bucești, county of Galați.

As psychomotor assessment methods, we used the Piaget Head spatial orientation test and the Harris laterality test [6].

The initial test was conducted at the beginning of the school year. After this test and after test analysis, we proposed that, during school year, one of the two classes of physical education should be dedicated to the development of psychomotricity by means of movement games.

After final testing, the results were statistically analysed by the absolute and relative frequency achieved through the program SPSS 23.

3. Results and discussions

In order to determine the subjects' spatial orientation index education level we used the spatial orientation test – Piaget Head, and the statistical results are presented in table 1 and table 2.

Table 1. The statistical results at the initial test in the space orientation test

Items	Frequency	Percent	Valid Percent	Cumulative Percent
Test successful	16	50.0	50.0	50.0
Test corrected spontaneously	3	9.4	9.4	59.4
Test unsuccessful	13	40.6	40.6	100.0
Total	32	100.0	100.0	

Table 2. The statistical results at the final test in the space orientation test

Items	Frequency	Percent	Valid Percent	Cumulative Percent
Test successful	18	56.3	56.3	56.3
Test corrected spontaneously	5	15.6	15.6	71.9
Test unsuccessful	9	28.1	28.1	100.0
Total	32	100.0	100.0	

In the Piaget Head test, conducted on 10-year old children (fig. 1), we noticed an improvement in task-solving of 22.7%, raising from 70.8%, within the initial test, to 93.5% within the final test.

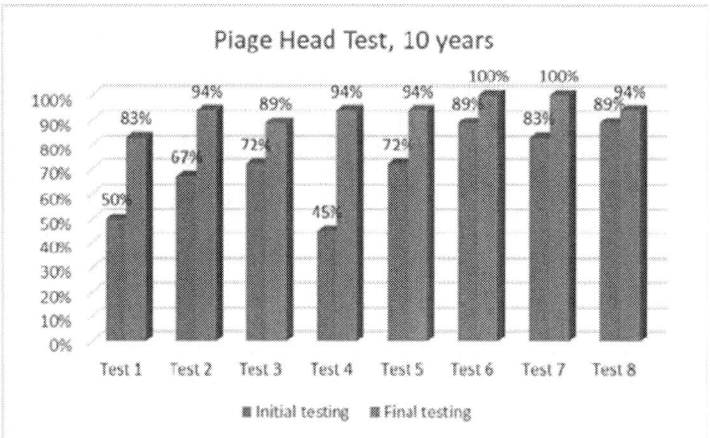

Fig. 1. Comparative results of the Piaget Head test at students in 10-year-olds

Together with an increase in age, due to a greater understanding ability, the difference in point of percentage between the two tests, the initial one and the final one, raises, reaching approximately 30%, the evolution of the students being from 63.2% within the initial test to 93% within the final test.

For the Harris laterality test, the statistical results were the ones presented in table 2 and, afterwards, graphically presented in the figures 1and 2.

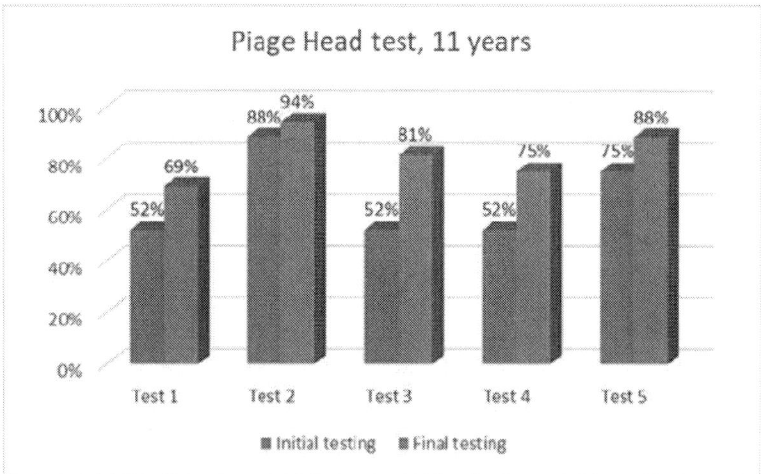

Fig. 2. Comparative results of the Piaget Head test at students in 11-year-olds

In the first step of the test (the initial test), right-handed people and cross laterality (figure 3), the 10-year old students presented numerical values, which were nearly equal (46%, 47%). After the final test, we notice the tendency to favour the development of the most used side (the right-handed students), this change becoming obvious for the students with cross laterality, the migration percentage being of 14%.

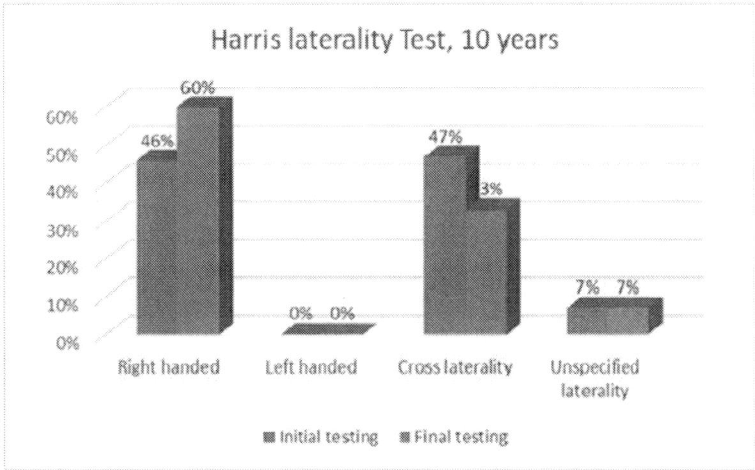

Fig. 3. Comparative results of the Harris laterality test at students in 10-year-olds

From the Harris laterality test graph, describing the 11-year old students (figure 4), we may draw the conclusion that the children's motor capacity improvement is obvious, starting from 12%, heading towards being ambidextrous and reaching 41%. This fact is due to the implementation of the movement game-based program in order to educate the psychomotor components.

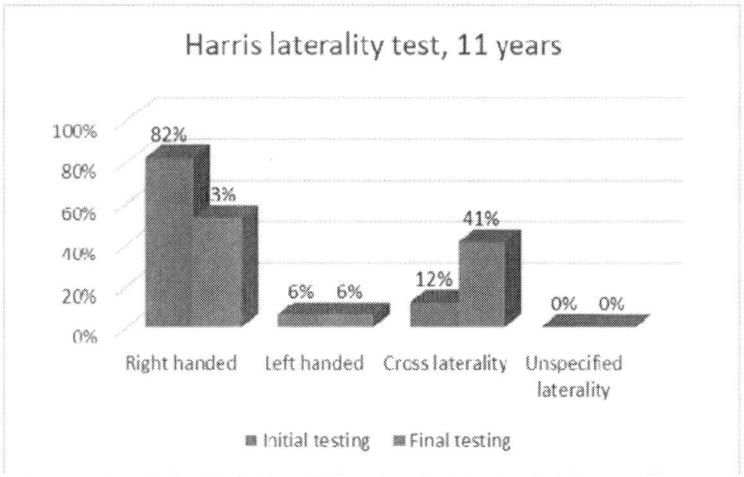

Fig. 4. Comparative results of the Harris laterality test at students in 11-year-olds

According to the results of the Piaget Head test, we discovered the fact that the participation in the program created for pre-school children's psychomotor ability education for the age of 10, succeeded in raising the spatial orientation indexes with an average of 22.7%, recording a value with 30% greater for 11-year old children. From here, we may deduce that the degree of involvement and awareness also increases depending on the age of the subjects involved in the research.

In the final test, by using the Harris laterality test, we find out the importance of the classmate environment influence, since the majority of the 10-year-old subjects (who are, obviously, more impressionable than 11-year-olds as far as the social and educational requirements are concerned), adapt and tend to use the right side as the dominant side, the laterality index moving from Cross laterality to right-handed in a percentage of 14%, whereas the 11-year-olds, are predominantly right-handed, the laterality index becoming, thus, stable.

4. Conclusion

Starting from the determination of the initial and final psychomotor levels, which resulted from the interaction of the morpho-functional factors (internal factors) and of the social and educational ones (external factors) with the motor education, we may draw the following conclusions:

- from a psychomotor point of view, the students follow the alternating stages of the biological factors' evolution and this is the reason why the results are different;
- in order to have a good relationship between efficiency and quality, the psychomotor education level and objective setting must be performed by taking into consideration the individual age and sex particularities as well as modern society requests;
- the stimulation of different age-specific processes, by means of an educational program based on the movement game method, such as: a harmonious physical development, the playful behaviour, the need for affirmation and competition successfully contribute to the education and formation of primary school student psychomotricity; the subjects' morpho-functional particularities require the use of certain tests, of specific methods and means, acknowledging the individual routes that are followed by psychomotor education and genetic evolution;
- by analysing the first results (the initial tests), we notice a negative influence from the part of modern civilization (the standard of living, technology, automation, sedentariness, the replacement of outdoor games with video games) on the motor age of pre-school children. This is the reason why we recommend an interventional strategy in the educational process, by means of movement-based games, in order to favour the development of primary school students' psychomotor abilities.

The main conclusion is that the use of game-based training program in the teaching activity leads to the acquisition of obvious and more valuable psychomotor abilities as compared to the simple use of methods based on simple strength training, sprint, long-distance (endurance) running, coordination capacity exercises, thus confirming the researched hypothesis.

References

1. A.C. Macri, *The role of the exercises in the improvement of the psychomotricity components in the development of the pupils,* Sport & Society / Sport si Societate, Special Issue, **14**, 155-162, (2014)
2. A.C. Cappellini, S. Mancini, S. Zuffellato, F. Bini, P. Polcaro, A.A. Conti, R. Molino Lova, C. Macchi, *Environmental effects on school age child psychomotricity*, Minerva Pediatrica, **60**(3):277-84, (2008).
3. C. Strujan, D. Bădău, A. Bădău – Physical education. Teacher guide, Publishing House Ria of Botosani, (2009).
4. D. Bădău, F. Dusa, A. Bădău, Physical education and sport.., Publishing University Press, Tirgu Mures, (2015).

5. Encyclopaedia Universalis, Edité par Encyclopaedia universalis France, (1990).
6. I. Lozincă, V. Marcu, Psihologia şi activităţile motrice, Oradea University Press pp. 125-136, (2005).
7. S. Pratesi, M. Fasano, A.C. Cappellini, Effects of a psychomotor education program on Body Mass index (BMI) in a group of school- aged Italian children, Journal of Anatomy and Embryology, **117**(2), 152, (2012).
8. V. Horghidan, Problematica psihomotricităţii, Editura Globus, Bucureşti. (2000).

Two focus interactive learning: Improving the quality of vocational training and the possibility of life self-fulfillment

Irina Loginova[1a]

[1]Krasnoyarsk State Medical University, Krasnoyarsk, Russia

Abstract. Currently the introduction of interactive learning due to two trends. The first follows from the general direction of the education development in forming mental activity, the ability to learn. The second follows from the modern requirements development to the quality of the individual graduate. The purpose of this study is to evaluate the possibilities of interactive learning at the same time hold two focus: improving the quality of vocational training, self-realization and life self-fulfillment of the educational process subjects. To assess the quality of training students the procedure of internal quality monitoring was used. Test Card has been developed to assess the implementation possibilities of the life self-fulfillment. Using interactive technologies in the organization of the training makes it possible to consider the issues of individual educational strategies, enhances the quality of learning and creates the opportunity for self-realization and life self-fulfillment.
Keywords: Vocational training; self-realization; life self-fulfillment

1 Introduction

Modern achievements of scientific and technical progress are accompanied by fundamental changes in the most diverse spheres of human life, including education. Today, the reserves for increasing the efficiency and quality of trainees training, based on traditional means of training, have actually been exhausted. Higher education is characterized by continued improvement, rethinking and revision of the conceptual framework and aggravation of competition in the market of educational services, increased requirements for the teachers innovative potential and the quality of the educational process. The improvement of international standards of training shows how important is the issue of highly qualified personnel training based on the use of the latest educational technologies and innovations [2, 8].

Currently the introduction of interactive learning due to two trends. The first follows from the general direction of the education development in forming mental activity and the ability to learn. The second follows from the modern requirements development to the

[a] Corresponding author: loginova70_70@mail.ru

quality of the individual graduate. Education subject's interact with each other, share information, jointly solve problems, simulate situations, evaluate each other's actions and their own behavior and immerse themselves in a real atmosphere of cooperation in solving problems in interactive learning [6].

Not all teachers and students are created for interactive methods. But their use provides an opportunity for quality training, professional growth, changing oneself and cooperative education [3].

In addition, education is the sphere of education subject's life self-fulfillment, therefore in the center of modern education there should be not so much academic subjects as the ways of thinking and the activity of the trainee.

Interactive learning is usually seen as learning immersed in communication. However, the term "immersed" does not at all mean that it is "substituted" by communication. Interactive learning retains the ultimate goal and main content of the educational process, but it modifies forms from traditional or translational (transfer) to interactive, that is, based on mutual understanding and interaction. Kurt Levin in the middle of XX century formulated the assumption that it is easier to change the individuals gathered into the group than to change any of them individually [7]. This is the most important feature of interactive learning: the learning process takes place in a group collaborative activity, being subordinate to the effects of group dynamics. The essence of interactive learning is that the learning process is organized in such way that virtually all trainees are involved in the process of cognition, they have the opportunity to understand and reflect on what they know and think. Cooperative activity in the learning process means that each subject contributes his own individual contribution, exchanges knowledge, ideas and methods of activity. This happens in an atmosphere of benevolence and mutual support, which allows not only to receive new knowledge, but also develops cognitive activity, translates it into higher forms of cooperation.

The logic of the educational process in an interactive training varies considerably: it does not follow from the theory to practice, and moves from the formation of a new experience to the theoretical understanding through the application. Student's interactive activities ensure the growth of the knowledge, skills, methods of work and communication, all of which determine the quality of training and opportunities for their life self-fulfillment.

2 Methods

The purpose of this study is to evaluate the possibilities of interactive learning at the same time hold two focus: improving the quality of vocational training, self-realization and life self-fulfillment of the educational process subjects.

The study involved teachers and students of the Clinical Psychology Faculty who have issued informed consent. The number of students is 238 people. The number of teachers is 47. The study was of a longitudinal character from 2012 to 2016.

The study was approved by a medical university ethical committee.

The procedure of internal quality monitoring was used to assess the quality of training students. The questionnaire of "Assessment of the teacher on student opinion" and "Assessment of students on teacher opinion", "Self-assessment of learning activities" and "Self-assessment of educational activities" were used in the monitoring. These questionnaires suggested assessment on a 5-point scale from 1 to 5.

Test Card has been developed to assess the implementation possibilities of the life self-fulfillment. The arithmetic mean of the number of possibilities and the degree of their implementation in percent during the lesson was calculated.

Mathematical processing of the obtained results was carried out using the SPSS Statistics 21 software package.

3 Results and discussion

Since 2010, the Clinical Psychology Faculty has implemented interactive learning technology, which began with a poll using SMS voting in classrooms (lectures, seminars). This technology allows to quickly getting information about the opinions of students in the group, to divide the students into groups according to their position, to use the results in the discussion. During the period of using this technology it can be stated that an interactive survey using SMS voting in training sessions is one of the control forms over the quality of education at the faculty.

The next step was the reduction of the non-imitative (used in the traditional forms of learning activities, lectures, classes, course and diploma design, etc.) and increase of simulation (gaming and non-gaming) technologies in the educational process.

The need for the introduction of interactive learning in the training practice was due to two trends. The first trend follows from the general direction of the development of education, its orientation is not so much to gain specific knowledge, but rather to develop skills of thinking activity, the ability to learn, the ability to process huge amounts of information. The second trend follows from the development of the requirements for the personality characteristics of the graduate, who must also have the ability of optimal behavior in various situations in the professional sphere.

Results of study show increasing satisfaction of all participants in the educational process [9].

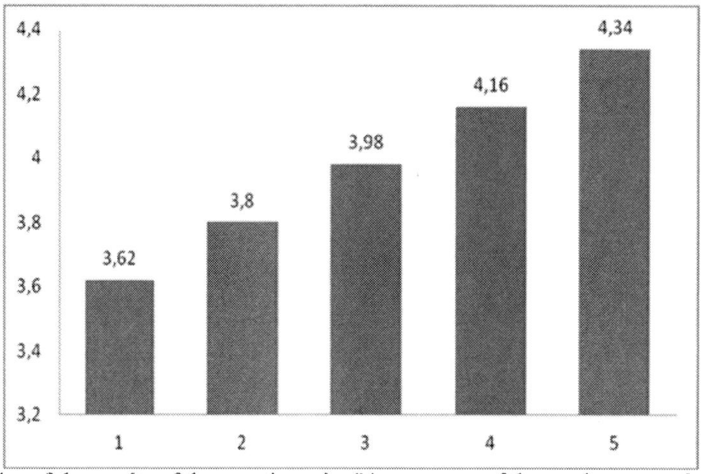

Fig. 1. Dynamics of the results of the questionnaire "Assessment of the teacher on student opinion" for 2012 - 2016

The results of questionnaire "Assessment of the teacher on student opinion" for 2012 - 2016 years show that the total assessment increased from 3.62 to 4.34 points.

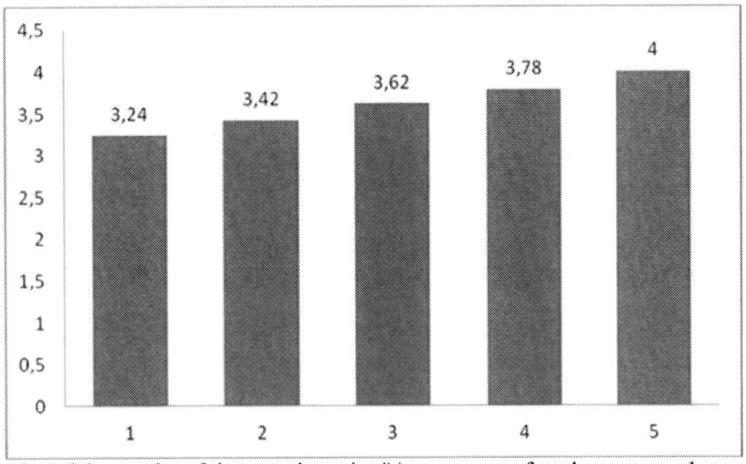

Fig. 2. Dynamics of the results of the questionnaire "Assessment of students on teacher opinion" for 2012 – 2016

The results of questionnaire "Assessment of students on teacher opinion" for 2012 - 2016 years show that the total assessment increased from 3.24 to 4.0 points.

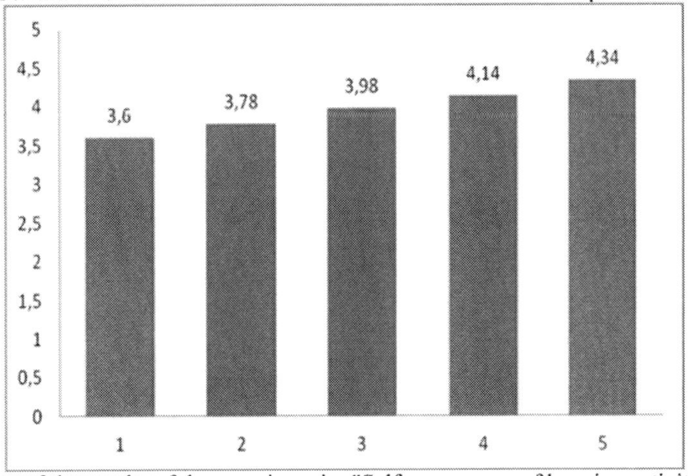

Fig. 3. Dynamics of the results of the questionnaire "Self-assessment of learning activities" for 2012 – 2016

The results of questionnaire "Self-assessment of learning activities" for 2012 - 2016 years show that the total assessment increased from 3.6 to 4.34 points.

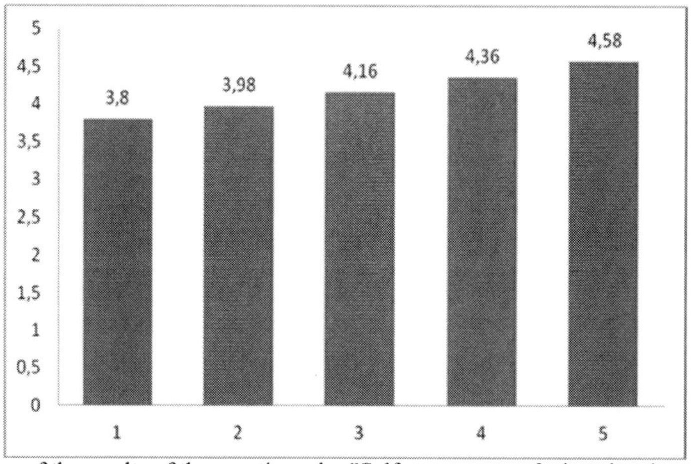

Fig. 4. Dynamics of the results of the questionnaire "Self-assessment of educational activities" for 2012 – 2016

The results of questionnaire "Self-assessment of educational activities" for 2012 - 2016 years show that the total assessment increased from 3.8 to 4.58 points.

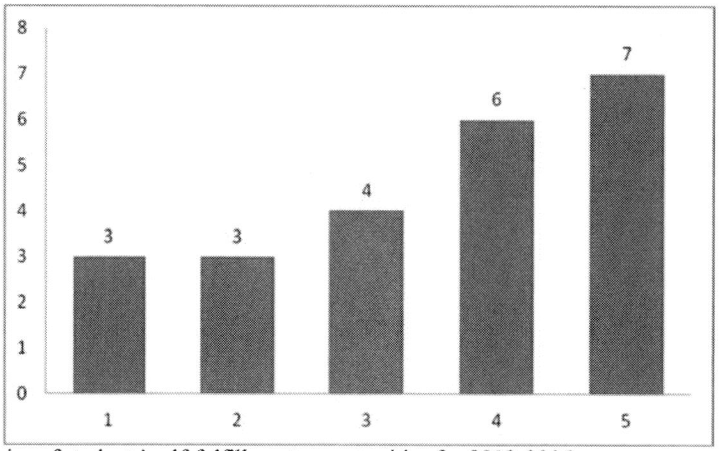

Fig. 5. Dynamics of students' self-fulfillment opportunities for 2012-2016

Evaluation of the implementation opportunities of the student's life self-fulfillment for 2012 - 2016 years show that the amount of detected opportunities in one lesson has grown from 3 to 7.

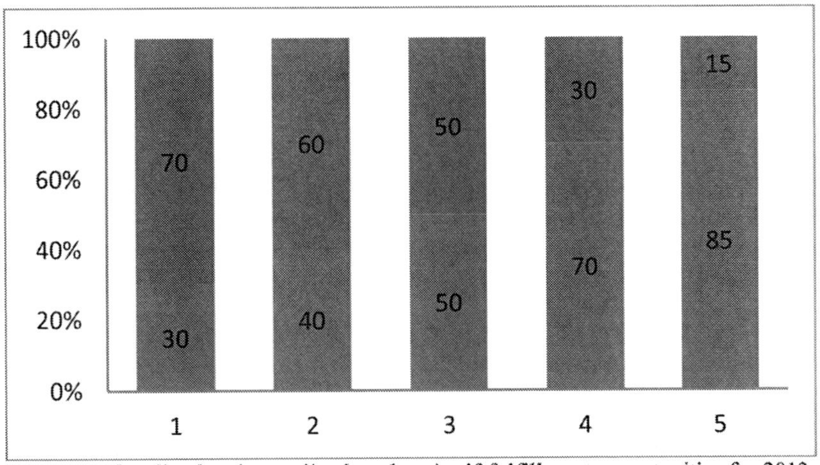

Fig. 6. Percentage of realized and unrealized students' self-fulfillment opportunities for 2012 - 2016

The percentage of realized opportunities of the student's life self-fulfillment for 2012 - 2016 years has increased from 30% to 85%.

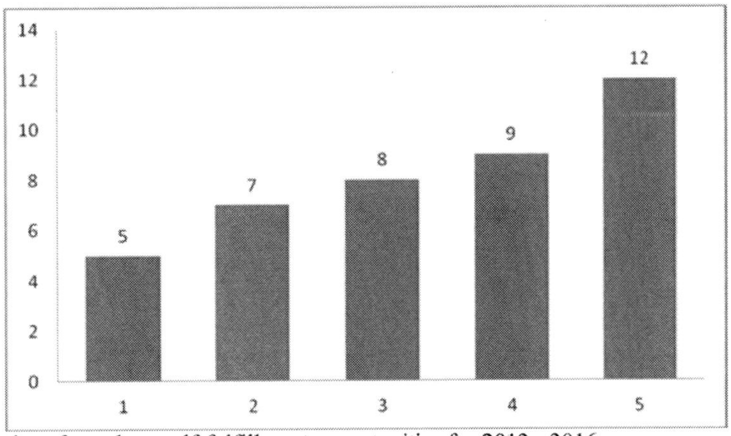

Fig. 7. Dynamics of teachers self-fulfillment opportunities for 2012 - 2016

Evaluations of the implementation opportunities of the teacher's life self-fulfillment for 2012 - 2016 years show that the amount of detected opportunities in one lesson has grown from 5 to 12.

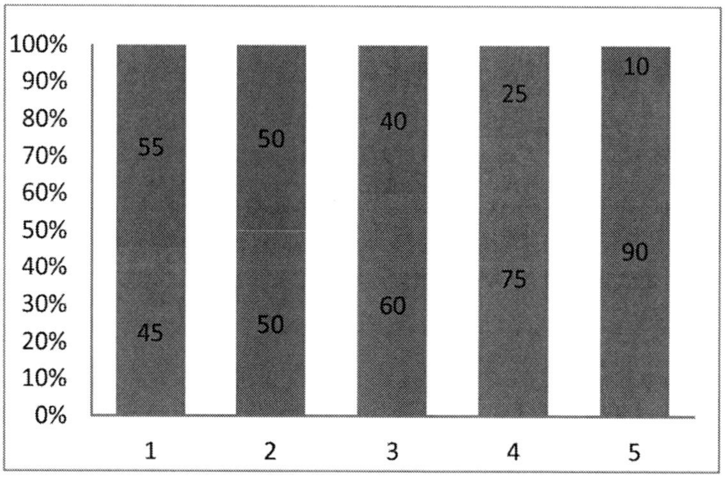

Fig. 8. Percentage of realized and unrealized teacher's self-fulfillment opportunities for 2012 - 2016

The percentage of realized opportunities of the teacher's life self-fulfillment for 2012 - 2016 years has increased from 45% to 90%.

According to scientists, the interactive training allows a sharp increase in the percentage of mastering the material compared to other types of learning activities. Thus, the memorization of the lecture is increased by 5%, reading by 10%, video or audio materials by 20%, demonstrations by 30%, discussions by 50%, practices by 75%, training others or application of the acquired knowledge by 90% [5].

T. Volfovskaya emphasizes the importance of interactive skills, which provide a harmonious and creative entry of a person into social life. The scientist unites them in two groups. The first group describes a person as a responsible personal autonomous human and embraces self-control, self-esteem, self-presentation, orientation to his own system of assessing various situations. The second group of interactive skills determines the socio-perceptual and operational-technological components of personal interaction. The ability to contact, the mood for consent and tolerance, the ability to design and use different models of behavior, the ability to be a leader and obey and the ability to maintain friendly relations (cooperative skills) are referred to the second group [1].

Our experience shows that interactive training allows:

- realize the subject - the subject approach in the organization of educational activity;
- form active-cognitive and intellectual activity of students;
- strengthen the motivation to study;
- create a favorable atmosphere in class;
- exclude monologic presentation of educational material and duplication of information that can be obtained from accessible sources;
- spontaneously memorize special terms and information;
- develop students' communicative competences in various forms [4].

The changes in the organization of communication among students occur.

This are a sincere and open behavior, the independence of the opinions, the independence of the evaluations produced, the initiative and the ability to lead others for themselves.

In addition, the self-assessment of the professional activities of teachers is growing in the interactive educational process. They are more appreciative of students, because they are not the object of evaluation, but full partners in cooperative activities.

We can assume that direct interaction, the cooperative creation of the students and the teacher, the formation of a professional world outlook and the expansion of reflective experience are the reasons for the growing opportunities for the students 'and teachers' life self-fulfillment and the degree of their realization from year to year.

4 Conclusions

The results of the research and the practice of introducing interactive technologies contribute to

- Growth the level of trust of external and internal consumers to the educational services quality, their effectiveness and effectiveness;
- Growth the competitiveness of faculty graduates in the labor market;
- Involving faculty members in the development of the educational and additional professional services, growth the commitment of employees to the idea of quality.

Using interactive technologies in the organization of the training makes it possible to consider the issues of individual educational strategies, enhances the quality of learning and creates the opportunity for self-realization and life self-fulfillment.

References

1. T.O. Volfovskaya. Determination of the level of formation of interactive personality skills at the stages of socialization. Pedagogic and Psychology. 3-4, 141-148 (2003)
2. P.P. Efimov, I.O. Efimova. Interactive teaching methods - the basis of innovative pedagogical technologies. *Innovative pedagogical technologies: materials of Intern. Sci. Conf. (Kazan, October 2014).* Kazan, 286-290 (2014)
3. I.O. Loginova, V.B. Chupina. *Technology of interactive learning in the university.* Krasnoyarsk: KrasSMU, 178 (2011)
4. I.O. Loginova, E.I. Chernova. Peculiarities of psychological and educational support for students' readiness to fulfillment their choice. Psychology of training, 4, 115-128. Access mode: http://www.edit.muh.ru/content/mag/jour3.php?link=po042013 (2013)
5. O.I. Pometun, L.V. Pirozhenko. *Interactive learning technologies: theory and practice.* Kiev: ASK, 136 (2002)
6. O.A. Sidorenko, I.O. Loginova. Possibilities of methods and technologies of simulation modeling in the preparation of students-psychologists. *Effective management and organization of the educational process in Modern Medical University (Pedagogical University).* Krasnoyarsk: Verso, 286-289 (2014)
7. K. Levin. Frontiers in Group Dynamics: Concept, Method, and Reality in Social Science. Human Relation, 1, 5-38 (1947)
8. I.O. Loginova, O.V. Volkova, J.V. Andrejeva, T.I. Serduk, I.O. Kononenko. International Accreditation of the Main Educational Program as Possibility of opening the New Educational Horizons. TOJET, 11, 1254-1258 (2016)
9. M.V. Sokolovskaya, E.V. Zamiralova, R.G. Buyankina. Self-evaluation as a tool of improving the quality management system of educational organization. Siberian medical review, 3, 80-84 (2014)

The verification of educational objectives in the chemistry education of the Czech Republic

Jan Tříska[1a], and Hana Čtrnáctová[1]

[1]Charles University, Faculty of Science, Department of Teaching and Didactics of Chemistry, Albertov 6, 128 42, Prague, Czech Republic

Abstract. The educational objectives in the Czech Republic are determined by so-called Framework Education Programs. For each individual subject, compulsory curriculum and expected outcomes of pupils are determined. Expected outcomes are defined by active verbs and they match the highest level of Bloom's taxonomy of educational objectives. For the pupils to reach these objectives, they first have to acquire the knowledge and skills of the lower levels. Our project is focused on the creation of indicators, by which we mean suitable learning exercises, which serve to verify the attainment of objectives of chemistry education at upper secondary school. These indicators are being created on the three levels of difficulty – acquisition of knowledge, the application of said knowledge, and reasoning and problem solving. The indicators are being tested in the school practice.
Keywords: Educational objectives; curriculum; Czech Republic

1 Introduction

In the year 2000, the preparations of the reform of the school system started in the Czech Republic. In 2004, they resulted in the introduction of the so-called Framework Educational Program on the level of preschool, primary, secondary school and higher vocational school. Since 2004 the school reform has been in progress. This project is focused on students between 15 and 18 years who study at upper secondary school. In the Czech Republic, this type of general education school is called "Gymnasium." The Framework Educational Program for gymnasiums [1] defines the educational objectives and reflects needs and trends in education of the 21st century [2]. In the scope of school's individual subjects, the subject of chemistry among them, the Framework Educational Program for gymnasiums defines the compulsory content of curriculum and the cognitive objectives. The educational objective is expressed by so-called expected outcomes of the student and these expected outcomes are defined by active verbs.

[a] Corresponding author: triskaja@gmail.com

DOI: 10.1051/shsconf/20173701073

1.1 The drawbacks of Framework Educational Programs

A certain trend, which was brought by the Framework Educational Program, is a departure from the cognitive objectives. However, the authors of this project are of opinion that the cognitive objectives occupy an irreplaceable spot in the secondary school education (gymnasium) and this reduction of the curriculum documents prevents the evaluation of the success in the education. The Framework Educational Program for the gymnasium mentions only 4 general cognitive objectives for the general chemistry:

- Student uses technical terminology for describing substances and explaining chemical processes,
- Student performs chemical calculations and applies them to solving practical problems,
- Student predicts the properties of elements and their behavior in chemical processes based on the knowledge of the Periodic System of Elements,
- Student uses knowledge of the particle structure of substances and chemical bonds to predict some physico-chemical properties of substances and their behavior in chemical reactions.

These objectives match the highest level of the Bloom's taxonomy of educational objectives [3] and they are introduced by words such as *"predicts, applies, and uses the knowledge for prediction"*. We assume that the student will reach these levels only after acquiring the knowledge and skills on the lower levels of the Bloom's taxonomy of educational objectives. We also think that the existence of a greater number of the cognitive objectives and tools for their verification will provide us with relevant data about the success of chemistry education at the upper secondary school. Currently, no such tools for the verification of the educational objectives at the gymnasium exist.

2 Methods

Our project is focused on the creation of the indicators, suitable learning tasks, which will test the attainment of the cognitive objectives of the chemistry education at the gymnasium [4]. Among other things, testing of 15 to 18 years old aged students is missing in the Czech Republic. The goal of the project is to prepare a set of indicators, which will reliably verify these objectives of general chemistry written in the Framework Educational Program.

2.1 Indicators of chemical education

An indicator is an observable fact which indicates the presence of unobservable fact [5]. Indicators are usually used for monitoring and controlling [6]. At school, we want to evaluate and verify educational results. Educational indicators are qualitative indicators that tell us about the characteristics, functioning and financing of the education system [7]. In curriculum, it is expected that students achieve certain objectives. As soon as we define the expected outcomes, we should say how to verify them. One way of verifying the expected outcomes of students is the creation of the indicators of the educational results. Learning tasks are good indicators for evaluating the quality of education [8]. The Created learning tasks validate various levels of subject matter and achievement of the expected outcomes of students.

2.2 Three levels of indicators

The indicators are created for three levels of difficulty – acquisition of knowledge, application of the said knowledge and reasoning and problem solving. The creation of indicators had been preceded by assessment of the similar objectives for the general chemistry. The recourse was an analysis of the documents, especially of the catalogue of requirements for the common part of the school-leaving chemistry exam [9]. If the suitable objective wasn't present in the catalogue, it was designed by the authors of this project. The created indicators are being consulted with focus group, who are able ascertain the suitability of the established objectives.

2.3 Example of designed indicator

Here is an example of a designed indicator (Fig. 1). The set is focused on phenomenon of radioactivity. The first tasks is about using radioactivity in medicine, especially in the spa treatment. The exercise is focused on the acquisition of knowledge and the expected outcomes of students are:

- The student describes the types of radioactive radiation and defines the differences between natural and artificial radioactive transformation of elements.
- The student describes the types of nuclear reactions and writes the equations of nuclear reactions in accordance with the weight conservation law.

Radioactive treatment in Jáchymov

In the Ore Mountains lies the town of Jáchymov, famous for its uranium mines and spa (Task fig. 1). For the treatment of diseases of the locomotoric system, peripheral nerves and vessels, radon water containing radon isotopes $^{222}_{86}Rn$ is used. The ionizing radiation that radon water produces has stimulating effects on the body. Radon isotope $^{222}_{86}\mathrm{Rn}$ is transformed into the polonium isotope $^{218}_{84}\mathrm{Po}$ during the radioactive conversion:

$$^{222}_{86}\mathrm{Rn} \rightarrow\ ^{218}_{84}\mathrm{Po} + \_\_\_\_\_\_$$

Task fig. 1 – Spa in Jáchymov, Czech Republic

Fig. 1a: The preview of indicator for the lowest level of acquisition

Question 1:
Which particles generate ionizing radiation?

a) Hydrogen isotope nuclei $^{1}_{1}H$
b) Helium isotope nuclei $^{4}_{2}He$
c) Radon isotope nuclei $^{222}_{86}Rn$
d) Polonium isotope nuclei $^{218}_{84}Po$

Question 2:
This type of ionizing radiation, which is the least penetrating and has the least energy, is also denoted by the Greek letter. What kind of radioactive radiation is it?

a) α-radiation
b) β^{-}-radiation
c) β^{+}-radiation
d) γ-radiation

Fig. 1b: The preview of indicator for the lowest level of acquisition

The task on the second level of the Bloom's taxonomy (the application of the said knowledge) is focused on thermonuclear fusion on the surface of the sun. The preview is shown in the fig. 2. The task on the highest level (reasoning and problem solving) is focused on the application of radioactivity in nuclear power engineering and the preview is shown in the fig. 3. We try to ensure that all indicators are applied to practical examples.

What is happening in the Sun?
The Sun is a star which is situated in the center of the Solar System. It is composed of hot plasma and constantly produces a tremendous amount of energy. This energy is generated in the Sun through thermonuclear reactions that have been, and still are, the basic prerequisite for life on Earth. The Sun supplies Earth with light and warmth.

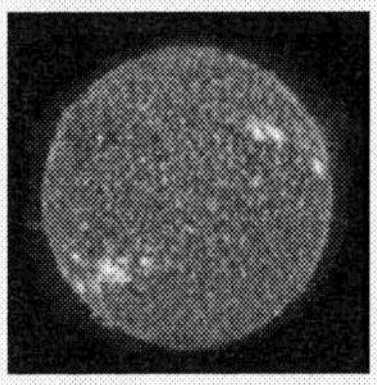

Task fig. 2 – The Sun

Question:
Sun's energy is produced by a particular thermonuclear reaction – so-called thermonuclear fusion. Which of the following reactions is an example of thermonuclear fusion that is consistent with the mass conservation law?

a) $^{2}_{1}H + ^{3}_{1}H \rightarrow ^{4}_{2}He$
b) $^{2}_{1}H + ^{3}_{1}H \rightarrow ^{4}_{2}He + ^{1}_{0}n$
c) $^{4}_{2}He + ^{1}_{0}n \rightarrow ^{2}_{1}H + ^{3}_{1}H$
d) $^{235}_{92}U \rightarrow ^{4}_{2}He + ^{231}_{90}Th$

Fig 2: The preview of indicator for the medium level of acquisition

How does the nuclear power station work?

Nuclear power stations (Task fig. 3) produce energy through a steam turbine that drives alternators to produce electricity. The steam is generated by evaporation of the liquid water in the steam generator. The heat that is needed for this transformation is a fissionable nuclear reaction. The basic type of fuel is uranium ore containing isotope $^{235}_{92}U$.

Task fig.3 – Nuclear power station Temelín, Czech Republic

Question:

The fission nuclear reaction that takes place in a nuclear reactor is schematically shown in the Task fig. 4. This reaction is initiated by neutrons which bombard uranium isotope $^{235}_{92}U$.

Describe the next course of this fission reaction in your own words: ....
....
....

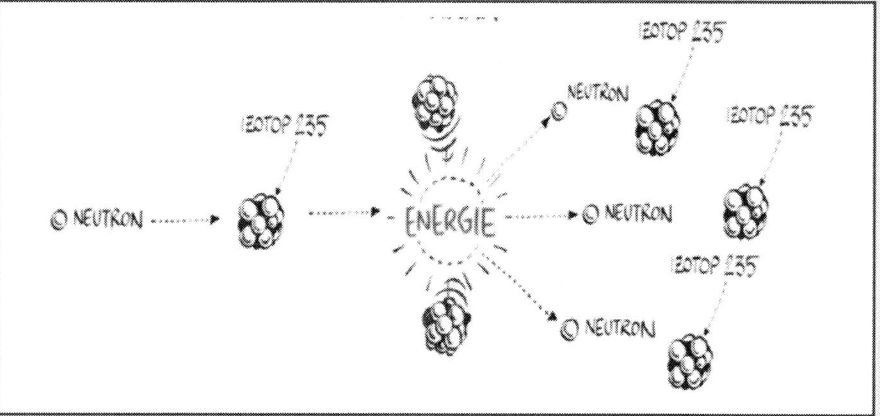

Task fig. 4 - Nuclear reaction in nuclear reactor

Fig. 3: The preview of indicator for the highest level of acquisition

The tasks are always followed by methodical comments. There we note the correct solutions and how the task should be evaluated. In the methodical comments, we also explain what part of the curriculum is verified by this task, and on what level (Fig. 4).

Methodical comments and evaluation of the task
The goal of the first task is to demonstrate the student's knowledge of radioactivity. From the task assignment, it is likely that the isotope of radon $^{222}_{86}Rn$ is transformed into the polonium $^{218}_{84}Po$ isotope, which releases radioactive radiation. In the second part of the task, the student demonstrates further knowledge of a fact that the helium helix current is also called α-radiation. Correct solution: 1 b); 2 a) The goal of the second task is to verify whether the student can apply this knowledge and correctly write the equation of a thermonuclear reaction based on its description. At the same time, they have to determine the proper reactants and reaction products (i.e. hydrogen isotopes), and also take into account the mass conservation law. Correct solution: b) The goal of the third task is to show the student's ability of reasoning and problem solving on an example of a practical application of nuclear reactions in nuclear power plants. The schematics of reaction should allow the student to determine and describe in their own words how the reaction will continue. Correct solution: The nuclear reaction is caused by a neutron that causes the nucleus of uranium isotope 235 to split. This results in two lighter nuclei and the release of three more neutrons. These neutrons cause the fission of more nuclei, which causes the reaction to continue on its own with increasing speed. Because of that, the power plants must control the reaction and capture excess neutrons in order to prevent a runaway reaction and explosion.

Fig. 4: Methodical comments and evaluation of the tasks

3 Results

We are currently finishing the design of indicators. We have designed 10 sets of indicators on different topics from general chemistry: Substances and Their Properties, Calculation from Chemical Equations, Solutions, Atomic Electron Shell, Radioactivity, Chemical Bonds, Thermochemistry, Speed of Chemical Reactions, Acid-base Processes, and Redox Processes. In 2018, we are going to verify the indicators in practice. Students who will solve the sets of indicator tasks will be rated according to their success and according to the input data, which they have provided to the reviewers. The input data will be obtained from a questionnaire, where we will focus on the understanding of the topics, the student's motivation, readiness, and self-confidence during problem solving. The results of our project will allow the establishing of more detailed cognitive objectives for curriculum of general chemistry at gymnasiums and the use of the designed tools – indicators – for the verifications of these objectives within the chemistry education in the Czech Republic. Sub-outcomes of the project will be data about the attitude of Czech students toward learning and solving tasks – which is 2 of the 6 key competencies defined by the Framework Educational Programs. The designed indicators, which will be verified on the sample of Czech students and evaluated by experts, will be further provided to other institutions, both domestic and foreign.

4 Discussion and conclusion

According to the Framework Educational Program, the students should achieve the highest level of educational objectives. However, we expect the reality to be different. We are going to test these students at their schools, after the teacher finishes their explanation of the topic. We suppose that the largest group of the students will be able to solve only the lowest level of indicators correctly. We also expect, that only very few students will be able to solve the highest level of the indicators, although it is compulsory according to the Framework Educational Program. This should prove that the current state of the Framework Educational Program was badly designed and it is not useful in practice. In our opinion, the Framework Educational Program should be remade to be more specific and it should include more cognitive objectives including the objectives of the lower levels of Bloom's taxonomy. We hope that our project will prove there is a need for these changes.

The main benefit of our project is that the designed indicators can be useful for gymnasium teachers. They will have the indicators available, accompanied by a list of expected student outcomes. The teachers can assign these indicators to their students and evaluate the results [10]. Based on the evaluation of the indicator, the teachers will be able to give feedback to their students and they can help them with improving their results in the future.

References

1. MŠMT (2007) *Rámcový vzdělávací program pro gymnázia* (RVP G). Praha: Výzkumný ústav pedagogický v Praze. ISBN 978-80-87000-11-3.
2. Delors, J. (1998). Learning: The treasure within – report to UNESCO of the International Commission.Paris : UNESCO
3. Anderson, L., W.; Krathwohl, D., R., eds. (2001). *A taxonomy for learning, teaching, and assessing: A revision of Bloom's taxonomy of educational objectives*. Allyn and Bacon.
4. Tříska, J., Čtrnáctová, H. (2016). *Indicators of Educational Results in Chemistry Teaching*. Proceedings of the 7th International Conference on Research in Didactics of the Sciences DidSci 2016, Kraków, Poland. ISBN 978-83-8084-037-9.
5. Bunge, M. (2003) *Philosophical Dictionary, Enlarged Edition*. New York: Prometheus Books. ISBN 1-59102-037-9.
6. Janoušková, S., Maršák, J. (2008). *Indikátory – významný prostředek našeho poznávání*. Pedagogika, 52 (1),s. 29-35.
7. Průcha, J., Walterová, E., Mareš, J. (2009) Pedagogický slovník. 6. rozšířené a aktualizované vydání. Praha: Portál, 395 s. ISBN 978-807-3676-476.
8. Čtrnáctová, H. (2009). *Učební úlohy v chemii 1. díl*. (2. vyd.) Praha, Karolinum.
9. MŠMT (2004) *Katalog požadavků ke společné části maturitní zkoušky v roce 2004: Chemie*. Praha: CERMAT.
10. Straková, J. (2013). *Jak dál s kurikulární reformou*. Pedagogická orientace, roč. 23, č. 5, s. 734-743.

Preschool and early school education of migrants and minorities in Poland. Teachers' competences in the light of regulations and practice

Justyna Wojniak[1a], Kinga Orzeł-Dereń[1]

[1]Pedagogical University of Krakow, ul. Podchorążych 2, 30-084 Krakow, Poland

Abstract. According to Polish Constitution all children, regardless of their nationality and legal status, have the right to education, and the obligation to study up to the age of 18 [1]. So far there have been no comprehensive solutions to support kindergartens and schools, as well as teachers and educators who are not prepared to work with children of different cultures, especially children with little or no knowledge of Polish language. Although Poland is still a relatively homogeneous from the ethnic and religious point of view, and ethnic minorities account for 2.5-3% (about 1-1.2 million) of the population, number of foreigners living in Poland makes their education an increasing challenge. The paper is divided into two sections. The first one is an overview of the EU regulations as well as national legal provisions concerning education of children of the migrant background. The second part discusses challenges and tasks indicated by teachers who work with students of foreign origin. They involve not only adjusting the teaching content to intercultural requirements, but also, more broadly, adaptation of working methods to specific needs of various participators of educational process. Work in such circumstances forces teachers and school management to seek new solutions and, above all, to acquire or develop new, intercultural competences.
Keywords: migrants, minorities, perception, early school education

1 Introduction

An increasing number of migrant pupils in European schools has implications for education systems. In the first instance, schools must be adjusted to their presence and take into consideration their particular needs, from the point of view of an equal right to education

[a] Corresponding author: jwojniak@up.krakow.pl

and its high quality. These conditions are vital for effective education, which is able to provide these pupils with instruments necessary to become integrated, successful and productive citizens of the host country.

2 Migrant and Minority Education in the European Union Law

According to the Green Paper by the Commission of the European Communities on Migration & Mobility, describing challenges and opportunities for EU education systems, a broad concept of the term "migration" should be adopted. Taking it into account, the terms "children from a migrant background", "children of migrants" and "migrant pupils" refer to "the children of all persons living in an EU country where they were not born, irrespective of whether they are third country nationals, citizens of another EU Member State or subsequently became nationals of the host Member State" [2]. The reason of such an attitude is that the specific educational issues might be applied to a significant number of individuals. Moreover, the data that exemplify these issues do not distinguish between the countries of origin, whether their citizens come from the EU member states or from the third countries [3].

In this context one must remember that these are Member States that are responsible for establishing general educational aims and policies. Nevertheless, the challenges of migrants' integration and education are common. An analysis of implementation of the Education and Training 2010 Work Programme proves an existing educational disadvantage of many migrant pupils. It particularly concerns the need of reducing the gaps in educational attainment between migrant pupils and other host peers as well as in the performance and scoring in such areas as science, mathematics and reading [4].

The European Union has already undertaken several different types of activities which impact, directly or indirectly, Member States' policies regarding these issues. The actions related to the issue comprise of: National Contact Points, the European Fund for the Integration of Third-country Nationals, aimed at facilitating integration measures for migrant youth and children. In addition, the Recommendation of the European Parliament and the Council on "Key Competences for Lifelong Learning" of 2006 lists the attitudes, knowledge and skills necessary to facilitate personal fulfilment and development, active citizenship, social inclusion and employment in modern Europe. Such competences as Social and Civic Competences and Cultural Awareness are particularly relevant for developing national educational approaches [5].

One of the most important instruments in this field is Directive 77/486/EEC on the education of the children of migrant workers. According to the Directive's provisions, "Member States shall ensure that free tuition to facilitate initial reception is offered in their territory [to the children of migrant workers], including, in particular, the teaching of the official language or one of the official languages of the host State", and "Member States shall in cooperation with the States of origin, take appropriate measures to promote in coordination with normal education, teaching of the mother tongue and culture of the country of origin" [6]. The impact of the Directive however is limited, as it allows some flexibility in the way these aims are achieved, and the Member States have all developed their own approaches to the teaching migrant children.

The issue of educating the children of migrants has also been addressed by the European Parliament in the Resolution of 2009. The Parliament, among others, "Calls on the Member State governments to ensure education for the children of legal migrants, including the teaching of the official languages of the host country and the promotion of their native languages and cultures" [7]. This institution also believes that preserving and promoting multilingualism must be a part of every school's curriculum, and language-learning should be encouraged from pre-school age to promote inclusion of migrants. The place given to teaching in the mother tongue within the curriculum and the organisation of this process must be however left to the Member States [8].

Projects related to intercultural education, school integration of migrant pupils and social inclusion for disadvantaged youth are supported in the framework of the Erasmus+ Programme (2014-2020), while Cohesion Policy, via the Structural Funds - in particular the European Social Fund - support social inclusion projects and measures at national and regional level.

3 Migrant and Minority Education in Polish Education System

In Poland, challenges and dilemmas concerning education of the children of migrants remain limited, as the country - from the national and cultural point of view - is a distinctively homogenous one. The groups of various cultural and national backgrounds are as follows:

1. National minorities: Belarusians, Czechs, Lithuanians, Armenians, Russians, Germans, Ukrainians, Jews, Slovaks;
2. Ethnic minorities: Roma, Lemkos, Tatars, Karais;
3. Children of migrants and refugees with different statuses of residence, i.e. tolerated stay, temporary protection, subsidiary protection;
4. Children of repatriates.

In 1990s, there were almost no students of migrant background in Polish schools. The problem began to grow with an increasing number of people applying for a refugee status. Since 2000, intensified immigration of Chechen refugees to Poland has been observed. This situation forced development of new systemic and legal solutions.

An institutional and legal framework for the education of children of migrants in the Polish system is established by the Act on the Education System [9], and the Regulation on Admission of non-Polish citizens to public kindergartens, schools, teacher education establishments and institutions and organizations of additional Polish language learning, additional compensatory activities and learning the language and culture of the country of origin [10]. In case of students with undetermined legal status, the right to education derives from the Constitution of the Republic of Poland of 1997, guaranteeing everyone the right to education, and from international commitments, including above all the provisions of the Convention on the Rights of the Child [11].

What is noteworthy, an amendment of the Act on the Education System of 2009 states that persons who are subject to compulsory education but are not Polish citizens and do not speak Polish or their level of speaking is insufficient to learn, have the right for an additional, free course of Polish, organized by a school authority, namely a commune, which is the smallest administrative district in Poland. The Act on the education system also includes provisions on organizing additional compensatory activities of individual teaching subjects, which are organized by the school authority as well, lasting no longer than 12 months. Non-Polish nationals subject to compulsory education who do not speak Polish at all or speak it at an insufficient level, have the right to be assisted by a person who speaks the language of their country of origin. Such a person is employed as a teacher's assistant by a school principal and this sort of support is also granted for maximum 12 months [12].

Polish legal acts concerning the education system are also addressed to national and ethnic minorities, as well as to the communities using the regional language [13]. These provisions are more detailed than those devoted to the pupils of migrant background. The reason of such an attitude are different educational aims of the mentioned groups. In case of migrant children, the goal is to provide them with the most effective instruments of assimilation and inclusion. Therefore, preserving the language and culture of origin becomes mostly the matter of parents and family members. Moreover, migrant groups in

Poland, as it was mentioned, are not numerous and usually dispersed – those who live in the refugee centres usually also represent different nationalities. Under such circumstances, opening courses of the language of origin or suitable cultural activities might be complicated from the organisational and financial point of view. On the contrary, in case of national and ethnic minorities in Poland, the aim is to preserve the linguistic and cultural diversity, as well as to sustain their sense of distinct identity.

The European Commission pursues an active policy to protect and support regional and minority languages in Europe. This is the main instrument of promoting multilingualism in the united Europe, based on the provisions of the Charter of Fundamental Rights of the European Union, which states that the Union respects cultural, religious and linguistic diversity [14]. The European Parliament, in its resolution of 2009 on multilingualism, stresses the importance of the languages of national and ethnic minorities used in Europe [15]. This issue was also undertaken by the European Charter for Regional or Minority Languages of 2003, which was signed and adopted by the Republic of Poland.

Effective implementation of these rights depends on diverse legal solutions, taking into account special educational needs manifested by the minority pupils. The Constitution of the Republic of Poland is the basic law regulating the sphere of rights and freedoms of national and ethnic minorities in Poland. Constitutional principles are supplemented by the Act of 2005 on national and ethnic minorities and the regional language.

Other executive acts relating to organization of the education system for children of national and ethnic minorities and those who use a regional language are: 1) Regulation of the Minister of National Education of 2009 on the admission of pre-school education programs and curricula in schools and for the use of school textbooks (in the development and use of textbooks for children and young people of national and ethnic minority groups and using regional languages); 2) Regulation of the Minister of National Education of 2007 on the conditions and manner of assessing, classifying and promoting pupils and students, and carrying out examinations of children and youth from national and ethnic minorities and using regional languages; 3) Regulation of the Minister of National Education of 2001 on requirements for the performance of examinations of children and adolescents from national and ethnic minorities and using regional languages.

This education primarily includes the ability to maintain the sense of identity. At the request of parents, this can be accomplished in separate groups, units or schools, or in groups, units or schools with additional language, history and culture classes. In this case, the inter-departmental group, composed of students of different units, must comprise of at least 7 students in elementary and lower secondary school, and 14 students in upper secondary school. Taking into account organization of the teaching process in combined classes, there should be at least 3 but not more than 14 students. Inter-school teaching groups are also applicable [16].

From the legal and practical point of view, recognition and meeting of educational rights of migrants and minorities in Poland might be also considered on the basis of special educational needs. International origins of this term may be found in the UNESCO Salamanca Statement and Framework for Action on Special Needs Education of 1994. According to its provisions, "Every child has unique characteristics, interests, abilities and learning needs; Education systems should be designed and educational programmes implemented to take into account the wide diversity of these characteristics and needs" [17].

In Polish education system, identification and satisfaction of the individual developmental and educational needs of a pupil, as well as their individual psychophysical abilities form a prerequisite for providing them with psychological and pedagogical assistance [18]. Among the origins of special educational needs, Polish Ministry of National Education indicates: disability, social maladjustment, special aptitudes, specific learning difficulties, disorder of linguistic communication, chronic disease, crisis or traumatic situation, adaptive difficulties related to cultural differences or changes in the educational environment resulting, for example, from earlier learning abroad. The last category may be perceived as a useful instrument of effective fulfillment of the needs of children with migrant backgrounds.

Overcoming learning difficulties that result from varied conditions, and adjusting the learning environment to individual developmental characteristics and capabilities of the group of students in question may concern the objectives, content, or methods used in the education process, as well as the organizational forms or teaching resources. These requirements could be hardly met without a wide range of assistance provided to the teachers by the psychological and pedagogical counselling centres. Professionals, who are employed in such institutions, recognize individual developmental and educational needs and psychophysical capabilities of children and adolescents. Another area of support for teachers is the planning and implementation of education and career counseling along with the development of student's interests and talents. Psychological and pedagogical counselling cooperates also with kindergartens, schools and institutions in provision and organization of psychological and pedagogical assistance, development and implementation of individual educational and therapeutic programs as well as individual programs of revalidation and education [19].

The main limitation of this solution is that in the first instance it is addressed to disabled or socially maladjusted pupils. Children from migrant backgrounds demand a more complex and more flexible attitude, depending on their individual situation. One of the instruments used in work with the migrant children is support of the cultural aide. Provisions of the Act on the education system enable to employ a person who speaks the language of the student's country of origin, and Polish schools have the opportunity to finance their employment from public funds. However, the cultural aides are employed on average in the framework of the school project implemented by non-governmental organizations. This situation often results in the lack of interest from the school authorities, namely the communes. The education subsidy received from the state budget is insufficient, and they must provide the financing from their own budget.

The competencies and responsibilities of such a professional are rather the matter of everyday practice than detailed legal regulations [20]. A cultural aide should demonstrate knowledge of Polish and the language spoken by the students under their care. Moreover, the ability to establish a fine contact with the child and the competence in interpersonal communication, ability to deal with difficult situations, knowledge of the culture of the pupils' country of origin, including cultural differences between Polish culture and the culture of origin are regarded as essential [21]. Scope of duties of a cultural aide is also based on expectations of class teachers, school principals and other teachers. Generally, it should include cooperation with teachers, parents and direct assistance to the child [22]

4 Interculturalism in Polish School

In many cases, especially taking into consideration the increasing number of migrants, such solutions may turn out to be insufficient. For this reason, one of the most important diversity support strategy within the school environment is building the professional capacity of the teaching staff. The teachers' role is to effectively influence students through the art of social communication. The teacher (…) should shape in their pupils the sense of value and openness to the emerging "otherness" [23].

For this reason, teachers should continually improve their qualifications including intercultural competences. They should pay particular attention to:

1. Basic knowledge concerning the psychological situation of the migrant child and its family, including the consequences of being refugee and migrant;

2. Skills to understand the consequences of using stereotypes, anti-bias and discrimination skills; skills of the equal treatment of all pupils, while tactfully supporting those children who need to be included in education process;
3. Knowledge of cultural differences, and the manner they affect the pupil's behaviour; understanding the behaviour of a pupil, which may result not only from their individual characteristics, but also from the culture of the country of origin;
4. Reliable cultural knowledge about the origins of pupils, including the most important traditions and customs, the most important holidays, cultural taboos, ways of behaving – for example, respecting specificity of education in the country of origin, roles of women, men and children;
5. Knowledge of existing legislation concerning various groups, such as refugees, migrants ethnic and national minorities, their rights and obligations, count of these groups;
6. Basic knowledge of acculturation, including: adaptation strategies, cultural stress, culture shock, cultural adaptation, intercultural communication challenges – verbal and nonverbal;
7. Ability to adapt materials to the needs and capabilities of migrant children, including the use of individualized methods [24].

The expected model is integration intended to build a common society rather than separate particular groups and marginalize them. However, it must be emphasized that it should be based on the multiculturalism concept, not on simple assimilation. Hence, teachers are expected to be competent in four key areas:

1. Intercultural knowledge;
2. Sensitivity and openness to others and cultural differences (ability of modeling specific situations of responding to cultural differences, creating intergenerational relations standards and building trust and sincere relations with parents);
3. Appropriate attitudes and behaviours resulting from the teacher's familiarization with theirpupils' cultural differences;
4. Language competence and linguistic skills necessary for effective communication with the children of minority or migrant background [25].

As the research proves, the teachers' attitude towards migrant pupils, described by themselves demonstrates ambivalence. On one hand, they declare fear and sense of insecurity, on the other – enthusiasm and willingness to work with foreign students. These attitudes are accompanied by lack of orientation in the specificity of the problems that teachers are supposed to face. As for their competencies, they estimate their level as very low, declaring lack of knowledge and skills, and inadequate preparation for this sort of assignments. When asked to describe their competencies in a more detailed way, the teachers point out a low level of knowledge on cultural diversity and experiences of the migrant children; they also mention insufficient knowledge of foreign languages, lack of knowledge on the problems of the migrants and refugees and rather poor skills in cooperation with parents of different cultural background. Teachers also stress the lack of knowledge on regulations concerning education of the foreign pupils, as well as insufficient preparation for work with culturally heterogeneous group [26].

Other research (carried out by the authors) confirms the pointed data. The research was performed in 2017 in urban primary schools that educate children of refugees, migrants and minorities children. The selection of research area was based on the urban character of the phenomenon of intercultural migration and on occurrence of high cultural diversity in these schools. Women predominated in the study group. The study was carried out in 50 schools. However, the sex parity was changing noticeably as they moved in the hierarchy: almost every fifth manager and every eighth teacher was a man. Long-term work experience was dominant in a group of teachers.

In the group of school educators there was a greater variation in length of service. When it comes to principals, most of them have short-term work experience. Questionnaires included among others questions related to the issues such as the problems and the need of children of minorities in the institution, the problems and needs connected with working with these students, the concerns of working with parents of these children, the opportunities and needs and resulting from working with these children, assessment of own competencies and skills in working with these children, training needs.

In the researched schools, there were 58 students in total (foreigners, children of minorities), 28 girls and 32 boys. In most schools, there were individual pupils or small groups of them (up to 6). Both the principals and the teachers describe presence of a foreign or a minority child at school as a challenge. The principals showed a friendlier attitude towards the presence of foreign children or migrants children at school than teachers. Teachers described presence of those children more as problem than an opportunity.

Respondents stressed the need to develop solutions to compensate program differences (in relation to migrants children). Cognitive values were pointed most often as a positive aspect of the presence of foreign children and migrant children. The most frequently reported negative impact of the presence of immigrant children and minority children was the unfavorable influence of these children on interpersonal relationships within the group. The most common social problems arising from attendance of migrants and minorities children were conflicts based on cultural differences, racist behavior, xenophobic behavior, intolerant behavior and exclusion of these children. The most important needs of multicultural education teachers were integration of children, adapting the work to specifics of the foreign and migrants children, the need to improve intercultural competences. Teachers also point to the need to contact a psychologist in the context of working in multicultural environment. A large majority of respondents emphasized lack of support from school and of other forms of aid. Most teachers indicated that there should be more classes of Polish for foreign students. The study clearly shows the need and teachers' willingness to participate in trainings and workshops on multicultural issues. The majority of the respondents do not know the specifics and characteristics of work in a multicultural environment. Nearly half of the respondents are unaware of the specificities of working in such an environment, and they are not aware of the needs of culturally diverse children. Teachers perceive differences in the behavior of migrant and minority children, take actions aimed at integrating such children with the group, but they do not feel that they have sufficient competences, which makes working in the multicultural environment stressful for them.

The guidance counsellors seem to be most inadequately prepared for work with migrant pupils – due to the specificity of their professional tasks, their everyday contact with the students is limited, they are concentrated on the formal aspects of their work, and they have only occasional contact with the parents. Another problem mentioned is lack of knowledge on migration processes, the problems and challenges that occur in the broad societal context. Last but not least – limited opportunities of professional development in this field. It is partly caused by the ad hoc actions and temporary projects used as the most popular tool for preparing a teacher to work with children from a migrant background. The latter problem is accompanied by the lack of effective supervision and certification of the competences acquired [27].

5 Conclusion

These attitudes and beliefs confirm that development of suitable teacher training programs is a vital condition for effective education of migrants, which results in their further integration and consistency of the entire society. Although every initiative in the field of professional teacher preparation for work with foreigners might be useful, one-day or short courses on diversity or non-discrimination issues are not a sufficient measure. Similarly to temporary projects, they do not lead to significant improvement of the teachers' performance. Poland has 5 public and 8 non-public higher education institutions dedicated to educating future teachers. Besides, there are a number of academic and non-academic institutions offering bachelor and master degrees in education. An analysis of their education proves that none of them provide programs or courses devoted to preparing to work in a culturally diverse environment. There are few institutions dedicated to special educational needs, as they are rather focused on work with disabled or socially maladjusted students, thus the gap existing in the Polish teacher education.

The most probable explanation for this situation is obviously a limited need of such initiatives due to Polish demographical specificity. However, it should be kept in mind that in the era of globalization and freedom of movement within EU, the social and educational institutions must be comprehensively prepared for the inflow of migrants and refugees, particularly taking into account the current political and economic crises. For these reasons the point of view expressed by the European Policy Network on the education of children and young people with a migrant background (SIRIUS) should be perceived as the most adequate. According to the SIRIUS report, "Teacher training programs that take diversity as a starting point and integrate the topic into the curricula of all courses – and address it from all perspectives – prepare teachers to become experts in the topic, capable of helping students from migrant backgrounds to achieve their full potential" [28], in favour of the host society as a whole.

References

1. Konstytucja Rzeczypospolitej Polskiej z dnia 2 kwietnia 1997 r., Dz.U. 1997 nr 78, poz. 483
2. Commission of the European Communities (2008), *Green Paper. Migration & mobility: challenges and opportunities for EU education systems*, Brussels, 2, retrieved: http://eur-lex.europa.eu/LexUriServ/LexUriServ.do?uri=COM:2008:0423:FIN:EN:PDF . (Accessed: 2.05.2017)
3. Ibid.
4. EU Council and the Commission, *2010 joint progress report of the Council and the Commission on the implementation of the 'Education and Training 2010 work programme'*, Official Journal of the European Union 2010/C 117/1 (2010)
5. European Parliament and the Council, *Recommendation of 18 December 2006 on key competences for lifelong learning (2006/962/EC)*, Official Journal of the European Union L 394/10, 30.12.2006, (2006)
6. Council Directive 77/486/EEC of 25 July 1977 on the education of the children of migrant workers, Official Journal L 199, 6.8.1977, (1977)
7. European Parliament, *EP resolution of 2 April 2009 on educating the children of migrants*, Official Journal of the European Union C 137 E/1, 27.5.2010 (2009a)
8. Ibid.
9. Ustawa z dnia 7 września 1991 r. o systemie oświaty, Dz.U. 1991 nr 95 poz. 425
10. Rozporządzenie Ministra Edukacji Narodowej z dnia 1 kwietnia 2010 r. w sprawie przyjmowania osób niebędących obywatelami polskimi do publicznych przedszkoli, szkół, zakładów kształcenia nauczycieli i placówek oraz organizacji dodatkowej nauki języka polskiego, dodatkowych zajęć wyrównawczych oraz nauki języka i kultury kraju pochodzenia, Dz.U. 2010 nr 57 poz. 361 (1991)
11. UN General Assembly resolution 44/25 of 20 November 1989, *Convention on the Rights of the Child*, retrieved: http://www.ohchr.org/Documents/ProfessionalInterest/crc.pdf (Accessed: 5.05.2017)
12. Ustawa z dnia 7 września 1991 r. o systemie oświaty, Dz.U. 1991 nr 95 poz. 425 (1991)

13. Ustawa z dnia 6 stycznia 2005 r. o mniejszościach narodowych i etnicznych oraz o języku regionalnym, Dz.U. 2005 nr 17 poz. 141 (2005)
14. European Union, *Charter of Fundamental Rights of the European Union*, Official Journal of the European Communities C 364/1, 18.12.2000 (2000)
15. European Parliament, *EP resolution of 24 March 2009 on Multilingualism: an asset for Europe and a shared commitment*, Session document A6-0092/2009, 24.2.2009, (2009b)
16. Ustawa z dnia 6 stycznia 2005 r. o mniejszościach narodowych i etnicznych oraz o języku regionalnym, Dz.U. 2005 nr 17 poz. 141 (2005)
17. UNESCO, Salamanca Statement and Framework for Action on Special Needs Education, Salamanca 1994, retrieved: http://unesdoc.unesco.org/images/0009/000984/098427eo.pdf (Accessed: 3.05.2017).
18. Rozporządzenie Ministra Edukacji Narodowej z dnia 30 kwietnia 2013 roku w sprawie zasad udzielania i organizacji pomocy psychologiczno-pedagogicznej w publicznych przedszkolach, szkołach i placówkach, Dz.U. 2013, poz. 532 (2013)
19. Ibid.
20. Ośrodek Rozwoju Edukacji, *Edukacja mniejszości narodowych i etnicznych oraz społeczności posługującej się językiem regionalnym w Polsce 2010-2011*, Warszawa,11 (2012)
21. Ibid., 10
22. K. Białek, *Międzykulturowość w szkole. Poradnik dla nauczycieli i specjalistów* (ed.), Ośrodek Rozwoju Edukacji, Warszawa, 48-49 (2015)
23. B. Czernecka, *Kształcenie nauczycieli zintegrowanej Europy* in: *Kształcenie nauczycieli w kontekście integracji europejskie,* M. Ochmański (ed.), Wyd. UMCS, Lublin, 38-40 (1997)
24. D. Misiejuk, *Dzieci imigrantów i mniejszości narodowych* in: *Małe dziecko w Polsce: raport o sytuacji edukacji elementarnej*, T. Szlendak (ed.), Fundacja Rozwoju Dzieci, Warszawa, 147 (2006)
25. Ibid, 148
26. K. M. Błeszyńska, *Dzieci obcokrajowców w polskich placówkach oświatowych – perspektywa szkoły*, Ośrodek Rozwoju Edukacji, Warszawa, 74-76 (2010)
27. Ibid., 76-79
28. S. Severiens, *Developing School Capacity for Diversity*, SIRIUS Network, 4 (2014).

Measuring the ICT competencies in Slovakia and in Serbia in the higher education

Gabor Kiss[1a]

[1]J. Selye University, Department of Mathematics and Informatics, Bratislavská cesta 3322, 945 01, Komárno, Slovakia

Abstract. The purpose of this study is to identify the levels of ICT Competencies of university students from two universities, one in Slovakia and the other in Serbia. The research type is quantitative and exploratory. The instrument consists of 14 items related to three types of competencies: Basic, Application and Ethical. The quantitative data analysis was performed with SPSS software using descriptive statistics and Mann-Whitney independent sample U test. The situation of education in Slovakia and Serbia is not so very different although each country has taken different paths in the field. The results referring to Slovakian and Serbian students' perceptions of their competencies in ICT indicate that they perceive themselves as having high levels of competencies in ICT. These results suggest the need to develop strategies that promote the effective use of technology resources by both students and teachers.
Keywords: ICT Competencies; Slovakia and Serbia; university students

1 Introduction

The purpose of this study is to identify the level of ICT Competencies of university students from Slovakia and Serbia.

The research type is quantitative. The methodological strategy used was the replication of the instruments used by one of the authors in another international research project where perceptions of teachers and students from two Mexican universities (Veracruzana University and Chihuahua University) and one Spanish university (Salamanca University) were compared [1]. However, in this paper the results of an exploratory study comprising just one dimension of the instruments that were applied are shown: Students' levels of ICT competencies.

The instrument for measuring students' ICT competency is composed of 14 items. The reliability of the questionnaire obtained by the Cronbach technique was 0.81. The design of the instrument included the Likert scale with four categories: "Not at all, A little, Quite a lot and A lot". For the purposes of this study it is assumed that students having a certain level

[a] Corresponding author: kiss.gabor@bgk.uni-obuda.hu

of competency fit into the categories "Quite a lot" and "A lot" while, the absence or deficiency in competencies is represented by "Not at all" and "A little".

Table 1. contains the types of competencies and their associated items following the analytical proposal of García-Valcárcel and Arras regarding the division into three types:

(1) Basic Competencies;
(2) Application Competencies; and
(3) Ethical Competencies.

Table 1. Types of competencies

Basic competencies	You use the main informatics and network resources. You use the applications in a productive way. You apply the digital tools to obtain information from varied sources. You make use of models and simulations to explore complex topics. You interact and collaborate with your partners, using a variety of digital recourses.
Application Competencies	You communicate in an effective way the information and ideas, using a variety of media and formats. You participate in groups that develop project for the production of original works or solve problems. You solve problems, and make decisions using the appropriate tools and digital resources. You plan and organize the required activities to solve a problem or make a project. You create original works as a medium of personal expression.
Ethical Competencies	You select, analyze, and make ethically correct use of the information obtained. You make rational, legal and responsible use of information using ICT You value ICT as an instrument of permanent learning. You value ICT as a medium of collaboration and social communication

2 ICT competencies

The training process of college students focuses on developing a set of competencies in order to acquire their college degrees. In this sense, we can point to at least two large blocks which are common at the international level: generic and specific competencies [2].

Within the preferred generic competencies that apply in most of the university educational programs on the international level, we find ICT competencies identified by various international education programs (UNESCO, ODM, EPT, DNUA, DEDS).

In this sense, according to Fuentes [3], we could say that competency is: A set of knowledge, skills, attitudes, and values that is needed to effectively perform an occupation or a productive role. Ina similar way Yañez-Galecio [4] affirms that competency could be seen as an attribute of a person: specifically competency can be related to his/her success in the performance of a task. In this way failure is seen as the absence or low level of development of one or several competencies associated with a specific activity.

Meanwhile, Tobón [5]. defines competency as the integrated actions performed by a person in order to carry out activities and solve problems, based on certain eligibility criteria, continuous improvement and ethics. So, it can be said that ICT competencies are a group of skills, knowledge and attitudes that are applied to the use of information and communication systems, as well as the devices that the activity involves and, according to NETS for Students [6], also the knowledge that people should have and be able to learn and transfer, effectively, in order to live productively in a digital world.

Thus, these ICT competencies are being taken into consideration in the educational standards that various countries have developed in the form of profiles, such as NETS in the United States, the Official certificate in Computing and Internet (B2i) in France, the

DOI: 10.1051/shsconf/20173701075

incorporation of ICTs indicators in the National Curriculum in England, as well the transversal integration of the ICTs in schools, in Belgium [1].

Also in Hungary and Slovakia national policies have even been working on increasing the development of these ICT competencies in their teachers and students. But the results are quite different as we will discuss later. We could say that Hungary has developed its own standards for developing ICT competency, but Slovakia followed a little bit other way to give more free hand for the teachers.

Hence many international authorities describe key points of the educational development of ICT-literate students. For instance, NETS includes: the ability to make Web designs, presentations, databases, and the ability to use graphics software, spreadsheets, databases, online applications, e-mail, chat applications and word processors, among others. Moreover, UNESCO [7] has presented the ICT competency standards for teachers, which combines the requirements for teachers and students in today's world and emphasizes the current importance of ICT for all countries, including the members of the OECD [8].

Finally it is relevant to say that according to UNESCO, Competencies in ICT can be classified as: (a) digital literacy competencies, (b) application competencies and (c) ethical competencies. So, the core competencies of digital literacy (a) are related to the use of ICT in classroom presentations and activities, and involve the use of digital tools to obtain information, and the use and development of materials obtained from various online sources. Meanwhile, application competencies (b) are related to the use of skills and knowledge to create and manage complex projects, solve problems in real-world situations, collaborate with others, and make use of information and networks of experts. Finally ethical competencies (c) are related to the ethical, legal and responsible use of ICT [9].

3 Information technology education in Slovakia

The education of Informatics from the 2nd grade has been compulsory since the school year of 2008/2009, since the introduction of the school reform but it also appears in the 1st grade as well as in the nursery school curriculum though not as a compulsory subject. It is compulsory to have 1 Informatics lesson a week in the junior section and 0.5 lesson a week in the senior section that can be raised by the schools' own programme. Some schools took the opportunity and increased it to 1 lesson a week. The National Educational Programme does not assign precisely what teachers have to teach in the various grades but announces the school leaving standards to reach at the end of the senior section. So it does not matter if programming is taught in the 6th grade in one school and in the 8th grade in another school; the aim is to reach the school leaving standards. It is part of the educational programme of the school how its students should reach these standards, how many lessons they have a week and at what pace they learn the material; this programme is accepted by the management of the school and its teachers together .

The National Educational Programme divides Informatics into 5 topics (it does not specify the number of lessons):

1. Information around us
2. Communication with the help of the means of the ICT
3. Problem solving, thinking with the help of algorithms
4. Basic principles of the operation of the ICT tools
5. IS society

These 5 topics are then to be divided into the school leaving standards.

4 Information technology education in Serbia

The education of Informatics from the 1nd grade has been compulsory since the school year of 2008/2009, following the National Educational Program. It is compulsory to have 1 Informatics lesson a week in the junior section (1st-4th grades) [10, 11]. The learning material include the basic knowledge about computer, Painting program, Word processing, Presentation and e-mail. In the senior section (7th-8th grades) is it just selectable on basic level. The learning material include programming, creating web pages and using multimedia devices. The students have to chance to choose the technical-informatics direction, in that case they spend 2 lessons a week with this subject.

In the secondary grammar school have the students more chance to learn more about ICT. In generally 2 lessons per week is the opportunity the learn ICT, except the students in Art school, where they learn ICT just in the first grade. The learning material include programming, database management and Web 2.0 materials. The students in a specialized secondary grammar schools (natural science and computer science) can spend 12 lessons per week with ICT. The problem is the learning material is not parallel with ECDL, it gives not same knowledge [8].

The Serbian students get more ICT lessons from the 1st grade to the end of the secondary grammar school, than the Slovakian students.

Our starting hypothesis after get to know the Serbian and the Slovakian ICT Education, the Serbian Students will reach better results.

4 Analyzing students' ICT competencies

The purpose of this study is to compare the ICT competencies of students from Slovakian and Serbian universities.

The number of participants: The sample consisted of 440 students, 226 Serbian and 214 Slovakian students (Table 2.).

Table 2. The number of participants by gender and country

	Male	**Female**	**Total**
Serbian	92	134	226
Slovakian	107	107	214
Total	199	241	644

4.1 Differences in Competencies by countries

The students filled out a self-reported questionnaire with 14 items. We have used Likert-type rating scales to measure the ICT competency level of students [12]. Likert scales are commonly used by self-reported questionnaire, providing a range of responses to a given question or statement [13].

The Likert scale is ordinary scale, and as such we can calculate mean, min, max, median, modus, std. dev. etc. We can use the non parametic tests where we need ordinary variables. We have two independent samples so we could use the Mann-Whitney-Wilcoxon test for 2 samples [14]. The Mann-Whitney-Wilcoxon test seems better choice versus t test by Likert-type data [15], because it is testing the medians of the samples.

We used the Mann-Whitney independent sample U test of SPSS to compare the means of scores taken by the students. Monitoring was held on p=5% significancy level in the whole analyzing process.

 DOI: 10.1051/shsconf/20173701075

Table 3. Levels of Competencies Questions by university and results of the Mann-Whitney-Wilcoxon test

Item	Media Global	Serbia	Slovakia	Sig.
You use the main informatics and network resources.	2,87	2,99	2,74	**0,00**
You use the applications in a productive way.	2,77	2,89	2,64	**0,00**
You apply the digital tools to obtain information from varied sources.	2,93	3,01	2,85	**0,00**
You select, analyze, y realize an ethic use of the obtained information.	2,69	2,82	2,56	**0,00**
You communicate in an effective way the information and ideas, using a variety of media and formats.	2,85	2,93	2,76	**0,00**
You make use of models and simulations to explore complex topics.	2,20	2,36	2,04	**0,00**
You interact and collaborate with your partners, using a variety of digital recourses.	3,00	3,01	2,98	0,56
You participate in groups that develop project for the production of original works or solve problems.	2,91	2,93	2,89	0,61
You solve problems, and make decisions using the appropriate tools and digital resources.	2,77	2,81	2,73	0,16
You plan and organize the required activities to solve a problem or make a project.	2,75	2,83	2,66	**0,01**
You create original works as a medium of personal expression.	2,20	2,33	2,07	**0,00**
You make a rational, legal and responsible use of the information through the ICT	2,72	2,77	2,68	**0,01**
You value the ICT as an instrument of permanent learning.	3,02	3,00	3,05	0,26
You value the ICT as a medium of collaboration and social communication.	2,82	2,92	2,70	**0,00**

According to the Mann-Whitney-Wilcoxon test significant differences were found in at least 10 different items.

Figure 1 shows an overview of the profile that exists in the various dimensions of ICT competencies levels. It is clear that similar levels exist between students from the two countries. However the dimension of Application Competencies presents a major difference

DOI: 10.1051/shsconf/20173701075

in favor of Serbian students. Basic and Ethical Competencies show very similar values, being slightly higher for the Serbian students.

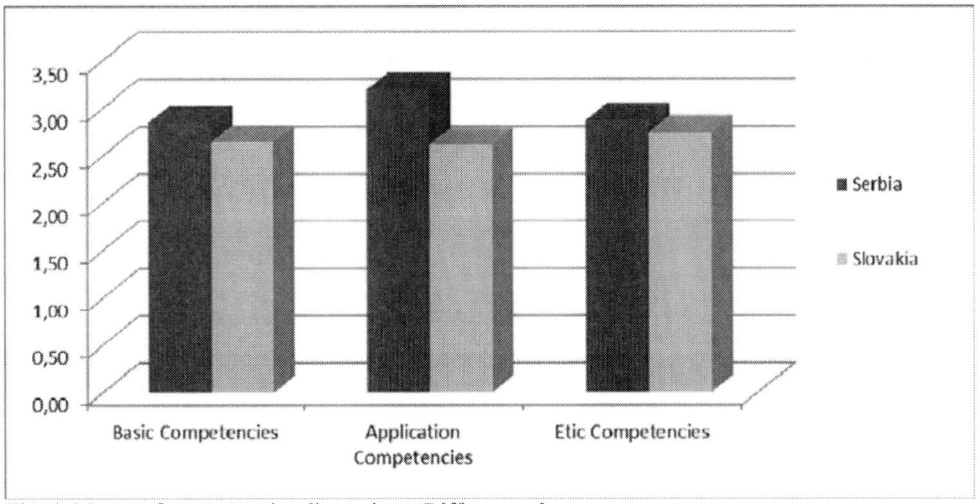

Fig. 1. Means of competencies dimensions: Differences by country

4.2. Creation percentages by dimension

To provide further details on the manner in which students from both countries recognize themselves as competent in various activities relating to the use of ICT, the percentages obtained for each item comprising the three different dimensions are presented. The activities in which students claim to be highly proficient (at or above 75% values) are also pointed out.

Basic Competencies can be considered basic for proper scholarly performance. This type of dimension is related to activities such as interaction with others through the digital media, the use of models to explore complex topics, the application of tools used to find information from various sources, the productive use of applications and the use of the main informatics resources (Fig. 2.).

The percentages obtained in this dimension, indicate the presence of an acceptable level of competency for the students of Slovakia and Serbia in many areas. However, in the item referring to the use of models to explore complex topics, a lower level of competence was obtained. The percentage was higher for the Serbian students (39.8%) in comparison to Slovakian students (19.2%).

Meanwhile in interaction through the use of digital resources, there is a higher level of competency for the Slovakians (80.8%) compared to the Serbians (79.2%). In the use and application of digital tools to obtain information from a variety of resources, a new there is a higher level of competency in the Serbian students (82.7%) than the Slovakian students (77.1%).

Finally, in reference to the productive use of the applications, and the use of the main informatics resources, we find that there is a major degree of competencies in the students from Slovakia (61.7% and 71.0%) compared to the students from Serbia (77.4% and 88.1%).

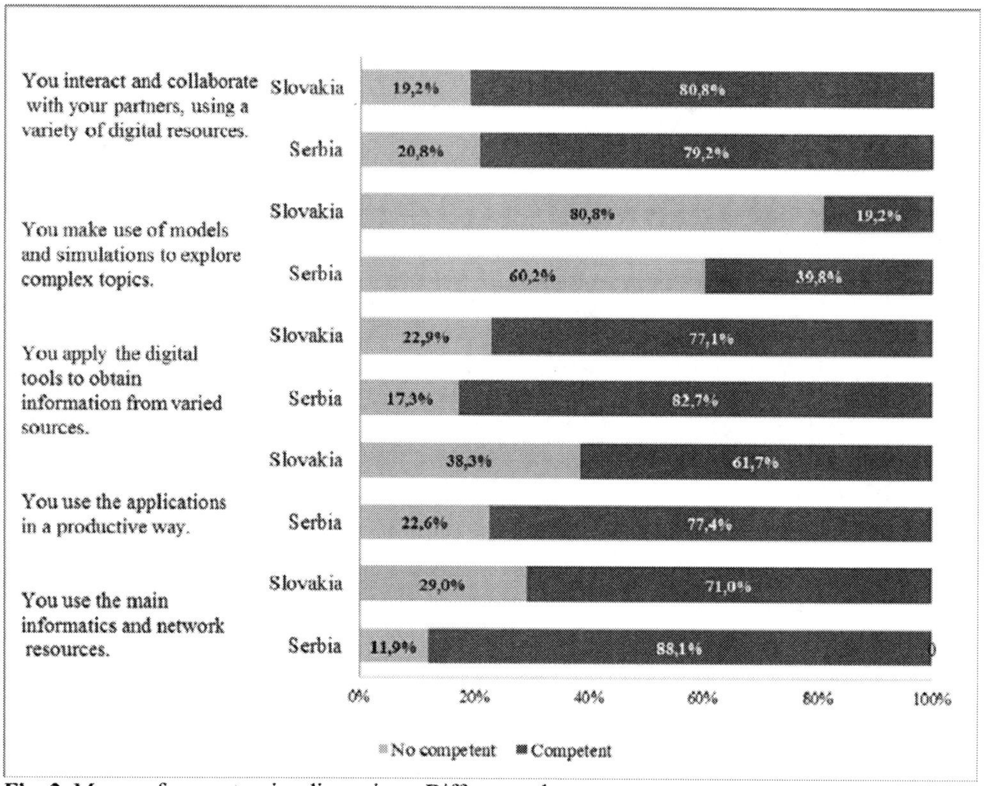

Fig. 2. Means of competencies dimensions: Differences by country

The items rated highest by the Serbian students are those related to the use of the main informatics and network resources and the application of digital tools to obtain information.

Meanwhile, their worst ratings are in the use of models to explore complex topics. For the Slovakians their highest levels of competency are in interaction and collaboration using digital resources and the application of digital tools to obtain information. The area where they receive the lowest evaluation is the one related to the use of models to explore complex topics.

According to this data we can say that Serbian students have higher levels of competencies in basic activities such as the use of applications and the use of the main informatics resources.

4.3. Application competencies

In the Application Competencies are the questions related to the use that is given to ICT in various fields. Activities such as the creation of work as a medium of expression, the planning, as well as the resolution of problems through digital resources, the participation in groups that use these tools and effective communication using a variety of informatics resources (Fig. 3.).

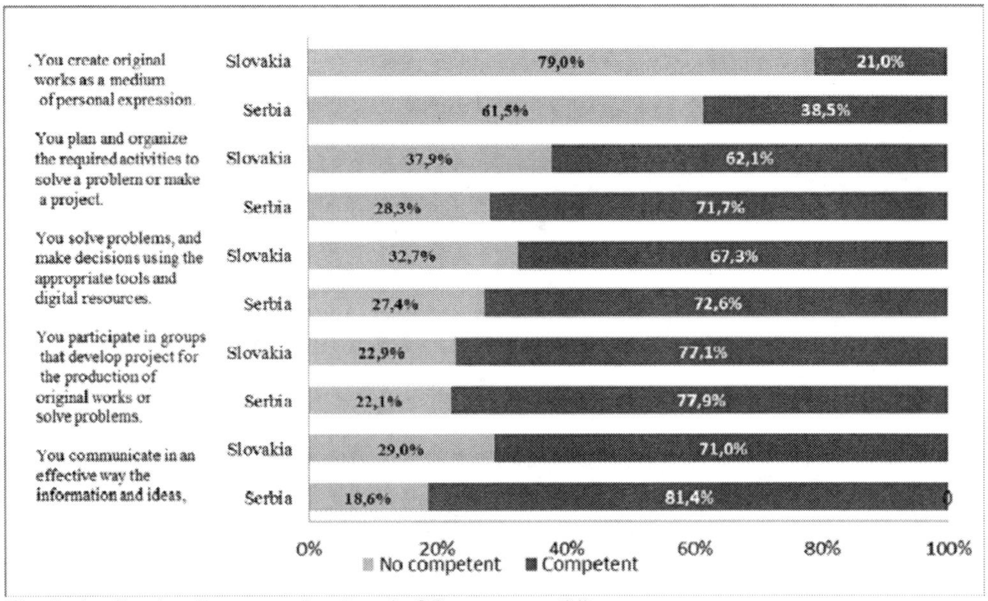

Fig. 3. Application Competencies: Level of Competency (%)

Within this dimension we find an acceptable level of competency for the students of both countries. An exception occurs regarding the creation of work as a medium of personal expression, where the Slovakian students (21.0%) show certain levels of non-competency, while the Serbian students consider themselves competent (38,5%), so the Slovakian students say that their major level of non-competency (79.0%) is in the participation in groups that develop projects for the production of original work. In this same item, the Serbians show an admissible level of non-competency (61.5%).

For the area concerning the planning and organization of activities for problem solving or carrying out projects the Serbian students (71.7%) are once more competent in comparison to their Slovakian counterparts (62.1%).

In relation to problem solving and decision making through digital resources, the Serbians (72.5%) are once more competent in comparison to their Slovakian counterparts (67.3%).

For effective communication through media and formats, the Slovakians (29.0%) are more non-competent in comparison to their Serbian counterparts (18.6%).

In relation to participate in groups that develop project for the production of original works or solve problems, the Serbians (77.9%) show same level of competency than the Slovakians (77.1%).

The Serbian students evaluate as their own highest level of competency the area of effective communication through media and formats while the area they rate as their lowest is the creation of work as a medium of personal expression.

Meanwhile, for the Slovakians, we find that their highest level of competency is participate in groups that develop project for the production of original works. Their lowest level of competency is same with the Serbians the creation of original work as a medium of communication.

4.4. Ethical competencies

Finally, for the dimension of Ethical competencies, we find the areas where we ask the students about their level of competency in ethical activities. These questions analyze the impression of the students about ICT as a medium of collaboration and as an instrument of learning, as well as the use that is given to the information obtained from ICT (Fig. 4.).

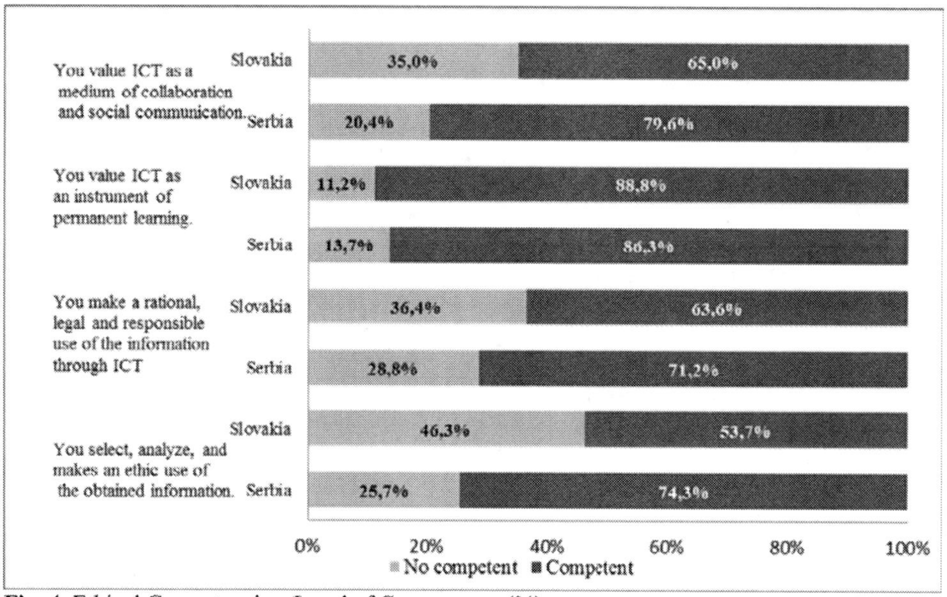

Fig. 4. Ethical Competencies: Level of Competency (%)

The results indicate the existence of a high level of ICT competency in the students of both countries. Referring to the question of ICT as a medium of collaboration and communication, there is a higher level of competency in Serbian students (79.6%) in comparison with the Slovakian students (65.0%). For the area of ICT as a permanent tool for learning, there are high levels of competency in both cases: Serbian students 86.3% and Slovakian students 88.8%.

Slovakian and Serbian consider using ICT as an instrument of permanent learning to be their area of highest competency. For Slovakian and Serbian students the area they felt least competent in was the legal use of the information obtained through ICT.

Serbian students show higher levels of competency in the area of ethical competencies than Slovakian students.

5 Conclusion

The situation of education in Serbia and Slovakia is not so very different although each country has taken a different path.

The results referring of Serbian and Slovakian Students' perceptions of their competencies in ICT indicate that they perceive a high level of competency in ICT. The students obtained a high degree of competency in the use of ICT as a permanent means of learning and as a means of social communication. The students also felt they made productive use of the various applications that are offered. The main use given to these tools is obtaining information, and they claim they make legal and responsible use of the resources.

Referring to the hypothesis we proposed, we could say that in some areas there were some significant differences between the two participating universities (University of Novi Sad and J. Selye University) in reference to the students' perceptions regarding their levels of ICT Competencies.

The differences between Slovakian and Serbian students found in the Mann-Whithey-Wilcoxon test include the selection of computer resources and the use of information obtained from the network, interaction with classmates through project developing, problem solving through the use of digital tools and the choosing ICT tools a for permanent

DOI: 10.1051/shsconf/20173701075

learning and social communication. In the rest of the areas no relevant differences were found.

Meanwhile, we found that eight questions do not receive significantly different answers.

In this document a proposed classification of Competencies in ICT (Basic, Applicationand Ethical) was presented. In these terms, the highest level obtained was for Ethical Competencies, followed by Basic Competencies and finally Application Competencies. These results suggest the need for developing strategies that promote the effective use of technology resources by students and teachers alike.

As for differences by university (J. Selye and Novi Sad), percentages indicate that there are higher levels of competencies in the Serbian students. By using the main informatics and network resources, developing project in group, using a variety of media and formats the Serbian students are more productive. The higher number of ICT lessons in Serbia shows a good way for the Serbian students to prefer teamwork over individual work what is more important in the future on the labor market.

Acknowledgements

Thank you for the teacher colleagues at University of Novi Sad for the collecting data from the students in Serbia.

References

1. García-Valcárcel, & A. Arras, Competencias en TIC y rendimiento académico en la universidad, Diferencias por género. México: Pearson, 2011
2. A. Aypay Information and communication technology (ICT) usage and achievement of Turkish students in PISA 2006. TOJET: The Turkish Online Journal of Educational Technology, 9 (2), 116-124, 2010
3. M. Fuentes, Las competencias académicas desde la perspectiva interconductual (Academic competencies from an interbehavioral perspective). Acta Colombiana de Psicología, 10(2), 51-58, 2007
4. J. Yañez-Galecio, Competencias profesionales del Psicólogo Clínico: Un análisis preliminar. Terapia Psicológica, 23(2), 85-93, 2005
5. S. Tobón. Metodología de gestión curricular. Una perspectiva socio-formativa.México: Trillas, 2013
6. NETS for students, ISTE Standards, 2007
7. UNESCO ICT competency standards for teachers, 2008
8. OECD, Education at a Glance 2013: OECD Indicators. OECD Publishing,http://dx.doi.org/10.1787/eag-2013-en, 2013
9. UNESCO Institute for Statistics International Standard Classification of Education. Canada,, 1997
10. Министарство просвете, науке и технолошког развоја (2008): Наставни програм за предмет Од играчке до рачунара за први и други разред основног образовања и васпитања. http://bit.ly/1scrO2j (2014. 03 26.)
11. Министарство просвете, науке и технолошког развоја (2008): Наставни програм образовања и васпитања за трећи разред основног образовања и васпитања. http://bit.ly/Ke3tHx (2014. 03 26.)
12. R. Likert, R, A technique for the measurement of attitudes, Archives of Psychology, Vol.: 27, No.: 140, pp 44–55, 1932
13. S. Jamieson, Likert scales: how to (ab)use them, Medical Education 2004; Vol.: 38, pp 1217–1218, 2004
14. W. Boonyasit, Appropriate statistical analysis for two independent groups of Likert-type data, Dissertation, American University Washington, 2011
15. J. C. F. De Winter and D. Dodou, Five-Point Likert Items: t test versus Mann-Whitney-Wilcoxon, Practical Assessment, Research & Evaluation, Vol.: 15, No.: 11, ISSN: 1531-7714, 2010

Analyzing of the self reported ICT literacy level of Slovakian and Serbian Students in the higher education

Gabor Kiss[1a], Peter Csiba[2]

[1]Obuda University, Institute of Mechanical Engineering and Safety Science, Becsi ut 96/b, Budapest H-1034, Hungary
[2]J. Selye University, Department of Mathematics and Informatics, Bratislavská cesta 3322, 945 01, Komárno, Slovakia

Abstract. The students generally use technology for communication in the European Union and outside of the Union. First of all we have to see in this research the ICT knowledge level of the students in the higher education to make decision about the application and retraining methods. It is important to know can we find any difference in ICT literacy between the Slovakian and the Serbian students to see how long is the way to finish the ICT revolution in these countries. On the other hand is it important to see which topic need more attention from the teachers in the high school to give a good knowledge for the student before they go in the higher education. We measured the ICT literacy level with a tool consisting of 15 items (Likert scaled). The data analysis was performed with SPSS software using descriptive statistics and Mann-Whitney test.
Keywords: communication, higher education, technology education

1 Introduction

Communication and technology have an important role in life and especially in education. Nowadays, students generally use technology for communication. When using technology in education, there may be some communication barriers.

An international comparison analysis tool is an effective way for understanding the situation between two or more different regions of the world. In this sense, literature shows the relevance of analyzing how ICT has been used in education to better understand educational strategies, learning methods and pedagogical techniques in order to effectively apply ICT in the classroom.

The purpose of this study is to identify the levels of ICT Competencies of students from two countries, one in Slovakia (in the EU Commission) and the other in Serbia (out of EU

[a] Corresponding author: kiss.gabor@bgk.uni-obuda.hu

Commission). First of all we have to see the ICT knowledge level of the students to make decision about the application and retraining methods.

It is important to know can we find any difference in ICT literacy between the Slovakian and the Serbian students to see how long is the way to finish the ICT revolution in these countries. On the other hand is it important to see which topic need more attention from the teachers in the high school to give a good knowledge for the student before they go in the higher education.

Some earlier research analyzed the ICT literacy of the students in Hungary on different levels [1], [2], [3], [4]. The current research analyses the ICT literacy level of the Serbian and Slovakian students in Higher Education.

2 Information technology education in Slovakia

The education of Informatics from the 2nd grade has been compulsory since the school year of 2008/2009, since the introduction of the school reform but it also appears in the 1st grade as well as in the nursery school curriculum though not as a compulsory subject. It is compulsory to have 1 Informatics lesson a week in the junior section and 0.5 lesson a week in the senior section that can be raised by the schools' own programme. Some schools took the opportunity and increased it to 1 lesson a week. The National Educational Programme does not assign precisely what teachers have to teach in the various grades but announces the school leaving standards to reach at the end of the senior section. So it does not matter if programming is taught in the 6th grade in one school and in the 8th grade in another school; the aim is to reach the school leaving standards. It is part of the educational programme of the school how its students should reach these standards, how many lessons they have a week and at what pace they learn the material; this programme is accepted by the management of the school and its teachers together .

The National Educational Programme divides Informatics into 5 topics (it does not specify the number of lessons):

1. Information around us
2. Communication with the help of the means of the ICT
3. Problem solving, thinking with the help of algorithms
4. Basic principles of the operation of the ICT tools
5. IS society

These 5 topics are then to be divided into the school leaving standards.

3 Information technology education in Serbia

The education of Informatics from the 1nd grade has been compulsory since the school year of 2008/2009, following the National Educational Program. It is compulsory to have 1 Informatics lesson a week in the junior section (1st-4th grades) [6], [7]. The learning material include the basic knowledge about computer, Painting program, Word processing, Presentation and e-mail. In the senior section (7th-8th grades) is it just selectable on basic level. The learning material include programming, creating web pages and using multimedia devices. The students have to chance to choose the technical-informatics direction, in that case they spend 2 lessons a week with this subject.

In the secondary grammar school have the students more chance to learn more about ICT. In generally 2 lessons per week is the opportunity the learn ICT, except the students in Art school, where they learn ICT just in the first grade. The learning material include programming, database management and Web 2.0 materials. The students in a specialized secondary grammar schools (natural science and computer science) can spend 12 lessons per week with ICT. The problem is the learning material is not parallel with ECDL, it gives not same knowledge [8].

The Serbian students get more ICT lessons from the 1st grade to the end of the secondary grammar school, than the Slovakian students.

Our starting hypothesis after get to know the Serbian and the Slovakian ICT Education, the Serbian Students will reach better results.

4 Analyzing students' ICT literacy level

The purpose of this study is to compare the ICT literacy level of students from Slovakian and Serbian universities.

The number of participants: The sample consisted of 440 students, 226 Serbian and 214 Slovakian students (Table 1.)

Table 1. The number of participants by gender and country

	Male	**Female**	**Total**
Serbian	92	134	226
Slovakian	107	107	214
Total	199	241	644

The students filled out a self-reported questionnaire with 15 items. We have used Likert-type rating scales to measure the ICT literacy level of students [9].

Liker scales are commonly used by self-reported questionnaire, providing a range of responses to a given question or statement [10]. There were 4 categories of response: 1 = basic level; 2 = medium; 3 = advanced, 4 = „master".

The reliability of the questionnaire obtained by the technique of Cronbach-α was 0.927 it means the reliability of the questionnaire is very good.

4.1 The results of Independent Samples Mann-Whitney U test

The Likert scale is ordinary scale, and as such we can calculate mean, min, max, median, modus, std. dev. etc. We can use the nonparametic tests where we need ordinary variables. We have two independent samples so we could use the Mann-Whitney-Wilcoxon test for 2 samples [11]. The Mann-Whitney-Wilcoxon test seems better choice versus t test by Likert-type data [12], because it is testing the medians of the samples.

We used the Mann-Whitney independent sample U test of SPSS to compare the means of scores taken by the students. Monitoring was held on p=5% significancy level in the whole analyzing process.

We used 3 different ways of comparison: by countries, by gender and by gender in Slovakia or in Serbia

4.1.1 The results of Independent Samples Mann-Whitney U test by countries

If we summarize the scores of all items and make the comparison can we see the ICT literacy level of students by countries. The result of Mann-Whitney U test on the total scores has shown significant difference between the 2 group of students by ICT literacy, p=0.000.

We calculated the mean scores by items and also calculated the difference between them grouped by countries. Then we can made analysis process with Mann-Whitney U test (Table 2.).

Table 2. The results of Independent Samples Mann-Whitney U test by countries

Number of item	Item	Serbian (Mean score)	Slovakian (Mean score)	p
1	Handling Operating System (OS)	2,66	2,10	0,00
2	Word processor	3,03	2,36	0,00
3	Spreadsheet	2,60	1,93	0,00
4	Database Management	2,04	1,56	0,00
5	Multimedia	2,57	2,06	0,00
6	Software specific to my degree	2,08	1,71	0,00
7	Using documentary bases (Such as EBSCO)	2,03	1,57	0,00
8	Web Browsing	3,24	2,80	0,00
9	Internet Communication	3,31	2,77	0,00
10	Internet Safety	2,65	2,05	0,00
11	Website design	1,82	1,38	0,00
12	Using learning platforms	1,69	1,28	0,00
13	Image Editing	2,58	2,06	0,00
14	Video Editing	2,03	1,61	0,00
15	Creating simulations and animations	1,73	1,31	0,00

According to the table we can see the scores of the students from different countries; we can see that the subjective ICT literacy level of Serbian students is significant higher than the Slovakian students by every items. It means the Serbian students can take the advantages of the higher number of ICT lessons.

4.1.2 The results of Independent Samples Mann-Whitney U test by gender

We have seen the Serbian students reached significant higher scores by every items. It is important to see, the difference is same by the genders too, or not. We calculated the mean scores by items and also calculated the difference between them grouped by genders. Then can we make analysis process with Mann-Whitney U test by boys (Table 3.) and girls (Table 4.).

Table 3. The results of Independent Samples Mann-Whitney U test by boys

Number of item	Item	Serbian boys (Mean score)	Slovakian boys (Mean score)	p
1	Handling Operating System (OS)	3,11	2,45	0,00
2	Word processor	3,22	2,50	0,00
3	Spreadsheet	2,78	2,07	0,00
4	Database Management	2,22	1,62	0,00
5	Multimedia	2,88	2,28	0,00
6	Software specific to my degree	2,24	1,76	0,00
7	Using documentary bases (Such as EBSCO)	2,10	1,53	0,00
8	Web Browsing	3,46	2,99	0,00
9	Internet Communication	3,45	2,90	0,00
10	Internet Safety	2,82	2,21	0,00
11	Website design	2,16	1,53	0,00
12	Using learning platforms	1,77	1,30	0,00
13	Image Editing	2,59	2,19	0,00
14	Video Editing	2,41	1,76	0,00
15	Creating simulations and animations	1,92	1,32	0,00

According to the table (Table 3.) we can find significant differences by every items as sooner. The subjective ICT literacy level of Serbian boys is higher as the Slovakian boys.

The situation is same by girls too (Table 4.). The Serbian girls achieved significant higher scores by ever items than Slovakian girls. It seems the higher number of ICT lessons have same influence on the ICK literacy level independently from the gender.

Table 4. The results of Independent Samples Mann-Whitney U test by girls

Number of item	Item	Serbian girls (Mean score)	Slovakian girls (Mean score)	p
1	Handling Operating System (OS)	2,35	1,75	0,00
2	Word processor	2,90	2,21	0,00
3	Spreadsheet	2,47	1,79	0,00
4	Database Management	1,93	1,50	0,00
5	Multimedia	2,35	1,84	0,00
6	Software specific to my degree	1,98	1,65	0,00
7	Using documentary bases (Such as EBSCO)	1,99	1,60	0,00
8	Web Browsing	3,10	2,61	0,00
9	Internet Communication	3,22	2,64	0,00
10	Internet Safety	2,53	1,88	0,00
11	Website design	1,58	1,23	0,00
12	Using learning platforms	1,64	1,26	0,00
13	Image Editing	2,57	1,93	0,00
14	Video Editing	1,77	1,47	0,01
15	Creating simulations and animations	1,59	1,30	0,00

4.1.3 The results of Independent Samples Mann-Whitney U test by gender in Serbia

The following steps are to see the difference in subjective ICT literacy level by gender in the countries.

We calculated the mean scores by items and also calculated the difference between the students grouped by genders in Serbia. Then we can make analysis process with Mann-Whitney U test by gender (Table 5.).

Table 5. The results of Independent Samples Mann-Whitney U test by gender in Serbia

Number of item	Item	Serbian girls (Mean score)	Slovakian girls (Mean score)	p
1	Handling Operating System (OS)	3,11	2,35	0,00
2	Word processor	3,22	2,90	0,01
3	Spreadsheet	2,78	2,47	0,01
4	Database Management	2,22	1,93	0,02
5	Multimedia	2,88	2,35	0,00
6	Software specific to my degree	2,24	1,98	0,04
7	**Using documentary bases (Such as EBSCO)**	**2,10**	**1,99**	**0,55**
8	Web Browsing	3,46	3,10	0,01
9	Internet Communication	3,45	3,22	0,04
10	Internet Safety	2,82	2,53	0,01
11	Website design	2,16	1,58	0,00
12	**Using learning platforms**	**1,77**	**1,64**	**0,16**
13	**Image Editing**	**2,59**	**2,57**	**0,84**
14	Video Editing	2,41	1,77	0,00
15	Creating simulations and animations	1,92	1,59	0,00

DOI: 10.1051/shsconf/20173701076

According to the table (Table 5.) we can find any significant differences in the subjective ICT literacy level of Serbian girls and boys. It means the Serbian girls and boys do not have same subjective ICT literacy level in the higher education, by the big part of items the scores of boys are higher. On other hand the subjective ICT literacy level of Serbian boys is same with Serbian girls by handling "Using documentary bases", "Using learning platforms" and "image editing".

4.1.4 The results of Independent Samples Mann-Whitney U test by gender in Slovakia

We calculated the mean scores by items and also calculated the difference between the students grouped by genders in Slovakia.

Then we can made analysis process with Mann-Whitney U test by gender (Table 6.).

Table 6. The results of Independent Samples Mann-Whitney U test by gender in Slovakia

Number of item	Item	Serbian girls (Mean score)	Slovakian girls (Mean score)	p
1	Handling Operating System (OS)	2,45	1,75	0,00
2	Word processor	2,50	2,21	0,00
3	Spreadsheet	2,07	1,79	0,01
4	**Database Management**	**1,62**	**1,50**	**0,52**
5	Multimedia	2,28	1,84	0,00
6	**Software specific to my degree**	**1,76**	**1,65**	**0,28**
7	**Using documentary bases (Such as EBSCO)**	**1,53**	**1,60**	**0,71**
8	Web Browsing	2,99	2,61	0,00
9	Internet Communication	2,90	2,64	0,02
10	Internet Safety	2,21	1,88	0,00
11	Website design	1,53	1,23	0,00
12	**Using learning platforms**	**1,30**	**1,26**	**0,47**
13	Image Editing	2,19	1,93	0,03
14	Video Editing	1,76	1,47	0,00
15	**Creating simulations and animations**	**1,32**	**1,30**	**0,85**

According to the table (Table 6.) we can find any significant differences in the subjective ICT literacy level of Slovakian girls and boys. It means the Slovakian girls and boys do not have same subjective ICT literacy level in the higher education. On other hand the subjective ICT literacy level of Slovakian boys higher as the Slovakian girls by handling operating systems, word processing, spreadsheet calculation, multimedia, web browsing, internet communication, internet safety, website design, image and video editing. They have same subjective ICT literacy level by the rest of items.

5 Conclusion

In this research we have tried to analyze the subjective ICT literacy level of the Serbian and Slovakian students in the higher education. We have used a self-reported questionnaire with 15 items) and Likert-type rating.

After the analyzing process we can say the subjective ICT literacy level of Serbian students by every items is higher than Slovakian students.

We have made more analysis by gender by countries. In the following we share the important information connection with it.

We have found significant differences by boys in same case then by countries. It means the subjective ICT literacy level of Serbian boys is higher as the Slovakian boys. The results by girls are the same. It shows the subjective ICT literacy level of Serbian girls is higher than the Slovakian girls in the higher education. The Serbian studenst can take the advantage of the higher ICT lessons from the primary school to the final exam independently from the gender.

We made the analysis by gender in countries too and we have found some interesting thing in that case. The Serbian girls and boys have same subjective ICT literacy level by "Using documentary bases", "Using learning platforms" and "Image editing", by the rest of items the Serbian boys reached higher scores.

The situation was a little bit different in Slovakia. The ICT literacy level of Slovakian boys is higher by handling operating systems, word processing, spreadsheet calculation, multimedia, web browsing, internet communication, internet safety, website design, image and video editing. By the rest of the items we could not find significant difference by gender in Slovakia. We have found more items where was not difference in the subjective ICT literacy level by gender in Slovakia it means the gender-gap is not so big in this country.

The Serbian girls did not have higher subjective ICT literacy level than boys by any items it means in Serbia would be more important to think over the by gender separated ICT education like it works in Germany where it was recognized the girls can catch same result in ITC but they need other teaching methods.

Acknowledgements

Thank you for the teacher colleagues at University of Novi Sad for the collecting data from the students.

References

1. G. Kiss, "The survey measuring the informatics skills of the entering Students at Budapest Tech, Bánki Donát Faculty of Mechanical and Safety Engineering", 7th IEEE International Symposium on Intelligent System and Informatics, Subotica, Serbia, 2009, ISBN: 978-1-4244-5348-1, pp:395-397, IEEE Xplore digital library Digital Object Identifier: 10.1109/SISY.2009.5291125
2. G. Kiss, "A comparison of informatics skills by genders of Hungarian grammar school students", 8th International Conference on Applied Informatics, Eger, 2010, ISBN 978 9894 72 3, Vol. 2., pp. 17-27
3. G. Kiss, "A Comparison of Informatics Skills by schooltypes in the 9-10th grades in Hungary", *International Journal of Advanced Research in Computer Science*, 2011, Vol.: 2, No. 2, ISSN: 0976-5697, pp. 417-428
4. G. Kiss, "Measuring Student's Computer Science Knowledge at the End of the primary stage in Hungary", *9th IEEE International Symposium on Applied Machine Intelligence and Informatics*, Smolenice, Slovakia, 2011, ISBN: 978-1-4244-7428-8, pp. 19-22, IEEE Catalog Number: CFP1108E-CDR, IEEE Xplore digital library Digital Object Identifier: 10.1109/SAMI.2011.5738880;
5. G. Kiss, "Measuring Hungarian and Slovakian Students' IT Skills and Programming Knowledge", *Acta Polytechnica Hungarica*, Vol. 9., No. 6, 2012, ISSN: 1785-8860, pp. 195-210,
6. Министарство просвете, науке и технолошког развоја (2008): Наставни програм за предмет Од играчке до рачунара за први и други разред основног образовања и васпитања. http://bit.ly/1scrO2j (2014. 03 26.)

7. Министарство просвете, науке и технолошког развоја (2008): Наставни програм образовања и васпитања за трећи разред основног образовања и васпитања. http://bit.ly/Ke3tHx (2014. 03 26.)
8. Zs. Námesztovszki, „IKT eszközök a Vajdaság iskoláiban", *II. „Trefort Ágoston" Szakmai Tanárképzési Konferencia*, Óbudai Egyetem, Trefort Ágoston Mérnökpedagógiai Központ, Budapest. ISBN: 978-615-5018-39-8, pp. 222-233.
9. R. Likert, „A technique for the measurement of attitudes", *Archives of Psychology*, 1932, Vol.: 27, No.: 140, pp 44–55
10. S. Jamieson, „Likert scales: how to (ab)use them", *Medical Education* 2004; Vol.: 38, pp 1217–1218
11. W. Boonyasit, „Appropriate statistical analysis for two independent groups of Likert-type data", Dissertation, American University Washington ,2011
12. J. C. F. De Winter and D. Dodou, „Five-Point Likert Items: t test versus Mann-Whitney-Wilcoxon, Practical Assessment", *Research & Evaluation*, 2010, Vol.: 15, No.: 11, ISSN: 1531-7714

Project-based learning in the teaching-learning process university. A longitudinal study

Leyla Angélica Sandoval Hamón[1a], Fernando Casani[1], Jesus Pomeda-Rodriguez[1], and Ricado Olmos Albacete[2]

[1]Autonomous University of Madrid, Faculty of Economics and Business Studies, Madrid 28049. Spain.
[2] Autonomous University of Madrid, Faculty of Psychology, Madrid 28049. Spain.

Abstract. The European Higher Education Area promotes the change in teaching-learning, where students have a more active role in their educational process. The main objective of this work is to analyse the use of an alternative proposal, focus in student-based teamwork activities, who seek to favour the acquisition and deepening of knowledge and skills. The implementation of this research was carried out by means of a longitudinal study in the subject of the degree of Economics, with the development of the methodology of Project Based Learning integrating the ICTs and improving the evaluation process (e.g. establishing headings and psychometric analysis of knowledge tests). The results of the research showed an improvement in the learning process from the observation, collection of works, analysis of knowledge tests and the official survey by students to assess the activity and the development of their competitors.
Keywords: Project-Based Learning; ICTs; Evaluation; Higher Education.

1 Introduction

The European Higher Education Area has presented a new university context that seeks to respond to the challenges of European educational convergence, with modifications that affect each of the elements that make up the teaching-learning process. Consequently, the changes are not only directed to learning, competencies, teaching methodologies or the incorporation of technologies, but also to transformations "in the evaluation, in all its approaches: object, agents, moments; as well as in the instruments and techniques that enable their implementation"[1].

This work focuses on analysing the use of an alternative methodology to the traditional one (project based learning), while promoting the use of information and communication technologies (ICTs); and taking into account the adaptation to this change in regard to the way in which the subject is evaluated.

From the above, some definitions are indicated that have served as a point of reference throughout the course:

[a] Corresponding author: angelica.sandoval@uam.es

Project-Based Learning: PBL is a learning and teaching approach that makes students search for new knowledge and skills, helps them overcome real-life questions, and makes them design their own studies and performances"[2]. The "need to know / need to do" principle also drives the learning process and inspires them to delve deeper into concepts [3]. Students are involved in learning authentic themes, asking questions, raising hypotheses, searching for relevant information, planning an inquiry, collecting data, thinking critically, discussing, sharing ideas, reasoning and decision-making, developing a product, and presenting it to an audience. [4].

Furthermore, PBL applications also contribute to equipping students with 21st century skills, identified as critical thinking, problem solving, creativity, access to and restructuring of information, usage of digital resources, taking responsibility, sharing ideas, self-control and reconciliation [5].

The use of ICTs in education according to UNESCO contributes, among other things, to equality in education, the exercise of quality teaching and learning and the professional development of teachers, as well as the management of more efficient management and administration of the educational system.

With regards to evaluation strategies, two main groups can be classified: traditional strategies (open and closed knowledge tests, work, projects and oral exams) to which summative assessment and innovative strategies are associated (self-evaluation, Portfolios, techniques of observation ...) that are associated to the formative evaluation.

In short, the literature indicates that using an active methodology (such as PBL) requires going hand in hand with an adaptation of the evaluation. This makes sense, considering that assessment is "the most powerful weapon teachers have in influencing how students respond to courses and behave as students" [6].

2 Method

2.1 Contextualization -Research Group

- Degree: Economy
- Course: Fourth grade. First semester academic year.
- Academic years: 2014-2015, 2015-2016, 2016-2017.
- Subject: Seminar of Business Administration (ADE in advance) and Socio-Political Environment.
- Nº Credits: 6 (150 hours)
- Total students: 110
- Course objective: This seminar aims to bring the student to fully comprehend the functioning reality of the economic system and the behavior of companies.

2.2 Design and development

Before beginning the first semester of each academic year part of the study, the teaching team of the subject met and planned all the class sessions sharing with the students (including the time of work outside of class). To verify that the students fulfilled the tasks proposed, they always had to make a delivery or presentation of some material to go evaluating the evolution of the construction of their knowledge.

The content was related to the development of two projects in teamwork (five students per team) throughout the course, one related to the analysis of a sector of activity and another specifically with the analysis of a company of the sector in order to use ICTs.

Table 1. Methodologies / Evaluation and their corresponding tasks.

Phase	Description	Tasks
1	Project learning	1.1 Preparation of proposals 1.2 Planning and instructions for doing the projects 1.3 Project monitoring 1.4 Verification of results 1.5 Evaluation of results
2	ICTs	2.1 Identify the technological resources. (Listing) 2.2 Share resources with students and influence how to use them with the proposed active methodology. 2.3 Promote the use of ICTs. 2.4 Supporting students in the use of ICTs.
3	Evaluation	3.1 Elaboration of rubrics for the two projects (Company and Sector). 3.2 Elaboration of two knowledge tests (peer-reviewed). 3.3 Psychometric analysis of knowledge tests (Test Analysis Program, TAP). 3.5 Students' evaluation questionnaire on the methodology, resources and form of assessment of the subject.

In line with the development of the active methodology (PBL) and with the process of change of the subject, the teachers adapted the evaluation, in such a way that the students:

(a) knew in advance the evaluation criteria of the activities and once delivered projects easily recognise their strengths and weaknesses, according to teacher guidelines and feedback, and

(b) have an aggregated test of knowledge testing.

2.3 Data Collection

The process of collecting information on the use of the PBL methodology, the incorporation of ICTs and the adaptation of the evaluation was integrated by different sources:

A source came from the continuous development of the two projects (where two deliveries of final reports were received and presented to the class, where the use of new ICTs was evidenced) and the behaviour of the team, both aspects are considered in the Items that were provided.

Another source that was considered was the summative evaluation, where, once the knowledge tests were adapted (two tests), in total 110 students completed them in the three academic courses. The results of the knowledge tests were taken as reference for the psychometric analysis.

2.4 Analysis of the Data

Statistical analysis was performed using the Test Analysis Program (TAP) software and complemented with SPSS v21. The TAP program addressed psychometric analysis. Cronbach's Alpha coefficient was used to assess the quality of the tests in terms of their reliability. In order to examine the quality of the items, the indices of difficulty and discrimination were used.

In particular, six test-type knowledge tests with 32 questions each and four response options were analysed. The tests are 2014 (two of them), 2015 (two others) and 2016 (the last two). With this psychometric study we tried to find out if there was an improvement in the reliability and the psychometric properties of the questions as an evolution to the good practices developed in the preparation of exams.

3 Results and suggestions

Psychometric analysis of the knowledge tests mentioned.

The following table shows the reliability coefficients of the six exams, the average difficulty of the questions (understood as proportion of hits on the total answers), the average discrimination of the questions (high discrimination indices inform that multiple choice questions distinguish between less and high competent students), and the number of students.

Table 1. Data of the psychometric analysis performed

Year	Test	Coefficient α	Difficulty	Discrimination	N
2014	Test 1	0,583	0,613	0,276	39
	Test 2	0,763	0,837	0,278	
2015	Test 1	0,533	0,646	0,212	36
	Test 2	0,664	0,798	0,264	
2016	Test 1	0,719	0,564	0,378	35
	Test 2	0,752	0,818	0,307	

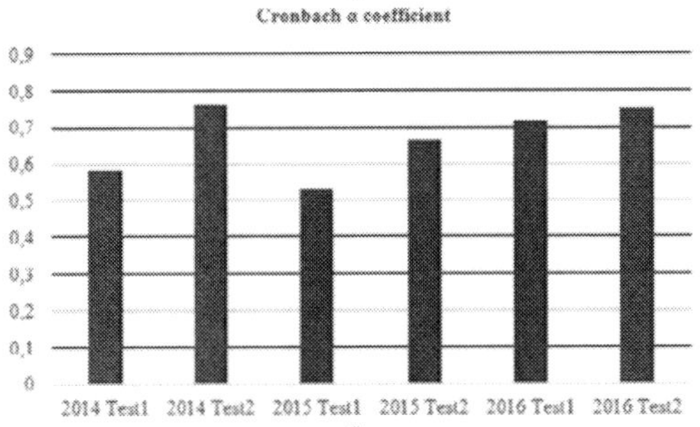

Fig. 1. Test reliability coefficients.

These results show that in the last two courses the two tests analysed exceeded the reliability of 0.70 (cut off usually used to consider that a knowledge test measures accurately). In the previous years, only in 2014 a test exceeded this value. In addition, the average discrimination of the questions exceeded the value 0.30 only in the two exams of 2016, sign that the questions were elaborated correctly and with the capacity to distinguish between the more and less competent students. Probably, the 2016 results are due to the fact that two judges independently examined the quality of the questions. The sample size was similar between the different exams.

The results in general indicate that the use of the active methodology (PBL), the favouring of the ICT and the adaptation of the evaluation have been positive for the construction of the learning, this is evidenced on the one hand by the psychometric analysis of the tests of knowledge that shows.

In short, the changes in the methodology of the subject have been useful, because it has been advanced in that the students are better prepared, not only in the theoretical knowledge about the organizations, but in that they are also able to act in them of and integrate ICTs in a practical, useful, responsible and ethical way. Evidence of this significant advance has been the improvement in the grades obtained by the students and, in addition, by the satisfaction shown by these with the subject (collected in the official survey conducted).

References

[1] M. . I. B. Alsina, F. Á. C. Rodríguez, "Estrategias de evaluación de los aprendizajes centradas en el proceso," *Rev. Esp. Pedagog.*, vol. 59, no. 218, pp. 25–48, (2001).

[2] O. D. Baysura, S. Altun, B. Yucel-Toy, "Perceptions of Teacher Candidates regarding Project-Based Learning," *Eurasian J. Educ. Res.*, no. 62, pp. 15–36, (2016).

[3] S. Jacques, S. Bissey, A. Martin, "Multidisciplinary Project Based Learning Within a Collaborative Framework: A Case Study on Urban Drone Conception," *Int. J. Emerg. Technol. Learn. IJET*, vol. 11, no. 12, p. 36, Dec. (2016).

[4] O. Goldstein, "A project-based learning approach to teaching physics for pre-service elementary school teacher education students," *Cogent Educ.*, vol. 3, p. UNSP 1200833, (2016).

[5] S. Bell, "Project-Based Learning for the 21st Century: Skills for the Future," *Clear. House J. Educ. Strateg. Issues Ideas*, vol. 83, no. 2, pp. 39–43, Jan. (2010).

[6] Gibbs, G., *Uso estratégico de la educación en el aprendizaje. Evaluar en la universidad: problemas y nuevos enfoque.* Narcea, (2003).

Cultural aspect in the course materials for the vocational training programs

Lilia R. Ismagilova[1a], Irina M. Solodkova[2] and Elena V. Grigorieva[3]

[1]Department of Foreign Languages, Institute of Management, Economics and Finances, Kazan Federal University, Russia
[2]Department of Foreign Languages, Institute of Management, Economics and Finances, Kazan Federal University, Russia
[3]Department of Foreign Languages, Institute of Management, Economics and Finances, Kazan Federal University, Russia

Abstract. Competitiveness on a labour market makes specialists be involved in self-development projects connected with widening their background knowledge. Vocational training programs provide foreign language education to help specialists be promoted in multinational companies as language and culture misunderstanding are seen as real career trials. The paper suggests the analysis of the cultural aspect in coursebook materials for the vocational training program at the Educational Center for Professional Communicative Training of Kazan Federal University. The research aims at collating the syllabus requirements to the cultural aspect in a coursebook materials. The data obtained throughout the analysis afforded ground for deciding on the coursebook that best meets syllabus requirements due to multi-aspect approach to cultural knowledge acquisition. At the end of the vocational training course students would demonstrate cultural knowledge which allows to adapt to foreign environment, to overcome mentality differences in doing business, traditions and customs thus satisfying learners' real-world professional demands.
Keywords: cultural aspect, vocational training programs, student, syllabus, coursebook material, socio-cultural competence, language education

1 Introduction

Globalization and the processes following it like off-shoring and great job migration,' the increase of international students in higher educational institutions, the flow of migrants from non-CIS countries into the territory of the Russian Federation' make environments become more multicultural [2]. Specialists are required to relocate and be able to embed themselves into a foreign culture adopting its rules, norms of behaviour and social

[a] Corresponding author: liliaismg@gmail.com

dimensions. English language serves as a lingua franca for professionals in different spheres allowing them to communicate successfully [8]. They should have 'English language ability at the level to guarantee successful professional communication' [8].

It has transformed itself into varieties of 'Englishes' and in fact communication between non-native speakers of English is far greater in frequency, amount, and significance as well as the number of speakers today [5,7].

Consequently, English language acquisition is inconceivable without acquisition of cultural knowledge as 'language and culture must be treated as inseparable constructs' [3, 10].

The importance of the matter is stressed in the report by the Modern Language Association Ad Hoc Committee on Foreign Languages. It highlights the equality of cultural knowledge and linguistic competence if 'one wishes to understand people and their communities' [13].

The crucial importance foreign language acquisition and cultural knowledge gained in Russia was due to 'the participation of Russia in international organizations as BRICS, WTO, APEC, SCO, as well as, involvement in foreign trade' [15]. Under these circumstances country needs specialists who can act in foreign environments regardless cultural and social differences. This made the government together with university officials brought up a question of updating the programs on foreign language teaching, changing the curriculum, renovating the tools and materials used for the language studies, developing vocational training courses to bridge the gap between what students want to know and what they really need to learn to become successful in the future career.

Vocational training programs delivered at tertiary educational institutions strive for graduating specialists who can use a foreign language primarily for communication and therefore incorporating multiple levels of language, including pragmatics [1].

Reviewed researches allow concluding that the issue of cultural aspect in teaching English as a foreign language is not a very recent trend. There could be observed the tendency of increasing the amount of teaching materials that would enable educators to implement the practices of combining language matters with cultural aspects in the classrooms. University executives and teaching community should choose those materials, textbooks, in particular, which incorporate the main theories of foreign language acquisition.

This research paper aims at providing the analysis of the cultural aspect in a course book materials for the vocational training program delivered at tertiary educational institution. Authors employed the features distinguished by the Common European Framework of Reference for Languages to trace the categories outlined in the examined textbooks.

1.1 Research question

Basing on literature review the authors of the study assigned a research question, that is:

1. To what extent is cultural aspect presented in the course materials for the vocational training programs?

1.2 Problem statement

Vocational training program at the Educational Center for Professional Communicative Training of Kazan Federal University supplies foreign language education to help specialists adapt to the cultural peculiarities and later be promoted in multinational companies. The target audience of the discussed vocational training program is the graduates of the business schools working for local or international companies and who have a necessity to be equipped with translation skills.

The significance of cultural aspect in teaching students of vocational training program is explained by the following:

- expansion and broadening of intercultural communications;
- development of self-awareness to overcome stereotypes and prejudices and establish intercultural understanding between nations;
- the formation of linguistic and cultural competence to integrate new experiences into one's own cultural system.

Thus, course materials are thoroughly selected to serve the above mentioned purposes providing comprehensive and complete perception of culture, language and career.

In higher education and especially in a foreign language classroom, "the textbook is one of the many tools used for learning" [14].

Undoubtedly, textbooks have considerable influence on classroom practice forming the core of the most teaching programs [5]. Some teachers use them as the main tool, others as supplementary resource that helps to get a flow of topics studied throughout the lesson. No matter what role textbooks have, they would always be 'the most powerful device' [12].

Printed textbooks are more frequently substituted by digital versions as they are more compact, comfortable and available everywhere, as well as easier to be used in large groups. Besides, 'textbooks are outdated as soon as they are printed, apps and websites can be constantly updated" [10]. We agree with Velde & Ernst who say that "print books are here to stay; e-books will enhance access to more science and research" [16].

The authors of the research opted for printed versions of the textbooks for several accounts: all our students are supplied with printed textbooks which are issued at the beginning of an academic year; it is easier to return to the cultural aspect that was studied before for revision or clarification; textbooks are rarely lost as handouts and are not dependent on Internet connection if stored online; they allow students to structure the material in no time referring to the necessary page and section.

A course book for teaching English presents a structured selection of topics suited to meet the needs of a certain category of learners, their level of language proficiency as well as the sphere of interests. Being divided into subsections, textbooks provide tasks to practice different language skills: reading, writing, listening, speaking. Following the theory of combining language competency and cultural one, each subsection of a studied unit should possess cultural aspect allowing students to immerse into foreign culture progressively, not necessarily of English-speaking countries. Considering the specificity of teaching a foreign language textbooks perform several interrelated functions: informative, motivating, pragmatic and controlling intended to optimize the achievement of goals. So, all tasks, containing cultural information have to envisage the discussed requirements.

The reviewed literature on the researched issue did not supply with the criteria used to estimate the quality and the scale of the cultural aspect presented in the course books for teaching English at vocational training programs. Basing on authors' experience and relying on their teaching flair they took a chance to form out the requirements to the cultural content used in the textbooks. First and foremost aspect is the authenticity of the material presenting cultural information; then comes association with the profession acquired and the various fields of science and technology correlating with it; all textbook materials should be designed to stimulate students' motivation for acquiring cultural information and later mastering it in communication in a foreign language in their professional field; the textbook's material should replenish the absence of foreign language environment, procure the conditions for communication, organizing the interaction of communicants as imitative authentic communication and serve as a basis for the future implementation of certain social roles by communicants as professionals; textbook's tasks with cultural content have to provide students with the availability of self-control and self-correction.

We are strongly convinced that all sections of the units included into a textbook could contain cultural aspect, no matter if it is a grammar exercise or filling in the gaps vocabulary practice. As long as there is a link between studied situations, real work and culture peculiarities students would get experiences that can enrich their language and cultural competency levels.

The provisions issued defined the motives for examining the course book materials used at vocational training program with the aim to distinguish the most affordable ones.

2 Method

The findings reported in this research are based on literature review aimed to clarify the problem statement and two stage survey. The first stage was supposed to provide the analysis of qualitative data for 3 Business English course books of upper-intermediate level produced by leading publishing houses: "Market Leader" by Pearson Longman, "Business Result" by Oxford University Press and "Intelligent Business" by Pearson Longman. The choice of this course books range was stipulated by co-decision of teaching staff for the vocational training program at the Educational Center for Professional Communicative Training of Kazan Federal University as they are among up-dated textbooks for Business English. The content of these course books was investigated from the social-cultural angle. The main data collection tool at this stage was SWOT analysis to reflect advantageous and disadvantageous features.

The second stage entailed analysis of socio-cultural features in course books creating the potential for researchers to generate quantitative data. In this context the researchers were particularly interested in the following features distinctively characteristic of a society adjusted by Common European Framework of Reference for Languages: everyday living; living conditions; interpersonal relations; values, beliefs and attitudes; body language; social conventions; ritual behaviour [4].

The data obtained throughout the above mentioned methods afforded ground for deciding on the course book that best meet syllabus requirements due to multi-aspect approach to cultural knowledge acquisition.

3 Findings

Having more than ten years of teaching experience as teachers of English, we could point several widespread drawbacks of the textbooks that are used at the lessons: cultural aspect in the textbooks is not presented in the amount that is adequate to meet the needs of the curriculum. Supplementary handouts are required. It provides extra workload for teachers and is time consuming to find worksheets matching the discussed topics; tasks lack real life expressions and vocabulary; there are usually no images which could help students visualize the cultural aspect; video support does not always supply students with the peculiarities of body language, gestures, mimics; from the audio tasks it is not always clear what country of origin the speaker's accent comes from; representatives of several countries are rarely presented in one task simultaneously.

The SWOT analysis gave the overall picture of cultural representation in the whole set of the courses as a set (including video support, supplementary books and DVD-ROMs) in Tables 1, 2 and 3.

Table 1. Market Leader SWOT

STRENGTHS	WEAKNESSES
- provides multiskills training of cultural awareness; provides video support to get patterns of behaviour and non-verbal means of communication; has a special section "Working across cultures" to teach the cultural difference in doing business; contains audio with different accents; has a special business skills section	- the business skills studied are westernized; not all topics highlight the cultural aspect of business; case studies do not give the background information on the business culture of the countries discussed
OPPORTUNITIES	**THREATS**
- provide useful web links skills; Youtube hosts international videos on the topics of the book; - English becomes an international language to build cultural dialogue; - skills and across cultural sections could be used as independent course; - continuous globalization of business; - does not give the comparison of cultures	- business realities are changing too rapid; - the textbook is not tailored to the cultural needs of individual student; - localization of business traditions -

Table 2. Intelligent business SWOT

STRENGTHS	WEAKNESSES
- cultural aspect is taught within the main topic of the unit; examples are not of abstract nature; - cultural aspect is presented in a separate section and within the text and listening tasks; - covers common, highly discussed topics; - has a video support to develop socio-cultural knowledge; - contains the comparison of cultures	- cultural aspect ranks the last place in the list of tasks; - the patterns of behavior are taken from the western business culture; - insufficient cultural information in the case studies briefs
OPPORTUNITIES	**THREATS**
- challenges students with out of book research; - business skills book does not depend on the content of the textbook; - has a website with updated texts	- tasks on cultural differences aren't based on students' needs; - demographic shifts change the culture of countries and the book doesn't keep up with that; - the change of economic environment and demography

Table 3. Business results SWOT

STRENGTHS	WEAKNESSES
- cultural aspect is represented in all activities: reading, writing, speaking, listening; - has "business communication skills" section based on cultural aspect; - section "practically speaking" – good opportunities for sounding more natural when students speak English; - a wide range of countries involved are used as examples	- some topics don't reflect the cultural aspect; - few comparisons of culture; some information is outdated; - doesn't have a separate skills book; contains discrepancy of students religious beliefs and content of the texts; - doesn't always consider the individual students cultural needs in group tasks
OPPORTUNITIES	**THREATS**
- considers business skills on a global scale that can help students communicate more accurately in real work situations; - possesses video support on YouTube, provides interactive workbook for practicing the language and skills in work and testing progress	- features of cultural knowledge are limited; - global changes in economy, culture, national identity, etc.; - orientalization of Europe

Examining the Strengths we have noted that all three coursebooks provide multi skills approach to cultural acquisition, contain audio provision to enhance cultural awareness and have video support giving details on body language, mimics and other behavioral information. Business skills sections in the textbooks enable obtaining and training communication skills necessary to be adequate in the real business situations, Intelligent Business even developed Skills books that could be used as an independent course. Market Leader, however, has a special section Working Across Cultures with an aim to encourage students to dialogue in the companies with international staff.

As for the Weaknesses we should note that in all three sets of coursebooks the business skills studied are westernized, though Intelligent Business gives some theoretical insight in the other cultures no practical output is followed. Some topics do not touch upon the cultural aspect of business directly and case studies do not give the background information on the business culture of the countries discussed that hurdles overall understanding the situation.

Considering the Opportunities, on the other hand, with English becoming lingua franca these business courses are getting additional value and the updates and YouTube support provide extra availability and recognitions. Thus, the materials produced by different cultures could be discussed and compared and English is shown in action as a language to build a dialogue of cultures.

The Threats revealed the overall problems of the course materials: the business realities are changing too quickly for any update to follow; the courses are not tailored to the cultural needs of individual student and may contradict and even hurt the cultural and religious perspectives; localization of business traditions that prevents unification of any rules in conducting business; demographic, cultural and social changes due to recent migration wave that make any value and cultural shifts unpredictable.

Hence, all three examined courses possessed high potential for study strategy with their individual advantages and drawbacks.

According to Common European Framework of Reference for Languages distinguishes social-cultural features as: everyday living (food and drink, meal times, public holidays; leisure activities); living conditions (living standards, welfare arrangements); interpersonal relations (relations between sexes, family structures and relations, relations in work situations); everyday living (race and community relations, relations among political and religious groupings); values, beliefs and attitudes (national identity, social class; occupational groups, minorities); body language; social conventions (punctuality, presents, dress, behavioral and conversational conventions and taboos); ritual behavior (birth, marriage, death, celebrations, festivals, dances, discos, religious observances and rites) [4]. We examined the textbooks only to define the percentage of cultural aspect features discussed above presence, but for the body language as this aspect is available with face-to-face communication or video content.

The results highlighted that cultural aspect is studied in the discussed textbooks in almost equal proportion (Market Leader – 46%, Intelligent Business – 40.2%, Business results 44.2%). Examining the features in Table 4, it is clear that across all three textbooks interpersonal relations consistently receive attention, particularly due to the sections devoted to working relations' establishment. Values, beliefs and attitudes got considerable amount of attention especially in the case studies and speaking sections. Everyday living and living conditions were presented merely equal and get far less attention as the main subject of the textbooks is business. And, finally, social conventions and ritual behavior received the least attention from the authors of the textbooks. The probable explanation is less conscious desire to focus on taboos and religious observances in fast changing world of demographic shifts.

Table 4. Socio-cultural knowledge features comparative analysis

Features	Market Leader	Intelligent Business	Business Result
everyday living	9.6%	7.4%	6.5%
living conditions	13.3%	14.3%	17.6%
interpersonal relations	44.3%	43.2%	48.8%
values, beliefs and attitudes	23.5%	25.8%	17.6%
social conventions	5.4%	5.8%	4%
ritual behaviour	3.9%	3.5%	5.5%

4 Discussion and conclusion

This study investigated business English textbook regarding cultural aspects they give attention to. It has been examined that the textbooks give most attention to interpersonal relations, values, beliefs and attitudes, while ritual behavior and social conventions gets minimal degrees of attention. It has also been distinguished that all studied textbooks envisage similar trend in presenting socio and cultural knowledge. The obtained results would help educators to enhance the amount of cultural information to provide comprehensive socio-cultural education.

It could be predicted that at the end of the vocational training course students would demonstrate cultural knowledge which allows to adapt to foreign environment, to overcome mentality differences in doing business, financial and law matters, get an insight of traditions and customs thus satisfying learners' real-world professional demands. As a result the graduates of the vocational program will acquire the cultural inhering, tolerance and become culturally responsive personalities. They would easily organize their speech and non-speech behavior adequate to the tasks of communication and in accordance with its terms and conditions.

References

1. Bardovi-Harlig. One functional approach to second language acquisition: The concept-oriented approach. In B. VanPatten & J. Williams (Eds.). Theories in second language acquisition: An introduction. New York: Routledge. pp. 57-76, (2007).
2. T. A. Baklashova, E. M. Galishnikova, L. V. Khafizova. Formation of Student's Tolerance in Multicultural Environment When Teaching a Foreign Language (KFU Experience, Kazan, Republic of Tatarstan, Russia. *The European Proceedings of Social & Behavioural Sciences*, Vol. 12, EpSBS e-ISSN: 23571330, pp. 38-44, (2016).
3. H. Byrnes. The cultural turn in foreign language departments: Challenge and opportunity. *Profession 2002*, pp.114-129, (2002).
4. Common European Framework of Reference for Languages: Learning, Teaching, Assessment, Cambridge University Press, ISBN : HB 0521803136 - PB 0521005310 www.uk.cambridge.org/elt
5. D. Crystal. English as a Global Language. Cambridge: Cambridge University press, (1997).
6. McDonough & Shaw. Material and methods in ELT. Oxford: Blackwell, (1993).
7. D. Graddol. The Future of English? British Council, (1997).
8. E. V. Grigorieva, L. R. Ismagilova , I. M.Solodkova. Comparative analysis of oral and computer based types of assessment in teaching English for students of economics, business and finance. ERPA INTERNATIONAL CONGRESSES ON EDUCATION 2015 (ERPA): *SHS Web of Conferences* Vol. 26, Art. №: UNSP 01131, (2016).
9. L. R. Ismagilova, O. V. Polyakova. The problem of the syllabus design within the competence approach based on the course “English for Master Degree Students in Economics (advanced level)”. *Procedia - Social and Behavioral Sciences* 152, pp.1095 – 1100, (2014).
10. C. Kramsch. Context and culture in language teaching. Oxford: Oxford University Press, (1993).
11. B. Lenon. Textbooks have a huge impact on education. http://www.telegraph.co.uk/education/educationopinion/11739310/Textbooks-have-a-huge-impact-on-education.html), (2015).
12. A. Littlejohn. The analysis of language teaching materials: Inside the Trojan Horse. In B. Tomlinson (Ed)., Materials development in language teaching. Cambridge: Cambridge University Press. pp.190-216, (1998).
13. Modern Language Association Ad Hoc Committee on Foreign Languages Foreign languages and higher education: New structures for a changed world. *Profession 2007*, pp.234-245, (2007).
14. A. J. Rockinson- Szapkiw*, J. Courduff, K. Carter, D. Bennett. Electronic versus traditional print textbooks: A comparison study on the influence of university students' learning. *Computers & Education* 63, pp. 259–266, (2013).
15. I.M. Solodkova, L.R. Ismagilova. Acquisition of Socio-Cultural Competence via Dynamic Learning Environment. *The European Proceedings of Social & Behavioural Sciences*, Vol. 12, .pp.389-395, (2016).
16. Velde & Ernst. The future of eBooks? Will print disappear? An end-user perspective. Library Hi Tech, 27, pp.570-583, (2009).

 DOI: 10.1051/shsconf/20173701079

The model of the first-year students' adaptation to vocational training: the example of foreign language

Elena M. Galishninkova[1] and Liliya V. Khafizova[1a]

[1]Kazan Federal University, Butlerov street, 4, Kazan, Russia, 420112

Abstract. The paper considers the problem of adaptation of the first-year students to professional activity by means of foreign language. To design the adaptation model, we developed four-block questionnaires to determine students' readiness for adaptation. The experiment resulted in the three groups of students with high, average and low levels of adaptation. Students with low level of adaptation become the target of our research. To remove the difficulties in studying a foreign language by the third group of students, an adaptation model was elaborated. Further, we identified the conditions for the effective implementation of the adaptation model of students to vocational training. In our view, these pedagogical conditions promote a more "sparing" transition of students to their main function as first-year students and increase the level of foreign language learning as well as improve the educational indicators.
Keywords: adaptation; vocational training; adaptation model; foreign language; communicative competence; component; extramural work of students; motivation.

1 Introduction

One of the fundamental conditions for the successful preparation of competitive professionals at the university is to develop students' interest in obtaining qualified knowledge, skills and competencies. To fulfill this condition, it is necessary to lay the foundations of expertise during the years of attendance in the university, to set up the need and readiness for continuous self-education in a rapidly changing economic environment. In this regard, the problem of future specialist's adaptation to the exercise of profession is brought to the forefront. It is from such specialists that a high level of activity, independence, flexibility, and the ability to quickly orient oneself to any environment are expected. At the same time, the development of international relations, the intensification of business contacts contribute to the demand for specialists who are fluent in a foreign language. The problem of training graduates with knowledge of foreign languages is conditioned by the social order of the society and is currently one of the important tasks in university teaching [8]. In this situation, the issue of adapting students to professional work

[a] Corresponding author :ptrlilia2004@mail.ru

with a means of foreign language acquires special significance and seems very relevant to us.

The analysis of scientific sources from different fields of knowledge has shown that adaptation is viewed by scientists from different angles. Adaptation is considered as a central concept in several major social disciplines, for example, G. Simonet emphasizes that there is a growing interest in adaptation in environmental science because of the acceleration of global environmental and socio-economic change [7].

Besides, adaptation is viewed by scientists [6, 9] from the perspective of sociology and psychology. It is also considered within the social, cultural and historical aspects [2].

While reviewing scientific sources, we came to the conclusion that in general there are some works devoted to various problems of adaptation in higher educational institutions [3, 4 and 1] and at the same time there are no scientific researches devoted to the first-year student's adaptation to vocational training on the basis of foreign language.

2 Method

For the purpose of our research we used such theoretical methods as theoretical analysis of philosophical, pedagogical, psychological literature on the subject of study, generalization, comparison, projection as well as such empirical method as the method of included monitoring and peer review, interviews, questionnaires, discussion, pedagogical experiment, the quantitative analysis of the results of the experiment.

2.1 Participants

The participants of the experiment were 124 first-year students of 2016-2017 academic year (the fall semester).

2.2 Procedure

Four block questionnaires to determine students' readiness for adaptation were developed. The obtained data was processed by the method of incidence of correspondences, when for each "effect" the frequency of its finding in all reviews was calculated. These blocks are: 1) motivating component of cognitive activity; 2) motivational and emotional block; 3) motivational and communicative block (as an important part of communicative competence),4) motivational activity block.

3 Discussion

In modern Russia, intensive studies of the adaptation of young people are conducted at different levels in philosophy, pedagogics and psychology emphasizing its philosophical, psychological and socio-pedagogical aspects. Based on the analysis of scientific sources, it can be concluded that adaptation is considered in sociology, as a form of human behavior that corresponds to personal qualities. In psychological concepts, adaptation appears as a process of active adjustment of an individual to certain material surroundings, norms and values of the social environment, as an indispensible part of the process of socialization.

The main characteristics of adaptation as a concept are: the process of interaction between the individual and the educational environment, and therefore, change in the lifestyle of the individual in accordance with the requirements of this environment; entry and adaptation to new conditions of the social and educational environment (university-hostel-social environment); acceptance of new social roles, norms and values; readiness to change personal qualities under the influence of the educational process and new external factors. And it is important to note that adaptation covers only the first months of the first semester, so it is advisable to consider it as a process of adaptation, assimilation that takes a relatively short period of time. It is known that the educational process is an organized, interrelated and purposeful activity of students and teachers with the aim to acquire vocationally important competences. Since the first component of this process is its goal, the second and, especially important one is its subjects and objects (teacher and student), forming a dynamic "teacher-student" system with the teacher having a leading role. The third component is the content of the educational process. The content is carefully selected and analyzed in accordance with the principles of content selection. As the fourth structural component of the educational process, we define its organizational and management unity involving the forms and methods of education and training, the fifth component is pedagogical diagnostics - testing knowledge and skills; expert assessments and characteristics. The sixth structural component of the educational process is extramural work of students, since public life is the most important factor in students' successful socialization.

In the process of mastering a foreign language for specific purpose, students gradually acquire knowledge and skills of professional speech behavior, ethical norms in various professional communications, they elaborate from artificially created situations to a natural professional speech, which determines the building of professional and communicative competence in foreign language. The content of teaching foreign languages to students of economic faculties should be aimed at their training as competitive specialists, which is ensured by a whole set of competences, among which a foreign language professional communicative competence acquires special significance. For the first-year students, at the very first stage of education, we consider it important to determine the "frontiers" of the cognitive aspect and the degree of readiness (motivation) for foreign communication as a first level of professional communicative competence (the skill of speaking in another language). Such "frontiers" and degree of readiness were determined on the basis of an analysis of expert assessments.

4 Findings

The responses were distributed by blocks. The following results were obtained: 1st block (motivating component of cognitive activity) – "I have no difficulties in learning a foreign language" (28%), "I have small difficulties with a foreign language" (39%), "Learning a foreign language causes me great difficulties"(33%). Since emotions are closely related to the motivational-cognitive component (knowledge varies and enriches which leads to the change in person's emotions and all levels of the language contain an emotional component [5], we singled out 2nd block (motivational and emotional) where the responses were - "I am interested in learning a foreign language" (36%), "I learn a foreign language to get a positive grade" (47 %), "I'm not interested in studying a foreign language" (17%). 3rd block - motivational and communicative (as an important part of communicative competence) that implies readiness for communication in foreign language classes was determined by students in accordance with the following parameters: "I try to communicate, I do it with pleasure" (68%), "I try to communicate on demand, as much as necessary" (25%), "I cannot speak English at all" (7%). In addition, we singled out a motivational activity block, which is related to the above-mentioned form of human behavior, which manifests itself most clearly in the desire and willingness of students to participate in certain tasks both during classroom and extracurricular activities, for example "to make a video clip on a certain topic with own soundtrack"(42% of respondents expressed their eagerness to perform the task), "to prepare and deliver a report on the topic" (23% of respondents), "to take part in extracurricular activities (English song party, thematic quiz, mini contest" (12%), while 23% ignored the tasks. Thus, during the ascertaining experiment, three groups of students were identified:

1st group – having a sufficiently high level of adaptation- 44% of respondents

2nd group – with an average level of adaptation - 30% of respondents

3rd group - low level of adaptation - 26% of respondents

The third group is the object of our study

To build an educational experiment, we designed an adaptation model of first-year students to vocational training by means of a foreign language. In general, the design method is practical or theoretical manipulation of the object in which the object under study is replaced by a natural or artificial analogue, through its research we penetrate into the object of cognition. Consequently, the model is an analog of the object of investigation. When designing a model, we have the opportunity to present this or that area of research in the form of a structure, determine its components, their characteristics and relationships, and monitor model's functioning. The obtained results will enable to determine the significance of the created model (environment), to choose the vector of its improvement, to predict the expected result. Accordingly, the goal of creating a theoretical model of vocational adaptation by means of a foreign language is the readiness of students of the economic faculties to professional work, overcoming difficulties in the new educational environment. To construct this model, we will rely on the components of the educational process identified and the above-mentioned components. The theoretical model is based on the following principles: scientific, professional orientation and interdisciplinarity, individualization of teaching, close interaction and mutual understanding between students and teachers.

When designing the model, we incorporate in its structure the basic components of teaching and educational process in the discipline of a foreign language: - target (consistent implementation of the revised goals and objectives), informative (informative content that means professional content in a foreign language and functional originality), activity-operational (methodical and technological mechanisms for the realization of educational tasks: ways, means of teaching, forms of organizing cognitive activity), ethical-behavioral (norms and rules of behavior, and the interaction of applicants- students both in the group and with the faculty), the diagnostic component (controlling and adjusting) (Figure1).

All the elaborated components of the model are designed on the basis of the discipline "Foreign Language". The main objective of studying "Foreign language" as an academic subject in the economics departments of the university is to possess a foreign language at the level that is sufficient for business communication in the framework of the selected profile and to build an individual development pathway, i.e., shaping of professional communicative competence in foreign language. The so-called framework of the selected profile is, in fact, vocational orientation of training, including conceptual and terminological apparatus of the future job, knowledge in the area of interest relying on interdisciplinary links, main categories and ideas, as well as studying some specifics related to the economics, for example, figures, graphs, diagrams, etc. and their description.

As the components of the content of language training in the first year, we consider

- means of communication (grammatical, lexical, stylistic, country knowledge);
- knowledge and skills acquired in the course of training and allowing the use of the language;
- general and professional themes and situations for oral and written communication.

Given the fact that some students come with a fairly high proficiency level and do not encounter any difficulties with adaptation, we shifted our attention to the category of students with a low level of adaptation in accordance with the data of ascertaining experiment. This includes the students from rural localities, students who are not motivated to learn a foreign language; students who came from neighboring countries. Based on our experiment and for effective adaptation process by means of a foreign language for this category of students, we developed the following (implementation) mechanisms: a) placement test which enables to divide students into groups according to the level of language proficiency; b) spiral learning during the first two months, based on the revision of school material and gradual expansion along the line - grammar, vocabulary, communication; c) "immersion" of yesterday's applicants in the student environment by using such teaching aids as preparing and viewing video clips, getting to know the city, the university, introducing and communicating with classmates, creating a friendly atmosphere in class, shifting the focus on topics close to yesterday's schoolchildren interests - My native city, My country, The main industries of my country; d) work with the so-called international words (economy, banking, management, marketing, company) e) work with the conceptual-terminological apparatus employing word formation exercises - to consume-consumption- consumer, consumer goods; to employ-employer-employee - employment-unemployment; f) work with "group of words" - antonyms and synonyms - goods-commodity, items, product; to fall, to go down, to drop, to rise-to-fall, to increase- to decrease: g)massive open online courses (MOOC) designed by teachers of the foreign language department - Job hunting , Great Britain, etc. with lexical, communicative material, tests and audio-visual training tools on relevant topics; h) development of communication skills through games – "your question - my answer", interviewing fellow students on different topics (question-answer system), organizing mini-dialogues and mini-speeches, role-playing games.

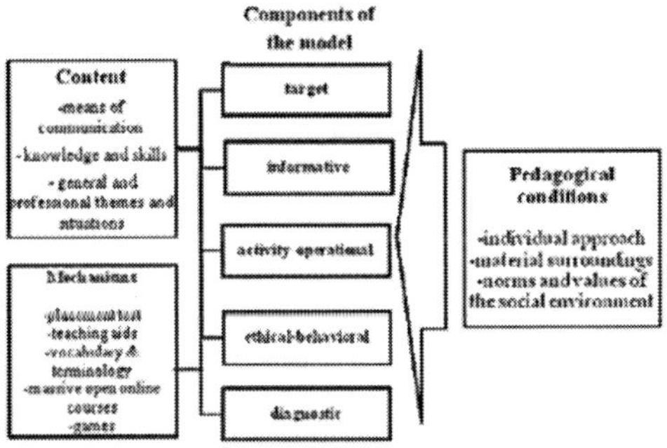

Fig.1. The model of the first-year students' adaptation to vocational training

When solving the problem of adaptation, we do not focus not on the whole "body" of students or a group of students, we pay attention to each of them, taking into account his/her individual characteristics, his/her level of preparedness. Hence, one of the conditions for the effective implementation of the adaptation model of students' to vocational training is the requirement for the teacher to follow an individual approach to each student, which implies, as already mentioned, a form of human behavior that corresponds to personal qualities, that is, 1) personality qualities of students: interests and motives (with the motivation for vocational training, learning a foreign language dominating), traits (activity, consciousness, responsibility, proactivity, the desire for independence, or the purposefulness of an individual or indifference) and temperament (mental ballast, activity, stress-resistance, impulsiveness, sensitivity, vulnerability); 2) the level of intellectual development and cognitive interests (sustained attention, developed imagination, greater integration of memory, the ability to process body of information, to clearly state one's thoughts, focus on the profession and learning a foreign language); 3) independence in the academic work - to make records, compose a mind-map based on the text read, work with reference sources, readiness for self-improvement. It is easier to take into account these parameters for teachers of a foreign language, since the number of hours devoted to this subject (6 hours a week) allows you to meet with them more often and work closely (the learning cycle is 10 - 14 people) both during classes and out-of-class activities (English days, mini-conferences, English language contests, quizzes, Christmas carols party, etc.)

The second condition for the effective implementation of the named model, as we noted above on the basis of the analysis of the scientific literature, is a process of active adjustment of an individual to certain material surroundings, norms and values of the social environment, as an indispensable part of the process of socialization. These certain material surroundings and the social environment are created on the basis of the discipline "Foreign Language", namely the creation of a local foreign language environment as part of the educational space, which in turn has a large measure of complexity and includes integrated content of curricula and disciplines, interdisciplinary connections , interaction of traditional and innovative technologies, material and technical base, provides for a close interaction of teachers and students. The teacher of a foreign language, especially if he/she is also the advisor of the group is fully able to carry out psychological and pedagogical support of adaptation. Extracurricular work in a foreign language (song contests, poster contests, watching movies etc.) plays a big role in the process of adaptation of first-year students to vocational learning, as it provides a wide range of development tools for their foreign language potential, cognitive interest, creativity and professional motivation.

Thus, the implementation of the adaptation model of first-year students to professional activity by means of a foreign language on the basis of fulfilling certain pedagogical conditions has made it possible to "build a bridge" that promotes a more "sparing" transition of students (43 students of the above category) to their main function as a first year student.

From the first block (cognitive), the following responses were received (they are selected already from the category defined above - 43 students of experimental groups): by parameters - means of communication - lexical and grammatical aspects were taken. In the experimental group – in lexics - 47% improved results, in control group - 16%, in grammar - experimental group - 38%, control - 12%.

By parameters - knowledge, skills and abilities that allow using the language - simple monologues and dialogues, the ability to ask and answer questions - the experimental group showed 29%, the control group - 11%.

By the topics and situations of general and professional oral and written communication, the results turned out to be more than modest, although there is a clear improvement in results compared to the control group - a summary of the main idea of the read text on the topic or a brief retelling - 34% versus 6% respectively (Figure 2).

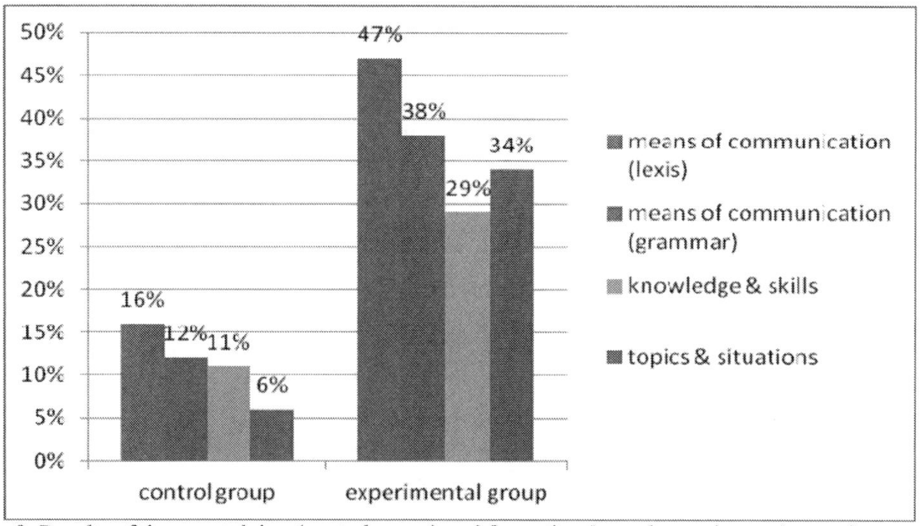

Fig. 2. Results of the ascertaining (control group) and formative (experimental group) experiments

4 Conclusion

The process of first year student's adaptation to vocational training by means of foreign language in higher education establishments will be effective if:

- to introduce adaptation model that consists of target, informative, activity-operational, ethical-behavioral, the diagnostic components
- to employ the implementation mechanisms
- to meet appropriate pedagogical conditions

The research resulted in the development of adaptation model, the mechanisms and conditions for its implementation. These contribute to effective inclusion of low-achieving students into educational environment by means of a foreign language.

References

1. Bathmaker, A.-M. & Avis, J. "How do i cope with that?" the challenge of 'schooling' cultures in further education for trainee FE lecturers. British Educational Research Journal, **33**(4), 509-532., (2007).
2. Baumeister, R. F & Muraven, M. Identity as adaptation to social, cultural, and historical context. Journal of Adolescence, **19**, 405–416., (1996). https://pdfs.semanticscholar.org/6fd3/b47efab8c3b1740e911c58fa729f4a71a3a9.pdf/
3. Cameron, K. S. Organizational adaptation and Higher education. Journal of Higher Education, **55**(2), 122-144., (1984).
4. Figuera, P. &Torrado, M. The transition to university of at-risk groups in Spain: The case of students from vocational education and training. Revista de Cercetare si Interventie Sociala, **49**(6), 23-40., (2015).
5. Goleman, D. The Emotional Intelligence: Why it can matter more than IQ? Bentam Books., (1997).
6. Jakubowicz, A. Psychological adaptation In Encyclopediae Universalis. 247-250., (2002).
7. Simonet, G. "The concept of adaptation: interdisciplinary scope and involvement in climate change", *S.A.P.I.EN.S* [Online], 3.1 | (2010)., http://sapiens.revues.org/997.
8. Solodkova Irina M. & Ismagilova Liliya R. Teaching English as a second language: an extent of socio-cultural knowledge. *Psychology and psychiatry, sociology and healthcare, education conference proceedings*, **1** (III), 1019-1025., (2016)
9. Taché, A. L'adaptation : un concept sociologique systémique. Éditions L'Harmattan,. (2003).

The Jordanian terms of address: Asocio-pragmatic study

Mahmoud Al-Qudah[1a]

[1]Princess Sumaya University for Technology, Jordan

Abstract. This study investigates the terms of address in Jordanian Arabic. It focuses on six major categories of address terms. The study identifies the most important forms under each category, their social meanings, and the governing factors that control their use. The participants of the study are 100 adult Jordanians who are chosen randomly from different public places. The data is collected by means of a questionnaire and participant interview. The results of the study show that Jordanian terms of address reflect the complex social relationship between the interlocutors. The choice of a given term is determined by a number of social factors such as age, gender, social status, formality, intimacy, and familiarity between the speaker and the addressee. Each category of address terms has its special uses in different social domains. The interpretation of each term is found to be context-dependent. Finally, the study concludes with restating the study objectives and the main findings of the study in addition to recommendations for further research.
Keywords: Pragramatics, Social Context, interlocutors, terms of address, Kinship terms

1 Introduction

A linguistic interaction is necessarily a social interaction during which the use of language entails more than simply exchanging information about thoughts and factual things between one person and another [1]. According to [2], when people participate in conversations, they consciously or unconsciously show their identities, their belonging to a specific culture or group and also their tendencies to become close or distant from others. A significant linguistic area in which all these functions are highlighted is "terms of address".

According to [3], terms of address are words or linguistic items used for addressing others to attract their attention or referring to them during interaction. They hold two types of meanings, i.e. lexical and social meanings which do not necessarily have a close connection [4, 5]. For example, the term sister refers to a woman or a girl of the same parents, but it could be also used to refer to a nun. Therefore, Braun [4] posits that the address behavior refers to how speakers use the repertoire of address variants available to them.

Terms of address can be investigated within the framework of politeness theory in which the choice of a particular address form is determined by how polite it sounds in a given situation. According to Brown and Levinson [6], terms of address are vital linguistic mechanisms by which a speaker's attitude toward, and evaluation of his or her relationship

[a] Corresponding author: mahmoudqudah58@gmail.com

 DOI: 10.1051/shsconf/20173701080

with another speaker is mirrored. Moreover, they argue that by the appropriate use of these terms, the speaker can identify himself/herself as part of a social group while an inappropriate choice of address is expected to impede or even cease good interaction. The significance of these terms lies in their function as an indicator of interlocutors' social status as well as their social distance, showing their emotions to the other side and a means of saving one's face. Thus, the more intimate the speaker is to the addressee, the more s/he will use familiar forms such as first names, and the more distant the speaker is from the addressee, the more s/he would be expected to use more formal ones such as titles.

Nominal forms of address include a wide range of categories. Dunkling [7] provides a good classification for terms of address: 1) kinship terms which are used to address members in the family, e.g. mum, cousin and uncle, 2) names, e.g. first, middle and last names which can be used with other terms of address as well, 3) religious terms, e.g. father in Christianity, imaam in Islam and Rabbi in Jewish, 4) titles, e.g. sir, madam and your majesty, 5) occupational terms, e.g. doctor, driver and waiter, 6) military ranks, e.g. sergeant and general, and 7) endearment and friendship terms, e.g. love, baby and angle. Afful [8] adds another category to this classification which is 8) zero address, i.e. terms used when the speaker is not certain how to address others, e.g. excuse me.

The usage of address terms is a rule governed process that mainly depends on the speaker, addresses and the context. However, these terms might be used in contexts other than the expected ones, where they are meant to convey a certain message [4, 9]. For example, a White police officer addresses a Black doctor by using the term boy instead of a title; this indicates a racial message by denying both the doctor's rank and age. The followings represent the most influential factors that affect the address system:

Who are the interlocutors? The speaker's as well as the addressee's age, gender, identity, and social relations influence address behaviors [9, 3, 10]. For examples, men use terms of address such as Old Boy, and Old Chap more frequently than women, and those who are superiors tend to use first name when addressing their subordinates [7].

What is the context? Setting, audience, and topic of the discourse are very important elements that may affect the choice of the proper terms of address [11]. For example, Esmae'li [12] reveals that the social context affects the way that Iranian spouses address each other. He reveals that Iranian couples do not use pet names in the presence of children or parents-in-law.

What is the culture? Terms of address are culture-dependent. Not only terms of address are different from one culture into another, but also their pragmatic meanings are different. For example, Hwang [13] observes the differences in the address system between Korean and American cultures. The results indicate that the American culture is first-name oriented, while Korean culture is family name and title oriented. Moreover, the use of kinship terms in the American society is limited to address relatives only, whereas Korean may use these terms to address elderly people.

What are the historical changes? Terms of address change in the course of time. In the sense that new forms emerge and other forms extinct or change its meanings [5]. For instance, Moghaddam, et al. [2] examine the changes in that Persian address terms in three different historical periods and suggest that there is a gradual and regular movement in the Iranian address system from formality to solidarity.

Due to the fact that the proper use of address forms may result in an effective communication, and since the usage of these terms is context-dependent, these term have been the subject of many studies which generally attempt at investigating their nature, major categories, and governing factors. Therefore, it seems plausible to explore the Jordanian terms of address from a pragmatic point of view. This paper is an attempt in this direction.

Specifically, the study seeks answer to the following questions:

- What are the social meanings and usages of Jordanian terms of address?
- What are the social factors that govern the usage of these terms?

2 Literature Review

Research on terms of address is generally agreed to have begun by Brown and Gilman's [14] article "The Pronouns of Power and Solidarity" which investigates pronominal terms of address in European languages and differentiates between two pronominal forms, i.e. T pronouns (second person singular pronouns) and V pronouns (second person plural pronouns). Brown and Gilman (ibid) find that "T pronouns" are used to address intimates or inferiors, whereas "V pronouns" are used with non-intimate or superiors. They conclude that the choice of pronouns is determined by the notion of power and solidarity between the speaker and the addressee. This piece of work has been followed by a number of influential studies which analyze the address systems in different languages and determine their pragmatic usage in different context.

Parkinson [15] investigates Egyptian Arabic (EA) terms of address. To collect natural data on EA address system. He analyzes the conversations of Egyptians individuals from different social classes. The results show that EA terms of address are chosen based on who is the addressee and what type is the relationship between the speaker and the receiver. Also, he notices two linguistic phenomena affecting EA address system, i.e. the first is borrowing from prestigious languages such as "boss" from English, and "monsieur" from French, and the second is phonological reduction such as ***uṣtaaz/ uṣta***.

Dickey [16] attempts to examine how terms differ in address and in reference and what factors control this difference. After observing and interviewing 28 informants who are native speakers of English, Italian and German. The study indicates that dimensions of power and solidarity between the speaker and the addressee influence terms of reference as well as terms of address. Keshavarz [3] explores the impact of social context, intimacy and distance on the choice of Persian address system. His study reveals that the Parisian language has two pronominal terms, i.e. the pronoun ***to*** which reflects inferiority and informality and s***ome*** which denotes distance and respect. Furthermore, the study suggests that context and social factors such as age, gender, education, social status and occupation have great influence on the choice of address forms.

Nevala [17] investigates terms of address and forms of reference in late 16th-century English correspondence from a socio-pragmatic point of view. The results of his study reveal that the reasons for the choice of an appropriate term are complex and the parameters set for, e.g., positive and negative politeness can no longer be seen as equally valid.

Afful [8] explores the address system of university students in Ghana based on spontaneous and deliberative spoken discourse. He highlights the strong relation between terms of address and variations in terms of gender, mood, domain, purposes, and setting. Salihu [10] also investigates the address system of Hausa society. The research gives a list of Hausa terms of address and shows that each class of address forms has its special usage for particular people under certain circumstances. The employment of address terms in Hausa is affected by age, gender, personality, social status, religion, and family relation. Furthermore, the results reveal that kinship terms in Hausa are sometimes used to address non- relatives.

In conclusion, many studies have investigated terms of address in different languages. However, to the best the researcher's knowledge, no research has tackled the Jordanian forms of address, the factors that govern their usage, and how can they be used to manifest interpersonal relationships. This highlights the plausibility of conducting a study to fill this research gap.

3 Methods

3.1 The participants

The sample of this study consists of 100 Jordanians who are chosen randomly from different public places and from different Jordanian governorates. The participants' age ranges from 18 to 73 years old. Fifty percent of the participants are males, and the other (50%) are females.

3.2 Data collection

The researcher designs a questionnaire to provide a large quantity of natural data concerning Jordanian terms of address. In addition, short interviews with 20 participants to support the findings are conducted.

The questionnaire designed to collect the data is made up of two sections; viz. the first collects personal information, including age, gender and educational level, whereas the second investigates Jordanian terms of address in various social contexts, i.e. family, neighbors, work, university and strangers. Then, the questionnaire is distributed, completed, and collected.

Moreover, twenty participants, i.e. 12 females, and 8 males are interviewed for 15 minutes each during which they are asked to justify their answers in the questionnaire and if there are any other alternative terms they would like to add and in which context they use them. Finally, the informants' responses are analyzed statistically and the terms of address figured out in the study are classified into six categories, i.e. kinship terms, tecnonyms, first names, titles, religious terms, and zero terms.

4 Findings and discussion

It has been argued that terms of address are almost never neutral in the interpersonal meanings they convey, so the choice of a particular form inevitably entails the expression of particular feelings and attitudes (Moghaddam, 2013). This section discusses the social uses of address terms, the factors governing the usage of these terms and the social meaning they convey within the framework of politeness theory. Each category is examined individually and discussed in terms of its pragmatic meaning and the factors governing its use.

4.1 Kinship terms

Kinship terms are used to address members in the family, e.g. mum, cousin and uncle. Table (1) below shows the percentage of kinship terms in each social domain.

Table 1. The percentage of kinship terms' usage in different social domains

Gender	Relatives	Neighbors	University	Work	Strangers
Male	100%	87%	20%	10%	50%
female	100%	93%	7%	15%	60%

Kinship terms are originally used to address relatives. The Jordanian kinship system distinguishes between maternal and paternal relatives as the following:

Baba, yabaa, ʔabuuy, waaldi, and babi for the father
Maamaa, yammaa, ʔummy walidti, and maami for the mother
ʕammi, and ʕammo for the father's brother
ʕammti, and ʕammto for the father's sister
Xaali, and Xaalo for the mother's brother
Xaalti, Xaalto, and anti for the mother's sister
Jiduu, jiddi, siidi, and siido for grandfather
Jiddah, jidity, teta, and sitoo for grandmother
ʔaxoy for a brother
ʔuxti for a sister

Table (1) shows that kinship terms are not only used to address relatives, but are also used to address people in other social domains. First, the terms ***ʕammi*** and ***ʕammti*** are widely extended to address parents-in-law. Married males and females reported that they use the terms ***ʕammi and ʕammti/xalti*** when addressing their father- and mother-in-law. This result might be attributed to the assumption that these terms of address are more polite than the original terms ***ħamaay*** (father-in- law) and ***ħamaati*** (mother-in-law).

Moreover, no differences are found in the use of address terms between male and female when addressing relatives. However, females use more Madani terms of address (the dialect of the urban areas in Jordan), such as ***xaalto, anti, mami, teta,*** than males do. The results also show that Jordanians do not use kinship terms to address siblings, brothers- and sisters-in-laws; instead, they use first names or tecnonyms to address them.

In addition, the findings of the study indicate that kinship terms are widely used to address neighbors. (93%) of females and (87%) of males reported that they use kinship terms (***ʕammi, xalti, and ʔuxtii***) to address neighbors. These terms can be used in combination with first name, or tecnonyms. Furthermore, the use kinship terms is found to be extended to include strangers: (60%) of informants use (***ʕammi,*** and ***xalti***) to address strangers who are older than them, and (40%) of informants use ***ʔxuii/ʔuxtii*** to address strangers who are of the same age of the speaker.

However, the results reveal that kinship terms are not frequently used at university and work. Their use is limited to address individuals who share the same or less amount of power. For example, (70%) of females informants use the term ***ʕammo*** to address a subordinate old age male at, but they do not use this term to address their boss at work. With regard to university domain, the results show that a very limited number of male informants reported that they use the term ***ʔuxt*** to address unfamiliar female students. Besides, some instructors reported that they use the terms ***binti*** (my daughter) and ***ibni*** (my son) to address their students in order to reflect intimacy and avoid formality. The results also indicate that elderly speakers in Jordan usually use the terms ***binti, ibni,*** when addressing young individuals in different social contexts.

However, they might also use the terms ***ʕammi, xaalii, ʕammto,*** and ***xaaluo***. This use is widely acceptable and polite.

It can be noticed that the use of kinship terms is affected by some factors; viz. the social domain, the addressee, age, and context. While these terms are considered polite and face-saving forms to address family members, and neighbors, they are not appropriate to be used in formal settings. Another important factor that governs the use of kinship terms is the age difference between the speaker and the addressee. For example, when a male speaker addresses someone who is older than him, he would most probably use the term ***ʕammi,*** whereas when the addressee is younger than him, he may use the term ***ibni,*** and if the addressee is of the same age, he may opt to use the term ***ʔxuui.*** At work old- aged subordinates are usually addressed with ***9ammi, xaali, or xalti,*** but young subordinates are addressed by their first name. Also, power relations are found to influence the use of kinship terms. For example, no one addresses his/her old-aged boss by ***9ammi,*** or ***xalii.***

In sum, kinship terms have two social meanings that contradict each other: the first denotes respect and politeness with family members, neighbors, and strangers in the street. The second, on the other hand, denotes inferiority or same level of power in formal settings such university and work.

4.2 Tecnonyms

Tecnonyms are terms used to address adults which are derived from the name of their eldest child. Arabic tecnonyms are a combination of the words ***abu*** + the name of the eldest male child. Table (2) below shows the percentages of tecnonyms' use in different social domains:

Table 2. The percentages of tecnonyms' useage in different social domains

Gender	Family	Neighbor	University	Work	Strangers
Male	80%	70%	10%	35%	4%
Female	70%	80%	0%	25%	0%

Table (2) indicates that tecnonyms are used by all informants for addressing relatives, friends, and neighbors. First, they are widely used to address family members. Most of the informants reported that they use tecnonyms to address married relatives with or without kinship terms. In addition, some informants reported that they use them to address their spouses in public. The results reveal that tecnonyms are also used to address neighbors; (70%) of male informants and 80% of females use tecnonyms when addressing neighbors.

As far as formal settings, i.e. university and work, are concerned, the findings point out a limited use of tecnonyms. Only (30%) of informants use tecnonyms at work, and (5%) of informants use them at university. The participants' responses also indicate that tecnonyms are used to address a colleague with the same or less level of power. However, they are rarely used to address a superior. Finally, the study detects a number of fixed tecnonyms that are used among male youth to address strangers, or friends such as ***abu-ḥmeid*** and ***abu-alshabaab***

In conclusion, the findings of the study show that tecnonymic terms are widely used in the Jordanian community. They are frequently used with family members, friends, and neighbors to indicate familiarity, intimacy, politeness and respect. Furthermore, the results point out that the age of the addressee, his/her maternal status as well as the social context are the most important factors that control the pragmatic meaning of tecnonyms.

4.3 First name

In Jordan, people rarely address each other with family names. In contrast, first names are widely used and embedded in the Jordanian society as a term of address. Table (3) presents the percentages of first names as they are found to be used in different social domains.

Table 3. The percentages of first names' use in different social domains

Gender	family	Neighbors	University	Work	Strangers
Male	90%	70%	60%	60%	5%
Female	80%	80%	70%	70%	0%

According to Table (3), first names are used to address people in different social domains except when addressing strangers. Among family members and neighbors, first names are used to address individuals in the same age of the speaker or younger. Most of the informants reported that they use first names to address their younger brothers and sisters. Moreover, married participants also stated that they address their brothers- and sisters-in-law who are also of the same age or younger by their first names.

Furthermore, (70%) of male informants and (90%) of females stated that they use first names when addressing their neighbors: 1) who are of the same age or younger, and 2) who have the same gender. However, in formal settings, first name is used according to hierarchal and symmetrical relationships. The questionnaire reveals that (96%) of informants use first name with their subordinate employees, (60%) of informants use first name with their colleagues without any title, whereas (0%) of informants use first name to address their boss.

It is important to be mentioned here that gender play a role in addressing others using first name. Both male and female participants reported that they use first names more freely when addressing people of the same gender. Females avoid addressing non-relative males with their first names without any title. Similarly, males tend to avoid addressing non-relatives females with their first names.

Besides, the familiarity between participants, even among males and females, affects the use of first names in all domains. The more familiar the addressee is, the more frequent s/he would be addressed by his/her first name.

In sum, it appears that there are four main social factors governing the usage of first names. These factors are the addressee's age, social rank, gender, and familiarity.

4.4 Titles

The findings reveal two types of titles in Jordan; viz. gender-oriented titles such as ***?anisah*** (miss), ***madaam*** (madam), ***sayeed*** (Mr.), and job-oriented titles such as ***muhandis*** (engineer), ***ductoor*** (doctor),***?ustzaz*** (instructor), and ***m9alim***(teacher). Table (4) below shows the percentages of titles' use as terms of address according to social domains:

Table 4. The percentages of title terms in different social domains

Gender	Family	Neighbors	University	Work	Strangers
Male	0%	15%	85%	90%	50%
Female	0%	20%	90%	95%	40%

A glance at Table (4) shows that titles are broadly most likely to be used at work and university. But, they are rarely used with family members and neighbors. The results reveal that (90%) of males and (95%) of females address their superior by using titles. Furthermore, all the informants use the title ***ductoor*** when addressing their professors inside and outside the lecture.

The data analysis also reveals that the use of ***?ustzaz*** (male instructor), and ***m9alim*** (male teacher) has been extended to indicate other meanings. ***?ustzaz*** is used to address school teachers, school master, employees in banks and companies and strangers who seem educated. The term ***m9alim***, on the other hand, is more commonly used to address people who have low-status jobs such as craftsmen, workers, grocers and even plumbers. Furthermore, the word ***m9alim*** is used by male informants but not females who prefer zero or kinship terms to address people with low-status jobs. Another observation, the borrowed word ***miss*** is used to address female teachers only. Finally, the findings reveal that job-oriented titles are used more frequently in the Jordanian culture than gender-oriented titles. Only (20%) of the participants use gender-oriented titles, while all participants use job-oriented titles.

The participants reported that that title terms would support negative face in formal situations where they express distance and formality. However, in some situations, they might be used to express irony. One of the participants in the interviews stated that once he had an argument with an uneducated man who expressed an opinion with which the participant dids not agree, so he addressed him by saying "***sho ya duktoor, khef ʕlina !***". Finally, the addressees' social status, familiarity, and the formality of the situation are found to be the most important factors determining the use of titles.

4.5 Religious terms Hadj/ Hadjah

The use of the term ***ḥadj*** to address old males and ***ḥadjah*** to address old females is very common among Jordanians. This term is used to address old people in general whether they have undertaken the pilgrimage to Mecca or not. Table (5) below shows the percentages of ***ḥadj/ ḥadjah*** as they are used in different social domain:

Table 5. The percentages of ḥadj / ḥadjah in different social domains

Gender	Family	Neighbors	University	Work	Strangers
Male	50%	70%	0%	0%	50%
Female	30%	60%	0%	0%	0%

The results show that ***hadj*** is used to address elderly relatives, neighbors, and strangers. (50%) percent of males and (30%) of females use ***ḥadj*** and ***ḥadjah*** to address their parents and grandparents. About (65%) of informants use ***ḥadj*** and ***ḥadjah*** when addressing elderly neighbors, and (50%) of male informants use ***ḥadj/ḥadjah*** when addressing elderly strangers. However, females avoid the terms ***ḥadj/ḥadjah*** to address elderly strangers, instead they reported that they opt to use the terms ***9ammoo*** and ***xaaltoo***.

Nevertheless, the findings show that religious terms are rarely used at university and work; informants do not use ***ḥadj /ḥadjah*** to address their colleagues at work and university even if the age difference is very big. The most significant factors that were found to determine the appropriatness of ***ḥadj*** and ***ḥadjah*** terms are the addressee's age, the social context, and speakers' gender.

4.6 Zero terms

Zero terms refer to the avoidance of using any term of address. According to Afful (2007), this can be achieved by two strategies; viz. the use of attention getters such as ***excuse me***, or the use of greetings such as ***hi***, and ***hello***. Table (6) below shows the percentages of zero terms of address as they were found to be used in different social domains.

Table 6. The percentages of zero terms in different social domains

Gender	Family	Neighbors	University	Work	Strangers
Male	0%	20%	40%	10%	80%
Female	0%	30%	50%	20%	100%

According to Table (6), Jordanians use zero terms mainly to address a stranger and rarely use them with an acquaintance. Moreover, the results show that females address strangers with zero terms more than males do. The results also reveal that the participants tend to use less zero terms with elderly strangers who are usually addressed with kinship terms or religious terms ***ḥadj*** or ***ḥadjah***. Furthermore, both attention getters such as ***law samaḥt*** (excuse me!), ***9afuan*** (pardon me!), ***m9lish*** (forgive me!), ***momkin laḥẓah*** (can you give me a minute?!), and ***min ba9id ?iZnak*** (if you allow me!), and greeting terms such as ***marhaba*** (hi), ***assalam alykum***, ***sallam***, and ***sbah alkheir*** (good morning) were found to be used by Jordanians to attract the recipients' attention.

Finally, the data analysis shows that zero terms are widely used to address the government's employees, police officers, and employees in banks. However, workers and grocers are more addressed with the term ***m9alim***, or with some kinship terms. This may indicates that zero forms in such contexts are considered more polite and more prestigious than kinship terms and the term ***m9alim***.

However, the participants reported that zero terms might be considered inappropriate when addressing a friend, a colleague or a family member.

In sum, zero terms are wildly used as a polite strategy for addressing strangers. Furthermore, it appears that the social domain, familiarity, gender, and social status affect the use of zero terms.

5 Conclusion

This paper is an investigation of the address system in Jordanian Arabic. It focuses on six major classes of terms of address and examines their social usages and meanings in different contexts. In addition, the study highlights the factors governing the usage of each category of address terms.

The study reveals that the social meanings of Jordanian terms of address are context-dependent. For instance, Kinship terms have peculiar behavior. They are used to address relatives and non-relatives to support positive face. For example, the kinship terms ***9ammi*** and ***xali*** are not limited to their literal meaning of relatives since these terms can also be used to address neighbors and strangers. Furthermore, Tecnonyms are found to be greatly embedded in the Jordanian culture as polite terms of address since they are nearly used in all social domains. First names and titles, on the other hand, reflect symmetrical and asymmetrical relationships between individuals. Jordanians are found to display great tendency in the avoidance of addressing strangers through the use of zero terms (attention getters, and greetings) instead they tend to address them with kinship or religious terms. Besides, males and females sometimes reveal some differences in the way they use terms of address.

In addition, the findings of the study reveal that the use of a given Jordanian term of address in a particular context is governed by the interlocutors' age, social rank, power, and social distance. The social domain is also found to affect the use of these terms to a great extent. Finally, the researcher recommends further research to be conducted in order to examine other categories of address terms such as pronominal, verbal, occupational, and friendship categories and see if these terms are used to achieve additional meanings in different contexts.

Getters, and greetings instead they tend to address them with kinship or religious terms. Besides, males and females sometimes reveal some differences in the way they use terms of address.

In addition, the findings of the study reveal that the use of a given Jordanian term of address in a particular context is governed by the interlocutors' age, social rank, power, and social distance. The social domain is also found to affect the use of these terms to a great extent. Finally, the researcher recommends further research to be conducted in order to examine other categories of address terms such as pronominal, verbal, occupational, and friendship categories and see if these terms are used to achieve additional meanings in different contexts.

References

1. Yule, G. Pragmatics. Oxford University Press: New York, (1996).
2. Moghaddam, A. S., Yazdanpanah, L., and Abolhassanizadeh, V. The Analysis of Persian Address Terms Based on theTheory of Politeness. SKASE Journal of Theoretical Linguistics, 10(3), p55 (2013).
3. Keshavarz, M. The role of social context, intimacy and distance in the choice of forms of address. International of the Soceity of Language, 148, 5-18 (2001).
4. Braun, F. Terms of Address: Problems of Patterns and Usage in Various Languages and Cultures. Berlin: Mouto De Gruyter, (1998).
5. Taavitsainen, I. and Jucker A. Diachronic Perspectives on Address Term Systems. Pragmatics & Beyond New Series. Amsterdam: John Benjamins, (2002).
6. Brown, P., and Levinson, S. Politeness: Some language universals in language use. Cambridge: Cambridge University Press, (1987).
7. Dunkling, L. A Dictionary of Epithets and Terms of Address. New york: Routledge, (1990).
8. Afful, J. Address Terms among University Students in Ghana: The Case of Descriptive Phrases. The International journal of Language Society and Culture, 20, 50 (2007).
9. Ervin-Tripp, S. Sociolinguistic Rules of Address. In J.B. Pride, & Janet Holmes (Eds.), Sociolinguistics (p.225-240). London: Penguin Education, (1970).
10. Salihu H. The Sociolinguistics Study of Gender Address Patterns in the Hausa Society. International Journal of Social Science and Humanity, 4 (1), (2014).
11. Mazzon, G. Pronouns and Normal Address in Shakespearian English. In Irma Taavitsainen, Andreas H. Jucker (Eds.), Diachronic Perspectives on Address Term Systems (p. 223- 250). Philadelphia: John Benjamines B.V., (2002).

DOI: 10.1051/shsconf/20173701080

12. Esmae'li, S. Terms of Address Usage: the Case of Iranian Spouses. International Journal of Humanities and Social Science, 1 (9) 183-188 (2001).
13. Hwang, S. Terms of address: in korean and American culter's. International Communication studies 1(2).http://web.uri.edu/iaics/files/08-Shin-Ja-J.-Hwang.pdf
14. Brown, R. and Gilman, A. The Pronouns of Power and Solidarity. In Thomas A. Sebeok (Ed.), Style in Language (p.253-276). Massachusetts: MIT Press, (1966).
15. Parkinson, D. Constructing the Social Context of Communication: Terms of Adress in Egyption Arabic. Berlin: Mouto De Gruyter, (1985).
16. Dickey, E. Forms of address and terms of reference. J.Linguistics, 33, 255- 274 (1997).
17. Nevala, M. Inside and out. Forms of address in seventeenth- and eighteenth-century letters. Journal of historical pragmatics, 5(2): 271–296 (2004).

Professional and communicative foreign language competence of future teachers

Valentina Panfilova[1], Alexej Panfilov[1], Alfia Gazizova[3,1a] and Nataliya Samarina[4]

[1,2] Kazan Federal University, Russia, 423600, Elabuga, Kazanskaya St., 89
[3] Kazan Federal University, Russia, 423810, Naberezhnye Chelny, pr. Mira, 68/19
[4] Kalashnikov Izhevsk State Technical University, Russia, 427960, Sarapul, Krasnoarmeiskaya St., 93

Abstract. Studying of foreign-language competence at the present stage of higher pedagogical education development acquires the increasing relevance. In this paper the requirements of federal educational standards of pedagogical education and teacher' professional standard to forming students' foreign language competence mastering non-linguistic pedagogical specialties are specified. Analysis of understanding of professional and communicative foreign language competence by researchers has been performed; the author's structure of future pedagogues' foreign language competence is presented. The following sub-competences are distinguished as its structural components: linguistic, discursive, colloquial, pragmatic, information-technological, strategic, socio-cultural, personal-creative. The results of the foreign language competence level of the first and second year students of non-linguistic pedagogical specialties are shown. It is determined that the key structural elements of students' foreign language competence are within the advanced level of development. The strategic sub-competence is in a zone of optimal development level that makes actual creation of the psychological and pedagogical conditions for their development.
Keywords: Foreign language competence, structural elements of foreign language competence, subcompetence

1 Introduction

1.1. The problem of future teachers' foreign language competence

New requirements for the quality of school education, Federal state educational standards and teacher' professional standard suggest the need for changes in organization, content, technology, and the scale of teacher training in educational institutions.

[a] Corresponding author: Alfgazva@mail.ru

The current Federal state education standard of higher education according to the academic bachelor program 44.03.01 - Pedagogical education calls for the revision of approaches to foreign language training of future teachers. Practical language skills not only as a language of international communication, but also as a means of professional and personal development are becoming increasingly relevant. It is the universal competence of future teachers that should be mastered: "...able to communicate in oral and written forms in Russian and foreign languages for solving tasks of interpersonal and intercultural interaction" [3]. It actualizes the development of foreign language professional and communicative competence of future teachers, which in its turn generates the need to clarify working definitions, structure of the studied competence and establish its relationship with the readiness to use foreign language opportunities for self-education and professional activities. Teacher' professional standard is defined as "the use of foreign language sources of information, translation tools, pronunciation together with the students" [14].

1.2 View on foreign language professional communicative competence

The study of professional communicative foreign language competence (PCFLC) is becoming increasingly important at the present stage of higher pedagogical education. PCFLC has been the subject of research studies of M.K. Kabardov [6], A.V. Khutorskoy [7], I.A. Zimnyaya [18], N.A. Proshjanz [17], I.I. Galimzyanova [4], A.I. Kurpesheva [9], M.D. Ilyazova [5], A.S. Andrienko [1], E.B. Mikhaylova [11]. As for T.A. Kostyukova, A.L. Morozova, it is not enough to be limited to linguistic and sociolinguistic aspects of foreign language competence, without paying proper attention to the professional orientation of future specialists' language training [8]. According to E.G. Nikitina, professional-foreign language competence is considered as the unity of three components: motivational-value; cognitive-pragmatic and emotional [13]. In studies of E.I. Baguzina the following foreign language components are specified: linguistic, discursive, strategic, socio-cultural, pragmatic and personal ones [2].

So, the analysis of studies show that foreign language competence is considered as a complex, multicomponent phenomenon, and scientists focus on the professional orientation of foreign language competence of future specialists. Non-linguistic competence is defined by authors differently, as "knowledge, skills and abilities", "abilities", "integrative personal and professional phenomenon ".

1.3. Author's understanding of professional and communicative foreign language competence

Structurally-substantial models of foreign language competence, despite common structural components, also have differences. There is a significant variability in component composition of foreign language competence, which is associated with the complexity and multidimensionality of foreign-language communication process. There is a need to identify the author's model of PCFLC of future teachers [15, 16]. At the heart of the author's model are the thesis of the importance of its professional orientation and singling out its components as separate subcomponents.

We understand PCFLC as an integrative personal and professional phenomenon that determines the ability and willingness of the student to creatively solve practice-oriented information and communication tasks in professional activities as well as tasks of professionally oriented communication with native speakers in corresponding environment. We distinguish sub-competences as PCFLC structural components: linguistic (mastering vocabulary, grammar, phonetics, orthography): discursive (mastering logical organization of speech and written texts); colloquial (ability to speak coherently, without effort, at natural tempo, without long pauses for seeking the linguistic forms in receiving and transmitting professional information); pragmatic (ability to deliver the communication content according to the social context); information-technological (ability to search for professionally relevant information from different sources, efficiently use the foreign language Internet-resources in professional activity); strategic (ability to use the verbal and nonverbal professional communication strategies for compensation of the missing knowledge in real linguistic communication); socio-cultural (knowledge of the socio-cultural context where the language is used, ability to establish the foreign language professional communication adequately); personal-creative (ability to increase the level of the foreign language proficiency, ability to self-development in research and creative activity).

2 Purpose and methods

The study determined the initial level of future teachers' PCFLC. As a subject of study the structural parts, criteria, indicators, evaluation methods of PCFLC were identified. Fixation of monitoring and evaluation of students' speaking and writing skills were conducted with the help of authors' "Students' linguistic competence assessment map".

The level of each sub-competence development was estimated according to the 10-point scale: "8-10" - high level of motivation, knowledge, skills, abilities and abilities, "6-7" – the advanced level, "3-5" - the optimal level, "1-2" - the initial level. The final level of PCFLC development was defined as the arithmetic mean obtained during the expert evaluation of students' performance in various types of assignments. Each subcomponent consists of cognitive, operational-effective, emotional, motivational-value and reflective components.

Linguistic and communicative tests, and peer assessment of students' speaking skills were applied in study of cognitive component of students' foreign language competence. Studying operational-efficient PCFLC component the communicative tests were applied, as well as expert assessment of speech and writing activity that evaluated the structural elements such as linguistic, conversational, pragmatic, information technological, strategic, socio-cultural and personal-creative ones. The final data were recorded in the observation maps and estimated as the arithmetic mean of the grades obtained while studying the researched competences.

Observing motivational-value PCFLC component the adapted methodology by M.I. Lukyanova and N.V. Kalinina was used [10]. The investigation of the emotional and reflexive PCFLC components was based on self-regulation method and evaluation of the training-professional activity [12].

3 Results

The first and the second year students of non-linguistic pedagogical specialties (739 students, bachelor level program "Pedagogical education") took part in the study of initial level of PCFLC structural elements. At the first research stage the students that demonstrated high level of foreign language skills according to the results of practice tests were identified (120 students, that makes 16,2% of the total sample). In the second stage the results reflecting the intensity level of each sub-competence were obtained. The average values of the indicators in groups were determined (Figure 1).

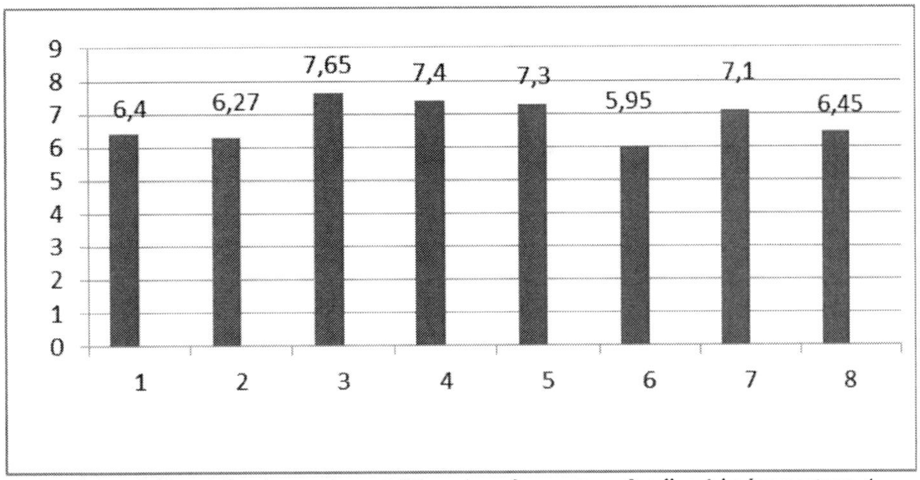

Conventional signs: 1. Linguistic subcompetence. 2. Discursive subcompetence.3. colloquial subcompetence. 4. Pragmatic subcompetence. 5. Information technological subcompetence. 6. Strategic subcompetence. 7. Sociocultural subcompetence. 8. Personal-creative subcompetence.

Figure 1. The initial level of future teachers' PCFLC

The analysis showed that most of the PCFLC structural elements fall within the area of the advanced development level – from 6,07 to 7,65 points. Higher level was identified in respect of the colloquial sub-competence representing the students' ability to speak coherently, without strain, at natural tempo, without long pauses for seeking the linguistic forms in exchanging professional information – 7,65 points; as well as the pragmatic sub-competence representing the student's ability to deliver the communication content according to the social context – 7,4 points. The strategic sub-competence representing the ability to use verbal and nonverbal communication strategies - 5,95 points. Thus, at the optimal level are the skills associated with the linguistic creativity of students, as the ability to show creativity when writing a report or a business letter (5.4 points); the ability to display the variability and uniqueness of speech solutions in oral speech and in written texts (5.8 points).

While analyzing the obtained data, the initial level of PCFLC components (cognitive, operational-effective, emotional-volitional, motivational-value and reflective components) as the arithmetic mean of indicators in studied group of students was defined (Figure 2).

4 Discussion

Analysis of future teachers' PCFLC components allows to conclude that the cognitive component reflecting professional and linguistic knowledge is at the advanced level of development (72,3 points), as well as the operational effective component, reflecting the ability to implement professional language communication (68,7 points), motivational and value component, reflecting educational and professional motives and values is 63,8 points. The highest level on cognitive component development was identified, that shows the dominance of "knowledge" model in foreign language learning. The PCFLC reflective component, representing the capacity to introspect, the ability to determine own educational route (set goals, bear responsibility for the final result of mastering foreign language) showed the optimal level (57,8 points).

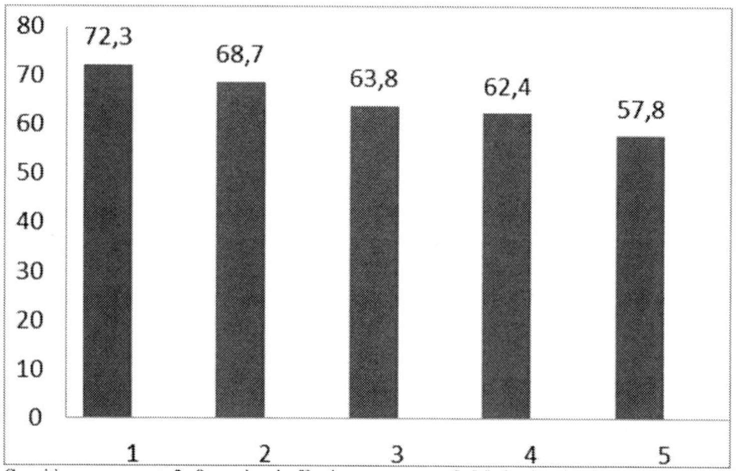

Conventional signs: 1. Cognitive component. 2. Operational-effective component. 3. Motivational value component. 4. Emotional component. 5. The reflective component.

Figure 2. The initial level of future teachers' PCFLC components

In group of students with the high level of foreign language proficiency according to the expert evaluation of oral and written activity the high level of linguistic and communicative skills were identified. However, only 60,3% of the first year students and 62,9% of the second year students demonstrated the high level of the linguistic creativity. 95.5% of students with a high level of language proficiency demonstrated dominance motivation to language learning, 93.3% – to mastery of profession.

5 Conclusion

Thus, the study identified the structural elements (linguistic, discursive, conversational, pragmatic, information technological, socio-cultural and personal-creative subcompetence) and components (cognitive, operational effective, motivational and value component, reflective) of future teachers' PCFLC. The initial level of such structural elements as linguistic, discursive, conversational, pragmatic, information technological, socio-cultural and personal-creative subcompetence is on advanced level according to the investigated group of students. Strategic subcompetence that reflects the ability to use verbal and non-verbal communicative strategies in light of linguistic communication, as well as the skills associated with the linguistic creativity is in optimal development level that causes the necessity of creating special psychological and pedagogical conditions for their development.

6 Summary

The practice of forming future teachers' PCFLC is largely determined by learning activities, forms and methods of engaging students to professional foreign language activities. The contents, forms and methods of work should provide optimal educational space for active, free and creative students' self-development providing variance and openness of the educational process. This view corresponds to the requirements of current state educational standard of teacher training. For students of non-language pedagogical specialties, the subject "Foreign language" is not profiling.

Teachers should clearly understand the role and place of foreign language in their life and future professional work, so the process of professional and communicative competence development will be effective and purposeful. The subject "Foreign language", being outside the sphere of direct relevant interests, acts as a tool of studying another subject area that causes a need for clarifying its content at the pedagogical university.

It is necessary to remove the discrepancy between: the increasing importance of students' practical foreign language in light of international educational space integration, the requirements of teacher professional standard and the "knowledge technology" of professionally communicative competence development. While learning the students to a greater extent master those competence components that are associated with the mastery of knowledge, the ability to operate them in foreign-professional communication, the ability to self-regulate educational and professional activities. The subject "Foreign Language" has the potential to develop professional and personal qualities of future specialists (communication, reflexivity, tolerance, ability to overcome a psychological barrier in communication, etc.) and their unsatisfactory in professional training. So, PCFLC reflective component as the ability to plan and monitor the intermediate and final results, the adequacy of self-assessment and assessing success of educational activities on subjective criteria, the autonomy performing tasks definitely needs further development.

References

1. Andriyenko, A.S. Development of the foreign language professional communication competence in students of a technical college (on the basis of the credit modular system of education): abstract of the Thesis of Candidate of Pedagogical Sciences: 13.00.08/ Andriyenko Anzhela Sergeyevna. – Rostov-on-Don, (2006).
2. Baguzina, E.I. Web-quest technology as the didactic method of formation of the foreign language communication competence: by the example of the students of a non-linguistic university, PhD thesis, Moscow State University, Moscow, (2012).
3. Federal state education standard of higher education according to the degree program 44.03.01 Pedagogical education (qualification (degree) "bachelor") (approved by the order of the Ministry of Education and Science of the Russian Federation d/d December 04, 2015 N 1426); URL:http://fgosvo.ru/uploadfiles/fgosvob/440301.pdf (access date 22.12.2016)
4. Galimzyanova, I.I. Pedagogical system of formation of the foreign language competence of future engineers: abstract of the Thesis of Doctor of Pedagogical Sciences: 13.00.08. – Kazan, (2009).
5. Ilyazova, M.D. Formation of invariants of the professional competence of students - sociologists: situational-context approach: methodological guidelines for teachers. Astrakhan, P.48, (2009).
6. Kabardov, M.K. Concerning diagnostics of the foreign language capabilities. Psychological and psychophysiological speech studies. Moscow, Nauka, PP. 176-202, (1985).
7. Khutorskoy, A. V. The key competences and education standards [Digital resource] / A. V. Khutorskoy; Center of distance education 'Eidos', Internet-magazine 'Eidos'. – (2002). Access mode: http:// www.eidos.ru/journal/ 2002/0423.htm.
8. Kostyukova, T.A. and Morozova, A.L. Development of the foreign language communication competence in students of non-linguistic colleges. Tomsk: Publishing House of the Tomsk Polytechnic University, P. 119, (2011).
9. Kurpesheva, A.I. Invariants of the foreign language communication competence in students of a technical college. Journal of AGTU. #1: 87-90, (2011).
10. Lukyanova, M.I. and Kalinina, N.V. Psychological-pedagogical indicators of the school activity: criteria and diagnostics. Moscow SC Sphere. P. 208, (2004).
11. Mikhaylova, E.B. Formation of the professional foreign language competence in students of the engineering specialties with the use of the information and

communication technologies: abstract of the Thesis of Candidate of Pedagogical Sciences: 13.00.08. Nizhny Novgorod, (2012).
12. Morosanova, V.I. Individual self-regulation style in the random human activity. Psychological journal. # 4: PP. 26-35, (1995).
13. Nikitina, E.G. Development of the foreign language competence of the university students by means of the modular education: by the example of the economic specialties: Thesis of the Candidate of Pedagogical Sciences: 13.00.08. Cheboksary, P. 292. Journal of Language and Literature, (2010). ISSN: 2078-0303, Vol. 6. No. 3. Iss.1, August, 2015 | 41
14. Order of the Ministry of Labor and Social Security of the Russian Federation №544n d/d October 18, 2013. 'Concerning approval of the professional standard "Pedagogue" (pedagogical activity in the sphere of the preschool, primary and secondary education) (kindergartener, teacher) http://www.rosmintrud.ru/docs/mintrud/ orders/129
15. Panfilov, A.N., V.M. Panfilova. Linguistic aptitude of students as the foundation for creation of the foreign language educational space. Nauka i mir, #3(7) (Volume 3): 87-90, (2014).
16. Panfilova V.M., Panfilov A.N., Merzon E.E. Organizational-Pedagogical Conditions to Form the Foreign Competence in Students with the Features of Linguistic Giftedness. International Education Studies, Vol. 8, #. 2: 176 - 185; (2015). ISSN 1913-9020 E-ISSN 1913-9039. doi:10.5539/ies.v8n2p176 URL: http://dx.doi.org/10.5539/ ies.v8n2p176 (access date 1.04.2015)
17. Proshyants, N.A. Formation of the foreign language linguistic competences within the professional discourse / N.A. Proshyants // Research work. - # 3 - PP. 34-38, (2010).
18. Zimnyaya, I.A. Competency-based approach. What is its place in the system of modern approaches to the issues of education? (Theoretical-methodological aspect). Higher education today, #8: 20-26, (2006).

Integration of health service with electronic nursery care process

Yeliz Doğan Merih [a], and Kerime Derya Beydağ [2]

[1] PhD, Dr. Zeynep Kamil Women and Child Research and Training Hospital, Istanbul/ Turkey
[2] Faculty of Health Science, Department of Nursing, Okan University, Turkey

Abstract. You This study aims to provide to integrate the health service with electronic nursery care process and so do create lingua franca. This research has been done between April 2010 and January 2012 in a teaching and research hospital where is specialized on obstetrician and gynecology. 280 nurse are the sample of the study. The datas are collected by using a survey with 22 questions. After the observations and evaluations, in case of standards 40 nursery care process about most experienced problems in gynecology, obstetrician and pediatry clinics is formed and its infrastructure for integrating these flow diagrams to the data processing system is prepared. For working the new system, instructive sessions is done. After the applications, the using of process approach in nursery care service and the pleasure of the nurses are analysed. The datas are analysed by using percentage calculation, t-test and variant analysis test in case of SPSS programme. In this study, 3 different application for the usage of process approach is used. These applications are done in different 15 bedded clinics and in different times. In the first application, empty forms which have standard format, are given to the nurses to complete.In the second application, the forms which special nursery activity has been wrritten on, are given to the nurses to sign their own activity and in the third application, the standard process approach which has been integrated to electronic system and which is special to patient, is requested to use. After all aplications, according to analysation of the results, the usage of the process' method rates are; 10% is for first method, 40% is for second method and 90% is for third method. Especially, the nursery process approach which has been integrated to electronic system is used more desirous. According to the nurses' opinion, this system increases the creation of lingua franca, data security and effective time management. It is determined that their pleasure is much more than the other methods and their belief to this system increases ($p<0.01$)

Keywords: Electronic Process, nursery, service

[a] Corresponding author: derya.beydag@okan.edu.tr

1 Introduction

The provision of health care has changed dramatically in recent years. Changing and evolving health care system affects the basic health needs of people and so the health care approach. All health professionals who are involved and take charge in this care approach must move with the changes and be open for improvement.1

The birth of nursing that is one of the oldest health professions goes back ancient times. The nursing history has started with the therapeutic (healing) role of women. Today, the goal of health care is to provide quality care. The nurses must give effective care to their patients with constantly updated information. In general, the purpose of nursing is to support, maintain the health of person or improve the level of health [1-4].

Today, the nursing profession has become a medical discipline that its theories and practices are based on the scientific basis by showing great improvements. The modern nursing adopts a systematic approach to organize and provide nursing care in all care environments of person with undertaken contemporary roles, by providing the best nursing care. This approach is the nursing process [3-4].

The nursing process that provides a professional identity to nursing profession is a systematic, scientific problem solving method that is used in determining the health care requirements of healthy / sick person and in individualized care [5]. The World Health Organization (WHO) defines the nursing process as a systematic approach of scientific problem solving method in nursing care [6].Various classification systems are using for nursing process that forms the basis of the scientific process. Some of those are North American Nursing Diagnosis Association (NANDA), Nursing Interventions Classification (NIC) and Nursing Results Classification (NOC) [7]. Nursing process includes these five stages; data collection, nursing diagnosing, determining the outcome criteria, planning / implementation and evaluation [8].

Nursing process is a systematic method that is used in determining care needs of sick or healthy person and in individualized care and it depends on interpersonal interaction. Because, this process is required to one-to-one, direct and constant interaction and communication with patient to meet the patient's needs. Nursing process is planned and goal-oriented. Between nurses and patients, in a planful manner, it is a creative tool to solve the patient's identified health problems. Nursing process focuses on feedback that provides to reveal the problem again and to revise the care plan again [9-11].

The duties and responsibilities of nurses are given relying on the nursing process in Article 4 of the Law No. 5634 which is related to making amendments on Nursing Act (No. 6283). According to Law No. 5634, nurses must ground their applications to nursing process. However, in the studies conducted on both nurses and students, it was determined that nurses did not use the nursing process at desired level [12].

Nursing diagnosis determined by the students on neurological patients, it was determined that students were insufficient in the selection of initiatives towards determined nursing diagnosis [13].

Literature and conducted studies indicate that the nursing process is not used enough in application. It was observed that the nursing process is used in some health facilities, but some difficulties were experienced when applying. To use the nursing process effectively in the service area; to properly teach the nursing process to students during basic nursing education, to provide training for using the process in service training for use nurse in the field, to activate application facilitating systems in order that nurses who work in institutions use the process approach in their service are important [4].

To organize the standards for nursing practices and becoming effective of process approaches provide the service to acquire a meeting the requirements, effective, suitable for time management, observing patient-employee satisfaction, has certain limits, provide access to objective and measurable property. In our study it is aimed to active use of processes and create a common language in service delivery by ensuring the integration of electronic nursing process approach to services.

2 Method

This descriptive study was conducted as a quasi-experimental study between 25 April 2010- January 2012, in a maternity and children's hospital on the Anatolian Side of Istanbul.

2.1 Participants

The research sample: The research sample has created by 280 nurses who actively work in working time in maternity and child clinics of the related hospital and agreed to participate in the study.

2.2. Procedure

The data were collected by 22 question survey that was formed by researchers to measure socio-demographic, occupational characteristics, views towards using of the nursing process (the first 10 questions) and the satisfaction about used maintenance process methods before and after application (12 question, 4 likert) of participants by researchers. The data of research were obtained by filling the surveys by talking face to face with nurses. Nurses had totally 20 minutes to fill the survey.

In research process in order to activate the process approach in the hospital nursing service before all nurses provided training for nursing process, scope, implementation steps, benefits and successful examples. After awareness training nurses were provided to use three methods at different times in process applications. The consulting and control approaches were activated by about subject experienced researchers on work in all applied processes.

Three different process application methods were applied at different times in our hospital's 15 inmate service.

• In the first method; the patient-based, manually using of forms was requested by giving in a standard format empty process forms to nurses. The first method has been provided to be used in all clinics of the hospital, evaluation surveys were applied to nurses before and after the usage to make them evaluate the application.

• In the second method; standard full forms in which diagnoses-specific nursery activities are written were provided to participants, and nurses were asked to mark the activities they did on patient basis. After the first method was ended, the second method was provided to be utilized in all clinics of the hospital for 3 months, evaluation surveys were applied to participating nurses before and after the usage to make them evaluate the application.

• In the third application; the third application process was activated after the first two application has ended.

The steps of third application are as follows.

- Following the evaluations, 40 nursery care process (data collection, diagnose, planning, application, evaluation) in total were created at first within the scope of standards for most common problems of nurses they encounter in gynecology and pediatric clinics.

- Researchers and IT employees started a joint working programme, together they creted the software steps of electronic nursery process.
- The created 40 nursery process were integrated into the configured electronic software process on step basis.
- Information meetings were held for the created system and operatability was provided.
- The integrated electronic care process was applied as pilot in a gynecology and pediatric service, healing processes were initiated after the application.
- The finalized electronic nursery process was integrated into service and started to be applied in all clinics for a period of 3 months.
- After the application, the usage of process approach in nursery services and satisfaction of the nurses were evaluated.

For the research, the required permissions were granted from the hospital's ethics committee and hospital administration. The participants were informed in writing that their identities would be kept hidden and the information would be used only for this research, consent was taken. In evaluation of the research; percentage calculation, t test and variance analysis tests were used within SPSS programme.

3 Findings

It was identified that 43.2% of the participants were in 20-25 age group, 81.8% of them had bachelor and master's degree and 36% of them had 2-5 years of professional experience (Table 1).

Table 1. Distribution of Participants According to Their Demographic and Professional Characteristics (n=280)

Characteristics		**Number**	**%**
Age groups	20-25	121	43.2
	26-31	81	29.0
	32-37	45	16.0
	38-43	19	7.0
	+44	14	5.0
Educational Status	High School	6	2.1
	Associate Degree	45	16.1
	Bachelor's Degree	192	68,6
	Master's Degree and Above	37	13.2
Professional Experience	0-1 year	39	14.0
	2-5 years	101	36.0
	6-10 years	59	21.0
	+ 10 years	81	29.0
Total		**280**	**100.0**

In order to determine the opinions of participants on the process issue before the application, it was identified that 68% of them had education on nursery process before, that 64% of them did not find themselves sufficient, and that 79% of the participants stated the electronic process approach in the first place in reply to question of which method they would prefer to apply the nursery process if they were to apply the process (Figure 1).

DOI: 10.1051/shsconf/20173701082

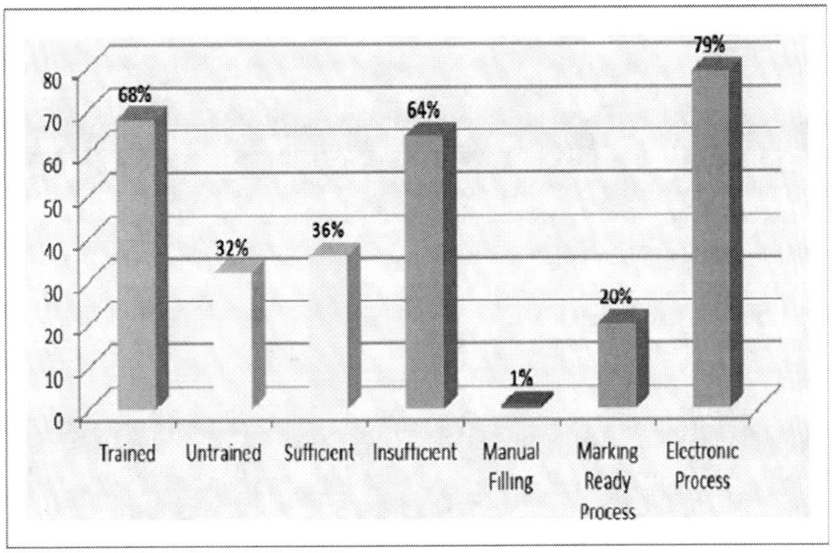

Figure 1: Opinions of Participants for Nursery Processes (n=280)

In result of the evaluation made after all the applications, it was determined that the using rates of process methods for participants were 10% in the first application whereas 40% in the second application and 90% in the third one. When test results before and after the application for the three methods were compared, it was determined that there was a significant increase only in electronic nursery application (p<0.01), and that satisfaction for nursery process application was at high level (Table 2).

Table 2. Evaluations of Participants for Process Applications Before and After The Application (n=280)

Form For Evaluating The Effectiveness of Process Applications		**Average**	**n**	**Std deviation**	**Std Error**	**Statistical Test (p)***
Manual Application	**Pre-test**	3,4899	280	0,46916	0,03979	t: 1,465
	Post-test	3,5065	280	0,19568	0,01660	p:0,243
Ready Process Forms	**Pre-test**	3,5125	280	0,54149	0,04593	t: 1,194
	Post-test	3,7094	280	0,24538	0,02081	P: 0,161
Electronic Nursery Process	**Pre-test**	3,5387	280	0,55397	0,04699	t: 9,211
	Post-test	3,9964	280	0,23634	0,02005	p: 0,000

(Paired Samples t-test= 0.000 p<0.01)

4 Discussion

In hospitals, which serve on a very critical and an important topic as human health, our entire information should be accurate and the process in our health related procedures should run accurately. Within this process, integration of service records of health team members into hospital information management system (HIMS) is quite important. Today, using of IT in service processes of nurses are not at desired level.

In order to exist in the changing and developing world order, nursery should keep all its channels open, get stronger by ongoing professional trainings, adapt the change by integrating its knowledge into HIMS. Here in this process, informatics and the records providing the professional visibility have great importance [4,14,15]. In our study, based upon the importance and necessity of process systems, it was aimed to provide the integration of electronic nursery care process approach into the service and use the processes actively and create common language in service presentation.

It was determined that 43.2% of participants were in 20-25 age group, 81.8% of them had undergraduate and higher education and 36% of them had 2-5 years of professional experience. It was determined that the majority of nurses participated in our study consisted of young group of nurses who had undergraduate study. When characteristics of participants were considered, it was set forth that it was a group having effective knowledge in nursery process topic. However, it was identified that the participants did not have awareness on nursery process topic as much as they were expected to. This circumstance brought us to the finding that the education of nurses on nursery process topic might be insufficient.

As the nursery students graduate by experiencing problems related to nursery process, their use of nursery process when they become nurses are also negatively affected. In a study conducted by Lea et al, it was identified that the information of students on nursery process was not at the level desired by the school [16]. Although students state that they find nursery process useful and apply it, this result shows that students have deficiencies and these have to be completed.

In the survey carried out in our study with intent to determine the opinions of participants on the process before application, it was identified that 68% of them had previous education on nursery process, that 64% did not find themselves adequate and that they stated electronic process approach in the first place with a rate of 79% in reply to question with which method they would apply the nursery process if they were to apply it (Figure 1).

The nursery process, which brings a scientific identity to nursery applications, has a lot of benefits for nurses and student nurses. One of such benefits is providing individual centered nursery care [17]. The other one provides that the nurse gives care in line with a plan and thus uses her time more effectively. Furthermore, it develops the communication between team members, creates written sources and proofs for nursery education and researches and thus makes nursery services visible [18-19].

The nursery process, which is a model that brings solution to nursery problems, is taught as an important element of nursery education. However, although the nursery process - the application of scientific method to nursery care - is taught to students in scope of nursery education, students still have difficulties in preparing care plan. Furthermore, he states in a more challenging aspect that it is remarkable as the students can not bring care plan even to application stage [20]. And this reveals that the education in such schools fail to accomplish this purpose. The students, who are graduated without learning to work with nursery process and understanding the importance of working with the process, do not use nursery process also when they are graduated or resist to use it [21-22]. In our study, the statements of nurses that they did not have sufficient education on process topic and find themselves inadequate about the process supports the study results.

As the result of evaluation made after all the applications in our research, the rates for participants' process method use was determined as 10% in manual process application whereas 40% in application of standard forms and 90% in electronic process application. When test results before and after the application for the three method are compared, it was determined that there was significant difference only in electronic nursery process application (p<0.01), and that there were much satisfaction from electronic nursery process application.

With the writing of nursery process, care plan is created. While writing the care plan, an applicable one should be prepared and this care plan should be up-to-date, effectual, right and compliant to environment. An ideal registration plan should have the features such as easy readability, easy to be filed, fast registration, applicability to computer, being in accordance with the institution's standards, easy to access information, allow to register the patient's needs from physical, psychological and sociocultural aspects, fit the purpose of health professional. The advantage of using standard care plans is that no new care plan is created for each patient and thus it saves time [23, 24].

In the study conducted by Yıldırım, it was revealed that the nurses had no sufficient information regarding nursery process, that nursery process was not handled as a whole but as individual function parts and not reflected to the application [25]. However, due to a large variety of reasons, nurses do not use nursery process in clinics. According to Yılmaz, the reasons why nurses do not use the process can be listed as follows; they do not want to use the nursery process, there are a great number of patients in the service that the nurses are responsible to care for, increase in workload; active clinics do not lean towards nursery process applications, think that it does not contribute to patient care, do not know how to apply it [26].

In our study, it was determined that electronically integrated nursery process approach was used more willingly by nurses among the process methods due to being standard and providing ease of use. It was determined that nurses stated as electronic process increased creating common language, registration security and effective time management, that their satisfaction from the system was more than the other methods and their commitment to the system increased, and that our findings were consonant with literature information and study results.

5 Conclusion and Suggestions

Using of care processes in nursery is important in terms of making effective decision, presenting integrated approach, providing effective team work, preventing medical faults and providing effective time management.

- In our study, it was determined that the participants had medium knowledge level regarding process approach, that they felt themselves insufficient regarding the application of nursery process and leant more towards electronic nursery process if they had to apply it.
- It was determined that the extensive nursery process training, which was provided for nurses before the three different processes in our hospital, was important for increasing the awareness of nurses and that the nurses behaved more willingly in process applications after the training.
- As the result of evaluation made after all the applications in our research, the rates for participants' process method use were determined as 10% in manual process application whereas 40% in application of standard forms and 90% in electronic process application.
- As the test results before and after the application for the three methods are compared, it is determined that there is significant increase only in nursery process application (p<0.01) and satisfaction from electronic nursery process is at high level.

In parallel to study results, the following suggestions are made:

- •To increase the time allocated for nursery process in nursery curriculum programmes and nursery in-service trainings in the field.
- •To provide references (book, magazine) which the students and nurses might benefit regarding the process.
- •By making cooperation between school and hospital, encouraging the students and nurses in the field for patient-oriented work.
- •To develop practical registration systems in health institutions for the use of all nurses; which are standard, provides ease of use and includes all steps of the process.
- •To create management supported electronic nursery registration systems in hospitals and provide continuous healing.

Acknowledgment

Regarding the research and/or authorship of this article, the authors didn't receive any financial

References

1. Esatoğlu AE, Ersoy K. Hasta Tatmininin Ölçülmesi. İçinde: Çoruh M, Editör. Sağlık Hizmetlerinde Toplam Kalite Yönetimi Ve Performans Ölçümü. Haberal Eğitim Vakfı; 61-71., (1997).
2. Kocaman G., Türkiye'de Hemşirelik Eğitim Sorunları. 12 Mayıs 2003 Dünya Hemşireler Günü. Özel Baskı: 71-91.,(2003).
3. 14. Sabuncu N., Editör. Hemşirelik Bakımında İlke Ve Uygulamalar. Ankara: Alter Yayıncılık Org. Tic. Ltd. Şti.; (2008).
4. Keski Ç., Karadağ A., Son Sınıf Hemşirelik Öğrencilerinin Hemşirelik Süreci Hakkında Bilgi Düzeylerinin İncelenmesi, Gazi Üniversitesi Sağlık Bilimleri Enstitüsü Hemşirelik Programı Yüksek Lisans Tezi, Ankara, (2009).
5. Birol L., Hemşirelikle İlgili Kuramlar, Hemşirelik Süreci (Editör: Leman Birol), Etki Matb. Yayıncılık Ltd. Şti, İzmir,51-102., (2005).
6. Velioğlu P., Hemşirelikte Kavram Ve Kuramlar, Alaş Ofset, İstanbul., (1999)
7. Carpenito L., Hemşirelik Tanıları El Kitabı (Çeviri: Firdevs Erdemir), Nobel Kitabevi, Ankara., (2004).
8. Corder J., Nursing Process As A Therapetic Frameworks. In: Delaune S C, Ladner P K (Eds) Fundamentals Of Nursing Standards & Practice, Delmar Publishers, Albany, Newyork, 297-306., (1998).
9. Sabuncu N., Editör. Hemşirelik Bakımında İlke Ve Uygulamalar. Ankara: Alter Yayıncılık Org. Tic. Ltd. Şti. (2008).
10. Bayat M., Öğretim Süreci Ve Hemşirelik. Sağlık Bilimleri Dergisi. (Ek Sayı: Hemşirelik Özel Sayısı)14: 66-72., (2005).
11. Sorrentino AS. Mosby's Textbook for Nursing Assistants. 6th Ed. Missouri: Mosby Company, (2004).
12. Sağlık Bakanlığı. Hemşirelik Kanununda Değişiklik Yapılmasına Dair Kanun. Kanun Numarası: 5634. Kabul Tarihi: 25.4.2007. Yayımlandığı Resmi Gazete: Tarih: 2.5.2007 Sayı: 26510.
13. Karadakovan A., Usta Yeşilbalkan Ö., Öğrencilerin Nörolojik Hastalarda Saptadıkları Nanda Hemşirelik Tanılarının İncelenmesi. Atatürk Üniversitesi Hemşirelik Yüksekokulu Dergisi, 7(3), 1-7., (2004).
14. Birol L. Hemşirelik Süreci. 8. Baskı. İzmir: Etki Matbaacılık; (2007).

15. Bayat M. Öğretim Süreci Ve Hemşirelik. Sağlık Bilimleri Dergisi. (Ek Sayı: Hemşirelik Özel Sayısı)14: 66-72., (2005).
16. Lea SF, Anema MG, Briscoe VJ, Allie H., The Nursing Process: What Do Students Know? The ABNF Journal, 12,1: 3-8., (2001).
17. Sorrentino As., Mosby's Textbook For Nursing Assistants, 6th Ed, Mosby Company, (2004).
18. Potter AP., The Nursing Process And Critical Thinking In Potter Ap, Perry Ag (Eds) Fundamentals Of Nursing Concepts, Process And Practice, 4th Ed, Mosby Company, St.Louis, (1997).
19. Boroski B., The Medical Surgical Nurse. In Burke Km, Lemone P, Mohn-Brown El (Eds), Medical- Surgical Nursing Care, Pearson Education Inc. (2003).
20. Uyer G., Türkiye'de Hemşirelik Yönetiminde Değişen Ve Gelişen Yaklaşımlar, III. Ulusal Hemşirelik Kongresi Kitabı, Esnaf Ofset Matbaacılık, Sivas, 133-136., (1992).
21. Güner P, Terakye G., Hemşirelik Yüksekokulları Son Sınıf Öğrencilerinin Hemşirelik Tanılarını Belirleyebilme Düzeyleri, Cumhuriyet Üniversitesi Hemşirelik Yüksekokulu Dergisi, 4(1), 9-15.,(2000).
22. Taşdemir, G., Kızılkaya, M. Sağlık Yüksekokulu Son Sınıf Öğrencilerin Ruh Sağlığı Ve Hastalıkları Hemşireliği Dersi Klinik Uygulamasında NANDA Hemşirelik Tanılarının İncelenmesi. International Journal of Human Sciences. (10)1, 246-257., (2013).
23. Lipe S., Beasley S. Critical Thinking İn Nursing A Cognitive Skills Workbook. Lıppıncott Wıllıams & Wılkıns United States Of America, 87–120., (2004).
24. Yıldırım B. Hemşirelikte Eleştirel Düşünme Uygulamalı Yaklaşım. Ed: Süheyla Altuğ Özsoy, Tuna Matbaacılık, Aydın., (2010).
25. Yıldırım A. Yataklı Tedavi Kurumlarında Çalışan Hemşirelerin Hizmetlerinde Yer Alması Gereken Hemşirelik İşlevleri Hakkında Bilgi Düzeylerinin Araştırılması. Yüksek Lisans. İstanbul: İstanbul Üniversitesi; (1988).
26. Yılmaz N. Hemşirelerin Hemşirelik Sürecine İlişkin Bilgi Ve Görüşlerinin İncelenmesi. Yüksek Lisans. İstanbul: Ege Üniversitesi; (2000).

The effects of women's satisfaction with their birth experience on breastfeeding sufficiency

Nilay Gökbulut [1a], and Kerime Derya Beydağ [2]

[1]Msc. Midwife, Malatya Doğanşehir State Hospital, Malatya/Turkey
[2]Faculty of Health Science, Department of Nursing, Okan University, Turkey

Abstract. Postpartum is the period when the family cares and creates a safe environment for the baby, communicates with the baby, adopts new roles, develops family awareness and copes with the problems of the baby. This study has been performed to define how the mothers assessed their birth experience and as a descriptive with intent to reveal the effects of this experience on the postnatal breastfeeding period. The sample of study was composed of 281 mothers who were in the postnatal clinic of İstanbul Okmeydanı Research and Training Hospital and agreed to participate the study between January-May 2015, literate and able to talk and understand Turkish, and also gave birth vaginally or by cesarean section. The survey form included the descriptive features of women and "The Scale Of Satisfaction" and The Scale of Breastfeeding Sufficiency" have been used for gathering data. SPSS 22.0 program was used to analyze the data. As a consequence, the mothers' satisfaction with their birth experience scale has been varied according to the delivery methods and the elapsed time after birth experience. Relatedly when the satisfaction level of them was varied, the breastfeeding sufficiency of them was also varied, too.

Keywords: Birth experience, Breastfeeding Suffiency, Satisfaction.

1 Introduction

Family is an indispensable, traditional and social institution of the society. In order to provide the continuance of humanity, raise conventionalized individuals, pass down from generation to generation; the family has a universal mission and responsibility. With fertility function, this universal mission is accomplished [1].

Postpartum is the period when the family cares and creates a safe environment for the baby, communicates with the baby, adopts new roles, develops family awareness and copes with the problems of the baby. This period may be either experienced as a very positive and satisfying period for the family that strengths the family bonds, or as a crisis period [2].

[a] Corresponding author: derya.beydag@okan.edu.tr

In social lives of couples, changes appear when they have children. If mother is working, she may have to keep her business life in the background for a time. The time she spends at home will also increase. Consequently, limitations that occur in social and business life may lead the mother to get stressed. Besides, it is possible for many fathers to get stressed since the interest and love of their spouses completely turn towards the baby. The old order in previous bilateral relationship of spouses may go bad, expectations of spouses from each other may change, an increase in their duties and responsibilities may be observed [3].

In our country, mothers are often discharged from the hospital 24 hours after they give birth. In order to prevent some complications which may be urgent during the first 24 hours, this period may be considered sufficient. However, this period may not be sufficient to support the mother to adapt herself for the new situation during postpartum period. In the first day after the birth, the care to be given from healthcare professionals as well as the family, particularly from delivery nurses/nurses, is very important for the mother to adapt herself for the postpartum period, who is intensively in contact with healthcare staff [4].

In order to allow the neonate to grow and develop healthy, he/she should have adequate and balanced nourishment during infancy. The properties which make breast milk the most suitable nutrient are that it changes according to neonate's requirements, has preventive property against infections, can meet the baby's physiological and psychosocial requirements by itself during the first 4-6 months, and is economic. During the first 4-6 months, it is recommended not to give even water in addition to breast milk and after 4-6 months, that breast milk should be continued with additional nutrition support until the baby is one year old [5].

Hospitals are suitable environments to provide training for the mother during prenatal and early postnatal periods. Following that; delivery nurses, nurses and physicians who were in charge during the first step have the most important part. They should be aware of the factors which may cause to leave breastfeeding in early period, and perform the required applications both during prenatal and postnatal periods to prevent those. Delivery nurses/nurses should give right and satisfactory information to mothers about self-care requirements and baby caring, and make sure that they understood those issues [6].

With this study, it was both intended to review from where birth experiences of mothers and breastfeeding self-sufficiencies are affected, and whether there is a relationship or not between birth experience and breastfeeding self-sufficiency.

2 Method

This study was conducted as descriptive in order to determine the effect of women's' satisfaction from birth to breastfeeding self-sufficiency, identify the factors which affect the satisfaction from birth experience and breastfeeding self-sufficiency

2.1 Participants

Population of the study consisted of puerperants who were registered in T.R. Ministry of Health Istanbul Okmeydanı Training and Research Hospital in 2014 (N=3043). Sample of the study consisted of 281 women who were identified by sampling formula with a known population, by considering the number of puerperants in 2014 in the abovementioned hospital.

DOI: 10.1051/shsconf/20173701083

2.2. Procedure

With regard to compatibility of the study with ethical principles, permission was taken from Aluş Tokat who created the Postpartum Breastfeeding Self-Sufficiency Scale and from Taşçı who created the scale of Satisfaction from Birth Experience. Before collecting data, ethics committee approval was obtained by applying to Ethics Committee of T.R. Okan University, then permission was taken from Beyoğlu Association of Public Hospitals which T.R. Ministry of Health Istanbul Okmeydanı Training and Research Hospital is a member of. All participants were informed about the aim of the study, eagerness and willingness to participation was cared and written consents were taken from all mothers participating the study.

Data were obtained from questionnaire form which includes the defining characteristics, and from "Satisfaction of Women from Birth Experience Scale" and "Breastfeeding Self-sufficiency Scale". The questionnaire form that includes the defining characteristics of women consisted of 10 questions. Satisfaction of Women from Birth Experience is a scale which has in 4 point likert type with 10 questions [2]. The lowest point to be obtained in the test shall be calculated as 10 and the highest as 40. As the points increase, level of satisfaction is interpreted as low. Breastfeeding Self-sufficiency is a 14 question scale. The lowest point to be obtained in the test is 14, while the highest is 70. If the points are high, it is interpreted as the breastfeeding self-sufficiency is high as well. The scale is 5 point Likert type and evaluated as 1=not sure at all 5=always sure.

In analyses of data SPSS 22.0 programme was used. In defining statistics; average, standard deviation, median, lowest and highest frequency and rate values were used. Distribution of variables was measured by Kolmogorov Simirnov test. In analysis of quantitative data, Kruskal-wallis, mann-whitney u test were used. In correlation analysis, spearman correlation analysis was used.

3 Findings

In Table 1, SFBES and PBSSS average points of mothers were calculated and presented. In our study, the average point was calculated as 21,5±5,2 in SFBES we applied to mothers. In our study, the average point was calculated as 54,7±11,9 in PBSSS we applied to mothers.

Table 1: Comparison of point averages between birth satisfaction of mothers scale and postpartum breastfeeding self-sufficiency scale (n=281)

	Min-Max		Median	Av.	±	s.s.
Satisfaction From Birth Experience Scale	10	38	21,0	21,5		5,2
Postpartum Breastfeeding Self-Sufficiency Scale	14	70	57,0	54,7		1,9

It was identified that there was a very weak and negative statistically significant relationship ($p<0,05$) between the SFBES point average and PBSSS averages of mothers (rs= -0,320) This result demonstrates that there is a negative relationship between satisfaction from birth experience and postpartum breastfeeding self-sufficiency (Table 2).

Table 2: Correlation coefficients of satisfaction from birth experience scale and postpartum breastfeeding self-sufficiency scale(n=281)

		Postpartum Breastfeeding Self-Sufficiency Scale
Satisfaction From Birth Experience Scale	R	-0,320
	P	0,000

Spearman Correlation

As the time after the birth gets longer, satisfaction level of mothers from birth has significantly increased (p<0,05). As the period after birth gets longer, since physical complaints reduce, adaptation to maternity increases and problems experienced during birth lose its freshness on the first day, it is considered that comfort and satisfaction will increase during postpartum. When the time that mothers gave birth and SFBES point average were observed, SFBES point average of the mother who gave birth before 0-30 days was identified as 54,8±12,1 and SFBES score did not present a significant difference according to time elapsed after birth (p>0,05) (Table 3).

Table 3: Comparison of point averages of satisfaction from birth experience scale and postpartum breastfeeding self-sufficiency scale according to how long ago the mothers gave birth (n=281)

		Min-Max		Median	Av.	± s.s.	P
Satisfaction From Birth Experience Scale							
How long ago did you give birth?	0-30 Days	10	38	21	21,6	5,2	0,016
	31-60 Days	19	32	25	24,4	4,0	
	More than 61 Days	13	32	19	19,9	4,9	
Postpartum Breastfeeding Self-Sufficiency Scale							
How long ago did you give birth?	0-30 Days	14	70	57	54,8	12,1	0,107
	31-60 Days	29	70	45	46,6	14,7	
	More than 61 Days	40	70	55	56,6	8,2	

Kruskal-wallis

SFBES score did not demonstrate a significant difference between the mothers who have given birth once and more than once (p>0,05). When number of times they gave birth and PBSSS point averages are compared, PBSSS score is found significantly higher for the ones who gave more than one birth than the ones who gave one birth (p<0,05) (Table 4).

According to breastfeeding of the previous baby, SFBES score did not demonstrate a significant difference (p>0,05). When mothers' state in breastfeeding of their previous babies and PBSSS point average are compared, PBSSS average point was found higher for the ones who breastfed their previous baby and PBSSS score demonstrated significant difference between the mothers who breastfed their previous baby and the mothers having the first baby (p<0,05) (Table 5).

Table 4: Comparison of point averages of satisfaction from birth experience scale and postpartum breastfeeding self-sufficiency scale according to how many times did the mothers give birth (n=281)

		Min-Max		Median	Av.	± s.s.	P
Satisfaction From Birth Experience Scale							
How many times did you give birth?	Once	12	37	20	21,2	5,2	0,357
	Two or More	10	38	21	21,7	5,2	
Postpartum Breastfeeding Self-Sufficiency Scale							
How many times did you give birth?	Once	23	70	54	52,9	11,0	0,011
	Two Or More	14	70	59	55,6	12,3	

Mann-whitney u test

Table 5: Comparison of point averages of satisfaction from birth experience scale and postpartum breastfeeding self-sufficiency scale according to mothers' state in breastfeeding of their previous babies (n=281)

		Min-Max		Median	Av.	± s.s.	p
Satisfaction From Birth Experience Scale							
Did you breastfeed your previous babies?	The First Baby	12	37	20	21,0	4,8	0,430
	Yes	10	38	21	21,9	5,4	
	No	14	32	21	21,0	5,1	
Postpartum Breastfeeding Self-Sufficiency Scale							
Did you breastfeed your previous babies?	The First Baby	25	70	54	53,1	10,6	0,000
	Yes	14	70	59	56,5	12,3	
	No	14	70	52	49,2	12,8	

Kruskal-wallis (Mann-whitney u test)

4 Discussion

In Table 1, 'de SFBES point average of mothers was calculated as 21,5±5,2. In the study of Taşcı (2005), SFBES point average was calculated as 21,8±4,3. SFBES point average was found in parallel to study finding [2]. PBSSS point average was calculated as 54,7±11,9. In the study of [6]. PBSSS point average of mothers was calculated as 59,49±8,46 while 55,88±10,85 according to study of Dennis (2003) and 60,09±8,2 according to study of Tokat (2009) [6-8]. PBSSS point averages were found parallel to study finding of Dennis (2003) while lower than study findings of Yenal et al. (2013) and Tokat (2009) [6-8]. It is considered that the reason why the study finding was found lower than the other study findings is the group which research was made on was selected from different regions.

In Table 2, SFBES averages of mothers according to their PBSSS points were evaluated with correlation aanalysis. It was identified that there was a very weak and negative statistically significant relationship ($p<0,05$) between SFBES point averages and PBSSS averages of mothers ($rs= -0,320$). This result reveals that there is a negatively relationship between satisfaction from birth experience and breastfeeding self-sufficiency. Before the study, a positive relationship was expected between birth experience and breastfeeding self-sufficiency. It is considered that the result might have occured since sample group did not show homogeneous didtribution and the mothers who participated the study consisted of people having different age groups and birth experience. Mother-baby interaction is an important factor that affects breastfeeding. The immediate start of mother-baby interaction in normal birth has an advantage on cesarean section. 56% of mothers who participted our study gave birth by cesarean section. Although the mothers who give birth by cesarean section do not feel pain during birth and pleased with the birth, when births take place by cesarean section; it may negatively affect the factors such as mother-baby interaction, the first breastfeeding period, stimulation of milk release; causes delay, and makes breastfeeding difficult, and this may reduce the mother's feeling of adequacy. Moreover, the reason of labor for mothers who give normal birth is that oxytocia increases uterus contractions. Increase in uterus contractions lead to mothers have child-birth pains, and reduce their satisfaction from birth. In the meantime, increase in oxytocia also raises the amount of prolactin and causes increase in milk release from breasts. Increase in milk release is considered as the mothers can breastfeed their babies easier and thus lead to increase in their level of satisfaction.

In Table 3, Wien how long ago the mothers in the study gave birth and their SFBES and PBSSS point averages are compared; it is observed that the time after birth gets longer, satisfaction level of mothers from birth significantly increases ($p<0,05$). As the time after the birth gets longer; since physical complaints reduce, adaptation to motherhood increases and the problems experienced during birth lose their freshness on the first day; it is considered that comfort and satisfaction will increase during postpartum period. When the time that mothers gave birth and PBSSS point average were observed, PBSSS point average of the mother who gave birth before 0-30 days was identified as 54,8±12,1 and PBSSS score did not present a significant difference according to time elapsed after birth ($p>0,05$). The reason for this was considered to arise from since majority of mothers in our study became willingly pregnant, this might lead to both increase in mother baby interaction psychologically and start the mother's breastfeeding of her baby earlier as well as provide the sustainability of breastfeeding.

In Table 4, when how many times the mothers gave birth and their SFBES point averages were compared, SFBES score did not reveal significant difference between the ones who gave one birth and who gave more than one birth ($p<0,05$). The mothers stated that they experienced the same pain regardless of times they gave birth. When their times of giving birth and PBSSS point averages were compared, PBSSS score is found significantly higher for the ones who gave more than one birth compared to ones who gave one birth ($p<0,05$). Breatfeeding self-sufficiency perception of mothers was evaluated who whether or not breasfeeding experience [9]. In the postnatal group, BSSP average of mothers having previous experience (X=62,9±6,6) was found higher than the ones having no experience (X=57.4±8.9) (t=.-4.276, P=0.00) [8]. This result had parallels with our study.

In Table 5, when SFBES point averages of mothers according to breastfeeding of their previous babies were compared, SFBES score did not reveal significant difference according to breastfeeding of previous baby ($p>0,05$). When mothers' state in breastfeeding of their previous babies and PBSSS point average were compared, PBSSS average point was found higher for the ones who breastfed their previous baby and PBSSS score demonstrated significant difference between the mothers who breastfed their previous baby and the mothers having the first baby ($p<0,05$). The mothers who breastfed their previous baby can breastfeed their present baby more easily.

5 Conclusion and Suggestions

Whether in the first step or delivery nurses, nurses and doctors working at hospitals have important responsibilities for being aware of the factors which may cause leaving the breastfeeding during early period, and perform necessary applications during both prenatal and postnatal periods to prevent those.

- Trainings to be given should be cared for being suitable for educational level of the mothers and in the way they can understand.
- In the literature, number of studies which reviewed the effect of satisfaction of mothers from birth on breasfeeding self-sufficiency are quite limited. We can suggest more studies to make on this topic.

Acknowledgment

Regarding the research and/or authorship of this article, the authors didn't receive any financial

References

1. Demirci H. İlk gebeliği olan kadınların psikolojik tepkilerinin incelenmesi (Tez). İstanbul Üniversitesi, Doğum ve Kadın Hastalıkları Hemşireliği Anabilim Dalı Yüksek Lisans Tezi; (1996).
2. Taşcı KD. Postpartum kendini değerlendirme ölçeğinin geçerlik ve güvenirlik çalışması (Tez). Dokuz Eylül Üniversitesi, Hemşirelik Ana Bilim Dalı Doğum ve Kadın Hastalıkları Hemşireliği Yüksek Lisans Tezi; (2005).
3. Taşkın L. Doğum ve Kadın Sağlığı Hemşireliği, 5. Baskı, Sistem Ofset Matbaacılık, Ankara, 365-366., (1997).
4. Taşcı KD, Mete S. "Postpartum Kendini Değerlendirme Ölçeğinin Geçerlik Ve Güvenirlik Çalışması" Atatürk Üniversitesi Hemşirelik Yüksekokulu Dergisi, 10(2): 20-29., (2007).
5. Tunçel EK, Dündar C, Canbaz S, Pekşen P. "Bir üniversite hastanesine başvuran 0-24 aylık çocukların anne sütü ile beslenme durumlarının saptanması" Cumhuriyet Üniversitesi Hemşirelik Yüksekokulu Dergisi, 10(1): 1-6., (2006).
6. Yenal K, Tokat MA, Ozan YD, Çeçe Ö, Abalın FB. "Annelerin emzirme öz-yeterlilik algıları ile emzirme başarıları arasındaki ilişkinin incelenmesi" Hemşirelikte Eğitim ve Araştırma Dergisi, 10(2): 14-19., (2013).
7. Dennis CL. "The Breastfeeding self-efficacy scale: psychometric assessment of the short form" Journal of Obstetric, Gynecologic and Neonatal Nursing, 32(6): 734–744.,(2003).
8. Tokat MA. Antenatal dönemde verilen eğitimin annelerin emzirme öz-yeterlilik algısına ve emzirme başarısına etkisi (Tez). Dokuz Eylül Üniversitesi, Doğum ve Kadın Hastalıkları Hemşireliği Doktora Tezi; (2009).
9. Kızılkaya S. Sezaryen ya da normal spontan doğum yapan primiparlarda doğum deneyiminin doğum sonu yaşam kalitesine etkisi (Tez). Marmara Üniversitesi, Doğum ve Kadın Hastalıkları Hemşireliği Anabilim Dalı Yüksek Lisans Tezi; (2013).

Participation of academics with disabilities in science using the example of AKTIF project

Sinem Ulutas[1], Susanne Groth[1], Wolfgang Thiems[1], and Mathilde Niehaus[1]

[1]Universität zu Köln, Lehrstuhl für Arbeit und berufliche Rehabilitation, Herbert-Lewin Straße 2, 50931 Köln

Abstract. This paper discusses the participation in the scientific world by referring to the AKTIF project. It introduces how the research team of AKTIF takes on the problems of academics with disabilities and reflects on the participation in one's own team. AKTIF project suggests that for a successful outcome of the participation in the academy, conditions of the recruitment process, employment intake, as well as the cooperation within the course of the project should be changed.
Keywords: AKTIF project; academics with disabilities; academy

1 Introduction

The relevance of the subject participation is based on the fact that in the future, academics with disabilities, as a result of a more inclusive educational and work system, will be increasingly represented in science. It is noticeable, however, that people with disabilities, even if they achieved a university degree, do not benefit as much from career advancement opportunities as people without disabilities who have an identical level of education ([1]; [2]). Therefore, this article concerns the inclusion or involvement of highly qualified people with disabilities in science.

Currently there is little information available in Germany concerning their involvement in scientific research, especially with regard to the area of participation and inclusion research. However, the available data and information material on the general labor market situation of persons with disabilities, on their participation in higher education [3], as well as on the observed interrelations of employment and educational opportunities suggests that the integration of this group into research enterprises is relatively weak. Even in the context of current participation and inclusion research, academics with disabilities seem to play a subordinate role as an active researcher as they are usually included as consultants. This paradoxical situation does neither meet the subject itself nor the requirements of full participation of people with disabilities. Furthermore, they could be far more engaged in the context of education and research in the field. From this point of view, the question as to which conditions must be met for a successful participation in the scientific work will be approached.

With the ratification of the United Nations Disability Equality Convention (UN-DEC) in 2009, Germany has committed itself to strengthening the autonomy and self-determination of people with disabilities, ensuring equal opportunities and accessibility as well as promoting full and effective participation in all areas of society. Article 24 (Education) and Article 27 (Work and Employment) provide for the establishment of concrete measures which should contribute to the participation in science in the future. In order to ensure this, besides addressing structural and technical issues, it is crucial to consider "barriers in the head" as well [1]. This indicates that all persons who are active in the field of science should break down prejudices and question stereotypes in order to make participation possible. Dealing with diversity in the field of science involves new challenges, which are described below. Yet, no research has shown how the participation of disabled academics in the scientific world can succeed, the challenges they face, and which prerequisites are needed for successful participation. First of all, this article shows how the research team of AKTIF takes on these problems and reflects on the participation in one's own team. Next, the relevance of this project and its initial situation will be clarified. Subsequently, the question of what constitutes participation in research and science will be discussed. In this way, the participatory development process can be exemplified in the course of the AKTIF project. Following a general reflection, the main findings are summarized in a conclusion and an outlook is given.

2 Background and starting point

Within the scope of the AKTIF project (academics with disabilities in participation and inclusion research), an inclusive, interdisciplinary network of researchers, who deal with issues of inclusion and participation research, is being developed at four locations throughout Germany. The main goal is to ensure that people with disabilities themselves and their organizations are involved in participation research as far as possible. At least half of the employees of the individual research teams have severe disabilities themselves. Within the framework of the project, funded by the German Federal Ministry of Labor and Social Affairs in 2015, scientists with and without disabilities jointly identify relevant research gaps and key issues. The aim of AKTIF is to promote opportunities for severely disabled academics in the scientific field: among other things, higher education, acquisition of and participation in inclusive externally funded projects and establishment in science at the university. It is expected that this will have an innovative thrust and a radiant power for the entire participation and inclusion research and will further promote research in the long term. In addition, the career prospects and the positions of qualified disabled academics in this future-oriented research area will be further developed, and insurable employment areas will be created for them. At the Cologne office, the Chair of Labor and Vocational Rehabilitation deals with issues related to the participation of people with disabilities in the scientific world. The chair represents an application-oriented and interdisciplinary approach to research and teaching. Pedagogical, psychological and social approaches of the vocational and social participation of people with disabilities and health problems are interlinked in science and practice.

The research approach is based on a participation-oriented understanding, which takes account of the perceptions and requirements of participating stakeholders and their involvement in the research process. Against this backdrop, a contribution was made by the AKTIF Cologne team, following a participatory research approach, to deal with the specific concern of participation in science.

3 What is meant by participation in science?

Essentially, scientists analyze the term "participation" and the concepts behind it by means of different approaches and systematization possibilities. Contingent on the subject and on the discipline one is socialized, the concept of participation is specifically accentuated. Participation does not refer solely to economic empowerment, but also to the political dimension (i.e. possibilities of influence) as well as to social dimensions (such as the degree of social inclusion or networking) [4]. Thus, participatory research is less an approach but a strategy and implies "to transfer the claim of participation to scientific research" [5]. Unger [6] extends that in order to change social reality, the diverse multitude of research approaches needs to be incorporated. An extension to target groups and individuals with special knowledge is quite possible [7]. Therefore, a distinction can be drawn between emancipatory research (active researchers with own research questions), participatory research (researchers are equally entitled), and research (active shapers of the research field and course) [8].

In participatory research, for example, academics with and without disabilities can cooperate or form alliances. The research question itself has to be in the (cognitive) interest of people with disabilities and research has to be conducted jointly by researchers with and without disabilities [9]. Thus, participatory research pursues the appropriate exploration of participation, but is also concerned with the realization of participation in the research process itself. . As educational scientists, psychologists, social scientists and sociologists, we will approach this particular perspective and way of thinking about participation. In this article, it is therefore assumed that participation in the research process increases the chances of academics with disabilities in research and science. Against this background, the work within the AKTIF project has highlighted three participation-oriented approaches and can be read as follows:

1. For equal opportunities in participation in science the creation of jobs is needed.
2. To ensure that academics with disabilities continue to participate in science, further qualifications are of particular importance.
3. To enable academics with disabilities to develop their potential in science, it is necessary that new steps will be taken to improve accessibility.

4 Conditions for successful participation in science – using the example of AKTIF

With regard to the realization and implementation of the three emerging approaches from the AKTIF project and a systematic evaluation of the experience reports created by the individual team members in 2015 and 2016 on the recruitment process at the university, the employment and cooperation in the course of the project, the following can be concluded for the location in Cologne: The original purpose of the experience reports was to document the problems with the formation of inclusive research teams and the possible solutions already exist (best practice examples). The reports were once again systematically evaluated for the research project with regard to the challenges and conditions for participation in science work for disabled academics. The analysis of the experience reports differentiated between individual and collective challenges. When working at the University of Cologne, academics with disabilities were confronted with numerous additional organizational tasks. These tasks were related both directly and indirectly to the pursuit of their activities. In order to be able to work in a barrier-free way, different workplaces were applied for participation in working life at the Federal Employment Agency. The application and the procedure took additional temporal resources, partly because some responsibilities were initially unclear. The inclusion of the new activity in the field of science also called for a particularly high degree of flexibility for the disabled. By relocating to a new city, the employees with mobility and visual impairment were particularly challenged to find themselves in a very short time in a new infrastructure and to seek a new support network. In the workplace, the requirement of barrier-free communication was one of the biggest challenges for the entire team. Two academics with visual impairments met team members who had little experience working with visually impaired people. Over time, the team has learned to verbalize visual information, talk in structured meetings, make PDF documents barrier-free, dispense with the use of software that is not barrier-free, and e.g. how to successfully plan and take barrier-free business trips. For all project members it was also shown that a forward planning is particularly important for participation. This means, for example, that internal and external meetings are announced at an early stage so that barrier-free travel and accommodation can be organized and the deployment of personnel / technical support can be organized. Through the influence and co-determination in the research and science enterprise, a high commitment and a high degree of engagement arose. Prerequisites for securing participation are contact management and the equal distribution of information [10].

Participation in science is a relatively recent research area. On the way to an independent discipline, the development of specific research questions on the topic of disability during studies is of great importance. In this way, a new sensibility is being developed and visions and actions for the aspects of inclusion and participation of people with disabilities are mediated. We work together as a multidisciplinary team of psychologists, educators, and social scientists in an interdisciplinary manner. We corporate as a team to apply for inclusive research projects and to develop an inclusive research network.

5 Reflection

Participation in the scientific community may initially pose an additional expense in terms of time and organization, but this is more than offset by the synergies due to the very supportive and good cooperation. Through the participation, a well-functioning team with flat hierarchical structures and a forward-looking research stint, which acts innovative, inclusive, participatory and networking, is experienced. There is room for the individual, as well as a collective implementation and organisation of tasks. In order to guarantee accessibility, more financial and temporal resources are needed, but the innovative nature of the topics and outputs, the effectiveness and the quality of the work in these researches are very fruitful and beneficial for science, politics and society. In order to meet requirements, a planning of additional organization and technical aids is necessary.

Organizational challenges arise from the fact that barrier-free work materials, teaching materials and learning materials are not standardized as a special requirement and have to be "initiated". Special technical preparations must be prepared before each meeting or social event. For a successful communication and a good social co-operation, each team member is required a great sensitivity and attention for his co-workers and a great discipline.

6 Conclusion

In the coming years, the topic of "participation in the scientific enterprise" will become more relevant in practice and in research. In this article it was shown that participation is not only concernced with the transformation of social structures, but also with the consciousness formation of individuals. Especially, communication with each other is particularly important to work equally, effectively and innovatively, and what is more, to build and stabilize teamwork, so that joint research will be possible and social reality can be changed. In this context, "barriers in the minds" can be dismantled, as a rethinking is necessary. The participation of academics with disability can be achieved in the research and in the scientific enterprise, as soon as the cooperation and the alliances are also used as an opportunity. The research question itself must be in the (knowledge) interest of people with disabilities. Considering that, the normality of one's perception has to be be recognized and traditional notions of normality must be questioned. This indicates that one's own communication styles and assumptions must be reflected [11].

In conclusion, it can be stated the AKTIF project sucessfully demonstrated that inclusive work teams, adequate communications styles, as well as reflected assumptions [11] mutually contribute to the redefinement of the participative concept of work performance.

References

1. M. Niehaus, J. Bauer, Chancen und Barrieren für hochqualifizierte Menschen mit Behinderung: *Übergang in ein sozialversicherungspflichtiges Beschäftigungsverhältnis - Pilotstudie zur beruflichen Teilhabe (Aktion Mensch e.V., ed.)* (2013).
2. H.W. Bach, Berufliche Partizipation blinder, sehbehinderter und mehrfach behinderter Hochschulabsolventen in Deutschland, der Einfluss von Beratung - eine empirische Studie (2011) Retrieved from http://www.hdba.de/uploads/tx_sbdownloader/Berufliche_Partizipation_Text.pdf.
3. H. Pfaff, Lebenslagen der behinderten Menschen. Ergebnis des Mikrozensus 2009. Wirtschaft und Statistik 3rd ed., 232-243 (2012). Wiesbaden: Statistisches Bundesamt. Retrieved from https://www.destatis.de/DE/Publikationen/WirtschaftStatistik/Sozialleistungen/Lebenslagenbehinde rte032012.pdf? blob=publicationFile.
4. G. Biewer, Grundlagen der Heilpädagogik und Inklusiven Pädagogik. 2nd ed. (2010).
5. P. Flieger, Partizipatorische Forschung: Wege zur Entgrenzung der Rollen von ForscherInnen und Beforschten. In: J. Kerg, K. Merz-Atalik, R. Thümmler & H. Tiemann (Eds.), *Perspektiven auf Entgrenzung. Erfahrungen und Entwicklungsprozesse im Kontext von Inklusion und Integration* 59- 171 (2009).
6. H. Unger, Partizipative Forschung: Einführung in die Forschungspraxis (2014).
7. P. Flieger, Partizipative Forschungsmethoden und ihre konkrete Umsetzung. In G. Hermes & S. Köbsell (Ed.), Disability Studies in Deutschland - Behinderung neu denken. Dokumentation der Sommeruni, 200-204 (2003).
8. S. Krach, Partizipative Evaluation als Beitrag zur Praxisentwicklung. Teilhabe. 1 (50), 11-16. (2011).
9. Chappell, Emergence of participatory methodology in learning difficulty research: understanding the context. In: British Journal of Learning Disabilities 28, S. 38-43 (2000).
10. F.C. Brodbeck, Anderson, N. & West, M. Teamklima Inventar (TKI) (2000).
11. C. Behrens, U. Sielert, N. Hofmeister, N., Difference Troubles – Pädagogik der VielfaltArbeitsgruppe Primäre Prävention von Gewalt gegen Gruppenangehörige. *Materialsammlung: Workshop Reader*, 13-20 (2003), Retrieved from http://www.kriminalpraevention.de/files/DFK/dfk-publikationen/2003_workshop_reader.pdf.

AUTHOR INDEX

AUTHOR INDEX